A. LAWRENCE KOCHER

Published by Applied Research and Design Publishing, an imprint of ORO Editions.
Gordon Goff: Publisher

www.appliedresearchanddesign.com
info@appliedresearchanddesign.com

Authors: Luis Pancorbo Crespo and Inés Martín Robles
Book Design: Luis Pancorbo Crespo and Inés Martín Robles
Project Manager: Jake Anderson

10 9 8 7 6 5 4 3 2 1 First Edition
ISBN: 978-1-961856-61-5

Prepress and Print work by ORO Editions Inc.
Printed in China

AR+D Publishing makes a continuous effort to minimize the overall carbon footprint of its publications. As part of this goal, AR+D, in association with Global ReLeaf, arranges to plant trees to replace those used in the manufacturing of the paper produced for its books. Global ReLeaf is an international campaign run by American Forests, one of the world's oldest nonprofit conservation organizations. Global ReLeaf is American Forests' education and action program that helps individuals, organizations, agencies, and corporations improve the local and global environment by planting and caring for trees.

APPLIED RESEARCH +DESIGN

A. LAWRENCE KOCHER

AMERICAN ARCHITECT

Luis Pancorbo Crespo, Ph.D.

Inés Martín Robles, Ph.D.

CONTENTS

Foreword. 6
A. Lawrence Kocher: American Architect. By Edward R. Ford

Introduction. 8
From Disassembly to Display: The Aluminaire House's Desert Resurrection. By Leo Marmol.

1930.
Aluminaire House: The Migrating Villa. 11

1920–1929.
Before Aluminaire: In Search of a New American Architecture. 61

1931–1933.
The Experimental Weekend House and Parallel Experiences. 99

1933–1935.
Building on Two Coasts: From the Subsistence Farmsteads to the Kocher-Samson Building. 149

1935–1941.
The Carnegie Tech and Black Mountain College Years. 203

1941–1969.
Innovation and Tradition: From Black Mountain to Williamsburg. 253

Conclusions and Notes on the Graphic Reconstruction. 311

Bibliography. 375

Illustration Credits. 379

FOREWORD

A. LAWRENCE KOCHER: AMERICAN ARCHITECT

Edward R. Ford
Professor Emeritus, Architecture. University of Virginia.

In April of this year, the reconstructed Aluminaire House was opened to the public at the Palm Springs Museum of Art. It is, one hopes, the final chapter in a long odyssey. Originally built and exhibited in 1931 at an architecture fair in New York, the house has literally taken a 90-year, 3,000-mile journey across the country that required that it be disassembled and reassembled five times on six different sites. But just as it has been moved about geographically, it has been moved about in history. It was one of only two American houses included in the 1932 Modern Architecture: International Exhibition (The International Style Exhibition) at the Museum of Modern Art, New York. The reason for its inclusion was no doubt its formal and stylistic similarity to the Le Corbusier houses in the same show rather than its experimental construction. The show, by its own admission "made little attempt to present…the technical… aspects of the style."[1]

The 1987 restoration and relocation of the house to the Long Island Campus of the New York Institute of Technology, well documented and well published, moved the house to a different location in history as well. It made it clear that the Aluminaire House was a true industrial product built of industrial materials with industrial methodologies. None of the other houses in the 1932 show were arguably as factory-ready, capable of automobile-like mass production. The Aluminaire House's "dry" construction enabled a rapid 10-day on-site assembly in contrast to the international-style houses of the 1932 show—typically built of stucco on block supported by concrete frame, a wet process requiring slow assembly. This restoration brought well deserved fresh attention to its designers, A. Lawrence Kocher and Albert Frey, whose historical position has been no less transient than the buildings, and its architects were thus historically relocated as well.

Joseph Rosa's 1990 book on Frey, published three years after the Long Island reconstruction, documented the striking desert modernity of the work he did in Palm Springs after leaving his partnership with Kocher. This elevated Frey's reputation from a minor to a major figure, but the foregrounding of Frey had the effect of pushing Kocher into the background. There are more than five books on Frey, two on the Aluminaire House but none on Kocher. This is of course unfair. As the book that follows makes clear, Kocher was not a junior partner. For example, the use of aluminum and the expertise to do so are not doubt due to Kocher. Frey was new to America and knew little of its building culture. Kocher's post-partnership work, while not always as photogenic as Frey's, is no less profound and aggressively modern.

But the trajectory of Kocher's career remains puzzling. Just prior to the Aluminaire House, Kocher was an adviser to Colonial Williamsburg, never a hot bed of modernism, then moved on to Black Mountain College, one of modernism's epicenters and later returned to Williamsburg full time. It is one of the great virtues of the text that follows that it does much to explain this. Kocher's work at Colonial Williamsburg and his extensive work in traditional American vernacular building seems to contradict his avowed interest in European modernism and the industrialization of building, but they were connected for him. To understand Kocher, one must understand the historic moment.

The year 1932 marked an end and a beginning. In Europe it marked the end of international-style modernism, at least for many of its key practitioners. It marked the beginning of an interest in the regional, the vernacular, even the primitive. The vernacular was already appearing in the work of the stars of the 1932 exhibition. Le Corbusier's work featured heavy timber framing and ruble stone walls. Alvar Aalto was beginning his exploration of a Finnish timber regionalism. In America, there was a passion, not just for the vernacular, but the American vernacular—the local, the traditional wisdom of building. It was an era not just of regionalism but of cultural nationalism—in literature, in painting and in architecture. One result was vast cataloging of the history of American vernacular. Alfred Kazin points out:

> Here, in the vast granary of facts on life in America put away by the WPA writers, the documentary reporters, the folklorists preparing an American mythology, the explorers who went hunting through darkest America with notebook and camera, the new army of biographers and historians—here, stocked away like a reserve against bad times, is the raw stuff of that contemporary mass record which so many imaginative spirits tried to depict and failed to master.[2]

The results are all around us—Colonial Williamsburg and countless American Colonial and Spanish Colonial revival buildings. But as Kazin warned, there is a danger of a nostalgia "too easily content with the trappings of sentimental autobiography and romance" and the need "to discriminate…between the need for the past and the comforting surface of that past."[3]

This is precisely what Kocher was doing in his compilations of traditional American architecture or *Architectural Record,* which began before the Aluminaire House and his work at Colonial Williamsburg. Kocher had been cataloging and collecting colonial details for many years. This was not just cataloging traditional images. In theory at least it was not a language of images but a study of traditional ways of building.

For these modern architects, the true vernacular had no style. It was as a kind of pure, innocent functionalism independent of style. The veneration of the vernacular is much older than modernism. Writers from John Ruskin to Viollet-le-Duc celebrated the untrained, innocent, pragmatic, non-architect builder. The vernacular designer is unencumbered by knowledge of precedent, and can solve the problem of building in a straightforward, commonsense way using the materials and methods at hand, the conditions of the site, and the local climate. The results, in the eyes of many, are superior to the work of the historically knowledgeable and aesthetically self-aware designer. The results of this type of design are not necessarily beautiful and often not refined, but the appreciation of the vernacular is the idea that someone can create something beautiful with no intention of doing so. If one designs something that is direct, functional, and unpretentious, quality will follow. For Kocher, and most of his modernist colleagues, the quality of the vernacular was not a question of style, forms, elements, or motifs. It was about a ways of building.

Modern American architecture was no less focused on the regional. Thus, the years of Colonial Williamsburg were also the years of Gropius's and Breuer's experiments with wood-framed, clear-finished, clapboard-sided houses, the years of Richard Neutra's switch from a language of steel and stucco to redwood and cedar, the years of Mies van der Rohe's Resor House with its raw cypress siding.

Kocher's design output following the end of the partnership with Frey was substantial, ranging from single-family houses to large academic buildings. While he employed the international-style forms, the materials he used and construction had changed dramatically. In the post-Aluminaire work of Kocher and Frey, and in Kocher's later work, formal similarities with the dry, industrialized, metallic language of Aluminaire, they used a different pallete—traditionally milled wood framing rather than steel for example. All these projects were industrial but there was little to no steel or metal siding. It was modernism informed by vernacular tradition.

So, is this the final definitive history of these two enigmatic architects? Probably not, but it is by far the most accurate to date. For obvious reasons, a primary cause for the misunderstandings and misguided histories of all these buildings was that in many previous publications their construction and technology were presented in glib ways, if at all, as in the *International Style* book with pictures and short written descriptions. There was very little explanation of construction.

The large quantity of information—graphic and factual—and the large number of original drawings explaining the actual construction of the buildings presented here, allow us to see and understand not just the real methods but the true ideologies of building. They add significantly to the body of knowledge of important buildings largely unknown and published only in small fragments. Its illustrations are as important as its text. As a result, this work expands significantly with more available to the existing scholarship regarding the realities of the industrialization of American building, and provides a primer for the historical period. But the great revelation of the text is reexamination of the various apparently contradictory aspects of the work of Kocher giving here yet another, far more complex and far more architecturally significant version of this history.

Endnotes

1 Henry-Russell Hitchcock Philip Johnson, The International Style (W.W. Norton, New York, 1966), 13.

2 Alfred Kazin. On Native Grounds (Garden City: Doubleday, [1942] 1956), 381.

3 Kazin, 381.

INTRODUCTION

FROM DISASSEMBLY TO DISPLAY: THE ALUMINAIRE HOUSE'S DESERT RESURRECTION.

The Final Stages of the Aluminaire House Reconstruction in Palm Springs, California

Leo Marmol, FAIA

It was a pleasure and an honor to collaborate with the Palm Springs Art Museum and the Aluminaire House Foundation to reconstruct the Aluminaire House as the most recent monument to Modernism in Palm Springs. My firm, Marmol Radziner, was established in 1989 with my business partner, Ron Radziner. Marmol Radziner has decades of experience restoring Modern architectural marvels such as Richard Neutra's Kaufmann House, John Lautner's Garcia House, and the Loewy House designed by Albert Frey.

The realization of the Aluminaire House in the early 20th century and the continuing conversation surrounding the house is a testament to the Modern movement's unceasing evolution. As we approach the centennial of the Aluminaire House, its resurrection in Palm Springs has allowed the architectural gem to return to its intended purpose as a public exhibition, encouraging critical dialogue about the enduring relevance of Modern ideas. The reconstruction of the Aluminaire House is an act of poetic justice for the structure's storied journey to culminate in Palm Springs—the same city transformed into an oasis of Modernism by the house's architects, A. Lawrence Kocher and Albert Frey, so many years ago.

Despite its widely accepted status as a significant artifact of Modern architecture, the Aluminaire House spent many years hidden from public view. The house was relocated, renovated, and threatened with demolition. Until now, it never truly found an enduring site, languishing in storage for decades. First exhibited at the 1931 Allied Arts and Architecture Exposition, Kocher and Frey developed the 1,100-square-foot home as a prototype for low-income housing. Its compact, modular design was conceived under the looming shadow of a drastic economic crisis. As an architect, managing editor of Architectural Record, and professor at Black Mountain College, Kocher devised numerous modular housing designs that were never built. The Aluminaire House realizes Kocher's dream of affordable, beautiful housing for all people.

As the lead coordinator of material donations and funding for the project, Kocher believed in the power of the press and education as tools to promote the Modern movement. Kocher's editorial and business connections are to thank for the Aluminaire's successful unveiling at the 1931 Allied Arts and Architecture Exposition and the wildly positive articles dubbing it "the house of the future." The prototype was also one of only two residential projects designed by American architects featured in the 1932 landmark exhibition at the Museum of Modern Art in New York entitled "Modern Architecture: International Exhibition." We honor the Aluminaire House by allowing it to exist as its creators intended: a vehicle that would transport the philosophy of European Modernism across the Atlantic to the United States.

Architects Michael Schwarting and Frances Campani recognized the home's historic and architectural significance and took action to preserve it, founding the Aluminaire House Foundation in 2011. Modern-architect Wallace K. Harrison purchased the house after its initial exhibition, altering the structure and using it as a primary residence for his family. After residing on the Harrison Estate for more than 40 years, the site faced redevelopment and the house was threatened with demolition. Schwarting and Campani rescued the Aluminaire House and coordinated its relocation to the New York Institute of Technology's Central Islip campus. The campus closed in 2004, rendering the house without a permanent site yet again. Michael and Frances then coordinated the disassembly of the house and meticulously stored and cataloged its components, awaiting the right time and place for its reassembly.

In 2014, Schwarting and Campani presented the Aluminaire House at Palm Springs Modernism Week. This introduction to a new audience quickly sparked significant interest among local Modernist enthusiasts. A committee was formed to bring the house to Palm Springs permanently. This committee, comprising a group of local preservation supporters including Beth Edwards Harris, William Kopelk, Tracy Conrad, Mark Davis, and Brad Dunning, among others, worked tirelessly to find a suitable location to reconstruct the house.

After the Palm Springs committee considered multiple sites across Palm Springs, the Palm Springs Art Museum expressed interest in harboring the Aluminaire House. This decision by the museum was both monumental and logical, given that the museum's existing collection includes Frey House #2 and Albert Frey's architectural archive. In 2020, the Aluminaire House Foundation officially gifted the house to the Palm Springs Art Museum. Finally, it was time to reassemble the exhibition.

Historical landmarks like the Aluminaire House typically occupy a singular site, but this structure has been erected at multiple locations. Moreover, the Aluminaire House was entirely disassembled when the museum acquired it. So, we have to ask, why should a museum accept an old pile of house components into its permanent art collection? How do we understand the notion of significance with something so transitory? How can the Aluminaire House be historically significant when it is nothing but a kit of parts? This ephemeral nature raises questions about the notions of significance and authenticity in architectural preservation. The Aluminaire House's lack of a permanent site is an important aspect of its significance. Designed to be at home anywhere, the home's flexibility aligns with Modernist principles of adaptability and functionality.

In preservation, "integrity" often refers to the presence of the original materials or "historic fabric." The Aluminaire House is exceptional in this regard, as most of its structural reconstruction comprises materials from its original 1931 installation. However, preserving a historical artifact while making it functional within contemporary building codes poses significant challenges.

The installation of the Aluminaire House at the Palm Springs Art Museum incorporates several established preservation standards by the U.S. Secretary of the Interior. It is a Preservation project because it retains the original materials, a Rehabilitation project because it updates aspects of the structure to meet current construction standards and building codes, and a Restoration project due to repairs and enhancements beyond the original exhibition setup. Moreover, it is a Reconstruction project since the house was literally reassembled from its stored components.

One of the substantial challenges in reconstructing the Aluminaire House was adapting its design to the harsh desert environment of Palm Springs. Establishing the house on its new site in the museum's south parking lot began by laying a new concrete foundation. Originally developed on the East Coast, the house's steel and aluminum structure required modifications to withstand the potential for earthquakes as well as the intense desert sun. This adaptation involved updating the house's structural system, introducing new thermal insulation, and adding a waterproofing system, as the original design was installed in an indoor exhibition hall. Heating and cooling equipment was also added as a continuous preservation effort for the building's original materials.

The Aluminaire House's century-long journey concludes with its installation at the Palm Springs Art Museum. Here, the house will continue to inspire conversations about the paradoxes of Modern architecture. Due to its small size and multi-story design, the house cannot accommodate contemporary accessibility standards, so there is no interior access to the exhibition. However, visitors are given ample opportunity to peer through the Aluminaire House's glorious windows and closely inspect the reflective walls to examine its materials.

The Palm Springs Art Museum honors the home's lasting impact on the architectural landscape by acquiring one of Frey's earliest works in the U.S. and one of Kocher's most-realized modular visions. The Aluminaire House's innovative design, revolutionary use of materials, and creative prefabrication process symbolize the convergence of European modernism and American ingenuity. While the house was never mass-produced, its influence is evident in Modern architectural movements, such as the tiny-house movement, contemporary prefabrication projects, and even the construction of low-income housing.

The power of mass production and prefabrication continues to resonate in today's architectural conversation. Inspired by Henry Ford's assembly lines ad popularized by Sears' mail-order homes, the practice's ethos aimed to make housing more efficient and affordable. Despite economic and practical challenges, the dream of prefabrication persists, promising new solutions for efficient, sustainable housing. The house's acquisition by the Palm Springs Art Museum offers an exciting opportunity to explore and debate the relevance of Modernist ideals in contemporary architecture.

The permanent exhibition of the Aluminaire House in Palm Springs celebrates the Modernist movement and epitomizes how advanced processes and collaboration can create captivating architectural outcomes. The Aluminaire House's journey from uncertainty to preservation in Palm Springs is a story of dedication, innovation, and the enduring relevance of Modernist architecture. The Aluminaire House is a living museum, a tangible reminder of human resilience in pursuit of a better, more sustainable future.

1930

ALUMINAIRE HOUSE: THE MIGRATING VILLA

For most people, their social existence and cultural environment are experienced through a shared series of values, ideas, conventions, and symbols of a given era. The social imaginary is often expressed not in theoretical terms, but rather is carried in images, stories, and legends—it is a mutual understanding that enables the existence of common practices and a widely shared sense of legitimacy.[1] The events that shape the social imaginary are diverse and independent for a majority of historical periods. These events rarely can be organized within a coherent system of cause and effect. On the contrary, these events frequently intermingle, creating a constellation, an atlas of images and narratives whose relations are established more because of their simultaneity than their objective links. On rare occasions, all the events of an era can be organized consistently around one unique historical phenomenon. The decade of the 1930s in the United States of America (USA) can objectively be included in this category, as all the main historical occurrences of the era gravitate around one central concept: the Great Depression.[2] These years can be considered as the first period of American history to be fully documented graphically. The technological advancements in photography and cinematography made it possible to replace the previously bulky equipment with lighter, portable cameras. Alongside the simultaneous improvements in printing and publishing, new technology allowed photojournalists and documentarists to produce a lasting body of work that permitted Americans to look at themselves as never before and future generations to more extensively see the past.

The 1930s were a watershed in the story of the United States, capturing an unusually consistent and centralized social imaginary.[3] The resulting imaginary of this era has enormous persistence and validity in contemporary American society due mainly to several aggregated circumstances. The decade witnessed the establishment of a new balance between government and people, public works and services , and business and labor. The government exceeded its caretaker role after the 1932 presidential elections; it took responsibility to ensure that every American would be able to earn at least the basic means of life for themselves and their families. As historian T. H. Watkins puts it, this is a "new intimacy so thoroughly in place today that it is difficult to remember that once it was a revolutionary concept."[4] Until today, many persistent legislations, federal institutions, and agencies were created during the first and second New Deals, facilitated by a more active role of government in the daily life of contemporary American population. The best example might be the Social Security Act of 1935. Moreover, the legacy of this era is not restricted to politics and government, it manifested materially in the built public works and infrastructures. A large percentage of the New Deal irrigation systems, dams, sanitation plants, pipelines, power plants, highways, national parks, public pools, schools, hospitals, post offices, courthouses, city halls, and housing projects are still in use today.[5] This era also produced a profound change in patterns of mobility and the relationship Americans established with the territory they inhabit. Although there had been large migrations prior in the United States—namely the Great Migration of African Americans leaving the South since 1910, along with westward migration after the cession of the Mexican territories at the end of the Mexican–American War in 1848—the forced migrations during the depression created the social acceptation of a more nomadic and less rooted life in the territory. Documented by the media and vivid in public memory, this transient way of life is still a very relevant component of American contemporary life.[6]

Paradoxically, the monolithic social imaginary of the Depression era goes hand in hand with an extraordinary cultural exuberance unexpected for a time of deep economic and social crisis. Although the cultural manifestations of the time seem to be extremely diverse, they can always relate to the central concept of the Great Depression and be classified in two main categories that occupy two ends of a spectrum: the documentary approach of those artists willing to denounce the economic hardship and social injustices, and the escapist entertainment approach that aims to alleviate the anxiety of the general public by helping them picture a more promising future. Under the first category can be classified the work of writers like John Steinbeck, Erskine Caldwell, Mike Gold, and James Agee; photographers like Walker Evans, Margaret Bourke-White, Dorothea Lange, Arthur Rothstein, Russell Lee, Carl Mydans, Ben Shahn, and Marion Post Wolcott; documentarists as Pare Lorentz; and crooners like Woody Guthrie. The paradigms of the second category are the glamorous movies produced in Hollywood during this era, but there are many other examples included in what literary historian Morris Dickstein labels as "the culture of elegance."[7]

Being a useful art, architecture positioned itself in an intermediate category between these two poles immediately after the 1929 crash. It became clear that the extravagant, market-oriented Art Deco style dominant earlier in the decade was inappropriate for a moment of profound social pauperization. Luxury might be accepted in a lavish Hollywood fiction, but it was unbearable in the material realities of everyday life. Thus, the Streamline style demonstrated the design

Figure 1.1. A. Lawrence Kocher and Albert Frey. Aluminaire House. "The Future." Popular Mechanics 56, no 2. (August 1931) Illustration by Logan U. Reaves.

shift from wealthy (private) clients and corporations to the design for mass consumption by ordinary people. This new style substituted the rich materials of Art Deco (mosaics, marble, and bronze) with industrial materials—like steel, chrome, aluminum, and plastic—suitable for manufacturing, but most importantly, for the continuous surfaces consistent with the machinal and aerodynamic aesthetics of an optimistic architecture entrusted in a utopian future. The Streamline style coexisted with the more severe, minimalistic, and radical International Style. Highly influenced by the European modern movement, the International Style also shared a confidence in the future, along with the material palette of the Streamline style, but it was more radical in terms of social commitment, obedience to functional requirements, and rejection of any kind of superfluous ornamentation. Some of the still-scarce specimens of this modern style were presented to the general public in the 1932 Museum of Modern Art (MoMA) exhibition, "Modern Architecture: International Exhibition," curated by Henry-Russell Hitchcock and Philip Johnson. Some of these Modern works were broadcasted also in a more popular kind of media, like the magazine *Popular Mechanics*, devoted to explaining to a lay audience how technological artifacts, existing or imagined, work.[8]

During 1931, although financial crisis of the crash was already at full steam, its effects were still not evident to large sectors of the population. President Hoover ensured in a speech on March 7, 1930, that the worst effects of the crash upon employment will have passed in months, considering the depression as a temporary economical setback. In the midst of the Great Depression's worst moment, with the government and part of the public still in denial, the magazine *Popular Mechanics* published an issue in August of 1931 distilling optimism and trust in a brilliant technological future. The 1931 cover was illustrated with a futuristic rendering of a monorail flyer able to reach speeds of 150 miles per hour. Notably, on page 277, there was a rendered drawing of the so-called "House of the Future." Much like the scientific representation depicting a submarine or an aircraft—typical in these kinds of popular periodicals—this technical illustration depicted the house through a trimetric projection. Sections of the house's external skin were peeled away to reveal its internal features, focusing especially on the use of innovative materials, configurable furniture, and early home-automation systems. The illustration itself was neither drawn by an architect, nor destined to be a set of instructions for potential construction—it was the graphic representation of an already existing artifact. **(Figure 1.1)**

The meticulously illustrated "House of the Future" was the Aluminaire House. While it was not a real home rooted in a real site, the Aluminaire House was initially a demonstration object—a home as a pavilion for the exhibition of new construction technology shaped by the modern way of life and the new domestic performance necessities. Exhibited at the annual convention of the Architectural and Allied Arts Exposition, held in New York's Grand Central Palace from April 18th to 25th in 1931, advertised as an alternative for traditional houses. The need for an external stair connected to the terrace and the outward-opening entrance door fulfilled the fire-code requirements of a public building along with other features, like the lack of bracing for lateral load, revealed the remoteness of the Aluminaire House from any realistic domesticity and its closeness to a purely exhibition object. Its façades were in fact partially and strategically unfinished during its stay inside the Grand Central Palace to expose the interior layers and material composition to the visitors, especially regarding the innovative use of aluminum foil as a thermal insulation material. Therefore, the illustration in *Popular Mechanics* was very accurate in the depiction of an object that was not a house, but an experiment in housing technology independent from any specific physical context.

The American public was somewhat familiar with modern, domestic gadgets thanks to a shared popular culture—like Buster Keaton's 1922 silent film, "The Electric House" (1922)—and various public exhibition events, like the Electrical and Industrial Exposition, also at New York's Grand Central Palace, held between October 12 and October 22 of 1927. Accessible publications, moving pictures, and public expositions, all demonstrate the larger interest and timely potential in such a project as the Aluminaire House—the awe *Popular Mechanics* readers must have felt when confronted with the spaceship-like external rendering of all those internal technological innovations. Its futuristic materiality and abstract shape, its modern convertible furniture and automatized devices, its transparency and lightness—*everything* contributed to making the Aluminaire House the very first specimen of modern domestic architecture ever seen on the East Coast. Nevertheless, for many, the house had also something oddly familiar, as the *Popular Mechanics* anonymous writer put it: "a house such as men on some other planet might build, yet undeniably American."[9]

The popularity of the house among the general public was extraordinary during the 1931 Architectural and Allied Arts Exposition. The coeval newspapers register many articles about the unexpected success of the Aluminaire House as "a museum of domestic invention."[10] Despite its status as an exhibition object aimed to propagate the use of new building technologies amid a lay audience, the impact of the Aluminaire House on a more specialized public is not less relevant. It was one of just six American works selected for Hitchcock and Johnson's "Modern Architecture: International Exhibition" at MoMA.[11] This exhibition was supplemented with a catalog that gave rise to the famous book, *The International Style*, published in the same year by the same authors.[12] The book featured 82 examples of International modern architecture and included only two examples of American residential architecture. Interestingly, these two American projects—the Aluminaire House and Richard Neutra's Lovell Health House in Los Angeles—shared the commonality of championing more an architectural manifesto than a realistic domestic architecture. Both houses were perfect illustrations of Hitchcock and Johnson's vision about modern housing as an industrial object, fulfilling the new needs for hygiene, a healthy environment that includes light and air, and a novel use of athletic recreation and leisure time.[13] This intent was evident even in the name of the Aluminaire House, which, as explained by Albert Frey, is a portmanteau combining the Latin word *lumina* (irregular plural of *lux*, "light" in Latin) and the word "air," synthesized with the name of the predominant material in the construction, aluminum.[14]

Despite its popularity and extraordinary diffusion in the publications of its time, the Aluminaire House was always subject to a certain marginalization, which left it away from the main currents of the evolution of modern architecture in the United States. The reasons for this strangeness can be better understood through the study

Figure 1.2. A. Lawrence Kocher and Albert Frey. Aluminaire House. Henry-Russell Hitchcock and Philip Johnson's book, *The International Style. Architecture Since 1922.* Page 163. 1936. Palm Springs Art Museum. Albert Frey Collection, 55-1999.2.

of a second image of the Aluminaire House, siting on its new location on Long Island, as illustrated in Hitchcock and Johnson's book. **(Figure 1.2)**

If the first image of the Aluminaire House—as the "House of the Future" in *Popular Mechanics*—was close to a descriptive scientific or technological illustration, this second iteration, in *The International Style*, was strongly bound to the imaginary of mechanical visual arts: photography and cinema. The photograph shows a frontal view of the access façade. In the picture, the house is represented as a blank canvas. The shadows of the trees on the house's reflecting surfaces, windows, and aluminum panels painted a series of changing abstract shapes. Like the photosensitive plate of a camera, the house was able to register and reveal the forms and movement of the surrounding natural context, but it was unable neither to effectively interact with, nor to produce any substantial alteration on it. In the picture, the house stands uncomfortably on the ground, an object imposed to the site; it does not dominate or reign over the surrounding landscape as magnificently as the Villa Savoye—one of its precedents. With its abstract and compact vertical volume, the Aluminaire House, its light and shiny materiality, seems to be precariously rooted, suggesting a transitional occupation of the space: the sensation of the domestic mobility.

Since images produced by a particular society are but symptomatic of an attitude towards the subjects of the images, these two images summarize the dual stance American architectural historians and critics have toward the Aluminaire House. On the one hand, the house has been studied as a laboratory for material and technological innovation, a mechanical object in which technology and functionality supersede any cultural implications—an experiment of housing production more than an exploration of house design. On the other hand, the house has been regarded by most critics as a brilliant yet isolated case, a curiosity without historic continuity. It has been interpreted as a graft of modern European architecture without connection to any American precedent, which, although it could take precarious roots, did not bear any fruit. Its novel materiality and formal structure also contributed to its consideration as an "erratic" object forcibly inserted in the context of the American East Coast.[15] Despite these biases, the Aluminaire House is a key component of the American modern architectural tradition, capable both of influencing its future and inducing a reinterpretation of its past.

If the Aluminaire House bears a false duality in the history of American modern architecture, the same can be said about the architectural critic's assessment of the design team that made it possible. The Aluminaire House was the first common design endeavor of two architects: Alfred Lawrence Kocher and Albert Frey. Since their first meeting, Kocher and Frey represented an uneven but complementary professional pair. A married, 45-year-old Californian, Kocher was already established professionally on the East Coast and had long ago consolidated a reputation as a practitioner, researcher, educator, and the managing editor of *Architectural Record.* With excellent technical skills achieved during his education in Switzerland and his workdays in several European architecture offices, including the office of Le Corbusier in Paris, the unmarried, 27-year-old Frey was a promising designer searching for his first job opportunity in New York. Kocher was a renowned specialist in American vernacular architecture; Frey was a newcomer carrying an idealized view of America. The false duality constructed by architectural historians and critics considers Frey the main designer and relegates Kocher to the secondary roles of front man for client relationships, and project administration. One was predestined for success, the other doomed to oblivion.

September of 1930 was a life-changing month in the professional biography of Lawrence Kocher. Early in the month, he received the commission to design a display for the 1931 Architectural League of New York exhibition. The institution's previous three years of modestly sized expositions were held at the American Fine Arts Society Building on West 57 Street in New York City. Decidedly, 1931 marked the 50th anniversary of the Architectural League's founding, and to celebrate, an upscaled event at the more spacious venue of the Grand Central Palace on Lexington Avenue was planned. This new venue demanded a much bigger public audience to become a success. To address this necessity, the administrative leaders of the league—Harvey Corbett, Raymond Hood, and Jacques Elli Kahn—suggested Lawrence Kocher as the exhibition manager of the 45th Annual Exhibition, a good option to attract the general public's attention. In the 1929 Architecture and Allied Arts Exposition, also held in the Grand Central Palace just three years prior, Kocher designed the interior finishes and the furniture for a "Modern Architect Office" alongside architect Gerhard Ziegler, which had been extremely successful in attracting a non-specialized audience.

Just days after the Architectural League commission that September, another event took place to deeply influence the architect's professional path. He received the visit of a young Swiss architect named Albert Frey, who had just arrived from Zurich via Ellis Island. Frey had been visiting several architectural offices looking for employment during his first week in the city, interested only in those firms who followed the modern trend. Using American architecture magazines as a refence, Frey was aware of Kocher's collaborative work with Ziegler, and was particularly impressed by the furniture they designed for the Architecture and Allied Arts Exposition, which was placed in Kocher's office at *Architectural Record* at the time of their meeting. Kocher was likely pleased with Frey's experience in Le Corbusier's atelier, as he had always been very fond of Le Corbusier's work and had advocated for its diffusion in the States since his arrival to *Architectural Record.* In fact, *Architectural Record* was the very first American magazine to publish a review of Le Corbusier's *Towards a New Architecture*, written by Henry-Russell Hitchcock, and a text by Le Corbusier himself, "Architecture, the Expression of the Materials and Methods of our Times."[16] These two pioneering articles ignited a series of publications by and about Le Corbusier in the magazine along with a fluid, epistolary relationship between the Swiss master and the American editor as revealed in the archives of both the A. Lawrence Kocher Collection at Colonial Williamsburg and the Fondation Le Corbusier in Paris.

Since Ziegler had recently departed from New York, Kocher was in need of help to develop the commissioned Architecture League exhibition while simultaneously attending his new responsibilities at *Architectural Record.* After chatting about their common Swiss ancestry, Kocher offered Frey a position to collaborate in the coming projects with a generous weekly stipend of 25 dollars. The offer also

Figure 1.3. A. Lawrence Kocher and Albert Frey. Aluminaire House. Preliminary project 1930. Perspective view.

included meals and board with him and his wife; they had a spare bedroom, bathroom, and workroom in their house on Park End Place in the Forest Hills neighborhood of Long Island. Frey accepted the offer, moved to Long Island, and immediately began conferring with Kocher on how to frame the Grand Central Palace exhibition project. Kocher explained to Frey his profuse research about American vernacular architecture, how each period's technical proficiency and ways of living were fundamental in determining the design of buildings.[17] Both architects were very aware of the coeval economical context as it had been nearly one year since the Black Tuesday stock market crash that ignited the Great Depression.[18] The financial crisis rapidly derived in nearly all housing construction coming to a halt in the United States and in the inability of millions of Americans to continue payments on their home mortgages, leading to foreclosures on bank loans.[19] Kocher and Frey started envisioning a domestic prototype as an exhibition object to test the use of new materials and modern prefabricated systems—a means to decrease construction cost and time to help solve the housing shortage. **(Figure 1.3)**

Aside from budgetary limits, the architects faced several restrictions regarding display placement within the available space at Grand Central Palace. They had a 22-by-28-foot footprint available and a maximum clearance of three stories. Of course, there was also the maximum load for the building slabs, along with the regular requirements regarding fire egress and security. Time was also an important parameter as there was a 10-day gap between exhibitions in the venue; meaning, the structure should be suitable for fast assembly and disassembly. The curator additionally required that if they were doing a demonstration house, "only one of each type of room could be included."[20]

After a period of analysis and conceptual framing, the actual design process of the Aluminaire House began in November of 1930, ending in April of 1931. Kocher and Frey drafted a basic set of documents—including plans, elevations, and sections—of an extremely light prefabricated house, allegedly, for a married couple. **(Figures 1.4 and 1.5)** Frey made a 1/4"=1'-0"-scale model of the Aluminaire House and, together with Kocher, presented it to the authorities, along with suppliers and manufacturers of materials and products incorporated into the house. The idea was to test new material applications that were considered unusual in residential construction, testing their suitability for low-cost housing projects. **(Figures 1.6 to 1.8)** The home was designed to be industrially reproduced for 3,200 dollars and built with materials donated by various companies.[21] Promoted by the Aluminum Company of America, the most outstanding features of the house were the extension of its glazed surfaces and the intensive use of aluminum. Aluminum was used as a façade cladding and in all visible structural elements; the remaining structure was made of steel. A pioneer in the multiple applications of aluminum, the house was also the first non-industrial building to use Ferrobord folded steel decks.

In the history of architecture, there are very few precedents that materially deploy aluminum, and with such variation, as the Aluminaire House.[22] The Roman church of *San Gioacchino* (1890–1898), by architect Raffaele Ingami, is the first recorded use of aluminum cladding a façade —specifically, an external covering for the dome. Aluminum was used by Otto Wagner in 1903 for the façade of the *Die Zeit* newspaper agency and in 1906 as an interior covering on the Vienna Savings Bank. In the United States, Francis Plym first established patents for aluminum window frames in 1905, which progressively replaced wooden frames. As for the structural use of aluminum in the field of architecture, the new spire for the Smithfield United Church in Pittsburgh, designed by Henry Hornbostel in 1926, represents only one precedent built in the United States. Richard Buckminster Fuller produced his designs for the Dymaxion House in 1929, prior to the Aluminaire House, but these designs did not actually materialize until after World War II with the Wichita House, constructed entirely of aluminum. The first prototypes of the aluminum monocoque Airstream caravan were manufactured in 1936, four years after the Aluminaire House was erected. Aluminum had, however, already been widely used in aircraft construction, especially in the structure of late-19th- and early-20th-century airships. Thanks to metallurgist Alfred Wilm's invention of *Duraluminium* in 1910, aluminum was established as a basic material in airplanes; from 1936 on, airplanes were built exclusively in this material.[23]

The extensive and innovative use of aluminum in the Aluminaire House was the result of Kocher's years of research on new materials. In the "Technical News and Research" section of *Architectural Record*'s October 1929 issue, Kocher's editorial team explored many of the building systems used in what would later be the Aluminaire House: industrial steel window sashes, pressed-steel decks, metal spandrels, and aluminum façades. Notably, the use of these façade solutions decreased the thickness of the exterior walls from 13 inches to an even two inches and their structural load from 90 pounds per lineal foot to a mere eight pounds per lineal foot.[24] Built with a total thickness of three inches, the external walls were a mix of a non-structural balloon frame and a frame composed of steel angles fixed to two-by-two-inch wood nailers with a one-foot separation. One -half-inch rigid insulation board covered the frame on each side, and a washable Fabrikoid fabric, manufactured by the DuPont Company, finished the interior board. The exterior board was covered with a layer of waterproof building paper and clad with three-by-three-foot sheets of vertically corrugated polished aluminum, fastened to the boards with aluminum screws and washers. The façade frame was not directly top-loaded on the perimetral girders and joists; instead, there were cantilevered connection pieces that linked the studs laterally to the beams. **(Figure 1.9 and 1.10)** These small cantilevers were made of double-channel profiles, a solution that allowed for a continuous aluminum wrap of the building's external surfaces without any interruptions and without thermal bridges. This construction method was possible due to the lighter weight of the façade, conveying insignificant torsion stress to the beams.

The Aluminaire House's structural dimensions are 28 feet, 9 inches, by 22 feet, 8 inches, and a net area of 1,098 square feet, which excludes the garage and 463 square feet of terrace.[25] It has three levels with a reduced distance between finished floors of 9 feet and a total height of 27 feet. According to archival documents, the material palette of the house makes it extremely light, weighing in at 47,310 pounds, including the appliances, furniture, and mechanical systems.[26] The structure is supported by six columns, five inches in diameter. On each floor, there is a set of three primary beams made of

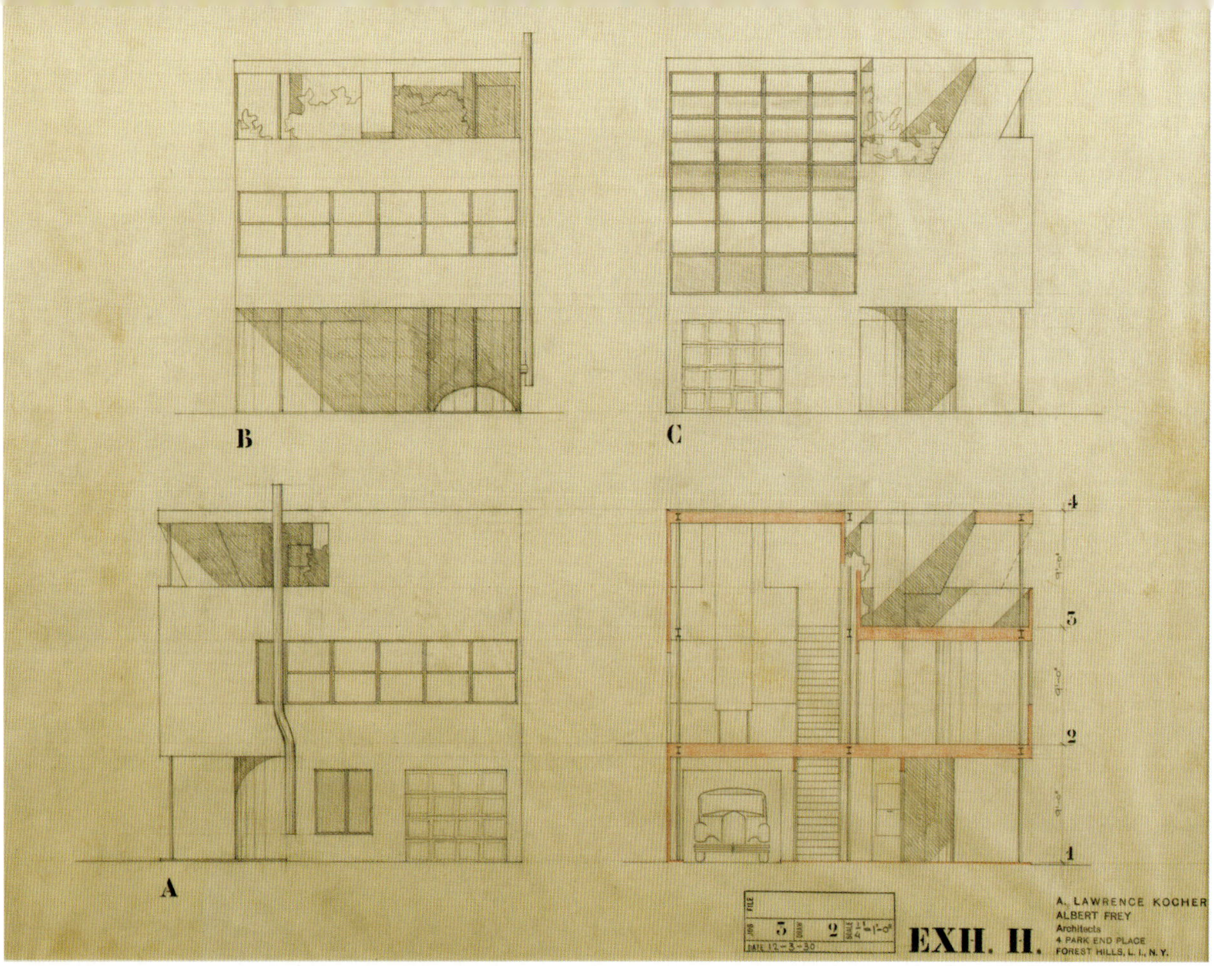
B
C
A
A. LAWRENCE KOCHER
ALBERT FREY
Architects
4 PARK END PLACE
FOREST HILLS, L. I., N. Y.
EXH. H.

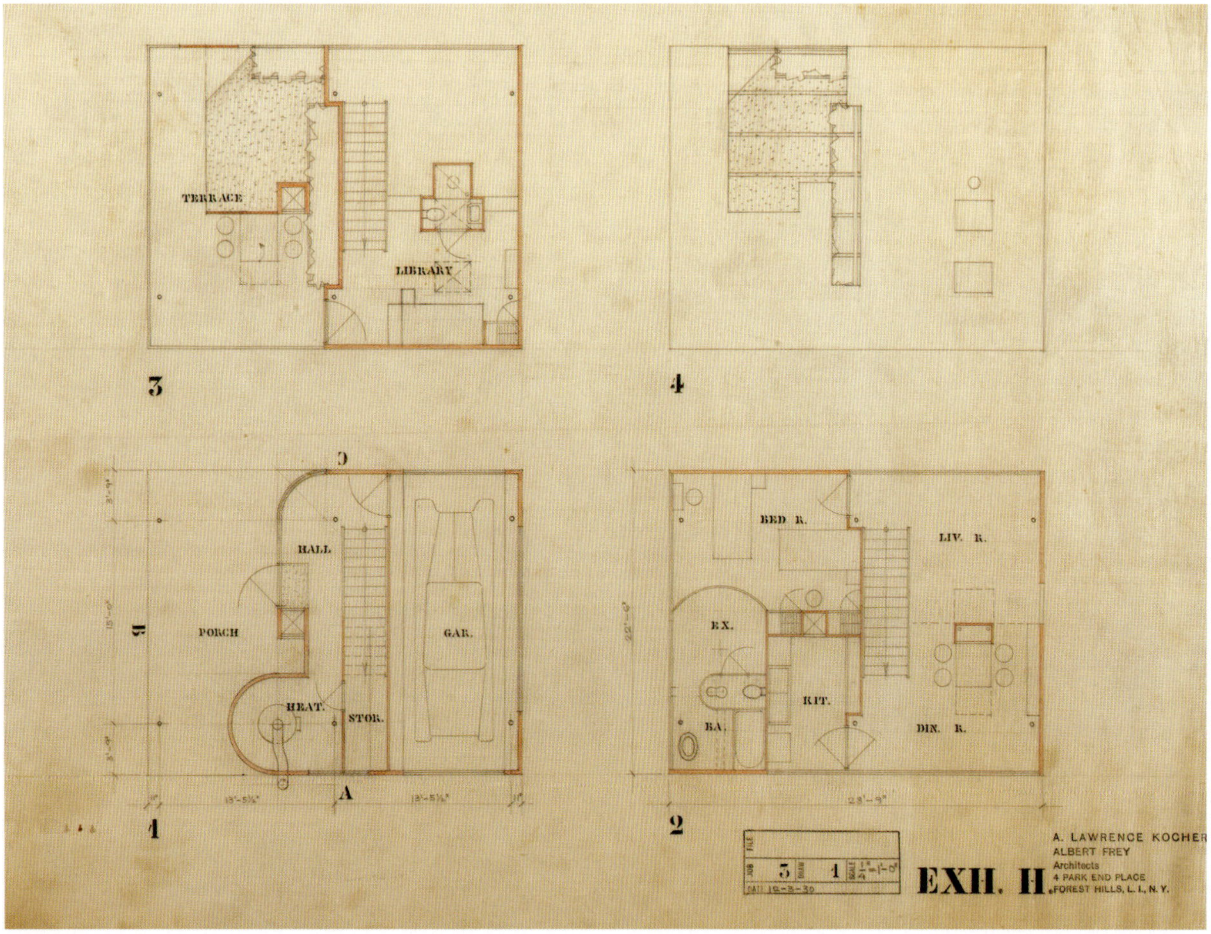
TERRACE
LIBRARY
3
4
HALL
PORCH
GAR.
HEAT.
STOR.
BED R.
LIV. R.
EX.
KIT.
BA.
DIN. R.
1
2
A. LAWRENCE KOCHER
ALBERT FREY
Architects
4 PARK END PLACE
FOREST HILLS, L. I., N. Y.
EXH. H.

double aluminum channels seven inches thick and 5-3/4-inches wide each attached laterally to these columns. The double girders, which are not exposed, are made of steel and have the same dimensions. The girders span two central bays of 14 feet, 10 inches, and they end in two lateral cantilevers of three feet, two inches. The secondary structure is made of channel and I-shape joists which span 13 feet, 4-1/2 inches from girder to girder and are normally three feet, two inches apart. All the structural elements were connected with bolted steel angles. These screwed connections allowed for a fast assembly and disassembly of the structure. **(Figure 1.11)** Above the joists sits a prefabricated steel deck from Truscon Steel Co.[27] called *Ferrobord* and measuring 1-3/4 inches thick, eight inches wide, and 12 feet long.[28] The decks are fire-proofed with one-foot panels of wood fiber supplied by the Thermax Corporation. The finished flooring is linoleum in different colors.

Another primary technological innovation of the house was the façade's glazing system, which held violet-ray glass, like that prescribed for the Sunlight Towers, an unbuilt high-rise housing project designed by Kocher and Ziegler years before. The Truscon Steel Company manufactured the Aluminaire House's industrialized sash window frames using a catalog of standardized rolled steel profiles. **(Figure 1.12)** Their reversible operation allowed maintenance from inside the house. The interior finishes were also highly innovative, designed for hygiene and low maintenance. Along with the profusely used Fabrikoid, the main bathroom walls were clad with black Vitrolite, a pigmented structural glass produced by the Pittsburgh Plate Glass Company. The bathroom's curved toilet compartment was made of white translucent Lumarith—an injection-molded cellulose acetate manufactured by the Celluloid Company—and supported with a polished aluminum frame. **(Figures 1.13 to 1.15)** The doors were steel-faced, the cabinets and fixed furniture were finished with glass and Bakelite. The stair had aluminum-painted steel risers and rubber treads with aluminum nosing.

The program of the house was distributed across its three floors. The first floor included a porch and an access hall that led to the circulating stair. The remaining area of this level was devoted to technical features: storage, a water-heater room, a drive-through garage with two automatized overhead doors, and a dumbwaiter that moved between the kitchen, main bedroom, and terrace. **(Figures 1.16 and 1.17)**

The most heavily programmed level was the second floor. **(Figure 1.18)** Occupying half of the floor area, a double-height living and dining area was slightly segregated by a glass and steel cupboard supported by two non-structural pipes and an extensible dining table. The other half of this level contained the kitchen, linked to both the dining room and the master bedroom suite with access from the living room. This L-shaped space is devoted not only to rest but also to exercise and hygiene. Everything in this room aimed toward efficiency and ease of maintenance. The beds and the dressing table were fixed in place and did not touch the floor; the beds were suspended, allowing easy access to clean below them, and the dressing table cantilevered from the spandrel under the windows, it's glass countertop and translucent drawers were made out of Lumarith, echoing the curved bathroom. An exercise room separated the resting spaces from the bathroom, which could further transition from the bedroom by deploying a folding partition on a curved track. The toilet was also separated from the rest of the bathroom with a hemicylindrical cubicle of translucent plastic. The disposition of all the elements in this bathroom was unconventional, and every piece was custom designed. The sink detached from the walls and was sustained by a central post, the deployable back-lit round mirror rotated and slid along a vertical pipe attached to the lintel and the spandrel of the longitudinal windows. The unconventional layout of the bathroom was also highly functional: it allowed for enough privacy to do various simultaneous activities without cross-disturbances and also to preserve an uninterrupted view through the panoramic window that spans across all the different spaces. **(Figures 1.19 to 1.23)**

Finally, the third floor of the house was limited in area due to the living room's double height. **(Figure 1.24)** The open stair connected to a mezzanine with a library and a smaller bathroom adjacent to the rooftop garden terrace, equipped with a lawn area and two elevated planters labeled as "flower boxes." The terrace included a covered dining space, served by the dumbwaiter, and connected with the second-floor entry hall and kitchen.

Detailed in the project's original documentation, the furniture within the house also merits special attention. The pieces that were actually fabricated and exhibited followed the canonical functionalist style to the furniture designed by Kocher and Ziegler for their display, "Office of a Modern Architect," in the 1929 Architecture and Allied Arts Exposition. In the Aluminaire House, there were many other highly experimental furniture elements that were never built. The storable, rotating bathroom mirror, easy chairs, inflatable rubber chaise lounges, spiral stools, fold-away terrace table, and hanging beds never left the drafting board, though some of these ideas did resurface in later designs. **(Figures 1.25 to 1.28)** Designs for hanging furniture were later repeated both in Frey's California projects, including his own house in Palm Springs (1956), and Kocher's later projects, such as the tables in the student rooms at Black Mountain College (1940–1941).

In just one week—from April 11th to 18th, 1931—the Aluminaire House was assembled in the Grand Central Palace exhibition hall and displayed from the 18th to the 25th. It was dismantled in just six hours on April 26th. Amazed by its ease for assembly and disassembly, several media outlets gave the house different names: *Time Magazine* called it the "Magic House," the *Brooklyn Eagle* named it "The Zipper House," while other periodicals dubbed it other names, such as "The All-Metal House," "The House of the Future," and "Peak-a-boo Domain."[29] The Architectural League exhibition had an admission fee of 75 cents and a large attendance—*The New York Times* reported more than 100,000 visitors during its one-week run. The show's success was not free of controversy: the only exhibited works from modern architects were those of Kocher and Frey, along with Howe and Lescaze. This provoked a response from various modern architects who, upon the rejection of their work, accused the Architectural League of being conservative, resulting in a parallel exhibition organized nearby at 903 Seventh Avenue, called the *Salón des Refusés*. Opening in tandem with the Architectural League's show, organizers of the *Salón des Refusés* exhibition offered free admission and advertised by picketing directly

Previous page:
Figures 1.4 and 1.5. A. Lawrence Kocher and Albert Frey. Aluminaire House. Preliminary project 1930. Plans, elevations, and section.

This page:
Figures 1.6, 1.7, and 1.8. A. Lawrence Kocher and Albert Frey. Aluminaire House. Preliminary project 1930. Model photos.

in front of the Grand Central Palace. Running until May 5th, their alternative exhibition aimed to educate the public on *real* modern style, especially after being confronted with the mostly conservative Beaux-Arts style of the Architectural League show. The architects participating in this parallel exhibition were: Clauss and Daub, Hazen Sise, William Muschenheim, Walter Baermann, and Elroy Webber—all from New York—along with Storonov and Morgen from Philadelphia.[30] Nevertheless, the *Salón des Refusés* organizers declared great appreciation for the Aluminaire House as the (almost) only modern work in the whole show.

The Aluminaire House's itinerant existence began upon the closing of the Architectural League exhibition.[31] Prior to the 1931 exhibition, architect Wallace K. Harrison—a partner at Corbett, Harrison & MacMurray, one of the firms that participated in the design of the Rockefeller Center in New York—and his wife Ellen purchased an 85-acre plot of land in South Huntington, Long Island. The property was a former farm, and while it included two granaries and various other farm buildings, the sprawling site lacked a house. Since they did not have enough money to build a new home, they opted for a ready, cheap solution and purchased the Aluminaire House. As friends of A. Lawrence Kocher, they bought the disassembled house for 1,000 dollars—its pieces numbered with chalk— and had it transported in a single truck to their plot on Long Island.[32] According to historian Joseph Rosa, the house was stored at its new location in the open air and a torrential rain washed off the chalk numbering. This incident, which brings to mind the events of Buster Keaton's film *One Week*, increased the time and cost of the reconstruction and determined that the (re)assembly of the house did not guarantee structural stability.[33] Other sources blamed the delay on the construction system of the aluminum skin.[34] Either way, what is certain is that instead of the 18 days estimated by the architects for reconstruction, it took several months and the house needed additional bracing to stiffen the structure against lateral loads. **(Figures 1.29 and 1.30)**

The couple lived in the reassembled house for eight years until they could complete the construction of their permanent residence. The Aluminaire House underwent numerous extensions during the Harrisons' occupation, reflecting the different construction phases. The first building addition was the cylindrical area of the new dining room, which connected to the ground floor in 1932. Shortly after, another cylindrical area, double in size, was added as a living room. Other successive additions adjoining the Aluminaire House included a new kitchen and bedroom wing; the Harrisons completed their home with the stables and garage by 1940.[35] **(Figures 1.31 and 1.32)**

Having played its part as a starter home, the Aluminaire House was slid or pushed on the slopes of a small hill elsewhere on the Harrisons' land. Adapting it to the pitch, Harrison shifted access to the second floor, leaving the first floor as a daylight basement and closing off the terrace. In its new location, the house was used both as a guest house and for storage, and slowly deteriorated over the course of more than 40 years. It thus fulfilled its function as a colonizing house, temporary refuge, and "chrysalis." Following this pattern established by its American precedents, it was cast aside and abandoned. Writer J.B. Jackson gives a cogent explanation of this typical pattern in American houses:

> The typical ramshackle frame house in the midst of abandoned fields that we find throughout contemporary America; and when we know America well, we find nothing really sad in the spectacle. The deserted house, nine times out of ten, is a chrysalis which its inhabitants have happily escaped to some brighter or more alluring prospect. Only in the Old World, with its dream of permanence, does the deserted house or the deserted field invariably speak of human tragedy.[36]

The Harrison property changed hands twice, and the Aluminaire House became forgotten and abandoned, until 1986, when a new owner asked for permission to demolish it. After a great media campaign led by historian Joseph Rosa, the house was purchased by the New York Institute of Technology. The Aluminaire House was disassembled once more, so that it could be restored to its original state. In 1987, it was rebuilt by professors and students on the campus of the New York Institute of Technology (NYIT) School of Architecture in Central Islip, Long Island. Nearly two decades later, in 2004, NYIT sold the land on which the Aluminaire House sat, casting its future into doubt. The house was eventually donated to the Aluminaire House Foundation, created in 2010. By 2012, it was dismantled again and stored in a shipping container. The Foundation had long been seeking a new site for the house's reconstruction and in March of 2023 reassembled it in the gardens of the Palm Springs Art Museum, California.

The unfortunate events befalling the Aluminaire House during its stay on the Harrisons' land revealed the advantages and disadvantages of its status as an architectural crossover between European and American architectural traditions. Though the house was easily disassembled and transported, it was difficult to modify and expand—like any of Kocher and Frey's houses, building additions proved challenging without distorting the architecture, destroying their essential abstraction, or diverging from the modern principle of regularity.[37]—The Aluminaire House's transportability and mobility stemmed from its allegedly North American ancestry, which includes a wide range of housing types, such as log cabins, plank houses, balloon frames, and primitive wooden prefabricated systems, like the Sears Roebuck catalog homes. It is arguable that because of their formal features, technology, material choice, and proposed way of life, the Aluminaire House and other subsequent domestic experiments by A. Lawrence Kocher and Albert Frey have another less evident yet assured lineage: the wagons of westward colonization, primitive camping trailers and caravans, and the first motor homes.

In fact, the lack of flexibility in Kocher and Frey's houses is seemingly derived from Corbusian ancestry, connecting it with the tradition of the European suburban villa, and the Aluminaire House showed this undeniable influence. To expand Le Corbusier's Villa Savoye or Andrea Palladio's Villa Capra would be to undermine their architectural integrity—their designs are frozen in a state of finished perfection, where stability and proportion play essential roles. To start with the obvious, the Aluminaire House's design is strongly linked to two of Le Corbusier and Pierre Jeanneret's residential works in which Frey collaborated most intensely: the Villa Savoye and the Maisons Loucheur.

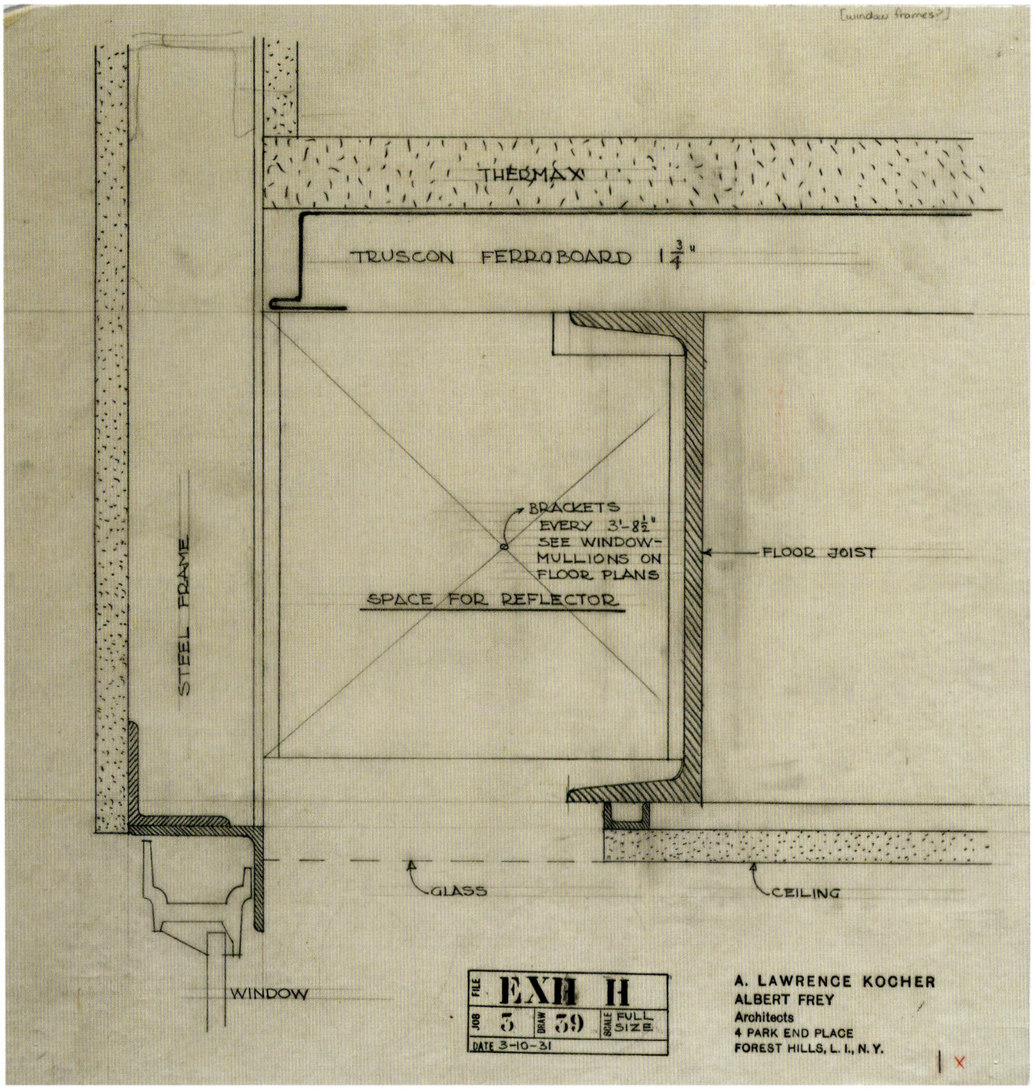

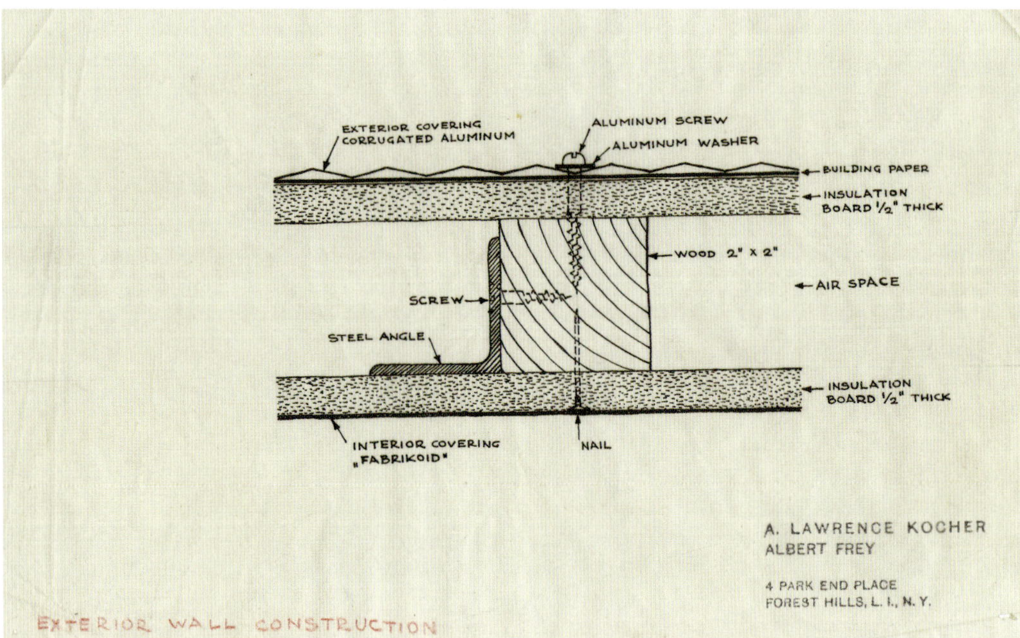

Figures 1.9 and 1.10. A. Lawrence Kocher and Albert Frey. Aluminaire House. Preliminary project 1930. Details for jamb and mullions and diagram of exterior wall construction.

Like the Villa Savoye, the Aluminaire House was a *machine à habiter*, and the perfect fulfillment of Le Corbusier's Five Points of Architecture. Columns lifted the house to free the ground plane, it had an independent structure allowing for a free layout of the inner partitions and spaces, its façade was liberated from load-bearing functions and solely dependent on the requirements dictated by the program, it made profuse use of horizontal windows, and it included rooftop gardens and terraces. Both the Villa Savoye and the Aluminaire House share a common tripartite division in section and a bilateral division in plan. This tripartite division in section is also a typical feature of Palladian villas, derived from a strict social stratification: peasant houses and other agricultural activities are hosted on the first floor, the second floor or *piano nobile* is the owners' private residence, and the attic contains the dwellings of their domestic servants.[38] In Le Corbusier's villas, despite the arrival of contemporary social practices, the sectional division is maintained but for other necessary reasons: in the case of Villa Savoye, the *piano nobile* remains as the second floor, yet the first floor reconsiders the new necessities of the modern mechanical world, especially given the fading agricultural industry and its manual laborers. Attached to the ground, this level hosts garages for the recently popularized automobiles and the surplus of machinery necessary to fulfill the new comfort standards in the modern cult of healthy living. Further, physical exercise dictated the transformation of the attic into a rooftop terrace and solarium.

Yet unlike Villa Savoye, the Aluminaire House did not have a roof solarium—it was replaced by an attic library—but it did have a roof garden connected to the communal areas of the house. The dematerialization of the uppermost floor did not affect the exterior cubic volume, as it did in Villa Savoye where the rooftop program is expressed as independent forms, like a still-life composition on top of the roof slab. Instead, the Aluminaire House's structure continues around the terrace.[39] The primary structure of the Aluminaire House remained visible from the interior, uninterrupted in the double-height living room. The form's completion can be attributed to the need for lateral bracing in construction based on the semi-rigid bolted connections, which contrasted with the complete structural stiffness of concrete in the Corbusian examples. **(Figures 1.33 to 1.41)**

Despite the deletion of agricultural servants for a novel mechanized lifestyle, the domestic servants still had a place in the layout of Villa Savoye's architecture. The design of the villa was not only for the leisure of the wealthy clients, Pierre and Eugénie Savoye, but also considered the workplace and home of a numerous domestic staff. Social segregation persists in the project, but it is not evident in the section; rather, it is formalized in the plan with a clear bilateral division between the domains of the servants and that of the owners on each floor. This division in plan forces two differentiated vertical cores: the main circulation ramp placed in the symmetrical axis of the plan and the secondary service core for servants.[40] Both houses have a centralized vertical circulation in plan. The Aluminaire House's reduced size drove tight-fitting solutions using a stair instead of a ramp. The stair operated in a strictly functional role, without achieving the spatial richness, processional importance, and visual connectivity of Le Corbusier's ramp at the Villa Savoye. Nevertheless, situating the circulation core close to the central axis in the Aluminaire House created a symmetry in the plan, one that organized a zig-zagging vertical sequence of main spaces: the entry porch, double-height living room, and garden terrace.

The influence of the Villa Savoye on the Aluminaire House pertains only to the formal aspects, without any similitude regarding their respective social concerns. The Aluminaire House can be interpreted as an experiment about how the professional middle class could achieve a lifestyle integrated with nature. It could also be understood as an exploration in minimal housing. Unlike the Villa Savoye, the Aluminaire House is meant to be inhabited by a family without servants, and in the context of the Great Depression, this may have been regarded as the extravagance of a privileged social class.

Beyond their formal differences and diverse scale, what sets the Aluminaire House apart from its French counterpart is the building technology. Le Corbusier relied heavily on the use of water and an intensive manual labor force: cast-on-site reinforced concrete structures, plastered masonry walls and partitions, and heavy pavements were construction techniques far from prefabrication or industrialization. Alternatively, the structure of the Aluminaire House was prefabricated entirely in a workshop and assembled on site, as were the rest of the materials and systems—from the framed partitions to the three-inch façades, the linoleum floors to the pressed steel decks.

Regarding its materiality and construction strategy, the Aluminaire House is reminiscent of Le Corbusier's Maisons Loucheur, a multi-family proposal for social housing in a program partnership with the French government to help stimulate the steel industry while providing necessary housing at the time. During his time in Le Corbusier's atelier, Frey participated in the design of the Maisons Loucheur. The third design proposal scheme revealed the construction of a steel framework over slender steel pillars, but different options were studied for the façade cladding—steel and zinc sheets, along with wood boards—all of which would attach to the structural frame with screwed connections. Much like the modular system of Corbusier's Maison Dom-Ino, the Aluminaire House replaced concrete with steel, and the three-story section is reduced to two horizontal planes creating a more minimal house elevation. Some authors establish relations between the Maisons Loucheur and other works by Le Corbusier and Pierre Jeanneret, such as the Maison Minimum and the Gardener's House of the Villa Savoye, but the materiality of the Maisons Loucher makes them a unique work amid the rest of Le Corbusier's oeuvre.[41] Frey was not the only one familiar with the Maisons Loucheur design; the August 1930 issue of *Architectural Record* included a complete dossier of the houses under the enthusiastic title, "The Minimal House: A Solution."[42] **(Figure 1.42)**

The Aluminaire House and the Maisons Loucheur share few formal similarities but are more connected to shared research on minimal domestic space and lightweight construction. The Maisons Loucheur are one of the clearest attempts by Le Corbusier and Pierre Jeanneret to "Americanize" their architecture through industrialized construction and furniture. In this project, the use of configurable elements could transform the house according to the needs of its inhabitants. Accompanying publications of these multi-family houses depicted a diagram demonstrating the diverse programmatic distributions by day and by night, achieved through the extensive

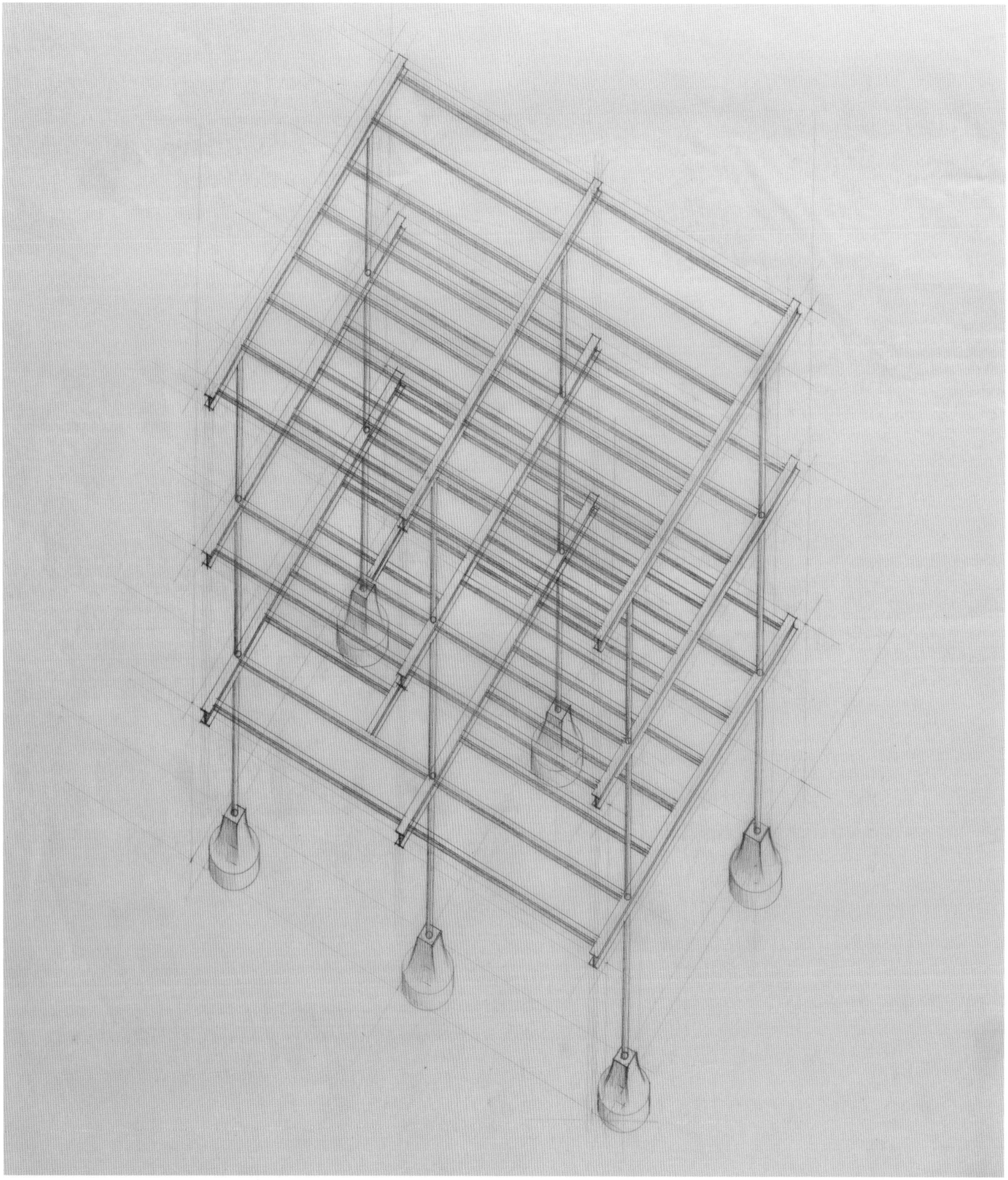

Figure 1.11. A. Lawrence Kocher and Albert Frey. Aluminaire House. Preliminary project 1930. Axonometric view of the structure.

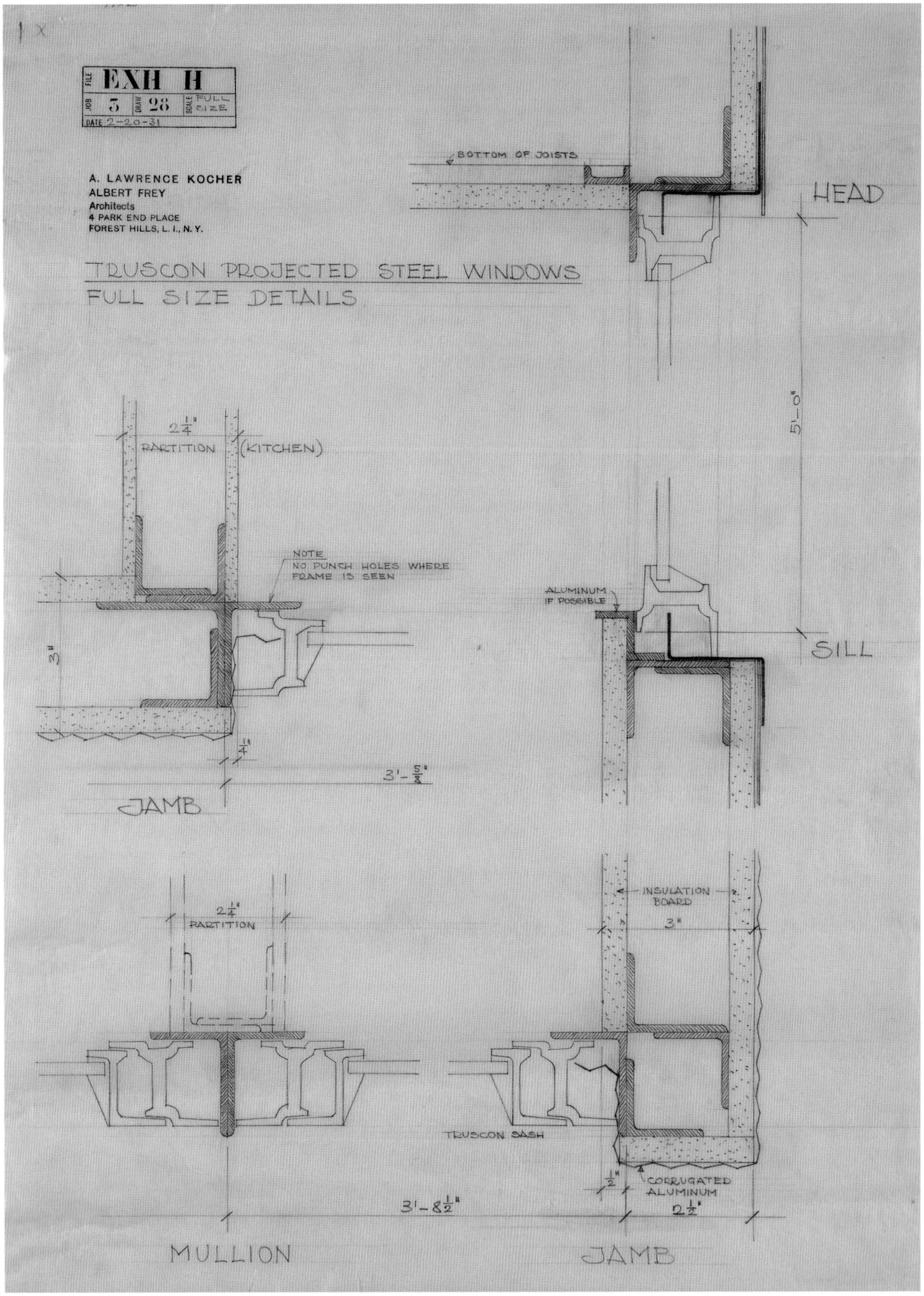

Figure 1.12. A. Lawrence Kocher and Albert Frey. Aluminaire House. Preliminary project 1930. Details for mullions and jambs.

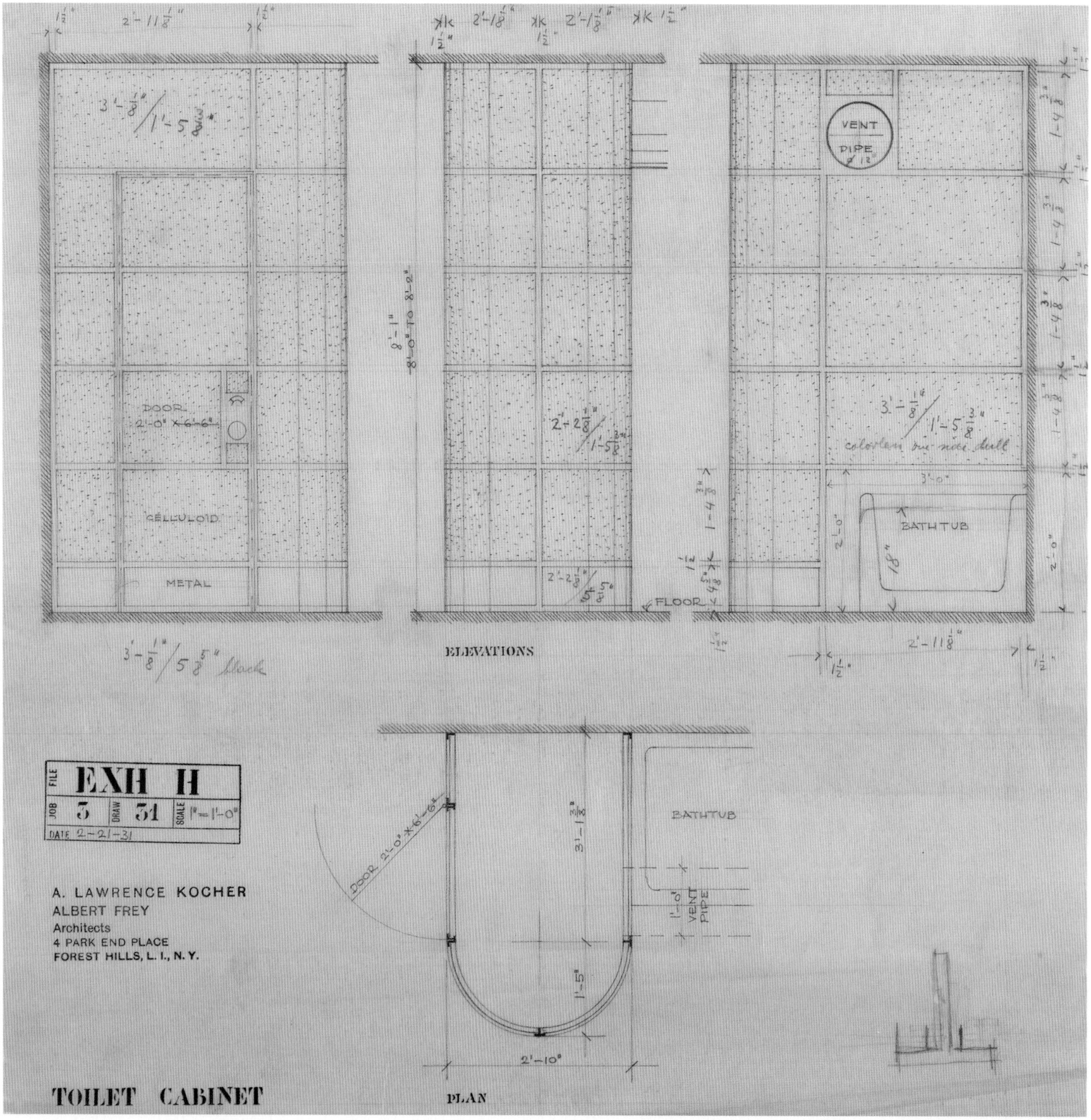

Figure 1.13. A. Lawrence Kocher and Albert Frey. Aluminaire House. Preliminary project 1930. Bathroom details. Toilet cabinet.

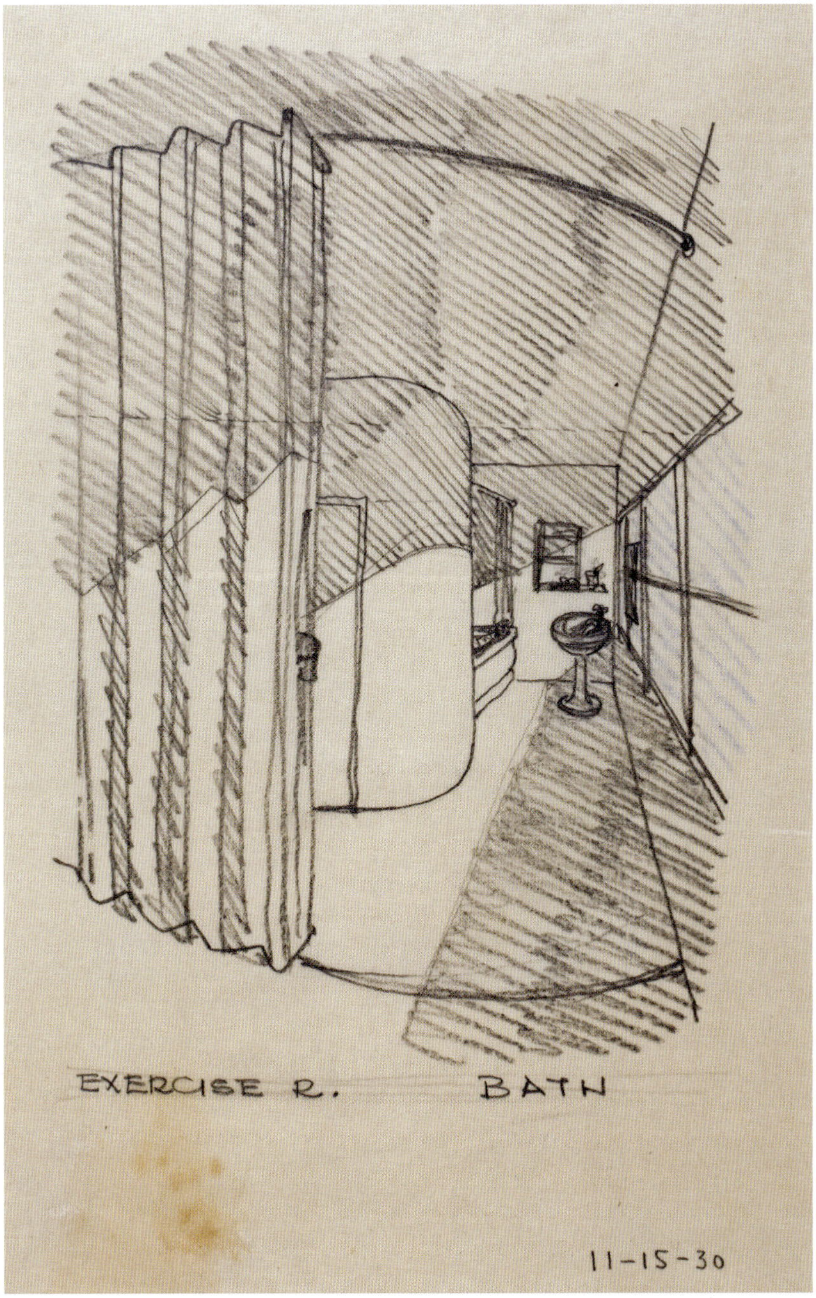

Figure 1.14. A. Lawrence Kocher and Albert Frey. Aluminaire House. Preliminary project 1930. Bathroom details. Exercise room. Sketch dated 11-15-1930.
Figure 1.15. A. Lawrence Kocher and Albert Frey. Aluminaire House. Preliminary project 1930. Bathroom details. Exercise room and bathroom. Sketch undated.

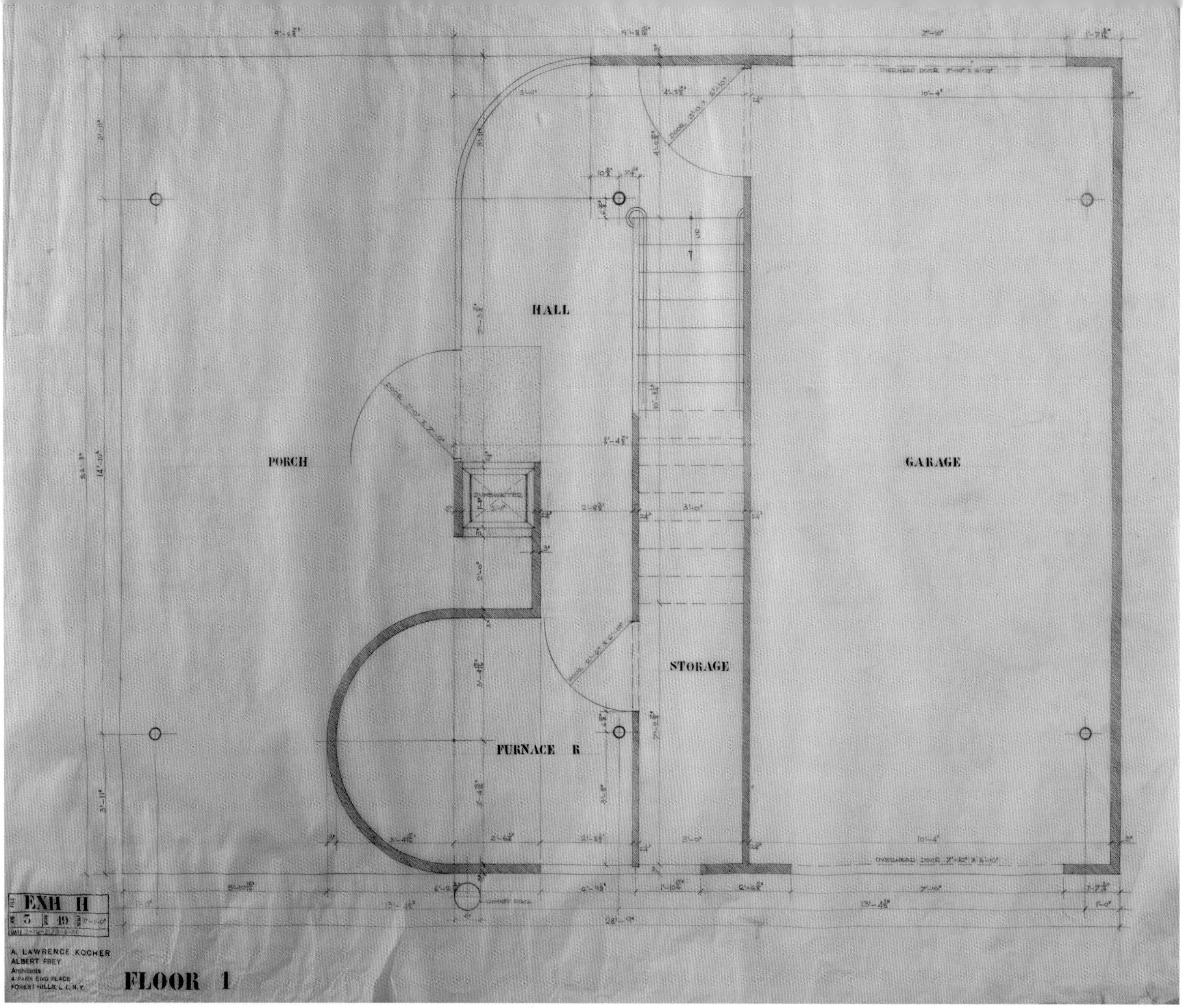

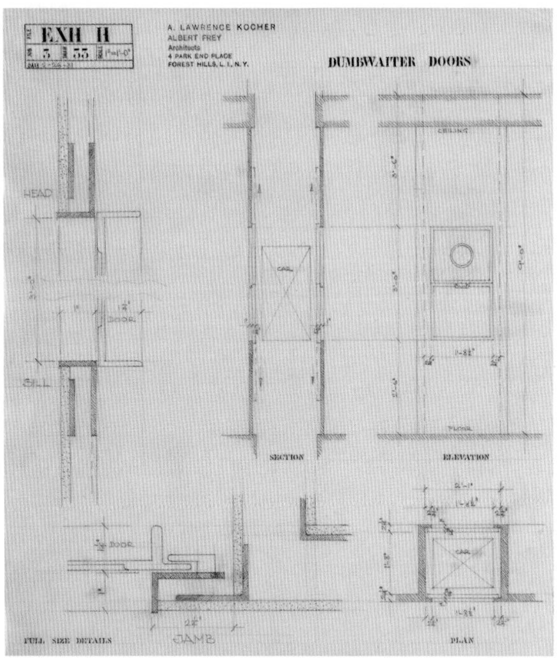

Figure 1.16. A. Lawrence Kocher and Albert Frey. Aluminaire House. Preliminary project 1930. First floor plan.
Figure 1.17. A. Lawrence Kocher and Albert Frey. Aluminaire House. Preliminary project 1930. Dumbwaiter details.

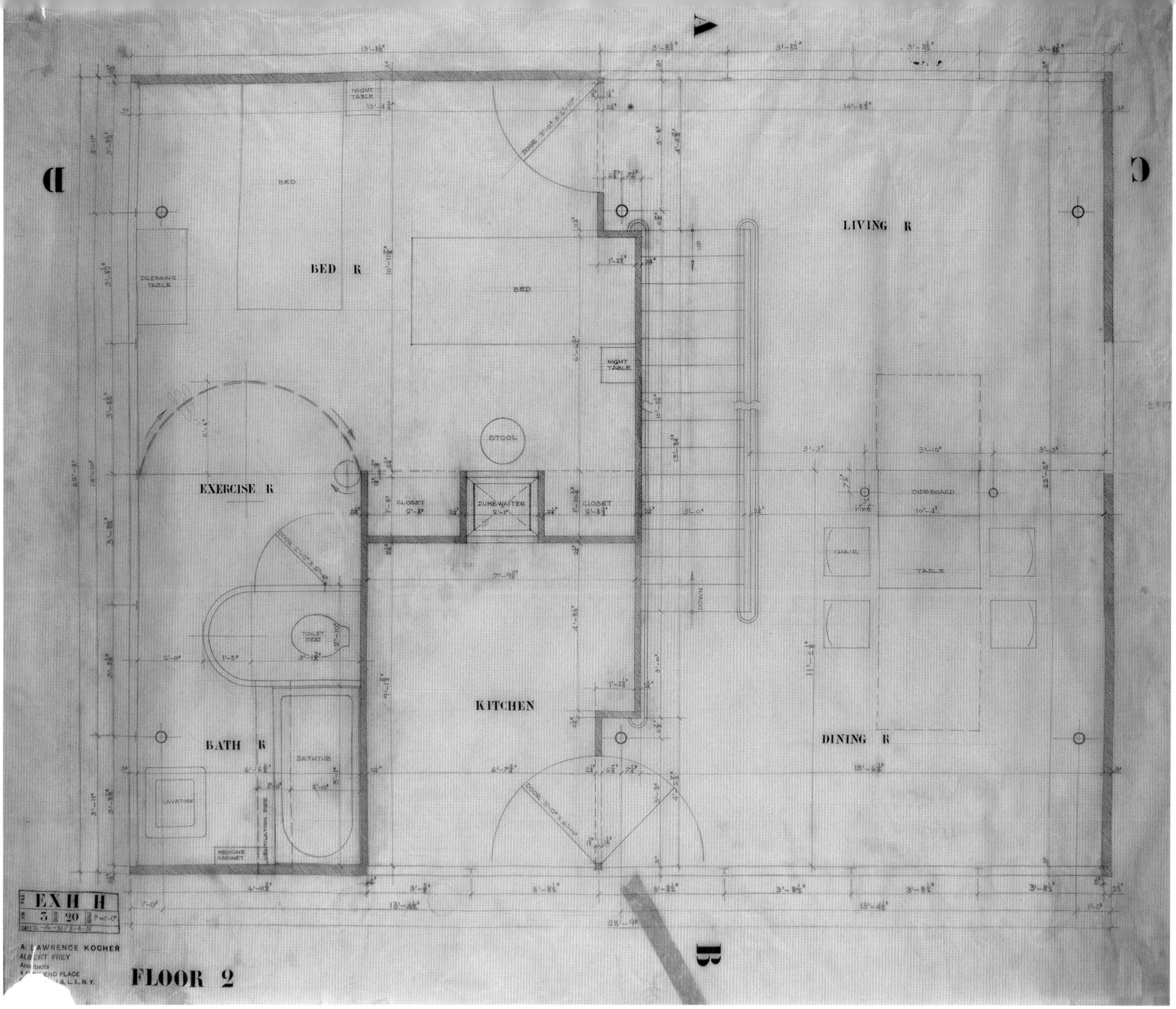

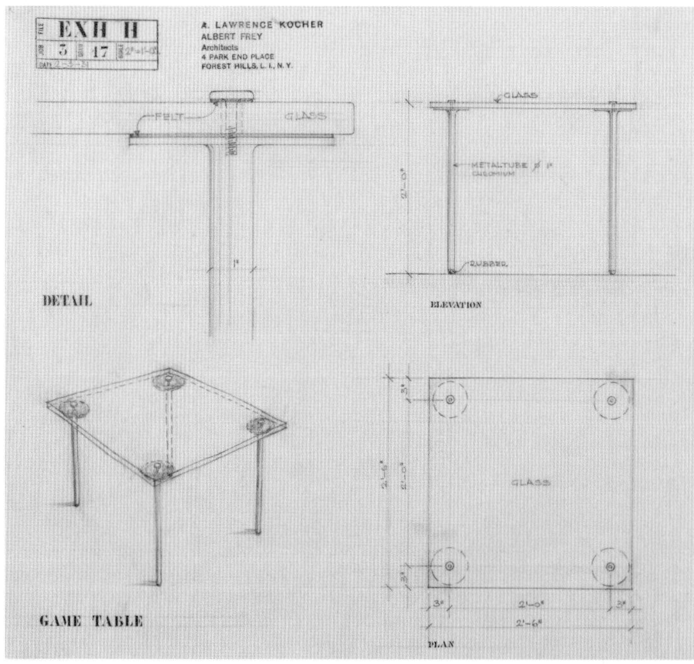

Figure 1.18. A. Lawrence Kocher and Albert Frey. Aluminaire House. Preliminary project 1930. Second floor plan.

Figure 1.19. A. Lawrence Kocher and Albert Frey. Aluminaire House. Preliminary project 1930. Living room. Game table details.

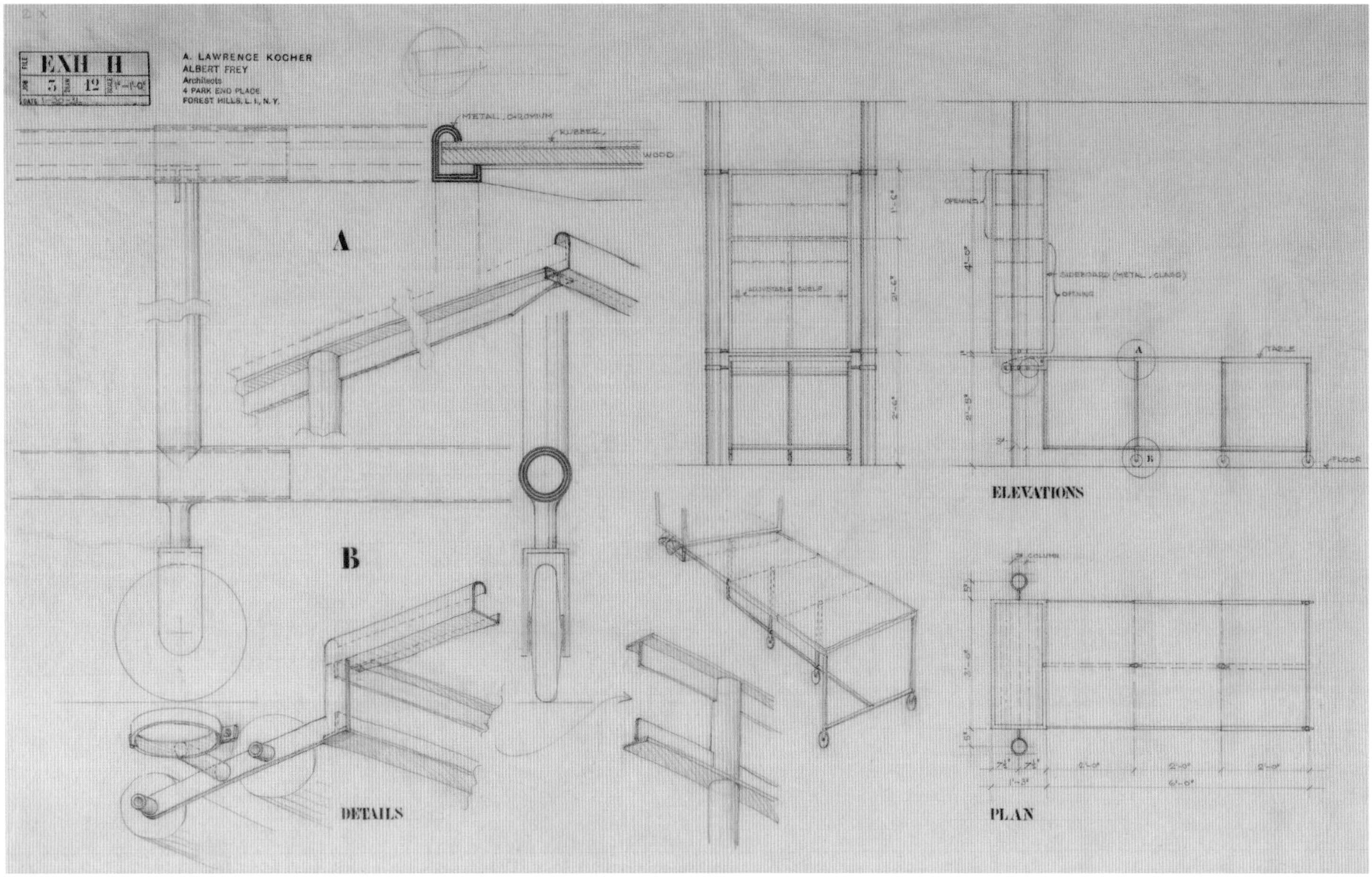

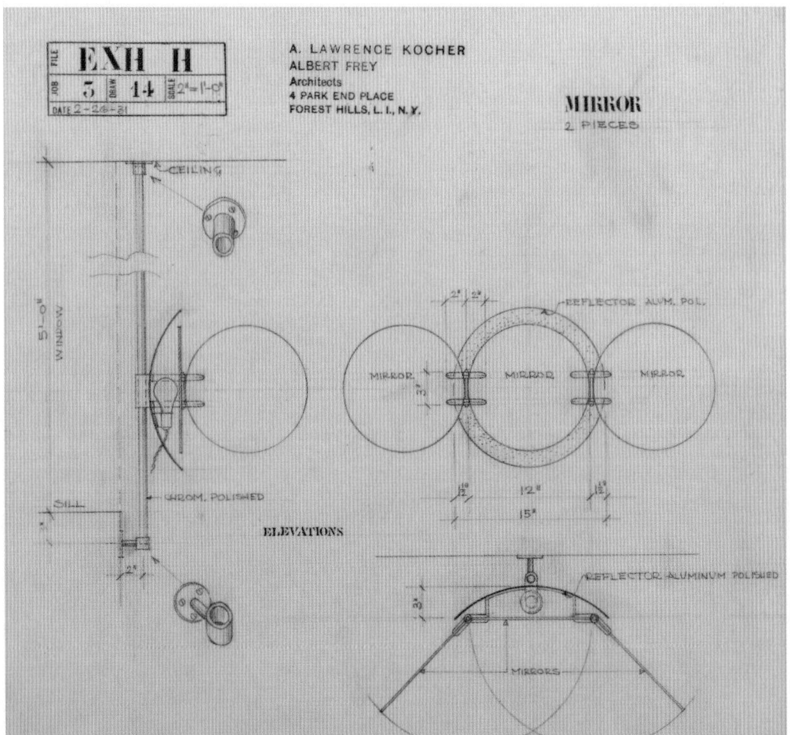

This page:
Figure 1.20. A. Lawrence Kocher and Albert Frey. Aluminaire House. Preliminary project 1930. Second floor plan details. Extensible dining table.
Figure 1.21. Second floor plan details. Rotating mirror of the bathroom.

Next page:
Figure 1.22. Second floor plan details. Dressing table.
Figure 1.23. Second floor plan details. Utility case.

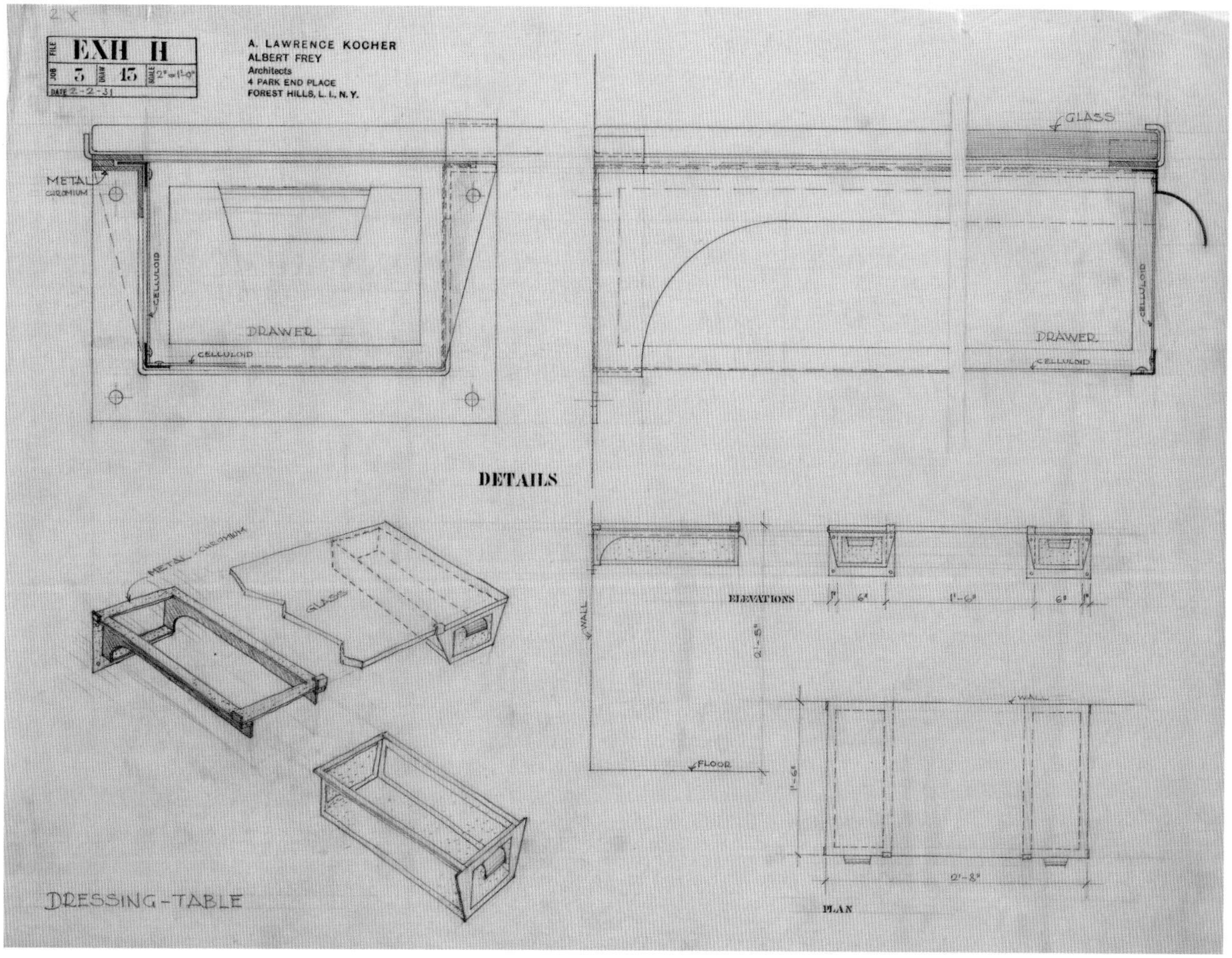
EXH H
JOB 3 DRAW 43 SCALE 2" = 1'-0"
DATE 3-2-31
A. LAWRENCE KOCHER
ALBERT FREY
Architects
4 PARK END PLACE
FOREST HILLS, L. I., N. Y.
METAL CHROMIUM
CELLULOID
DRAWER
GLASS
DETAILS
ELEVATIONS
WALL
FLOOR
PLAN
DRESSING-TABLE

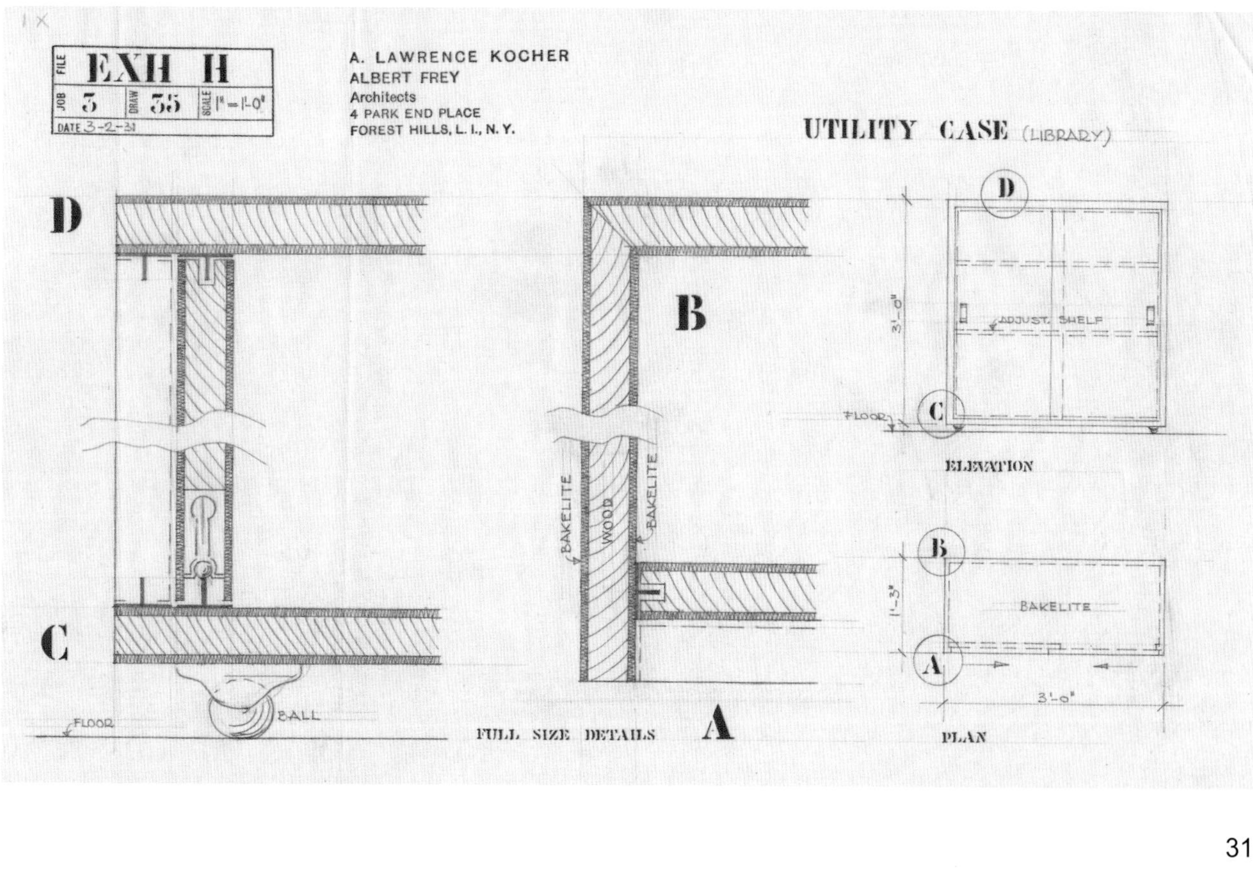
EXH H
JOB 3 DRAW 35 SCALE 1" = 1'-0"
DATE 3-2-31
A. LAWRENCE KOCHER
ALBERT FREY
Architects
4 PARK END PLACE
FOREST HILLS, L. I., N. Y.
UTILITY CASE (LIBRARY)
D
B
C
A
BAKELITE
WOOD
BALL
FLOOR
FULL SIZE DETAILS
ADJUST. SHELF
ELEVATION
PLAN
3'-0"
1'-3"

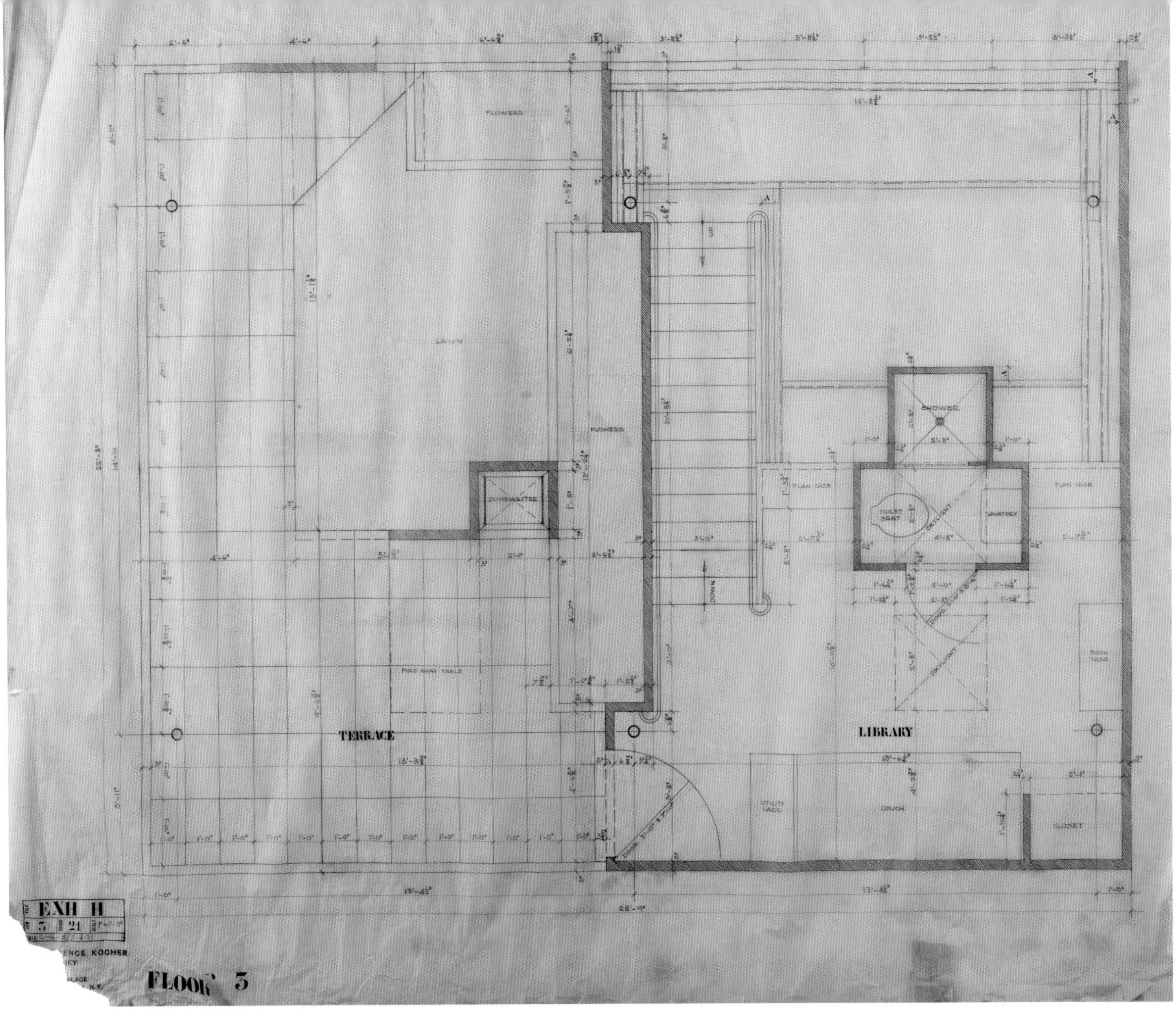

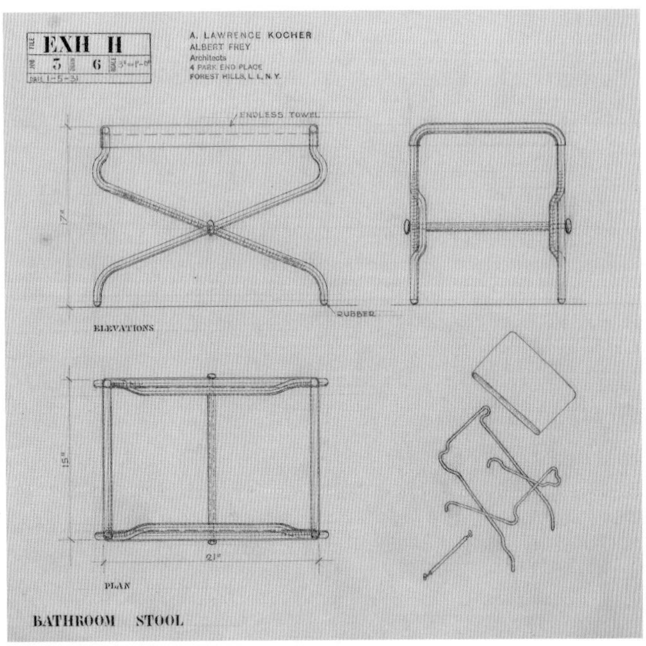

Figure 1.24. A. Lawrence Kocher and Albert Frey. Aluminaire House. Preliminary project 1930. Third floor plan.
Figure 1.25. A. Lawrence Kocher and Albert Frey. Aluminaire House. Preliminary project 1930. Details. Bathroom stool.

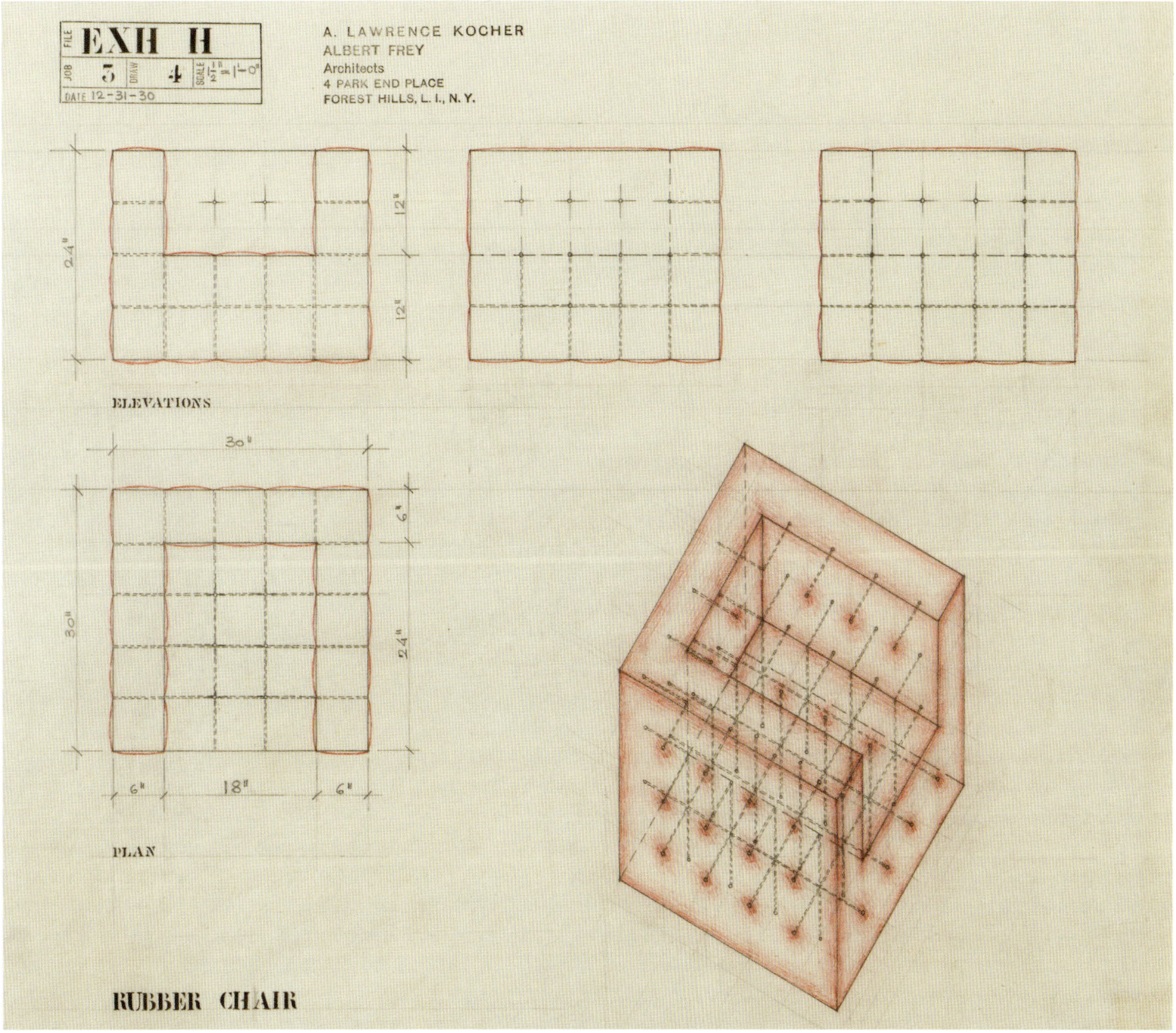

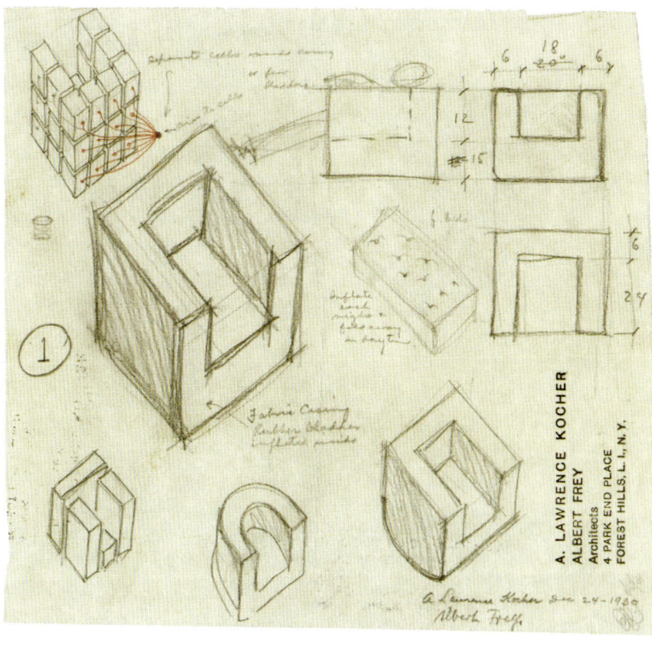

Figures 1.26 and 1.27. A. Lawrence Kocher and Albert Frey. Aluminaire House. Preliminary project 1930. Furniture details. Inflatable rubber chaise lounge.

Figure 1.28. A. Lawrence Kocher and Albert Frey. Aluminairc House. Preliminary project 1930. Cut-away axonometric view through the library, kitchen, bedroom, and bathroom, showing hanging furniture.

use of folding beds, sliding partitions, and extensible tables. It was estimated that an inhabitant could enjoy a usable space of 71 square meters even though the actual net area of the house was only 46 square meters. This strategic spatial optimism to make the most of a minimal space coincided with parallel research conducted by the American motorhome industry and was be replicated—to a slightly lesser extent—in the Aluminaire House. In Kocher and Frey's subsequent projects, there are numerous documents detailing similar operable devices. Despite the resemblances, only two traits can still be found in the Maisons Loucheur that are not present in the Aluminaire House: the aggregation to form a dense urban condition and the stone walls anchoring the houses to the terrain, meant to keep the local stonemasons involved in the construction.

Both the building technology and the leaps in the Aluminaire House's migratory biography speak clearly of an industrial object completely alienated from geographical specificity, from arising constraints, a climate, or a given cultural medium. The Aluminaire House is not an architectural object; it is a technical object which—like an automobile, a motor home, or a prefabricated house sold via catalog—does not undergo any formal alteration to accommodate a specific site. In the case of the Aluminaire House, a place must be transformed in order to accommodate the object, for it to settle without modification, and measures must be taken to ensure that it functions correctly.

There are various characteristics that explain the Aluminaire House's constant fluctuation between assembly and disassembly, and they can all be classified as "technological." Such descriptions include experimentation with new construction materials; the use of prefabricated construction subsystems that are assembled *in situ*; a low level of technical complexity in the design assembly, which enables non-specialized workers; and a production process with interchangeable parts that are coordinated yet independent. Two peculiar facts cast light on the Aluminaire House's status as a technical object. The first is that at no point during its many lives has a construction company ever been involved in its configuration. It is also the only architectural work included in the National Register of Historic Places that is protected without the site on which it stands. These facts reinforce the migrant nature of the house and its detachment from any specific location. The house was designed to be assembled and disassembled in a short period of time; the architects coordinated with various manufacturers who provided them with the materials for the work exhibited in the New York Architectural League show. The list of manufacturers appears on the exhibition brochure and catalogs a total of 46 participating companies. All the house's subsystems were coordinated in order to form a technological collage in which every joint is secured with screws.

Alienation from the site does not suppose independence from tradition. As we have argued, the Aluminaire House is not only related to European precedents, but is also well situated in the coeval American domestic tradition. From a technological standpoint, the house can be placed amid the numerous examples of prefabricated houses sold by catalog and shipped unassembled to the erection site.

It is possible to trace the genealogy of the American home, observing its trend towards an increase in mobility. Following the improvised, foundationless slab houses and log cabins of the pioneers who colonized the Midwest, housing construction in the United States arrived at the balloon-frame system by the mid-1800s, and this system remains an omnipresent construction technology to this day. The balloon frame, invented by carpenter Augustine Taylor in 1833 in the nascent city of Chicago, developed as a result of two prior technical innovations: mechanized saws and industrially produced nails.[43] It quickly became the most widespread construction method in North America due to the lack of specialization required in its assembly. Furthermore, its lightness, economy, and potential for prefabrication enabled the delivery of box-packed house kits with pre-assembled and numbered parts for construction on any site.

Following the invention of the balloon frame, two parallel developments in American housing resulted in even greater mobility: the prefabricated house and the box house—also known as the plank house. Simpler to construct than the balloon framed house, the plank house was deployed in temporary worker settlements, housing workers in the mining industry, agricultural businesses, timber, railway, and civil engineering companies.[44] It used an extremely cheap and makeshift system that had neither foundations nor bracing for lateral loads. Instead, it entrusted its stability entirely to a rigid exoskeleton composed of thick, 1 1/4-to-2-inch, vertical planks nailed to horizontal 2x4 beams, secured by an interior layer of vertical wooden planks of a lesser thickness. This type of house was either constructed on site or prefabricated and was easily transported by train due to its dimensions and lightness.

Beyond the invention and proliferation of these construction systems, there was not significant development in the design of prefabricated houses in the United States prior to the Aluminaire House. The technological and material advances of these dwellings were not accompanied by design developments. Sears Roebuck was the primary developer of prefabricated houses, offering a catalog of over 450 variants, yet based all their designs on the balloon-frame system. Sears sent its houses in boxes with numbered parts, which were typically shipped in two railway boxcars, and included nails, paint, door and window frames, tiles and other building materials, accompanied by 3/8" = 1'-0"-scale plans for assembly. Sears entered the prefabricated housing market in 1908 but went bankrupt in 1934 due to the Great Depression. At the time, there were numerous other companies selling similar pre-fabricated products, including Montgomery Ward, which operated between 1921 and 1931.

The historic precedents to the Aluminaire House in the field of prefabricated homes produced technological innovations but, above all, they investigated the methods of housing production. They neither created new residential types nor conducted formal research beyond what was essential to the deployment of a particular system or material. The stylistic variation of these prefabricated houses covered a broad range of traditional American styles and made them formally indistinguishable from houses built in a non-industrialized way. In all cases, technological research was conducted such that the formal design of the house occupied a subordinate position to their means of production. The only pre-1931 exceptions to this that we might cite are the unbuilt projects of the Diatom, Diatalum (1923) and the One Plus Two (1926) houses of Richard Neutra, along with the first versions of R. Buckminster Fuller's Dymaxion House, which were published between 1927 and 1930 but never built.[45]

Figures 1.29 and 1.30. A. Lawrence Kocher and Albert Frey. Aluminaire House. 1931. Photos of the house in the Harrisons' estate, first location.

Along with the genealogy of the American prefabricated house, we argue that it is also feasible to situate the Aluminaire House amid a more alien domestic tradition: that of the mobile home in North America. There are peculiar formal similarities between the Aluminaire House and several members of this technological lineage, like the Airstream travel trailer, whose production started in 1936.[46] These coincidences begin with the aluminum cladding of the exterior skin, and include many common features: the framed construction system that holds the thin and lightweight enclosure; the design of the windows as a continuum with the façade membrane; the prefabrication and industrialization of all the components using replaceable standardized pieces; the flexibility of the minimal interior spaces; the compacity of the design that drives to the impossibility of addition, aggregation, or expansion; the multifunctional performance of the fixed furniture; the proposal of a more natural lifestyle; and a transient relationship with the site. Most importantly, even before the 1930s all of these nomadic domestic solutions fostered innovation of new materials, building technology, and production systems, just like the more conservative American prefabricated housing companies. They also produced formal research beyond the purely technical, daring to create design proposals that responded to the new need derived from the modern lifestyle.

A token of these formal convergences can be found in the series of articles published by *The New York Times* in 1915, following the Conklin family, who traveled cross-country in their rattletrap motorhome. The series was not only an account of their travels, but a simultaneous advertisement for the Gas-Electric Motor Bus Company, owned by Roland Conklin. **(Figure 1.43)** His family's domestic experiment was covered extensively by the media, and it catalyzed the founding of new companies that subsequently produced similar mobile living solutions. The Conklins had a hand in activating the "Tin Can Tourism" trend, turning cars into personal campers by making spaces for sleeping or space to supplement a tent.[47] Most of these customizations were made to the Ford Model T; numerous records from the United States Patent Office between 1920 and 1932 detail intermediary inventions, all classified in the camping trailer category, linking the trailer, camping tent, and canvas-covered wagon.[48]

A purely visual examination of the photographs capturing the Conklin motorhome reveals many similar features to those of the Aluminaire House: the metal frame structure, a light enclosure, tripartite division, windows-as-membranes continuous with the external cladding, use of the rooftop as a terrace, compact shape, impossibility for aggregation or addition, transient relationship to the site, and minimal living spaces shaped through multi-functional and transformable furniture. In summary, the Conklin motorhome is strictly compliant with the fundamental principles touted by Hitchcock and Johnson in their book as the essential features of modern architecture.[49]

The Aluminaire House bears common characteristics with many of the informal constructions produced during the Great Depression. It anticipates the precarious ways of living yet to come within the decade, and is oddly consistent with many images of the Great Depression social imaginary. During the 1930s, the combined effect of droughts, unemployment, farm and home foreclosures, bank failures, loss of private deposits, and school closures increased drastically as did the number of homeless individuals and families in the USA. Many turned into transient laborers lodged in autocamps, much like those memorialized in John Steinbeck's seminal book, *The Grapes of Wrath*. Many others resided in improvised roadside camps—in their cars or in makeshift trailer homes towed behind the automobiles—continuously moving in search of work, using the donations of private and public relief agencies for gasoline. Still, others built more stable informal shelters, forming shantytowns on the outskirts of many cities, later dubbed as Hoovervilles. Corrugated metal sheets, flattened oil cans, metal advertising panels, and dismantled cars and trucks were all used as building materials in the Hoovervilles, producing what in many cases looked like a precarious makeshift version of the Aluminaire House. These unintended similarities reveal Kocher and Frey's interest in creating not only a vacation villa, but an affordable social dwelling.

Although the Aluminaire House has all the features of a detached villa, Kocher and Frey had in fact envisioned it as a construction destined for mass production, to be replicated and likely aggregated. This second possibility was explicitly explored by the designers in a 1931 article that gave two alternative plans for houses with a similar spatial distribution to the Aluminaire House, and adapted to form a dense aggregation through repetition.[50] The article completely contradicted the original thinking behind the Aluminaire House; according to the exhibition leaflet, the house aimed to create the conditions for a new suburban way of living in direct contact with nature. While the explanatory texts about the house, written by the architects, indicate otherwise, the notion of aggregation seems implicit in the design. This underlying intention would explain why the house has an elevation consisting of a wall without openings. This elevation is not included in any of the available project documents, and is listed only as "Elevation C." The blank façade is inexplicable when considering that the house was not designed for a specific place or orientation, but as an object to be displayed inside an exhibition hall. A hypothetical continuation, total or partial, of the panoramic window in Elevation A would have been absolutely in keeping with the functionality and general order of the project. Its use as a structural shear wall is also not explicit in any of the documents available, and the lack of diagonals embedded in the wall precludes its structural performance. The only reasonable explanation for the existence of this blank wall would be for division and aggregation—a party wall between two houses, as in the Maisons Loucheur. **(Figure 1.44)**

Contrary to the specific writing on the Aluminaire House, the article "Real Estate Subdivisions for Low-cost Housing" seems to reflect Kocher and Frey's actual intentions in their design. The text presents a proposal in response to the demand for cheap, small-sized houses in the suburbs of New York City and mentions Queens specifically. To meet the growing demand for housing in these suburban areas, real estate speculators produced housing plans based on long, narrow lots measuring 25 feet by 100 feet to build narrow houses, monotonously grouped into rows with little space between buildings. This type of land division and grouping of houses produced neighborhoods without typological variation, full of dark dwellings, vulnerabile to fires, and with little privacy. Their gardens were divided into two, a condition that diminished their usefulness and was further exacerbated by the placement of garages at the rear

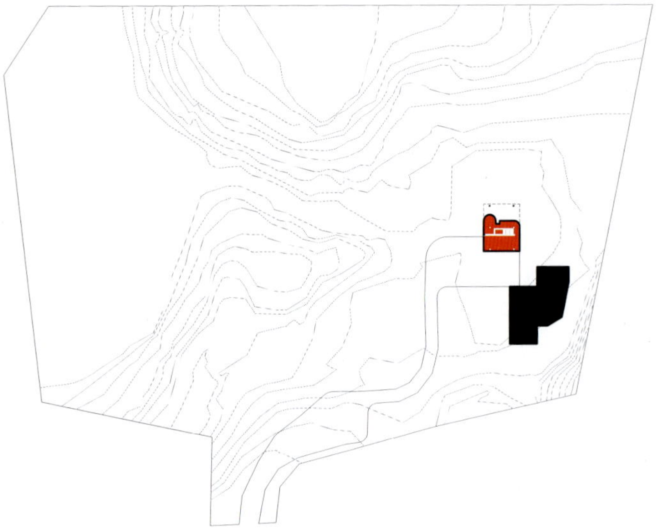

Original location at the Harrisons' estate. 1931–1940.

10' 50' 100'

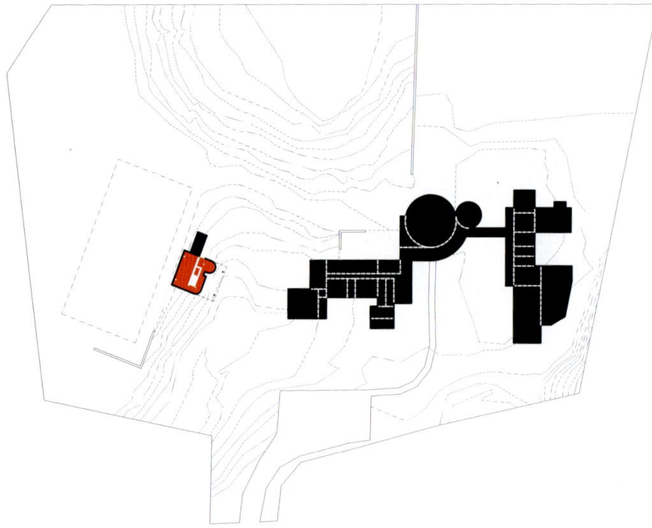

Final location at the Harrisons' estate. 1940–1986.

10' 50' 100'

Map of Aluminaire House's itinerance in the state of New York.

- A. Lawrence Kocher's residences
- Aluminaire House locations

Km 10 20 30 40

Miles 5 10 15 20 25

Figure 1.31. A. Lawrence Kocher and Albert Frey. Aluminaire House. Map of Aluminaire House's itinerance. 1931–1940.

1931

1. Aluminaire House
2. Existing farm buildings. Garage

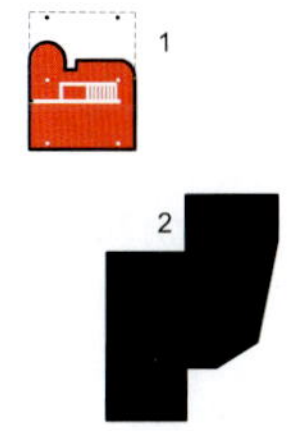

1932

1. Aluminaire House
2. Existing farm buildings, garage
3. Dining room

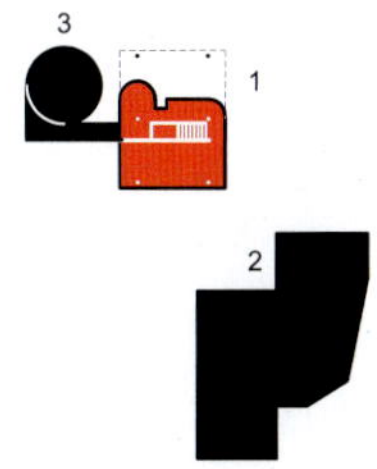

1933

1. Aluminaire House
2. Existing farm buildings, garage
3. Dining room
4. Living room

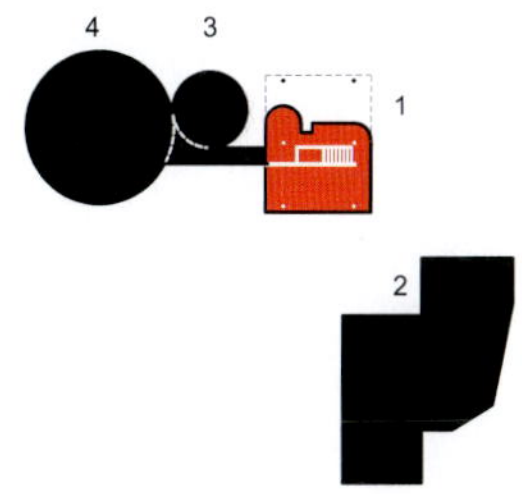

1935

1. Aluminaire House
2. Existing farm buildings, garage
3. Dining room
4. Living room
5. Greenhouse
6. Bedrooms
7. Kitchen

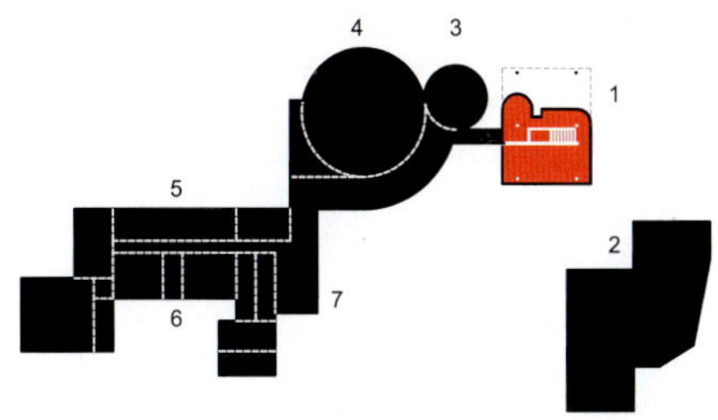

1940

2. Drafting room.
3. Dining room
4. Living room
5. Greenhouse
6. Bedrooms
7. Kitchen
8. Caretaker's apartment
9. Guest rooms
10. W.K. Harrison's Office.

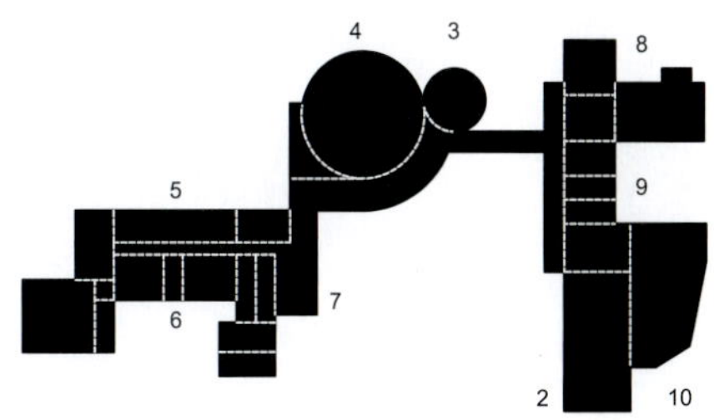

Figure 1.32. A. Lawrence Kocher and Albert Frey. Aluminaire House. Photo of the house with the first W.K. Harrison's additions. Wurts Brothers Photography. Collection, National Building Museum, Washington D.C.

patio, consuming a large area of the garden to meet the need for a private driveway. This type of neighborhood completely lacked common or public spaces for services or leisure.

Kocher and Frey redrew the lots with the same surface area, given this was an economic constant, but changed their shape to make them square. The new lots, measuring 50 by 50 feet, facilitated a series of functional improvements whilst maintaining equivalent density and economic viability. The volume of the proposed houses became wider and shorter, thus further improving the possibilities for their programmatic distribution. The gardens were located at the sides of the houses, providing better light and more privacy. Meanwhile, garages were absorbed into the volume of the house itself, meaning that the driveways could be shared by four residential units, thereby freeing significant space for gardens. **(Figures 1.45 to 1.47)**

The architects suggested several possible configurations for the grouping of this house type, which was a simplified version of the Aluminaire House. In Option A, the modules were positioned as independent houses, set in a row with more distance between them. Option B consisted of a row of attached houses, forming a continuous front along the street. In Option C, the plans of the houses were oriented at right angles, forming a grouping with more spatial variation. Their "Real Estate Subdivisions for Low-Cost Housing" article features an axonometric projection illustrating a combination of the three variants. This drawing, the house types, and their varied arrangements bear strong resemblance to those made by Le Corbusier and Pierre Jeanneret for the Cité Frugès in Pessac, the worker housing commissioned by industrialist Henri Frugès in 1924.

The aggregated houses by Kocher and Frey were longer and narrower than the Aluminaire House but retained a similar volume. The dimensions of the basic module were 18 by 35 feet, resulting in a surface area of 630 square feet; the Aluminaire House was 22 feet, eight inches, by 28 feet, nine inches,, having an overall footprint of 652 square feet. The low-cost houses did not have the double height that characterized the Aluminaire House; instead, they were structured with a denser program more suited to a typical family home. The spatial program included a porch, garage, boiler room, and entrance on the first floor; a hallway, kitchen, dining room, living room, master bedroom, and a complete bathroom on the second floor; and two bedrooms, storage space, and a terrace on the third floor.

The basic volumetric plan consisted of a single space occupying the entire second floor and two spaces on the first and third floors—each occupying half of the square footage—resulting in two squares measuring 18 by 18 feet. On the divided floors, the two spaces were at opposite ends of the house, freeing space for a porch on the first floor and a terrace on the third floor. Despite their differences, these proposed low-cost houses form part of the same typological family as the Aluminaire House. They include the same elements, such as the terrace and porch, despite a varying arrangement due to the specified staircase and its position within the plan. The façade finishes also appear to be similar, though in the aggregated scheme, the houses had two blank sides, increasing the possibilities for grouped configurations. Furthermore, the architects stated their intention in the text accompanying their drawings to produce prefabricated, industrialized architecture that explored the minimum dimensions needed for domestic elements—a statement closely relating this theoretical housing proposal to the Aluminaire House.

Public attention transformed the Aluminaire House into a catalyst for a new architectural sensibility. The effect of this house combined with Kocher's work in *Architectural Record* and the early governmental efforts under Hoover's presidency to overcome the house shortage—like the National Conference on Home Building and Home Ownership (1930) and the Emergency Relief and Reconstruction Act (1932)—generated a bulk of privately funded research on low-cost, minimal housing, along with the development of prefabricated systems and the use of new building materials in the United States.[51]

As an example of this sensibility toward the new architecture, modern homes were a key attraction at the 1933 World's Fair Century of Progress Exposition in Chicago, with nearly 50 million visitors. More specifically, the fair dedicated a large area to the theme of contemporary prefabricated housing, featuring complete houses demonstrating new materials, building technologies, and designs. Many of them were presented by prefabricated housing companies or by architects, such as George Fred Keck. Keck's House of Future and Crystal House, and Robert Law Weed's Florida Tropical House were the most architectonically innovative.[52] Keck had been greatly influenced by Hitchcock and Johnson's book, in which the Aluminaire House appeared. More conservative in form yet technologically innovative projects also included in the *House of Tomorrow* exhibition at the World's Fair were the Armco-Ferro House, Stran-steel House, and the Wieboldt-Rostone House. The work of Kocher and Frey and the domestic experiments of the World's Fair carried on through other inventive housing projects, like those fabricated by the companies American Motorhome, General Houses, American Rolling Mills, and American Houses during the 1930s. Kocher and Frey's work continued to influence other experiments on residential industrialization, such as the Packaged Houses by Walter Gropius and Konrad Wachsmann or Carl Strandlund's Lustron Homes, which developed into a fully modern language by in the 1940s. The influence of the Aluminaire House can be further traced to such relevant experiments as the Case Study Houses, with a shared preference for lightweight material systems and prefabrication technologies—these were the first projects on the West Coast to use constructive solutions already tested in the Aluminaire House, including the Ferrobord steel decking and the standardized industrial sash produced by Truscon Steel Co.

The syncretism and transient nature of Kocher and Frey's house make it a point of inflection between European and American domestic architecture. If the Aluminaire House is examined through the conceptual framework of the International Style as it was theorized by Hitchcock and Johnson, it absolutely fulfills each of its fundamental principles of *Volume*, *Regularity*, and *Suppression of Ornament*. The Aluminaire House replaces mass with volume by adhering to a strict separation between the structural system and its enclosure. The abstract condition of the planes that enclose the volume is accentuated by continuous surfaces of light and thin materials, which may be aluminum or painted canvas. Through the use of large windows acting as light membranes covering the entire façade, the architects comply with the second corollary to the principle

Figure 1.33. A. Lawrence Kocher and Albert Frey. Aluminaire House. Preliminary project 1930. Perspective view of the living room. Undated.

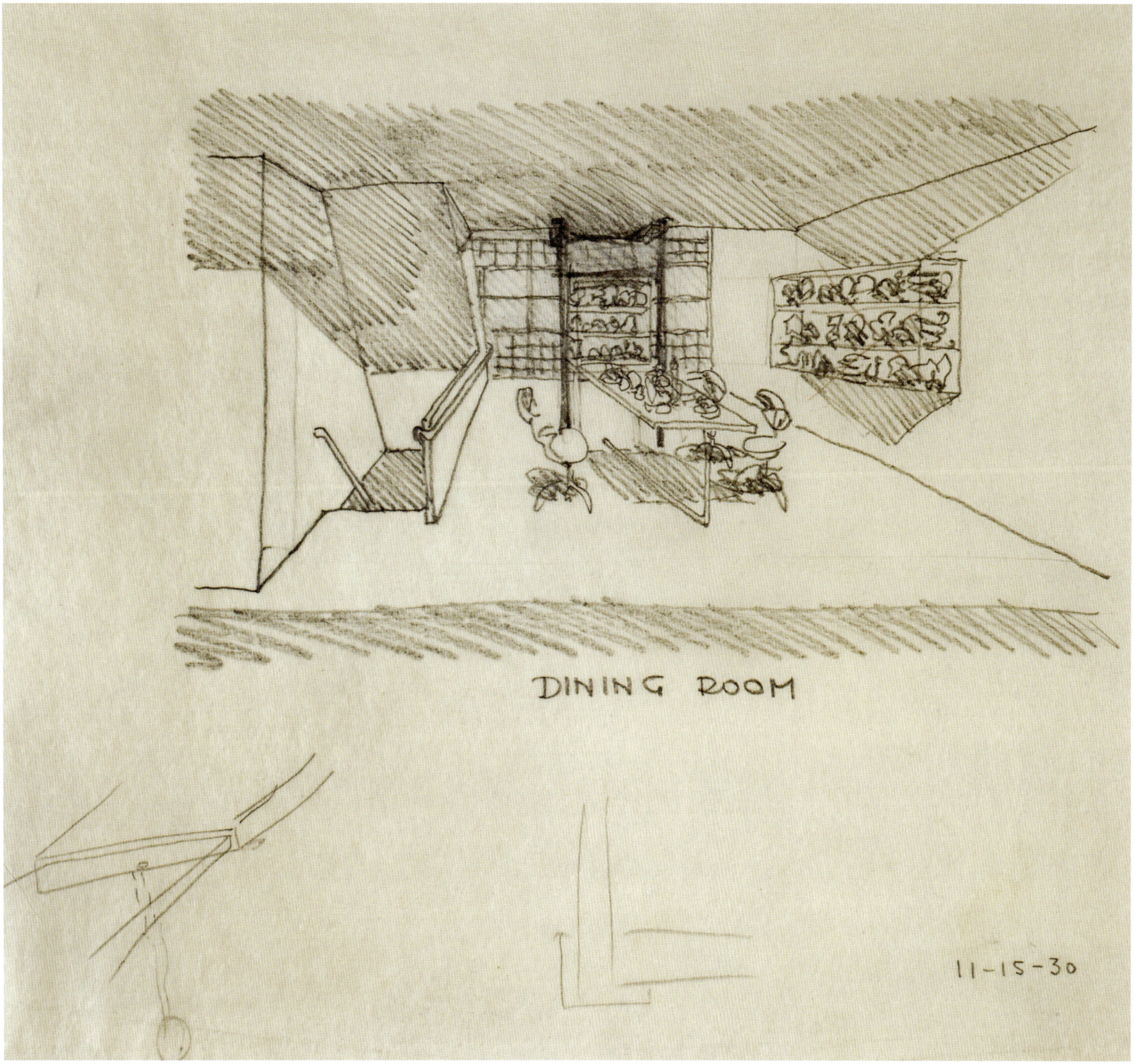

Figure 1.34. A. Lawrence Kocher and Albert Frey. Aluminaire House. Preliminary project 1930. Perspective view of the living room. Dated 11-15-1930.

This page:
Figure 1.35. A. Lawrence Kocher and Albert Frey. Aluminaire House. Preliminary project 1930. Perspective view of the kitchen. Dated 11-15-30.
Figure 1.36. Perspective view of the kitchen and axonometric view of the furnace room and entry hall. Undated.
Figure 1.37. A. Lawrence Kocher and Albert Frey. Aluminaire House. Photo of the terrace.

Next page:
Figure 1.38. A. Lawrence Kocher and Albert Frey. Aluminaire House. Preliminary project 1930. Perspective view of the library. Dated 11-15-30.
Figure 1.39. A. Lawrence Kocher and Albert Frey. Aluminaire House. Preliminary project 1930. Perspective view of the terrace. Dated 6-10-30.

glass
LIBRARY

6/10/30

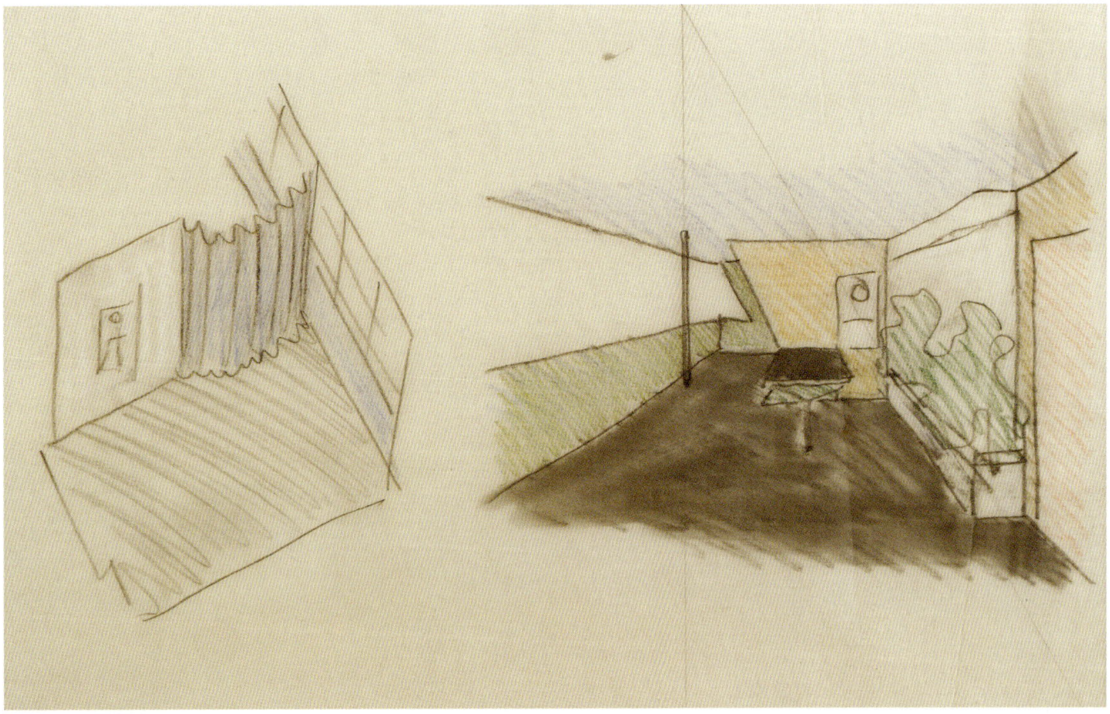

Figure 1.40. A. Lawrence Kocher and Albert Frey. Aluminaire House. Preliminary project 1930. Perspective of the terrace and axonometric view of the exercise room. Undated.
Figure 1.41. A. Lawrence Kocher and Albert Frey. Aluminaire House. Preliminary project 1930. Perspective view of the terrace. Dated 6-10-30.

of Volume.[53] **(Figures 1.48 to 1.51)** They surpass the first corollary to the same principle through the implied use of "continuous materials that produce an effect like skin tightly stretched over a supporting skeleton," and by embodying it in a literal sense through the use of a thin aluminum membrane pulled taut over a steel frame.[54] **(Figures 1.52 and 1.53)**

In addition to the complete adherence to the principles of the International Style, the Aluminaire House is completely immersed in the constructive and technological traditions of American transient domesticity. Its syncretic nature calls upon us to revisit its significance; the work by Kocher and Frey has a common lineage with many subsequent proposals for mobile, prefabricated, and transportable accommodation in North America. The relevance of this fact simply cannot be understated in the social context of a country in which one-tenth of all dwellings are now portable, with nearly all of the remainder built using lightweight and transportable systems derived from the balloon frame.[55] Kocher and Frey animated the modern movement with qualities of instability, provisionality, and ethereal materiality stemming from the American vernacular. They created, via the technification of the itinerant domesticity, a new kind of architecture aligned with a possible future for the American dwelling, as the one eloquently described by writer J.B. Jackson:

> It is tempting to analyze the dwelling entirely in socioeconomic terms; certainly, dwellings do not lend themselves to analysis in terms of architecture or folk art. But the real significance of the temporary dwelling, of the box house, to take an example out of many, lies elsewhere. I think it has always offered, though for a brief time only, a kind of freedom we often undervalue: the freedom from burdensome emotional ties with the environment, freedom from communal responsibilities, freedom from the tyranny of the emotional home and its possessions; the freedom from belonging to a tight knit social order; and above all, the freedom to move on to somewhere else. Now that environmentalism has become accepted establishment philosophy, the values we stress are stability and permanence and the putting down of roots and holding on to our architectural heritage; and no doubt it is as it should be. Still, we cannot help but be reminded that, whenever we look at our rapidly changing landscape and study our changing attitudes toward the home, we have a second architectural tradition, a tradition of mobility and short-term occupancy that is stronger and more visible than ever.[56]

The Aluminaire House, along with the rest of Kocher and Frey's domestic works, engages physical territory minimally, highlighting the desire for transient occupation. Perhaps the best proof of this ephemerality is the disappearance of most of these works. Not one of their houses remained in its original location, and none of them were inherited by the next generation. Following innumerable conservation efforts, only the Aluminaire House remains for future generations to explore in Palm Springs, California. There, more than 2,600 miles from any of its previous sites of assembly, it went through metamorphosis again. Its last transformation removed it from the world of functional objects, isolating it from any sort of domestic life and the construction of a quotidian narrative. Once more, the Aluminaire House becomes what it always was: a museum piece, a manifesto constructed to evidence what American residential architecture could have been and what, perhaps one day, it could be again.

Chapter endnotes

1 Charles Taylor, *Modern Social Imaginaries* (Durham: Duke University Press, 2004), 23–30.

2 A listicle of events following the stock market crash of 1929 include: the Smoot-Hawley Tariff Bill of 1930, the evictions , the "Hooverville," the factories and schools closures, the hunger, unemployment, and forced economic migrations of 1931, the sidewalk apple sellers and the soup lines, the Battle of River Rouge and the Bonus Expeditionary Force skirmish in Washington, D.C,. of 1932, the first Hundred Days of F. D. Roosevelt's administration in 1933, the unionization, the arrival of the "Okies" to California and political unrest of 1934, the Second New Deal of 1935, the Memorial Day Massacre of 1937, the "Roosevelt Recession" of 1938. Even nature contributed its share to the general collapse with the massive draught of 1930 to 1932 that ruined American agriculture and partially caused the Dust Bowl.

3 See Tom H. Watkins, *The Great Depression: America in the 1930s.* (New York: Back Bay Books, 1995), 350.

4 Watkins, *The Great Depression: America in the 1930s*, 248.

5 Watkins, 163.

6 This transient way of life intensified through the 1980s and has slowly decreased in recent decades. Some statistics from the US Census Bureau and American Community Survey (ACS) data supporting this statement include: more than 22 million Americans living in mobile or manufactured homes and over 580,000 were homeless in 2020; 20.2% of the American population moved during the year 1948; 13% moved in 2018 (last year available). This transient way of life has recently been put under public scrutiny by Jessica Bruder's 2018 fiction novel, *Nomadland*, and its homonymous 2020 film by Chloé Zhao. Jessica Bruder, *Nomadland: Surviving America in the Twenty-First Century* (New York: W. W. Norton & Company, 2018).

7 Morris Dickstein, *Dancing in the Dark: A Cultural History of the Great Depression* (New York: W. W. Norton & Company, 2009), 408.

8 The magazine is brilliantly defined by scholar Thomas Burns as a convergence of cultural imperatives, visual rhetoric, useful fictions, and technical communication. Burns explains the terms used in this definition. Cultural imperatives: a concept initially developed in the popular imagination and promoted in popular media until the concept is finally brought to practical function by industry. Visual rhetoric: any graphical artifact containing a set of visual symbols created for the purpose of communicating. Useful fiction: a discourse, statement, or piece of information that contains parts that are literally false, but nevertheless worth uttering in certain contexts, since the presence of that such portions are true is worthwhile for various theoretical purposes. Technical communication: the process of creating, designing, and transmitting technical information so that people can understand it easily, and use it safely, and effectively. Thomas Burns, "Useful Fictions: How Popular Mechanics Builds Technological Literacy through Magazine Cover Illustration" (PhD Diss, Texas Tech University, 2015), https://issuu.com/tomkburns/docs/burns_dissertationreview.

9 *Popular Mechanics* (August 1931): 277.

10 Ibid., 277.

11 Only six American buildings were presented out of a total of 82 works. See *Modern Architecture: International Exhibition, New York, Feb. 10 to March 23, 1932, Museum of Modern Art* (New York: Plandom Press, 1932).

12 "Five-thousand copies of this catalog were printed for the trustees of the Museum of Modern Art." *Modern Architecture: International Exhibition, New York, Feb. 10 to March 23, 1932, Museum of Modern Art*, 200.

13 Paraphrasing the exhibition catalog, *Modern Architecture: International Exhibition, New York, Feb. 10 to March 23, 1932*, Museum of Modern Art, 179.

14 Frey explains the meaning of the name in his foreword: "We called the house we designed for the League Exposition 'Aluminaire,' expressing our design concept of light

THE MINIMAL HOUSE: A SOLUTION

By LE CORBUSIER and P. JEANNERET, ARCHITECTS

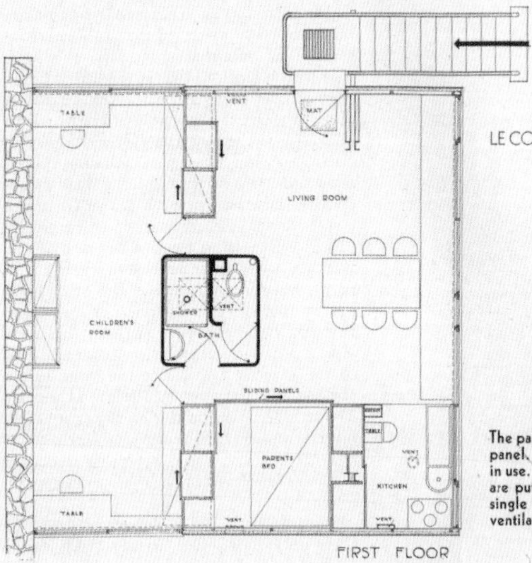

A MINIMAL HOUSE
LE CORBUSIER AND P. JEANNERET
ARCHITECTS

BY DAY

The parents' bed is shut off by a sliding panel. Likewise the kitchen when not in use. In the children's room the beds are put away and the children have a single large playroom and study, well ventilated and lighted

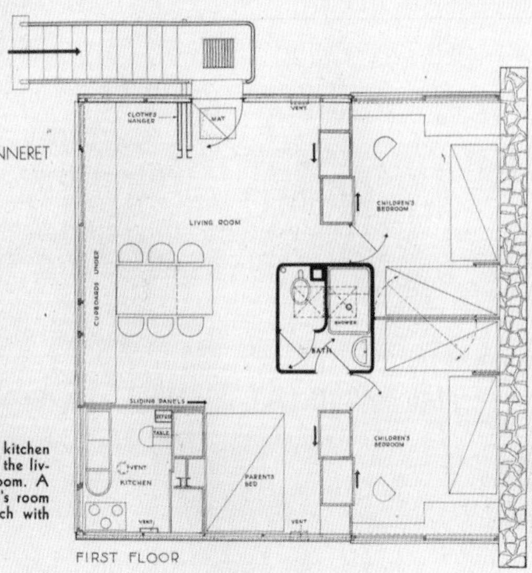

A MINIMAL HOUSE
LE CORBUSIER AND P. JEANNERET
ARCHITECTS

BY NIGHT

A sliding panel shuts off the kitchen and allows the parents to use the living room as part of the bedroom. A partition divides the children's room into two separate rooms, each with two beds

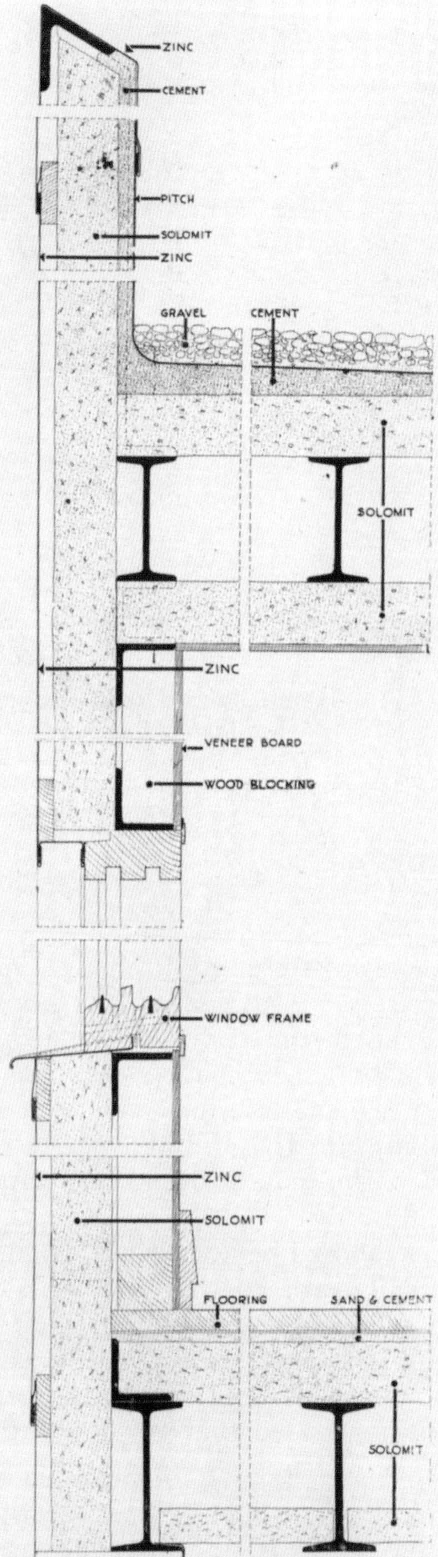

CONSTRUCTION DETAIL

A MINIMAL HOUSE
LE CORBUSIER AND P. JEANNERET
ARCHITECTS

Figure 1.42. Architectural Record August 1930. Le Corbusier and Pierre Jeanneret, "The Minimal House: A Solution."

and air. The house would feature large windows and open-air living, and be a durable structure with siding of aluminum." See Cynthia Zignego Stiverson, *Architecture and the Decorative Arts: the A. Lawrence Kocher Collection of Books at the Colonial Williamsburg Foundation* (West Cornwall, CT: Locust Hill Press, 1989), xvi.

15 An "erratic" is a boulder transported and deposited by a glacier; it has a lithology different than the bedrock upon which it sits.

16 Henry-Russell Hitchcock, "Towards a New Architecture. Le Corbusier," *Architectural Record* (vol. 63, no. 1, 1928): 90. Le Corbusier, "Architecture, the Expression of the Materials and Methods of our Times," *Architectural Record* (vol. 66, no. 2, 1929): 123–128. The title of Le Corbusier's article for Architectural Record was actually suggested by Kocher according to a letter at the Fondation Le Corbusier, dated May 8th, 1928. (FLC C3(5) 251). Cited in: F. Zaparaín Hernández, J. Ramos Jular, and P. Llamazares Blanco, (2020). "Le Corbusier: publicaciones en Estados Unidos, 1925-1939," *LC. Revue de recherches sur Le Corbusier* No. 02 (2020): 42–61.

17 Albert Frey, "Foreword," xv.

18 Black Tuesday was October 29, 1929, the last day of the stock market crash. By 1933, 40 to 50 percent of all home mortgages in the United States were in default.

19 Charles N. Glaab and A. Theodore Brown, *A History of Urban America* (New York: Macmillan Publishing Company, 1983), 299.

20 H. Ward Jandl, *Yesterday's Houses of Tomorrow* (Washington D.C.: The Preservation Press, 1991), 105.

21 The list of manufacturers appearing in the exhibition brochure includes 46 participating companies. The main suppliers: Jones & Laughlin Steel Corp. and McClintic-Marshall Corp. supplied the steel structure; Truscon Steel Co. installed all the window steel frames and decks; American Window Glass Co. and Mississippi Glass Co. supplied the glasses; and Aluminum Company of America supplied the aluminum elements.

22 These historic precedents have been obtained from José Benito Rodríguez Cheda, "El Aluminio en la construcción," *Tectonica 22, Aluminio* (Madrid: ATC Ediciones, 2006), 4–23.

23 Duraluminium is an alloy of aluminum, magnesium, and copper with a mechanical strength similar to that of medium-strength steel.

24 Robert L. Davison. "Technical News and Research," *Architectural Record* (October 1929): 362–385. The article offers another precedent in the use of aluminum in architecture: the pyramid-shaped roof of St. Louis' Civil Court House designed in 1928 by Klipstein & Rathmann Architects and built in 1930.

25 The dimensions of the house only respond to the needs of the exhibition space where it was sited. In the project documentation, there is a plan and a section of the external stair used to create direct public access to the terrace. It offered an alternate access and exit to the visitors to avoid crossings in the public circulation.

26 This figure does not include the Alberene Stone pavement for the ground floor (8,000 pounds) as it sits directly on the ground. To give a reference for the weight of the Aluminaire House, a classic Airstream trailer weighs 10,000 pounds including furniture, appliances, and full water tanks.

27 These dimensions are not coincident with those provided by the existing publications. The dimensions have been extracted from the structural assembly plans drafted by the Steel Frame House Co. Pittsburgh. In these documents, the distances in between joists are slightly adjusted to the necessities of the inner layout.

28 On project sheet 39, it is incorrectly labeled as "ferroboard."

29 *Time Magazine*, April 27, 1931.

30 "Young Architects Stage Rival Show," *The New York Times*, April 21, 1931.

31 Paraphrasing from the brief timeline offered by the architects in their candidacy for the R.S. Reynold Memorial Award of 1960. Box 4, Folder "Aluminaire House, List of Materials, Description, Handwritten notes, Typed transcripts of news and periodical articles," A. Lawrence Kocher Collection, Colonial Williamsburg Foundation, John D. Rockefeller Jr. Library.

32 Wallace K. Harrison's professional activities led him to work on important projects such as Lincoln Center, the headquarters of the United Nations, and both the La Guardia and John F. Kennedy airports of New York. He is responsible for the designs of notable buildings, such as the Time and Life Building) and the New York Hall of Science for the 1964 World's Fair.

33 As Joseph Rosa explains in his book about Frey. Joseph Rosa, *Albert Frey, Architect* (New York: Rizzoli International Publications, 1990), 28.

34 Jandl, *Yesterday's Houses of Tomorrow*, 113.

35 V. Newhouse, *Wallace K. Harrison, Architect.* (New York: Rizzoli, 1989), 60–66.

36 J. B. Jackson, "The Movable Dwelling and How It Came to America," *Landscape in Sight. Looking at America* (New Haven-London: Yale University Press, 1997), 217–18.

37 As established by Johnson and Hitchcock as a basis of the International Style. Henry Russel Hitchcock and Philip Johnson, *The International Style: Architecture Since 1922* (New York: W.W Norton and Co. Inc., 1932).

38 This scheme is observed in the history of the villa with certain modifications. For example, in the Virginian Jeffersonian villas, like Monticello in Charlottesville, Virginia, the first floor is inhabited by both the agricultural activities and the domestic service—composed entirely by enslaved laborers—and the attic is used to host the guests and the extended family of the owners. In the Italian Renaissance agricultural villas, the attic used to function as a granary.

39 Regarding this external compact appearance, the Aluminaire House is closer to other houses designed by Le Corbusier and Pierre Jeanneret, like the Maison Cook (1925) or the villa for the Weissenhof colony in Stuttgart (1927), than to the complex articulation of masses of the Villa Savoye, despite both examples four floors instead of three, as in the Aluminaire House and Villa Savoye.

40 This feature is more evident in the original plan of Villa Savoye, published in Le Corbusier's first volume of his complete works, than in the version that was finally built and published in the second volume. In this final version, the lineal service stair is substituted by a more open semi-cylindrical core. The kitchen moved to a position for a more fluid relation with the living room, and the laundry services disappeared from the roof level.

41 For a more comprehensive analysis on the critical reception of these houses, see: Alfonso Díaz Segura and Guillermo Mocholí Ferrándiz, "Les Maisons Loucher. la máquina para habitar se industrializa (The Machine for Living In Becomes Industrialized)," *Proyecto, Progreso, Arquitectura*, no. 6 (May, 2012): 34–49.

42 Le Corbusier and Pierre Jeanneret, "The minimal house: A Solution," ed. A. Lawrence Kocher, trans. N. Rice Norman, *Architectural Record*, Volume 68, Number 2 (August, 1930): 133–137.

43 For a history of the balloon frame, see: Walker Field, "A Re-examination into the Invention of the Balloon Frame," *Journal of the Society of Architectural Historians*, vol. 2, no. 4 (October 1942): 3–29. Also see: Paul E. Sprague, "The Origin of Balloon Framing," *Journal of the Society of Architectural Historians*, vol. 40, no. 4 (December 1981): 311–319.

44 The plank house has precedents within Native American architecture, see Peter Nabokov and Robert Easton, *Native American Architecture* (New York-Oxford: Oxford University Press, 1989).

45 The first built examples of industrialized, transportable, and prefabricated houses designed by Richard Neutra are dated to 1935 and include three small houses on an orchard in Los Altos, California, along with his Plywood Model House, dated 1936. Barbara Lamprecht and Julius Shulman, *Richard Neutra: Complete Works*, ed. Peter Gössel (Koln: Taschen, 2010).

46 The first aluminum model produced by Airstream was the Airstream Clipper, which was essentially a redesign of the Bowlus Road Chief. Also using aluminum, the first Bowlus Road Chief was designed and built independently by designer and aerospace engineer Hawley Bowlus in 1934.

47 Warren James Belasco, *Americans on the Road* (Cambridge: MIT Press, 1991).

48 The origin of the trailer home can be found long ago in the geographic and temporal background of certain nomadic cultures, such as the Romani. Many pioneering experiments in the United States, however, took place in the 1910s—such as the Aerocar designed by the aviation magnate Glenn Curtiss in 1919. In addition to Curtiss's company, two other major innovators started to operate in this sector by 1931: Covered Wagon of Detroit, incorporated in 1929, and Airstream, founded in Culver City, California in 1931. The founders of both companies, Arthur Sherman and Wally Byam, had similar beginnings. Both founders began by creating mobile houses for their own personal use, and both were initially inspired by the covered wagons of those who had emigrated to the West. Before the early 1930s, neither founder had taken the leap outside of the one-off manual fabrication, producing personal orders and publishing plans in specialized magazines for self-build mobile homes. It was nearly two decades later, following the Second World War, that motorhomes were produced on a larger scale.

49 Henry-Russell Hitchcock and Philip Johnson, *The International Style: Architecture Since 1922* (New York: W.W. Norton, 1932).

50 A. Lawrence Kocher and Albert Frey, "Real Estate Subdivisions for Low-Cost Housing," *Architectural Record*, vol 69 (April 1931): 323–327.

51 "The Conference on Home Building and Home ownership was announced by President Hoover on August 30, 1930. Its primary purpose was to bring together facts concerning housing throughout the United States; to determine the factors that influence housing, favorably or unfavorably, and how they are inter-related in cities, in smaller communities, and in rural areas; to focus attention upon the problems of home ownership and to suggest means of meeting them (...) More than 540 individuals served as volunteers on the study committees. Funds for research in preparation for the Conference and for publication of final reports were privately provided." See: "President's Conference on Home Building and Home Ownership (1931 : Washington, D.C.) Records," *Online Archive of California*, Hoover Institution Library and Archives, https://oac.cdlib.org/findaid/ark:/13030/tf1w1001jf/entire_text/. The Emergency Relief and Construction Act (ERCA), signed by President Hoover on July 27, 1932, appropriated $300 million in funds for federal relief loans to the states and $322 million for public works construction. See: Josephine Brown, *Public Relief, 1929–1939* (New York: Henry Holt and Company, 1940).

52 The Crystal House was exhibited in the second edition of the Fair in 1934, the same year that the Congress adopted the National Housing Act establishing the Federal Housing Administration (FHA).

53 "The ordering of the openings in the wall surface is quite as important as the avoidance of apparent reveals in the preservation of the integrity of the wall plane. (…) Contemporary buildings often have entire walls of transparent glass constituting one enormous window." Hitchcock and Johnson, *The International Style; Architecture Since 1922*, 46–47.

54 "Thus, a corollary of the principle of surface of volume there is the further requirement that the surfaces shall be unbroken in effect, like a skin tightly stretched over the supporting skeleton." Ibid., 45.

55 Allan D. Wallis, *Wheel State: The Rise and Decline of Mobile Homes* (New York-Oxford: Oxford University Press, 1991), 13.

56 J. B. Jackson, "The Movable Dwelling and How It Came to America," 222–223.

This page:
Figure 1.43. Conklin family's motorhome.

Next page:
Figure 1.44. A. Lawrence Kocher and Albert Frey. Aluminaire House. Photo of the blank façade.

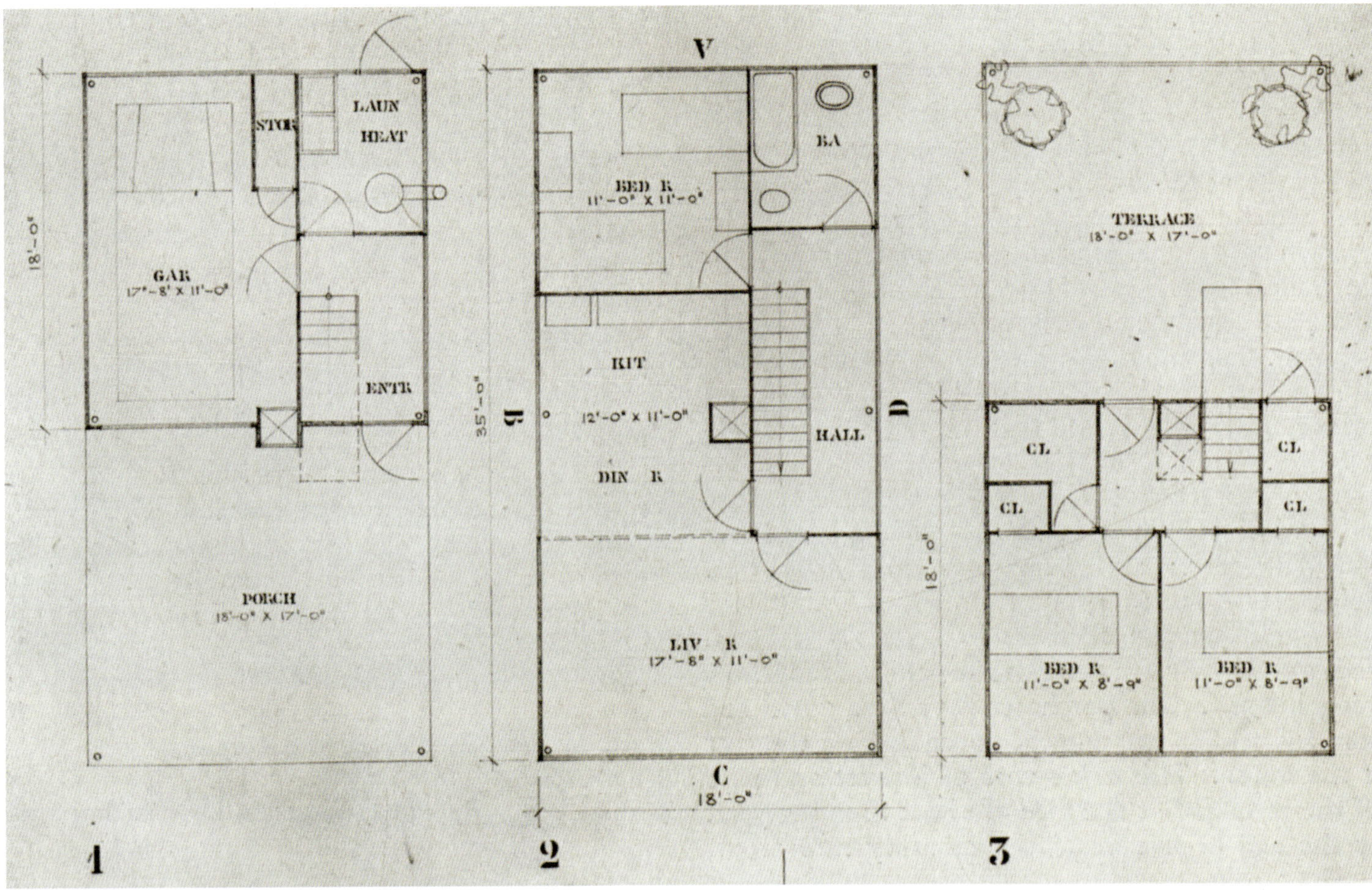

Figure 1.47. A. Lawrence Kocher and Albert Frey, 1931. "Real Estate Subdivisions for Low-Cost Housing." First, second, and third floor plans of the houses.
Figure 1.48. A. Lawrence Kocher and Albert Frey. Aluminaire House. Preliminary project 1930. Interior perspective of the living room looking at the window.

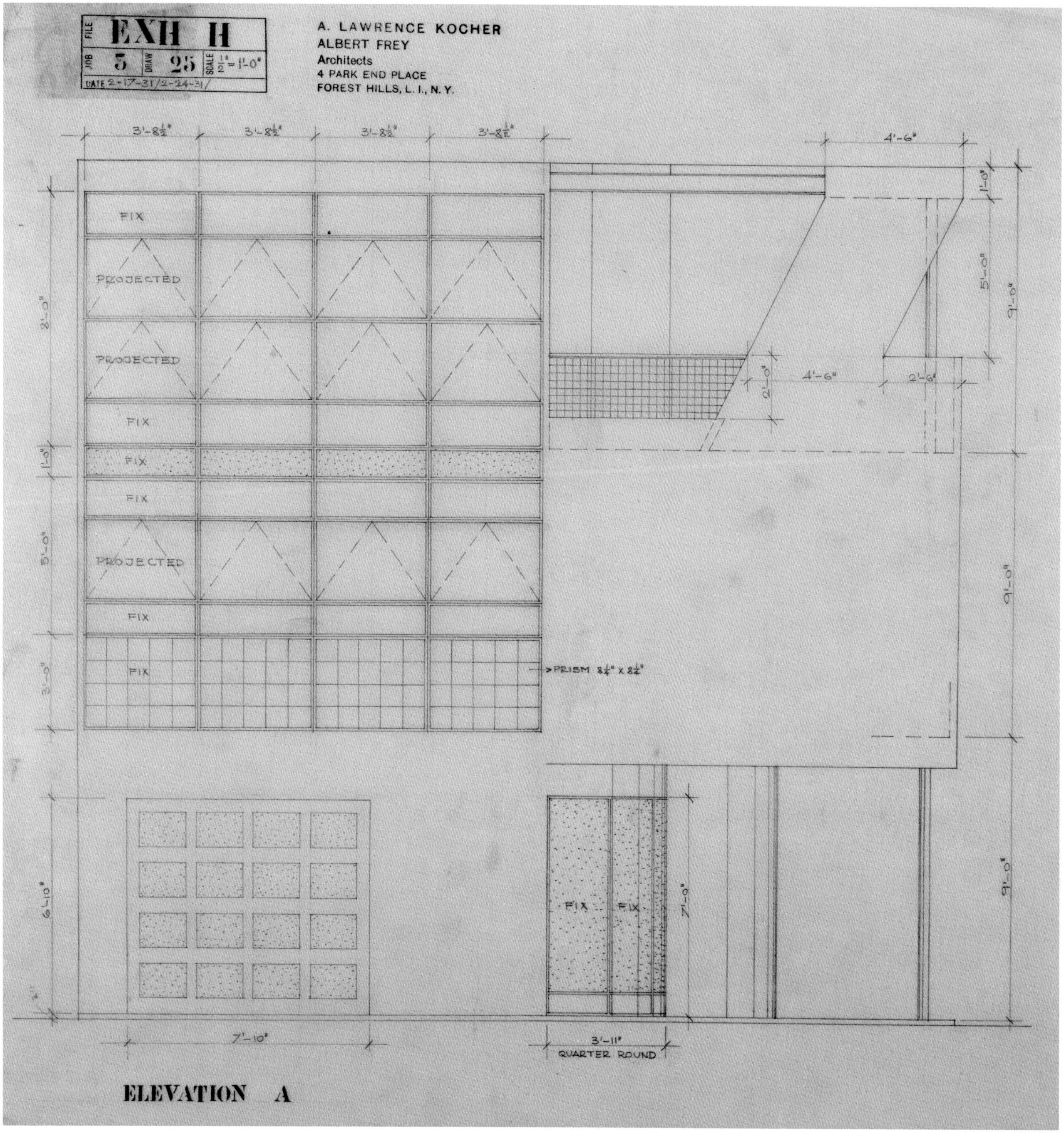

Figure 1.49. A. Lawrence Kocher and Albert Frey. Aluminaire House. Preliminary project 1930. Elevation A.

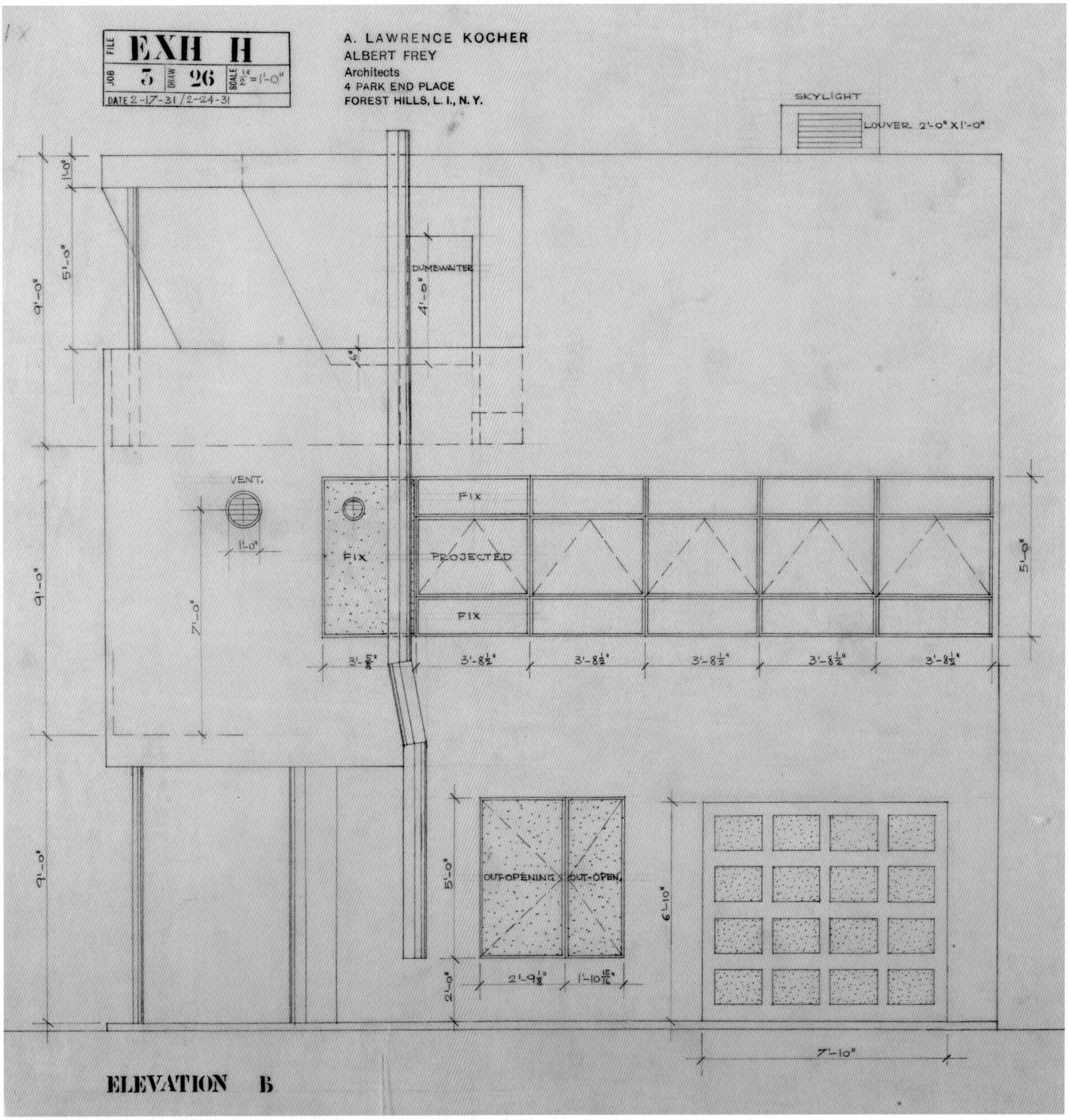

This page:
Figure 1.50. A. Lawrence Kocher and Albert Frey. Aluminaire House. Preliminary project 1930. Elevation B.

Next page:
Figure 1.51. A. Lawrence Kocher and Albert Frey. Aluminaire House. Preliminary project 1930. Elevation D.

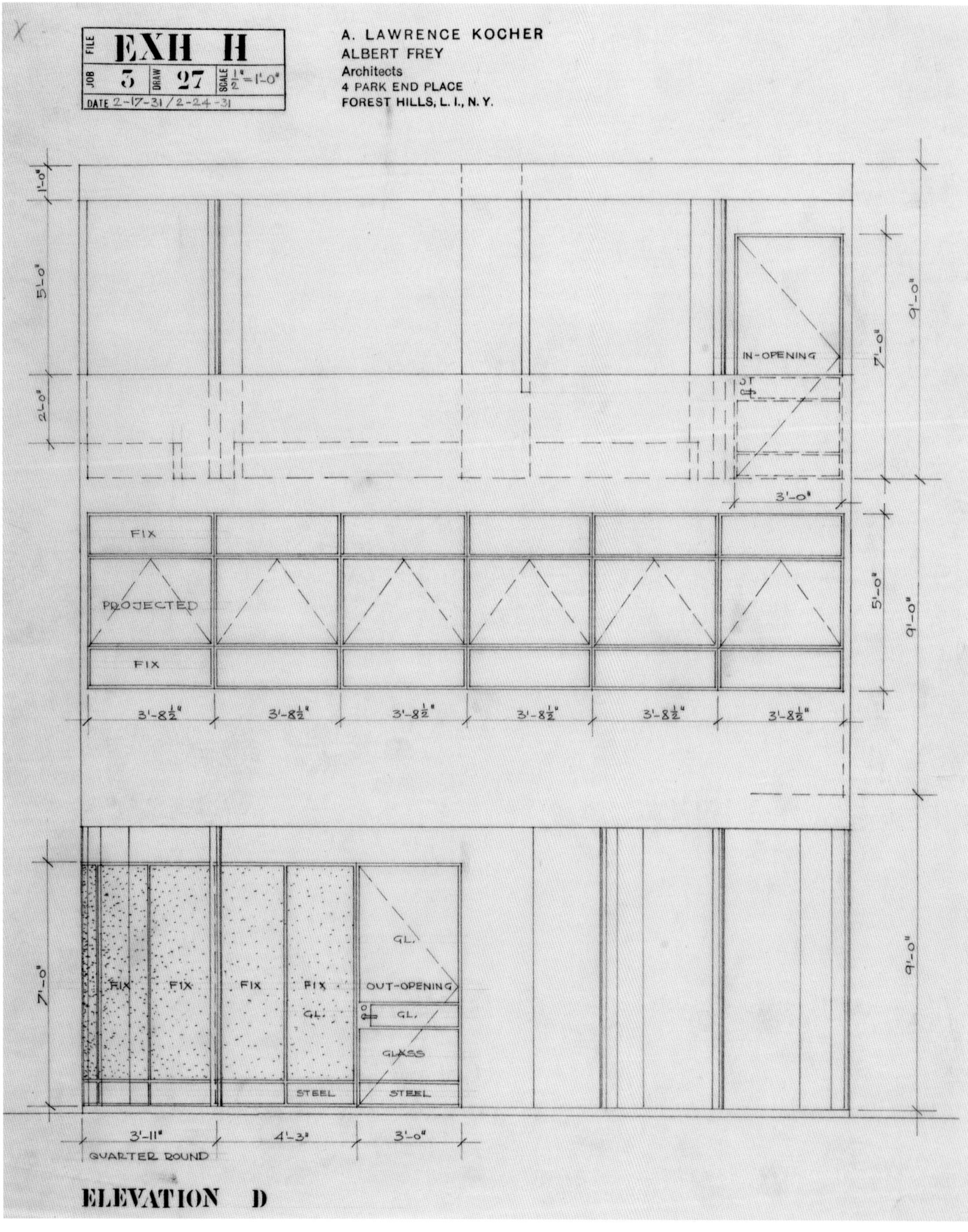
FILE EXH H
JOB 3 DRAW 27 SCALE 1/2" = 1'-0"
DATE 2-17-31 / 2-24-31
A. LAWRENCE KOCHER
ALBERT FREY
Architects
4 PARK END PLACE
FOREST HILLS, L. I., N. Y.
1'-0"
5'-0"
2'-0"
IN-OPENING
7'-0"
9'-0"
3'-0"
FIX
PROJECTED
FIX
5'-0"
9'-0"
3'-8 1/2"
3'-8 1/2"
3'-8 1/2"
3'-8 1/2"
3'-8 1/2"
3'-8 1/2"
7'-0"
FIX
FIX
FIX
FIX
GL.
GL.
OUT-OPENING
GL.
GLASS
STEEL
STEEL
9'-0"
3'-11"
4'-3"
3'-0"
QUARTER ROUND
ELEVATION D

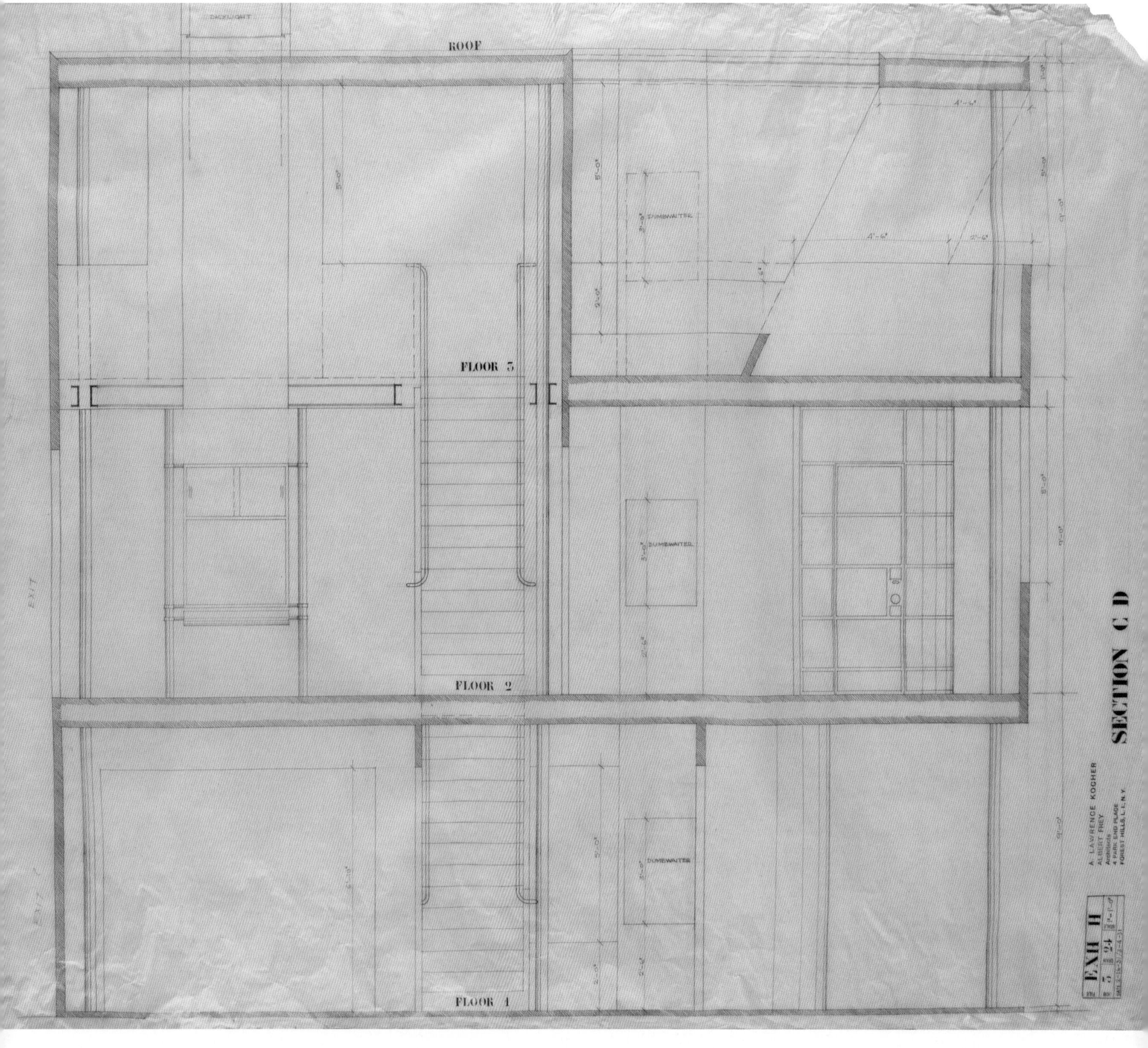

Figure 1.52. A. Lawrence Kocher and Albert Frey. Aluminaire House. Preliminary project 1930. Section through the living room double-height and the terrace.

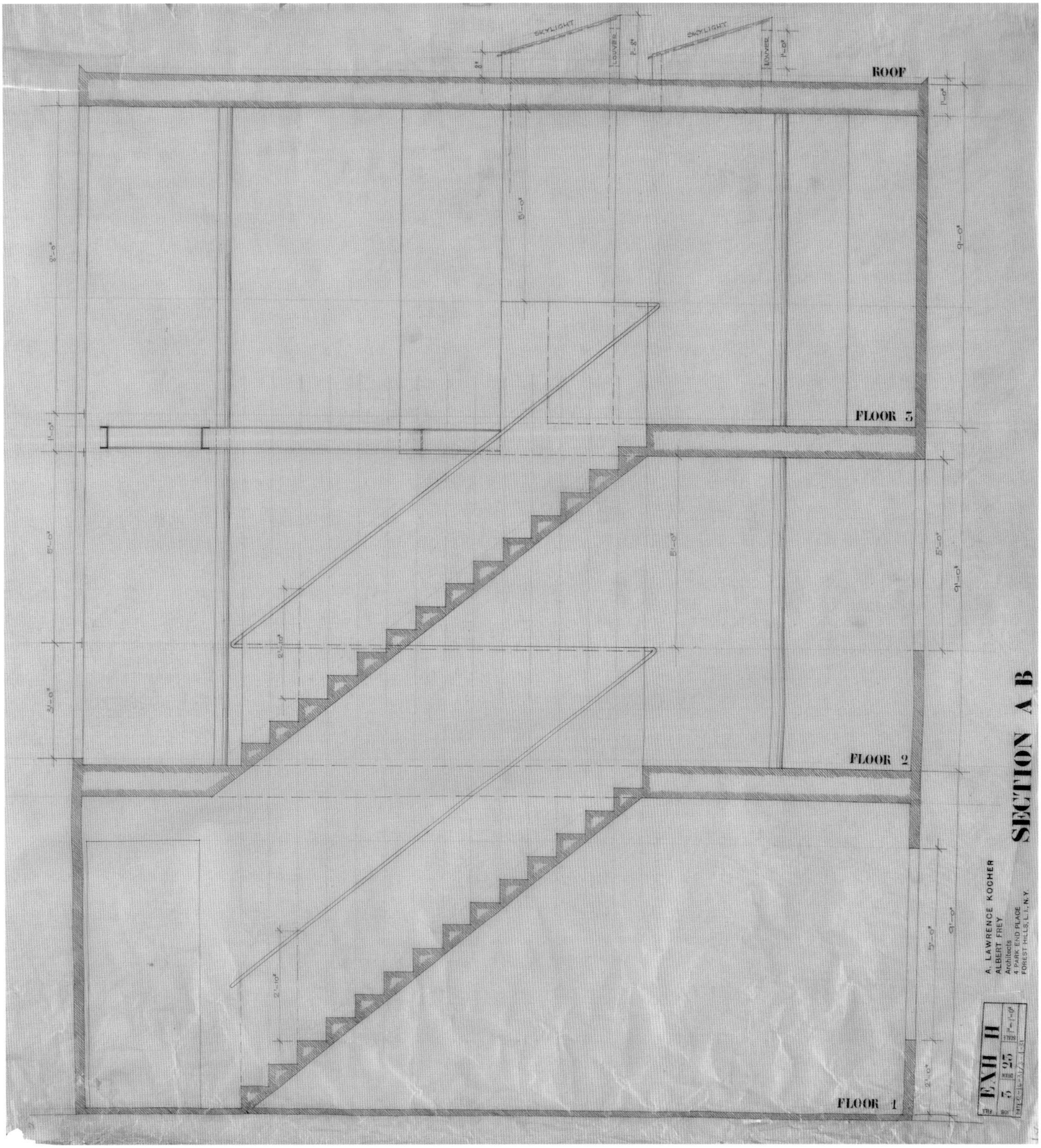

Figure 1.53. A. Lawrence Kocher and Albert Frey. Aluminaire House. Preliminary project 1930. Section through the stairs.

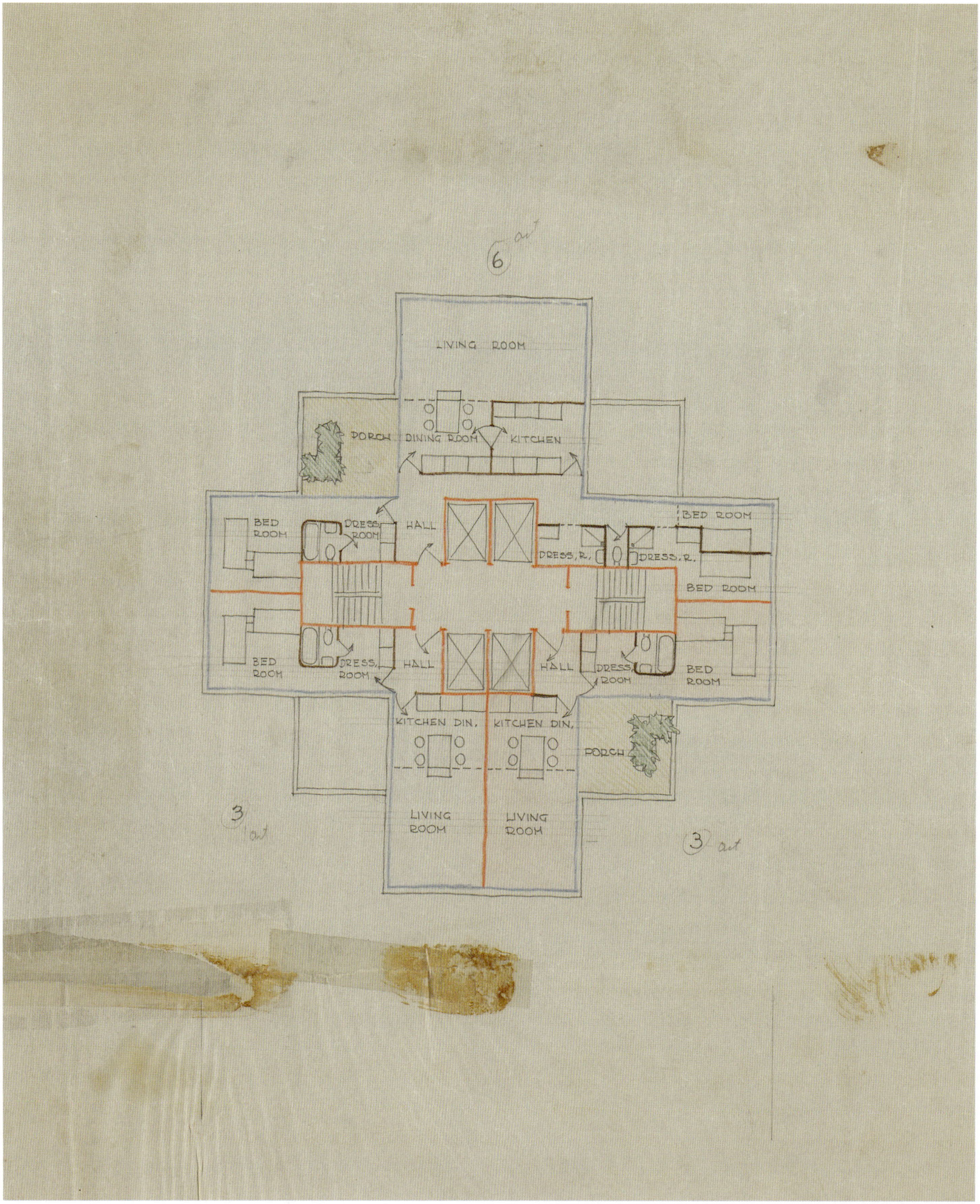

6 apt
LIVING ROOM
PORCH
DINING ROOM
KITCHEN
BED ROOM
DRESS. ROOM
HALL
DRESS. R.
DRESS. R.
BED ROOM
BED ROOM
BED ROOM
DRESS. ROOM
HALL
HALL
DRESS. ROOM
BED ROOM
KITCHEN DIN.
KITCHEN DIN.
PORCH
LIVING ROOM
LIVING ROOM
3 apt
3 apt

1920–1929

BEFORE ALUMINAIRE: IN SEARCH OF A NEW AMERICAN ARCHITECTURE

No matter how much we examine the objective facts of a life, they are always insufficient to fully explain the behavior of a non-fictional character. The contingent component of human life is so powerful that any coherent behavior is continuously truncated not only by the whim, physiology, and personal circumstances of the individual under study, but also by disturbances coming from the mutable historical context. This comes with a caveat that a given serious biographer shares: any human life is unfathomable. If the subject of the biography is not a person but a building, like the Aluminaire House, the task becomes even more complex. There are two main considerations to take into account in this case. First, the multiplicity of actors that have agency over the vicissitudes of the house's lifetime—how the extended life span of the architectural object, compared to human life, makes it more exposed to changes in historic or social context. Second, the dual condition of any architectural object, which can simultaneously be considered either a built material object or a potential object defined with a set of graphic representations. The wanderings of the Aluminaire House as a constructed object and its biography as a conceptual object, existing only on paper, has become indecipherable without analyzing the biographies of its designers and the historical context in which they worked. Before focusing on the rest of Kocher and Frey's domestic experiments, it is necessary to address these two matters—the designers' biographies and their historical context—prior to the design of the Aluminaire House. This expanded view will help clarify the crossing of European and American architectural traditions in a specific building as well as the many outstanding particularities of their future work as partners.

The historical context in which Kocher and Frey worked independently during the 1920s differs completely to what they faced during their professional association in the following decade. In the United States, the 1920s was a period of extraordinary social optimism fueled by solid economic growth. World War I accelerated the industrial production and profit. Prosperity and a seemingly endless stream of mass-produced goods were within reach for most of the population, improving their everyday life with millions of automobiles, telephones, radios, affordable electricity, heating, and household appliances. General prosperity, the material dream, and a self-centered consumerism had a relevant impact over American democracy. Apathy, individualism, and conformism were the root of decay in the public interest in political reform and politics. During the decade, Americans saw three consecutive conservative administrations with a record of low participation; Warren G. Harding won the 1920 elections with only 49.2 percent of the electorate. After Harding's death in 1923, Calvin Coolidge took office. Finally, in the 1924 elections, Herbert Hoover was elected as the third Republican president in a row, with a participation of 48.9 percent.

Isolationism and xenophobia also boosted in this decade. The United States failed to ratify the Treaty of Versailles and did not join the League of Nations. Much of the now-prosperous middle class feared immigration. A general mistrust of foreigners was ignited by the success of the Bolshevik revolution in Russia and the fear that American democracy would be subverted by foreign agents. A more racially focused xenophobia was caused by the massive arrival of immigrants after the war. Almost one million Europeans and 175,000 Mexicans arrived in the United States of America between 1919 and 1924. Further, these waves of immigrants arrived in communities that had already received an influx of African Americans in the millions during the Great Migration of the previous decade. Policy makers responded to this public fear with the passage of the 1921 Emergency Quota Act (also known as the Johnson Quota Act) and the even more restrictive 1924 Immigration Act (National Origins Act or Johnson-Reed Act). According to the National Census, the Immigration Act established a two-percent quota for the number of people from each nationality's total population present in the United States in 1890 and banned immigration from any Asian country.[1] The fear of "strangers" produced both the resurgence of Ku Klux Klan, especially in the rural Midwest, and the government's repression of any sign of subversion or social unrest.

Yet foreign immigration was not the only migratory flux happening in the 1920s. There were also massive internal population shifts, like the arrival of over 1.3 million new inhabitants to California during these years. The needs of these new residents made urbanization and house construction increase exponentially. Consequently, speculation went hand in hand with entrepreneurship as a defining feature of this particular era. The speculative craze found a perfect vehicle in the stock exchange market, driving a mass madness for investment—a frenzy that reached its peak during 1928 and 1929, when the extent of investments made the market nearly engulf the entire American economy. By the time the market crashed in 1929, this investment loss coupled with other confluent circumstances—the instability of the world economy after World War I, American protectionism, overproduction, over mortgaging, and a weak banking system lacking guaranties for the deposits—produced the deepest and most durable economic crisis of American history.

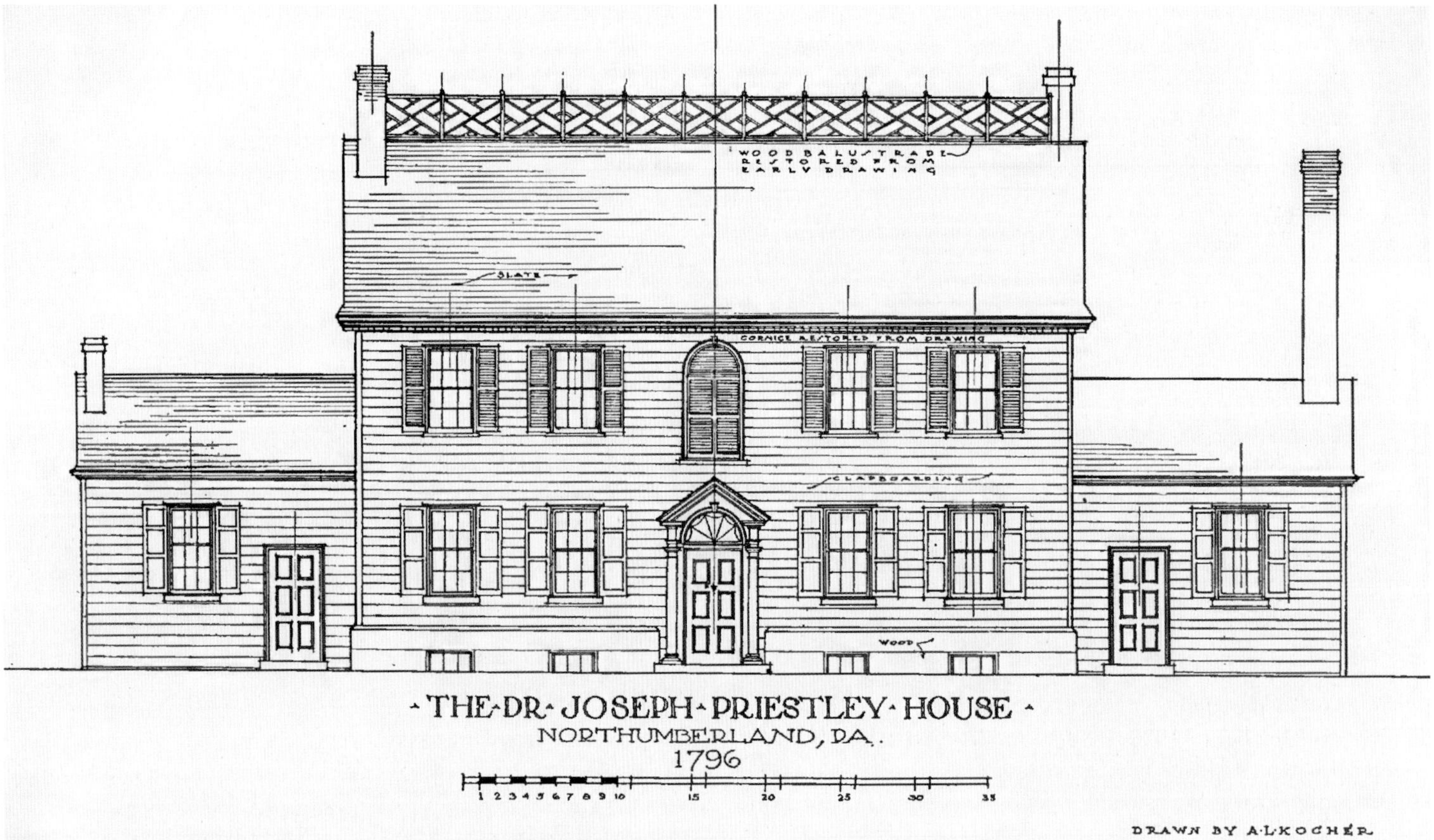

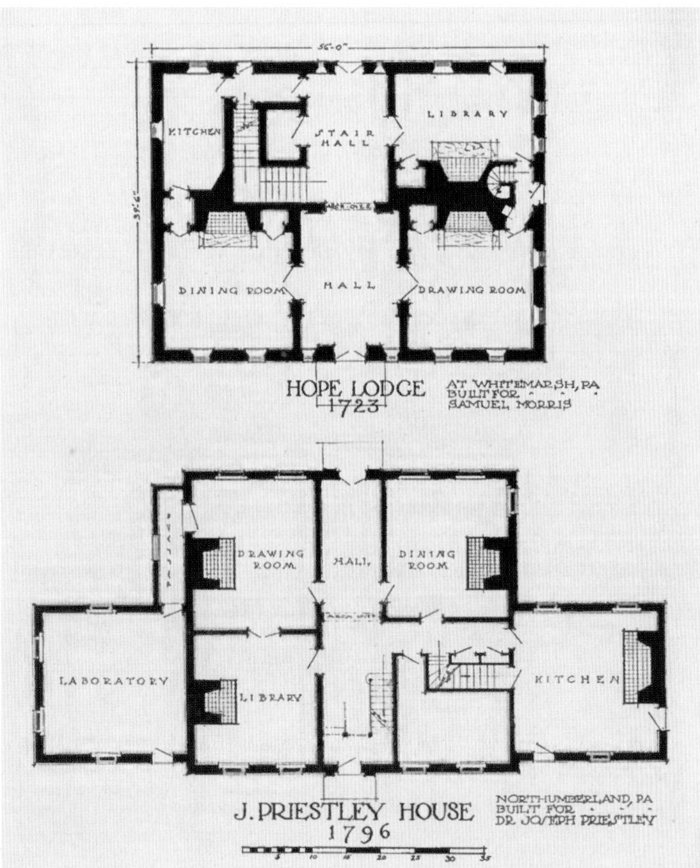

Figure 2.1 and 2.2. A. Lawrence Kocher, "Early Architecture of Pennsylvania, Part II." Published in Architectural Record, Vol. 49, No. 1 (January, 1921. J. Priestley House 1796. Elevation. J Priestley house, 1796, and Hope Lodge, 1723, plans. Drawn by A.L. Kocher.

Albert Frey did not experience the 1920s in the United States firsthand, but nevertheless he was embedded with the American optimism of the decade. Like many architects in Europe at the time, America was the synonym of progress and the technological avant-garde to Frey; the concepts of standardization, Taylorization, scientific management, and Fordism impregnated this generational ideology. Frey was part of the second wave of architects who emigrated to the United States; he arrived in New York in 1930 and started working on the East Coast before moving west in 1935. Born in Zurich, Switzerland, in 1903, Frey studied architecture at the Technological Institute of Winterthur, graduating in 1924. He worked in Brussels with architects Eggericx and Verwilghen from September 1925 to February 1927. After his stay in Brussels and before he started working for Le Corbusier, Frey developed a theoretical proposal for an affordable minimal metal house in 1928. The layout had no corridors. All the rooms were adjacent to a central core, composed by the living room and the kitchen. The living room opened to the exterior through a series of sliding glass doors. He envisioned a corrugated metal sheet as the sheathing material for the façade. This proposal is an interesting precedent to the work he would later develop with Kocher in the 1930s.

Undoubtedly, Frey's professional arrival was marked by his employment in the studio of Le Corbusier and Pierre Jeanneret, beginning in October of 1928. He was employed at the atelier until July of 1929, and his time coincided with that of Josep Lluís Sert, Nikolai Kolli, Ernest Weissmann, Kunio Maekawa, and Charlotte Perriand. In the office of Le Corbusier and Pierre Jeanneret, Frey collaborated on many notable projects: Villa Savoye in Poissy, the Centrosoyus Building in Moscow, Villa Church, Maisons Loucheur, Cité de Refuge, and Asile Flottant in Paris, the second project of the Société des Nations building, the Mundaneum of Geneva, and the project for the Prager Factory. Frey was deeply involved in the work for the Villa Savoye, for which he developed the construction details and the interior cabinetry. The details of the door connecting the terrace and the living room were based on hardware drawings for a barn sliding door in the *Sweets Architectural Catalogue*, modified for adaptation by local manufacturers. Frey also drew up various floor distribution and construction system proposals for the standardized Maisons Loucheur.[2] For a long time, Frey was interested in American architecture and technology—his perception of America was based on popular magazines, travel books, Eric Mendelsohn's book *Amerika,* and Richard Neutra's *Wie Baut Amerika?*, yet he was completely unfamiliar with the vernacular.[3] In fact, he chose to work with Le Corbusier because he was "building more along the American technique than Frank Lloyd Wright."[4]

Frey applied for a visa for travel to the United States, which was granted at the beginning of 1929. In order to earn money for the trip, he left Le Corbusier's office, where his wages didn't allow him to save any money; for a second time, he worked in Brussels for the office of Jean-Jules Eggerickx and Raphaël Verwilghen between October 1929 and August 1930. He arrived in New York City via Ellis Island on September 5, 1930, and within his first week in America, he started working for A. Lawrence Kocher for a generous wage of 25 dollars per week.[5] Frey fondly remembered the time his friendship with Kocher began:

> Lawrence Kocher was a great teacher. The articles we wrote together for the "Architectural Record" helped me tremendously with learning to express myself in English. He also taught me to drive in his air-cooled Franklin convertible. We enjoyed outings, some with his wife who was unfortunately ailing...Special treats were when Lawrence, his wife, and I went for Sunday dinners at Long Island duck farms or shore restaurants.[6]

Of the pair, A. Lawrence Kocher is the figure we must recover from obscurity. He remains undervalued by the majority of critics who have analyzed his works alongside Frey, overlooking his deeper contributions.[7] Kocher was a scholar of both vernacular American architecture and modern industrialized construction.[8] Born in 1885 in San José, California, he studied and was awarded a bachelor's degree in history at Stanford University in 1909. He then attended MIT as a graduate student from 1910 to 1912 without completing his degree. Kocher was hired as instructor in the Architectural History and Design program at Pennsylvania State University in 1912, where he was awarded a master's in architecture degree in 1916. At Penn State, he was promoted to Full Professor by 1918 and later became head of the department.[9]

During the 1920s, Kocher published numerous studies on vernacular American architecture. In 1920, he published an article about the historic architecture of Lancaster County, Pennsylvania, followed by a 15-part, serialized article in *Architectural Record* that ran from 1920 to 1922, titled "Early Architecture of Pennsylvania."[10] In this series, Kocher analyzed the development of the vernacular architecture in the region, producing a chronological division and defined three stages of stylistic evolution. **(Figures 2.1 and 2.2)** The first attempts of constructed structures were carried out by the pioneers before 1720, which then evolved into the mature architecture of the Pennsylvania Colonial style due to the arrival of specialized workers and artisans from Great Britain between 1720 and 1800, and finally arrived as the Federal Period after independence, with a more monumental and classical style architecture to better represent the institutional needs of the new state. Kocher highlights how the first constructions of the pioneers only slightly resembled their countries of origin. According to Kocher, the new manner of living, hostile environment, and diverse material availability caused methodological reformation of how to work and construct: "Their houses and public buildings came to be unconscious expressions of the new conditions, colored by their new living: and the results at first could scarcely come under the exacting term 'architecture.'"[11]

Although not studied enough, Kocher considered the first pioneering phase to contain the most fertile ground for the invention of original forms and architecturally constructive elements, which were maintained later as design invariants in the successive stages of architectural evolution. He poses the *pent-roof* or *Germantown hood* as an example of this survival in technological forms and "in the more permanent architecture which followed."[12] For the first time in Kocher's texts, the notion of impermanence in vernacular architecture emerges—one that will be central in his posterior thought about the creation of a new American domestic architecture. Within the same page of text, Kocher continued, differentiating two

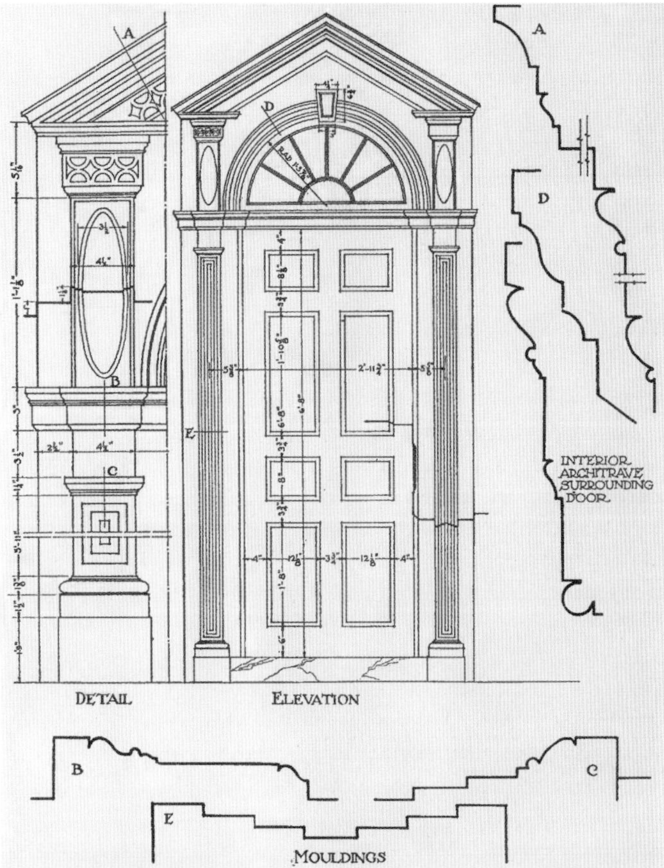

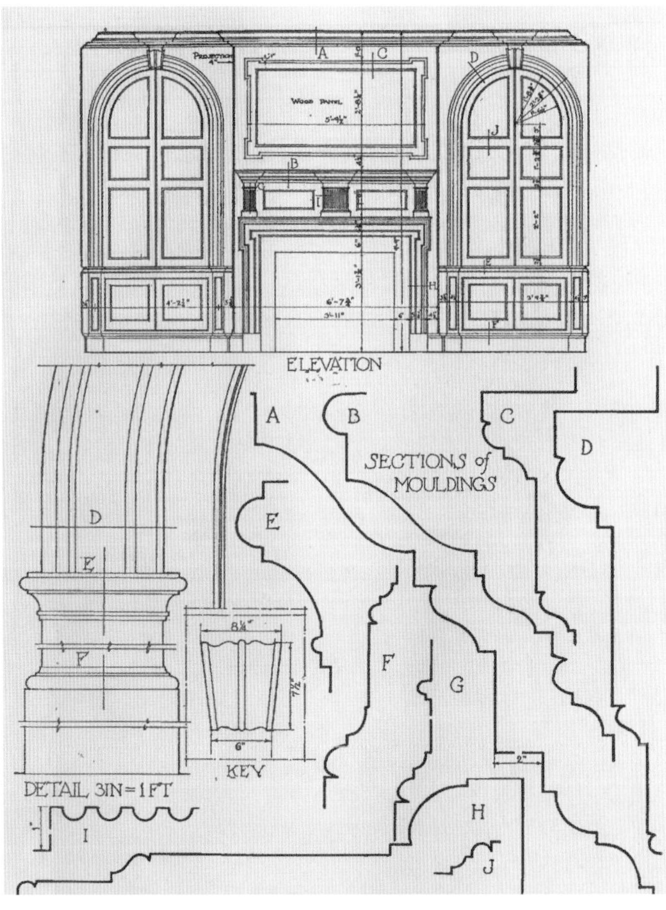

Figure 2.3. A. Lawrence Kocher, "Early Architecture of Pennsylvania, Part III," 1920. The Roxborough doorway. Philadelphia. **Figure 2.4.** Ibid. Main entrance Dickinson College. Carslyle, PA. By B. H. Latrobe, 1804. **Figure 2.5.** A. Lawrence Kocher, "Early Architecture of Pennsylvania, Part I," 1920. Linden Hall Tavern, circa 1800. Mantel and wall treatment. Measured and drawn by A. L. Kocher. **Figure 2.6.** Ibid. Doorway of R. Curtin House. Bellefonte, PA, 1804. Measured and drawn by A. L. Kocher, assisted by Lieut. E. C. Seibert.

traditions in the history of American architecture: the vernacular made by anonymous builders and the acculturate tradition designed by architects. He uses the duality between functionalism and beauty to make the divide between traditions. In his own words, "These first essays in building, then, are not to be classed as architecture, for true architecture has its inception in beauty, as well as usefulness."[13]

The earliest of these traditions, the primeval American vernacular, is embodied by a series of impermanent, provisional, precarious constructions not ascribed to any historical style and built with a strictly functional aim using locally available materials by low-skilled yet inventive anonymous builders.

> America has the results and not the names of country carpenters and masons who built up a style which outlived its age by recognized merit and which brought forth men gifted with the recognition of the worth and appropriate use of materials and who understood the proprieties and the limitations of architectural design.[14]

The subject of anonymous architecture is of special interest and it is underscored by Kocher many times in these articles. His enthusiasm completely aligned with the pioneers of the European modern movement, who saw a source for formulating their architectural functionalist theories in the Mediterranean and Japanese popular architecture, along with the "anonymous" American industrial architecture and engineering. This vernacular of industrial silos, factories, and warehouses appeared as a desirable model for modern architecture specifically because of their technical and economic adequacy, compositional naturality, structural clarity, and their use of new materials. Among the publications of the early modern movement featuring vernacular industrial structures, the most important are: *Jarhbuch des Deutschen Werkbundes* by Walter Gropius (1913), *Vers une architecture* by Le Corbusier (1923), *Der Moderne Zweckbau* by Adolf Behne (1923), *Funktsionalnyi metod i forma* by Moisei Ginzburg (1926), *Amerika* by Erich Mendelsohn (1926), and *Von Material zu Architektur* by Laszlo Moholy-Nagy (1929).

Kocher's interest in non-authored architecture reveals the fertile common ground that made the collaboration between Kocher and Frey possible. As a European architect and disciple of Le Corbusier, Frey was educated with the same interest for anonymous builders. Frey's 1939 book, *In Search of a Living Architecture*, is full of photographs taken during his trips between the American East and West Coasts in the early 1930s, illustrating his interest in Native American architecture, alongside gas tanks, radio antennas, airplane beacons, and other structures of an industrial landscape. The renewed interest on the topic of anonymous builders took a hold starting in the late 1940s—almost three decades after Kocher's writings in *Architectural Record*—with titles such as J.M. Richards' *The Castles on the Ground* (1946), Sigfried Giedion's *Mechanization Takes Command* (1948), Sybil Moholy-Nagy's *Native Genius in Anonymous Architecture* (1957), and Bernard Rudofsky's *Architecture Without Architects* (1964), along with *The Prodigious Builders* (1977). In the 1970s, another revival of vernacular architecture occurred, including authors like Henry Glassie in the U.S. or R.W. Brunskill in the UK.[15]

Another outstanding feature of Kocher's *Architectural Record* article series about early Pennsylvania architecture is the cataloging of standardized construction elements from the vernacular tradition. This cataloging effort is carried on in the articles through Kocher's own very technical and comprehensive drawings of cornices, doorways, windows and shutters, mantel pieces and fireplaces, and stairways. Not only does he catalog the elements but also the processes and methods of construction with different materials, like iron and stone. All drawings are scaled and dimensioned demonstrating the intention to find generalizable forms, standard patterns, and traces of a primitive prefabrication system within vernacular construction methods. Kocher's articles additionally catalog standardized construction elements and techniques, completely embedded in the prefabrication and industrialization character of the new modern architecture.[16] **(Figures 2.3 to 2.6)**

With a broad knowledge of the stylistic characteristics of vernacular architecture, Kocher also had a deep understanding of building technology and constructive systems. This focus on building technology was key for his future endeavors. Kocher saw in the American vernacular tradition a possible foundation to build a new national architectural identity; its rationalism could add a distinctive American character to an international modern architecture. In Kocher's vision, American vernacular architecture embodied the elements of functionalism, material economy, and constructive rationality—a prelude to the standardization and prefabrication that would facilitate the European modern movement and take root in America. In a text about Kocher, Frey clearly states the range of interests of his former partner:

> During discussions on modern architectural design, Lawrence told me that his extensive research on important traditional buildings, particularly vernacular American structures, convinced him that in each period technical proficiency and modes of living were fundamental in determining the design of buildings.[17]

Through his articles of the 1920s and his later work at *Architectural Record*, Kocher played an essential role in the connection between vernacular and modern architecture as well as the creation of a national modern movement in the United States. The same task was assumed in the 1930s in the British context by James Maude (J.M.) Richards with his own writings and work as editor of *Architectural Review*. Richards published several articles linking the vernacular architecture and the modern movement of authors like Philip Morton Shand, whose 1934 series, "A Scenario for Human Drama," preceded the publication of Nikolaus Pevsner's *Pioneers of the Modern Movement* in 1936. In his 1946 book, *The Castles on the Ground*, Richards posed the idea that:

> Modernism grew out of the tradition of British architecture with an argument that vernacular architecture — meaning that produced by and for ordinary people rather than architects — offered lessons about the place of the architect in culture and about how modernism could develop into a universal idiom.[18]

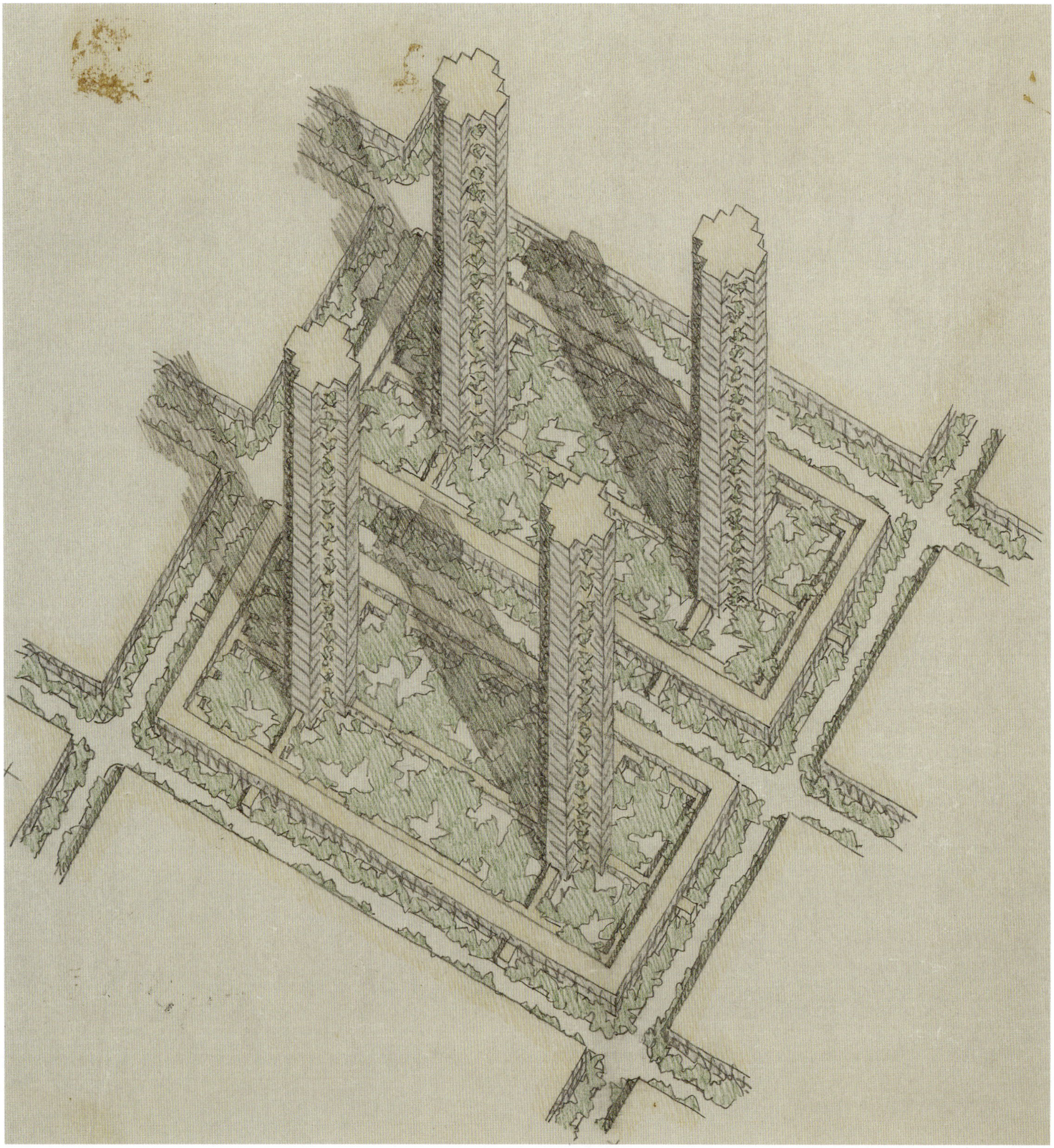

Figure 2.7. A. Lawrence Kocher and Gerhard Ziegler. Sunlight Towers. 1929. Unbuilt. Original sketches.

Although the examples of vernacular design he used were often industrial and even mass-produced, Richards used a more cultural approach for his "naturalization" of the British modern movement. He explored the concept of "vulgar" architecture and the role of the architect in the satisfaction of the social needs of the ordinary man. In return, Kocher used a more technical approach, one founded on the exploration of optimizing processes in building production through standardization, industrialization, and prefabrication in both vernacular and modern traditions.

The second tradition Kocher identified within his 15-part series is cultured architecture after 1720, composed mainly of public buildings but also of country and urban houses for the more affluent social strata. These buildings maintain certain formal elements from the anonymous vernacular yet are authored by architects and specialized workers trained mostly in Great Britain. The influence of Palladio on British architecture is based on the knowledge of Palladio's drawings; a distinguishing characteristic of these neo-Palladian architects was the adoption of the villa as the most distinctive Palladian type. The neo-Palladian Georgian style had three main sources: Palladio himself, the built works of Inigo Jones, and the *Ten Books of Architecture* by Vitruvius.[19]

Palladio's books were translated into English numerous times—like Giacomo Leoni's *Four Books* edition of 1715-1716 or the Issac Ware edition of 1738—emphasizing the publication of "new" books on both Palladio and Vitruvius.[20] Mostly sponsored by the Earl of Burlington, the list of publications start with the very influential 1727 *Vitruvius Britanicus* by Colin Campbell, and the 1728 *Books of Architecture* by James Gibbs.[21] The work of Inigo Jones was also published in the 1727 book *Designs of Inigo Jones* by William Kent. All these publications were done before the actual archeological excavations of the Roman ruins that happened after the middle of the 18th century and produced a great amount of measured and accurate drawings of these monuments.[22]

All this disciplinal body was exported to North America, where Palladianism took root as the new dilettante and professional American architects designed their buildings using the Neo-Palladian style illustrated in these architectural handbooks. As Kocher states:

> Many of these handbooks found their way to the colonies and were generally used as a guide. The vogue of these books meant that anyone with reasonably good taste could design a house and that, by following rules, his proportions would probably be pleasing. Carpenters and certain of the educated class alike are to be given the credit for the design of the buildings of that time.[23]

In an article from 1921, Kocher studies the use of various architectural handbooks by Samuel Rhoads, the master builder and designer of the Pennsylvania Hospital, one of the best examples of early American public architecture built between 1751 and 1781.[24] After the discovery of Rhoads' complete library, three treatises on architecture, published in England, were found with his name written in the title page from 1724, 1754, and 1768. Kocher reviews the content of the treatises, which were all similar and devoted to basic geometrical problems, plates of the classic orders, details of construction, and architectural elements, such as windows, doors and mantels, with a complete absence of suggestions for plan and façade design. He finally draws as a conclusion that these books used by American amateur constructors were,

> with rare exceptions, merely books of "the orders" and were not manuals of English architectural practice, nor did they include (as a rule) drawings of extant buildings of the British Isles. Therefore, our early architecture was not molded by buildings of the mother country so much as by the engraved specimens of the Italian Renaissance and Roman orders; or, rather, by the spirit of classic proportion.[25]
>
> This excerpt sets apart the ingenious, first generation of vernacular builders of the American colonies from the English traditions, creating a new vernacular origin related directly to classical sources.

Although Kocher only makes the case for the state of Pennsylvania in his article series, a broader view helps to understand the wider American context of local and imported design influences during this time. While there are several examples of this early American Palladianism along the East Coast—such as Peter Harrison's 1749 Redwood Library in Newport, Rhode Island, which culled illustrations from the Hoppus edition of Palladio's books for its design—Neo-Palladianism reaches its real starting point with Thomas Jefferson.[26] Having owned the British Palladian publications, Jefferson was familiar with Palladio; he also visited some of the classical buildings in Europe. During his 1784 diplomat missions in France, Jefferson studied several Roman ruins in the south of the country. He was especially fond of the Maison Carrée at Nîmes, along with the Roman remains at Lyon (Roman Theatre, the Temples of Cybele and Odeum) and Vienne (Temple of Augustus and Livia), the Triumphal Arch and Roman Theatre at Orange, and the Roman ruins of Glanum at Saint-Rémy-de-Provence.[27] Jefferson also had the opportunity to be acquainted with the French-stylized Palladianism used for the design of Pierre Rousseau's 1786 Hôtel de Salm and Jean-François Chalgrin's 1772 church of Saint-Philippe-du-Roule, in addition to the architectural avantgarde represented by the architects Étienne-Louis Boullée and Claude Nicolas Ledoux.[28] Further, Jefferson toured 19 English landscape gardens with John Adams, using Thomas Whately's seminal *Observations on Modern Gardening* (1770) as a guidebook.

Jefferson developed his own body of work that combines this diverse background in very different modes. His style ranged from the serene Roman classical style of the Richmond Capitol to the Palladian Academic Village in Charlottesville, though he usually situated his designs in a delicate equilibrium between French influences and Palladian sources.[29] This assessment is especially accurate for Jefferson's domestic architecture, the bulk of his architectural production. American architectural historian James S. Ackerman established a series of similitudes and differences between Palladio's and Jefferson's villas: though luxurious, both were modest in scale and were the headquarters of large agricultural exploitations. They were, however, different in two distinct ways: Palladian villas are situated in the outskirts of cities, immersed in highly humanized landscape, where-

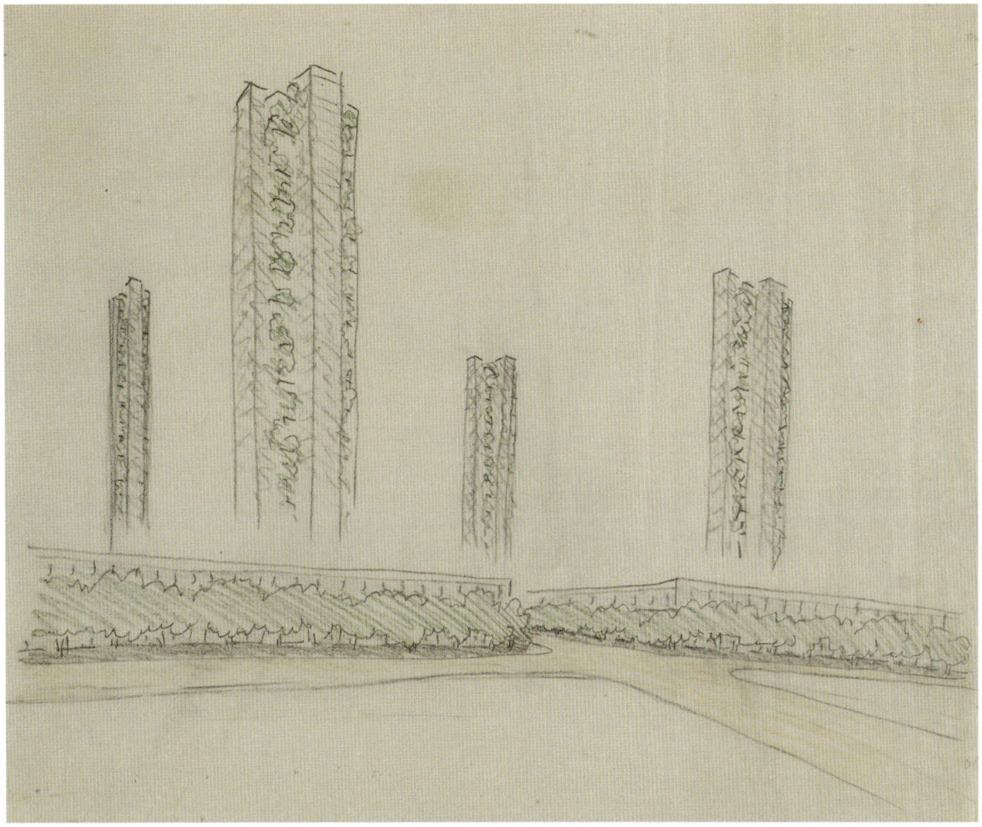

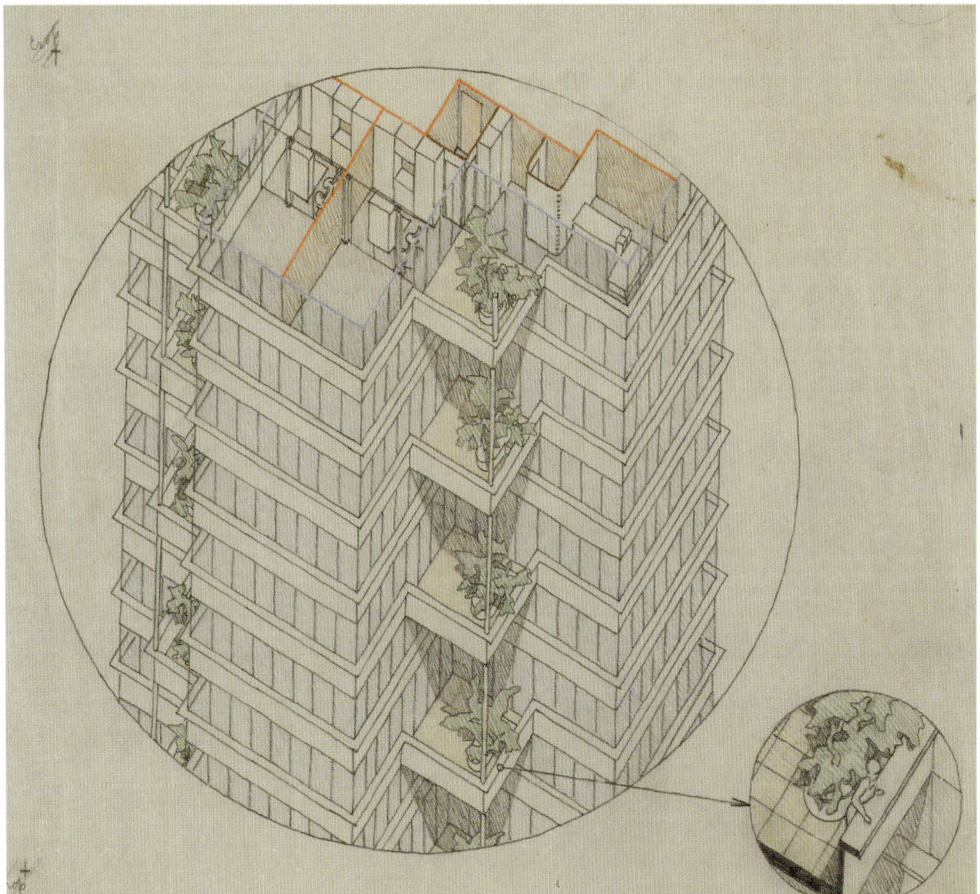

Figures 2.8 and 2.9. A. Lawrence Kocher and Gerhard Ziegler. Sunlight Towers. 1929. Unbuilt. Original sketches.

as Jeffersonian villas were in "the wilderness of a virgin land."[30] Unlike their European counterparts, another significant difference was the role slavery played in the design of Jefferson's villas, wherein enslaved laborers were the primary labor force in the villas' construction and during their operative years.[31]

Jefferson finished the construction of his first Monticello design likely prior to his French diplomatic mission in 1784. This first villa followed a clearly Palladian scheme. Upon his return home in 1794, Jefferson began planning a reconstruction to enlarge the villa. In 1796, the work started in Monticello with removing the second floor, shifting the architectural style to a mixture of Roman influence and the more contemporaneous French.[32] Jefferson designed at least five more villas for himself and for his friends between 1798 and 1817: Edgemont in 1796 (attributed to Jefferson); Edgehill, before 1798; Farmington in 1803; Poplar Forest, from 1804 to 1806; and Barboursville in 1817.[33]

Kocher's relationship with Jeffersonian architecture is fueled by his tenure at the University of Virginia, his work in Williamsburg, and his later academic appointment at The College of William and Mary, Jefferson's alma matter.[34] His lifelong friendship with architectural historian Sidney Fiske Kimball also reinforces Kocher's link to the Jeffersonian architectural tradition; there are 48 books listed as owned by or associated with Jefferson in Kocher's library.[35] Furthermore, Kocher's library includes many copies of the handbooks and copybooks used by colonial builders and carpenters, including Palladio's books.[36] As author Cynthia Z. Stiverson states in her book devoted to Kocher's library:

> He therefore sought out books purchased by the gentry of Colonial Virginia and the other colonies, which were in turn based upon copy-books of eminent British architects who strongly influenced the Colonial world—James Gibbs, Robert Adam, or William Chambers. Works by Charles Louis Clérisseau and Colen Campbell were purchased because they gave Jefferson precedents for the Virginia State Capitol at Richmond. Monticello was based upon the designs of Palladio, so Kocher purchased eight different copies of Palladio's *I Quattro Libri*, and seven copies of Vitruvius's *De Architectura*.[37]

1926. A Professional Turning Point.

The year of 1926 was crucial in Kocher's professional career; he earned a doctoral degree at New York University, which he had been pursuing since 1924, and he resigned as the head of the Department of Architecture at Penn State. On June 14, the Board of Visitors at the University of Virginia (UVA) confirmed his appointment as Professor and Department Head at the McIntire School of Architecture and Fine Arts.[38] In addition to his administrative and leading duties in the school, Kocher taught courses on Problems in Design, Problems in Advanced Design, and the History of Art.[39] Moreover, Kocher's academic appointment at UVA included his nomination as a member of the Virginia State Art Commission. The successor of Joseph Hudnut, Kocher's hire was highly recommended by the former head of the department, Sidney Fiske Kimball.[40] Kimball was chair of the AIA Preservation Committee and Restoration of Historic Sites and Buildings and director of the Pennsylvania Museum. Since the beginning, Kimball was involved in the restoration of Colonial Williamsburg, drawing Kocher to the project with his appointment at the Virginia State Art Commission.

Coincidentally, 1926 was precisely the year in which author William A.R. Goodwin showed the old city of Williamsburg to John D. Rockefeller, Jr., who proposed and funded its complete restoration. In turn, Williamsburg became a revolutionary experiment that changed the methodology of historic preservation in the United States. The drafting room at Williamsburg became the first de facto school of architectural restoration in the country. Charles B. Hosmer, Jr.—a historian of historic preservation—notes Williamsburg's importance for the emergent discipline:

> The decision of John D. Rockefeller, Jr. to restore the whole city of Williamsburg had the effect of broadening the base of support for preservation all over the country (...) The use of expert advice within the Rockefeller organization soon led to the foundation of other advisory boards, most notably in the National Park Service. The special needs of restorers and interpreters culminated in the formation of two new professional groups, the American Association for State and Local History and the Society of Architectural Historians.[41]

The advisory board of the Williamsburg restoration was created in 1928 and consisted of Sidney Fiske Kimball, Thomas Tallmadge, Edmund Campbell, Finlay Ferguson, Milton Medary, Robert E. Lee Taylor, Robert Bellows, and A. Lawrence Kocher.[42] Kimball and especially Kocher, acting as chairman, pioneered the collaboration between different disciplines: architects, archeologists, historians, and landscape architects collaborated on the restoration with a methodology based on local fieldwork.[43] Still in use today, they established a decalogue of precepts for restoration that assured the accuracy of the construction details and systems with respect not only for the original individual structures but also for the overall layout of the city's urban fabric.[44] Kocher was consistently involved with Williamsburg and its ongoing preservation work in diverse capacities until his death in 1969.

The first of three articles exploring vernacular architecture was published in November of 1925 within a monographic issue of *Architectural Record* dedicated to the Country House. In the article, Kocher states that the desire for a national art is one of the most critical of contemporary American society. He goes on to define the Country House as a "peculiar problem, with distinctly individual requirements, and with specialized and almost systematic treatments" that embodied the desire of American architects seeking independence from the historic European models to overcome the neglect of native styles. With drawings and photographs, the entire issue illustrated different examples of country houses in the United States; Kocher summarizes that the best examples are the result of a functionalistic approach combined with the use of vernacular styles. This novel, functional approach is due, in Kocher's opinion, to the fact that the character of the country house has been modified by modern social, technological, and economic developments.

Figure 2.10. A. Lawrence Kocher and Gerhard Ziegler. Sunlight Towers. 1929. Unbuilt. Original render by Hugh Ferriss.

As a result of both urban and rural changes, a new pattern of dwelling came: city land values and unprecedented development of transportation, especially the automobile, led to the obsolescence of the middle-class town house. Scarcity and unaffordability of manual agricultural labor led to abandonment of no-longer-productive agricultural land. The country house then became neither a stable housing option for the landowners nor a summer retreat for an urban aristocracy, but instead evolved into a new dual-pattern of middle-class living. Abandoning their urban and suburban stable houses to establish a more itinerant way of life, this middle-class lifestyle was further supported by the shortened distances between city and country, now permitted by new transportation technologies. The possibility to maintain a smaller apartment in the city, complemented with a country house where they could expend leisure time not only in summer, but any time of the year, was the class standard. The country house became a satellite of the city with a simplified distribution and a functional construction containing all commodities available in the city; new domestic components, like the garage, enhanced the relationship between internal and exterior spaces. In Kocher's words:

> In our earlier history the country house was a place of seclusion, to which one retired with some deliberateness and for a fairly long period of time. Its isolation made a degree of self-sufficiency necessary, and this in turn imposed conditions as to size and elaborateness. But the modern country house is really an extension and modification of the city itself. One might think of it, in part, as an urban residence set down in a rural park, and made readily accessible by convenient motor and electrical transportation. In point of time many of the estates of Long Island and Westchester are as near the business center of New York as the town houses on upper Fifth Avenue used to be.[45]

Kocher was interested in presenting the country house as the center of the new American-style architecture, yet in his writings, he also had the preoccupation to establish a genealogy for this architectural type. As we read in his articles: "The country house as an architectural type traces its ancestry to the French *manoir*, the English *country seat*, the German *Landhaus* and the Italian *villa*."[46] He also considers that most of the country houses of the 18th century consist of "buildings of stereotyped plan enclosed in a Palladian veneer."[47]

When establishing a lineage of the country house to help trace the later characteristics of Kocher and Frey's domestic architecture, the aforementioned relationship with the Italian villa (in general) and with the Palladian villa (in particular) must be highlighted. Substantially, as the head of the School of Architecture and a Charlottesville neighbor, Kocher's firsthand knowledge of Jeffersonian architecture must be taken for granted. His knowledge of Palladian country houses and their derivatives—like Monticello, Poplar Forest, and others surrounding Charlottesville—is also key to understanding the hybridization of traditions in Kocher and Frey's domestic architecture.

1927. A. Lawrence Kocher in *The Architectural Record*.

The University of Virginia student magazine, *College Topics*, announced Kocher's resignation in its June 14, 1927, issue, yet he seems to have remained involved in activities at UVA until 1928. By 1927, Kocher had already joined *Architectural Record* as an associate editor, and after his UVA resignation, he became managing editor. During his editorial tenure, between 1928 and 1938, he transformed the magazine into a forum for modern architecture. Of course, this was a progressive endeavor that matured in the early 1930s, but already in the first issue of January 1928, after explaining the magazine's format change for the sake of standardization, the chief editor Michael A. Mikkelsen made a cryptic statement about the changes to come:

> In the early nineties, when The Record was founded, American architecture was opening a new chapter, just as it is now...The chapter in architecture which closed with the War, and which was illustrated and praised in The Record,...is historically significant partly for certain origins of modernism but more specifically for the diffusion of cultured taste and technical excellence in architectural practice...We shall be content if the new chapter is promptly and competently recorded in the standard-size magazine. That it will be interesting we cannot doubt, but upon this Delphic utterance we are not prepared to expand very much. There will be probably something about ferro-concrete, about architectural polychromy, about a more effective direction and use of allied arts and the crafts. Possibly the impulse originated by Sullivan, developed by Frank Lloyd Wright and amplified abroad will bring repercussions from Europe. No doubt standardized shapes and machine-made surfaces will find their logical place in design. That there will be movement, enterprise, new feeling is clear from the evidence we—more particularly my colleague A. Lawrence Kocher—have taken pains to bring together in the present number.[48]

Founded in 1891, *Architectural Record* is the oldest surviving architecture magazine in the United States. Since its beginnings, the magazine had a dual focus. First, it fostered the inclusion of articles on history and criticism in traditional architecture and the extended allied arts and crafts written by renowned scholars. Second, the magazine had consistently been seeking a closer relationship between architecture and technology, paired with the Sweet's Indexed Catalogue of Building Construction, founded in 1905 and also published by the F.W. Dodge Corporation. This duality created a neat distinction between the original *Architectural Record* and other more portfolio-oriented competing journals at the time. In the early 1910s, with the appointment of a new editor-in-chief, Michael A. Mikkelsen brought the focus closer to a professional magazine, featuring more reviews of contemporary buildings, including photographs, and decreasing interest for pieces of architectural criticism.

Noting Kocher's experience in the fields of history, construction technology, and heritage preservation, it is clear how he was considered a good fit for the magazine's editorial focus. *Architectural*

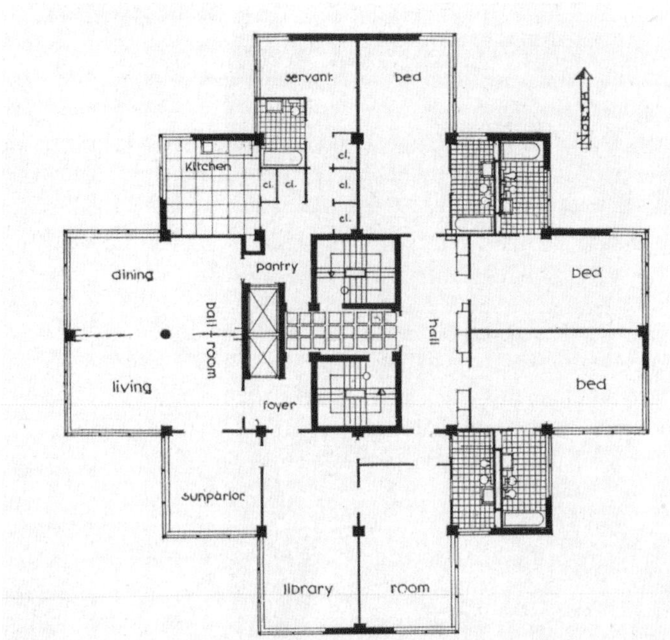

ALTERNATE C. Ten-room apartment. Living-dining rooms convertible to ballroom.

A

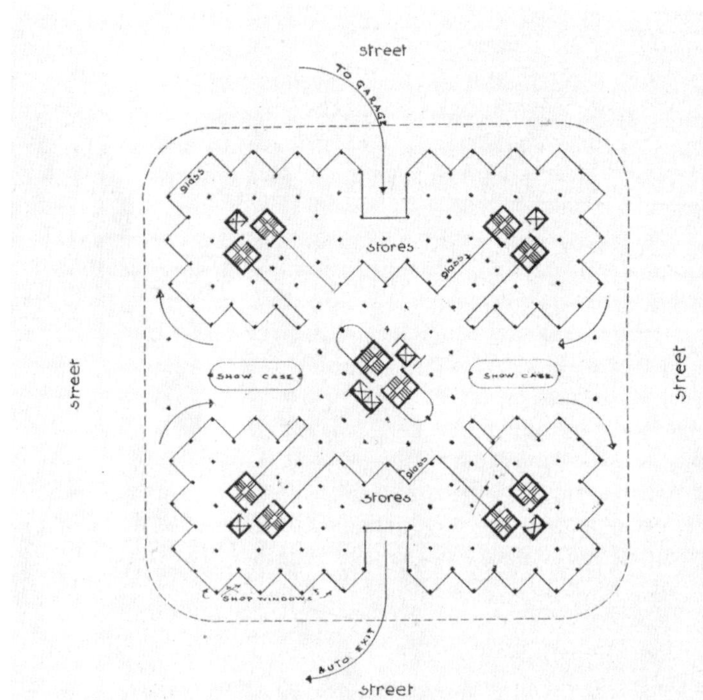

B

C

Figure 2.12. A. Lawrence Kocher and Gerhard Ziegler. Sunlight Towers. 1929. Published version. *The Architectural Record*, Volume 65, Number 3, March 1929. Various diagrams:
A. Typical floor plan. B. Ground floor plan. C. Sketch of ground floor shops.

It is a radical departure, occasioned by profound industrial and social readjustments (…) Not a partisan of any single school of experimenters, Record nevertheless assumes that the keynote of modern design is to be found in all those experiments which frankly employ the artistic qualities inherent in machine-made units, and achieve their effect through an economy of line, form and color. An interest in modern design thus soundly based is not incompatible with continued respect for principles of composition established and embodied in the past.[55]

Besides all these academic, editorial, and scholarly activities, Kocher never gave up his professional practice as an architect. During his time at Penn State, he designed three houses in The Highlands neighborhood of State College: the J.W. Henszey house at 320 East Hamilton; the E.C. Woodruff house at 234 West Fairmount; and his own home at 357 East Prospect, which was built in 1922. All three houses were representative of the type of American country house described by Kocher in his topical articles. His own house is especially interesting because he used several architectural elements reclaimed from demolished historic houses: a doorway from Dr. Constans Curtin home in Bellefonte (c. 1806), a bedroom mantel from the Hetherington house in Milton (1803–1804), and a living room mantel from the William Diller House on South Queen Street in Lancaster (1804).[56] The other two houses were designed in an American modern colonial style.

In addition to his interest in traditional architecture, Kocher advocated for modern architecture both in his own designs prior to his association with Frey and in a series of articles about standardized construction elements, minimal housing, and prefabrication. These specific articles were published in *Architectural Record* and, in many cases, were co-authored by Frey. Kocher's first completely modern project was the unbuilt design for the Sunlight Towers, published in *Architectural Record* three times: in March of 1929, March of 1930, and again in October of 1936. Kocher developed the design of these high-rise apartments associated with the German-born architect Gerhard Ziegler. Kocher and Ziegler collaborated together from 1928 to 1930, the year in which Ziegler returned to Europe. The 1929 published article and design illustrate Kocher and Ziegler's interest in natural ventilation and light as basic features for housing design. The 45-degree rotation of the housing units within the towers allowed for exposure and views in two directions, promoting cross ventilation for each apartment. The architects began the text by summarizing the advantages of a high-rise building in terms of ground occupation and functional benefits, like the avoidance of street noise and improved air quality, sun exposure, and outward views from within. The tower program was vertically divided with sunrooms, a gymnasium, and a swimming pool on the roof levels; restaurants and coffee shops on the second floor; completely glazed storefront on the ground floor; and subterranean parking. The drawings in the publication include three alternate typical floor plans, a hand drawing depicting the stores at the ground level, a typical plan and ground floor plan for an aggregation of five towers, and the aggregation drawn in perspective by the architect and illustrator Hugh Ferriss. Kocher and Ziegler also state their interest in innovative building systems and new materials: "Exterior walls are precast slab construction of aerated concrete. The interior surface of outer walls is lined with insulating material. Steel casement windows with violet-ray glass slide vertically in grooves, thus permitting complete opening and ventilation control."[57] **(Figures 2.7 to 2.11)**

The building rendered in the second published version, in 1930, created a complete separation of pedestrian and car circulation on the lower levels, which included the restaurants and retail stores. **(Figures 2.12 and 2.13)** The main part of the tower shaft is occupied by the residential program, composed by modular apartments of one, three, six, and 10 bedrooms. Each unit was given a porch with the possibility for planting—a feature that was not in the original 1929 proposal. In addition to a typical floor plan, a diagram of the lower levels, and a perspective of the building rendered in an urban setting, there is a perspective of the building in the country similar to the drawings of Le Corbusier for his Ville Contemporaine in the early 1920s. The caption of this drawing states the convenience of this country location for the inhabitant and the advantages the tower has for the surrounding landscape, preventing its own destruction due to the intensive land use typical of low-density suburbs. **(Figure 2.14)** Finally, the published 1936 iteration of the tower project was limited to simply a typical floor plan and included in an article entitled, "The Apartment Interior: Its Planning and Furnishing," authored by William Muschenheim.

Kocher and Ziegler's first materialized work was a display booth for the F. W. Dodge Corporation in the 44th annual exhibition of the Architectural League at Grand Central Palace in New York City in 1929. The booth showcased the complete office design, including furniture, for the head of a hypothetical architectural firm.[58] **(Figures 2.15 to 2.23)** The office was divided into three functional areas: the office proper with the desk of the architect for meetings with clients and employees, a reception area with couches for more informal client meetings, and a drafting space with an adjustable drawing table. The architects explained their will to renounce antique furniture and period ornamentation in favor of a functional, neutral, and calm design. The furniture was executed with chromium-plated steel tubes and Bakelite surfaces. The exhibit attracted many visitors during its week-long run and was additionally published in *Architectural Record*.[59] After the exhibition ended, many of the furniture pieces, like the desk, ended up in Kocher's office at the magazine. These light and functional tubular pieces are an important precedent to the more inventive furniture designed by Kocher and Frey for the Aluminaire House one year later.

In 1929, Kocher and Ziegler also designed the residence for Rex Stout, a famous writer of detective fiction. **(Figures 2.24 to 2.28)** The preliminary design of the house should actually be attributed to Stout, who did seven plywood models of the design, then hired Kocher and Ziegler to develop the project further. Stout also supervised the seven-month construction in Fairfield County, Connecticut, which finished in 1930. He additionally designed and executed all of the wood cabinetry. **(Figures 2.29 and 2.30)** The house is only one floor—except for the guest rooms and studio area—stepped to accommodate the hillside slope and arranged around a garden court to the east. The living room, kitchen, and primary bedroom are oriented to capture views of the rural Connecticut valley to the west. These rooms

Figure 2.13. A. Lawrence Kocher and Gerhard Ziegler. Sunlight Towers. 1930. Published version. *The Architectural Record*, March 1930. Render.

each have a terrace attached and striped corner windows similar to those of the Sunlight Towers. The spaces that relate interior with exterior are completed with a glass-roofed stepped conservatory on the south side, linking the garage and the entrance hall. The most interesting features of the house are its construction technology and color pattern. A significant contribution by the architects was the development of an innovative construction technique—an in-situ double-cast reinforced concrete façade. The Rex Stout house is considered the first poured-concrete residential construction on the American East Coast. The two cast walls are four inches each with an intermediate air space for thermal insulation, tied together with thin steel rods every two feet, and cast using Van Guilder steel molds. **(Figures 2.31 and 2.32)** The differentiating layers of poured concrete are emphasized in a way that is reminiscent of R. M. Schindler's Pueblo Rivera Court Apartments, designed in 1923 and built in 1924 in La Jolla, San Diego, California. The January 1933 issue of *Architectural Record* describes the role of color in the house, which is meant to "emphasize the third dimension"; the walls are painted in light gray when they are the background of a terrace and in black when they are a "terminating face." Steel casement windows and doors facing the exterior are painted in an orange-red color, while projecting window frames and windowsills are aluminum. Some interior walls are painted in canary yellow. The use of color, closely related to colonial architecture, will become a consistent feature in Kocher's future works.

In a 1928 article about the use of color in early American architecture, Kocher explains that paint was imported from England after a 1765 bill was introduced to Parliament, imposing a duty in the colonies on painters' colors, glass, and tea. **(Figure 2.33)** This bill triggered revolt in many parts of the colonies and encouraged local manufacturers to find new natural sources for paint production. After 1800, it was easy to find paints in more than 22 different paint colors—of which yellow was especially remarkable. Kocher states that:

> It is not possible to associate specific colors exclusively to the early or to the late periods of our native architecture. Color fashions changed so slowly and gradually that while new colors were introduced the older favorite ones were continued. The following statements indicate the prevailing tendency: Stone color, walnut-tree color, cream, gray, wainscot color and white are frequently mentioned for exterior work during the early eighteenth century. Interiors, until after the Revolution, are usually more brilliant with occasional use of intense blues, yellows, reds, olive and other greens. Exteriors of the last half of the eighteenth century continue the earlier shades but include an increasing use of white. Shutters and exterior doors were given a finish of intense green or of blue-green produced with a copper oxide. For interiors after the Revolution, pale shades and white are preferred. Moldings in churches are sometimes picked out in gilt. Ceilings are in white, cream and light green.[60]

This traditional combination of colors in façades, window frames, and doors of the exterior, along with the partitions, ceilings, and floors of the interior, can be found in most of Kocher and Frey's domestic work—the Kocher Canvas Weekend House is an outstanding example in this regard.

The last design developed by Kocher prior to his association with Frey is especially remarkable in relation to the later development of his architectural ideas. It is a miniature golf course designed between September and October of 1930, around the time Frey arrived at the office and right after Ziegler's departure. The original colored-pencil drawings are signed by Kocher and another architect whose name is indecipherable due to Kocher's sometimes illegible calligraphy.[61] **(Figures 2.34 to 2.36)** Some scholars, such as Joseph Rosa, attributed this project to Frey, but upon analyzing the design dates and the signatures on the original documents, this attribution seems conflictive. The graphic style of the original pencil drawings is extraordinarily consistent with other projects designed by Kocher before, during, and after his collaboration with Frey as those of the Sunlight Towers, the Donut Shop, and the Darien Guild Hall. Furthermore, the completeness of the design process and intent established by the drawings in the Kocher archive drives to this same conclusion: that Frey's hand was not part of these project drawings. The project was likely catalyzed by Kocher's well-documented fondness for golf.[62] The design process is documented in a series of axonometric drawings starting from a single large tent where Kocher probably observed as a means of weather protection for an existing miniature golf course. From this original tent, Kocher makes a series of iterations to reach the final solution, starting with the idea of covering each hole of the golf course with an independent tent. **(Figure 2.37)** The subsequent steps in the design process on September 27 achieve the connection among all these individual tents following the progression of the player from one hole to the next, yet still leave several gaps in between. **(Figure 2.38)** In this drawing, the tents, originally rectangular in plan, take on the shape of the different fairways and have a half-cylindrical section.[63] The last drawing in the series is dated October 1, 1930, and shows a completely developed scheme with one continuous semi-tubular canvas canopy, including all 18 holes. The canopy meanders through the lot, leaving interstitial spaces for gardens with trees. The roof coverture is complete, but the lateral canvas sometimes disappears to produce cross views of the entire golf course. **(Figure 2.39)** The structure is a metal tube frame with diagonal cross-bracing. Some free-standing perforated metal fire pits contribute modestly to the environmental conditioning of this open space. **(Figures 2.40 and 2.41)** The design of this mini golf course is an important precedent for several later works within Kocher's body of work, which incorporated canvas elements supported by light tubular skeletons in domestic designs. It is also the first evident hint, later exacerbated, of Kocher's growing propensity toward the domestic schemes and the light structures of transient American dwelling, including the motor camp and the roadside cabins. Kocher considered these modes of inhabitation as a new vernacular architecture tightly related to the automobile production and ownership boom in the United States.

Although their interests would eventually converge, Kocher and Frey had very different backgrounds and ideologies before first meeting. Kocher's profound knowledge on the realities of industry and American construction traditions contrasts with Frey's exaggerated and idealized Americanism. Upon his arrival in America, Frey was

Figure 2.14. A. Lawrence Kocher and Gerhard Ziegler. Sunlight Towers. 1930. Published version. *The Architectural Record*, March 1930. Perspective in a country location and alternate floor plans.

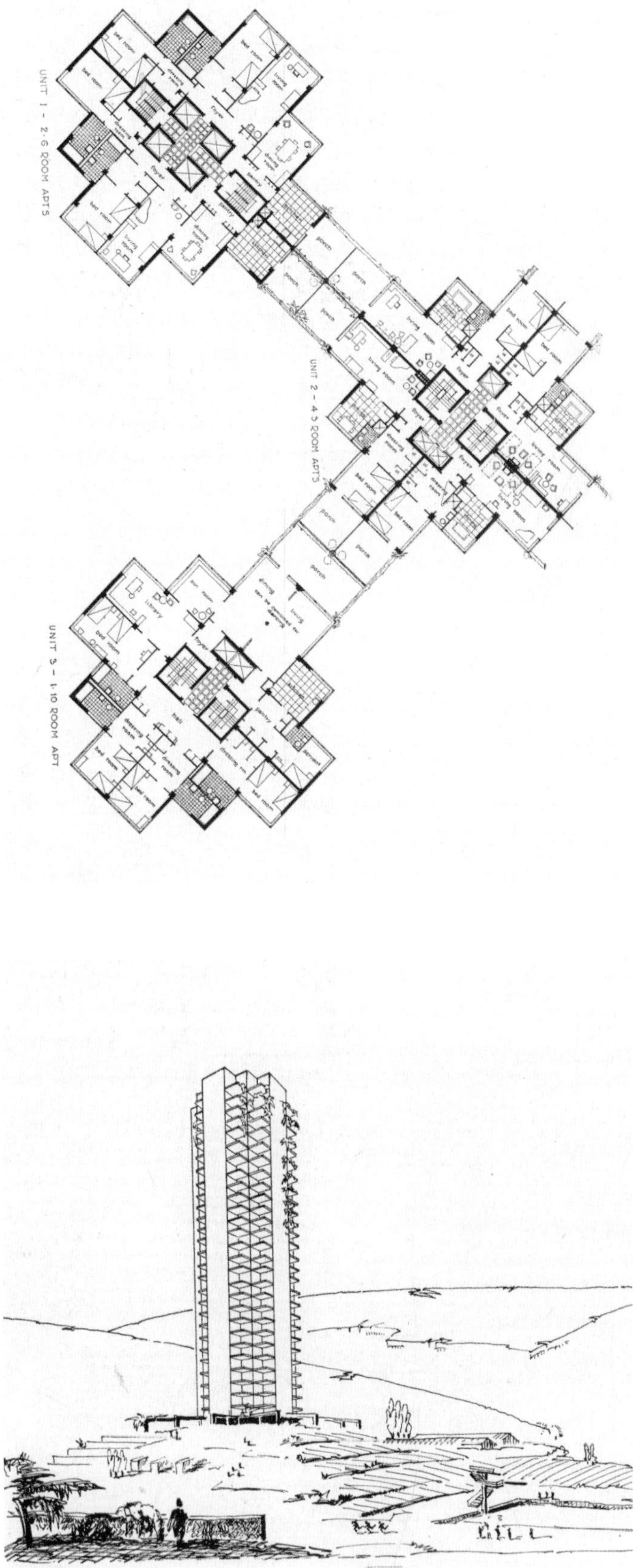

steeped in Le Corbusier's machinist ideology, knowing little about the tradition, functionality, methods, and resources of his adopted country—especially the technology in contemporary American construction. Like the rest of the European rationalist architects, Frey sought to distance himself from neo-classicist architecture, in machines specifically and purely technical objects in general. These self-proclaimed "Fordist" architects, led by Gropius and Le Corbusier, found a new vernacular in the American industrial buildings on which they could build a new tradition based on an image of functionality—far removed from industrial efficiency as the experiments of the contemporary plastic avant-garde. The photographs of American grain elevators published in the modern manifestos of Gropius and Le Corbusier were manipulated to eliminate any element belonging to the classic tradition, including pediments and friezes. Used as models for a new architecture, the factories were obsolete objects at the time of their publication and had long ago been replaced by more-efficient buildings with functional plans; otherwise, they were technically inefficient architectural objects, an effective means of propaganda for a new aesthetic of mechanical architecture.[64] Therefore, Kocher and Frey's collision exemplifies two ways of understanding the interaction between industry and architecture, which occurred with the arrival of numerous European architects in North America. The objective of the European modern movement could be summarized as plastic experimentation to obtain new forms and architectural types compatible with novel ways of living. The design objective for European rationalists and, by extension, Frey, is the architectural object itself, as industrial production becomes subordinate to the demands of its design. Industry would play a dual role as the facilitator of these formal experiments and as an abstract reference for the new forms.

In contrast, American architecture through the 1930s, maintained an alignment with the rest of the country's productive activities, which were secondary to industrial efficiency. From the formation of the American System of Manufacture to the arrival of Fordism, the focus of innovation in the U.S. shifted from the design of the produced object to the design of the production system.[65] Constant improvements in the means of production meant the objective of the design ceased to be the "production of a better object" and became a question of "how to better produce an object."[66] An emphasis on the subjective quality shifted to quantifiable measures of speed, cost, and volume. In an article about Kocher, there is an interesting quote concerning his main objective as an architect, teacher, and researcher verifying this hypothesis about the character of American architecture within his architectural thought. Sent to Walter Gropius in 1937, Kocher defined his professional activity as a "fact-finding investigation of the meaning of 'architecture' and 'the architect' with a view of discovering how architectural design may best be produced."[67] This quote indicates that Kocher's emphasis is on the forms and means of producing architecture, rather than the design itself. The technical dimension of architecture occupies a preeminent place in all facets of his activity. His penchant for testing new technological means or re-evaluating traditional building technologies guides both his professional practice as well as his writing and teaching. Unlike the European modern architects who wanted to start a new architecture by deleting historical precedents except those pertaining to anonymous industrial architecture, Kocher's appreciation of American vernacular architecture can be seen as an attempt to graft modern architecture to an existing tradition for the creation of a new national style. Kocher considered that this union could succeed on a common ground of knowledge in both traditional building techniques and cutting-edge modern material science.

Kocher and Frey's collaborative work resulted in the practice of a new type of American architecture, one that attempts to simultaneously answer two questions: "How do you design new architectural forms and objects based on industry?" and "How do you optimize the industrial production of architectural objects based on design?" Furthermore, their partnership also occurred precisely at a crucial point in United States history, beginning in the Great Depression, as the immediacy of the market crash heightened the need to answer both questions simultaneously and drove a push for the reduction in costs, increased production, and a shortening of residential construction time. This single event catalyzed their collaboration of experimental projects into the ensuing decade.

Chapter endnotes

1 The 1921 Emergency Quota Act banned all Asian immigrants—with the exception of Japanese and Filipino immigrants—and established a three percent quota for each nationality using the census of 1910. The use of the 1890 census favored immigrants with Anglo-Saxon and Western-European ancestry and penalized those of South- and Eastern-European heritage.

2 Joseph Rosa, *Albert Frey, Architect* (New York: Rizzoli International Publications, 1990), 16–17.

3 Rosa, *Albert Frey, Architect*, 17.

4 Ibid., 17.

5 Albert Frey, "Foreword," in Cynthia Zignego Stiverson, *Architecture and the Decorative Arts: the A. Lawrence Kocher Collection of Books at the Colonial Williamsburg Foundation* (West Cornwall, CT: Locust Hill Press, 1989), xv.

6 Frey, "Foreword," *Architecture and the Decorative Arts*, xvii.

7 For instance, author Joseph Rosa, quoting Phillip Johnson: "It was commonly known that, "Frey was the designer and Kocher was the writer and the front man," Rosa, *Albert Frey, Architect,* 26.

8 Ibid., 26.

9 K. Edward Lay, Professor Emeritus in Architecture of the University of Virginia states that Kocher attended to the Bauhaus, although he does not provide dates. We have not found any other evidence of this fact in any of the studied documents. K. Edward Lay, "History of the A. School. A School Built Upon the Foundation of Mr. Jefferson's Principles of Architecture," https://issuu.com/uvaschoolofarchitecture/docs/aschoolhistory_pages.

10 A. Lawrence Kocher, *The Early Architecture of Lancaster County, Pennsylvania: Being an Account of the Origin and Development of Architectural Forms in Lancaster County During the Eighteenth Century* (Lancaster, PA.: Lancaster County Historical Society, 1920).

11 A. Lawrence Kocher, "Early Architecture of Pennsylvania, Part I," *Architectural Record*, Vol. 48, No. 6 (December, 1920): 515.

12 Kocher, "Early Architecture of Pennsylvania. Part I.," 515.

13 Ibid., 518.

14 A. Lawrence Kocher, "Early Architecture of Pennsylvania. Part III," *Architectural Record*, Vol 49, No 2 (February, 1921): 136.

15 Almost contemporary to the earliest of these publications is A. Lawrence Kocher and Howard Dearstyne's book depicting the restoration procedures and reconstructed outcome of the old British colonial capital in Williamsburg, Virginia, published in 1949 and whose relevance we will treat more in depth later in this book.

16 Further, these catalogs are a precedent for the technical articles that Kocher published both as managing editor and as author (many alongside Albert Frey) in *Architectural Record* during the 1930s.

17 Frey, "Foreword," xv.

18 Jessica Kelly, "Vulgar Modernism: J. M. Richards, Modernism and the Vernacular in British Architecture," *Architectural History*, Vol. 58 (2015): 229–259.

19 Notably, these drawings were purchased and brought to the British Isles by the architect Inigo Jones 30 years after Palladio's death in 1580.

20 Another very popular edition in the U.S. is Edward Hoppus and Benjamin Cole, *Palladio, Andrea Palladio's Architecture in Four Books: The Whole Containing 226 [i.e, 222] Folio Copper Plates,* 1736. Benjn. Cole engraver the corner of Kings-Head-court, near Fetter-lane, Holbourn, & John Wilcox opposite the new church in the Strand.

21 Alexander Pope's Epistle to Burlington is the main text of the Palladian propaganda. Alexander Pope, *An Epistile to the Right Honourable Richard Earl of Burlington* (London: printed for L. Gilliver, 1731). Burlington additionally sponsored the publication of Robert Castell's 1728 *The Villas of the Ancient Illustrated*, an attempt to recreate Roman country houses and their gardens.

22 For a list of these publications, see: James Sambrook, *The Eighteenth Century: The Intellectual and Cultural Context of English Literature 1700-1789* (Abingdon: Routledge, 2016), 162.

23 A. Lawrence Kocher, "Early Architecture of Pennsylvania, Part I," *Architectural Record*, Vol 48, No 6 (December, 1920): 517.

24 A. Lawrence Kocher, "Hand Books of Samuel Rhoads, Carpenter-Builder," *Architectural Record*, Vol 50, No 6 (December, 1921): 507–509. The treatises were: William Halfpenny, *Tract on Practical Architecture, or a Sure Guide to the True Working According to the Rules of that Science; Representing the Five Orders, with their several Doors & Windows taken from Inigo Jones and other Celebrated Architects*, 1724; Batty and T. Langley, *The Builder's Jewel: or, the Youth's Remembrancer. Explaining Short and Easy Rules, Made familiar to the meanest Capacity,* 1754; Francis Prices, *The British Carpenter: or a Treatise on Carpentry. Containing the most Concise and Authentic Rules of that Art, in a more Useful and Extensive Method than has been made Public*, 1768.

25 Kocher, "Hand Books of Samuel Rhoads, Carpenter-Builder," 507–509.

26 For a more comprehensive list of these pioneer works, see: Walter Muir Whitehill and Frederick Doveton Nichols, *Palladio in America* (Milan: Electa Editrice, 1976), 104–110.

27 For a more detailed narration of Jefferson's visits to Roman ruins in France, see: https://www.francetoday.com/learn/history/jefferson_amid_the_ruins/.

28 Whitehill and Nichols, *Palladio in America*, 111.

29 Although its overall style is Palladian (designed after the drawings of Villa Trissino in Meledo de Sarego, present in the *Four Books of Architecture*, according to some historians), there are some influences that may be noted in the design of the Academic Village. The rotunda is obviously based on the Roman Pantheon. The historian Sidney Fiske Kimball first suggested the idea that the Château de Marly served as the model for the University of Virginia in his 1923 article, "The Genesis of Jefferson's Plan for the University of Virginia." Other historians, such as Michelle Benoit and Richard Guy Wilson think that "there is no one ultimate source for the design of the University of Virginia. Instead, it is unique among earlier American colleges because it draws from a variety of sources. Jefferson began forming ideas for his ideal university years before seeing the Château de Marly. He would have certainly been familiar with the oldest models of the American college — Harvard, which was established in 1636, William and Mary (1693), Yale (1701) and Princeton University (1746). Many of the earliest American colleges were connected to religious institutions, and architecturally resembled nothing more than large houses. Out of all of the American models, William and Mary was the most influential in forming Jefferson's vision of the ideal college, since he studied there from 1760 to 1762." Michelle Benoit and Richard Guy Wilson, "Jefferson and Marly: Complex Influences," *Bulletin du Centre de recherche du château de Versailles* (2012): http://journals.openedition.org/crcv/11936 ; DOI : 10.4000/crcv.11936.

30 James S. Ackerman, *The Villa: Form and Ideology of Country Houses* (Princeton: Princeton University Press, 1990), 186.

31 To study deeper this issue, see the works of UVA scholar Louis P. Nelson, especially Maurie D. McInnis and Louis P. Nelson, *Educated in Tyranny: Slavery at Thomas Jefferson's University* (Charlottesville: University of Virginia Press, 2019), and "The Architecture of Democracy in the Landscape of Slavery: Design and Construction at Jefferson's University" in Mabel O. Wilson, Lloyd Dewitt, and Corey Piper, *Thomas Jefferson, Architect: Palladian Models, Democratic Principles, and the Conflict of Ideals* (New Haven: Yale University Press, 2019). Pages 98–118.

32 Further reading about Monticello, see Ackerman, *The Villa: Form and Ideology of Country Houses*, 188–206.

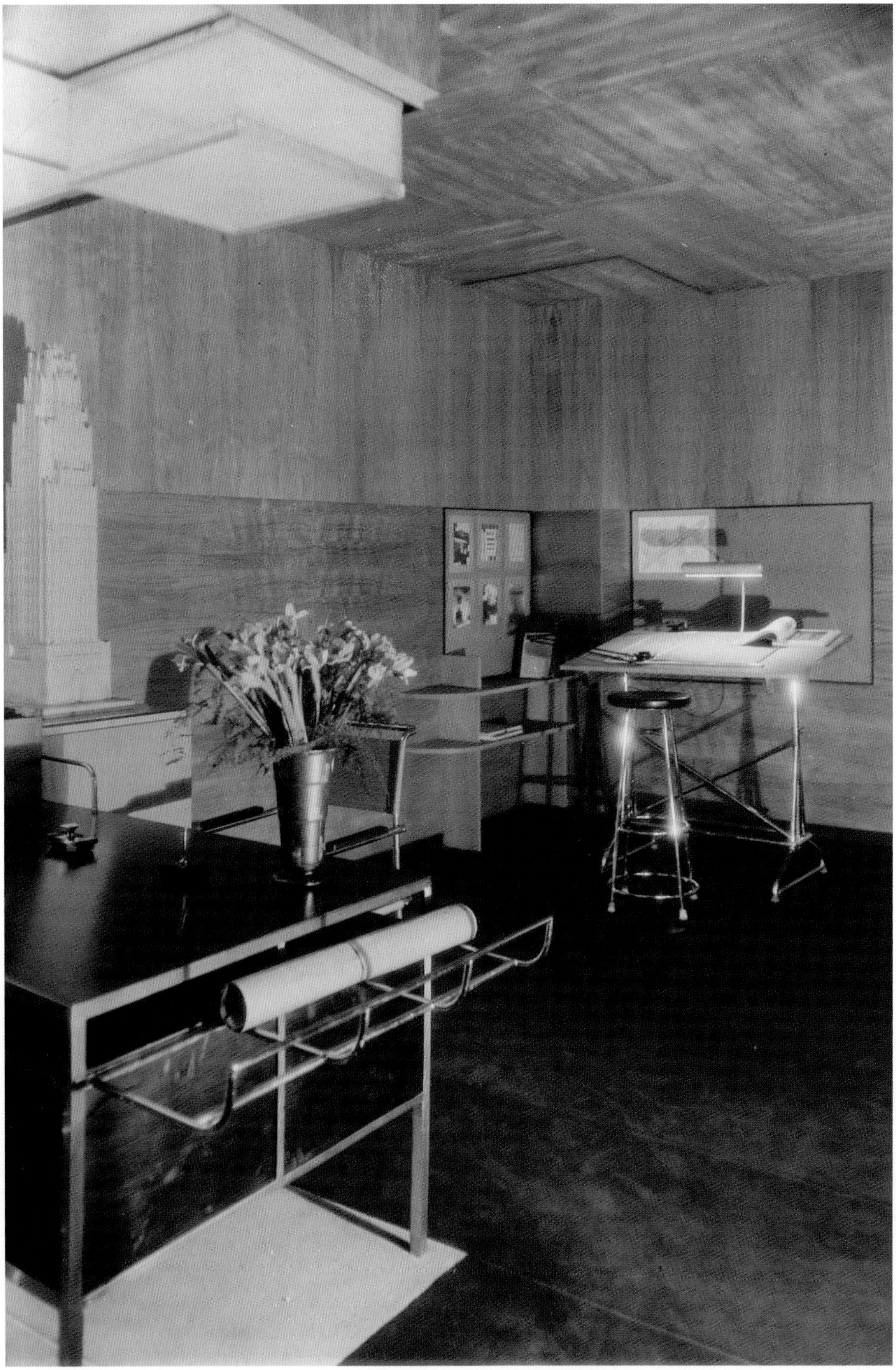

Figure 2.15. A. Lawrence Kocher and Gerhard Ziegler. Hypothetical architectural firm furniture and interior finishes for F. W. Dodge Corporation in the 44th annual exhibition of the Architectural League at Grand Central Palace in New York City. 1929. Photo.

33 There is still a sixth villa that some scholars have attributed to Jefferson, Upper Bremo, built between 1817–1820. The most updated research on Jeffersonian architecture seems to be against this attribution and leans toward the theory that Jefferson just advised and assisted his neighbor, associate, and friend, General John Hartwell Cocke (1780–1866), who was the owner of Bremo Plantation and authored the villa's design. The original drawings of the villa were done by John Neilson, who had worked for Jefferson at both Monticello and the University of Virginia.
34 The University of Virginia (UVA) was founded in Charlottesville by Thomas Jefferson, who designed the buildings of the academic village and lived nearby in his house at Monticello.
35 Stiverson, *Architecture and the Decorative Arts: The A. Lawrence Kocher Collection of Books at the Colonial Williamsburg Foundation*, 236.
36 Kocher, "Hand Books of Samuel Rhoads, Carpenter-Builder," 507–509.
37 Ibid.
38 According to Lawrence Wodehouse, Kocher's hiring by UVA was advertised in the university journal, *College Topics*, in its October issue of 1926. His resignation was published in the same magazine on June 14, 1927, although he stayed related to the University until 1928. Lawrence Wodehouse, "Kocher at Black Mountain," *Journal of the Society of Architectural Historians*, Vol. 41, No. 4 (December, 1982): 328.
39 The correspondence between university administrators regarding the negotiations of Kocher's contract date from March to July of 1926. A. Lawrence Kocher Collection, John D. Rockefeller Jr. Library, Williamsburg, Box 1.
40 Letter dated March 8th, 1926 from W.A. Lambeth, Superintendent of Buildings and Grounds to Kocher. A. Lawrence Kocher Collection, John D. Rockefeller Jr. Library, Williamsburg, Box 1.
41 Charles B. Hosmer, Jr., "Preservation Comes of Age: From Williamsburg to the National Trust, 1926-1949," *Bulletin of the Association for Preservation Technology*, Vol. 12, No. 3 (1980): 20–27.
42 Travis C. McDonald, "The Fundamental Practice of Fieldwork at Colonial Williamsburg," *Perspectives in Vernacular Architecture*, Special 25th Anniversary Issue: Vernacular Architecture Forum, Vol. 13, No. 2, (2006/2007): 36-53.
43 There is a text about the work in Williamsburg signed by Kocher as Chairman of the committee on the Williamsburg Restoration, the Preservation of Historic Monuments in Valley Forge Park, the Betsy Ross House, and several other activities in New York, Massachusetts, New Jersey, Indiana, Oklahoma, Chicago, Kentucky, Texas, and Oregon; see A. Lawrence Kocher, *American Architect and Architecture*, Vol. 135 (May 1929): 674.
44 The decalogue: 1. That all buildings or parts of buildings in which the colonial tradition persists should be retained irrespective of their actual date. 2. That where the Classical Tradition persists in buildings or parts of buildings great discretion should be exercised before destroying them. 3. That within the "Restoration Area" all work which no longer represents Colonial or Classical tradition should be demolished or removed. 4. That old buildings in Williamsburg outside the "Restoration Area" wherever possible should be left and if possible, preserved on their original sites and restored there rather than moved within the "Area." 5. That no surviving old work should be rebuilt for structural reasons if any reasonable additional trouble and expense would suffice to preserve it. 6. That there should be held in the mind of the architects and in the marketing of buildings the distinction between preservation where the object is scrupulous retention of the surviving work by ordinary repair, and restoration where the object is the recovery of the old form by new work; and that the largest practicable number of buildings should be preserved rather than restored. 7. That such preservation and restoration work require a slower pace than ordinary modern construction work and that in our opinion a superior result should be preferred to more rapid progress. 8. That in restoration the use of old materials and details of the period and character, properly marked, is commendable when they can be secured. 9. That in the securing of old materials there should be no demolition or removal of buildings where there seems a reasonable prospect that they will persist intact on their original sites. 10. That where new materials must be used, they should be of a character approximating the old as closely as possible, but that no attempt should be made to "antique" them by theatrical means. A.Lawrence Kocher and Howard Dearstyne, *Colonial Williamsburg: Its Buildings and Gardens; A Descriptive Tour of the Restored Capital of the British Colony of Virginia* (Williamsburg, VA: Colonial Williamsburg, 1961), 48–49.
45 A. Lawrence Kocher, "The Country House. An Analysis of The Architect's Method of Approach," *Architectural Record*, Vol. 62, No. 5 (November 1926): 337.
46 A. Lawrence Kocher, "The Country House. Are We Developing an American Style?" *Architectural Record*, Vol. 60, No. 5 (November 1926): 386.
47 A. Lawrence Kocher, "The Country House. An Analysis of The Architect's Method of Approach," 340.
48 Michael A. Mikkelsen, "A Word About the New Format," *Architectural Record*, Vol. 63, No. 1 (January 1928): 2.
49 *House & Garden Magazine*, 1972, quoted in Paul Makovsky, "Knud Lonberg-Holm: Bucky Fuller's Mentor, Modernism's Invisible Architect," *Metropolis Magazine* (June 17, 2017): 102–118. https://www.metropolismag.com/architecture/knud-lonberg-hold-bucky-fuller-mentor-modernism-invisible-architect/
50 His photographs were uncredited in the first edition of 1926; only in the 1928 expanded edition is Lonberg-Holm credited for 17 of the images.
51 Paul Makovsky, "Knud Lonberg-Holm: Bucky Fuller's Mentor, Modernism's Invisible Architect," 102–118.
52 Lichtenstein, Susanne (1990) "Editing Architecture: Architectural Record and the growth of modern architecture: 1928-1938," (PhD dissertation, Cornell University), 133.
53 Michael A. Mikkelson, "Expansion of Architectural Record for 1930," *Architectural Record*, Vol 66 (November, 1929): 502. Although Mikkelsen is listed as the only author of this text, some authors—such as Hyungmin Pai—have concluded that Kocher was a co-author of most, if not all, of the editorials published in this early series. Hyungmin Pai, *The Portfolio and the Diagram: Architecture, Discourse, and Modernity in America* (Cambridge: MIT Press, 2006), cited by: Anna Goodman, "Making Prefabrication American. The Work of A. Lawrence Kocher," *Journal of Architectural Education*, Vol 71, No 1 (January 2017).
54 Henry Russel Hitchcock, *Modern Architecture: Romanticism and Reintegration* (New York: Payson & Clarke Ltd., 1929).
55 Mikkelson, "Expansion of Architectural Record for 1930," 502.
56 Jacqueline Melander, "An American Style: Three State College Houses by A. Lawrence Kocher," *Centre County Heritage*, Issue 30 (Centre County Historical Society, 1994).
57 The use of radiation-protective glass, along with the color pattern depicted as "black for low buildings" and "light green for the tower," are precedents for the later domestic works of Kocher with Frey, including the Aluminaire House. The interest in light and ventilation is a consistent preoccupation in Kocher's work, who came up with the name of the Aluminaire House as a portmanteau combining the terms aluminum, air, and light. A. Lawrence Kocher and Gerhard Ziegler, "Sunlight Towers," *Architectural Record*, Vol 65 (March, 1929): 307–10.
58 *American Architect and Architecture*, 563.
59 A. Lawrence Kocher and Gerhard Ziegler, "An Architect's Office, A. Lawrence Kocher and Gerhard Ziegler, Architects," *Architectural Record*, Vol. 66, No. 3 (September, 1929): 262–268.
60 A. Lawrence Kocher, "Color in Early American Architecture, with Special References to the Origin and Development of House Painting," *Architectural Record*, Vol 64, No 4 (October, 1928): 278–290.
61 The most probable guess these authors were able to make is architect H.G. MacHeys.
62 "For recreation and exercise, Lawrence played some tennis and golf, and we would take walks along the beaches and in the woods of the island." Albert Frey, *Architecture and the Decorative Arts: The A. Lawrence Kocher Collection of Books at the Colonial Williamsburg Foundation*, 236.
63 In golf terminology, the "fairway" is the closely mown area of grass between the teeing ground and the green on a golf hole.
64 This is the case of the Ford factory at Highland Park, which was already obsolete at the time of these publications and replaced by the new Ford plant at River Rouge. The Fiat Lingotto factory in Torino, designed by engineer Giacomo Mattè-Trucco, was an exact replica of Highland Park. The factory inverted the gravity system implemented in the American factory in order to locate a car-test circuit on the roof. This made the factory highly inefficient even compared to the production of the obsolete factory in Highland Park.
65 David A. Hounshell, *From the American System to Mass Production, 1800-1932: The Development of Manufacturing Technology in the United States* (Baltimore: John Hopkins University Press, 1984).
66 The best example of this phenomenon is the Ford Motor Company, which produced the same model—the Ford-T—for 19 years, annually increasing production from 10,666 units in 1909 to 1,911,705 units in 1925, and decreasing the price of the product from the initial $850 to $260 in 1925. R.E. Houston, "Ford Production Department, August 3rd, 1927," *Model T Ford Production*, https://www.mtfca.com/encyclo/fdprod.htm.
67 A. Lawrence Kocher, "Letter to Gropius, Tentative Memorandum for Dr. Walter Gropius, Circa December 24, 1937," Box 1, Series 1: General Correspondence, Folder: Gropius, Walter, Lawrence Kocher Collection, John D. Rockefeller Jr. Library, Williamsburg. Quoted in Anna Goodman, "Making Prefabrication American: The Work of A. Lawrence Kocher," *Journal of Architectural Education*, Vol 71, No 1 (January, 2017): 22.

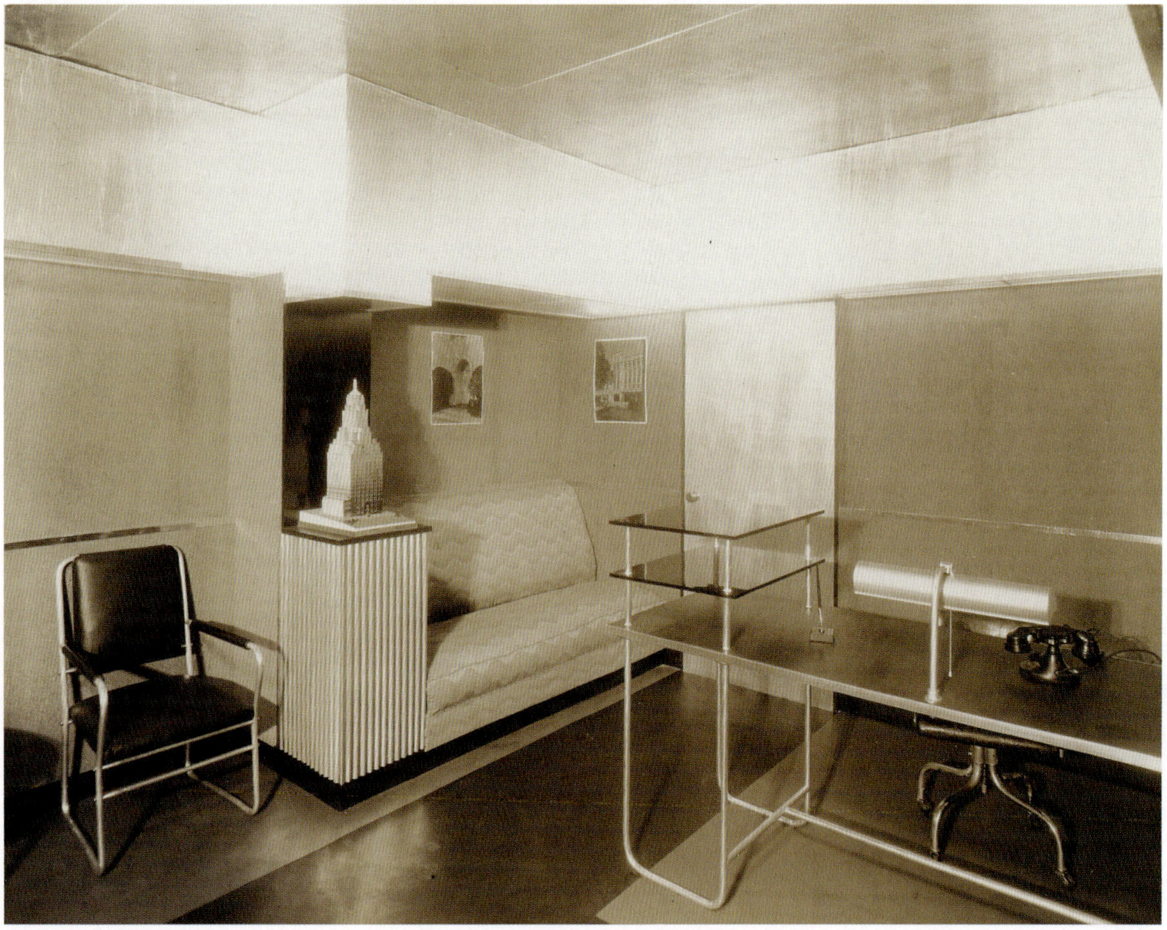

Figures 2.16 and 2.17. A. Lawrence Kocher and Gerhard Ziegler. Hypothetical architectural firm furniture and interior finishes for F. W. Dodge Corporation in the 44th annual exhibition of the Architectural League at Grand Central Palace in New York City. 1929.

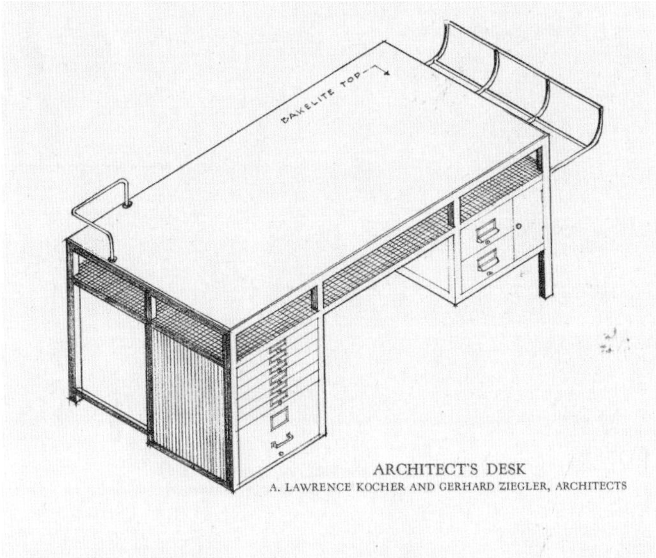

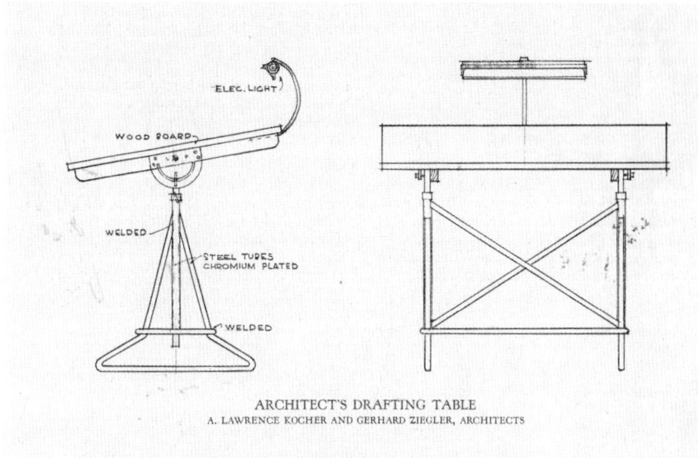

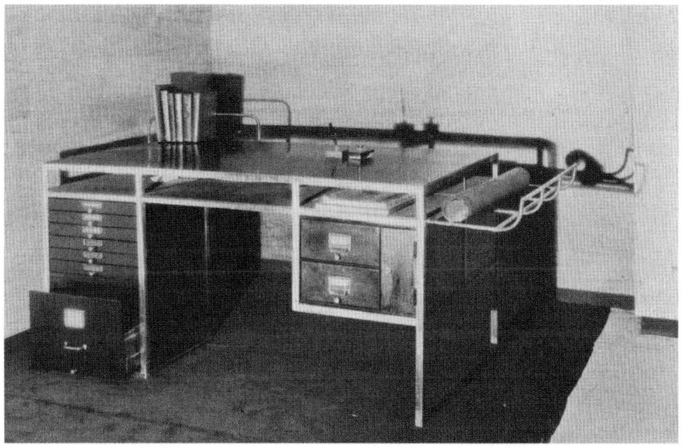

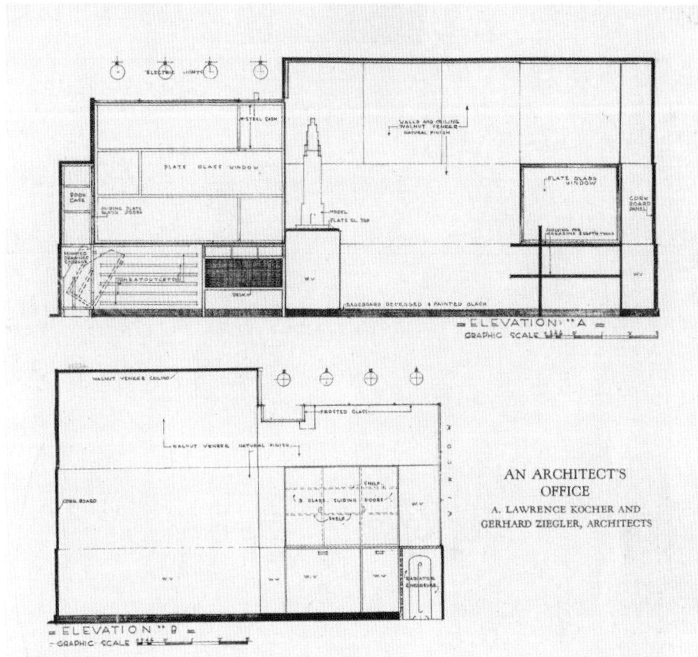

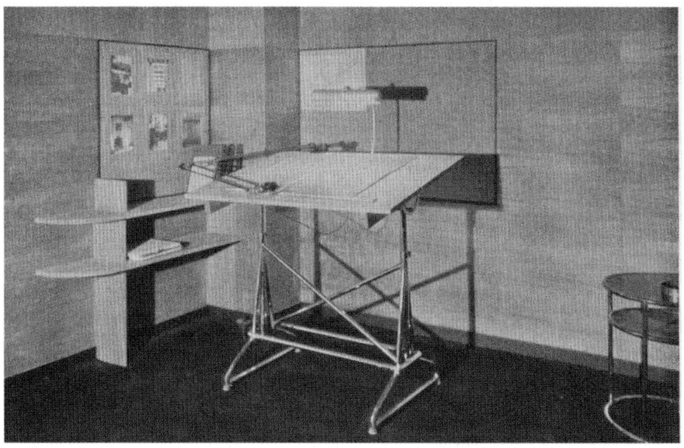

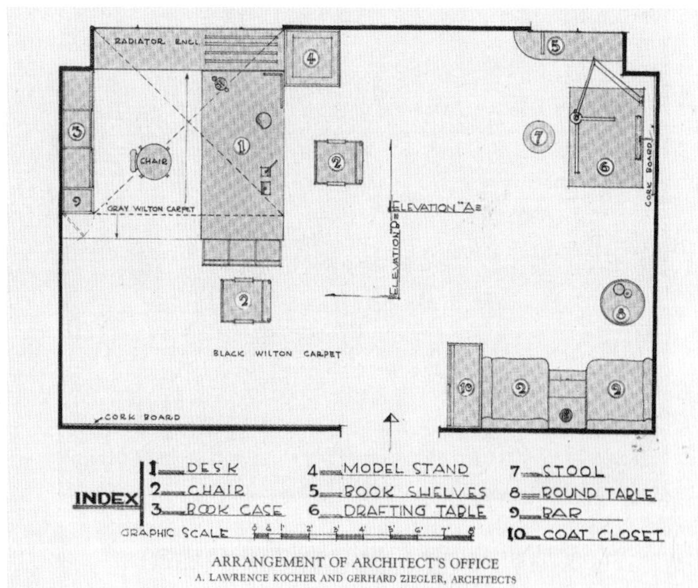

Figure 2.18 to 2.23. A. Lawrence Kocher and Gerhard Ziegler. Hypothetical architectural firm furniture and interior finishes for F. W. Dodge Corporation in the 44th annual exhibition of the Architectural League at Grand Central Palace in New York City. 1929. Drawings published in "An Architect's Office, A. Lawrence Kocher and Gerhard Ziegler, Architects," *Architectural Record*, Vol. 66, No. 3 (September, 1929): 262–268.

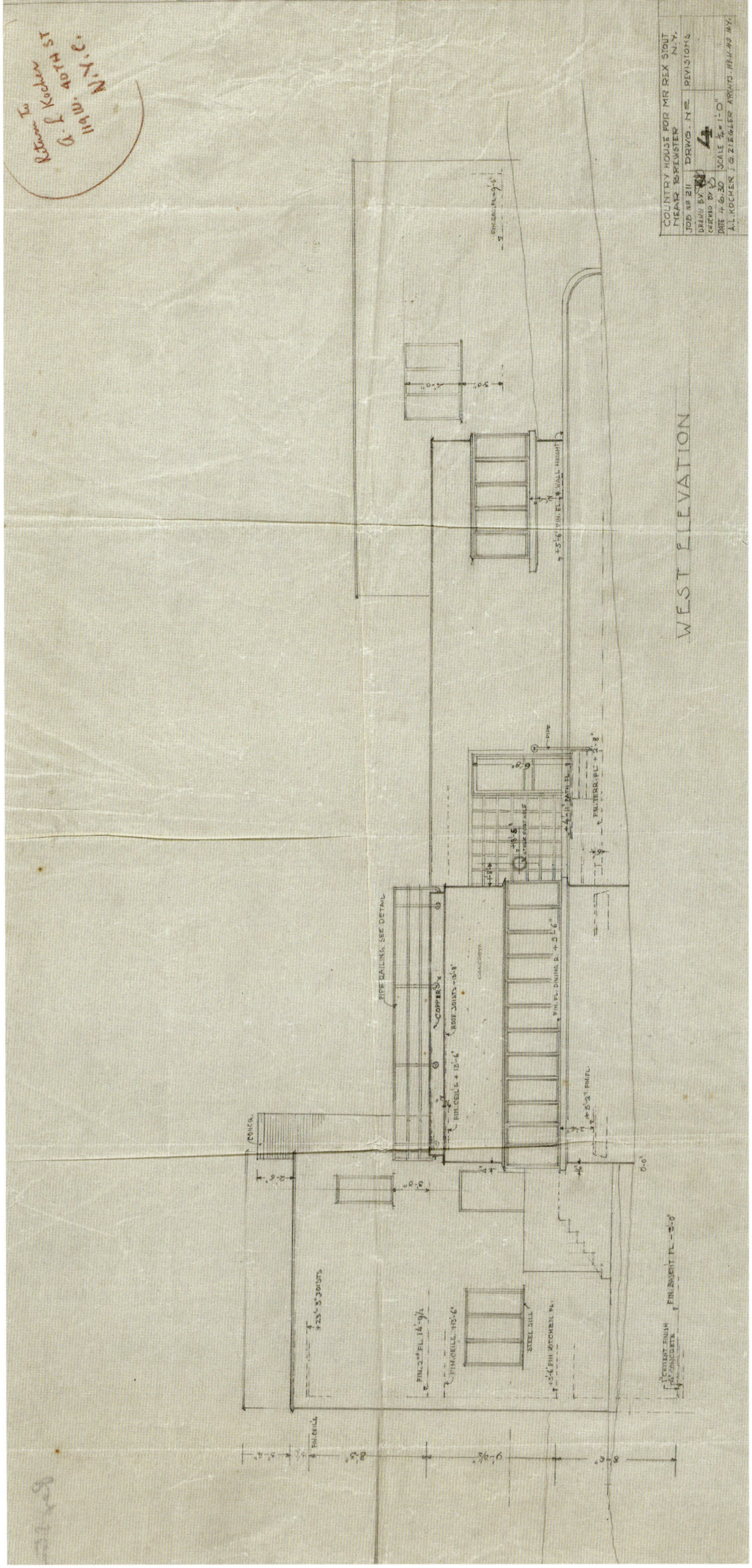

This page:
Figure 2.24. A. Lawrence Kocher and Gerhard Ziegler. Rex Stout House. Fairfield County, Connecticut. 1929–1930. Original project, west elevation.

Next page:
Figure 2.25. A. Lawrence Kocher and Gerhard Ziegler. Rex Stout House. Fairfield County, Connecticut. 1929–1930. Exterior photo by F. R. Lincoln.

This page:
Figure 2.26. A. Lawrence Kocher and Gerhard Ziegler. Rex Stout House. Fairfield County, Connecticut. 1929–1930. Exterior photo by F. R. Lincoln.

Next page:
Figure 2.27. A. Lawrence Kocher and Gerhard Ziegler. Rex Stout House. Fairfield County, Connecticut. 1929–1930. Exterior photo by F. R. Lincoln.

Figures 2.28 and 2.29. A. Lawrence Kocher and Gerhard Ziegler. Rex Stout House. Fairfield County, Connecticut. 1929–1930. Interior photos by F. R. Lincoln.

Next page:
Figure 2.30. A. Lawrence Kocher and Gerhard Ziegler. Rex Stout House. Fairfield County, Connecticut. 1929–1930. Kitchen cupboard and linen closet.

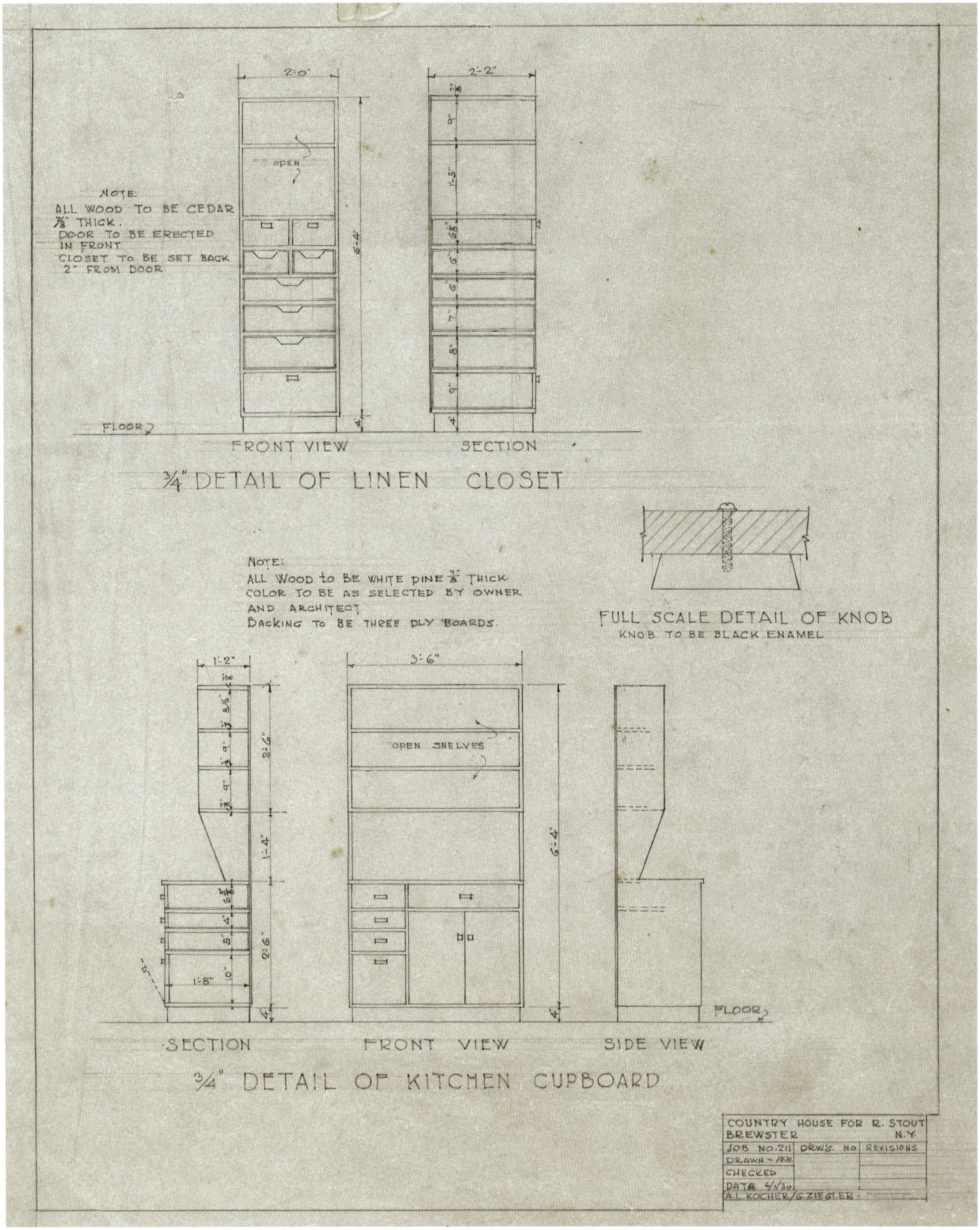
NOTE:
ALL WOOD TO BE CEDAR ⅞" THICK.
DOOR TO BE ERECTED IN FRONT
CLOSET TO BE SET BACK 2" FROM DOOR
OPEN
FLOOR
FRONT VIEW
SECTION
¾" DETAIL OF LINEN CLOSET
NOTE:
ALL WOOD TO BE WHITE PINE ⅞" THICK.
COLOR TO BE AS SELECTED BY OWNER AND ARCHITECT
BACKING TO BE THREE PLY BOARDS.
FULL SCALE DETAIL OF KNOB
KNOB TO BE BLACK ENAMEL
OPEN SHELVES
FLOOR
SECTION
FRONT VIEW
SIDE VIEW
¾" DETAIL OF KITCHEN CUPBOARD
COUNTRY HOUSE FOR R. STOUT
BREWSTER N.Y.
JOB NO. 211
DRWG. NO
REVISIONS
CHECKED
A.L. KOCHER / G. ZIEGLER

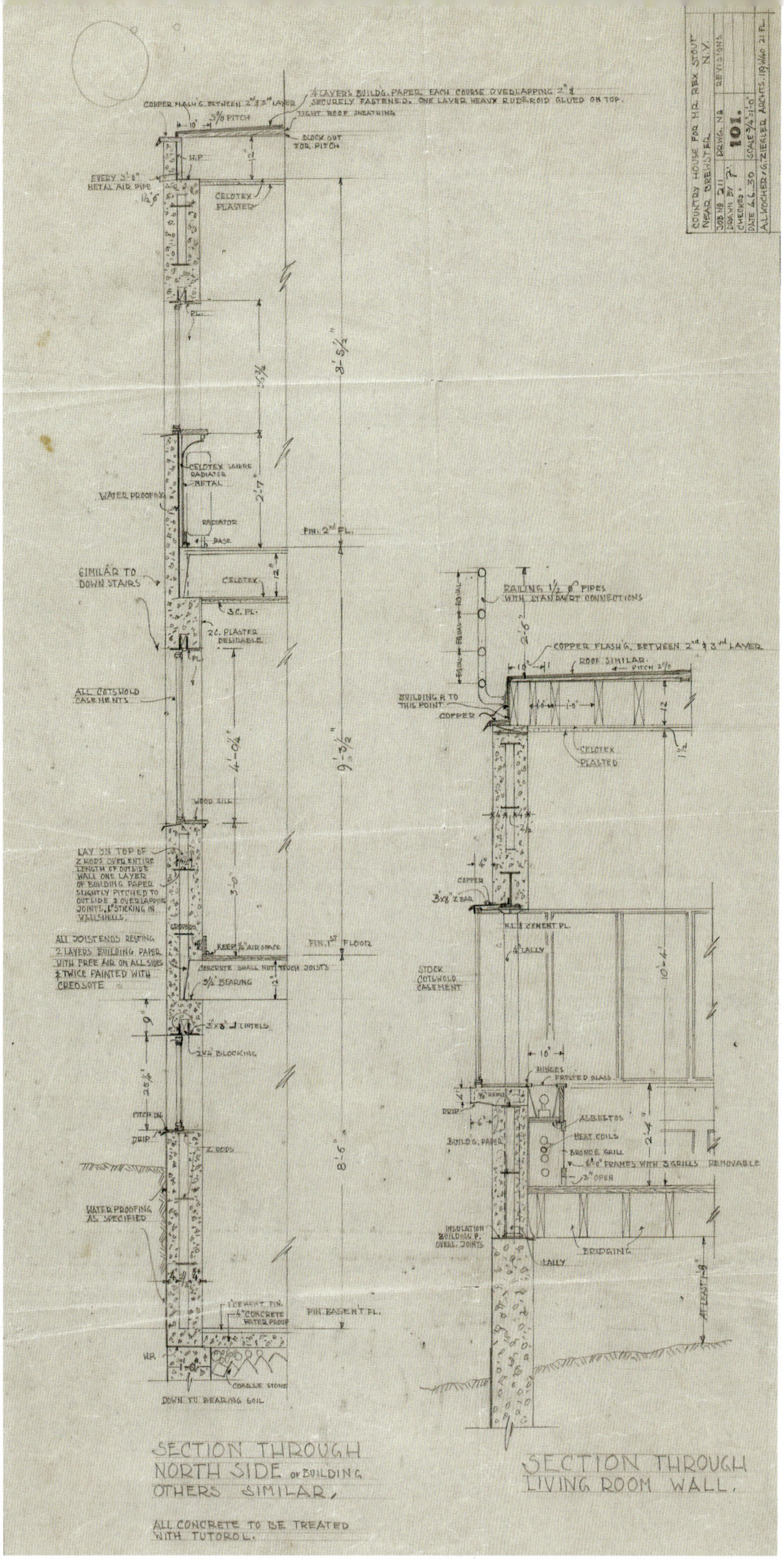

This page:

Figure 2.31. A. Lawrence Kocher and Gerhard Ziegler. Rex Stout House. Fairfield County, Connecticut. 1929–1930. Construction section of the exterior walls.

Next page:

Figure 2.32. A. Lawrence Kocher and Gerhard Ziegler. Rex Stout House. Fairfield County, Connecticut. 1929–1930. Exterior photo by F. R. Lincoln.

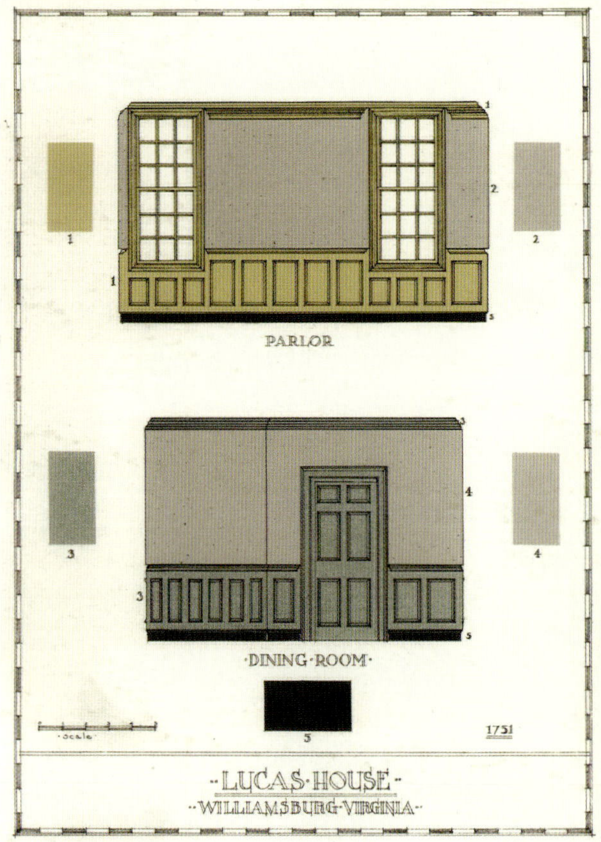

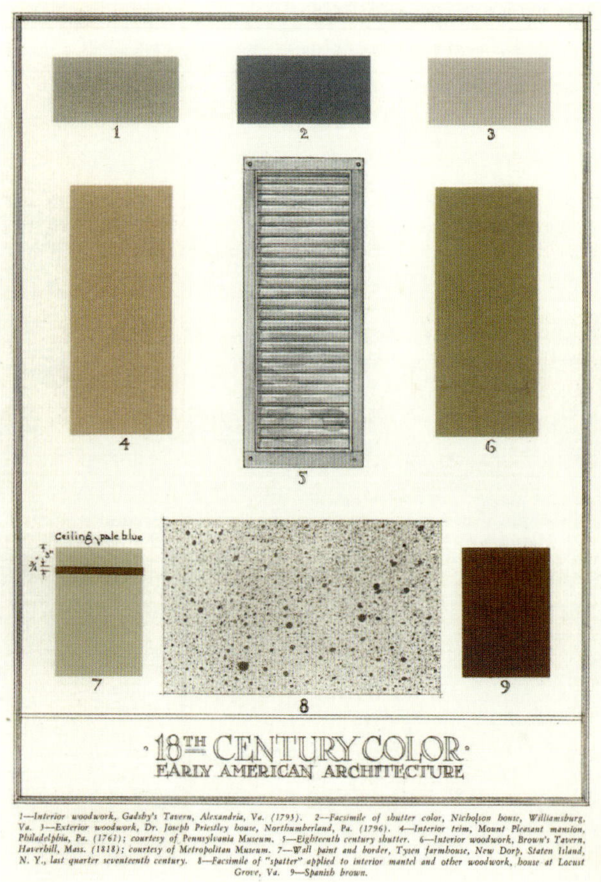

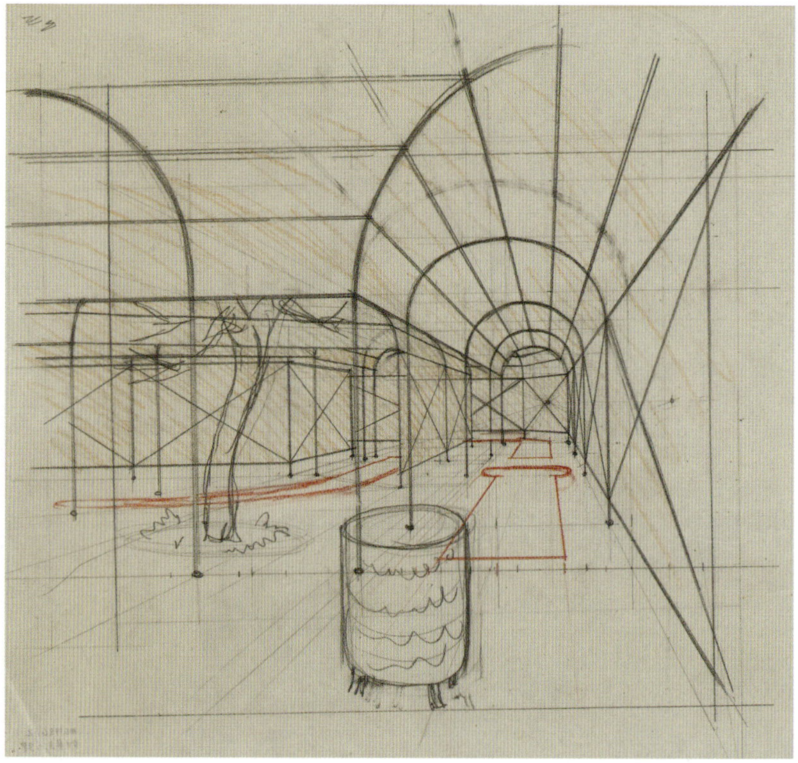

Figure 2.33. A. Lawrence Kocher. Article. "Color in Early American Architecture." *The Architectural Record*, October 1928. Page 17.

Figure 2.34. A. Lawrence Kocher. September and October of 1930. Miniature golf course.Preliminary perspective sketch. Undated.

Figure 2.35. A. Lawrence Kocher. September and October of 1930. Miniature golf course. Preliminary perspective sketch. Undated.

Figure 2.36. A. Lawrence Kocher. September and October of 1930. Miniature golf course. Final perspective sketch. Dated 10-1-30.

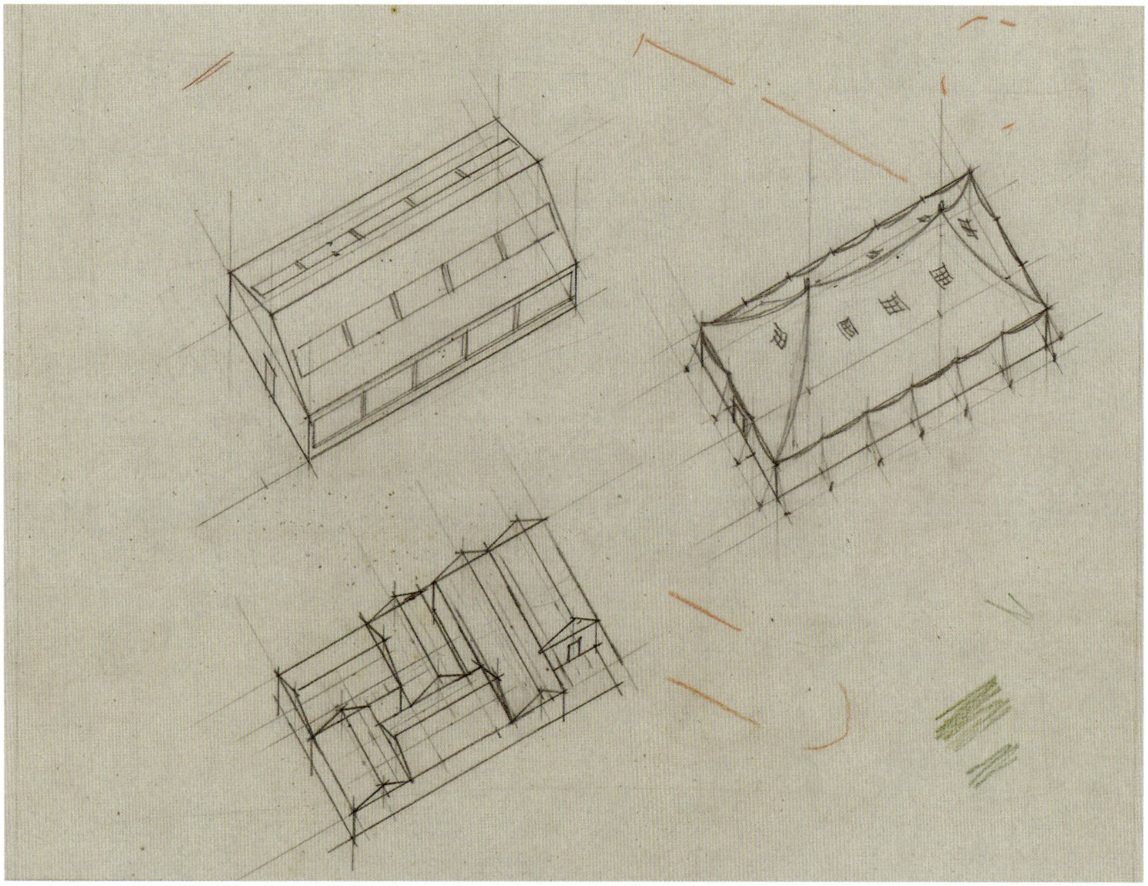

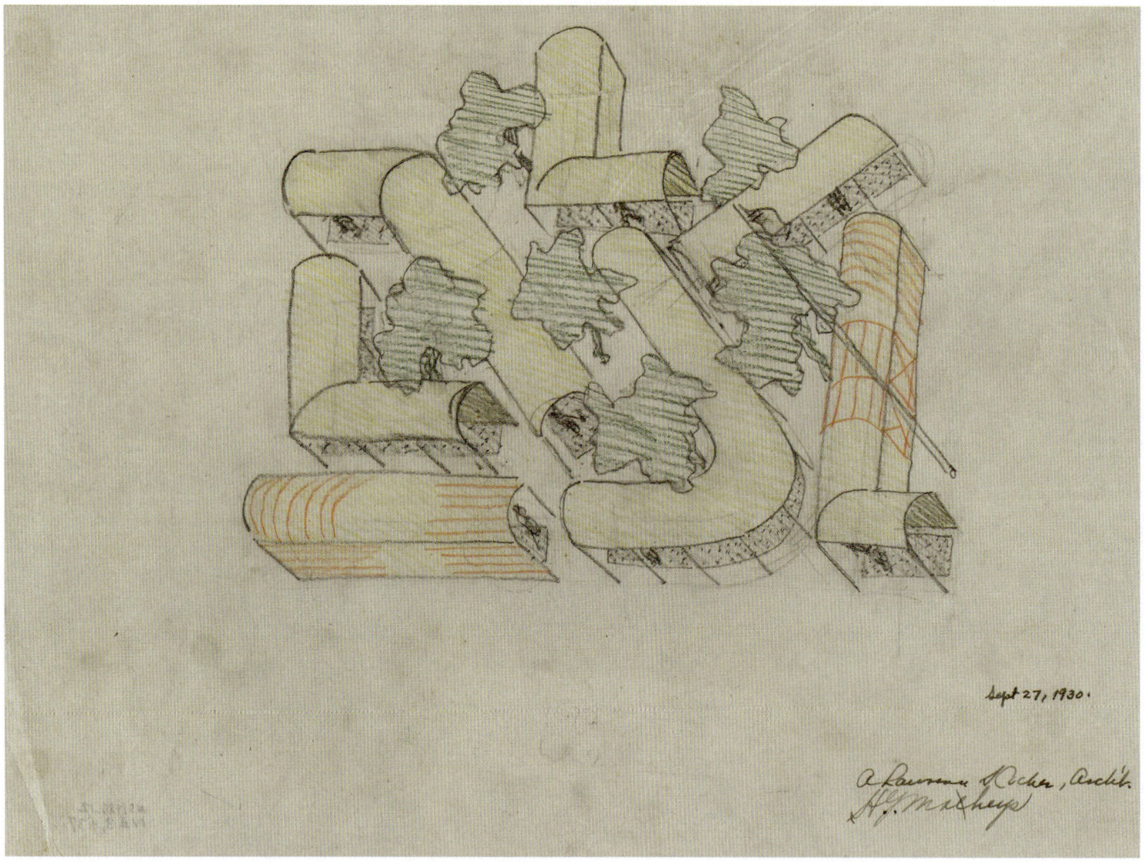
Sept 27, 1930.
A Lawrence Kocher, Archt.

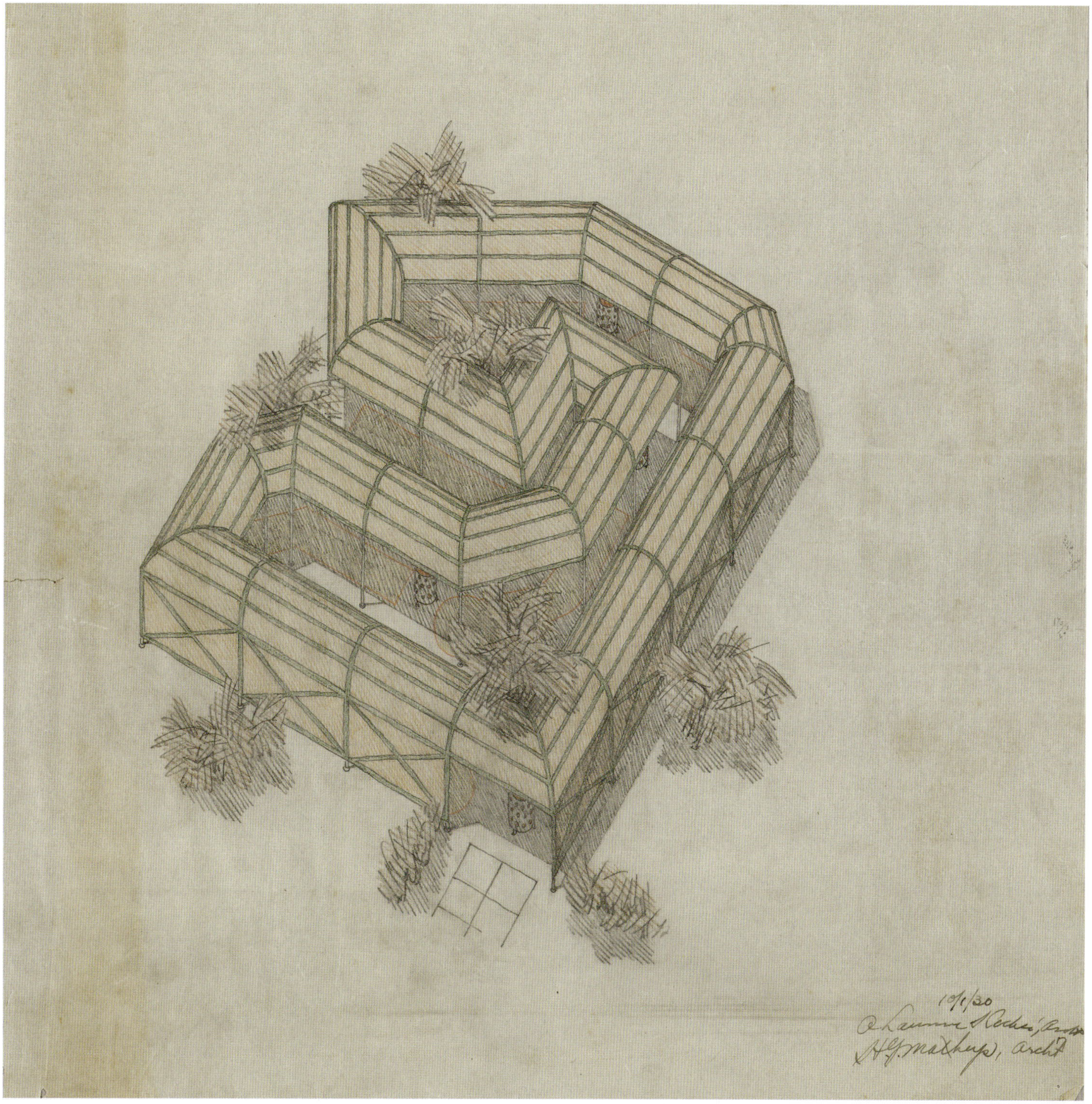

Previous page:
Figure 2.37. A. Lawrence Kocher. September and October of 1930. Miniature golf course. Initial scheme axonometric sketch. Undated.
Figure 2.38. A. Lawrence Kocher. September and October of 1930. Miniature golf course. Intermediate scheme axonometric sketch. Dated 9-27-30.

This page:
Figure 2.39. A. Lawrence Kocher. September and October of 1930. Miniature golf course. Final scheme axonometric sketch. Dated 10-1-30.

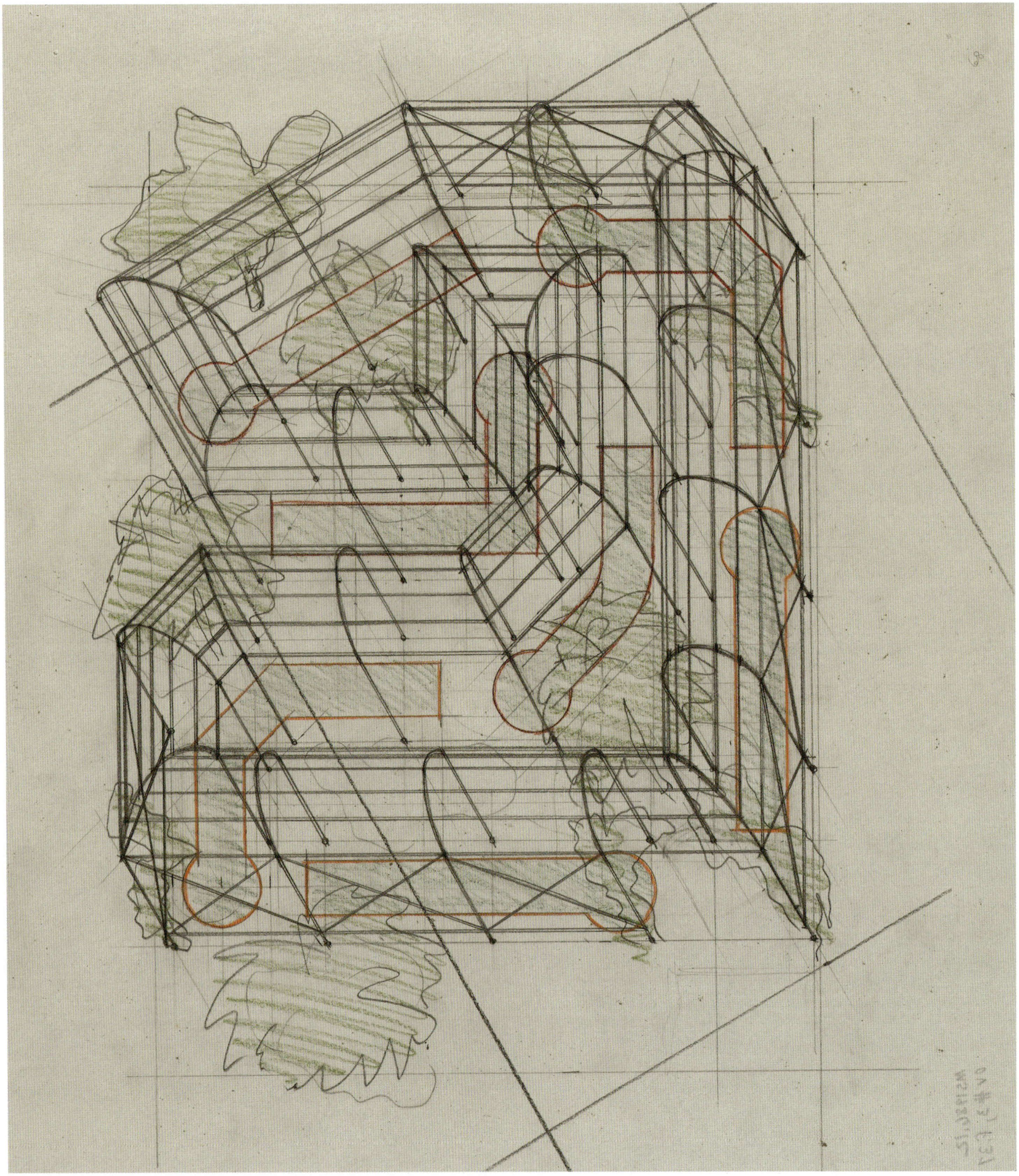

Figure 2.40. A. Lawrence Kocher. September and October of 1930. Miniature golf course. Final scheme preliminary axonometric sketch. Undated.
Figure 2.41. A. Lawrence Kocher. September and October of 1930. Miniature golf course. Final scheme definitive axonometric sketch. Dated 10-1-1930.

10/1/1980

1931–1933

THE EXPERIMENTAL WEEKEND HOUSE AND PARALLEL EXPERIENCES

After the Aluminaire House, A. Lawrence Kocher and Albert Frey produced their designs in a transitional social and political context: before and after F. D. Roosevelt's inauguration on March 4, 1933.[1] At the end of 1931, the depression was evident for the majority of the American population. Skyrocketing unemployment rates, along with the failure of banks, businesses, and farms, shattered the optimism of a once-prosperous United States and its middle-class dream.[2] The United States government, presided by Herbert Hoover, based its anti-crisis strategy in the dogma of self-reliance deeply rooted in American individualism and the belief that the federal government should stay out of the personal lives of citizens even in cases of dire necessity. Hoover firmly believed that direct aid to the individual was not the business of the federal government but of private enterprise, charity institutions, and local governments.

While unsuccessful in the long run, many private institutions created temporary relief programs, like the sidewalk apple sellers who organized in November of 1930 by the International Apple Shippers Association. Similarly, the Seattle-founded Unemployed Citizens League (UCL) formed in July of 1931; financed by the mayor's office, UCL organized self-help projects, like cutting wood on donated land, picking unwanted fruit, and distributing food and wood for those most in need. Other private charity institutions and wealthy individuals set up soup kitchens and bread lines for the starving crowds. All of these efforts soon proved to be just a temporary relief—completely inefficient in a scenario of long sustained economic hardship. Adding to the general calamities, in July of 1930, a drought of biblical proportions occurred in the Great Plains, the South, and the Midwest, and Hoover—following his politic of nonintervention instead of using federal means—delegated disaster relief to the Red Cross.

Although faithful to his self-reliance credo, Hoover nevertheless authorized $700 million in public works projects and created a series of agencies to deal with the depression in 1931. A number of them were completely useless and many collapsed in just a few years, like the National Business Survey Conference, the National Credit Corporation, and the President's Emergency Committee for Employment (PECE)—restructured within a year as the President's Organization for Unemployment Relief (POUR). Other organizations set up by the Hoover administration were more durable and successful, such as the Reconstruction Finance Corporation (RFC) that carried on operations during the New Deal years and had been funded by Congress with two billion dollars "to provide emergency financing facilities for financial institutions, to aid in financing agriculture, commerce, and industry, and for other purposes."[3] Contemporaneous to RFC's founding was the White House Conference on Home Building and Home Ownership, which was privately funded and occurred from December 2 to December 5 in 1931. The conference's aim, and the role of the government within it, was explained by President Hoover:

> To undertake the organization of an adequate investigation and study, on a nationwide scale, of the problems presented in homeownership and homebuilding, with the hope of developing the facts and a better understanding of the questions involved and inspiring better organization and the removal of influences which seriously limit the spread of homeownership, both town and country...It, obviously, is not our purpose to set up the Federal Government in the building of homes. But the Conference will, I believe, afford a basis for the development of a sound policy, and inspire better voluntary organization to cope with the problem.[4]

A planning committee of approximately 20 voluntary associations formed to conduct studies and set up a national conference to analyze and assess the data and recommendations compiled by expert committees.[5] For one year prior, about 400 persons prepared studies for the conference, and 1,000 individuals related to building and housing were enlisted to participate in the White House Conference. Twenty-five committees oversaw the study of specific fields within the general problem of housing covered by the conference.[6] Six correlating committees dealt with any issue of aim and method that may have been raised, coordinating the initial 25 committees. These correlating committees were devoted to standards and objectives, legislation and administration, education and service, and organization programs—local and national—and technological developments.[7] Most of Kocher and Frey's speculative and research-oriented work during 1931 was directly or indirectly related to several of these committees.

In November of 1931, Kocher and Frey designed a proposal for two low-cost farmhouses, published in 1932 and again in 1934 in Architectural Record.[8] The publication included only two plans, model pictures, and a partial axonometric-cutaway view of the construction system. This project was commissioned by the Committee on Farm and Village Housing of the White House

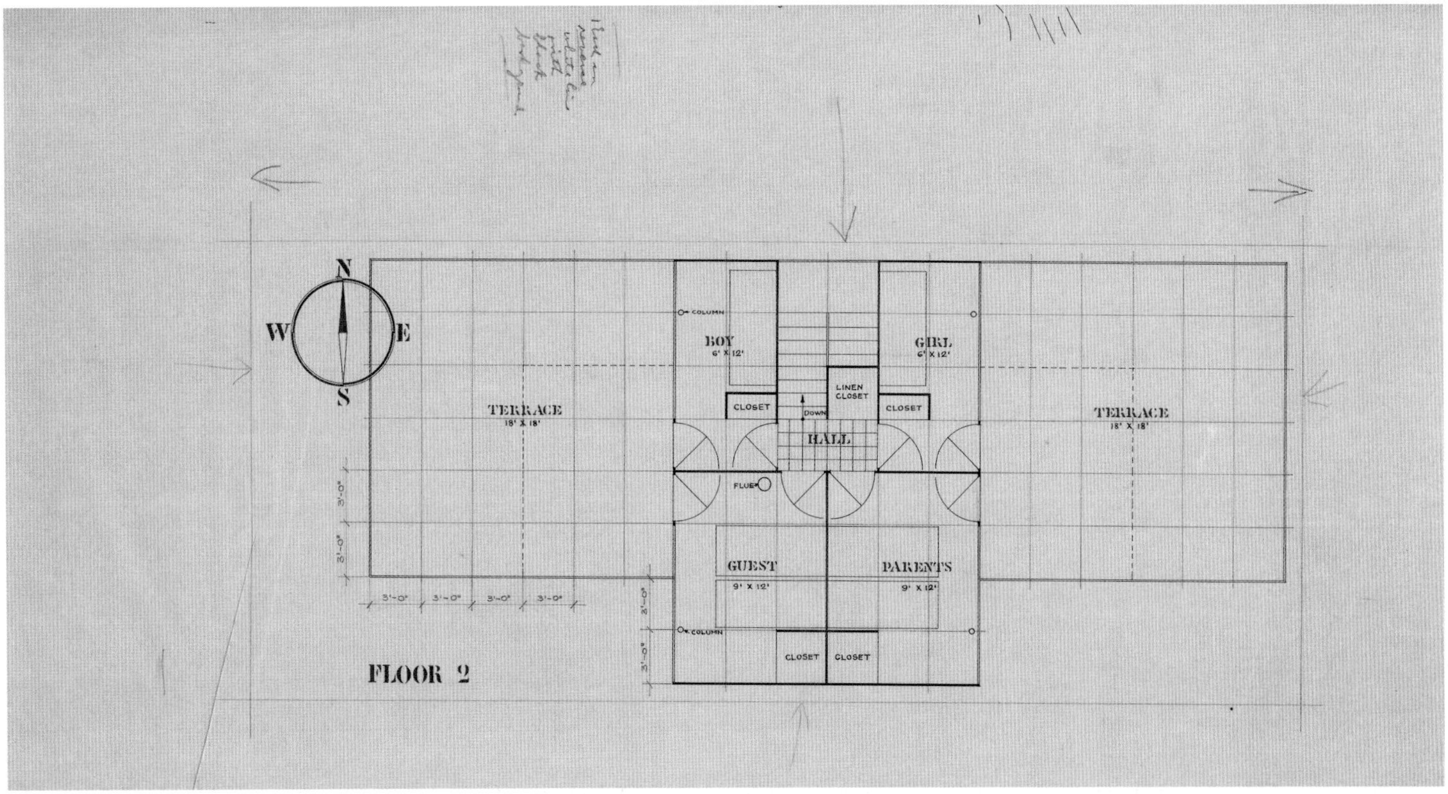

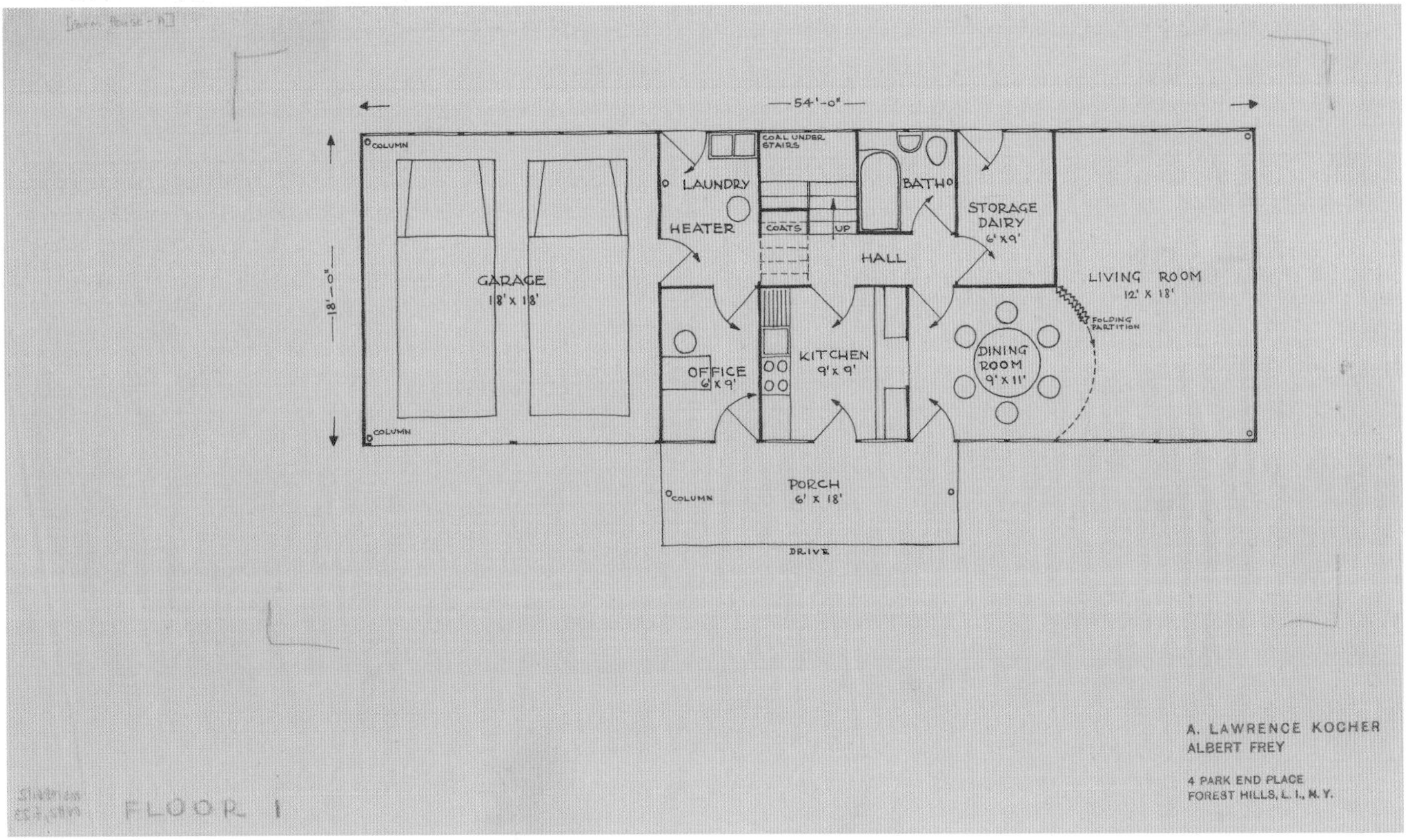

Figure 3.1 and 3.2. A. Lawrence Kocher and Albert Frey. 1931. Low-Cost Farmhouse type A. Original drawings. First and second floor.

Conference on Home Building and Home Ownership.[9] Through this unbuilt proposal, the two architects attempted to demonstrate the viability of a house construction method that used readily available industrially manufactured materials, an idea they had studied and demonstrated in the Aluminaire House. The program was determined by a group of sociologists specializing in rural life; the aim was to build a type of prefabricated, low-cost dwelling that could be disassembled, transported, and reassembled in a short period of time without using specialized labor. A requirement of the project specified that all components had to be completely reusable and recyclable. Furthermore, the system had to allow for the extension and replacement of its elements. Both houses are distributed across two floors to minimize the footprint and budgetary costs on foundations. Following recommendations by the Committee on Farm and Village Housing, the expected lifespan of the construction would last a full generation given the proposal was fully protected from fire, tornado, and earthquakes, along with termites, vermin, and corrosion.

Farmhouse A was designed for the Midwest and Farmhouse B for the temperate zone. Each design had a strict three-foot modulation and a similar construction. The main structure was composed of standardized rolled-steel I-shape beams. These girders spanned 18 feet and connected easily to the circular columns slightly set back from the façades, a system already used in the Aluminaire House that allows a perfectly even modulation in every elevation. These I-beams cantilever three feet to create a porch on the south façade in both farmhouse iterations. The main structure holds a secondary system of prefabricated steel open-web trusses, also spanning 18 feet and set three feet apart. On top of the open-web trusses there was a prefabricated steel deck, similar to the *Ferrobord* used in the Aluminaire House. Cork insulation and linoleum flooring were then laid on this platform. The façade was constructed using T-shaped rolled-steel studs cladded with rigid insulation and three-foot-by-eight-foot-by-one-inch boards with an interior and exterior metallic finish that were adjusted and fixed by a continuous exterior vertical staple to ensure water tightness. A common feature in the two farmhouse types was the orientation of the generously glazed façades. On the first floor, glazing was exclusively placed in the north- and south-facing façades, leaving the west- and the east-facing sides completely opaque. The opposite happened on the second floor, where all the windows face east and west, connecting bedrooms and terraces. Kocher and Frey placed awnings (in type B) and fabric walls (in type A) on the terraces to alleviate the excessive sun radiation exposure to the second-floor windows.

With overall dimensions of 18 by 54 feet and a gross area of 1,134 square feet—which did not include a 108-square-foot porch, 684 square feet of terraces, and an enclosed 324-square-foot garage—the Type A had a $3,000 cost. **(Figures 3.1 and 3.2)** This farmhouse iteration had its longest façades oriented both north and south and was laid out in three squares, each subdivided into 36 three-by-three-foot modules. The first floor (216 square feet) was organized in a garage using the entirety of the west square with capacity for two vehicles; a central square contained all services (kitchen, bathroom, laundry, and heater room) and a steep stair with only 14 risers was placed in the center of the north side. The placement of the stair required the use of load-bearing walls to make the structure feasible. The central section also included an office for farm use with independent exterior access. The columns of this section were shifted three feet to the south façade to create a porch under a three-foot cantilever. The girders also cantilevered to the north side in an attempt both to maintain a consistent span and to improve structural behavior through symmetry. The first floor's east square included a dining and living room separated by a curved folding partition, recalling the Aluminaire House's exercise-room division. This east section also incorporated a dairy storage room accessible from the hall and the exterior. While the house has six possible means of access, there is an entry procession that is potentiated by the distribution: starting from the garage, occupants would cross the laundry-heater room, reaching a work clothes closet under the stairs, then use the hall to access the rest of the rooms. This sequence, determined by the Committee on Farm and Village Housing, enabled farm workers to remove their boots and work clothes and wash up before accessing the proper home. On the second floor, along the east and west sections, are two large (18-by-18-foot) terraces accessible from the bedrooms. The central section cantilevers to the south using eight-by-six square modules to form a rectangular shape that contains two individual (six-by-12-foot) and two double (nine-by-12-foot) bedrooms with built-in closets. The circulation spaces were kept spatially minimal with only 18 square feet on the second floor and 36 square feet on the first.

A smaller alternative to the Type A, the architects estimated that the Type B would cost about $1,500 to order; it could be built in 200 hours and disassembled in only 12. The Type B house fit into one and a half 18-by-18-foot squares with a footprint of 18 by 27 feet and a gross area of 702 square feet, plus a 162 square-foot garage fitting one vehicle, a 54-square-foot porch, and a 162-square-foot terrace. **(Figures 3.3 and 3.4)** These tighter dimensions pushed the designers to use more creative solutions for spatial distribution, sowing the seed for future developments in their work. The first floor is quite conventional, including the kitchen, a nook, the bathroom, a laundry-heater room, and a storage room only accessible from the exterior of the house. Here, the stairwell was shifted from the center to the northwest corner of the main section, yet the stair itself was dysfunctional, as the placement of the linen closet on the second floor did not leave enough clearance to be used unless its bottom followed the slope of the stair, and its placement conflicted with the main structural beams running along the west side of the main square. The second floor contained a feature that became common in Kocher and Frey's subsequent designs: to solve the lack of a living room on the first floor, the architects set up a flexible multi-purpose area on the second floor. This area can be swapped from a living room during the day to two double bedrooms during the night thanks to a folding partition in the middle of the space. A profusion of closets in the west wall of this area serves to store beds and furniture, allowing for a swift change in the way the inhabitants used the space. More sophisticated iterations of this feature come later in the Weekend Experimental House (1932) and the Kocher Canvas Weekend House (1934).

These two farmhouse designs clearly had strong ties to the Aluminaire House, and although deeply rooted in the American prefabrication industrial standards in construction, the stylistic influences of Le Corbusier are evident, but may not be exclusive. **(Figure 3.5)**

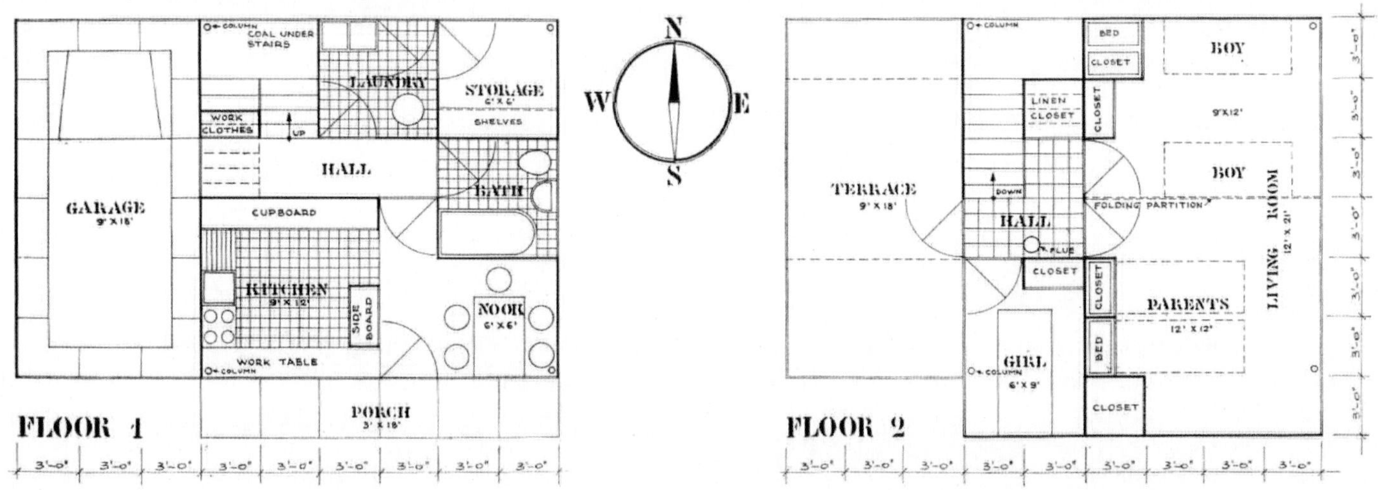

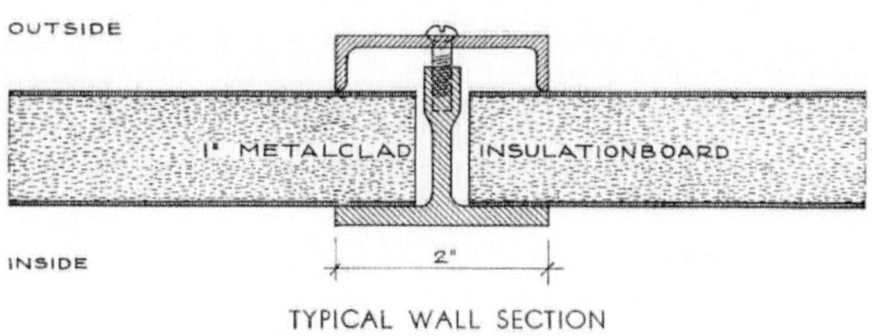

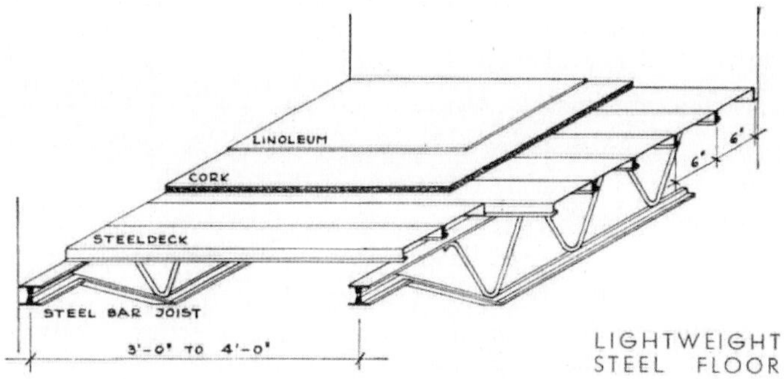

Figure 3.3. A. Lawrence Kocher and Albert Frey. 1931. Low-Cost Farmhouse type B. Published in *Architectural Record*, Vol. 75, No. 1 (January 1934).

Some researchers such as Joseph Rosa pointed out a conceptual relation with Walter Gropius' prefabricated experimental house in the *Weisenhofsiedlung* of Stuttgart, built in 1927 and visited by Frey that same year. Although both Gropius' house and Kocher and Frey's farmhouses have a very strict modulation in plan, each with two stories and a very light construction system, the similarities end there. The structure proposed in the two farmhouses was a post-and-beam system with open-web trusses for the roof and floor beams. This kind of construction was more similar to the Eames House (1949), for example, than to Weissenhof housing of the Werkbund Exhibition in Stuttgart, which was built with load-bearing frame walls using Z-shaped steel profiles as studs in the non-load-bearing walls, and I- and C-profiles in the load-bearing walls and beams. In Gropius' design, slabs were built with wood decking directly on top of the steel beams instead of the more sophisticated steel deck of the farmhouses. The façade systems were also completely different: Gropius's building used the structural Z-studs supplemented with wood stripes to nail two layers onto the façade, with the external sheathing made of Eternit (asbestos-cement panels), and the internal of Enso and Celotex light fiberboards. Water tightness of the external cladding is ensured by nailing vertical stripes of Eternit board, and thermal insulation was achieved through an intermediate compressed cork board. The Gropius façade system is very different from the one depicted for the farmhouses with the non-load-bearing walls composed of one insulation board pressed between a T-shaped profile and a U-shaped external continuous vertical staple. Other scholars, like Neil Jackson, have pointed out the lack of appreciation demonstrated by Albert Frey after visiting Gropius's building and thinking that "they looked as old boxes and had no articulation to them."[10]

Real Estate Subdivisions for Low-Cost Housing was published in April 1931, followed by *Model of Farmhouse of Low Cost* in May 1932, which was developed during 1931 for the White House Conference in December of that same year. Regardless of constructability and any functional problems we may find in these projects, they were key investigations in the development of A. Lawrence Kocher and Albert Frey's design methodology. When trying to position *Real Estate Subdivisions for Low-Cost Housing* within their larger body of work that appeared in *Architectural Record* during the 1930s, it is clear that the article relates to the research from the White House Conference's Subdivision Layout Committee.[11] These two articles were also considered part of a larger set of Kocher and Frey's writings published in *Architectural Record*, which explored aspects of architecture central to residential design. A. L. Kocher and A. Frey's articles fall into two basic categories defined by interrelated themes: first, the study of minimal housing produced by sizing architectural elements using functional criteria; and second, the research on the use of new construction materials and methods. Both themes align perfectly with many of the investigations developed during their work for the White House Conference on Home Building and Home Ownership. Our guess is that all these articles were developed or at least initiated during 1931 in close relation with the Washington, D.C., meeting and published sequentially during the following years.

Following their research and publications for the presidential conference, Kocher and Frey continued publishing articles for *Architectural Record* between 1931 and 1933 on the sizing of spaces and everyday furniture. They featured a large number of drawings that illustrated the standard dimensions of different elements such as: the domestic garage (January, 1931), windows (February, 1931), closets (March, 1931), stairs and ramps (July, 1931), kitchens (January, 1932), bedrooms and bathrooms (February, 1932), and the dimensions of chairs and tables (April, 1932). **(Figures 3.6 to 3.13)** This research series was later compiled into an extensive article, published in October of 1934 and titled, "Check List for New Construction and Modernization of Houses including Dimensions of Essential Equipment and Furniture." Importantly, this article series pioneered the graphic standardization of architectural elements in the United States. Kocher and Frey were the first to include modern furniture alongside industrialized and standardized architectural elements in this type of construction catalog.[12]

In the second thematic category of Kocher and Frey's theoretical works, their 1933 article titled "New Materials and Improved Construction Methods" reviewed innovative uses of new materials, emphasizing the need to reduce labor and transport costs in residential construction by using prefabrication and lighter materials.[13] The authors also examined various construction systems for roofs along with floor structures and façades, analyzing them through a series of axonometric projections. **(Figure 3.14)** This article is complemented by another appearing in the same issue, titled "Technical Research. Wood, Textiles, Paper," which contemplates numerous construction applications for materials, such as waterproof plywood produced using phenolic resin glue, fire-proof wooden panels, various types of connectors for construction elements, and paper impregnated with latex to make it damp resistant.[14] Thanks to their collaboration on the Aluminaire House, this substantial body of theoretical research on minimal housing, prefabrication, new materials, and industrialized construction systems formed the substrate on which the rest of Kocher and Frey's houses were designed. They generated an experimental framework through which we can not only understand their work, but also the adjacent projects developed by other architects working at that time.

Alongside their theoretical and research work, Kocher and Frey also collaborated on private commissions. Simultaneous to the design of the Aluminaire House, they worked on a Guild Hall in Darien, Connecticut.[15] **(Figures 3.15 and 3.16)** Due to budgetary difficulties, the Guild Hall project was never executed, but it was exhibited in New York City at the Architectural League's annual Allied Arts Show in April of 1931.[16] The project's design intent used an aggregation of different pre-designed volumes around a central multipurpose space dedicated to either the auditorium or exhibition space. The aggregated volumes took the size, proportions, and shape optimized for each varying program and attached to the central core, with functional requirements determining the best adjacencies. **(Figures 3.17 and 3.18)** Because its limits are solid, except when an entrance is dictated by the adjacency of another piece, the central volume of the auditorium/exhibition hall allowed for multiple ways of attachment; a clerestory set back from the façade line, supported by two lines of round columns, naturally lit the space. The system of aggregation allowed the designers to take full advantage of the site, shifting each piece vertically until it fit the topography. The

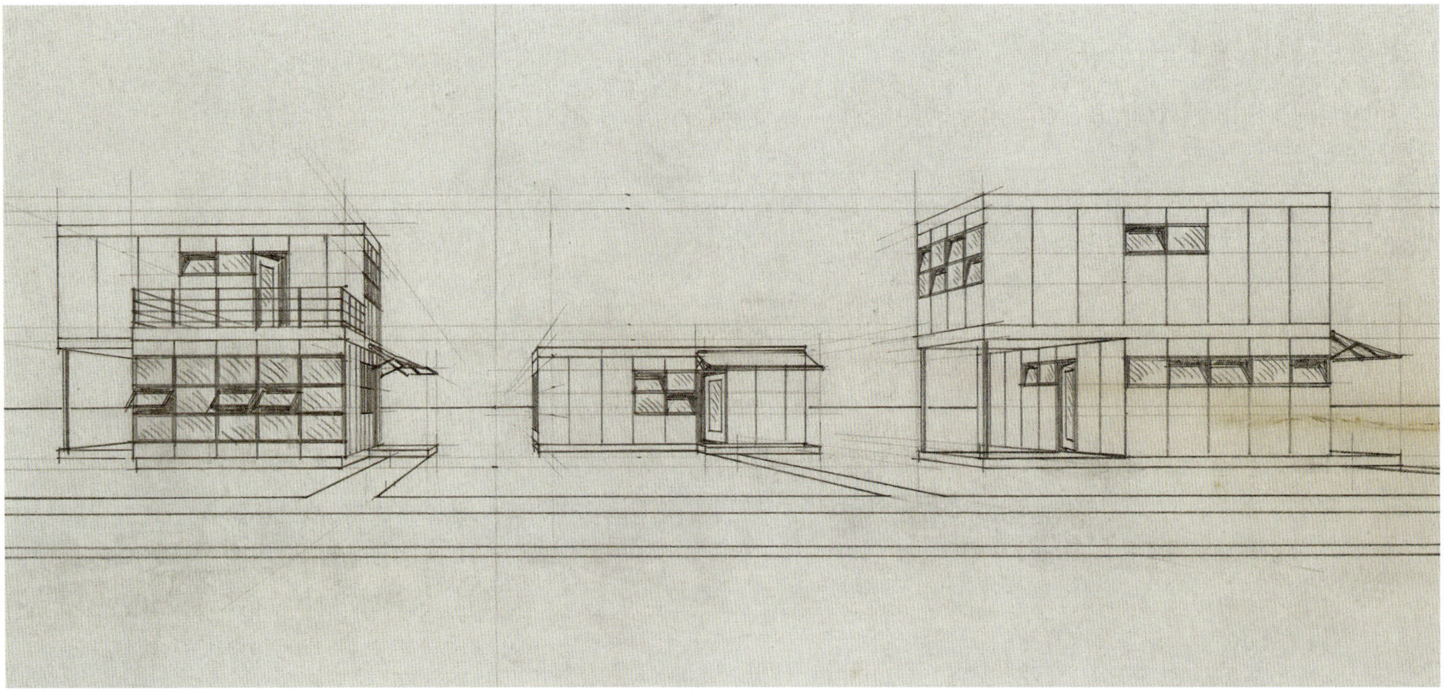

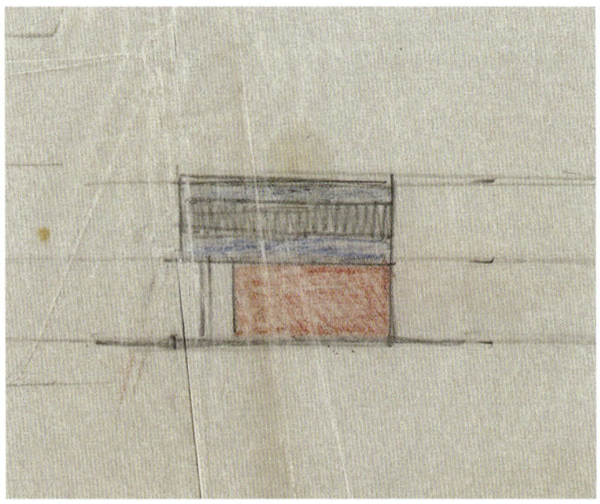

Figure 3.4. A. Lawrence Kocher and Albert Frey. 1931. Low-Cost Farmhouses. Original drawings. One-point perspective of the farmhouses.
Figure 3.5. A. Lawrence Kocher and Albert Frey. 1931. Low-Cost Farmhouse type A. Original drawings. Color Patterns in the façades. Details.

program's main entrance was placed on the lowest level of the site, under a bridge containing the main stair and lobby, and included ancillary services as restrooms, coat room, and the ticket and information office. The remaining secondary programs serving the auditorium/exhibition hall—the stage and studio, a furniture storage room, kitchen, and the dressing rooms—were placed vertically and horizontally for the most adequate situation regarding both site and program. **(Figures 3.19 to 3.30)**

In February 1931, Kocher incorporated Frey as designer into an ongoing furniture and interior design project, assisted by the architect R.L. Davison who advised on materials. After Kocher and Gerhard Ziegler's successful booth design at Architectural League's 44th Annual Exhibition at Grand Central Palace in New York City in 1929, F.W. Dodge Co. commissioned a new exhibition display booth for the 1931 Southern Architecture and Allied Arts Exposition in Memphis, Tennessee. Designed in February and March of 1931, the design concept was for a small architectural office that included a reception and furnishings used by an architect, such as desks, chairs, model-display stands, and bookshelves. The material finishes used for the interior walls and floor were consistent with Kocher's previous material research, prescribing rubber flooring, and walls combining cork and aluminum foil. The design of the furniture is decidedly modern and very similar to his 1929 designs and to the furniture of the Aluminaire House.[17] **(Figures 3.31 to 3.35)**

In June of 1931, five months before the design of the two farmhouses, Kocher and Frey produced the design documents for a site-less prototype: a Downyflake Donut Shop. After acquiring Adolph Levitt's automated doughnut machine in the early 1930s, the Donut Corporation of America launched the Downyflake franchise. They wanted to understand how a standardized shop could be designed and reached out to Kocher. In terms of building technology, the Downyflake Donut Shop could be considered a precedent for the farmhouses; both share all the main constructive features: a similar structural system, façade composition, and modulation. Architecturally, the Downyflake project resembled Darien Guild Hall, with a compelling volumetric interplay including a setback clerestory to monitor the main dining room while hiding views to the back service area with a completely opaque wall. The building offers a long porch to the adjacent main street with an entry, a sales window, and large plate glass at the end—where the donut machine stood publicly on display. On top of this window, a three-dimensional donut advertising Downyflake popped out of the façade on the second floor. This commercial project, of secondary relevance within Kocher and Frey's body of work, is nevertheless a token of their design ideology in which the means of production are as important as the product itself. **(Figures 3.36 to 3.51)**

Despite all of this work, the earnings of Kocher and Frey's office were still scarce, and the economic distress of the Great Depression was still ramping up. Kocher was able to supplement his income with the salary from *Architectural Record,* where he spent his afternoons, devoting the morning to the architectural office. However, Frey had to take additional part-time work for his fellow countryman William Lescaze.[18] While working for Howe and Lescaze, Frey collaborated on the Chrystie-Forsyth Street Housing Development, The River Garden Housing Project, and the Museum of Modern Art (MoMA), some of the office's most important designs. Frey kept both employments until July 1932:

> "While continuing to live and collaborate with Lawrence Kocher, I started to work afternoons with the architect William Lescaze, and I was able to buy a Model A Ford convertible. Driving into New York from Forest Hills, I could park near Lescaze's office at the east end of 42nd Street near the river."[19]

Immediately following Aluminaire House's inaugural exhibition in April 1931—concurrent with the research articles published in *Architectural Review* and the design of the Downyflake Donut Shop—Kocher received a commission from Charles Everett of the Cotton-Textile Institute to research the potentials of cotton as a building material. The client posed three questions, which were later stated in the design brief provided by the architects: With the aid of building-materials manufacturers, is it possible to improve and cheapen the construction of a house using derivatives of cotton? Can faulty existing building materials be improved by fabric application or reinforcement? Are there possibilities for mill owners to increase the value of their products with new processing methods that could serve building materials manufacture?[20] To answer these questions, the architects researched the use of cotton as a construction method in buildings. Everett had already initiated some experiments that applied fabric to pulp board, which were shared with the architects. Kocher and Frey contacted many institutions for their ongoing research, such as Algoma Plywood Co., Haskelite Manufacturing Co., Harnischfeger Corp., The U.S. Forest Products Laboratory, and the Pierce Foundation for House Research.[21] They also found a system used by the United States Navy for finishing, waterproofing, and fireproofing the ship decks with painted cotton fabric. In addition to decks, this marine treated canvas had also been used for roofs. Frey was no stranger to canvas; he had built canoes with waterproofed fabric when he was in Switzerland.

With the main idea of using canvas as an exterior sheathing material, Kocher and Frey worked on two different concept houses using canvas for the façades. They planned to present their work in an exhibition in Washington, D.C., sponsored by the Cotton-Textile Institute. According to Frey's own words, the exhibition was scheduled to be installed during Kocher and Frey's attendance to the President Hoover's Conference on Housing, then inaugurated immediately following the program.[22] At the beginning of 1932, Kocher and Frey presented two residential proposals for an exhibition named *Cotton Houses,* listed as *Cotton-Steel Houses* in the description sheets archived at the A. Lawrence Kocher Papers in Williamsburg. One residence was an Experimental Weekend House, while the other was the more conventional Experimental Five-Room House—a larger single-family residence. According to the existing photographs, the exhibition was very modest and included: a single table displaying each model, four pictures of the models, plan drawings, and a diagrammatic site plan demonstrating an aggregation of five units from the Experimental Five-Room House. **(Figure 3.52)** Both residential proposals shared a lightweight construction system and presented an exhaustive experiment in

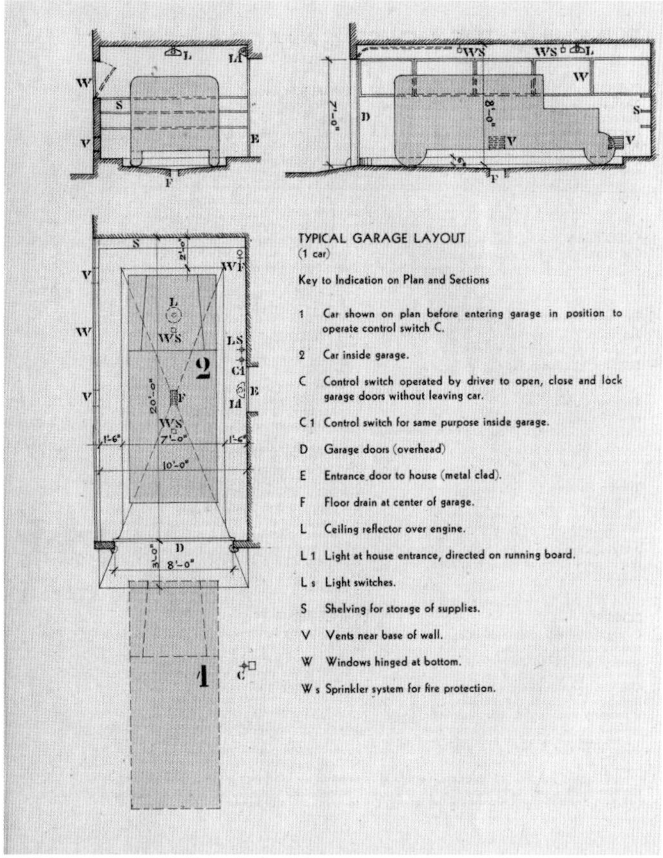

TYPICAL GARAGE LAYOUT
(1 car)

Key to Indication on Plan and Sections

1 Car shown on plan before entering garage in position to operate control switch C.

2 Car inside garage.

C Control switch operated by driver to open, close and lock garage doors without leaving car.

C 1 Control switch for same purpose inside garage.

D Garage doors (overhead)

E Entrance door to house (metal clad).

F Floor drain at center of garage.

L Ceiling reflector over engine.

L 1 Light at house entrance, directed on running board.

L s Light switches.

S Shelving for storage of supplies.

V Vents near base of wall.

W Windows hinged at bottom.

W s Sprinkler system for fire protection.

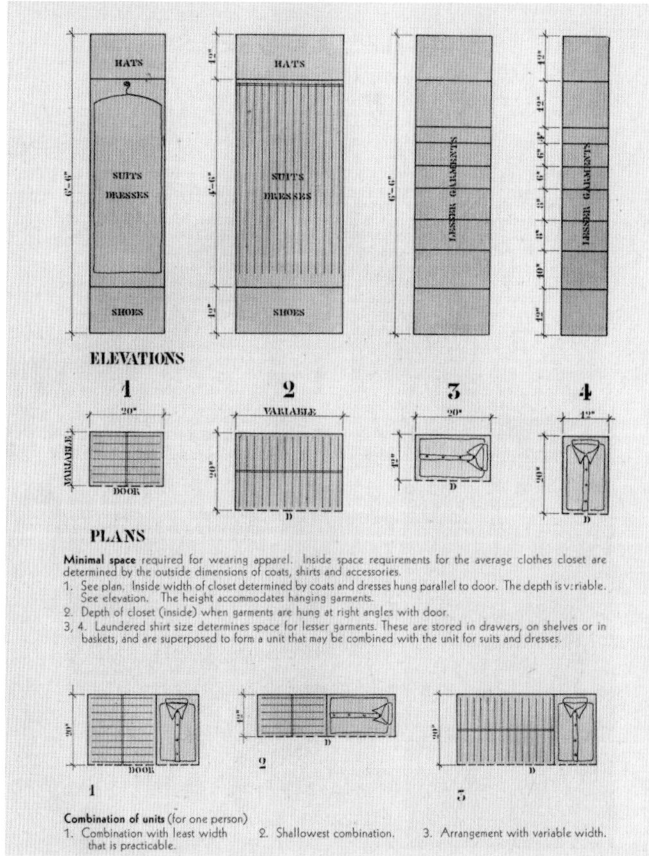

ELEVATIONS

PLANS

Minimal space required for wearing apparel. Inside space requirements for the average clothes closet are determined by the outside dimensions of coats, shirts and accessories.

1. See plan. Inside width of closet determined by coats and dresses hung parallel to door. The depth is variable. See elevation. The height accommodates hanging garments.
2. Depth of closet (inside) when garments are hung at right angles with door.
3, 4. Laundered shirt size determines space for lesser garments. These are stored in drawers, on shelves or in baskets, and are superposed to form a unit that may be combined with the unit for suits and dresses.

Combination of units (for one person)

1. Combination with least width that is practicable.
2. Shallowest combination.
3. Arrangement with variable width.

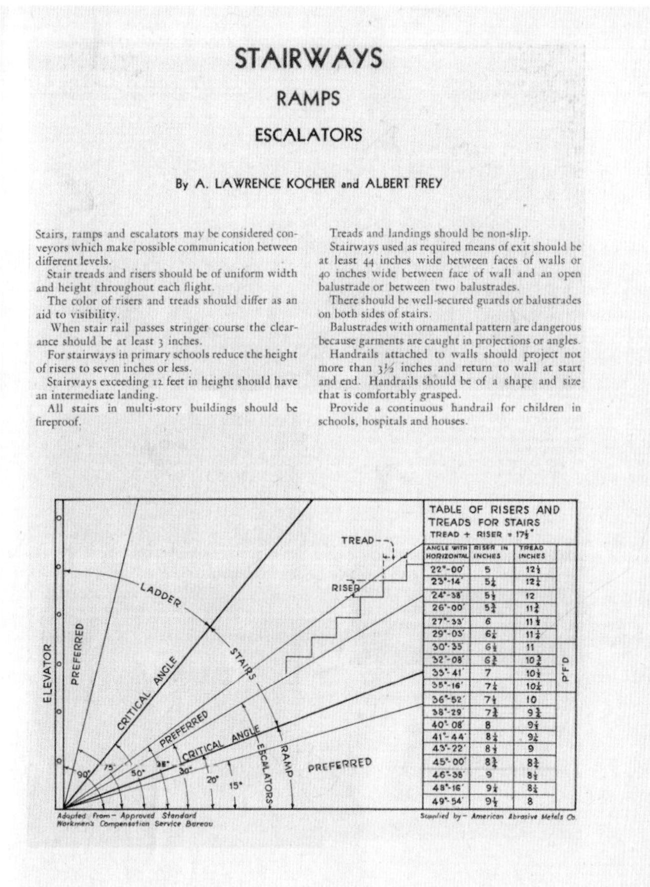

STAIRWAYS

RAMPS

ESCALATORS

By A. LAWRENCE KOCHER and ALBERT FREY

Stairs, ramps and escalators may be considered conveyors which make possible communication between different levels.

Stair treads and risers should be of uniform width and height throughout each flight.

The color of risers and treads should differ as an aid to visibility.

When stair rail passes stringer course the clearance should be at least 3 inches.

For stairways in primary schools reduce the height of risers to seven inches or less.

Stairways exceeding 12 feet in height should have an intermediate landing.

All stairs in multi-story buildings should be fireproof.

Treads and landings should be non-slip.

Stairways used as required means of exit should be at least 44 inches wide between faces of walls or 40 inches wide between face of wall and an open balustrade or between two balustrades.

There should be well-secured guards or balustrades on both sides of stairs.

Balustrades with ornamental pattern are dangerous because garments are caught in projections or angles.

Handrails attached to walls should project not more than 3½ inches and return to wall at start and end. Handrails should be of a shape and size that is comfortably grasped.

Provide a continuous handrail for children in schools, hospitals and houses.

TABLE OF RISERS AND TREADS FOR STAIRS
TREAD + RISER = 17½"

ANGLE WITH HORIZONTAL	RISER IN INCHES	TREAD INCHES
22°-00'	5	12½
23°-14'	5¼	12¼
24°-38'	5½	12
26°-00'	5¾	11¾
27°-33'	6	11½
29°-03'	6¼	11¼
30°-35'	6½	11
32°-08'	6¾	10¾
33°-41'	7	10½
35°-16'	7¼	10¼
36°-52'	7½	10
38°-29'	7¾	9¾
40°-08'	8	9½
41°-44'	8¼	9¼
43°-22'	8½	9
45°-00'	8¾	8¾
46°-38'	9	8½
48°-16'	9¼	8¼
49°-54'	9½	8

Adapted from—Approved Standard Workmen's Compensation Service Bureau

Supplied by—American Abrasive Metals Co.

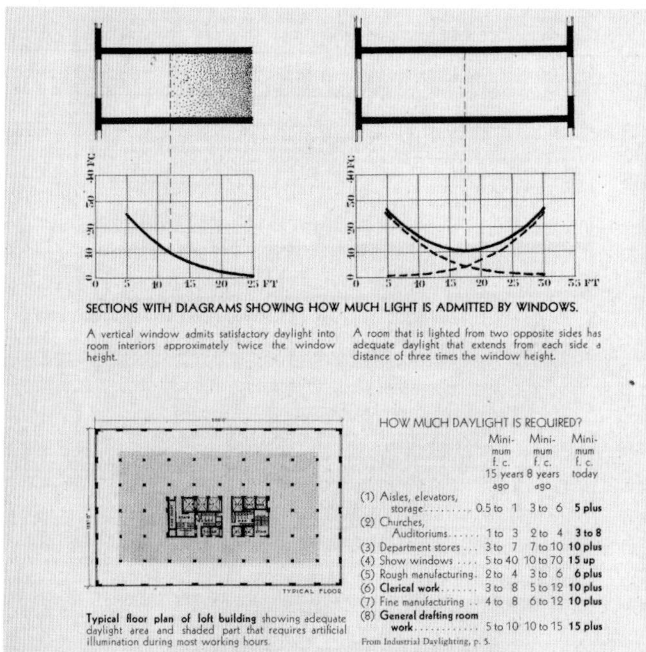

SECTIONS WITH DIAGRAMS SHOWING HOW MUCH LIGHT IS ADMITTED BY WINDOWS.

A vertical window admits satisfactory daylight into room interiors approximately twice the window height.

A room that is lighted from two opposite sides has adequate daylight that extends from each side a distance of three times the window height.

Typical floor plan of loft building showing adequate daylight area and shaded part that requires artificial illumination during most working hours.

HOW MUCH DAYLIGHT IS REQUIRED?

	Minimum f. c. 15 years ago	Minimum f. c. 8 years ago	Minimum f. c. today
(1) Aisles, elevators, storage	0.5 to 1	3 to 6	**5 plus**
(2) Churches, Auditoriums	1 to 3	2 to 4	**3 to 8**
(3) Department stores	3 to 7	7 to 10	**10 plus**
(4) Show windows	5 to 40	10 to 70	**15 up**
(5) Rough manufacturing	2 to 4	3 to 6	**6 plus**
(6) **Clerical work**	3 to 8	5 to 12	**10 plus**
(7) Fine manufacturing	4 to 8	6 to 12	**10 plus**
(8) **General drafting room work**	5 to 10	10 to 15	**15 plus**

From Industrial Daylighting, p. 5.

Figures 3.6 to 3.9. A. Lawrence Kocher and Albert Frey. Standard dimensions of housing elements published in *The Architectural Record.* From top to bottom and left to right: the domestic garage (January 1931), closets (March 1931), stairs and ramps (July 1931), and windows (February 1931).

Next page: **Figures 3.10 to 3.13.** Idem. From top to bottom and left to right: kitchens (January 1932), bedrooms (February 1932), bathrooms (February, 1932), and chairs and tables (April 1932).

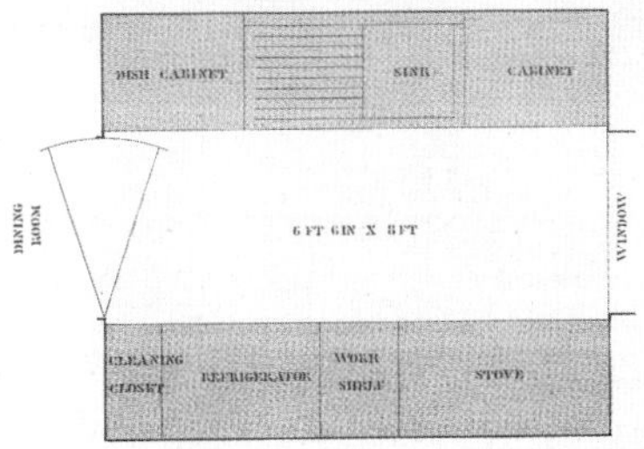

PLAN OF KITCHEN OF MINIMUM SIZE, suited to small family or apartment. "The size of the kitchen is determined by the equipment it must contain to carry out the activities of the family." From report of Committee on Kitchens and Other Work Centers, the President's Conference on Home Building and Home Ownership.

A MINIMAL KITCHEN

Kitchen				Pantry	
Design	Width	Length	Sq. ft.	Width	Length
Wall	4'8" 4'8" 4'6" 4'8" 5'	8'3" 8' 9' 9'3" 9'6"	38.5 37.3 40.5 43.5 47.5		
Small Apartment	6'9" 7' 5'6"	7' 8'6" 7'	46.6 59.5 38.5		
Apartment or Small Single House	6'6" 6'6" 6'8"	8'6" 8' 8'	55.25 52. 53.3		
Larger One-Family House—no maid	6'6" 7'	10'6" 12'	68.25 84.		
Rural	9'	11'6"	103.5		
(With breakfast nook) (With breakfast nook)	7'6" 9'3"	18' 20'	117. 192.5		
Rural	7'6"	12'	90.		
With work room. Dimensions do not include workroom	8'6" 9' 8'6"	13' 11' 11'	110.5 99. 93.5		
Rural	7'	12'3"	85.75	6'	7'6"
Apartment (with maid)	7' 7' 7'	9' 8' 8'	63. 56. 56.	7' 6' 6'6"	8' 7' 8'
Detached House (with maid)	7' 7'	8' 12'	56. 84.	4'9" 6'	8' 9'

TYPICAL KITCHENS AND SPACE REQUIREMENTS as listed by the Committee on Kitchens and Other Work Centers of The President's Conference on Home Building and Home Ownership.

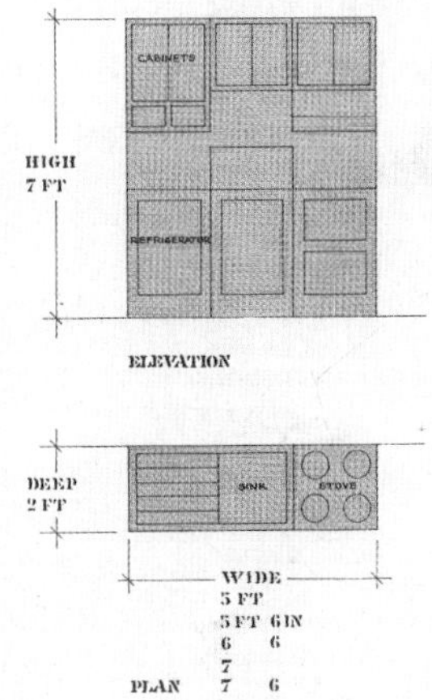

KITCHEN UNIT

DIMENSIONS

PART TWO

BEDROOMS • BATHROOMS

By A. LAWRENCE KOCHER and ALBERT FREY

Bonney

Bedroom with all furniture correct in size and in location for convenient use. The sitting-room area is made possible by the ample width of room. Cheerful lighting is obtained with windows at long side of room.

MINIMAL BEDROOMS

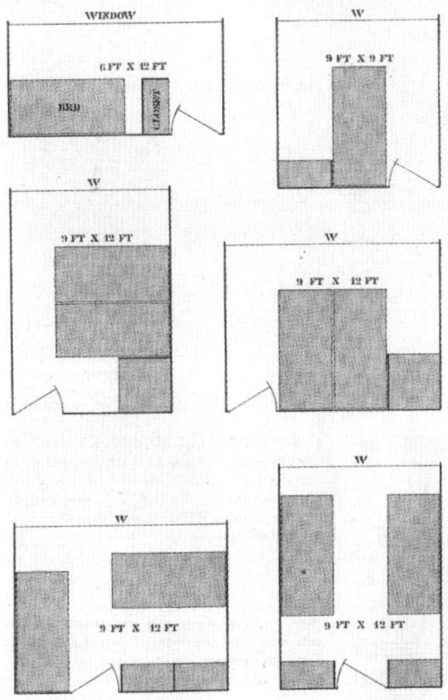

BEDROOMS OF MINIMAL SIZE are determined by the dimensions of:

(a) One or more beds.

(b) Single or double closet.

(c) Furniture (dresser, chairs, table) and required space for walking about and dressing in a room.

The accompanying plans indicate a variety of possible arrangements for rooms of small size with single or twin beds. The full-size bed (4'6" wide) can be substituted for the twin bed so as to obtain increased floor area. In all cases entrance doors are opposite windows because access to rooms is from hall or corridor. In the suggested rooms there are two shapes: (1) with windows at broad side; (2) with windows at narrow end of room. Closets of double size are indicated for rooms occupied by two persons.

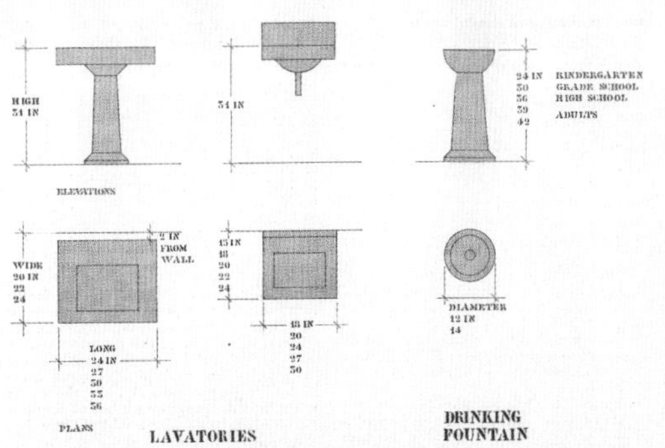

LAVATORIES

DRINKING FOUNTAIN

LAVATORIES OF PEDESTAL AND WALL TYPE AND DRINKING-FOUNTAIN SIZES for general use. The recommended height for the lavatory is 31 inches. Drinking fountains vary in height from 24 inches to 42 inches, accommodating all school grades from kindergarten to adults. Wash basins may be obtained with oval, circular or semi-circular bowls. Corner basins are also obtainable.

THE DIMENSIONS FOR FIXTURES IN DRAWINGS are for adults. The height of the toilet seat for kindergarten and for the nursery toilet should be a maximum of 9 inches. For junior high school grades the recommended seat height is 13 inches.

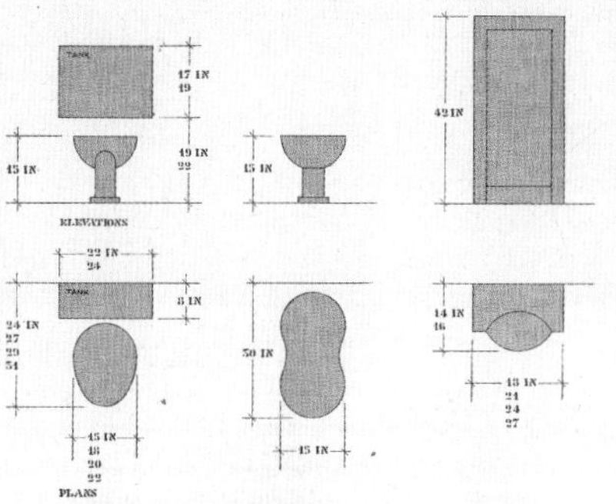

TOILET BIDET URINAL

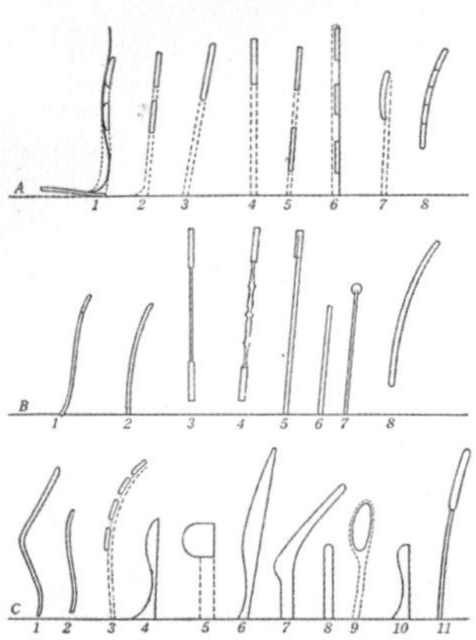

Various types of back supports used on school seats. First row: slat or cross-strip backs. Second row: vertical spindles or solid backs. Third row: various types used in European schools. All are sections along the center line. From "School Posture and Seating" by H. E. Bennett.

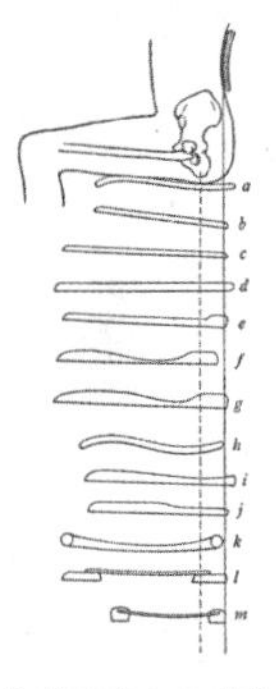

Seat forms in use on school furniture. Diagram at "a" shows relation to person seated. The seat shape that is concave toward back as shown at "a" is most desirable. There should be convex lumbar support to back of sitter.

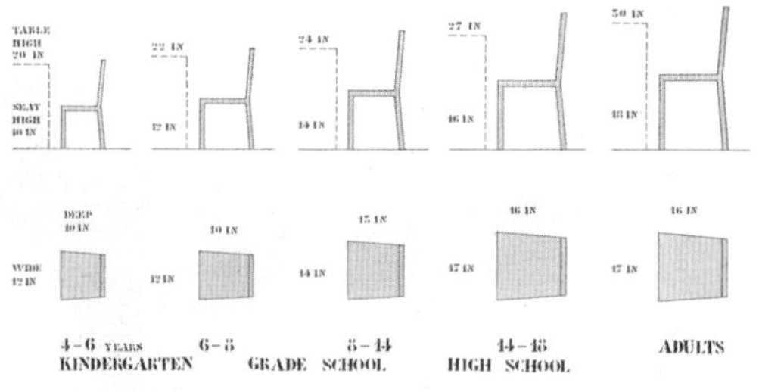

Dimensions of available chairs of same type for different school grades and for adults. The seat height is adjusted to height of table. Tables used for reading and writing should have sloping tops.

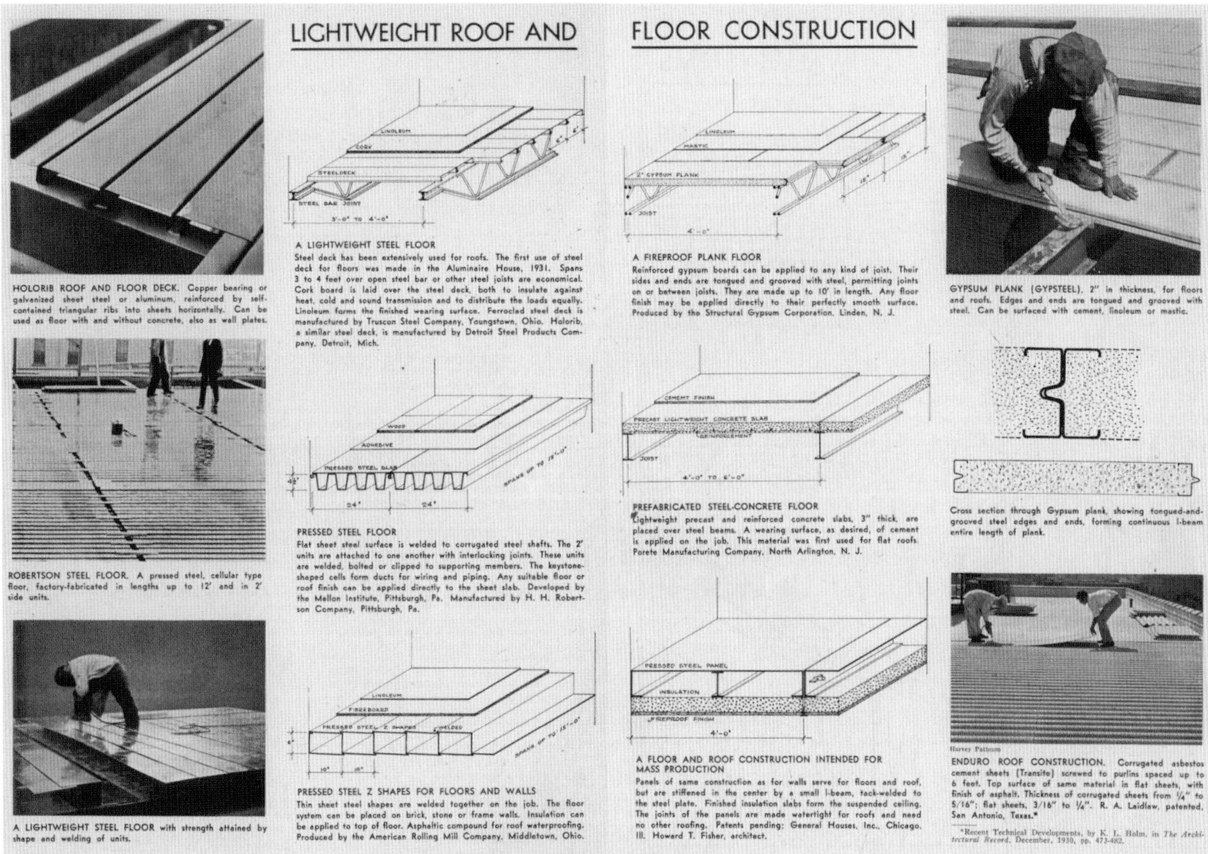

LIGHTWEIGHT ROOF AND FLOOR CONSTRUCTION

HOLORIB ROOF AND FLOOR DECK. Copper bearing or galvanized sheet steel or aluminum, reinforced by self-contained triangular ribs into sheets horizontally. Can be used as floor with and without concrete, also as wall plates.

ROBERTSON STEEL FLOOR. A pressed steel, cellular type floor, factory-fabricated in lengths up to 12' and in 2' side units.

A LIGHTWEIGHT STEEL FLOOR with strength attained by shape and welding of units.

A LIGHTWEIGHT STEEL FLOOR

Steel deck has been extensively used for roofs. The first use of steel deck for floors was made in the Aluminaire House, 1931. Spans 3 to 4 feet over open steel bar or other steel joists are economical. Cork board is laid over the steel deck, both to insulate against heat, cold and sound transmission and to distribute the loads equally. Linoleum forms the finished wearing surface. Ferroclad steel deck is manufactured by Truscon Steel Company, Youngstown, Ohio. Holorib, a similar steel deck, is manufactured by Detroit Steel Products Company, Detroit, Mich.

PRESSED STEEL FLOOR

Flat sheet steel surface is welded to corrugated steel shafts. The 2' units are attached to one another with interlocking joints. These units are welded, bolted or clipped to supporting members. The keystone-shaped cells form ducts for wiring and piping. Any suitable floor or roof finish can be applied directly to the sheet slab. Developed by the Mellon Institute, Pittsburgh, Pa. Manufactured by H. H. Robertson Company, Pittsburgh, Pa.

PRESSED STEEL Z SHAPES FOR FLOORS AND WALLS

Thin sheet steel shapes are welded together on the job. The floor system can be placed on brick, stone or frame walls. Insulation can be applied to top of floor. Asphaltic compound for roof waterproofing. Produced by the American Rolling Mill Company, Middletown, Ohio.

A FIREPROOF PLANK FLOOR

Reinforced gypsum boards can be applied to any kind of joist. Their sides and ends are tongued and grooved with steel, permitting joints on or between joists. They are made up to 10' in length. Any floor finish may be applied directly to their perfectly smooth surface. Produced by the Structural Gypsum Corporation, Linden, N. J.

PREFABRICATED STEEL-CONCRETE FLOOR

Lightweight precast and reinforced concrete slabs, 3" thick, are placed over steel beams. A wearing surface, as desired, of cement is applied on the job. This material was first used for flat roofs. Porete Manufacturing Company, North Arlington, N. J.

A FLOOR AND ROOF CONSTRUCTION INTENDED FOR MASS PRODUCTION

Panels of same construction as for walls serve for floors and roof, but are stiffened in the center by a small I-beam, tack-welded to the steel plate. Finished insulation slabs form the suspended ceiling. The joints of the panels are made watertight for roofs and need no other roofing. Patents pending: General Houses, Inc., Chicago, Ill. Howard T. Fisher, architect.

GYPSUM PLANK (GYPSTEEL), 2" in thickness, for floors and roofs. Edges and ends are tongued and grooved with steel. Can be surfaced with cement, linoleum or mastic.

Cross section through Gypsum plank, showing tongued-and-grooved steel edges and ends, forming continuous I-beam entire length of plank.

ENDURO ROOF CONSTRUCTION. Corrugated asbestos cement sheets (Transite) screwed to purlins spaced up to 6 feet. Top surface of same material in flat sheets, with finish of asphalt. Thickness of corrugated sheets from 1/4" to 5/16"; flat sheets, 3/16" to 1/4". R. A. Laidlaw, patented, San Antonio, Texas.*

*Recent Technical Developments, by K. L. Holm, in *The Architectural Record*, December, 1930, pp. 473-482.

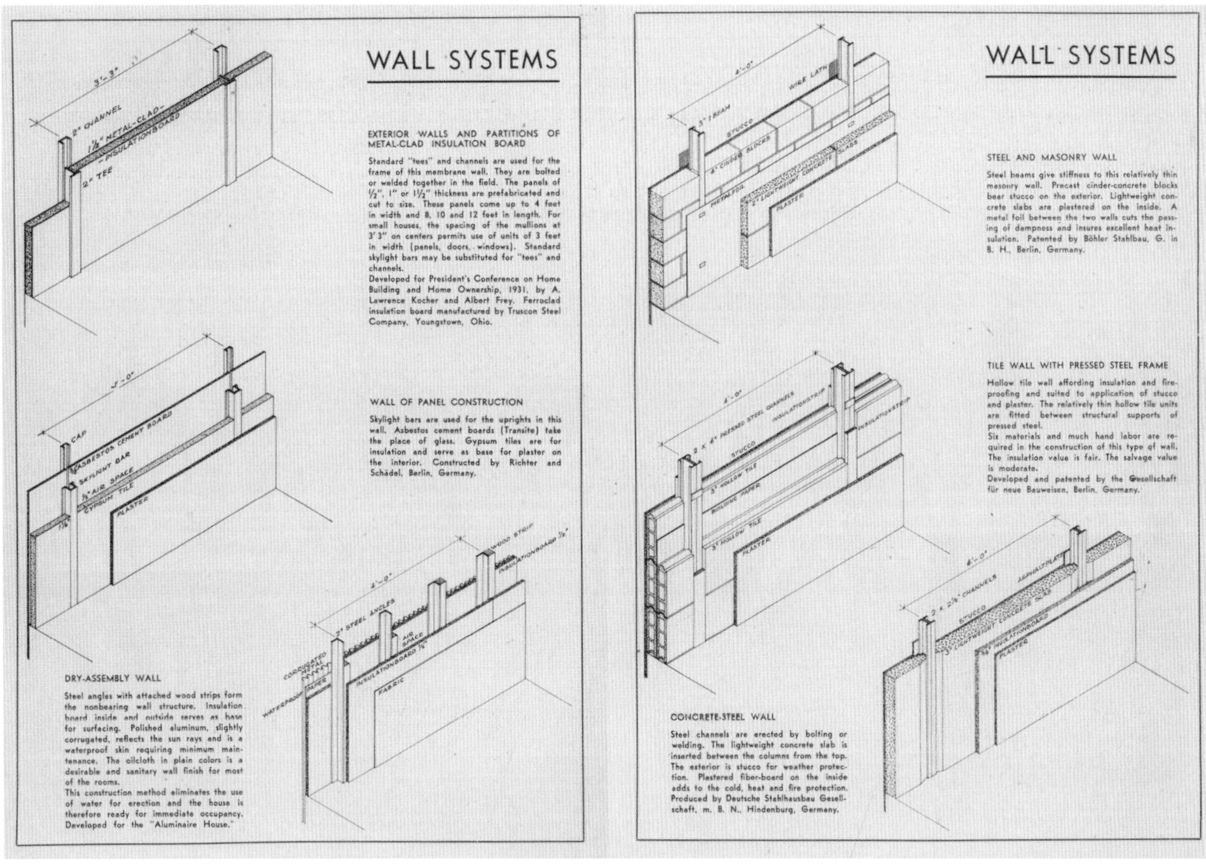

WALL SYSTEMS

EXTERIOR WALLS AND PARTITIONS OF METAL-CLAD INSULATION BOARD

Standard "tees" and channels are used for the frame of this membrane wall. They are bolted or welded together in the field. The panels of 1/2", 1" or 1 1/2" thickness are prefabricated and cut to size. These panels come up to 4 feet in width and 8, 10 and 12 feet in length. For small houses, the spacing of the mullions at 3' 3" on centers permits use of units of 3 feet in width (panels, doors, windows). Standard skylight bars may be substituted for "tees" and channels.

Developed for President's Conference on Home Building and Home Ownership, 1931, by A. Lawrence Kocher and Albert Frey. Ferroclad insulation board manufactured by Truscon Steel Company, Youngstown, Ohio.

WALL OF PANEL CONSTRUCTION

Skylight bars are used for the uprights in this wall. Asbestos cement boards (Transite) take the place of glass. Gypsum tiles are for insulation and serve as base for plaster on the interior. Constructed by Richter and Schädel, Berlin, Germany.

DRY-ASSEMBLY WALL

Steel angles with attached wood strips form the nonbearing wall structure. Insulation board inside and outside serves as base for surfacing. Polished aluminum, slightly corrugated, reflects the sun rays and is a waterproof skin requiring minimum maintenance. The oilcloth in plain colors is a desirable and sanitary wall finish for most of the rooms.

This construction method eliminates the use of water for erection and the house is therefore ready for immediate occupancy. Developed for the "Aluminaire House."

WALL SYSTEMS

STEEL AND MASONRY WALL

Steel beams give stiffness to this relatively thin masonry wall. Precast cinder-concrete blocks bear stucco on the exterior. Lightweight concrete slabs are plastered on the inside. A metal foil between the two walls cuts the passing of dampness and insures excellent heat insulation. Patented by Böhler Stahlbau, G. in B. H., Berlin, Germany.

TILE WALL WITH PRESSED STEEL FRAME

Hollow tile wall affording insulation and fireproofing and suited to application of stucco and plaster. The relatively thin hollow tile units are fitted between structural supports of pressed steel.

Six materials and much hand labor are required in the construction of this type of wall. The insulation value is fair. The salvage value is moderate.

Developed and patented by the Gesellschaft für neue Bauweisen, Berlin, Germany.

CONCRETE-STEEL WALL

Steel channels are erected by bolting or welding. The lightweight concrete slab is inserted between the columns from the top. The exterior is stucco for weather protection. Plastered fiber-board on the inside adds to the cold, heat and fire protection. Produced by Deutsche Stahlhausbau Gesellschaft, m. B. N., Hindenburg, Germany.

Figure 3.14. A. Lawrence Kocher and Albert Frey. "New Materials and Improved Construction Methods. *Architectural Record*, Vol. 73 (April 1933).

the use of cotton. The project description stated that the architects researched the characteristics, advantages, and limitations of cotton derived from its production—whether in mills or in factories—then adopted the different uses accordingly. The uses of cotton in the project is impressive, listing exterior and interior facing for the walls, surfacing for the floors and roof, waterproofing for the walls of the house (flashing), interior doors and partitions, surface material for the furniture, and enlarged uses for various house furnishings (like hangings, carpeting, accessories). Of course, in this last category, the project also included more traditional uses for cotton, such as curtains, roller window shades, parapets, and awnings.

The architects' final aim was the ability to fabricate and assemble two demonstration houses proving the functional advantages and budgetary feasibility in new construction methods to both builders and the public. These houses would have been erected with a steel skeleton and a steel frame, modulated with uniform 40-inch sections—based on 40-inch prefabricated panels for the façade, including windows, doors, insulation, and attached hardware—delivered to the site, along with assembly instructions, once the foundation and necessary connections to public services were completed. The assembly of the frame would require less than 70 man-hours, allowing six men to finish the task in less than two days. The complete construction could be accomplished in seven more days with the same work force.

The Harnischfeger Corporation was the proposed manufacturer for the steel frame system. The 40-inch modular sections had three-inch pressed steel channels, spaced 20 inches on center. The façade had two layers applied in the shop: the outer layer comprised of a half-inch insulation board while the inner layer was half-inch plywood board with a half inch of (air) space between both layers. The exterior board was later finished on site with a layer of six-ounce cotton fabric with a special adhesive manufactured by William L. Barrell & Co.; the fabric was then given three coats of canvas deck paint, sourced from the Devoe and Reynolds Co. The inner walls, partitions, and ceilings were prefabricated quarter-inch waterproofed plywood boards (fir, poplar, or southern gum wood) faced with fabric applied with a cresol-formaldehyde resin binder, hot-pressed and tempered. Finally, the partitions were painted on site. The use of this material system was extended to furniture to ensure the ease of washing all surfaces with regular water and soap. The framing of the floors and roof were made out of eight-inch pressed-steel channels, also in 40-inch modules. Nailed at the top of the channels, there was a one-inch insulation board for the floors, and a half-inch fir plywood board (Harbor Plywood Corp.) for the roof. The roof was finished with an eight-pound fabric and the same paint as the walls, whereas the floors were finished with a medium-weight tarred felt and half-inch plywood panels with a veneered surface of eight-ounce canvas. In the factory, one-inch steel casement windows were attached to the façade panels but glazed and painted later on site. The doors were board-coated with Bakelite paint. In the design brief, there is special emphasis on the specification of cabinets, closets, and furniture design—similar to that in the design of the Aluminaire House.

The Experimental Five-Room House was divided in plan into two rectangles forming an L-shape with a broken corner. **(Figures 3.53 to 3.56)** The bigger rectangle, measuring 20 by 35 feet, contained two bedrooms, one bathroom, a kitchen, a foyer, and flexible dining and living space that could be divided or integrated using a folding partition. The smaller nine-by-27-foot rectangle contained the garage, the furnace, coal storage, and general storage. The house and the garage had a gross area of 700 and 243 square feet respectively. The house is generously glazed, especially on the side opposite to the entrance, and this entirely glazed operable wall extends to the outside in an elevated deck, connecting the landscape through a longitudinal stair. To improve the house's thermal behavior, avoiding unnecessary solar exposure of the windows, there was a deployable awning covering the deck; the entrance path is also covered with a semi-cylindrical fabric canopy. Stylistically, the house could be identified as modern, timidly adhering to Le Corbusier's Five Points: it is raised off the ground using eight round steel columns, but lifting only about three feet—enough to avoid dampness, yet not enough to enable the garden to extend beneath the residence; panoramic horizontal windows, interrupted by structural steel studs every 20 or 40 inches; and a roof garden, accessible by a spiral staircase, featuring a solarium with a fabric parapet and a fabric semicircular partition. The only Corbusian principle that is absolutely lacking is the free composition of the plan and the façade, due to the chosen structural system. The use of the steel frame and the overall dimensions of the house drives to the unavoidable need for load-bearing partitions in the interior, compromising the freedom of the plan and façade design. The same can be said of a façade bearing the load of the roof along the perimeter of the house. The project description clearly stated that the demonstration house was not designed to be isolated but aggregated in a "subdivision or as a group of houses for workers in industry."[23] The pencil-drawn aggregation diagram depicted in Kocher and Frey's picture of the exhibition shows a series of five houses organized in a row. The volumes of the garages enhanced privacy between houses by dividing the front yards while simultaneously reducing the length of the driveways. As in the case of the Aluminaire House and the related aggregation of the unit in subdivisions for low-cost housing, Kocher and Frey's designs always tried to transcend the individuality of the detached home, reinforcing their position to the social realm of architecture by taking advantage of replication and standardization possibilities in America's mass-production industrial civilization.

The second house shown in the exhibition shared all the constructive characteristics of the Experimental Five-Room House. It was a very appealing piece of architecture and one of the most relevant designs within Kocher and Frey's body of work. Yet unlike the Experimental Five-Room House, the Experimental Weekend House was a radically modern kind of artifact with a clear Corbusian lineage. **(Figure 3.57)** The design was almost fully compliant of Le Corbusier's five architectural precepts: it was elevated on stilts, had a roof terrace, ribbon windows—although they were slightly compromised by the 20-inch modulation of the structural steel frame—and thanks to its small size, the house had a free plan. In its spatial simplicity, the Experimental Weekend House was more closely related to Le Corbusier's Loucheur Houses and the Gardener's House than to Villa Savoye. Therefore, it can be understood as an evolution of the Aluminaire House, moving toward minimal housing. Like the Loucheur Houses, the layout of this house was able to be completely

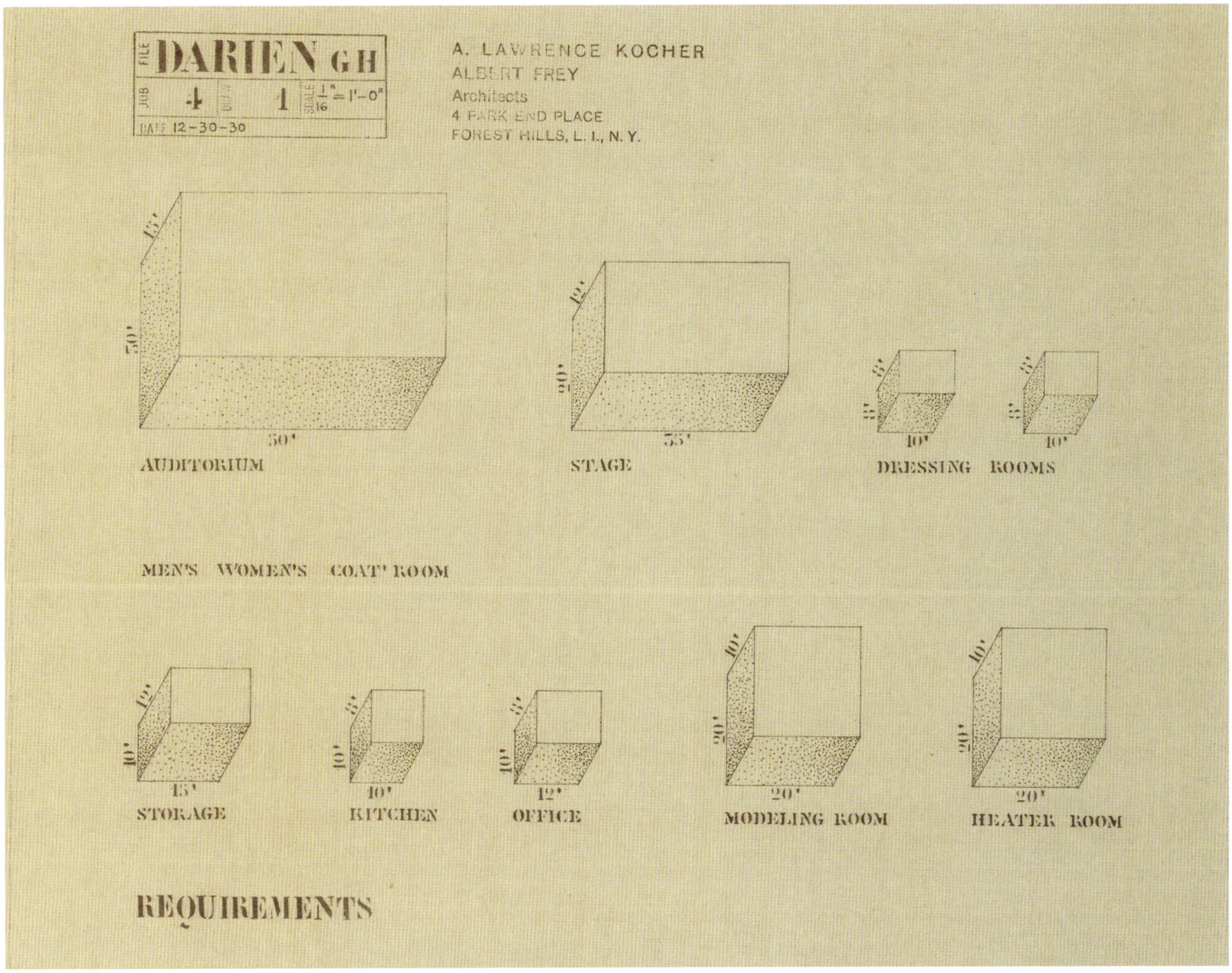

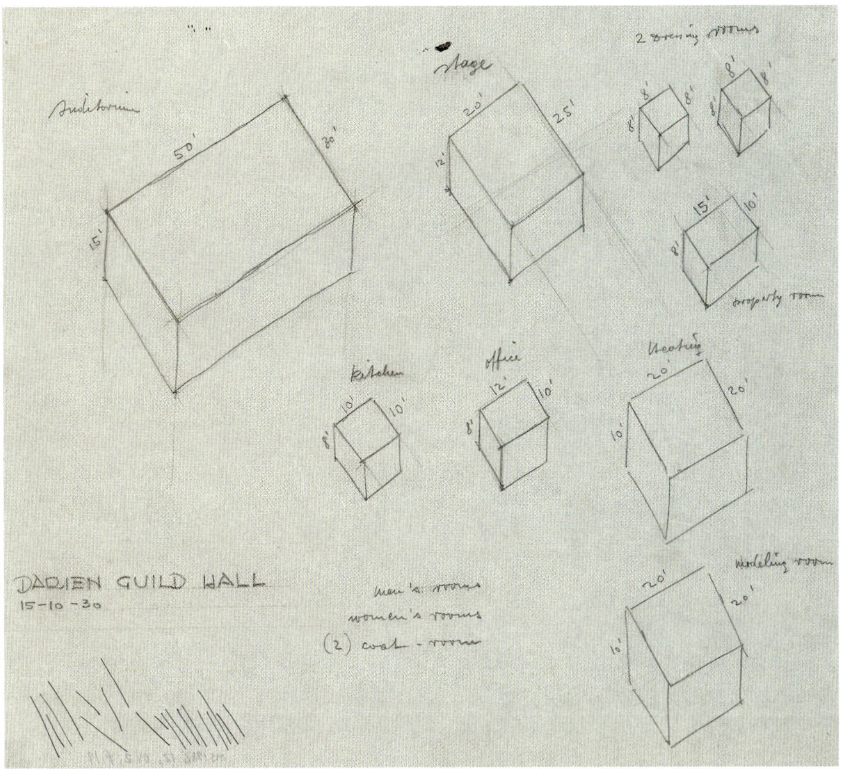

Previous page:
Figures 3.15 and 3.16. A. Lawrence Kocher and Albert Frey. 1930. Guild Hall in Darien, Connecticut. Unbuilt. Model Photos.

This page:
Figure 3.17. A. Lawrence Kocher and Albert Frey. 1930. Guild Hall in Darien, Connecticut. Unbuilt. Design intent diagram as published in Architectural Record in December 1936.
Figure 3.18. A. Lawrence Kocher and Albert Frey. 1930. Guild Hall in Darien, Connecticut. Unbuilt. Design intent diagram. Original preliminary drawing. Dated October 1930.

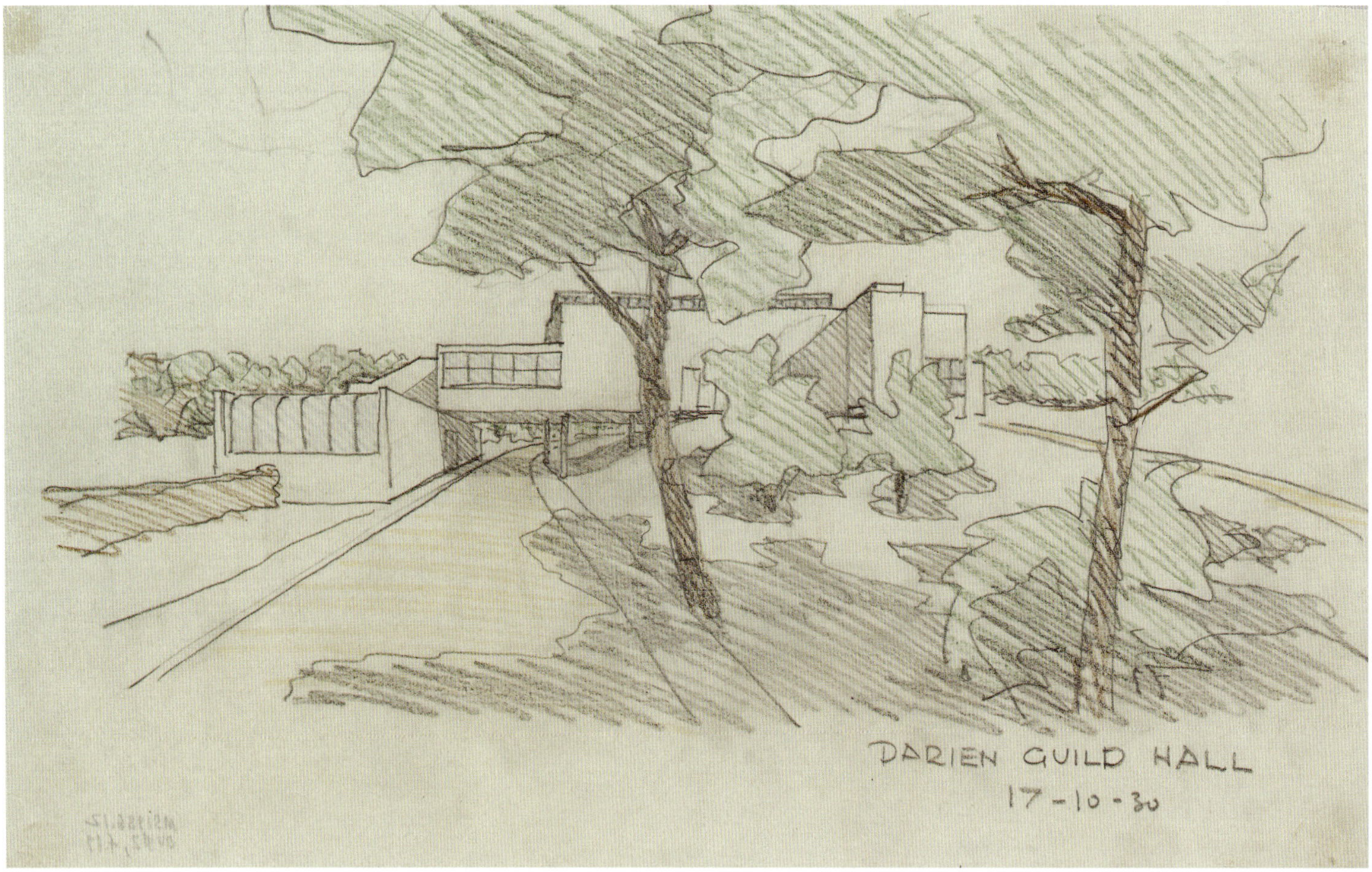
DARIEN GUILD HALL
17-10-30

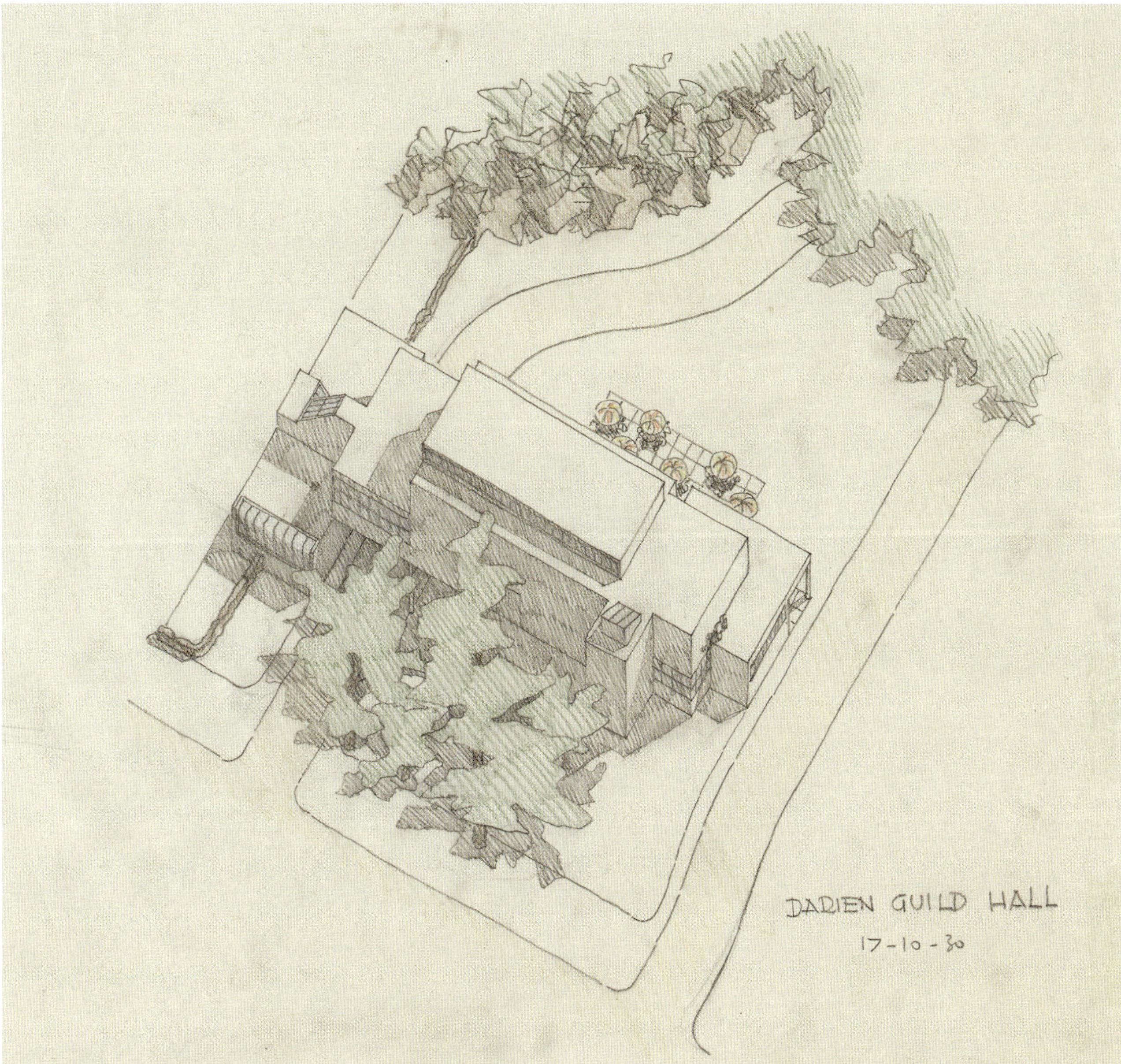

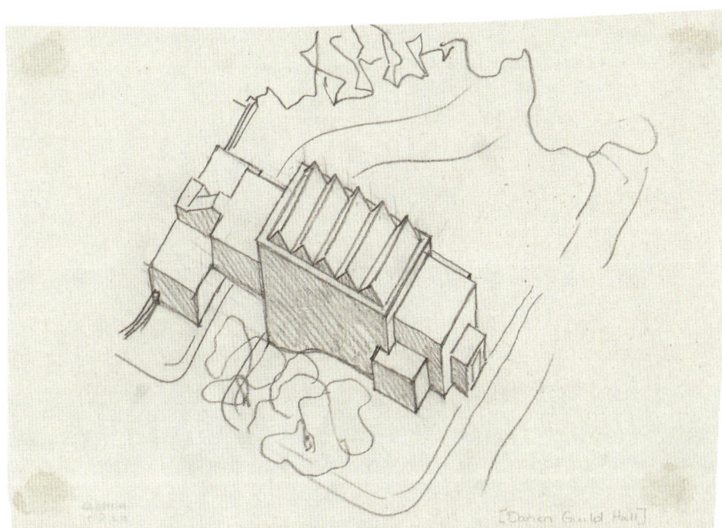

Previous page:
Figure 3.19. A. Lawrence Kocher and Albert Frey. 1930. Guild Hall in Darien, Connecticut. Unbuilt. Preliminary perspective. Dated 10-17-30.
Figure 3.20. A. Lawrence Kocher and Albert Frey. 1930. Guild Hall in Darien, Connecticut. Unbuilt. Final perspective. Dated 10-17-30.

This page:
Figure 3.21. A. Lawrence Kocher and Albert Frey. 1930. Guild Hall in Darien, Connecticut. Unbuilt. Axonometric view. Dated October 1930.
Figure 3.22. A. Lawrence Kocher and Albert Frey. 1930. Guild Hall in Darien, Connecticut. Unbuilt. Preliminary version with sawtooth skylights. Axonometric view. Undated.

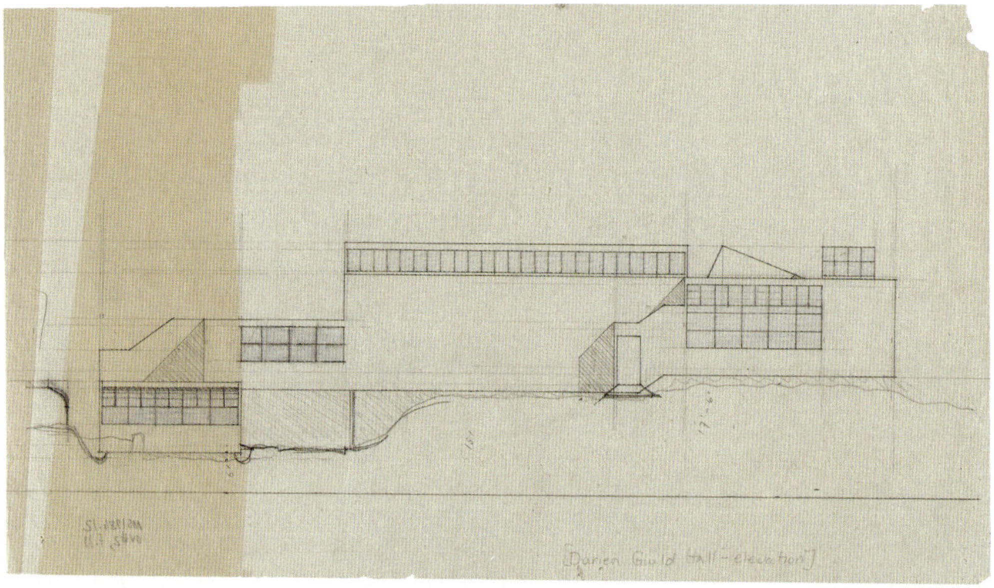

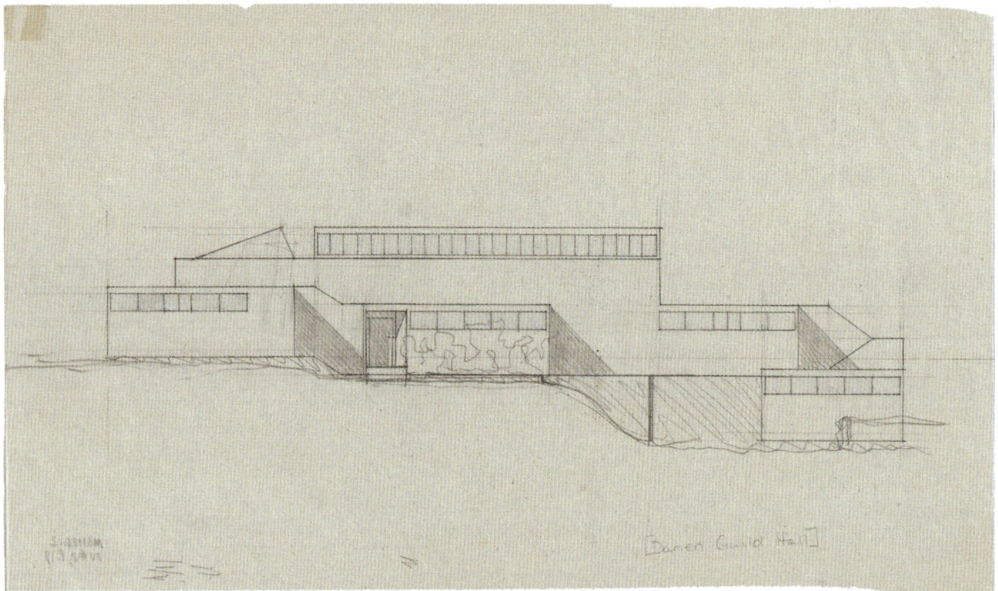

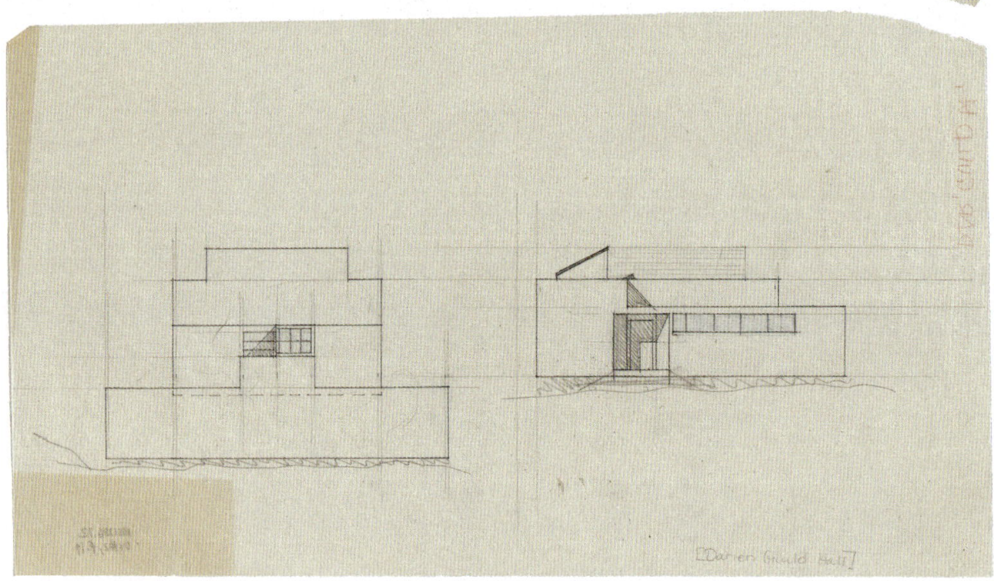

This page:
Figures 3.23 to 3.25. A. Lawrence Kocher and Albert Frey. 1930. Guild Hall in Darien, Connecticut. Unbuilt. Elevations. Undated.

Next page:
Figure 3.26. A. Lawrence Kocher and Albert Frey. 1930. Guild Hall in Darien, Connecticut. Unbuilt. Floor Plans of upper and lower levels. Dated November 1930.
Figures 3.27 to 3.29. Preliminary sketches. Dated October 1930.

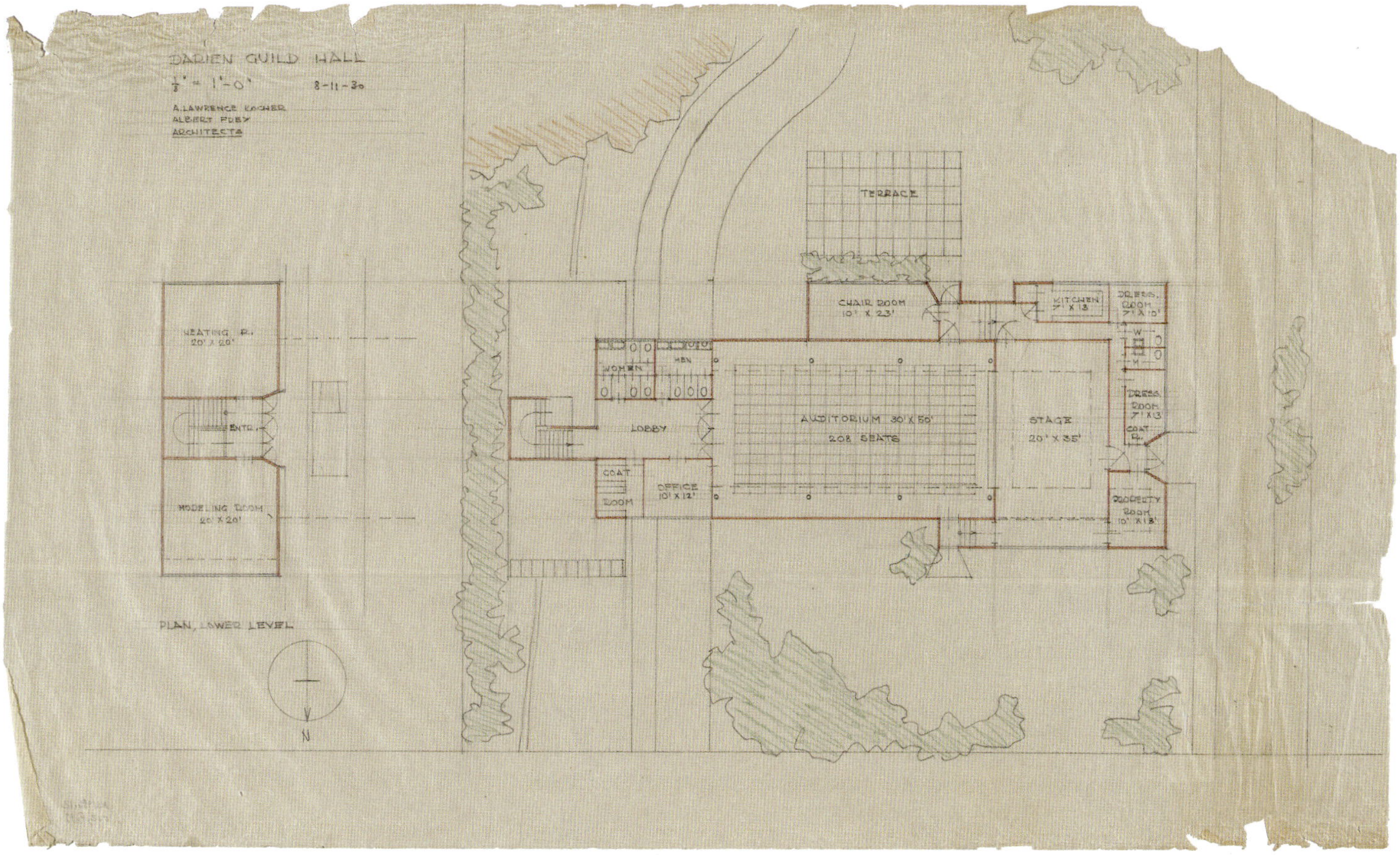
DARIEN GUILD HALL
1/8" = 1'-0" 8-11-30
A. LAWRENCE KOCHER
ALBERT FREY
ARCHITECTS
TERRACE
CHAIR ROOM 10' X 23'
KITCHEN 7' X 13'
WOMEN
MEN
LOBBY
AUDITORIUM 30' X 50'
208 SEATS
STAGE 20' X 35'
COAT ROOM
OFFICE 10' X 12'
PROPERTY ROOM 10' X 18'
HEATING R. 20' X 20'
ENTR.
MODELING ROOM 20' X 20'
PLAN, LOWER LEVEL
N

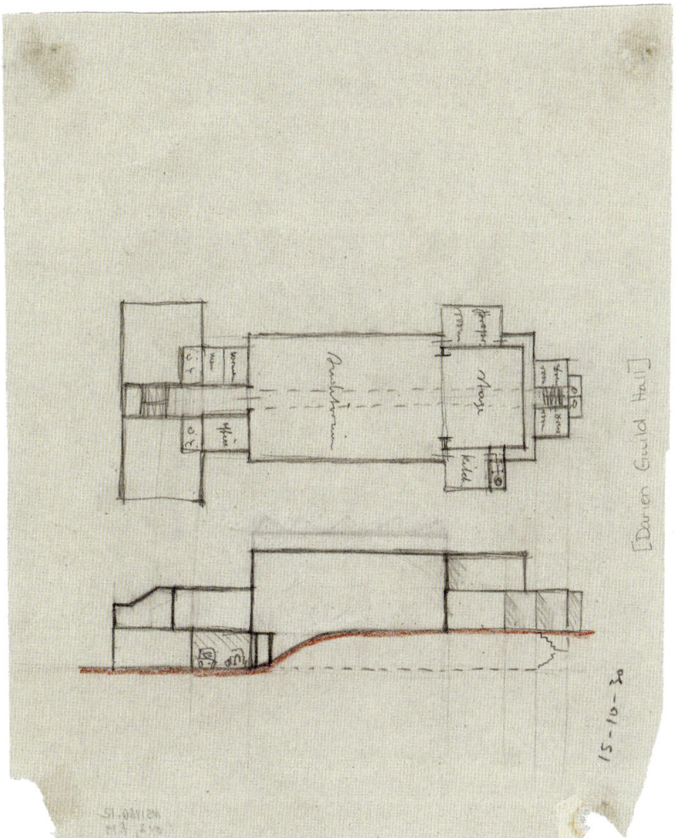
Auditorium
Stage
[Darien Guild Hall]
15-10-30

[Darien Guild Hall - perspective]

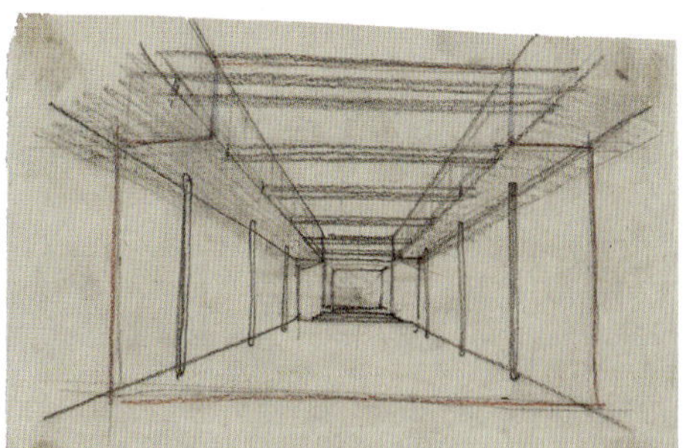
[Darien Guild Hall]

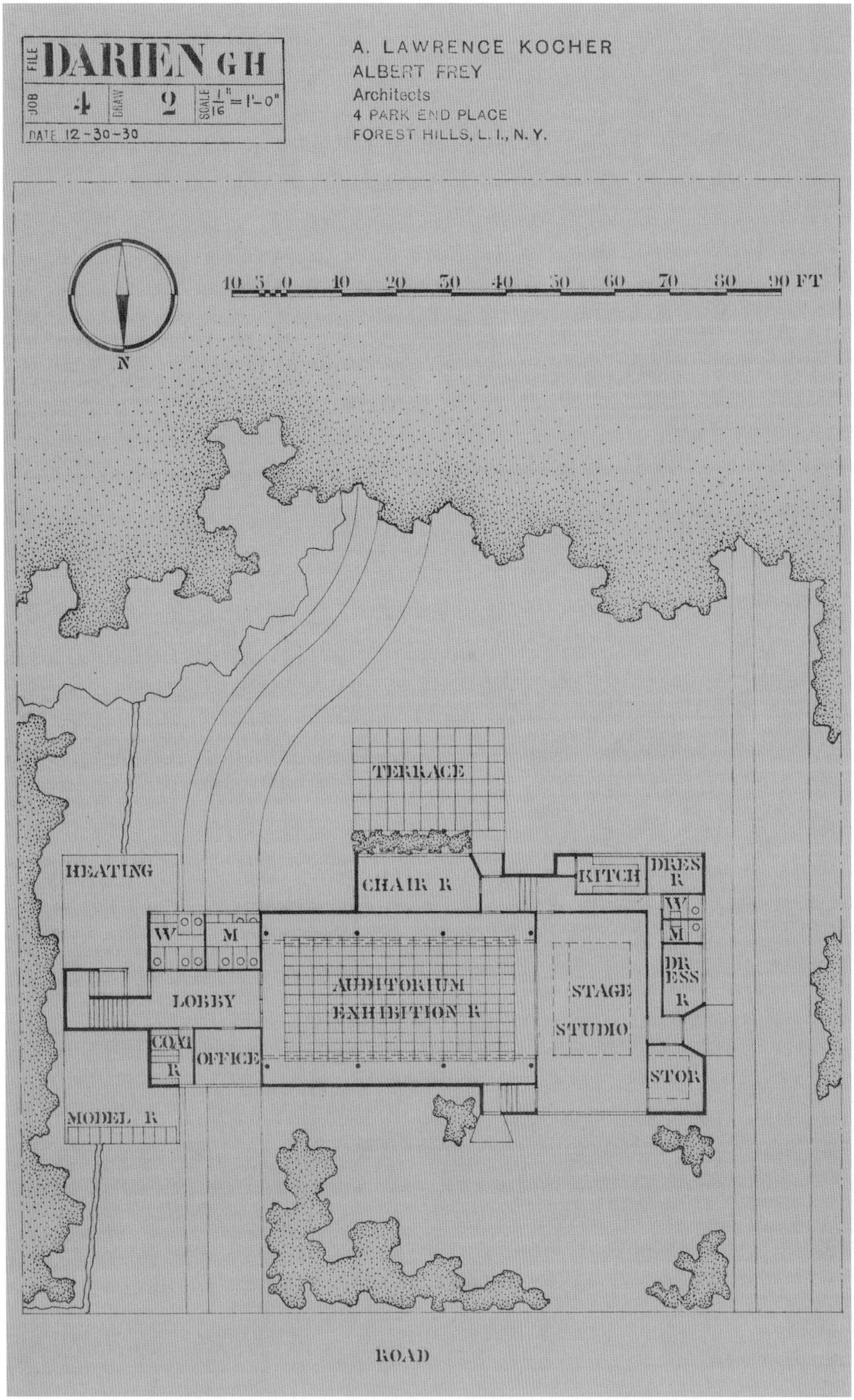

Figure 3.30. A. Lawrence Kocher and Albert Frey. 1930. Guild Hall in Darien, Connecticut. Unbuilt. Upper-level floor plan as published in *Architectural Record* in December 1936. Dated December 1930.

changed when swapping from day to night scenarios (living rooms to bedrooms), conceptually increasing the square footage of the house by enforcing time management over everyday activities. Kocher had published the Loucheur Houses in *Architectural Record* (August 1930), including alternate plans of the house during the day and the night, praising them as true "dwelling machines."[24] With the aim of minimizing the spatial needs and therefore the cost of housing units, Kocher and Frey designed a domestic Taylorism, breaking every task in the household down into its essential motions and creating a specific schedule for each.

The layout of the Experimental Weekend House was completely symmetrical and featured a bathroom and kitchen of the same size—the only spaces within the project that were enclosed by static walls and the only spaces with doors. Like in Le Corbusier's Gardener's House at the Villa Savoye, the short elevations of the house were windowless, and the long sides were glazed with a sliding window featuring a parapet and lintel. The steel-frame exterior walls were structural and supported a roof terrace shaded with curved canvases similar to the covered wagons of the American West during the colonization. In the scale model presented by Kocher and Frey in the exhibition, the bedroom window included roll-up fabric awnings with an aluminum finish as protection against the sun. Due to its use of previously patented devices and systems, along with its lack of specific design, the house formed a technological collage in an even more pronounced way than its antecedent, the Aluminaire House. This methodology of the technical collage was extended years later to its immediate typological descendent, the Kocher Canvas Weekend House, designed and built in 1934.

The Experimental Weekend House was raised off the ground by six round steel columns that did not continue through to the second floor. The space liberated under the house has enough clearance to be used as a covered porch or as a car port. The pictures of the scale model show an automobile parked underneath the house, probably to depict the functionality of that space or to relate the design to the machinal paradigm, central to the ideology of modern architects of that time. As a weekend house, a temporary dwelling located far from the urban environment, the automobile can be perceived as an extension of the house, vital to its basic functionality.

The house's second floor was a 24-foot-by-19-feet-and-six-inches (468-square-foot) rectangle and featured a minimalist program that included a kitchen, bathroom, dining room, and a flexible space that could be used as a living room or two bedrooms, much like the second-floor design of Farmhouse B. Yet unlike in its precedent, the storage space is very tight in the Experimental Weekend House; the closets were strictly dimensioned to fit the beds and do not leave much room for anything else to be stowed. The lack of a full-time living room space amplified the importance of the upper terrace—the house's de facto main social zone. **(Figure 3.58)** The home's overall spatial flexibility was achieved through the use of folding canvas partitions deployed radially from a central post aligned with the closets. The volumetric simplicity and its radical detachment from the landscape made possible the complete and uniform wrapping with treated canvas of all parapets, façades, terrace floor, and porch ceiling. This material continuity provided the design with a high level of abstraction, very different to the functional and programmatic compromises of the Experimental Five-Room House. This disconnection of the house from the surrounding landscape was so thorough that the scale model does not have any visible means to reach the second floor from the ground. In fact, the house does not have a regular permanent stair. Access to the second floor and roof terrace occurred via two motorized Bessler foldable stairs. The stairs were situated with one on the ceiling and the other on the floor of the second floor, adjacent to the kitchen and bathroom walls. This kind of mechanism was patented in 1931 and has since become a very common feature in many American homes, typically used to access attic storage. The house could therefore be totally isolated from the ground, resolving potential security concerns in a home that was designed for occasional occupation. As in most of Kocher and Frey's productions, the use of catalog solutions for these houses related to the use of builder's handbooks in American vernacular architecture of the 18th century. This strategy implied not only an ease for construction, supply, and budgetary accuracy, but it also methodologically linked modernism with local vernacular in the search of a new national style. The most exciting feature of the Experimental Weekend House that sets it apart from the Experimental Five-Room House was not its formal boldness, but its timely connection to the historic context and the changes in lifestyle it entailed.

The Experimental Weekend House was profoundly intertwined with the main political and social debates and preoccupations of its age and pioneered social trends that would be later developed and officially established by legislation. Although Henry Ford instituted a five-day, 40-hour workweek extended to all employees nationwide in 1926, an immense majority of American workers remained with a one-day weekend at the beginning of the 1930s. During the Depression-focused presidential campaign of 1932, shorter work hours were a major voter issue, and both candidates Hoover and Roosevelt had converging ideas on the matter. Hoover positioned shorter hours as a means of redistributing labor among the unemployed—everybody would earn less, but everybody would have work. He additionally urged the voluntary reduction of hours; major businesses such as Kellogg's, Sears Roebuck, General Motors, and Standard Oil followed this path as an alternative to firing part of their workforce. After losing the election in November 1932, the democrat senator Hugo Lafayette Black introduced a bill backed by the American Federation of Labor to temporarily shorten the workweek drastically to only 30 hours, six hours a day, five days a week. It had Roosevelt's support and after he took office on March 4th in 1933 with the claim that reducing workhours would reduce production, and thus oversupply, and help to create six million jobs, the Senate passed Black's 30-hour-week bill 53 to 30 in a bipartisan vote a month later. Arguments for the relevance of leisure and the right of workers to free time reinforced this cause. Later in the decade, increasing industry resistance to reduced hours doomed the bill and President Roosevelt abandoned the 30-hour effort, no longer challenging the two-day weekend. By 1938, the Fair Labor Standards Act limited the workweek to 40 hours, and a two-day weekend allowing for workers' leisure time.[25] The new two-day weekend and the use of automobiles allowed the American middle-class to afford enough leisure time to take advantage of a second temporary residence in the near countryside.

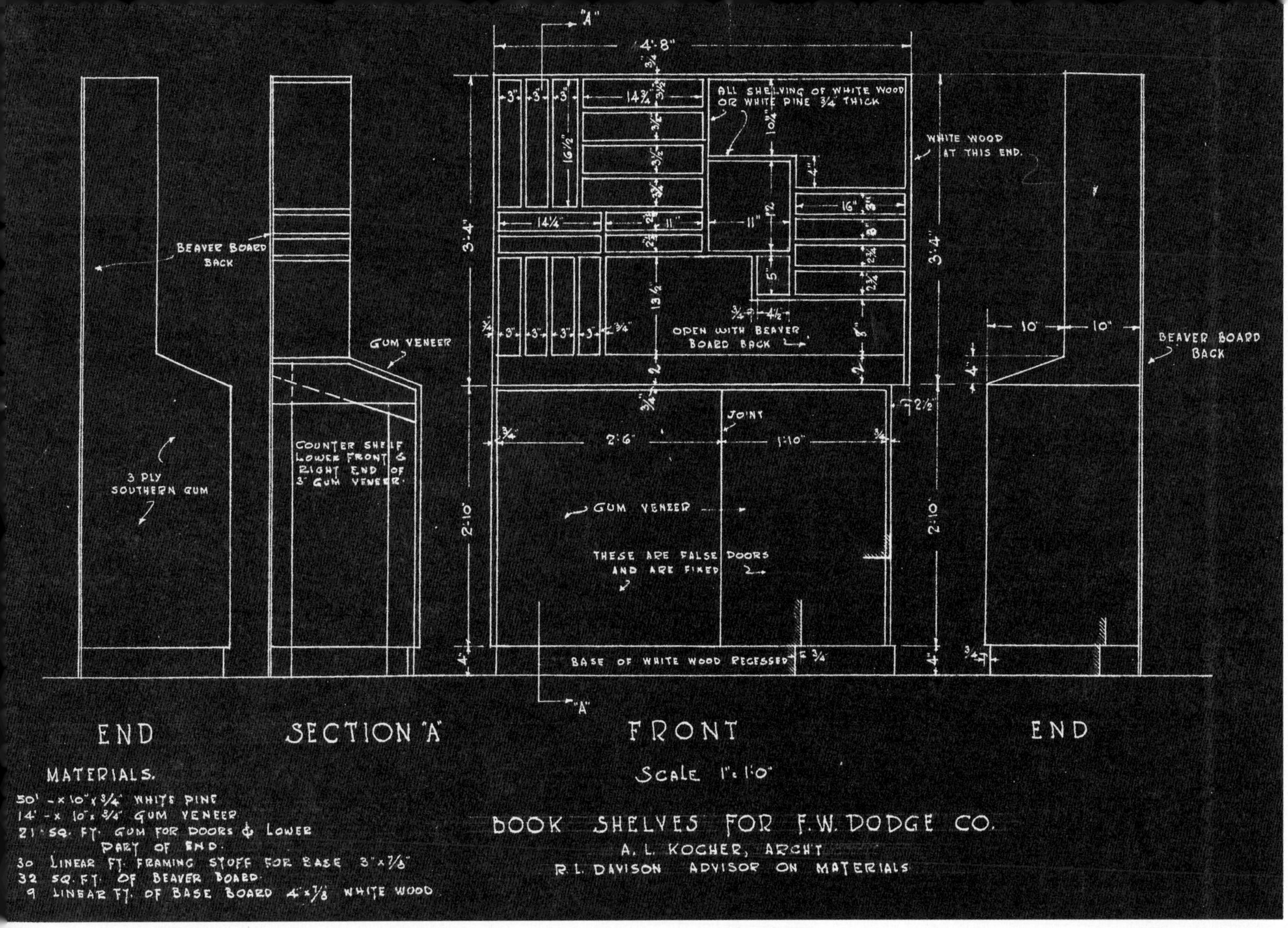

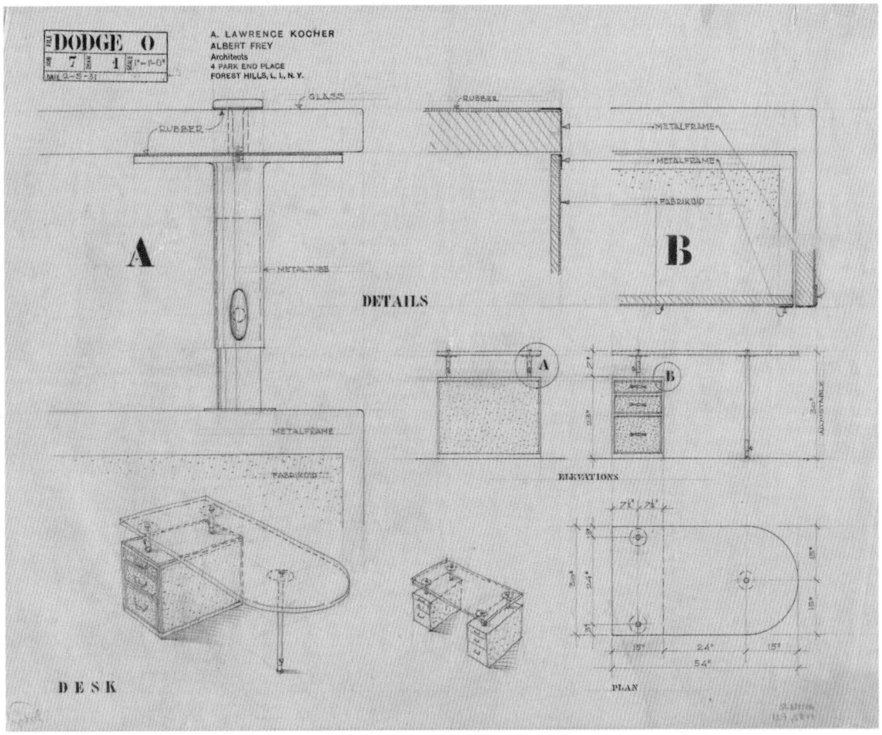

Figure 3.31. A. Lawrence Kocher, R.L. Davison, and Albert Frey. F.W. Dodge Co. exhibition display booth for the 1931 Southern Architecture and Allied Arts Exposition in Memphis, Tennessee. Book shelves details. Undated.

Figure 3.32. A. Lawrence Kocher, R.L. Davison, and Albert Frey. F.W. Dodge Co. exhibition display booth for the 1931 Southern Architecture and Allied Arts Exposition in Memphis, Tennessee. Architect desk details. Dated 2-05-1931.

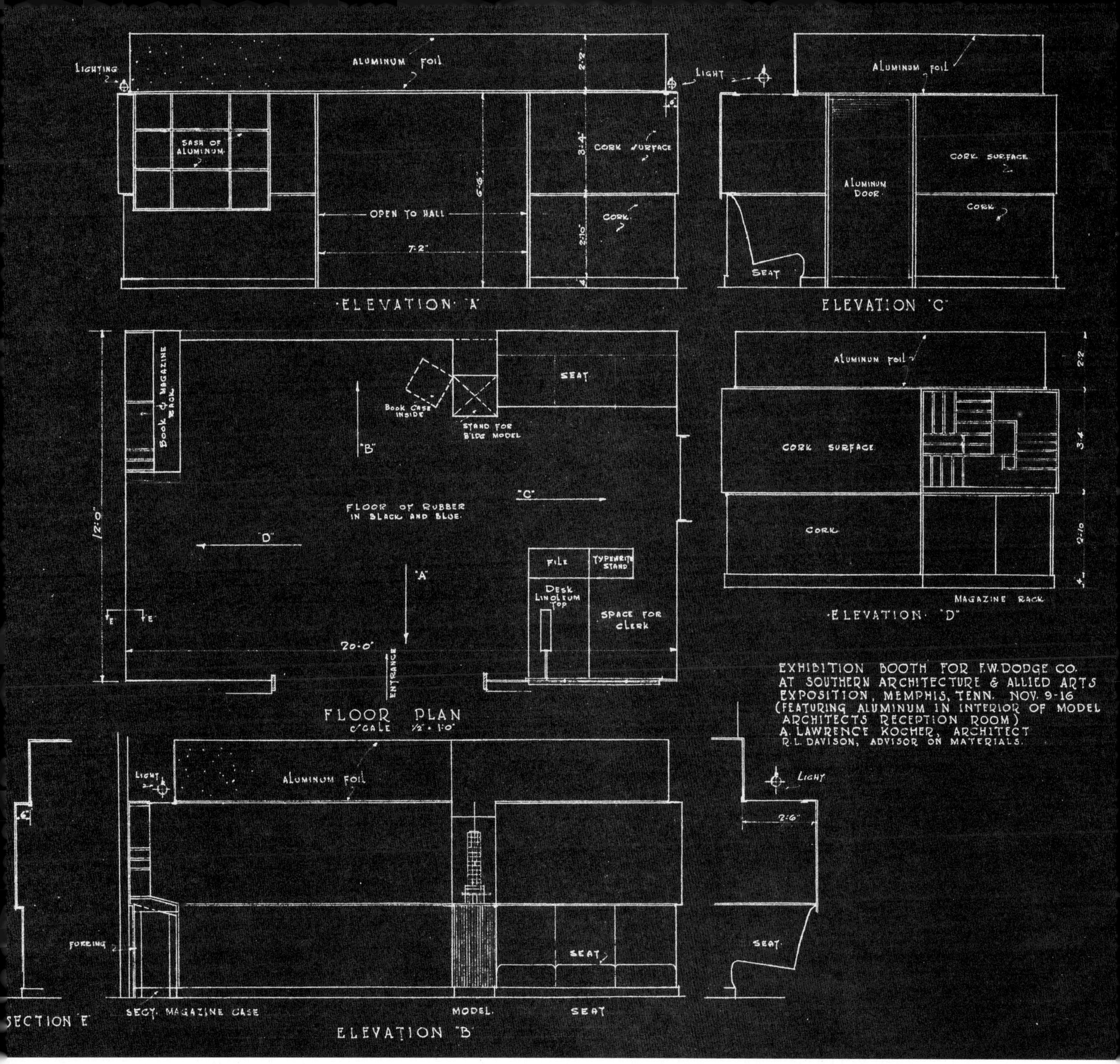

Figure 3.33. A. Lawrence Kocher, R.L. Davison, and Albert Frey. F.W. Dodge Co. exhibition display booth for the 1931 Southern Architecture and Allied Arts Exposition in Memphis, Tennessee. Floor plan and internal elevations. Undated.

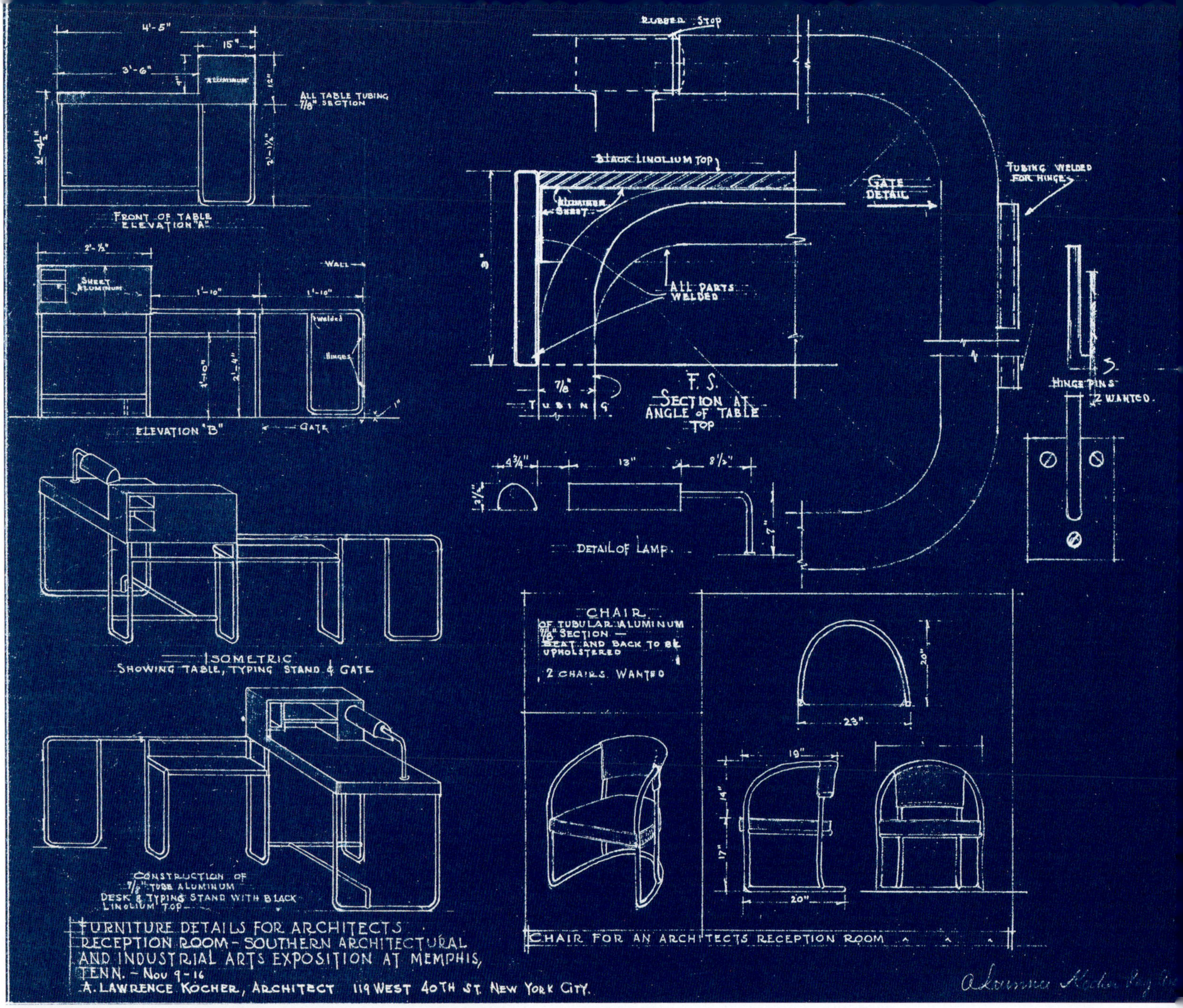

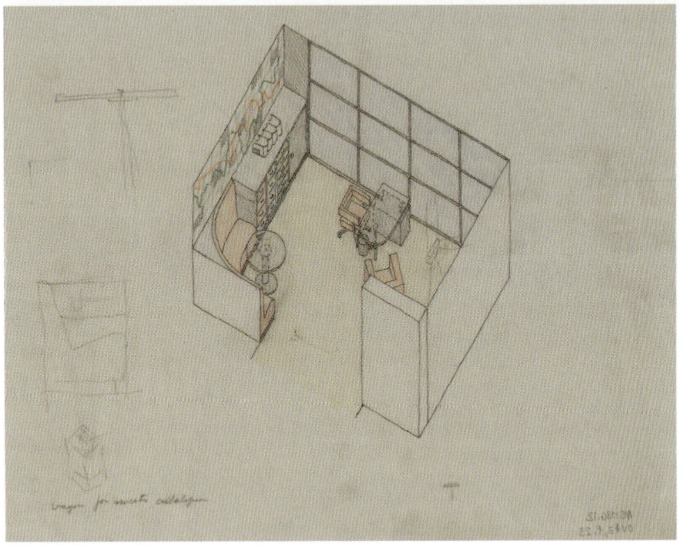

This page:

Figure 3.34. A. Lawrence Kocher, R.L. Davison, and Albert Frey. F.W. Dodge Co. exhibition display booth for the 1931 Southern Architecture and Allied Arts Exposition in Memphis, Tennessee. Reception room furniture including typing stand, table, gate, and chairs. Undated.

Figure 3.35. A. Lawrence Kocher and Albert Frey. Adaptation of the F.W. Dodge Co. exhibition furniture for a train wagon. Axonometric view of the wagon. Undated.

Next page:

Figures 3.36 and 3.37. A. Lawrence Kocher and Albert Frey. June 1931. Downyflake Donut shop prototype. Axonometric views.

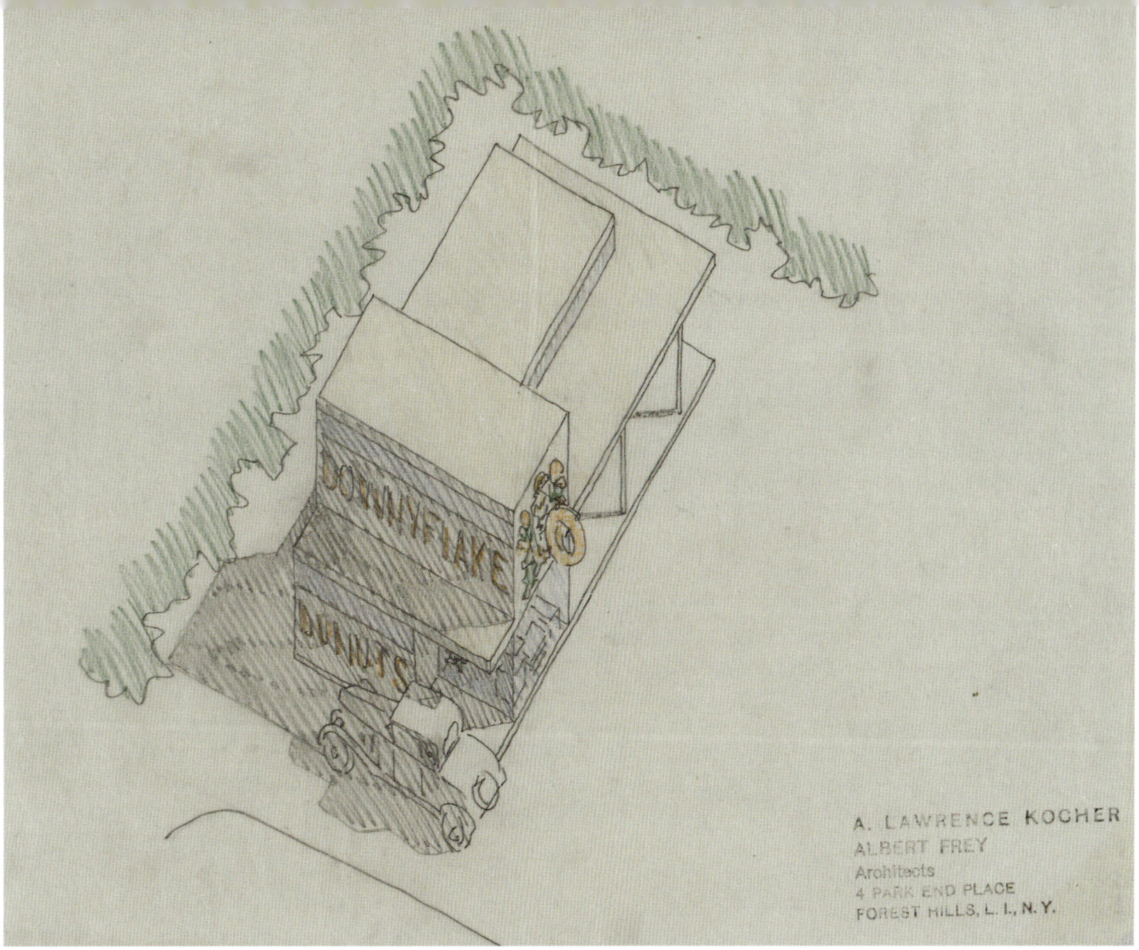

DONNYFLAKE
DONUTS
A. LAWRENCE KOCHER
ALBERT FREY
Architects
4 PARK END PLACE
FOREST HILLS, L. I., N. Y.

A. LAWRENCE KOCHER
ALBERT FREY
Architects
4 PARK END PLACE
FOREST HILLS, L. I., N. Y.

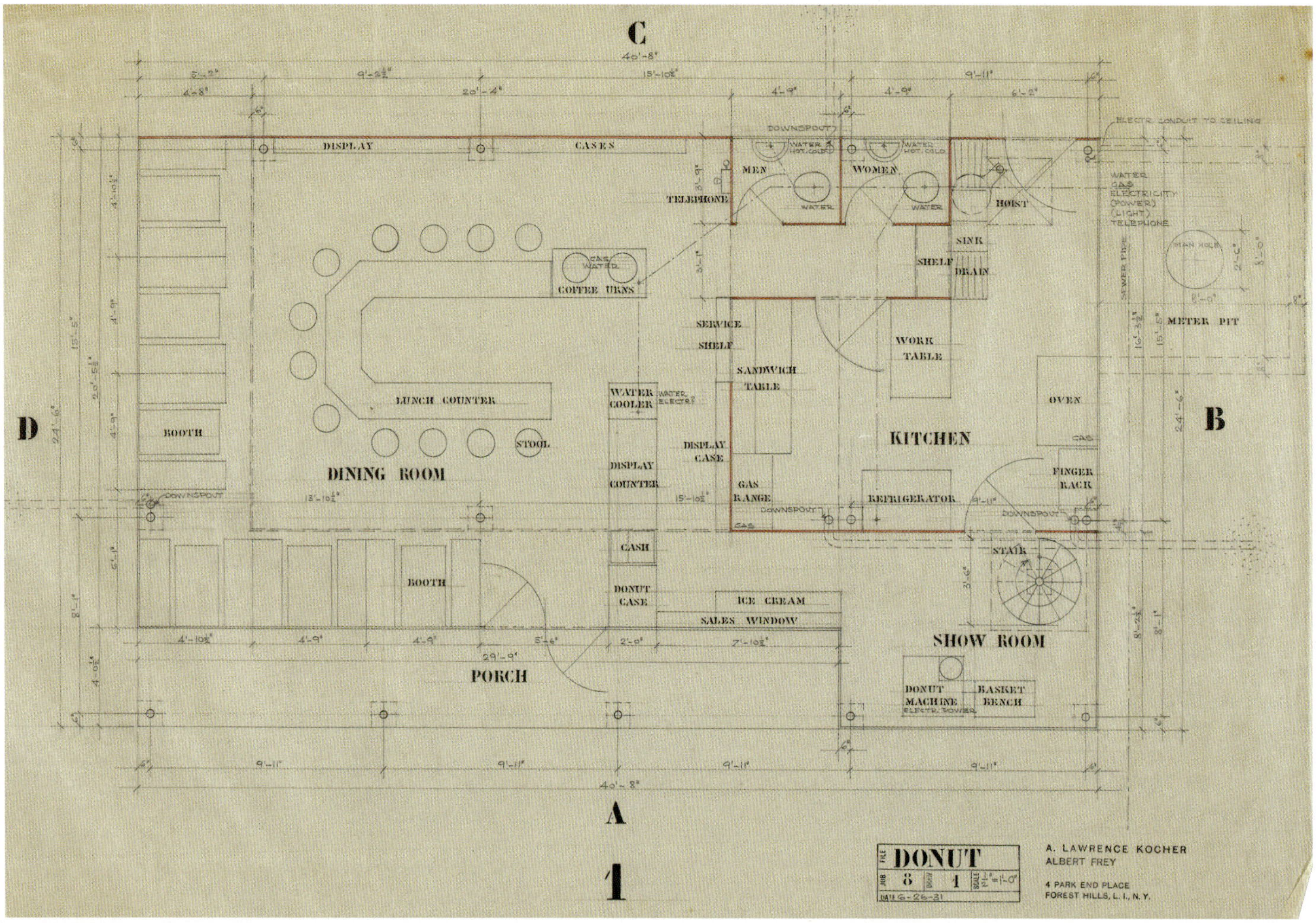
C
D
B
A
DISPLAY
CASES
MEN
WOMEN
TELEPHONE
HOIST
SINK
SHELF
DRAIN
COFFEE URNS
SERVICE
SHELF
SANDWICH
TABLE
WORK
TABLE
METER PIT
OVEN
BOOTH
LUNCH COUNTER
WATER
COOLER
KITCHEN
DISPLAY
CASE
DISPLAY
COUNTER
STOOL
DINING ROOM
FINGER
RACK
GAS
RANGE
REFRIGERATOR
CASH
STAIR
BOOTH
DONUT
CASE
ICE CREAM
SALES WINDOW
SHOW ROOM
PORCH
DONUT
MACHINE
BASKET
BENCH
1
DONUT
A. LAWRENCE KOCHER
ALBERT FREY
4 PARK END PLACE
FOREST HILLS, L. I., N. Y.

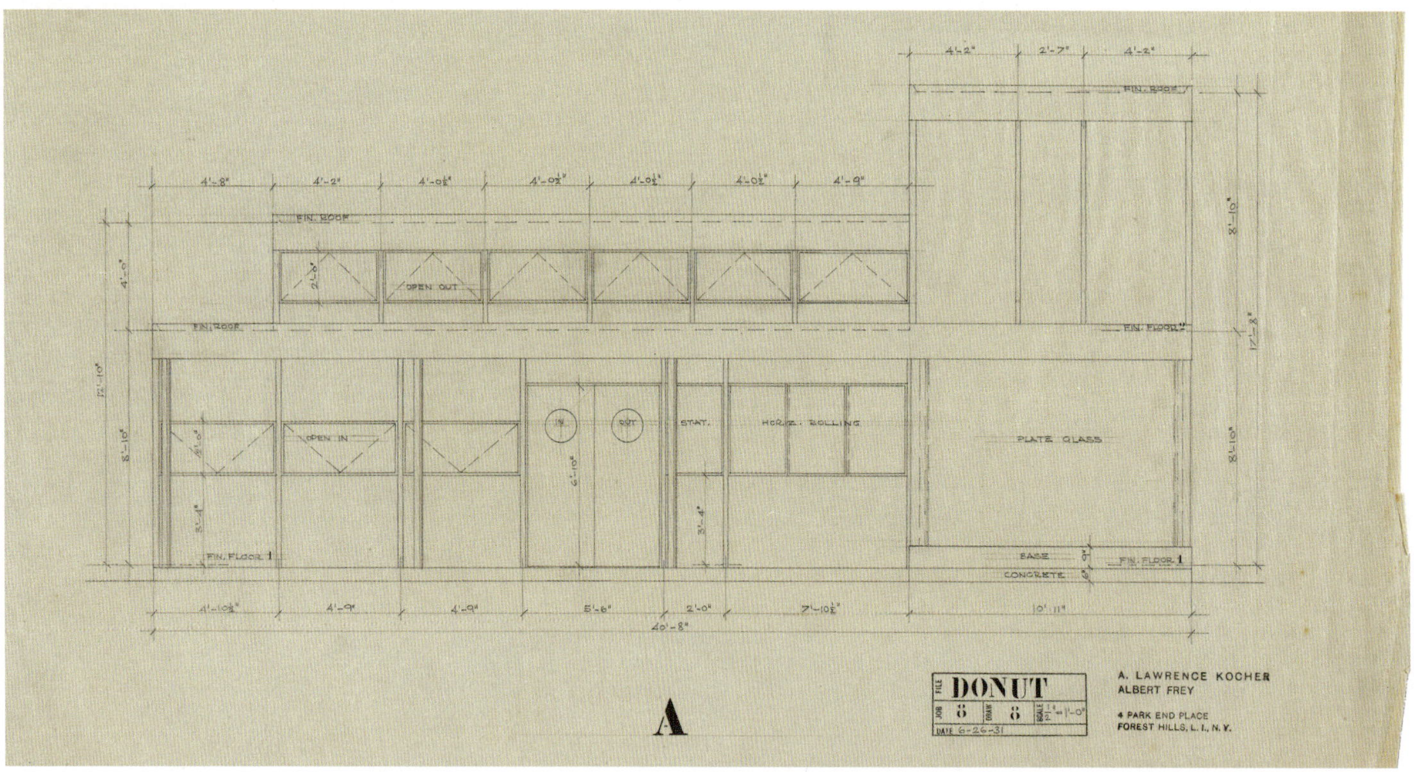
PLATE GLASS
A
DONUT
A. LAWRENCE KOCHER
ALBERT FREY
4 PARK END PLACE
FOREST HILLS, L. I., N. Y.

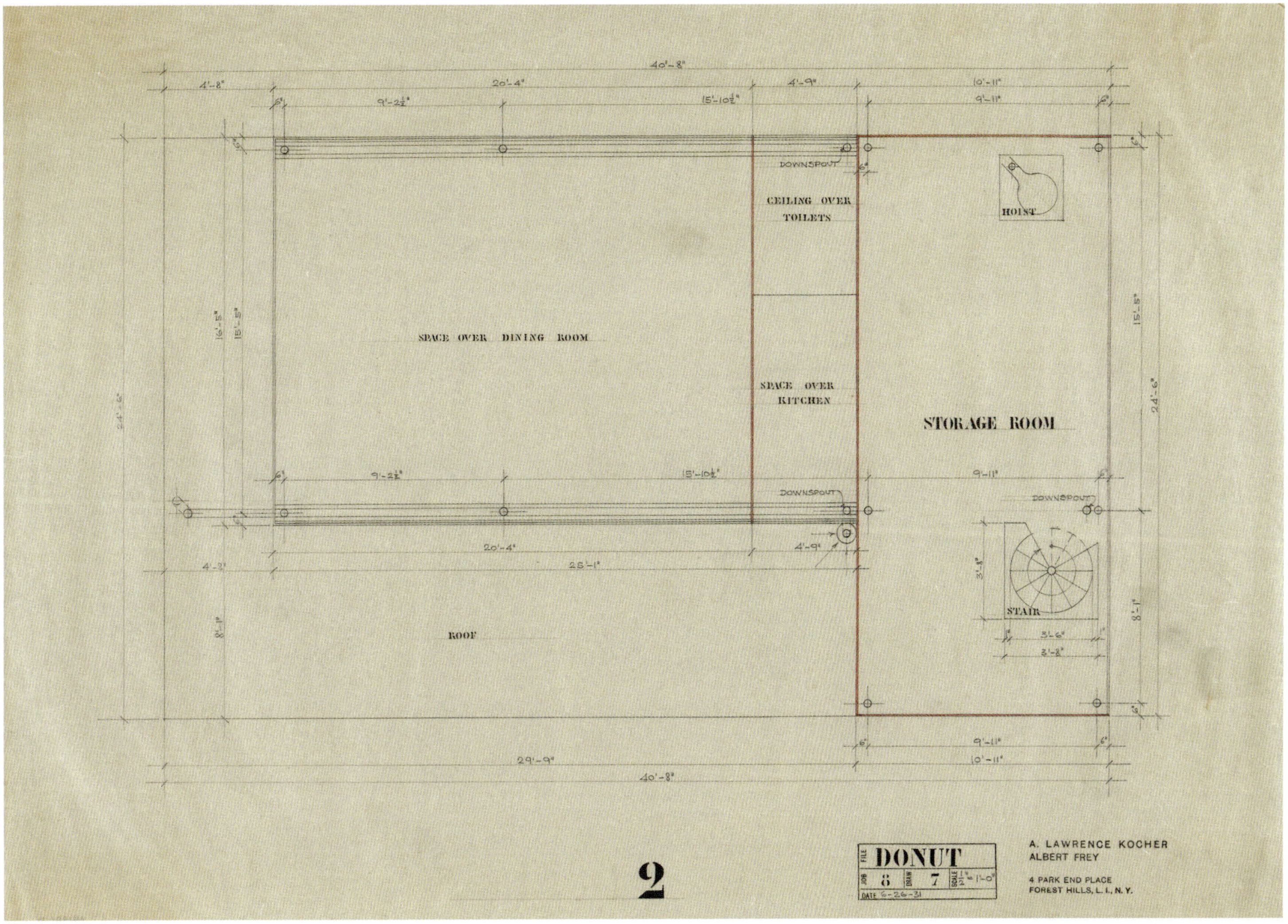

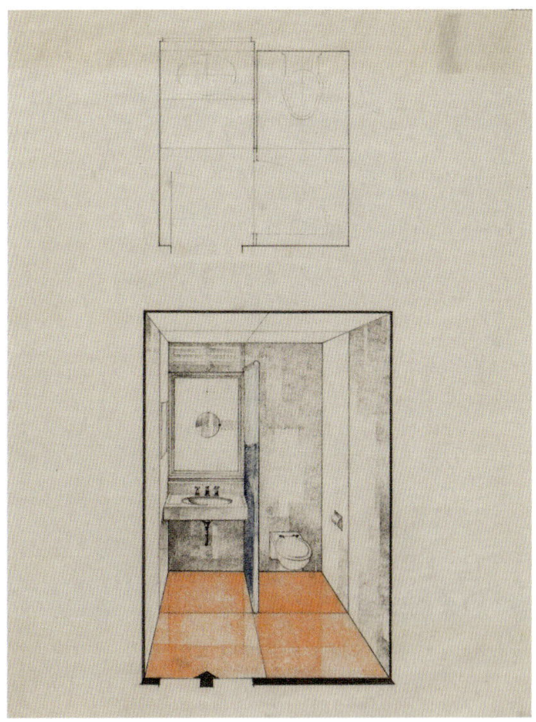

Previous page:
Figure 3.38. A. Lawrence Kocher and Albert Frey. June 1931. Downyflake Donut shop prototype. Ground floor plan. Dated 6-26-31.
Figure 3.39. A. Lawrence Kocher and Albert Frey. June 1931. Downyflake Donut shop prototype. Front elevation. Dated 6-26-31.

This page:
Figure 3.40. A. Lawrence Kocher and Albert Frey. 1931. Downyflake Donut shop prototype. Roof and mezzanine plan. Dated 6-26-31.
Figure 3.41. A. Lawrence Kocher and Albert Frey. 1931. Downyflake Donut shop prototype. Rest rooms, floor plan, and perspective view. Undated.

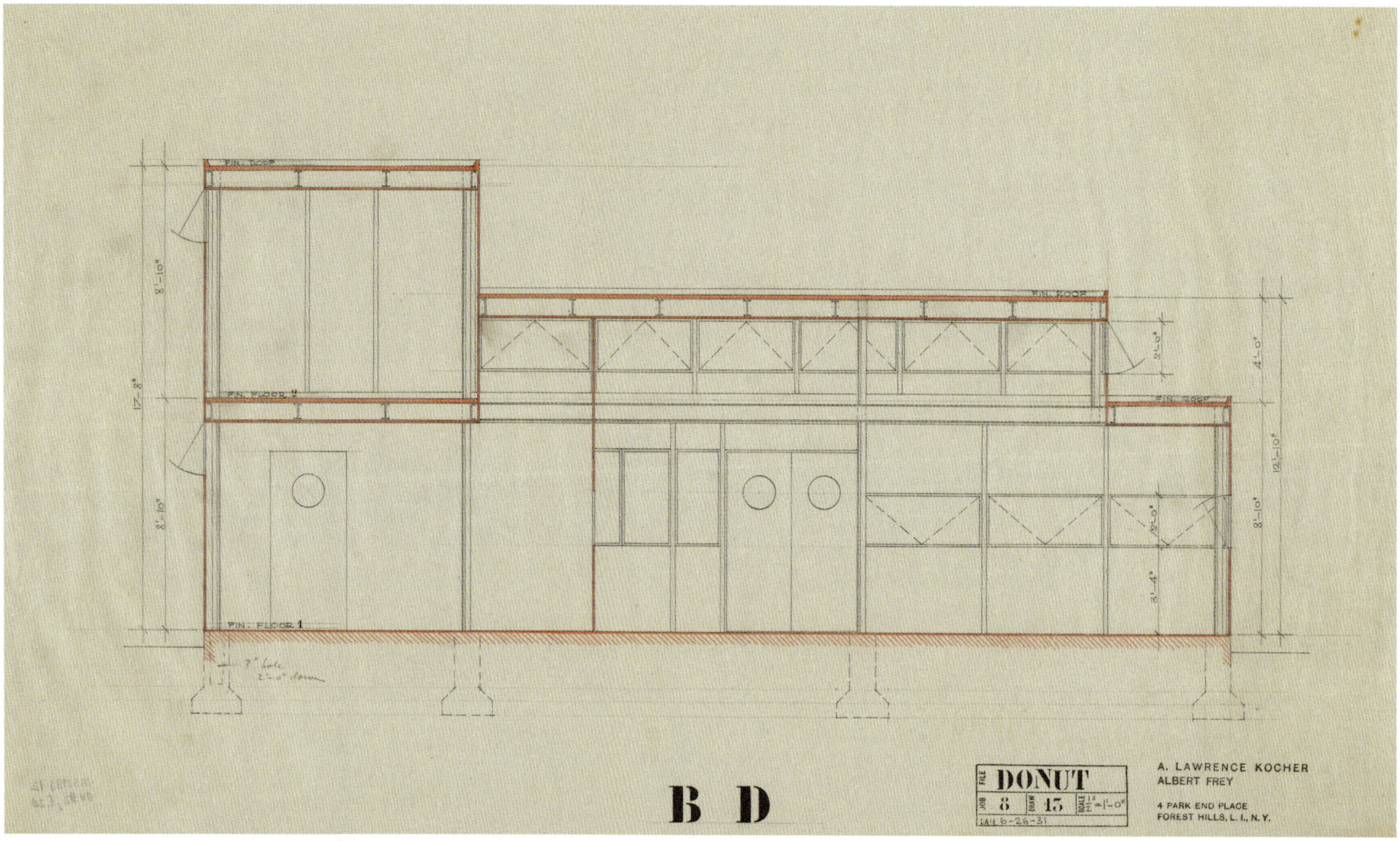
FIN. ROOF
FIN. FLOOR 1
B D
DONUT
JOB 8 DRAW 13
DATE 6-26-31
A. LAWRENCE KOCHER
ALBERT FREY
4 PARK END PLACE
FOREST HILLS, L. I., N. Y.

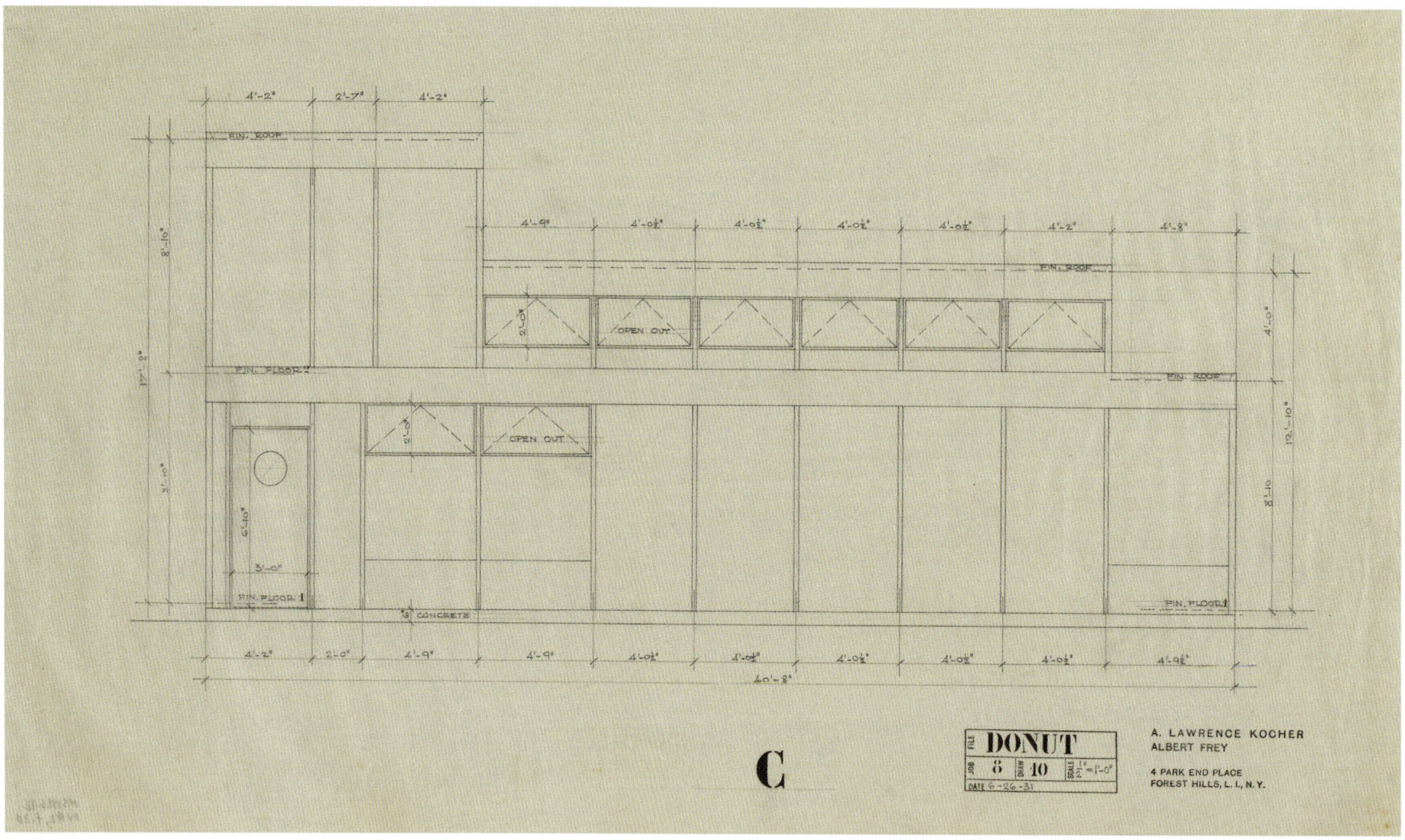
FIN. ROOF
OPEN OUT
FIN. FLOOR 1
CONCRETE
C
DONUT
JOB 8 DRAW 10
DATE 6-26-31
A. LAWRENCE KOCHER
ALBERT FREY
4 PARK END PLACE
FOREST HILLS, L. I., N. Y.

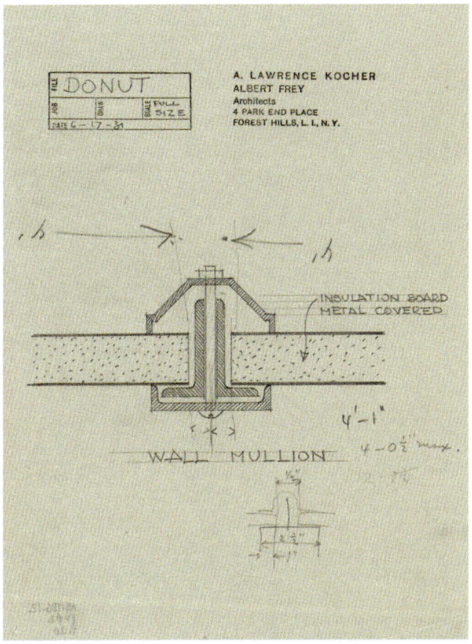

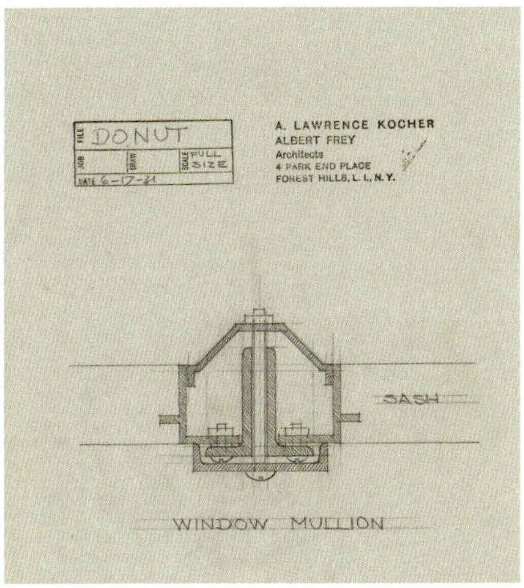

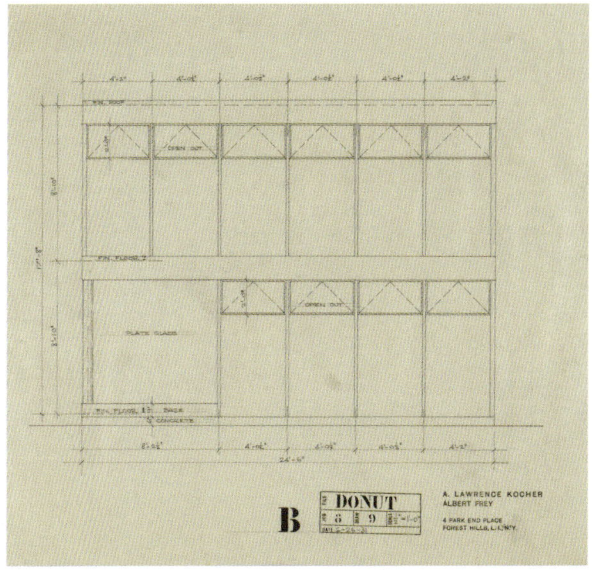

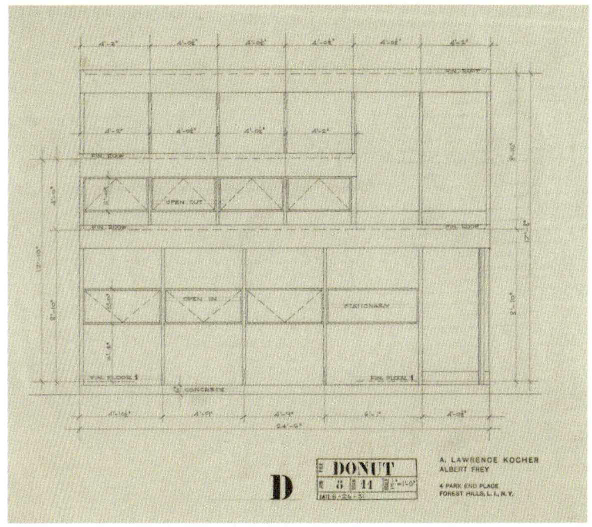

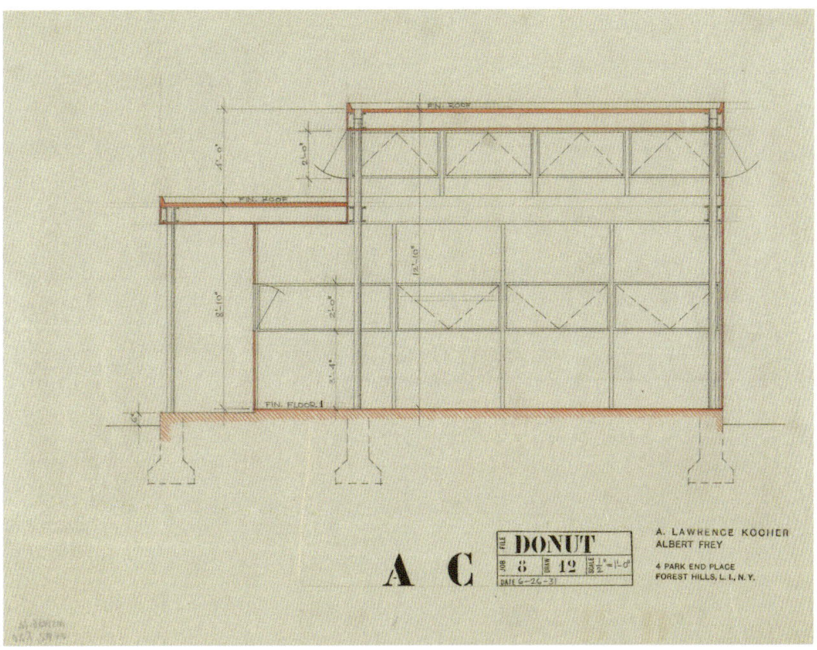

Previous page:
Figure 3.42. A. Lawrence Kocher and Albert Frey. 1931. Downyflake Donut shop prototype. Longitudinal section. Dated 6-26-31.
Figure 3.43. A. Lawrence Kocher and Albert Frey. 1931. Downyflake Donut shop prototype. Elevation. Dated 6-26-31.

This page:
Figure 3.44. A. Lawrence Kocher and Albert Frey. 1931. Downyflake Donut shop prototype. Wall mullion detail. Plan. Dated 6-17-31.
Figure 3.45. A. Lawrence Kocher and Albert Frey. 1931. Downyflake Donut shop prototype. Window mullion detail. Plan. Dated 6-17-31.
Figures 3.46 and 3.47. A. Lawrence Kocher and Albert Frey. 1931. Downyflake Donut shop prototype. Lateral elevations. Dated 6-17-31.
Figure 3.48. A. Lawrence Kocher and Albert Frey. 1931. Downyflake Donut shop prototype. Cross section. Dated 6-26-31.

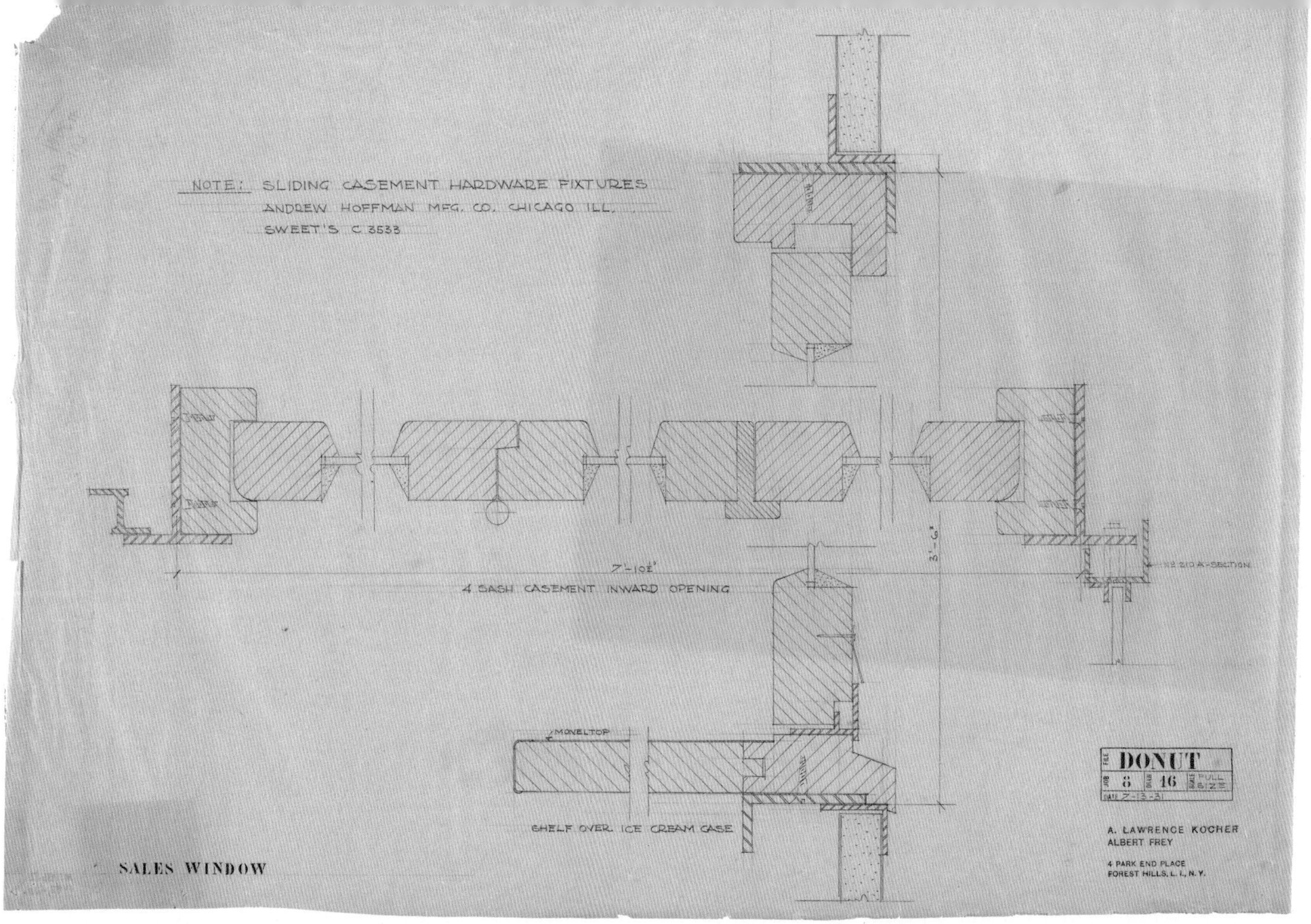

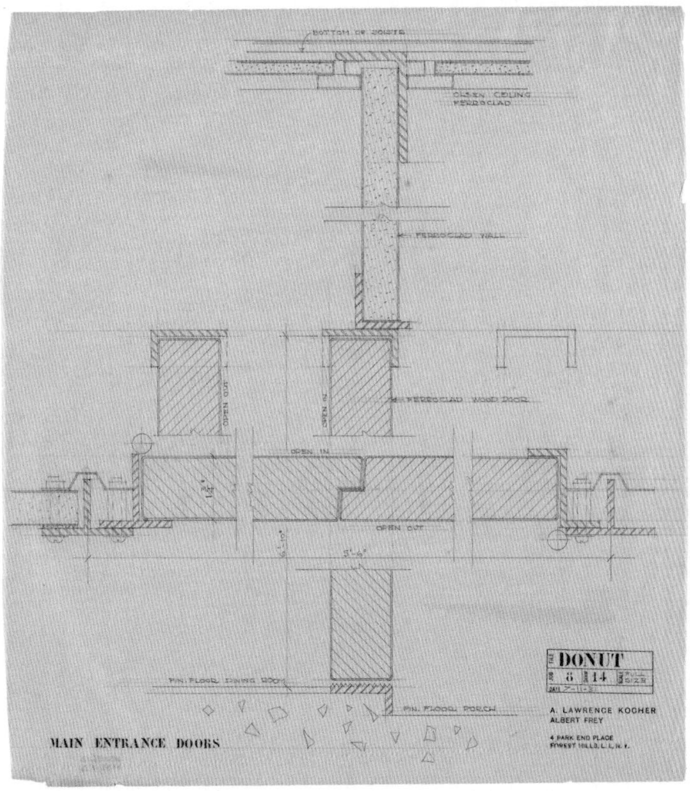

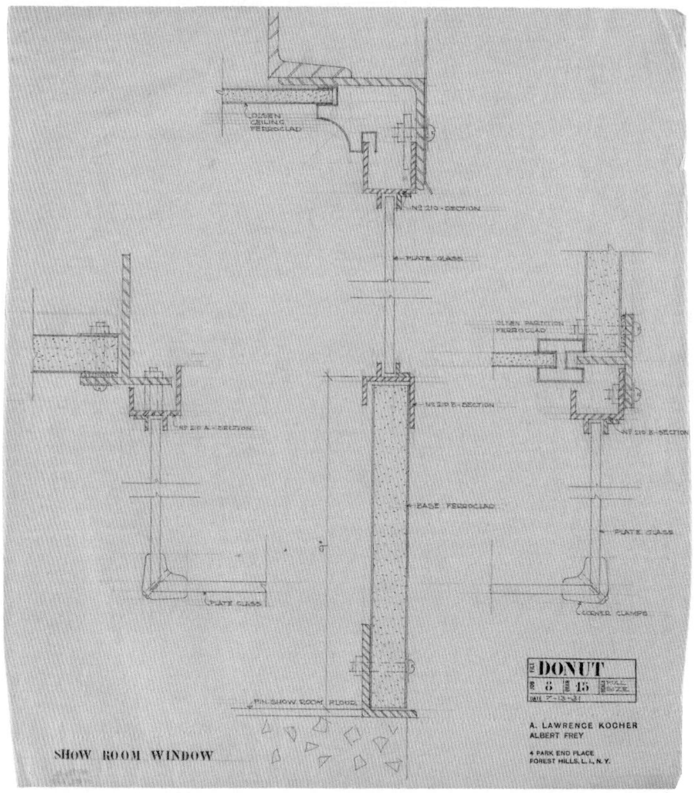

Figures 3.49 to 3.51. A. Lawrence Kocher and Albert Frey. 1931. Downy-flake Donut shop prototype. Various windows and doors details. Dated 7-13-31.

The difference between the Experimental Five-Room House and the Experimental Weekend House was as sharp on the formal front as it was in their proposed domestic lifestyles. There was a radically different ideology behind each design. On the one hand, the Experimental Five-Room House was based on a very traditional conception of family life. As with many of Le Corbusier's villas, it was a house designed for a bourgeois middle-class with a conservative setting including back and front yards, and permanent spaces designated for a unique and unchangeable activity with set furniture. On the other hand, the Experimental Weekend House explored a life more closely related to the natural environment; it reinforced a less stable, more nomadic, and less introverted kind of life ignited by the establishment of the two-day weekend, new ideas about leisure and health, and the popularity of the automobile.

In the same way that the Aluminaire House was a part of the lineage of prefabricated and mobile housing solutions in the USA, the Experimental Weekend House had a number of formal and conceptual features consistent with a social propensity, forced by the Depression, for new kinds of temporal roadside habitational solutions based around the car. Whether the car was a substantial part of or a necessary detachable complement to the domestic space, this affinity may have been due either to contingent factors, voluntary design decisions, or to the zeitgeist that transformed what was a fad in the 1920s to a solution for transient ways of life in the 1930s. The fact was that auto-camping, roadside cabins, and other types of minimal temporary shelters were on Kocher and Frey's radar, as well as that of their colleagues at *Architectural Record.* Therefore, the Experimental Weekend House can be situated as part of the ongoing investigations about the new car-related typologies that *Architectural Record* published in the early 1930s under Kocher's direction. Immediately after his appointment as managing director of *Architectural Record*, Kocher inaugurated the magazine's section "Technical News and Research," and put Knud Lonberg-Holm in charge. Both architects envisioned the articles of the section to be technically sound and didactic. Using the model of the 18th-century builder's handbooks, they nevertheless "initiated a fundamental break from traditional architectural discourse" by exploring the implications of the modern way of life to architectural design.[26] These implications essentially came from two sources: mass production and the adjustment of architectural practice to "the conditions created by modern technics in the useful arts, including commerce and industry."[27] Within these two categories, the automobile was identified as the mass-produced apparatus with the highest potential of influence over a modern lifestyle.

Consequently, the automobile was introduced as a subject of intense and sustained architectural research in *Architectural Record* and considered the main catalyst for the production of new kinds of buildings. This was a trend shared by other magazines, like *American Architect* and *Architectural Forum.* Despite an initial drop in early Great Depression, the sales of cars started to gradually increase again after 1932 due to new patterns in transient work and the potential of the car to not only be used as a means of transportation but also as a temporary dwelling option. The impact of the car over architecture and urbanism seemed to multiply during these years, and the specialized magazines saturated their pages with auto-related case studies, news, editorials, technical updates, and portfolios.[28]

Along this line of inquiry, many projects related to automobiles in varied degrees appeared in *Architectural Record.* Lonberg-Holm published an article in 1930 entitled "The Gasoline Filling and Service Station."[29] By precisely defining the functions to be accomplished in the building and use-economy of form and material, he attempted to give a modern alternative to the mimicry of traditional styles happening in the design of a new building typology—the gas station. In February of 1931, Stadium Consultant Myron W. Selby published a paper on "Stadium Planning and Design." It included a speculative design for a building that combined the stadium with the parking garage, including five levels of parking spaces adjacent to the seating areas and additional roof parking where spectators could follow sporting events directly from inside their cars. The designers of this hybrid typology were Lonberg-Holm and his former student from the University of Michigan, Seiichi Washizuka.[30] One month prior to Selby's paper, Kocher and Frey published their article, "Planning the House Garage," in which they state that the garage should be considered as the entrance of the house, readily accessible from the stair hallway, and reached as directly as possible from the street.[31] Later, in August of 1931, *Architectural Record* published an unattributed article about possible new fields of design for architects. The listed new design opportunities were almost exclusively based on air or terrestrial traffic: filling and service stations, roadside inns and refreshment stands, auto-restaurants, bus stations, and airplane hangars. Further, the article pushed that these emerging typologies should be erected by architects using a modern, rational criteria similar to those used in the design of the Experimental Weekend House: "suitability to purpose, portability, ease of assembly, disassembly, and maintenance, interchangeability of units, high salvage value, low production costs, substantial, although not necessarily permanent, construction."[32] Although many more examples can be found in *Architectural Record* during the early 1930s, these brief examples provide an overview of the automobile's relevance to architectural design of the time.[33] Nevertheless, two articles in particular are especially relevant to understanding the design of the Experimental Weekend House and its connection with automobile-related dwelling solutions. Each article is devoted to a type of building, namely weekend houses and roadside cabins, whose combination can presumably be considered as the conceptual and formal base of the Experimental Weekend House.

The first article, written by Lonberg-Holm and published in August of 1930—the same *Architectural Record* issue in which the Loucheur Houses by Le Corbusier and Jeanneret were published—explored the weekend house as an emerging building type, explicitly differentiated from a "city residence transferred to the country, or a suburban bungalow reduced in scale." The main differences from the precedent typologies that derived into a completely different formal developments are nevertheless based on further ideological questions. Carefully choosing each of the words used, the article defines the weekend house as the "minimum stationary setting for a family life reduced to its simplest terms in close contact with sun, soil, and sky and freed from obsolete social and architectural forms."[34] The set of graphic references used in the article included, among others,

THE COTTON HOUSE

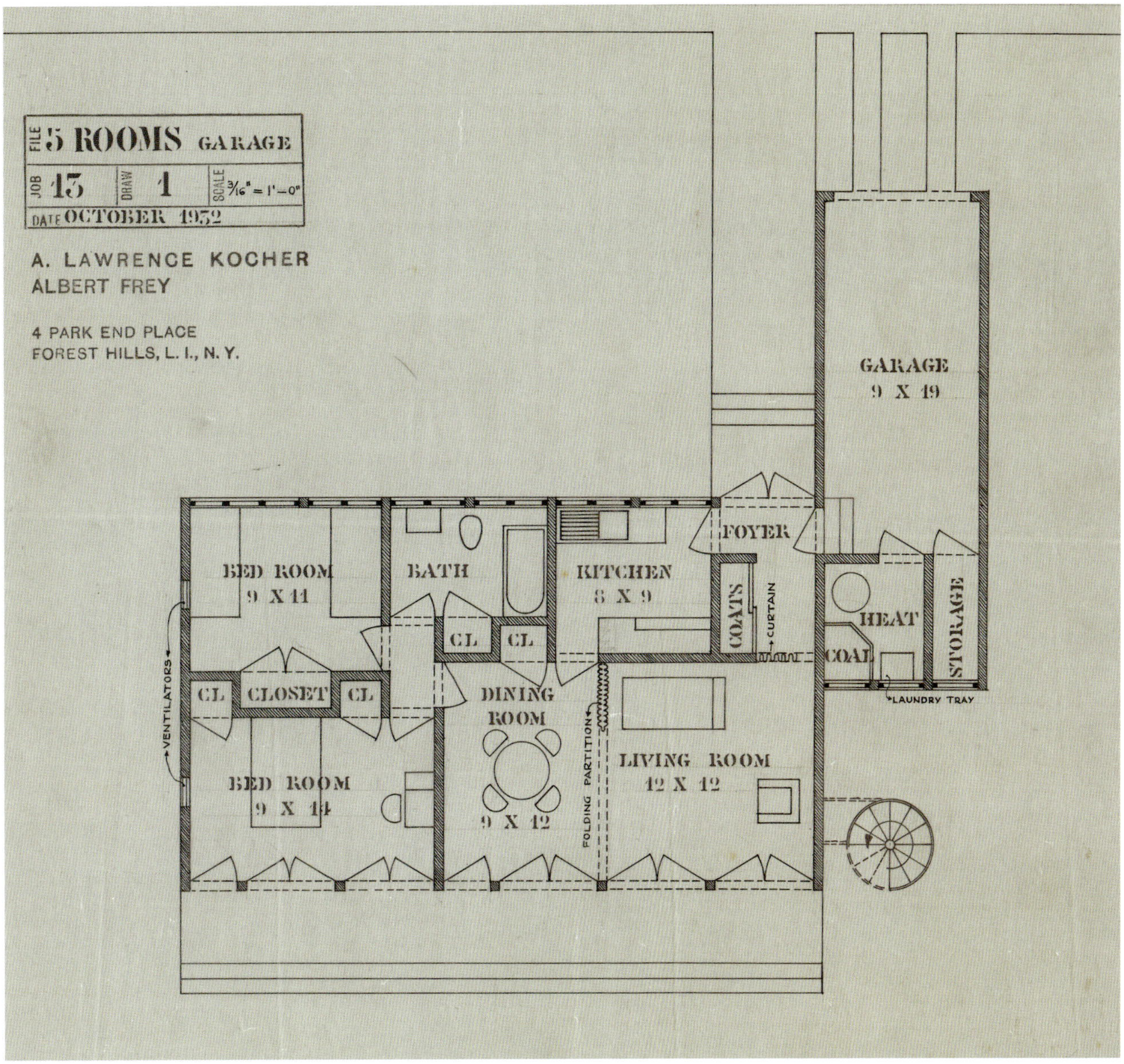

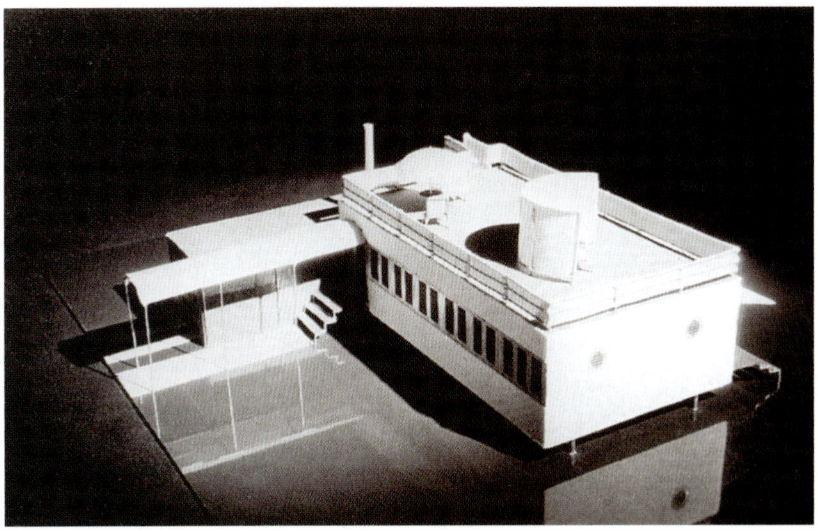

Previous page:
Figure 3.52. A. Lawrence Kocher and Albert Frey. The Cotton House Exhibition in Washington D.C. sponsored by the Cotton-Textile Institute. January 1932. Picture of the exhibition.
Figure 3.53. A. Lawrence Kocher and Albert Frey. 1932. Experimental Five-Room House. Picture of the model.

This page:
Figure 3.54. A. Lawrence Kocher and Albert Frey. 1932. Experimental Five-Room House. Floor plan. Final version.
Figure 3.55. A. Lawrence Kocher and Albert Frey. 1932. Experimental Five-Room House. Picture of the model.

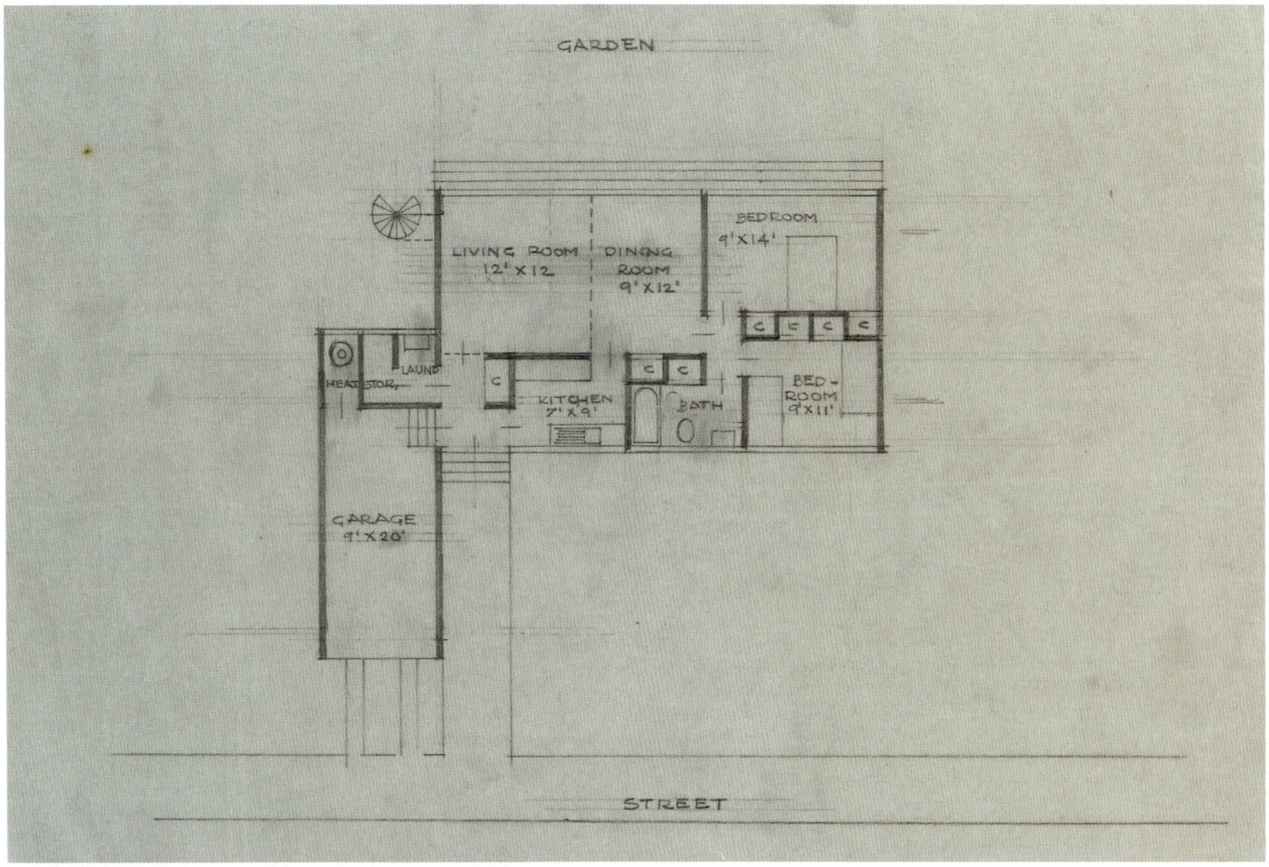

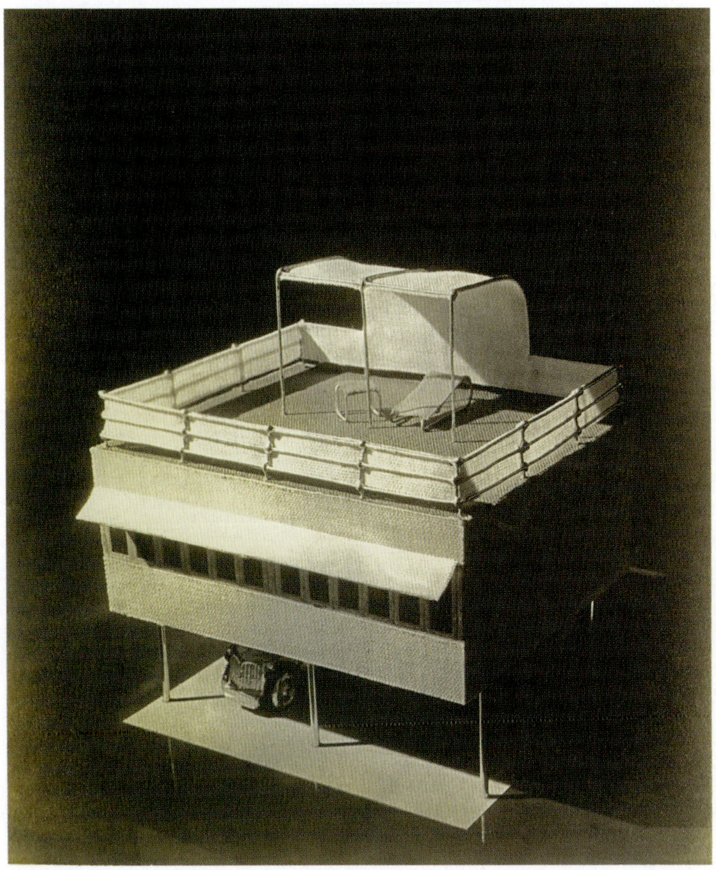

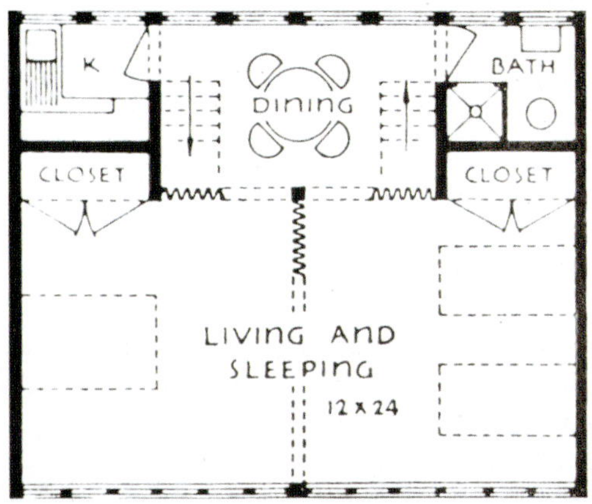

Figure 3.56. A. Lawrence Kocher and Albert Frey. 1932. Experimental Five-Room House. Floor plan. Preliminary version.
Figure 3.57. A. Lawrence Kocher and Albert Frey. 1932. Experimental Weekend House. Picture of the model.
Figure 3.58. A. Lawrence Kocher and Albert Frey. 1932. Experimental Weekend House. Floor plan.

the Dymaxion House by Richard Buckminster Fuller, a minimum modular weekend house by Richard Weber, the Ocatilla desert camp by F. L. Wright, a weekend camp in the mountains by Karl Meinhardt, along with the anonymous architectures of a revolving bath house and a single camping tent. Eight of the 10 references listed in the article's bibliography were devoted to summer camps. These facts are a hint to the direct relationship between the new weekend house typology and camping, according to Lonberg-Holm. The article defined a basic layout of the weekend house, determined by different daily activities—like eating, sleeping, dressing, washing, cooking, sunbathing, storing baggage and food supplies, and sheltering from inclement weather and insects. Of course, the layout also included a toilet and a parking space for automobiles, either in an open parking space with a canvas cover or as a covered parking space under the house—if raised from the ground. The author recommended a minimum of 50 square feet and 500 cubic feet per person and that "the space used during the day should be convertible for use by night in order to reduce the cost of the structure."[35] To provide the required contact with the exterior, the house had a suggested maximum of windows screened against insects and excessive sun exposure. Additional space for guests could be provided by means of screened porches, roofed sleeping porches, or temporary tents. During the long vacancy periods of the off-season, it was advised that the house should be made secure and inaccessible, and all textile parts—like awnings, canopies, screens, and tent extensions—must be removed and stored. The house was as an easy assembly performed by the owner or local unskilled labor of industrial ready-made and easily handled elements. The coincidences between Lonberg-Holm's article and Kocher and Frey's Experimental Weekend House are so radical we conjecture that the Experimental Weekend House is the architectural product of the fulfillment, and occasionally the exacerbation, of the ideological and functional program provided by the text published 16 months prior to the design's inaugural exhibition.

Published in December of 1933, almost one year after the Experimental Weekend House design was complete, the second article was an anonymous reaction to a story published weeks earlier in the November issue of *Harper's Magazine* about the touristic cabins that began proliferating American roadsides in the 1930s. The article's nameless authors regarded this uptick as "not only a new industry, but an important change in American ways of living, and are, furthermore, one of the few features of the American landscape which the depression is causing to grow by leaps and bounds."[36] The text explains how the convenience of this new building type, bred by the Depression for millions of wanderers, would eventually make the business grow even more in the following years. The *Architectural Record* responded to *Harper's Magazine* with a case study of several motor camps, including pictures of Moro Bay motor camp in California, along with drawings and pictures of Coronado Tent City (California), Raton Motor Camp (New Mexico), and Kingman Motor Camp (Arizona). **(Figures 3.59 to 3.62)** Frey was credited as the author of the motor camp pictures; they were taken during his trip across the United States in the summer of 1932, later described in detail in this chapter. The drawings were also attributed to Frey by some researchers, with detailed floor plans of the residential units of Kingman and Coronado and the general layout of the Raton and Kingman camps using a bird's-eye axonometric.[37] The drawings depicted the aggregation of cabins around central services that included a gas station, sanitary services, grocery store, and playgrounds that strongly recalled encampment layouts of the westward-bound covered wagons of the 19th century. The article pointed to their dependence on the automobile and praised the architectural simplicity, functionality, anonymity, and lack of decoration, almost as if they were part of the American vernacular.

These kinds of small buildings were usually completely prefabricated and assembled on site by the owner with little extra help, and therefore, depended on the car not only for its commercial capacity but also for the construction process. Some companies, like the Economy Housing Company of Iowa, offered kits with instructions on how to erect their cabins.[38] Do-it-yourself magazines, like *Popular Mechanics,* carried assembly plans and instructions.[39] This close relation with automobiles and roadside camping is illustrated with a picture of a camping tent and a car, captioned as: "Healthful outdoor living with comfort and convenience and with lightweight, movable shelter has been made possible by the automobile and highway."[40] In actuality, everything—from the building layout to the individual unit—was designed using the car as a basic module. The floor plan of the Kingman Camp depicts the units as reduced to a simple bedroom without a bathroom, revealing a usable interior area of the room that is exactly the same area needed for covered parking. It is the scale of the car, and not the human, that dictates the proportions and square footage of the complete unit. The units of Coronado Tent City had a floor plan more consistent with the requirements established for a weekend house in Lonberg-Holm's article; with a small kitchen and bathroom, a wardrobe, and a transformable 10-foot-and-six-inch-by-14-foot space (147 square feet) for living and dining during daytime and sleeping during the night. The use of curtains to divide the space was very similar to the folding canvas partitions of the Experimental Weekend House.

It is significative that Kocher and Frey were involved in all of these investigations of car-dependent, lightweight minimal construction, providing basic space for temporary occupation in close contact with nature. Their collaborative articles can be interpreted as a functional and ideological program for the Experimental Weekend House and a formal influence for the later Kocher Canvas Weekend House. This connection is further reinforced by the evidence of a typological kinship between the Experimental Weekend House and all the dwelling solutions illustrated in the articles. Both the published materials and speculative designs are a reaction to a common yet challenging historic moment, sharing not only morphological and technological coincidences, but also proposing a similarly fresh understanding of domesticity and everyday life for the users. Consequently, the typical weekend house—as envisioned by Kocher, Frey, and Lonberg-Holm—does not belong to the modern European tradition of the functionalist minimal house. Rather, it is a purely American type that can be inserted within the formal evolutionary line established by many scholars, binding together autocamps, tourist homes, cabin camps, cottage courts, motor courts, motor inns, and highway motels.[41]

It's likely that from this convergence with the most current topics of its time, the Experimental Weekend House was one of the

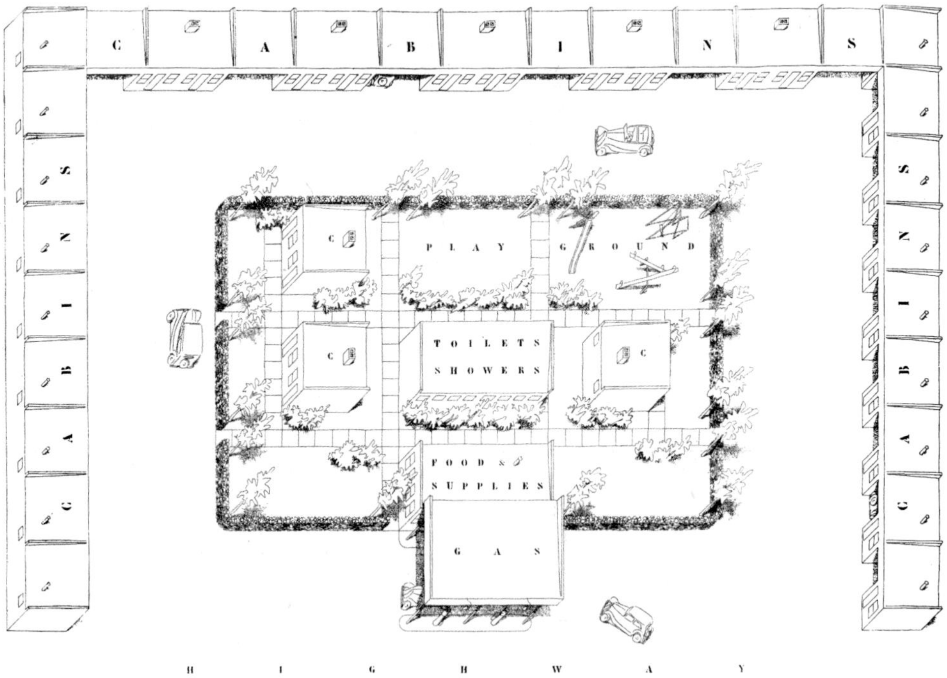

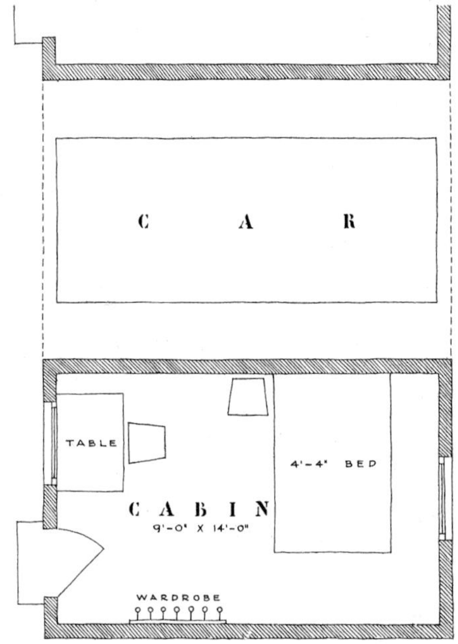

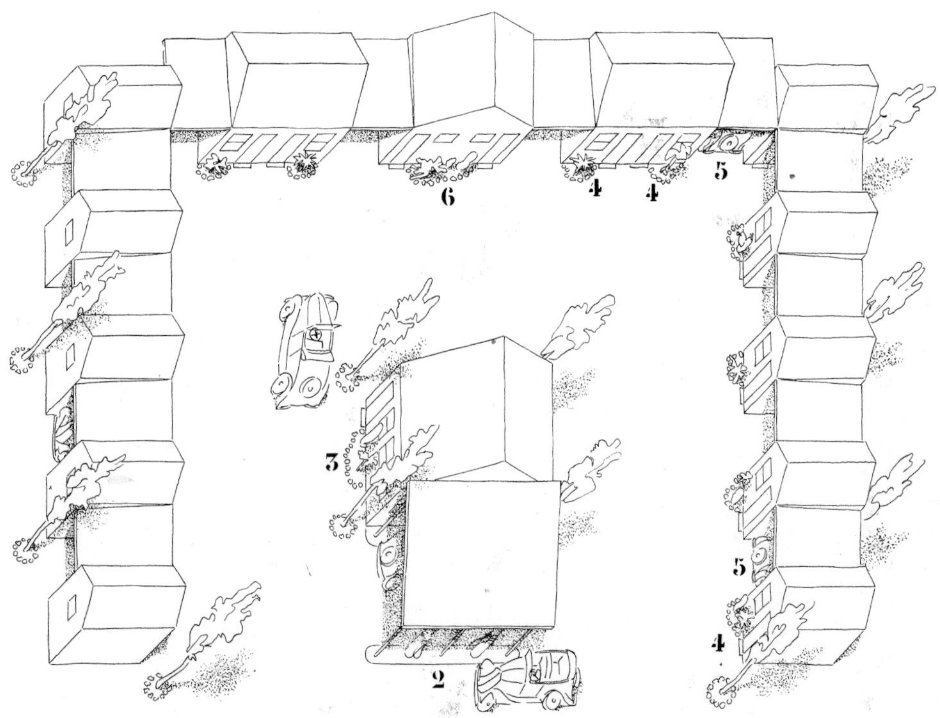

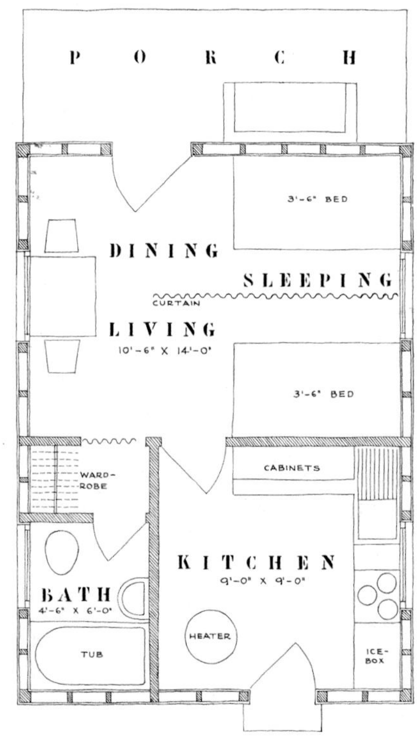

Figure 3.59 and 3.60. Architectural Record. December of 1933. Roadside Cabins for Tourists. Axonometric views of the cabins.
Figure 3.61 and 3.62. Architectural Record. December of 1933. Roadside Cabins for Tourists. Detailed floor plans of the cabins.

most published designs of the firm, second only to the Aluminaire House and followed by the Kocher Canvas Weekend House, its closest relative within Kocher and Frey's complete body of work. Despite all of this media attention, it must be pointed out that the radical experimentation and extreme degree of abstraction in the Experimental Weekend House seriously compromised its functionality and constructability. The fact was that the Cotton-Textile Institute never gave the green light to the fabrication of the prototypes due to financial problems. Furthermore, the kind of steel construction proposed by Kocher and Frey, similar to what was already executed in the fabrication of the Aluminaire House in the last months of 1930, was economically unaffordable in 1932, due to a scenario of rapid deterioration of American economy.[42] This was a fact that the architects would learn in their next project, the Ralph-Barbarin House near Stamford, Connecticut.

The clients were Georgia Ralph and Gabrielle Barbarin, who wanted a house either as a summer home or a permanent residence. Ms. Barbarin was a retired educator acquainted with the work of Le Corbusier; she had seen publications on the Aluminaire House and wanted Kocher and Frey to design a modern-style house for her and her friend Georgia. The clients also asked for an apartment to accommodate guests or rental with an independent entry. The lot had views over an artificial lake, and surrounding hills to the east, and was densely wooded. The program agreed upon by both the clients and the architects consisted of a first floor with a garage for one vehicle, a heater room, laundry storage, and a porch that could be used as an auxiliary garage. The second floor included the two-bedroom, one-bathroom house of the owners. The penthouse was a one-bedroom apartment. The need for independent access to the penthouse provided the architects with the first project restriction: the stairwell needed to be independent and external to comply with their requirement.

Kocher and Frey presented a first design scheme to the clients clearly influenced by Le Corbusier's architecture. The architects revealed two perspective views of the house; both were rather abstract drawings with highly contrasting black and white areas and a lot of care in the depiction of the cast shadows to reveal the play of the white masses brought together in light. **(Figure 3.63)** Although the base volume of the house was a quite regular geometry, a three-floor rectangular parallelepiped measuring 22 feet, six inches, by 36 feet, six inches, it looked like an irregular aggregation of masses due to the addition of the stairwell volume protruding in the north corner, along with the operational subtractions for the porch and attic terraces. White continuous surfaces, long horizontal glazed areas, and slender circular columns supporting the porch and carport on the first floor completed the set of Corbusian features. The plan was no less influenced by the work of Le Corbusier than the elevations: the second-floor layout was very similar to one of the alternate designs of the Loucheur Houses. The Ralph Barbarin House had a central living room and library open to the opposing northeast and southwest façades through two large horizontal windows. Symmetrically opposed on both sides of this central area were two bedrooms packed together with a bathroom on the southeast, and on the northwest side, the kitchen and dining alcove were located near the stairs. **(Figures 3.64 to 3.72)** The drawings didn't define any specific construction method or materials, but according to the architects, they planned to replicate the coetaneous building technology of the Cotton-Steel Houses with a steel structure and façades sheathed with a continuous material. When contacting the local contractors, the architects realized that they were very reluctant to use a building technology unfamiliar to them. The construction budget skyrocketed, and Kocher and Frey were forced to find a more commonly used building technology for the house. Frey explains this clash with reality they had during the development of the project in this way:

> Lawrence and I had found that while metal construction was accepted and competitive in industrial buildings, in houses, particularly in the country where contractors and carpenters were accustomed to wood framing and siding, the new methods were resisted, and costs were increased. Since the Ralph-Barbarin House had to be built within a set budget, we decided to adhere to the building methods of the locality. In designing the house, we provided the ladies with the desired comforts of space and convenience.[43]

Due to economic circumstances at that time, the abstract qualities and the modern look of the original project were impossible to realize. The house was ultimately built with exposed concrete block walls on the first floor and a wood-frame structure above. The façades were insulated with aluminum foil and faced with shingles. Decks were covered in canvas. The factory-made steel frames were changed for vertical wood double-hung windows aligned in the façade but interrupted by the structural frame. Only the slender circular steel columns of the first floor survived, adding a slightly bizarre counterpoint to the banal look of the remaining construction.

While keeping the same overall square footage, volume, footprint (now 21 feet, nine inches, by 37 feet, four inches), and floor programing, the shift in the construction method also changed the layout of the spaces inside the house. Wood-frame floors cannot span as much distance as steel beams, so the openness and free design of the floor plan was interrupted with internal load-bearing partitions. The second floor was especially affected, changing the scheme radically from a double-oriented living room into a divided living space and kitchen-dining room. Probably looking for the vertical and horizontal vicinity of the service rooms, the kitchens and bathrooms were all relocated near the northeast façade, partially blocking the lake view, and disturbing the transversal transparency of the house. **(Figures 3.73 to 3.90)**

The lessons learned in the Ralph-Barbarin House were retroactively applied to the ongoing publication of previous work. For example, when the Experimental Weekend House was published and began circulating profusely, the structure depicted was no longer metallic; rather, it was designed to be built with balloon frame walls and wooden floor structures utilizing double two-by-two-inch studs set one foot apart—a kind of construction similar to that of the Ralph-Barbarin House and also to the roadside cabins studied in their 1933 article. Acting as thermal insulation a sheet of thermo-reflective aluminum was trapped between the studs, which were then covered in quarter-inch to 3/4-inch laminated wood panels with an interior and exterior finish of cotton fabric. On the exterior, the fabric

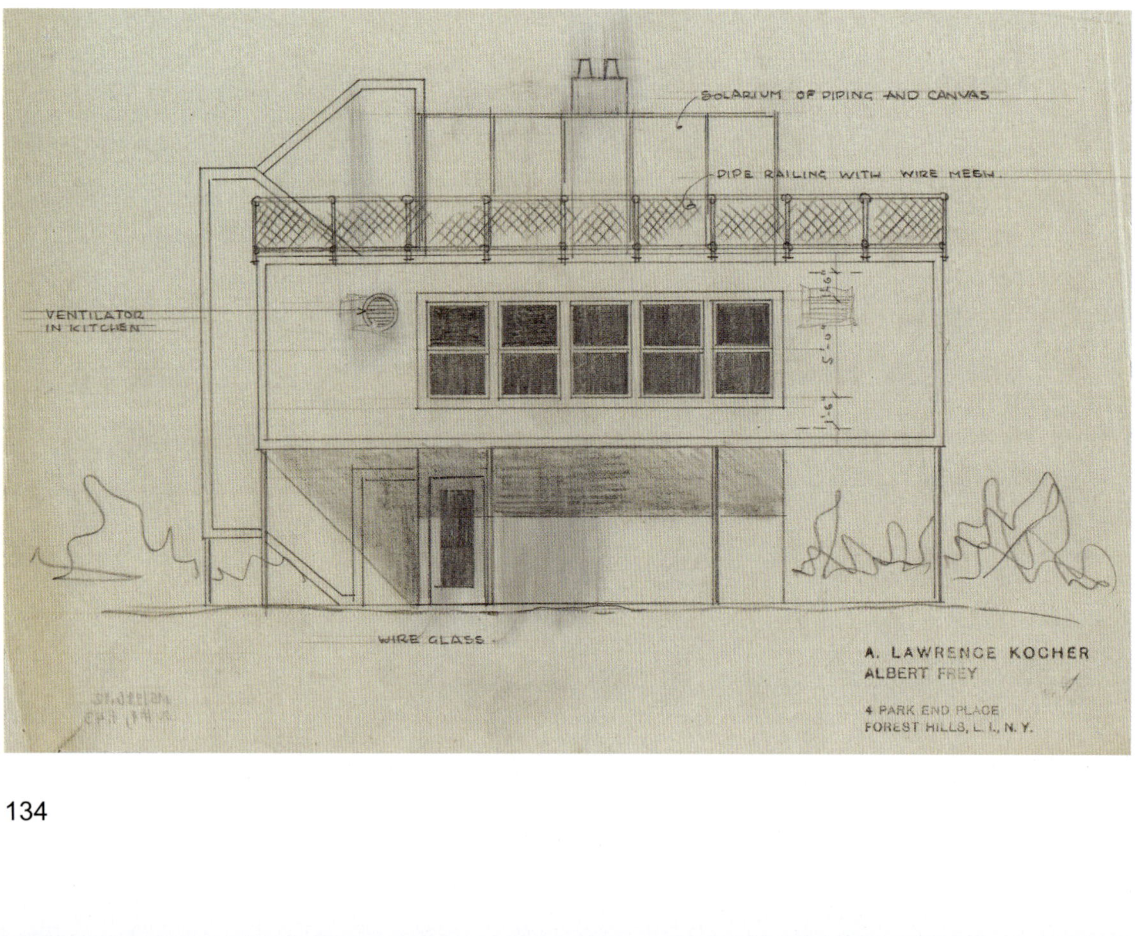

Figure 3.63. A. Lawrence Kocher and Albert Frey. 1932. Ralph-Barbarin House. First version. Pencil perspectives of the house seen from the street and from the garden. Dated April 1932.

Figure 3.64. A. Lawrence Kocher and Albert Frey. 1932. Ralph-Barbarin House. First version. Elevation from the garden including a solarium with canvas instead of a penthouse. Undated.

was waterproofed, fireproofed, and finished with aluminum paint. The floor structures were made of simple two-by-six-inch wooden beams, which supported a platform formed of laminated tongue-and-groove wooden decking, over which linoleum flooring was applied. Plywood sheets were nailed to the underside of the joists for the finish application. The ceiling structure included an intermediate sheet of aluminum for thermal insulation and an upper finish of water- and fire-proofed painted cotton fabric. Drawings of these changes and detailed constructional explanations were published in the first edition of *The Modern House*, by F.R.S Yorke in 1934.[44] The Experimental Weekend House was never built, neither in its steel version nor in its wood-frame option.

The circumstances surrounding the construction of Kocher and Frey's first site-specific work caused a profound change in the way the architects approached their next commissions. Although the Ralph-Barbarin House was a design of second order within the architects' body of work, it produced a fissure in their preconceptions derived from their previously monolithic adherence to the principles of the modernist European architecture. Kocher and Frey acknowledged the dire situation of the country in 1932—one that demanded immediate solutions from professionals of any field to remedy a social emergency and discard any innovation that could not be easily applied in the context of economic penury. This general social emergency affected the volume of work in the office for the remainder of 1932 and added to the worsening health of Kocher's wife.

After finishing his contract with William Lescaze, and with Kocher's office workload below minimum, Frey decided to take a two-month vacation. In July 1932, wanting to discover more about his host country, he started a photographic round trip to the West Coast.[45] Alongside a friend from the F. W. Dodge Corporation, he drove his Ford-A to Chicago and Wisconsin, where he visited Frank Lloyd Wright at Taliesin. Camping on the roadside, they traveled through Yellowstone Park, Yosemite, and San Francisco. Driving south, they visited the Kocher House in San Jose, and met several of his relatives. In the Los Angeles and San Diego areas, Frey met many modern architects, including Rudolph Schindler and Richard Neutra. On the return trip, they visited the Grand Canyon of Arizona, the Mesa Verde cliff dwellings in Colorado, and the Indian *pueblos* of New Mexico. They then proceeded to New Orleans and along the Gulf Coast to pay a visit to the Spanish remains of St. Augustine, Florida. Then they drove north through Savannah, Charleston, Richmond, and finally back to Kocher's home in Forest Hills.[46] As previously mentioned, some of the photographs documenting this trip were later published in *Architectural Record* as part of a research article about new car-derived architectural typologies. Some others were compiled and published in the 1939 book, *In Search of a Living Architecture*—a documented corroboration of the importance assigned by Frey to anonymous American architecture, completely aligning with Kocher's appreciation of vernacular American architecture. After Frey's return at the end of August 1932, he continued collaborating with Kocher in finalizing the construction of the Ralph-Barbarin House and in some articles for *Architectural Record*. During these months Kocher's wife, Amy Agnes Moerder, passed away.

The general picture of the country did not help in alleviating Kocher and Frey's personal and professional situation. Social discontent had already devolved into two dramatic episodes of social violence in the previous months of 1932. In March of 1932, the American communist party labor arm, the Trade Union Unity League (TUU), and the Detroit Unemployment Council organized a demonstration against the wage drop at the Ford Motor Company. On March 7th, thousands of Ford workers started a "hunger march" to the employment office at the Ford River Rouge Plant in Dearborn, Michigan. Confronted violently by Dearborn Police and Ford's private security forces, tear gas was thrown, stones were hurled, shots were fired, and the result was four dead and more than 60 marchers wounded. The second episode was even more concerning as it involved war veterans and state violence. Since June 1932, 15 to 25 thousand marchers of the Bonus Expeditionary Force (BEF) were camping in 27 informal settlements around the edge of the District of Columbia. They were veterans demanding the advanced payment of the bonus for their services during World War I. The bonus was scheduled for payment in 1945, but the unemployed veterans demanded its immediate payment to feed and shelter their starving families. After a vote in the Senate, the approval of the payment was defeated, and President Hoover signed a transportation loan bill to send the marchers back to their hometowns. Eight to 10 thousand veterans remained in Washington, D.C., crossed the Potomac River, and occupied several buildings in the city. Fearing a social revolt, Hoover sent the army under the orders of General Douglas MacArthur. On July 28th, the troops set fire to the encampments around D.C. and entered in direct conflagration with the BEF members, the outcome of which involved two dead veterans and the BEF driven out of Washington.

These two violent episodes marked a turning point in public opinion as they revealed both the failure of private companies to provide economic security and the failure of the government to find ways to reverse the steep decline of the country. In times of peace, the government used the U.S. Army against unarmed citizens. This fact and the Great Depression were the sole topics of the 1932 presidential campaign. On election day, November 8th, Franklin Delano Roosevelt received 22,800,000 popular votes (57.3 percent) to Hoover's nearly 15,750,000 (39.6 percent). The electoral vote was 472 to 59. As a punishment, not just to Hoover but also to the Republican Party, Americans elected substantial Democratic majorities to both houses of Congress, ending the almost complete (save two terms) Republican dominance since 1860.

The United States was on the verge of a new era, but in the months between Roosevelt's election and his inauguration on March 4th of 1933, the economic situation worsened further. The breadlines and Hoovervilles grew in all American cities, foreclosures continued, and unemployment boosted. With Kocher mourning his wife and without any prospective commissions arriving to the office, Frey decided to temporarily return to Switzerland. In January of 1933, Frey's oldest sister and her husband asked him to design a modern house for them near Zurich. He accepted the invitation and spent nine months in Switzerland working on the project and directing its construction. The Gut-Frey House was a work developed independently by Frey, and therefore not a subject of this investigation, but as the only European work for either of them, it provides an interesting contrast to Kocher and Frey's American work. Although the distribution of

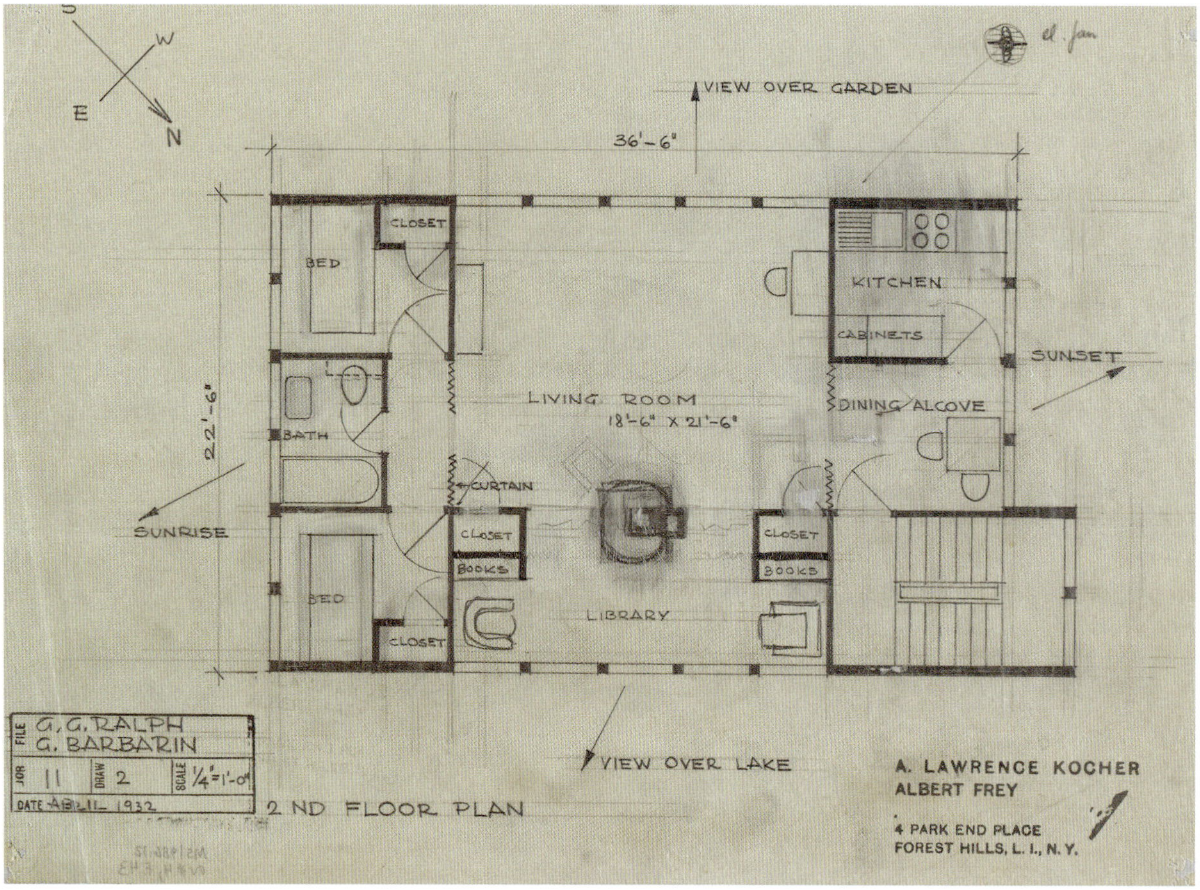

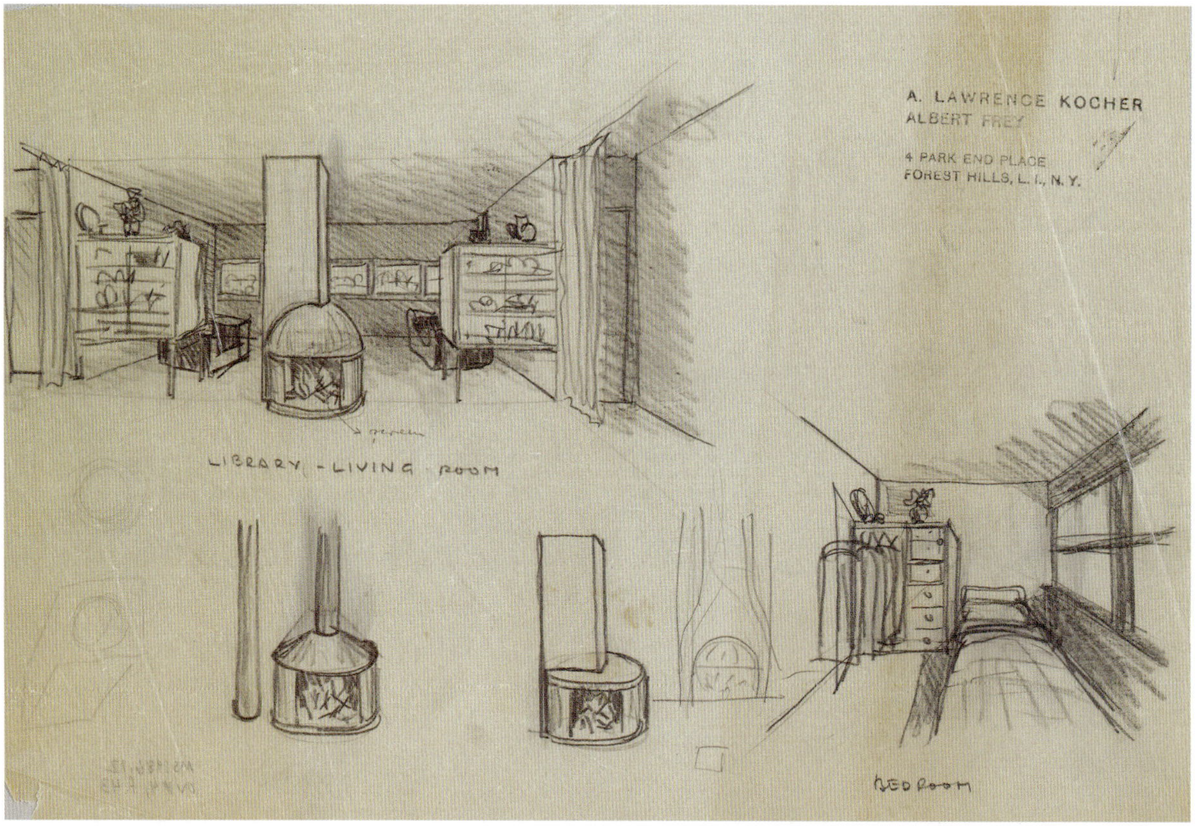

Figure 3.65. A. Lawrence Kocher and Albert Frey. 1932. Ralph-Barbarin House. First version. Second floor plan. Dated April 1932.

Figure 3.66. A. Lawrence Kocher and Albert Frey. 1932. Ralph-Barbarin House. First version. Interior pencil perspectives of the living room and bed- room. Undated.

the plan had some common features to previous designs, like the Aluminaire House or the Ralph-Barbarin house (attic terraces, porch, situation of the stair), the construction methods and the materiality of the house are radically different. The Gut-Frey House used a heavy, monolithic, and hyperstatic reinforced concrete structure. An orthogonal structural grid dominated the composition of all the façades, filled with solid walls or windows of the same size for all levels and orientations. The material consistency is absolute. Every surface is covered with the same light stucco, without any articulation between structural and non-structural parts. The lineage of this house is neither American, nor can it be traced to Le Corbusier, as is the case of the previous houses, but instead it relates more directly to Adolf Loos' 1930 Villa Müller in Prague or Wittgenstein's House in Vienna designed by Paul Egelmann in 1928.[47] It is therefore a regression to more European references unique to Frey's body of work. This house is also a token to the relevance of Kocher's contributions within the team; without his experimental approach to building methods and materials, and his reevaluation of American vernacular architecture, the architecture of the office would have been quite different.

During the construction of the Gut-Frey House from March to October of 1932, Frey worked part-time with his friend, Alfred Roth, from his time at Le Corbusier's office. With Roth, Frey visited Le Corbusier and Pierre Jeanneret as well as Mondrian's atelier in Paris; Mondrian was later a big influence for his Californian works. Frey also wrote two articles that were published in the Swiss architectural magazine *Werk*, illustrating them with photographs of his collaborative architectural work with Kocher, and from his 1932 American trip.[48] During the period that Frey spent in Europe, Kocher became engaged to his second wife, Margaret Taylor. When Frey came back to attend to the wedding in Forest Hills in October 1933, he found a renovated Kocher and a brand-new America.

Chapter endnotes

1 F.D.R. was elected in November of 1932 but did not take office until the following March.

2 The following numbers provide a glimpse into the deep impact of the Depression. 1930: 1,352 bank failures, 853 million dollars of deposits lost, 4.3 million unemployed, 26,355 businesses collapsed. 1931: 2,294 bank failures, 1.7 billion dollars of deposits lost, 8 million unemployed, 28,285 businesses collapsed. 1932: 1,453 bank failures, 706 million dollars of deposits lost, 12 million unemployed, 31,822 businesses collapsed. The value of farm property declined from 57.7 million dollars in 1929 to 36.2 million dollars in 1933. Unemployment in 1933 was 24.9 percent of the civilian labor force. Per capita, income fell from 681 dollars in 1929 to 495 dollars in 1933, and an estimated 28 percent of the population had no income at all. Gross national production fell from 104 billion dollars to 41 billion dollars from 1929 to 1933. Bank deposits were uninsured until 1934. Roosevelt signed the Banking Act on June 16, 1933. Section 8 aimed to create the Federal Deposit Insurance Corporation, which was increasingly implemented on January 1, 1934. Sources: Lester V. Chandler, *America's Greatest Depression, 1929-1941* (New York: Harper-Collins College Division, 1970); Ben J. Wattenberg, *The Statistical History of the United States: From Colonial Times to the Present* (New York: Basic Books Publishers, 1976); *Federal Deposit Insurance Corporation*: www.fdic.gov/bank/historical/managing/chronological/pre-fdic.html.

3 President Hoover signed the Reconstruction Finance Corporation Act on January 22, 1932, establishing the Reconstruction Finance Corporation.

4 Herbert Hoover, "Statement Announcing the White House Conference on Home Building and Home Ownership," Ed. Gerhard Peters and John T. Woolley, *The American Presidency Project* (UC Santa Barbara), www.presidency.ucsb.edu/node/207591.

5 Included among the associations represented on the Planning Committee: American Civic Association, American Farm Bureau Federation, American Federation of Labor, American Home Economics Association, American Institute of Architects, Associated General Contractors Association of Life Insurance Presidents, Better Homes in America, Chamber of Commerce of the United States, General Federation of Women's Clubs, National Association of Builders' Exchanges, National Association of Real Estate Boards, National Congress of Parents and Teachers, National Farmers Union, National Grange, National Housing Association, Russell Sage Foundation, Savings Bank Division of the American Bankers Association, United States League of Building and Loan Associations, and Women's National Farm and Garden Association.

6 The complete list of committees is as follows: Types of Dwellings, Fundamental Equipment, Kitchens and Other Work Centers, Utilities for Houses, Subdivision Layout, Business and Housing, Industrial Decentralization and Housing, Blighted Areas and Slums, Reconditioning, Remodeling and Modernizing, Construction, Design, City Planning and Zoning, Finance, Taxation, Home Ownership and Leasing, Home Furnishing and Decoration, Landscape Planning and Planting, Household Management, Housing and the Community, Farm and Village Housing, Negro Housing, Home Information Centers, Homemaking, Large Scale Operations, and Relationship of Income and the Home. A politely critical review of the conference proceedings can be found in Michael A. Mikkelsen, "Findings and Suggestions of the Housing Conference," *Architectural Record*, Vol. 71, No. 1 (January, 1932): 39–43.

7 Hoover, "Statement Announcing the White House Conference on Home Building and Home Ownership."

8 A. Lawrence Kocher and Albert Frey, "Model of Farmhouse of Low Cost," *Architectural Record*, Vol. 71, No. 5 (May, 1932): 297. A. Lawrence Kocher and Albert Frey, "Low-Cost Farmhouse," *Architectural Record*, Vol. 75, No. 1 (January, 1934): 30–31.

9 Although author Joseph Rosa says that Kocher was a committee member, we have not found any prove of this statement neither in the member list published in the final report of the committee nor in the archive of A.L. Kocher Papers. Joseph Rosa, *Albert Frey, Architect* (New York: Princeton Architectural Press, 2000), 31.

10 Albert Frey quoted by Neil Jackson. Neil Jackson, *The Modern Steel House* (London: Routledge, 1996), 25.

11 A. Lawrence Kocher and Albert Frey, "Real Estate Subdivisions for Low-Cost Housing," *Architectural Record*, Vol. 69 (April, 1931): 323–327.

12 The closest competing example is the classic book *Architectural Graphic Standards* by Ramsey and Sleeper from the second half of 1932. Some precursors can be named, such as Clarence Martin's *Details of Building Construction* (1899), and Philip Knobloch's two-volume *Good Practice in Construction* (1923–25), but none of them reached the level of standardization, precision, and thoroughness of Kocher and Frey's articles. Partly due to the lag-time of publishing, these precursors lacked any connection to industrial production or modern architecture. There were also innumerable construction handbooks used in America during the Colonial and early-Republic days, of which Kocher was an avid collector, and he studied their implications on America's architectural development in several published and unpublished texts. For example, the unpublished paper: A. Lawrence Kocher, "Use of Architectural handbooks in the Colonies," Box 2, Subseries B: Lectures, folder: Use of Architectural Handbooks in the Colonies, A. Lawrence Kocher Collection, Colonial Williamsburg Foundation, John D. Rockefeller Jr. Library.

13 A. Lawrence Kocher and Albert Frey, "New Materials and Improved Construction Methods," *Architectural Record*, Vol. 73 (April, 1933): 281–287.

14 Included among these material examples, is an experimental house Kocher and Frey developed for the Cotton-Textile Institute

15 Published years later in *Architectural Record*: A. Lawrence Kocher and Albert Frey, "A Community Exhibition Building Proposed for Darien, Conn.," *Architectural Recor*d, Vol 80 (December 1936): 425.

16 Note that this was the same exhibition as the one showcasing the Aluminaire House, but different gallery space—on display from April 18 through April 25.

17 The design of the architect's desk was reused in an undated proposal for a train wagon for the Sweets Catalog.

18 William Lescaze was born March 27, 1896, in Geneva, Switzerland, and died February 9, 1969, in New York, United States.

19 Albert Frey, "Foreword," in Cynthia Zignego Stiverson, *Architecture and the Decorative Arts: The A. Lawrence Kocher Collection of Books at the Colonial Williamsburg Foundation* (West Cornwall, CT: Locust Hill Press, 1989).

20 A. Lawrence Kocher Collection, Colonial Williamsburg Foundation, John D. Rockefeller Jr. Library.

21 Although it was originally a company dedicated to mining machinery, Harnischfeger sought ways to diversify during the Depression, making welding machines, welding electrodes, diesel engines, and even prefabricated houses. Haskelite Manufacturing Corporation was a conglomerate of multiple Michigan-based companies that manufactured Haskelite plywood for a wide variety of applications. The John B. Pierce Foundation was established in 1924 by John B. Pierce, then Vice President of the American Radiator & Standard Sanitary Corporation. Its Housing Research Division was established in 1931.

22 "One memorable trip was visiting Rex Stout in his new house. Another was a trip to Washington, D.C., to install an exhibit on contemporary architectural features and to attend President Hoover's Conference on Housing. Yet another was a trip to the site of the future Ralph-Barbarin House in Stamford, Connecticut." Frey, "Foreword," *Architecture and the Decorative Arts: The A. Lawrence Kocher Collection of Books at the Colonial Williamsburg Foundation.*

23 A. Lawrence Kocher Collection, Colonial Williamsburg Foundation, John D. Rockefeller Jr. Library.

24 Le Corbusier and Pierre Jeanneret, "The Minimal House. A Solution." *Architectural Record,* Vol. 68, No. 2 (August 1930): 133–137.

25 Benjamin Hunnicutt, *Work Without End: Abandoning Shorter Hours for the Right to Work* (Philadelphia, PA: Temple University Press, 2010).

26 Quoting: Hyungmin Pai, *The Portfolio and the Diagram. Architecture, Discourse, and Modernity in America* (Cambridge, MA: The MIT Press, 2002), 152.

27 As stated by Architectural Record's leadership in: Michael A. Mikkelsen, "Two Problems of Architecture," *Architectural Record* Vol. 66 (January 1929): 65.

28 Gabrielle Sperdy, *American Autopia: An Intellectual History of the American Roadside at Midcentury* (Charlottesville, VA: University of Virginia Press, 2019), 54.

29 Knud Lonberg-Holm, "The Gasoline Filling and Service Station," *Architectural Record*, Vol. 67, No. 6 (June, 1930): 561–584. As to reinforce the line of research, the article was preceded by a short study by Henry-Russell Hitchcock Jr., titled "Traffic and Building Art," found on pages 555 to 560.

30 Myron W. Selby. "Technical News and Research. Stadium Planning and Design," *Architectural Record*, Vol. 69, No. 2 (February 1931): 151–176.

31 A. Lawrence Kocher and Albert Frey, "Planning the House Garage," *Architectural Record*, Vol. 69, No. 1 (January 1931): 52–57.

32 The need for a substantial construction was a basic requirement to apply for a bank loan. The Editors, "New Fields for Architects," *Architectural Record*, Vol. 70, No. 2 (August 1931): 116–117.

33 Other examples include: "Multiple Service Station in Detroit," *Architectural Record*, Vol. 70, No. 6 (December 1931): 455–457. "A Standardized Filling Station Unit," *Architectural Record*, Vol. 70, No. 6 (December 1931): 458. "Service Station at Ann Arbor Michigan and Gasoline Station Designed by R. M. Schindler," *Architectural Record*, Vol. 74, No. 2 (August 1933): 142–144. "Parks and Highways in Long Island," *Architectural Record*, Vol. 74, No. 6 (December 1933): 429–438.

34 Knud Lonberg-Holm, "The Week-End House," *Architectural Record*, Vol. 68, No. 2 (August 1930): 177.

35 Lonberg-Holm, "The Week-End House," 179.

36 John J. McCarthy and Robert Littell, "Three Hundred Thousand Shacks: The Arrival of a New American Industry," *Harper's Magazine*, Issue 167 (July 1933): 180–188.

37 The attribution seems to be sound due to the stylistic qualities of the drawings, "since the plans and aerial perspectives have the nervous graphic energy and the charette stencil lettering (this typeface was then uncommon in the United States) that Frey learned from Le Corbusier." Sperdy, *American Autopia: An Intellectual History of the American Roadside at Midcentury*, 54, 59.

38 John A. Jakle, Keith A. Sculle, and Jefferson S. Rogers, *The Motel in America,* (Baltimore: Johns Hopkins University Press, 1996), 38.

39 "Tourist Cabins That Get the Business," *Popular Mechanics*, Vol. 64, Issue 1 (July 1935): 151–154.

40 The Editors, "Roadside Cabins for Tourists," *Architectural Record*, Vol. 74, No. 6 (December 1933): 457–462.

41 For instance: Warren J. Belasco, *Americans on the Road: From Autocamp to Motel, 1910–1945*, (Cambridge MA: The MIT Press, 1981); and Jakle, Sculle, Rogers, *The Motel in America.*

42 Kocher received the commission for the Aluminaire House in September of 1930; the design must have happened in the following months to give enough time for the fabrication and installation of the house in April of 1931.

43 Frey, "Foreword," *Architecture and the Decorative Arts.*

44 F. R. S. Yorke, *The Modern House* (London: The Architectural Press, 1934), 184.

45 Some scholars suggest that the photographic trip was commissioned by Kocher to obtain graphic materials for the articles published during those years at *Architectural Record*, exploring the role of the car as a catalyst for the design of new types of buildings. For example, Frey's pictures of motor camps were published in the article, "Roadside Cabins for Tourists," *Architectural Record* (December, 1933). Also, see: Sperdy, *American Autopia*, 59.

46 This description of Frey's trip freely paraphrases parts of his own recount; Frey, "Foreword," *Architecture and the Decorative Arts.*

47 Some scholars credit Wittgenstein and even Adolf Loos as inspiration, co-authors, or design consultants for this house.

48 Albert Frey, "Amerikanische Notizen," *Werk* (October 1933): 312–317. Albert Frey, "Gebrauchsarchitektur in U.S.A.," *Werk* (October 1933): 382.

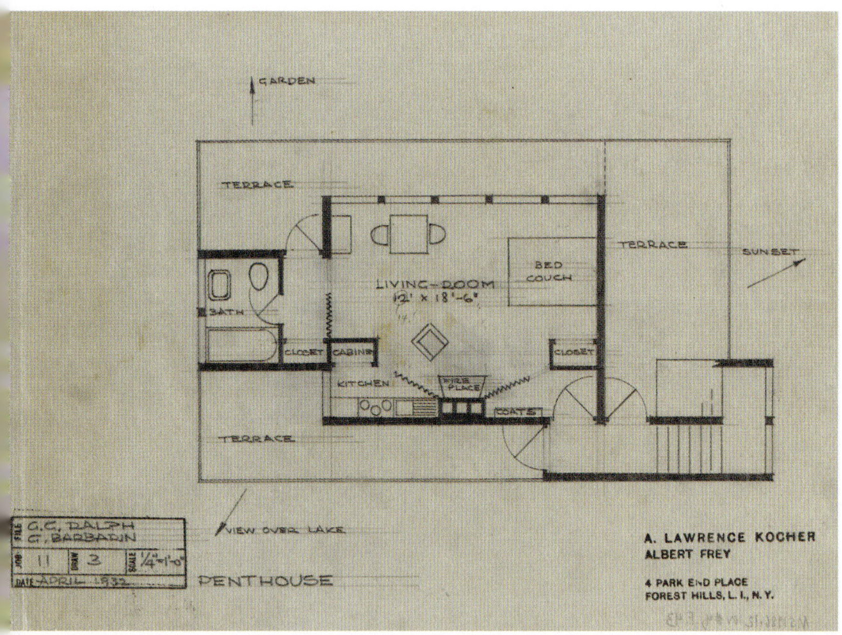

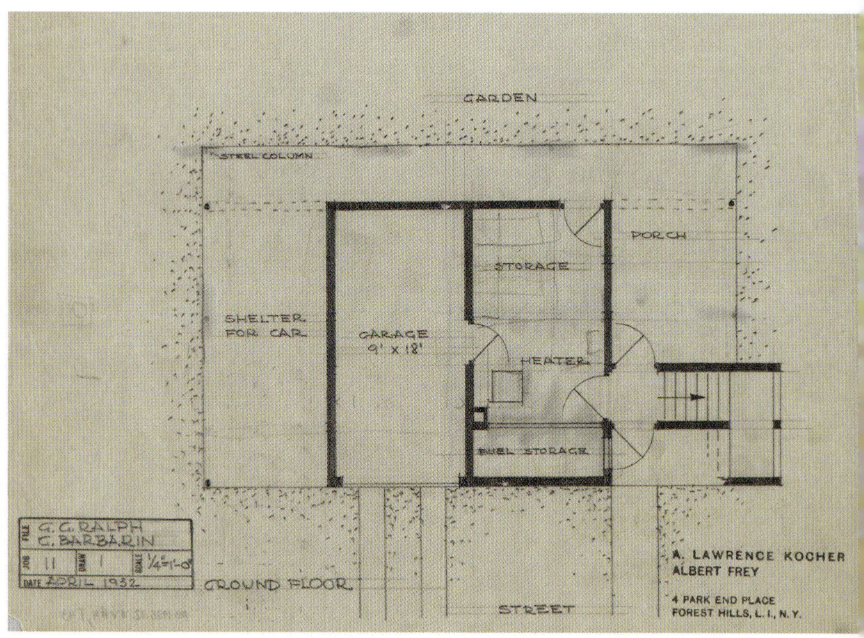

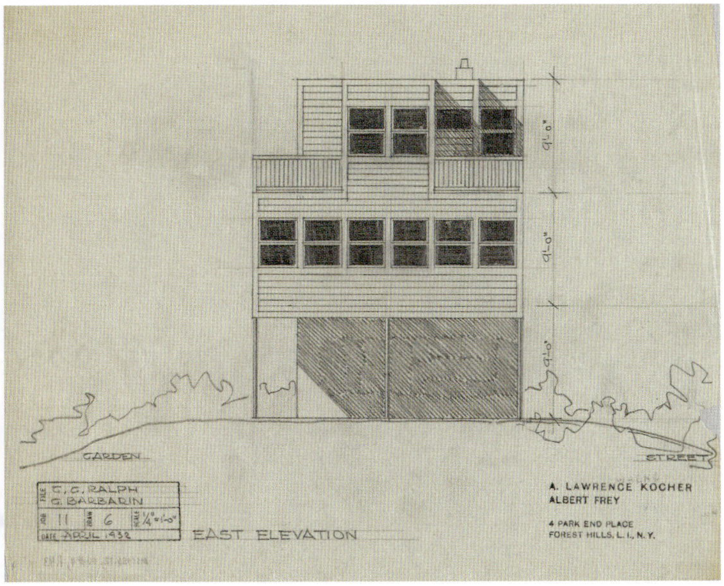

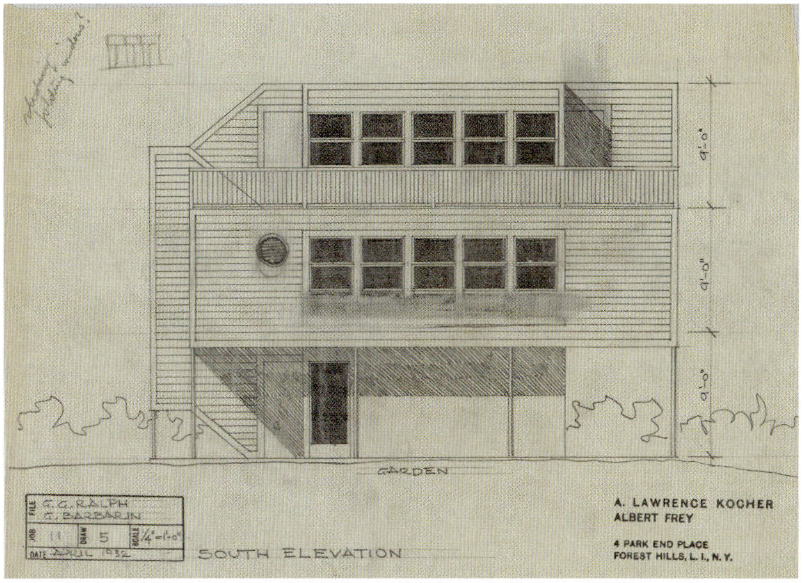

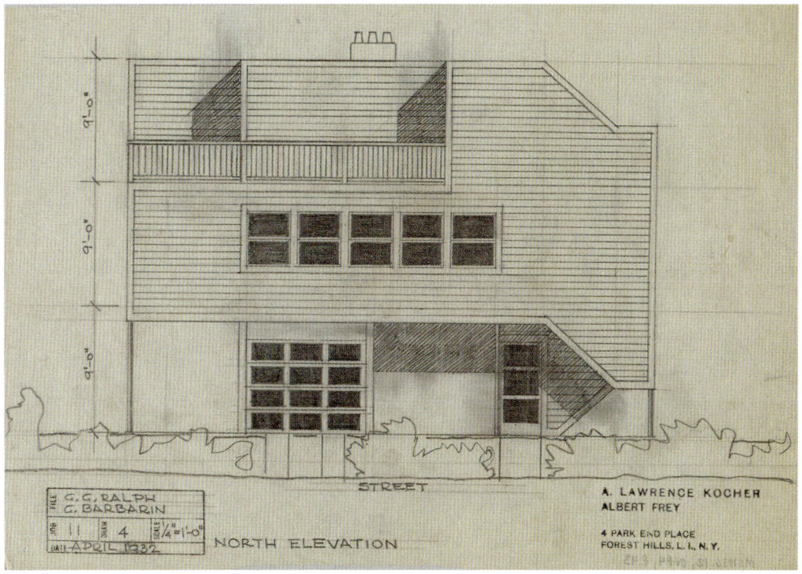

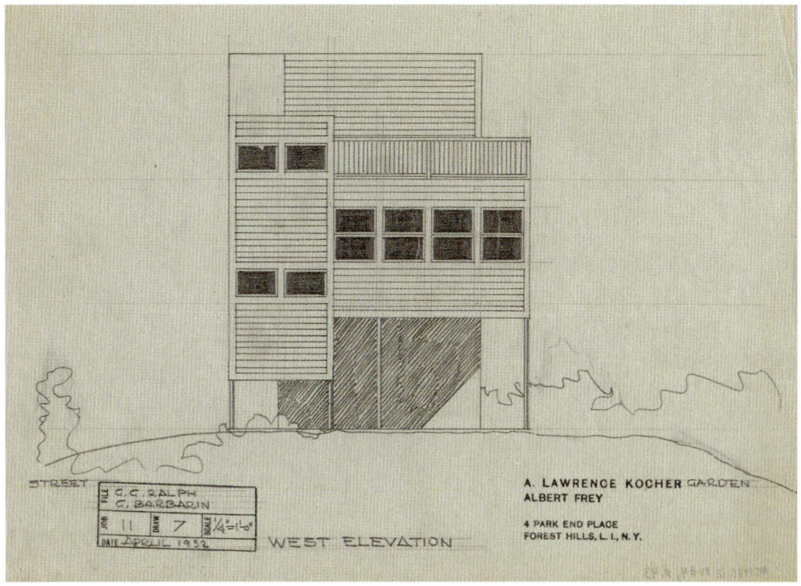

Previous page:
Figure 3.67. A. Lawrence Kocher and Albert Frey. 1932. Ralph-Barbarin House. First version. Penthouse plan. Dated April 1932.
Figure 3.68. A. Lawrence Kocher and Albert Frey. 1932. Ralph-Barbarin House. First version. Ground floor plan. Dated April 1932.

This page:
Figure 3.69. A. Lawrence Kocher and Albert Frey. 1932. Ralph-Barbarin House. First version. East elevation. Dated April 1932.
Figure 3.70. A. Lawrence Kocher and Albert Frey. 1932. Ralph-Barbarin House. First version. South elevation. Dated April 1932.
Figure 3.71. A. Lawrence Kocher and Albert Frey. 1932. Ralph-Barbarin House. First version. North elevation. Dated April 1932.
Figure 3.72. A. Lawrence Kocher and Albert Frey. 1932. Ralph-Barbarin House. First version. West elevation. Dated April 1932.

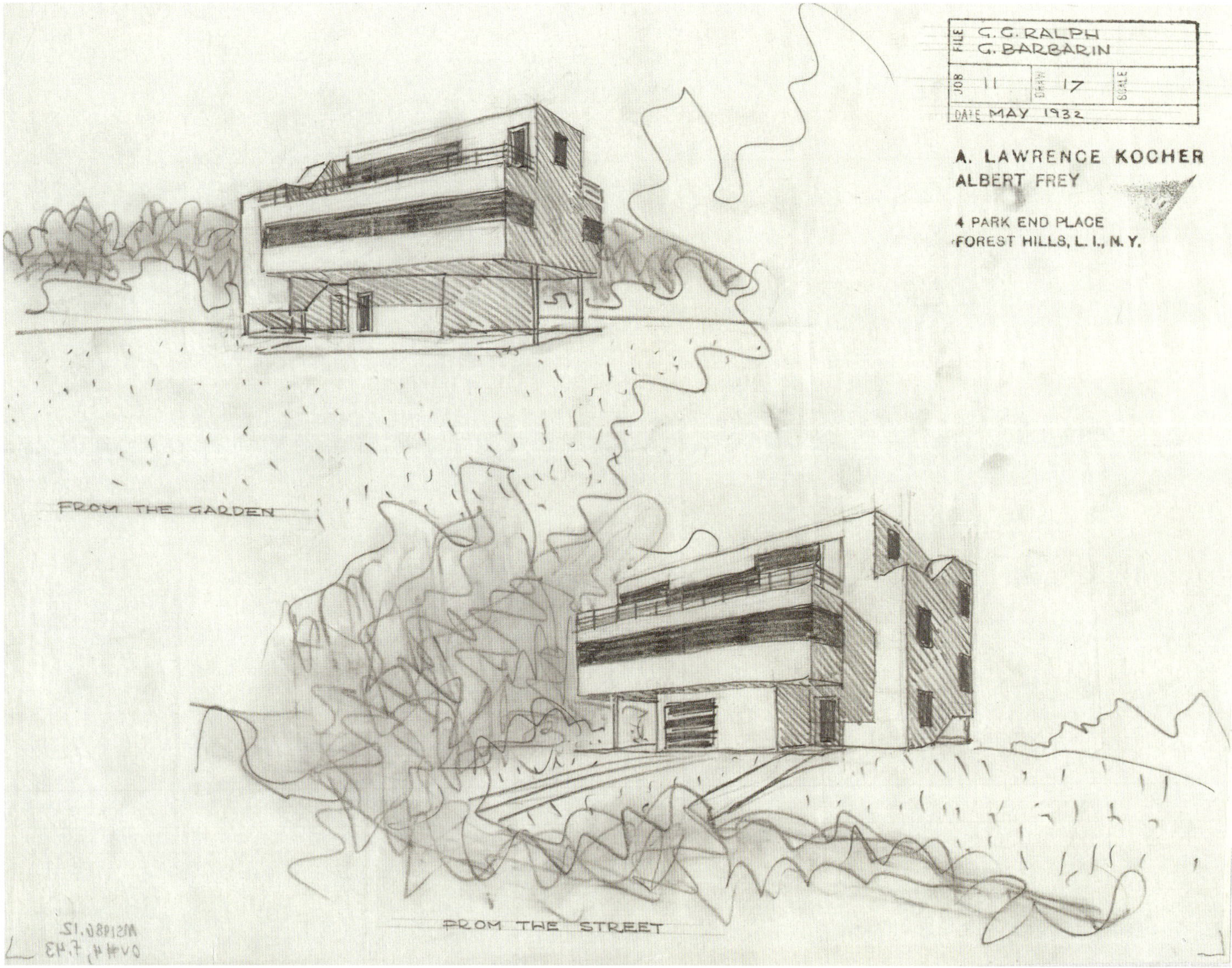

Figure 3.73. A. Lawrence Kocher and Albert Frey. 1932. Ralph-Barbarin House. Final version. Pencil perspectives from the garden and from the street. Dated May 1932.

Figure 3.74. A. Lawrence Kocher and Albert Frey. 1932. Ralph-Barbarin House. Final version. Photo of the construction. Undated.

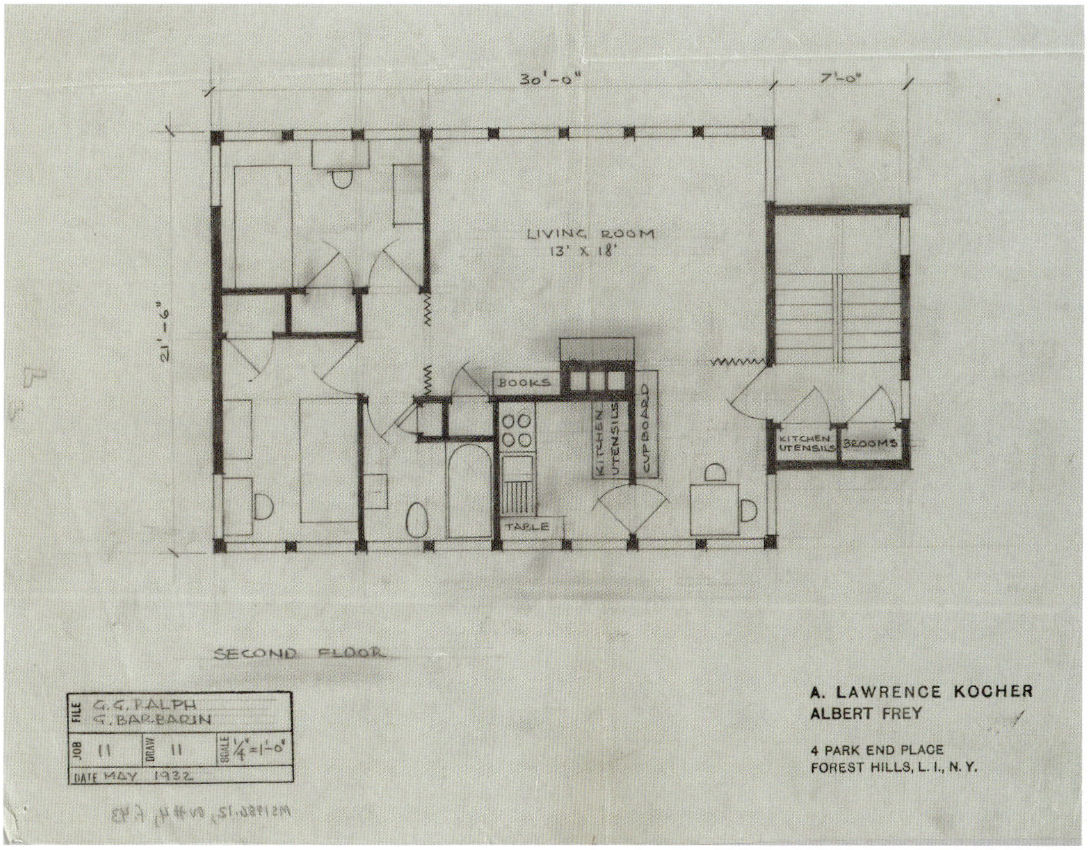

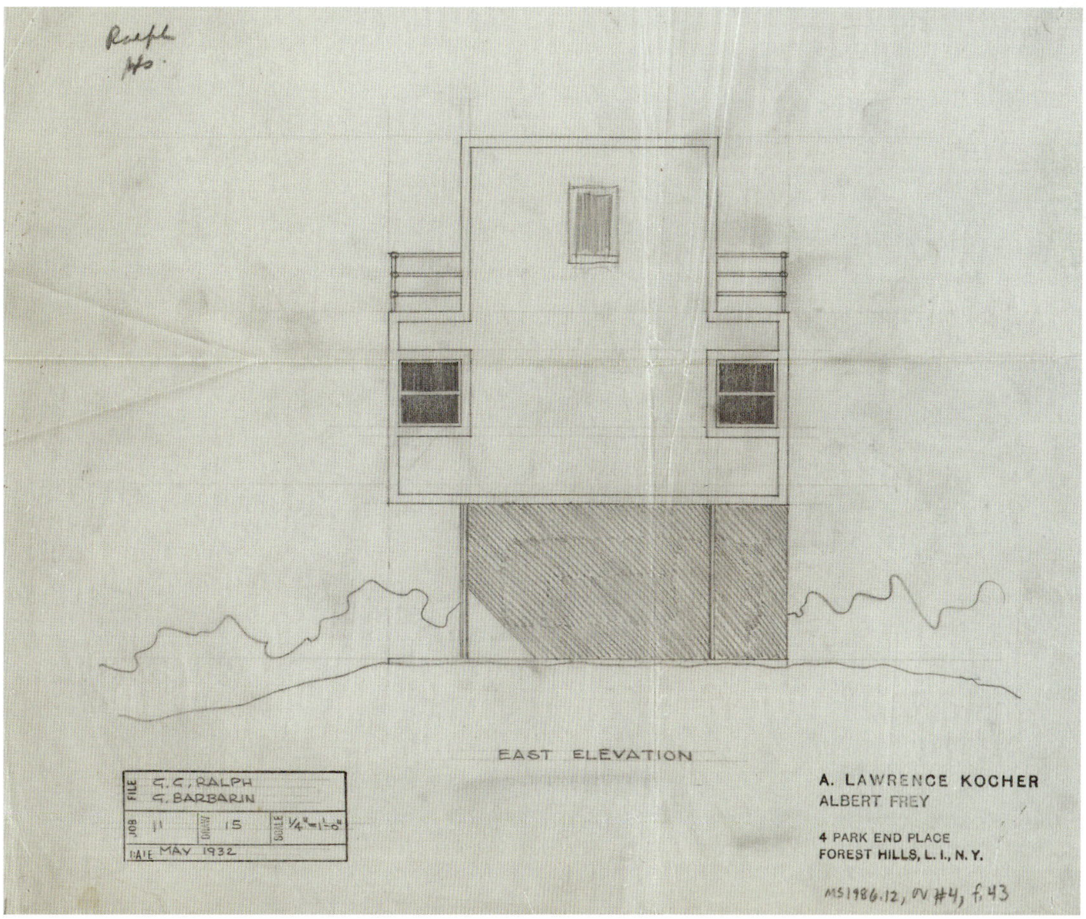

Figure 3.75. A. Lawrence Kocher and Albert Frey. 1932. Ralph-Barbarin House. Final version. Second floor plan. Dated May 1932.
Figure 3.76. A. Lawrence Kocher and Albert Frey. 1932. Ralph-Barbarin House. Final version. East elevation. Dated May 1932.

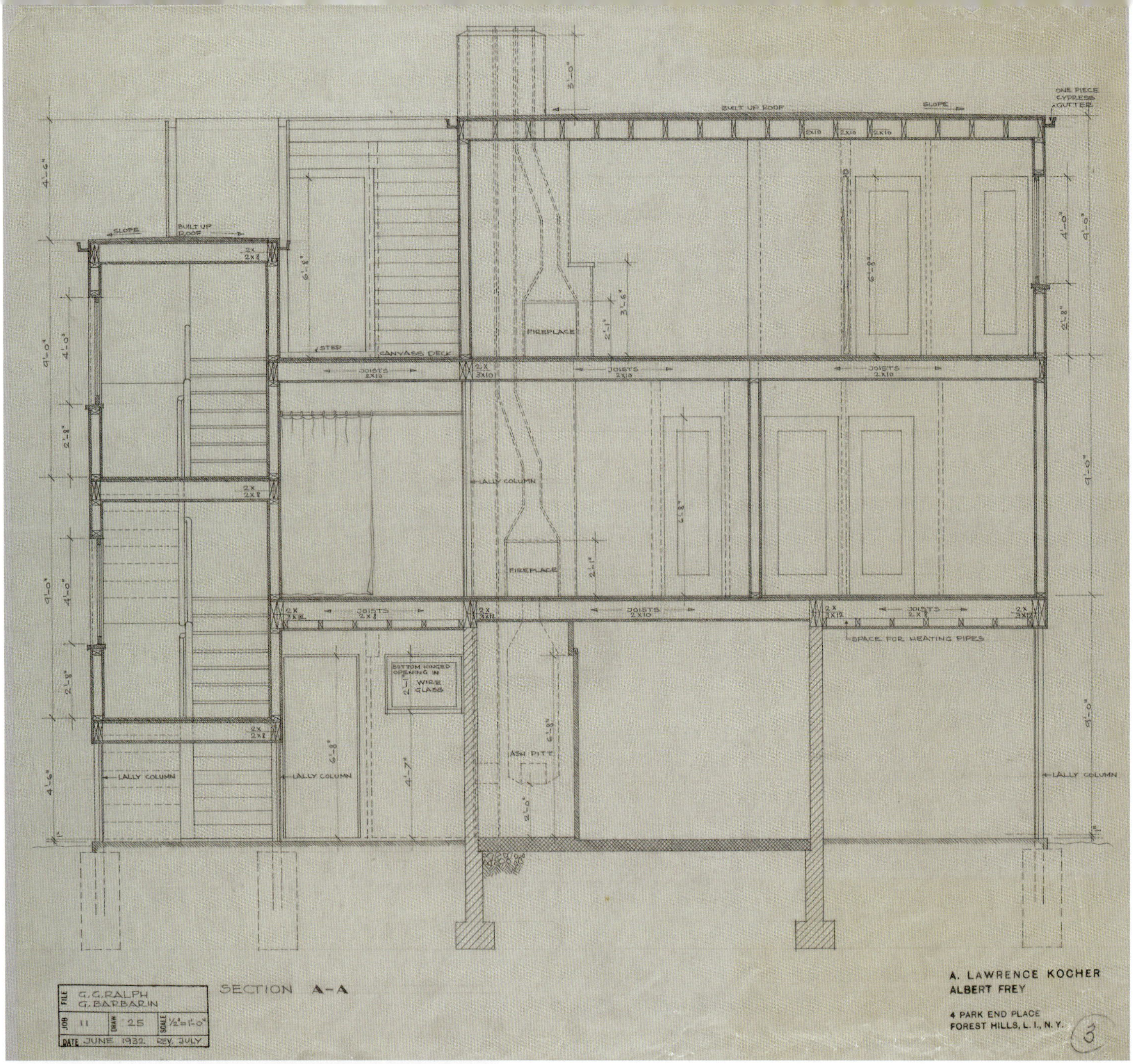

This page:
Figure 3.77. A. Lawrence Kocher and Albert Frey. 1932. Ralph-Barbarin House. Final version, construction documents. Constructive section. Dated June 1932.
Figure 3.78. A. Lawrence Kocher and Albert Frey. 1932. Ralph-Barbarin House. Final version. Photo of the construction. Undated.

Next pages:
Figures 3.79 and 3.80. A. Lawrence Kocher and Albert Frey. 1932. Ralph-Barbarin House. Final version. Dated May 1932. Floor plans and elevations. Dated May 1932.

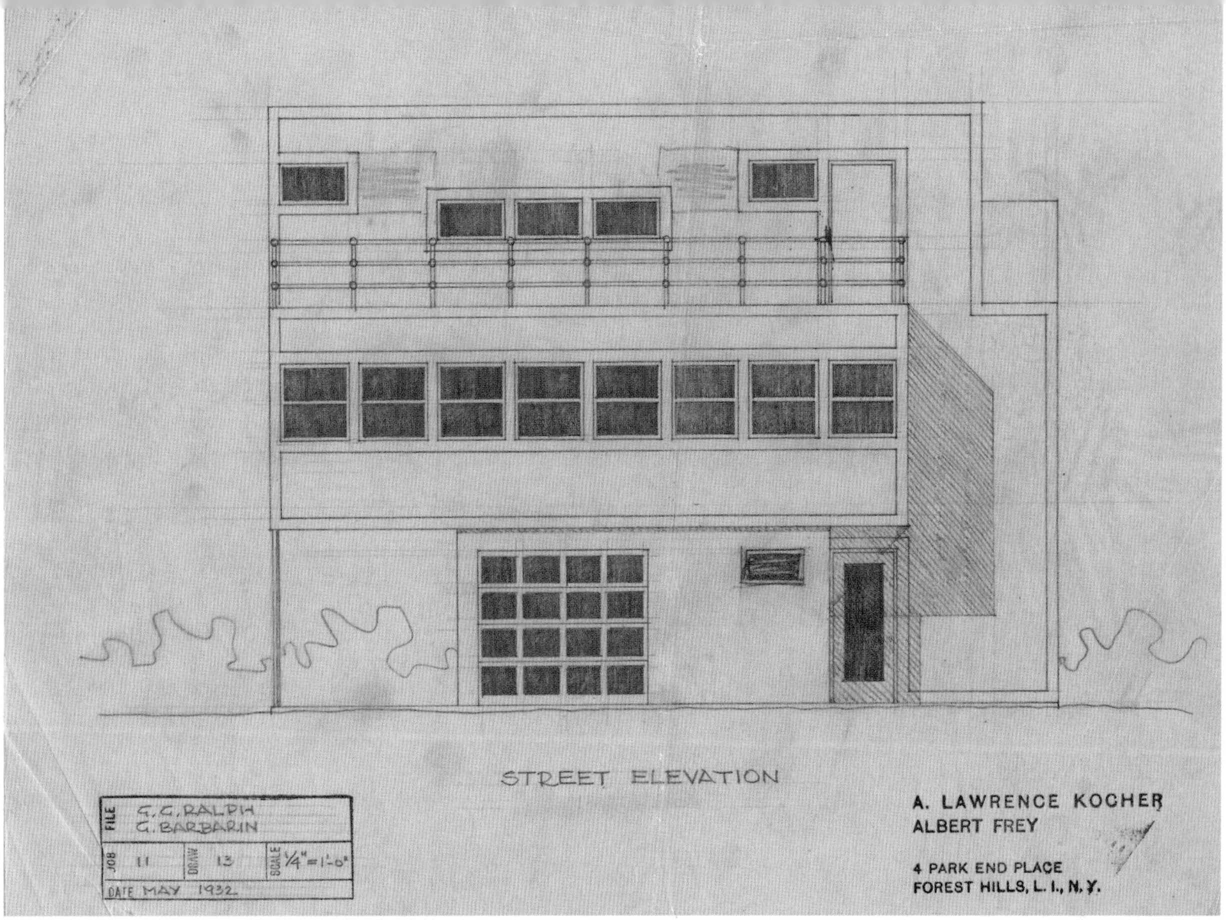
STREET ELEVATION
FILE G.G. RALPH
G. BARBARIN
JOB 11 DRAW 13 SCALE 1/4"=1'-0"
DATE MAY 1932
A. LAWRENCE KOCHER
ALBERT FREY
4 PARK END PLACE
FOREST HILLS, L. I., N. Y.

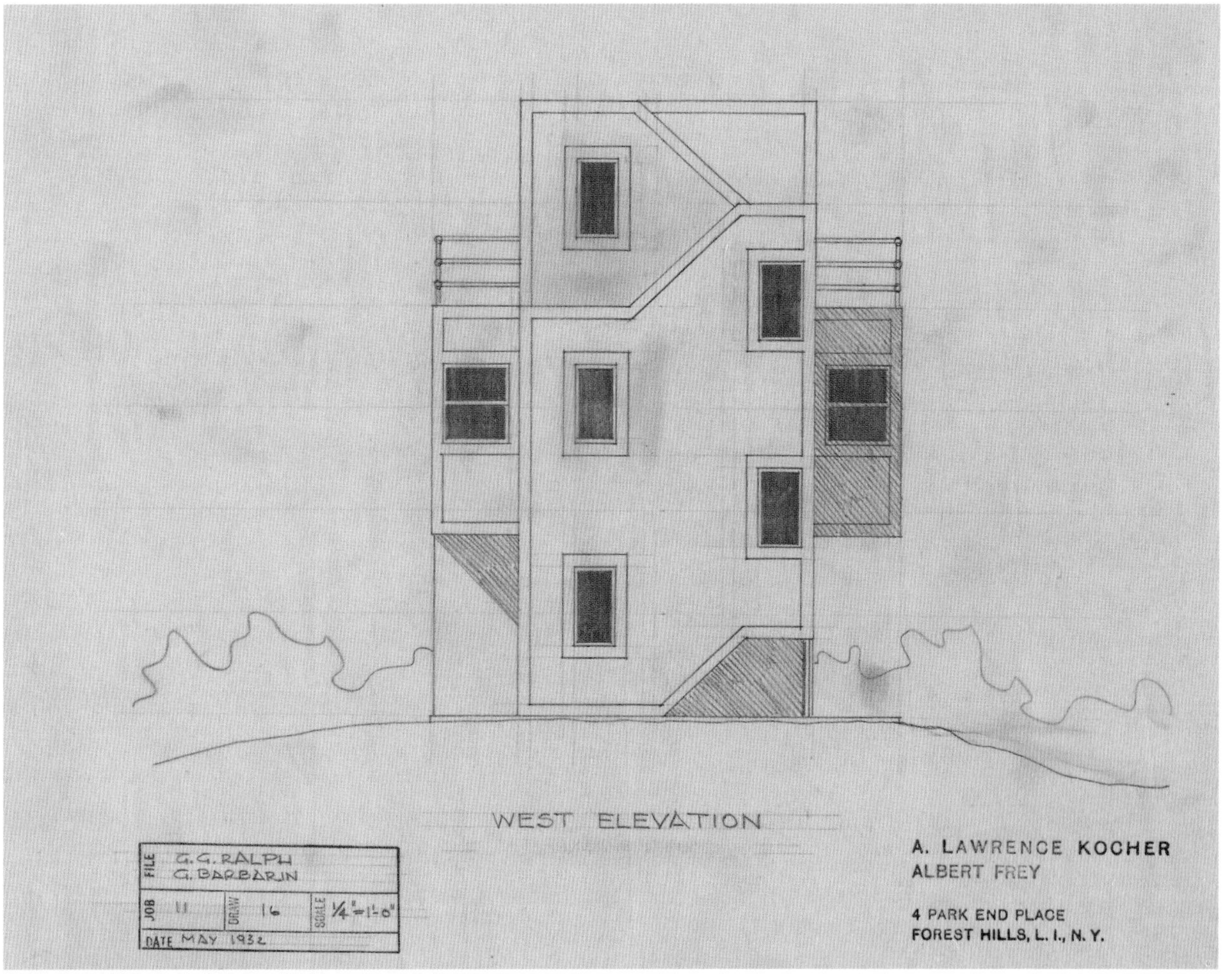
WEST ELEVATION
FILE G.G. RALPH
G. BARBARIN
JOB 11 DRAW 16 SCALE 1/4"=1'-0"
DATE MAY 1932
A. LAWRENCE KOCHER
ALBERT FREY
4 PARK END PLACE
FOREST HILLS, L. I., N. Y.

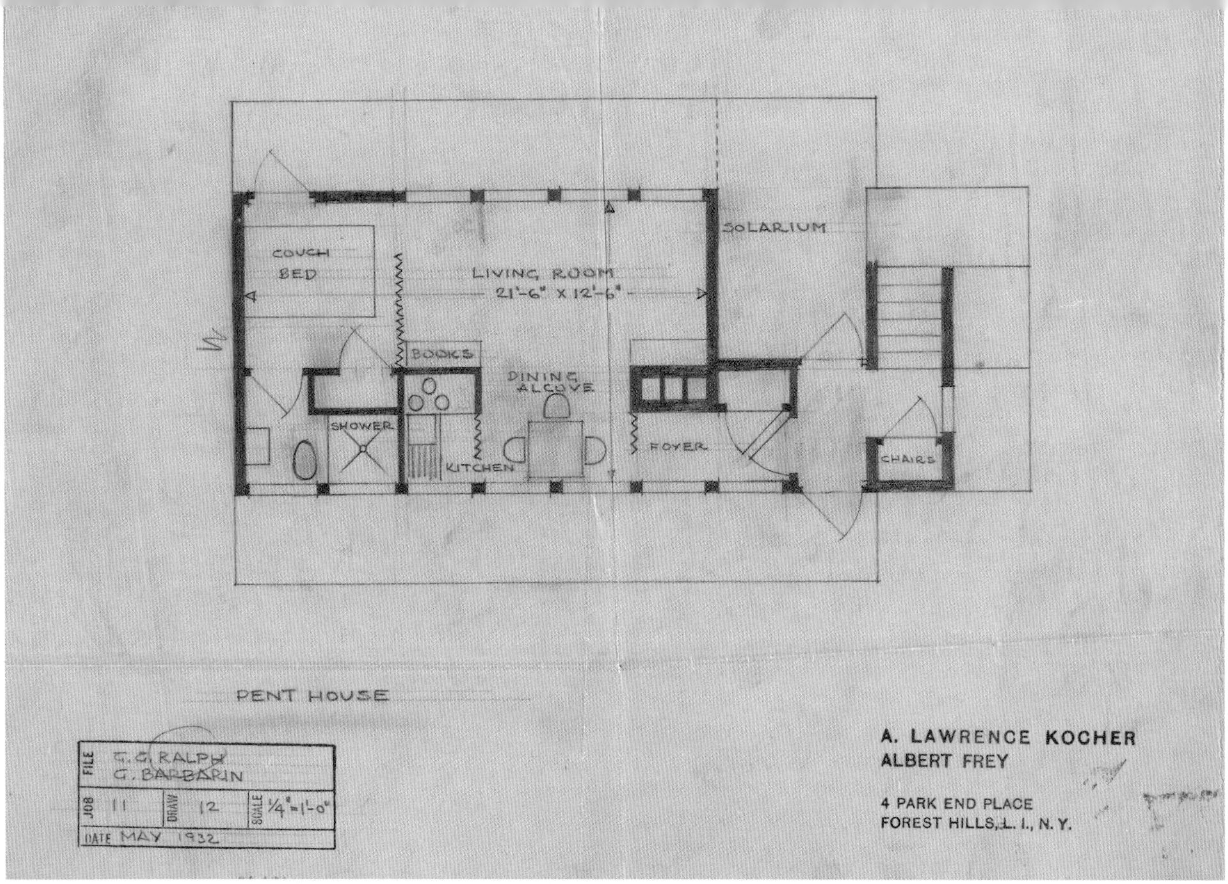
COUCH BED
LIVING ROOM
21'-6" X 12'-6"
SOLARIUM
BOOKS
DINING ALCOVE
SHOWER
KITCHEN
FOYER
CHAIRS
PENT HOUSE
FILE C. G. RALPH
G. BARBARIN
JOB 11
DRAW 12
SCALE 1/4"=1'-0"
DATE MAY 1932
A. LAWRENCE KOCHER
ALBERT FREY
4 PARK END PLACE
FOREST HILLS, L. I., N. Y.

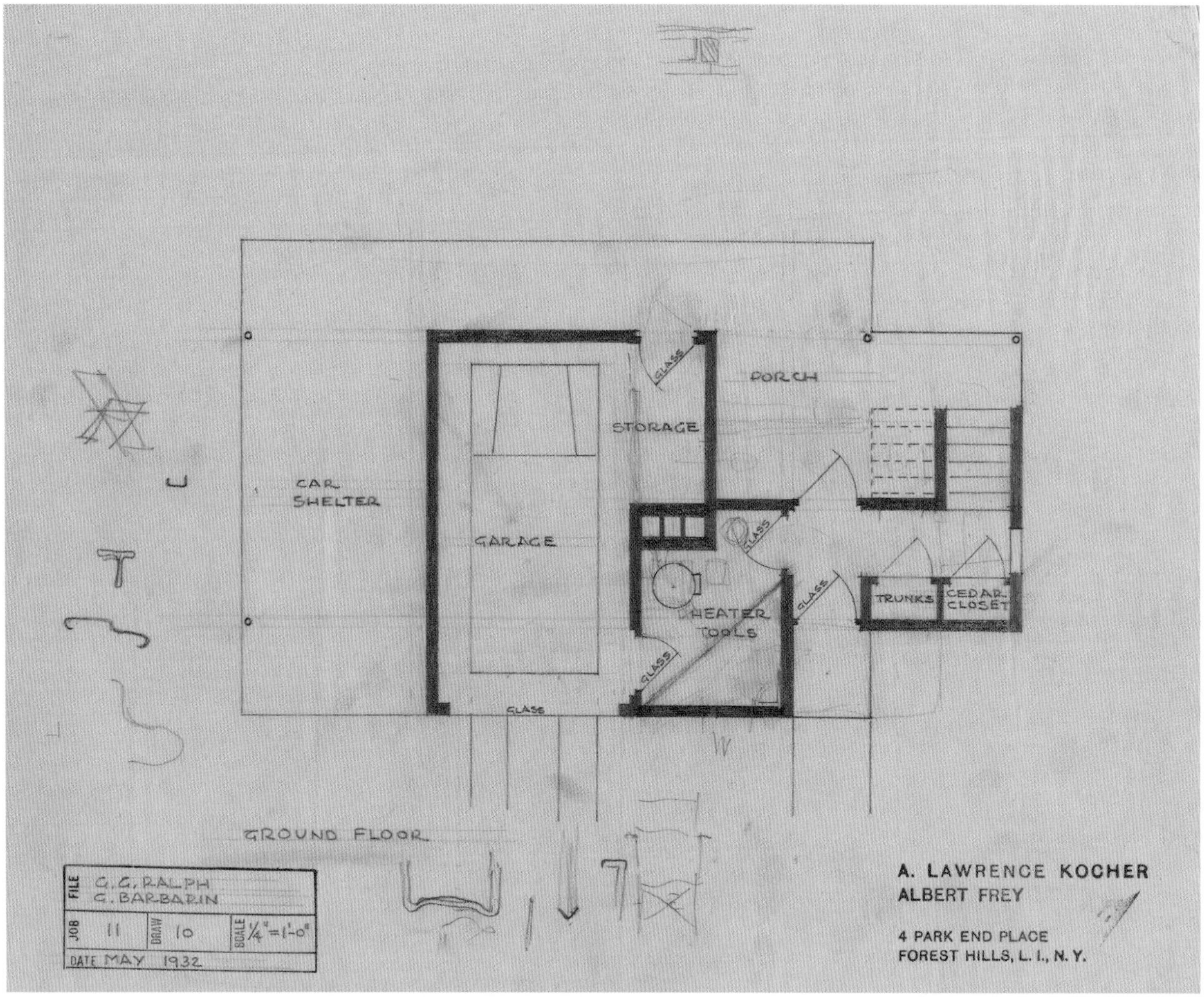
PORCH
GLASS
STORAGE
CAR SHELTER
GARAGE
GLASS
HEATER TOOLS
GLASS
TRUNKS
CEDAR CLOSET
GLASS
GLASS
GROUND FLOOR
FILE C. G. RALPH
G. BARBARIN
JOB 11
DRAW 10
SCALE 1/4"=1'-0"
DATE MAY 1932
A. LAWRENCE KOCHER
ALBERT FREY
4 PARK END PLACE
FOREST HILLS, L. I., N. Y.

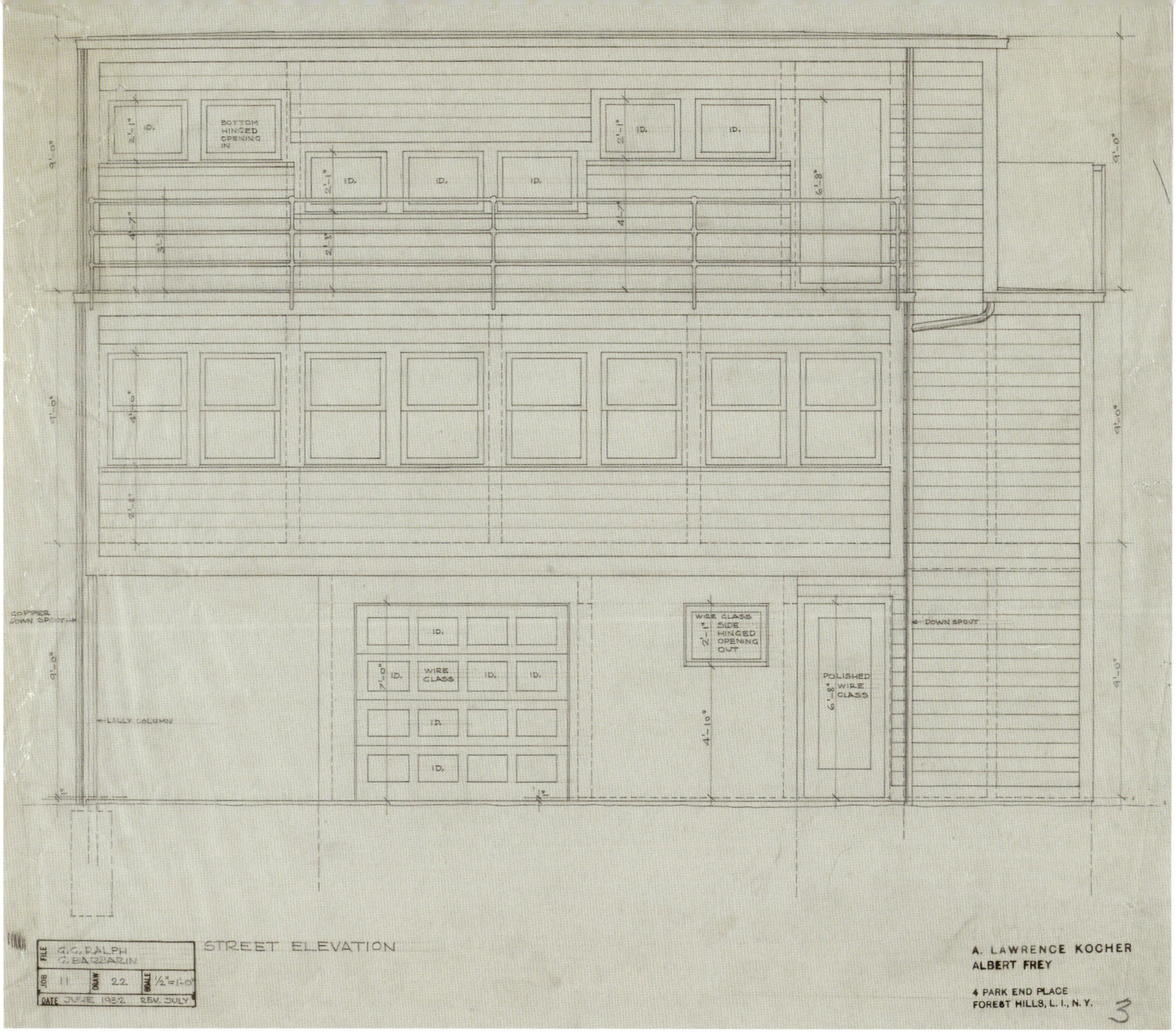

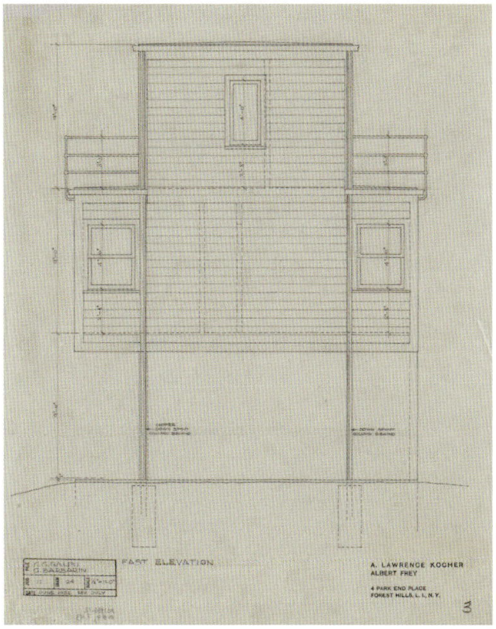

Previous page:
Figure 3.81. A. Lawrence Kocher and Albert Frey. 1932. Ralph-Barbarin House. Final version. Penthouse floor plan. Dated May 1932.
Figure 3.82. A. Lawrence Kocher and Albert Frey. 1932. Ralph-Barbarin House. Final version. Ground floor plan. Dated May 1932.

This page:
Figure 3.83. A. Lawrence Kocher and Albert Frey. 1932. Ralph-Barbarin House. Final version. Construction documents. Street elevation. Dated June 1932.
Figure 3.84. A. Lawrence Kocher and Albert Frey. 1932. Ralph-Barbarin House. Final version. Construction documents. East elevation. Dated June 1932.
Figure 3.85. A. Lawrence Kocher and Albert Frey. 1932. Ralph-Barbarin House. Picture of the construction. Application of aluminum foil on the ceiling of the porch. Published in *Architectural Record* in April 1933.

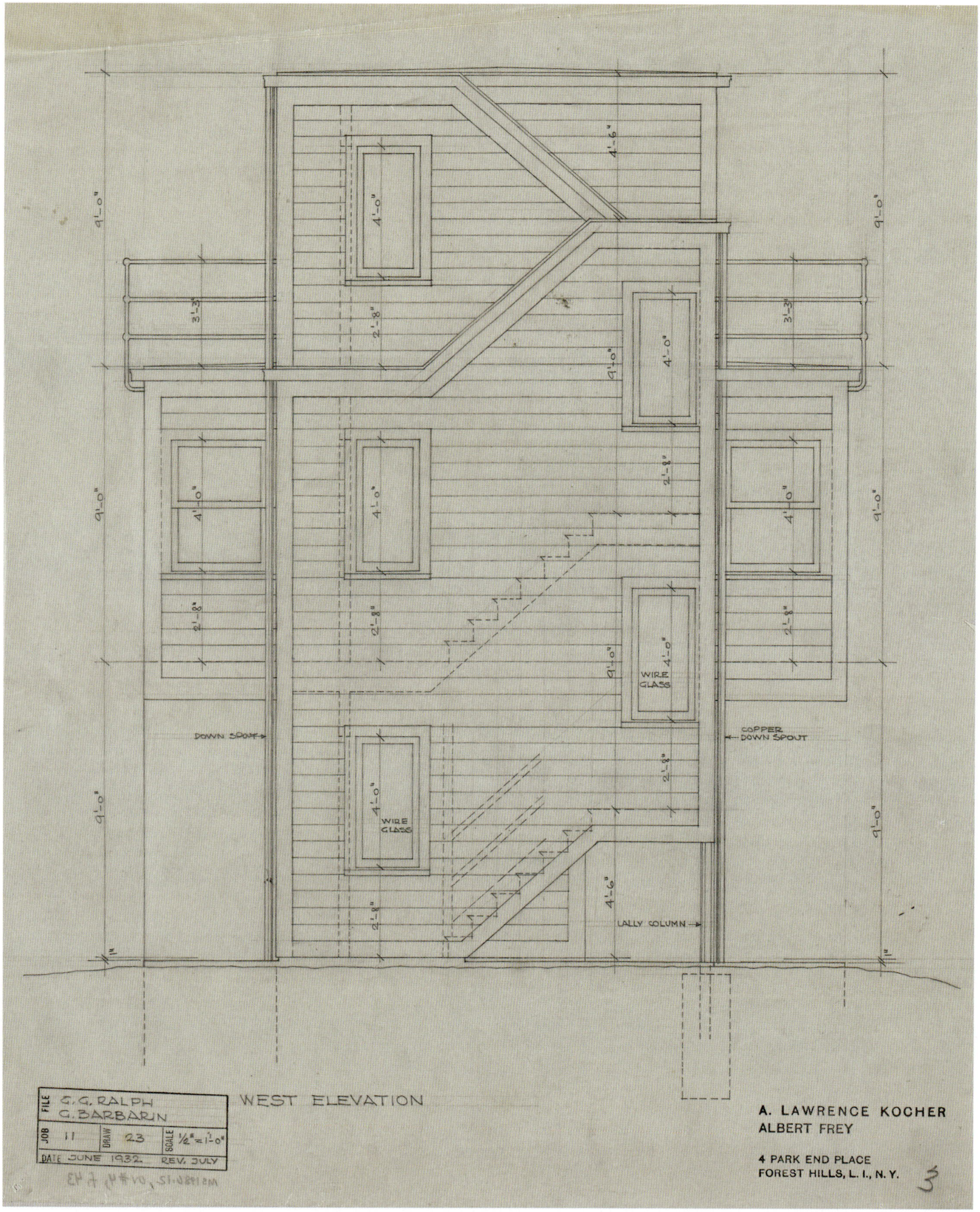

DOWN SPOUT
COPPER DOWN SPOUT
WIRE GLASS
LALLY COLUMN
WEST ELEVATION
FILE G.G. RALPH G. BARBARIN
JOB 11
DRAW 23
SCALE 1/2" = 1'-0"
DATE JUNE 1932 REV. JULY
A. LAWRENCE KOCHER
ALBERT FREY
4 PARK END PLACE
FOREST HILLS, L. I., N. Y.
3

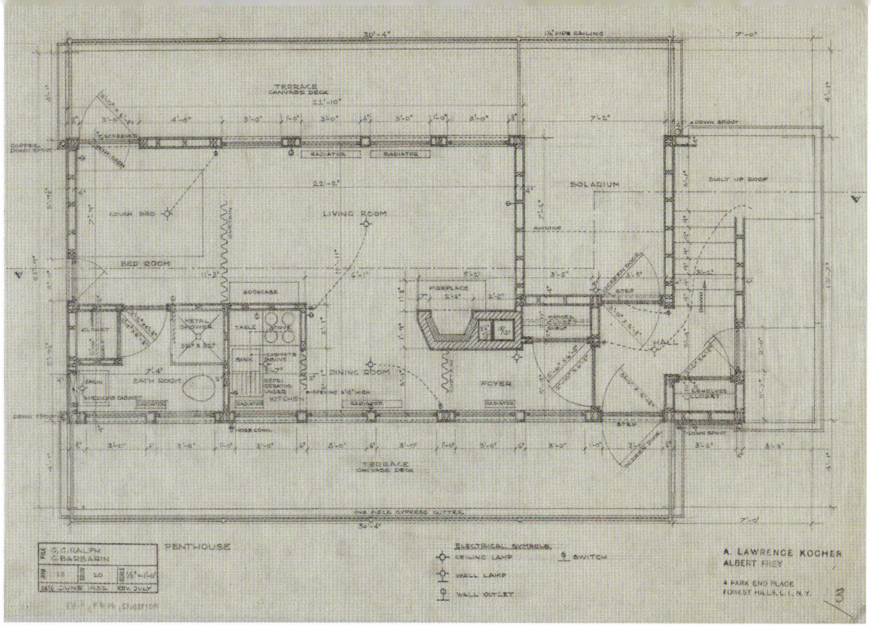

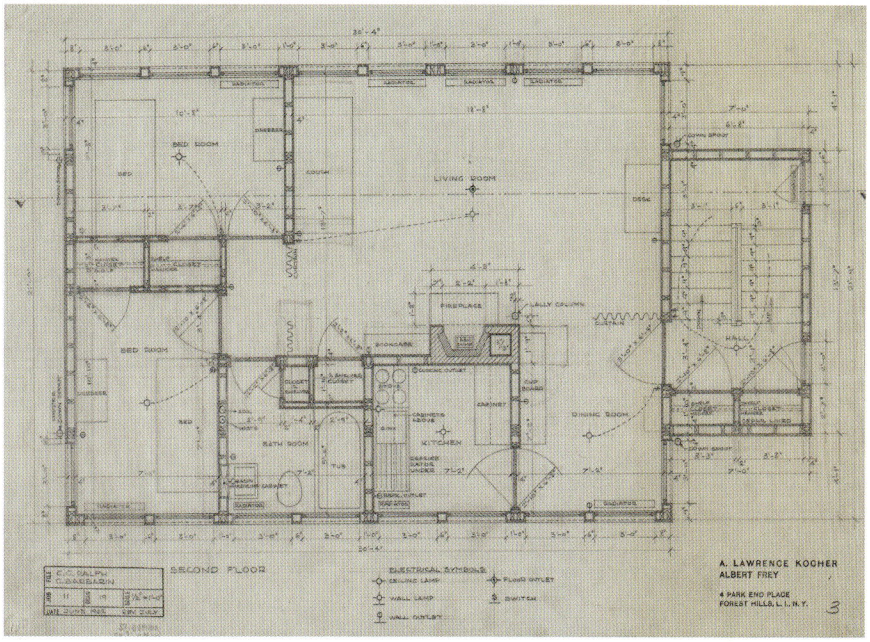

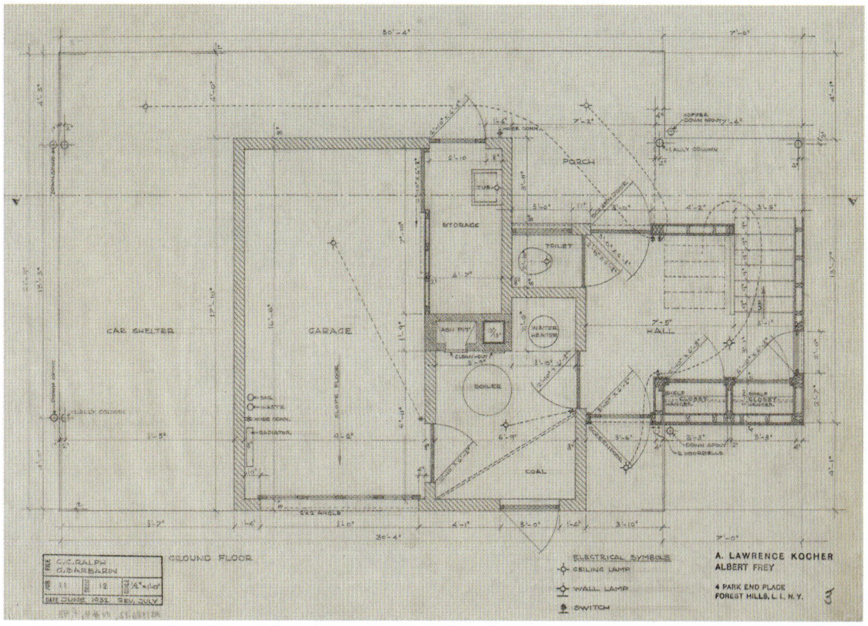

Previous page:
Figure 3.86. A. Lawrence Kocher and Albert Frey. 1932. Ralph-Barbarin House. Final version. Construction documents. West elevation. Dated June 1932.

This page:
Figure 3.87. A. Lawrence Kocher and Albert Frey. 1932. Ralph-Barbarin House. Final version. Construction documents. Penthouse floor plan. Dated June 1932.
Figure 3.88. A. Lawrence Kocher and Albert Frey. 1932. Ralph-Barbarin House. Final version. Construction documents. Second floor plan. Dated June 1932.
Figure 3.89. A. Lawrence Kocher and Albert Frey. 1932. Ralph-Barbarin House. Final version. Construction documents. Ground floor plan. Dated June 1932.
Figure 3.90. A. Lawrence Kocher and Albert Frey. 1932. Ralph-Barbarin House. Photo of the built house. Undated.

1933–1935

BUILDING ON TWO COASTS: FROM THE SUBSISTENCE FARMSTEADS TO THE KOCHER-SAMSON BUILDING

As the final months of 1932 rolled into early 1933, periods of deep crisis slowed down all economic activity in the United States. Commissions for Kocher and Frey had been scarce during 1932, but now they were completely nonexistent. With Frey abroad since January 1933 and still recovering from his wife's passing, Kocher decided to pause his professional practice and focus on his work at *Architectural Record*, his ongoing research, and his role as cultural catalyst in New York's architectural scene. Before Frey's departure, they had been working together in the organization of a modern architecture exhibition for the Sears Roebuck and Company Art Gallery in Washington, D.C., Inaugurated on December 6, 1932, "New Trends in Architecture" lasted for two weeks and exhibited international works by John Russell Pope, Hamilton and Gwenydd Beatty, Antonin Raymond (Tokyo, Japan), Ellis and Clack in association with Owen Williams (London, U.K.), Howe and Lescaze, Joseph Emberton (London, U.K.), Clauss and Daub, and the engineer O. H. Ammann. Kocher and Frey's own designs were generously represented in the exhibition with the President Hoover's Conference Farmhouses, the Ralph-Barbarin House, the Darien Guild Hall, the Experimental Five-Room House, and the Experimental Weekend House. The exhibition brochure additionally included texts by Le Corbusier, Clive Bell, and Frank Lloyd Wright.[1] According to *The Washington Post*, the exhibition contained 50 items that "illustrate low-cost mass production of modern buildings, including homes, skyscrapers, and apartment houses."[2] Some of the materials (boards and models) from this exhibition seem to have been recycled by Kocher and Frey for a new use. Once they removed the international examples, the remaining materials served as a base for a new exhibition on "Modern American Architecture" inaugurated on January 22, 1933, on the third floor of the New School for Social Research in New York City. The venue for this second exhibition was strategically chosen, as it was an example of the International Style—designed by Austrian-born Joseph Urban, built in 1931, and published in *Architectural Record* that same year.[3] As the curators, Kocher and Frey explicated in the *New York Herald Tribune* that the exhibition demonstrated how modern architecture responded to the new manners of living, including building materials and construction methods, improved ideals of comfort and convenience, health factors, and the overall modern trend toward efficiency, restraint, and economy.[4] Side-by-side pictures of "good" (modern) and "bad" architectural solutions for interior and exterior spaces for different programs, revealed the exhibition's didactic stance. While many were unbuilt, the included designs exhibited were by Walter Baermann, Robert M. Brown, Alfred Clauss, Hamilton and Gwenydd Beatty, Howe and Lescaze, Norman Herreshoff, Alfred Kastner, Norman Rice, William Muschenheim, Richard C. Wood, and of course by the architect of the host space, Urban, along with the curators, Kocher and Frey. The participant list reads as a *Who's who* of modern architecture on the East Coast.

Concurrent with the exhibition, Kocher had been working on an article about new materials and construction methods developed to reduce the labor on site, lightening material weight to streamline transportation and assembly with the ultimate goal of lowering the cost of construction. Published in *Architectural Record*'s April 1933 issue, the article was profusely illustrated with construction photos and a series of axonometric views with peeled-back layers to show alternative material solutions for different floor, roof, and wall systems.[5] A highly relevant example of how Kocher and Frey's research and practice were completely intertwined—both retrospectively and prospectively—some of the article's photographs documented the construction of their previous designs, like the Ralph-Barbarin House. Other suggested systems had already been used in the Aluminaire House, like the decks manufactured by Truscon Steel Company. In describing these novel systems and methodologies, a hint of future developments for their practice emerges. For example, the details described in the article as "an improved flat roof over wood construction" and "improved wood frame wall" have the exact composition of the systems later used in the Kocher Canvas Weekend House, built in 1934. Resolved in the form of a didactic catalog, the article draws parallels to the builder's handbooks that informed architects and builders during the Colonial through the Early Republic Periods in America how to design walls, roofs, doorways, windows, balconies, and fireplaces.[6] By this time, Kocher had gathered an extensive collection of such practical books, known to have been in the libraries of prominent citizens of that era, like Thomas Jefferson.[7]

The curation of these exhibitions and the work on the research paper for *Architectural Record* were the product of both the economic crisis and the personal circumstances that slowed down Kocher's practice, while Frey was in Switzerland. But these circumstances were about to change drastically and affect Kocher's upcoming professional life. First, during the last months of 1932, Kocher's personal life took a new direction with his matrimony to his second wife, Margaret Taylor Kocher. Further, the political milieu

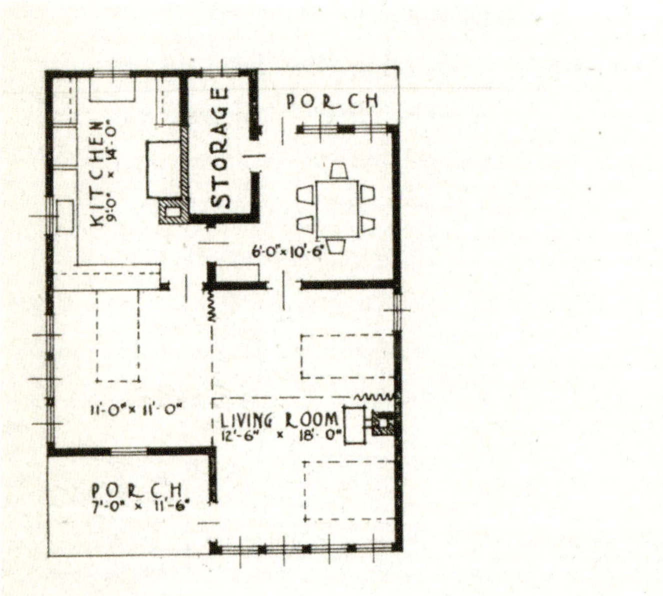

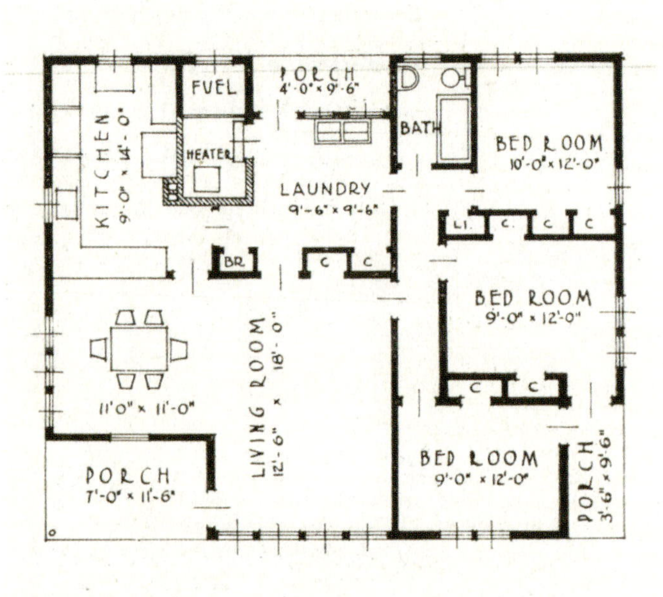

Figure 4.1. Albert Frey. 1934. Farm House 6531. *Farmers Bulletin*, No. 1738 (Washington D.C.: U.S. Department of Agriculture, October 1934): 40–43. Floor plan. First stage.
Figure 4.2. Albert Frey. 1934. Farm House 6531. *Farmers Bulletin*, No. 1738 (Washington D.C.: U.S. Department of Agriculture, October 1934): 40–43. Floor plan. Second stage.
Figure 4.3. Albert Frey. 1934. Farm House 6531. *Farmers Bulletin*, No. 1738 (Washington D.C.: U.S. Department of Agriculture, October 1934): 40–43. Exterior perspectives with different material options for the façade.

of the United States was in full effervescence and about to suffer a paradigm shift: between Franklin D. Roosevelt's (FDR) election on November 8, 1932, and his inauguration on March 4, 1933, there was an interregnum in which the depression grew worse by the day. That winter was the most devastating with a quarter of the workforce unemployed. More than 2,000 banks had failed during 1931; with no insurance for their deposits, people were reticent to pump any more money into the system and were very eager to withdraw their savings instead. In February of 1932, President Hoover created the Reconstruction Finance Corporation (RFC) whose purpose was to lend directly to banks and other financial institutions. That same year, the Glass-Steagall Banking Act reformed the Federal Reserve's role in providing credit during economic downturns.[8] The measures did not have the expected effect and soon some state governors declared bank holidays to prevent further massive fund withdrawals. During the interregnum, Roosevelt refused to support any of these initiatives or endorse any part of the Republicans' programs; nevertheless, when he took office on March 4, 1933, his first action was to declare a four-day bank holiday, shutting down the banking system, including the Federal Reserve. Days later, on March 9, he passed the Emergency Banking Act, a legislation that provided the reopening of banks as soon as they were financially sound; by March 13, banks started to reopen, overcoming public mistrust and reducing panic-driven withdrawals to a minimum. To solidify this renewed trust in the banking system and its reliability, Roosevelt signed another banking act three months later, creating the now-familiar Federal Deposit Insurance Corporation (FDIC).

After momentarily mitigating the banking crisis, Roosevelt aimed to reorganize the federal government to streamline superfluous bureaucracy to begin a legislative effort later known as the One Hundred Days. For many historians, it was "the most intensive period of reform legislation in American history."[9] During this time, the administration carried out a number of perdurable initiatives, like the creation of the Public Works Administration (PWA), which financed more than 34,500 public construction works over its first six years. From dams and highways to public schools and local post offices, the PWA employed more than half a million workers in any given year. A large percentage of the legislation was devoted to solving the agricultural emergency—farms had already suffered years of economic crisis with a steep drop in agricultural product prices since the 1920s. This fact, added to general deflation, drove many farms to foreclosure during 1932 and 1933. These foreclosures were opposed with violence in some cases and in others with hardly more sophisticated means of intimidation like the "Penny Auctions."[10] These desperate reactions against extraordinary economic hardships ignited the government's fear of a social upheaval in the Midwest.

By May of 1933, Congress created the Federal Emergency Relief Administration (FERA) whose most urgent objective was agriculture; to affect forthcoming crops, the government needed to act promptly as spring had already arrived in many regions of the country. The Agricultural Adjustment Bill was approved with the objective of raising the final price of farm products using government-subsidized scarcity. On May 12, 1933, Roosevelt signed the Agricultural Adjustment Act and the Emergency Farm Mortgage Act and forged the Agricultural Adjustment Administration (AAA) that immediately moved into action. The AAA asked farmers to reduce cultivated acreage and to slaughter a percentage of their livestock in order to stabilize the prices. As these measures were unpopular, Roosevelt's administration created the Federal Surplus Relief Corporation to purchase and redistribute overproduction guaranteeing farmers a fair price. The National Industrial Recovery Act (NIRA)—the same legislation that facilitated the Public Works Administration— passed on June 16, 1933, included the following narrative in Title II, Section 208, under the title of "Subsistence Homesteads":

> To provide for aiding the redistribution of the over-balance of population in industrial centers $25,000,000 is hereby made available to the President, to be used by him through such agencies as he may establish and under such regulations as he may make, for making loans for and otherwise aiding in the purchase of subsistence homesteads.[11]

The scheme of returning people to the land to help supplement their regular income with the grown products from their garden tracts for their own consumption was very much embedded in Roosevelt's own longing for the Jeffersonian arcadian ideal as a cure for the ills of urbanization and industrialization. In April 17, 1933, a month before the passing of the NIRA, Roosevelt wrote to a U.S. senator: "I would really like to get one more bill, which would allow us to spend $25 million this year to put 25,000 families on farms at the average cost of $1,000 per family."[12]

The Division of Subsistence Homesteads was created within the Department of Interior to coordinate and direct the effort; its explicit purpose was to promote the decentralization of the population from large industrial centers, to provide economic stability for families by proving the worth of a system that combined payroll employment with farming and gardening upon small plots of carefully selected land, and to raise living standards and overall social welfare.[13] The Subsistence Homesteads mitigated future effects from recurrent periods of industrial crisis. They also focused on attenuating the effects of labor conditions during the Depression that included seasonal unemployment, a shorter workday and work week, prematurely retired workers, and stranded industrial groups due to relocation or closures. Within the vicinity of industrial centers, "garden homes" furnished a place of refuge in times of crisis and reduced dependence upon a cash income. Funds were allocated not for individual families, but solely for the creation of full communities. The aggregation of homesteads into larger communities was expected to encourage private industry to move into areas where a worker group was readily available, and to foster innovative forms of livelihood.[14] The clearest definition of these homesteads is provided by the General Counselor for the Subsistence Homesteads Corporation, Philip M. Glick:

> As conceived by the administrators of the Federal program, a subsistence homestead is a plot of land, on which is located the family dwelling, and which is tilled to supply a substantial part of the food needs of the family to supplement, together with the production of such other articles for

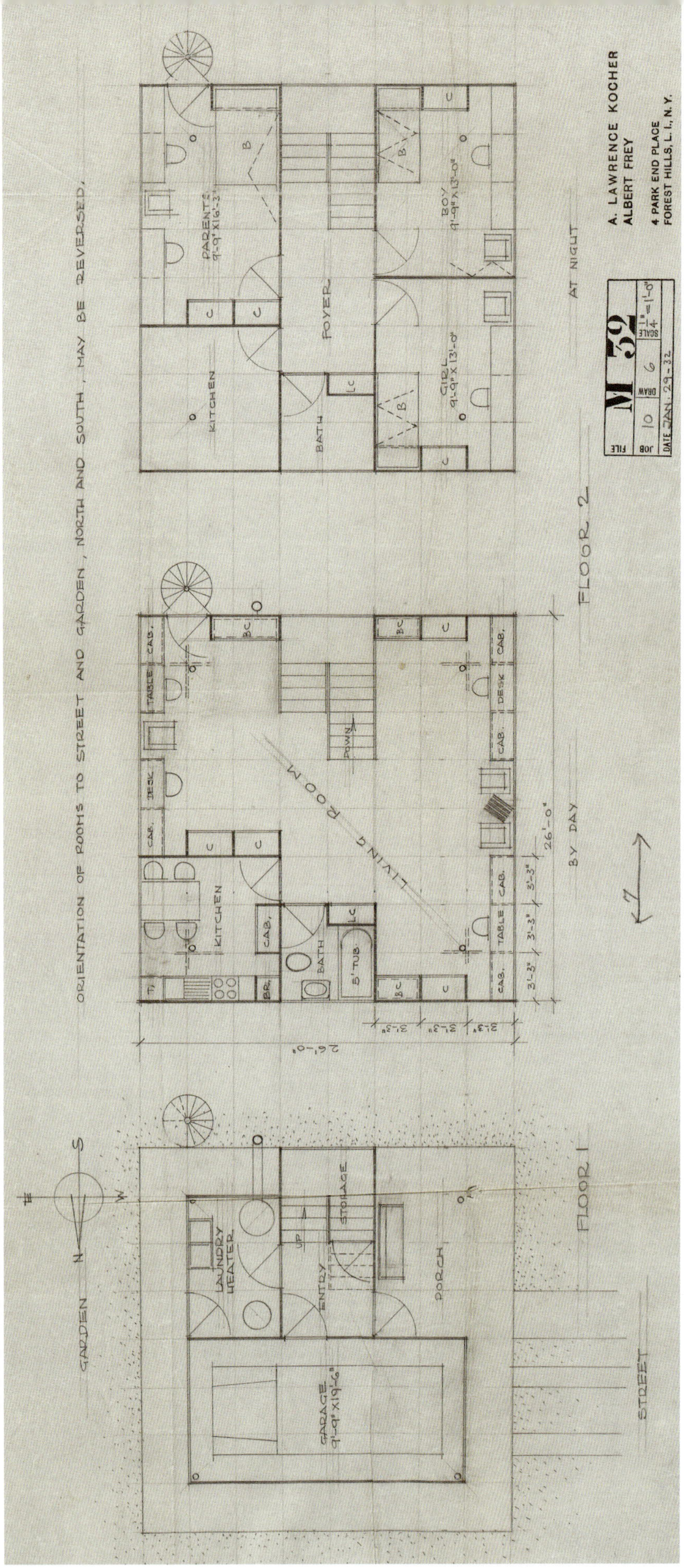

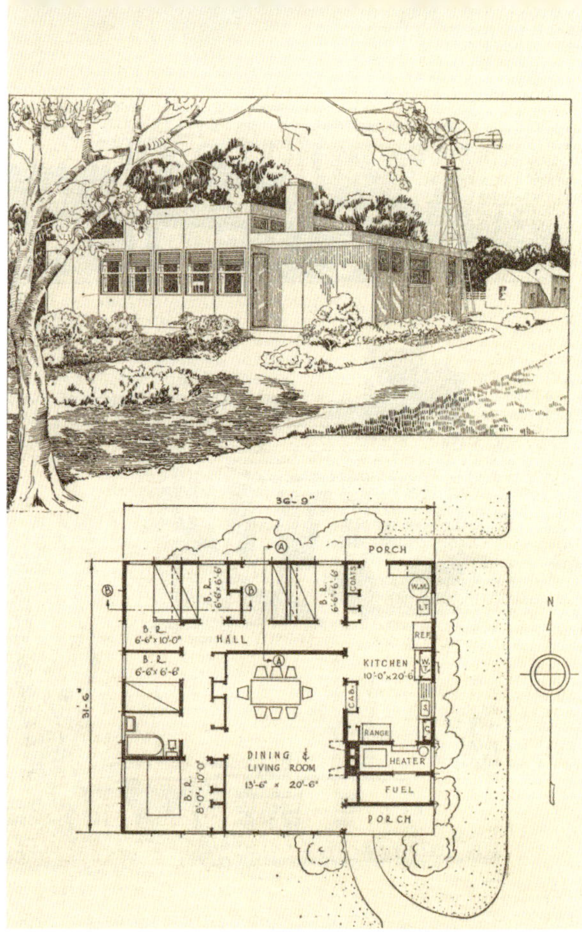

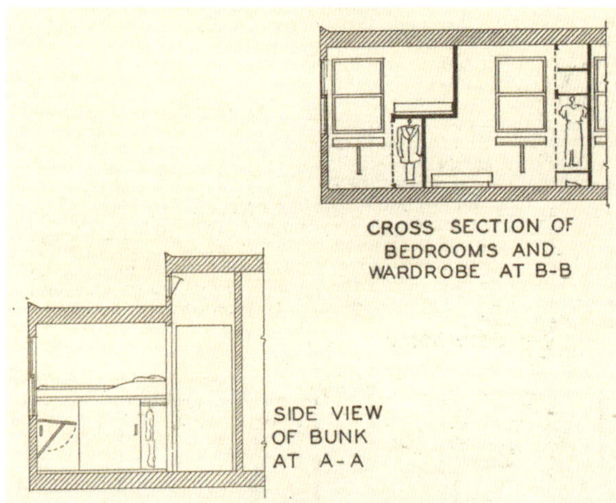

Figure 4.4. Albert Frey. 1934. Farm House 6532. *Farmers Bulletin*, No. 1738 (Washington D.C.: U.S. Department of Agriculture, October 1934): 40–43. Exterior perspective and floor plan. Sections of bedrooms.

Figure 4.5. A. Lawrence Kocher and Albert Frey. 1932. Intermediate proposal between the Low-Cost Farmhouses (1931) and the Subsistence Farmsteads (1934). The plan seeks for flexibility using movable interior partitions allowing for different day and night configurations of the domestic spaces.

consumption as may be produced in the home or a domestic workshop, cash income received from industrial or other outside employment.[15]

The newly created Federal Subsistence Homesteads Corporation would act as the operating agency of the Division of Subsistence Homesteads and asked for the cooperation of local interest groups and citizens to join the advisory board. Through the Corporation and its subsidiaries, the Division purchased the land, constructed the homesteads and outbuildings, and sold the completed buildings to families that complied with the necessary prerequisites. In a move typical of Roosevelt's political endeavors, the Division of Subsistence Homesteads and the Department of Agriculture asked stakeholders, interest groups, specialists, and leaders in the field to prepare a series of agreed joint proposals and studies before beginning the official work. Since this was not the first such exploration in the United States, the U.S. Department of Agriculture commissioned a compilation of prior background, resulting in the exhaustive 1934 publication "Bibliography on Land Settlement, with Particular Reference to Small Holdings and Subsistence Farmsteads," which included more than 2,700 examples from the U.S. and other countries.[16]

Additionally, the Federal Subsistence Homesteads Corporation and the Department of Agriculture commissioned two independent studies from a number of selected architects. The subsequent catalog developed by the Corporation consisted of 32 houses designed by both unidentified authors from the Architectural Unit of the Construction Section within the Division of Subsistence Homesteads and unidentified private architects associated with the Division.[17] With the requirements established by the Subsistence Homesteads Program, these commissions explored various design possibilities for compliant homestead floor plans. Ultimately, the Corporation would own a catalog of pre-designed homes to be used by the subsidiary corporations to develop and maintain new communities.[18] The guidelines for the designs were defined in advance by the bulletin: the cost was restricted to a minimum of $2,000 and a maximum of $3,000, ranging from three to six bedrooms. The three-bedroom houses, however, needed to be constructed in a way that they could be expanded with minimum alteration. All house plans had to be adapted to the local climatic conditions of the settlement community, taking into account features such as cross ventilation, the use of dual-purpose rooms wherever programs may be suitably grouped, and direct connection between bedrooms and bathrooms.

Enter Kocher and Frey into this defining moment of the Subsistence Homesteads Program. While Frey was abroad, Kocher reworked their article, "New Materials and Improved Construction Methods" (April 1933), and presented a paper for the National Conference on Low-Cost Housing in Cleveland that same year.[19] Organized by the Cleveland Engineering Society, this was a pioneering effort in studying social housing in the United States and preceded the first federal attempt to create a public housing corporation by months.[20] The conference had a strictly technological focus, with the bulk of the papers devoted to cost-saving solutions in construction and mechanical systems, materials, and environmental comfort. As published in the conference proceedings, Kocher's paper utilized select drawings from the *Architectural Record* article yet was more a summary of findings and conclusions about the convenience in use of new materials and building technologies. Using the example of the Sears, Roebuck and Company's catalog houses, Kocher advocated for a supervised partial-or-complete self-construction of single-family houses as a solution to reduce labor cost and give the owners agency over their living spaces. Kocher advocated for the convenience of wood as construction material over other options such as steel, concrete, clay, and non-ferrous metals. He also provided a cursory inventory of essential to low-cost construction materials and methods akin to a technological and functional program for the subsequent buildings of the office. This summary recommended an unprejudiced approach to the homes and their design including:

> Maximum use of plan area and cubage, by incorporating communication parts of the house, such as stairs, halls, vestibules, into living spaces. Reduce areas and height of service rooms, such as kitchen, bath, and closets, and with different floor levels. Units of construction and parts of the house serving multiplied purposes as follows: walls and windows being enclosures as well as supporting members, roofs serving as terrace, air space under house converted into outdoor shelter, outside walls forming screens for outdoor living or wind protection for plants and shrubs, rooms serving two or more purposes, furnishing and fixtures with combined functions requiring little space, furniture, if possible, of folding or disappearing type, and converting several small rooms into a large one when desired.[21]

Kocher's list combines certain Corbusian components with others pertaining to Kocher's knowledge of the construction industry and his practical sense. The use of load-bearing wood façades and partitions contradicted the principles of free façade and free plan but were perfectly adapted to the economic and technological reality of the given geographical and historic context. Kocher supplemented part of the documentation presented during the conference with designs for the low-cost farmhouses and featured this new examination in *Architectural Record*'s 1934 January issue.[22] Combined, these previous experiences and additional publications in non-architectural magazines put Kocher and Frey on the U.S. Department of Agriculture's radar.[23]

Following his European stay, Frey came back to the United States in October of 1934—though not in time to attend the conference in Cleveland—living again with Kocher and Kocher's new wife, Margaret, in Forest Hills, New York. Around this time, the Department of Agriculture contacted Kocher and Frey, inviting them to collaborate on a catalog of floor plans for subsistence homesteads. Kocher was too busy with editorial work at the magazine and making plans for a potential new school of architecture, but Frey accepted the challenge since the office did not have much work at that time. In his own words:

> The research and projects Lawrence and I had done on farm houses led to a stint at the U. S. Department of Agricul-

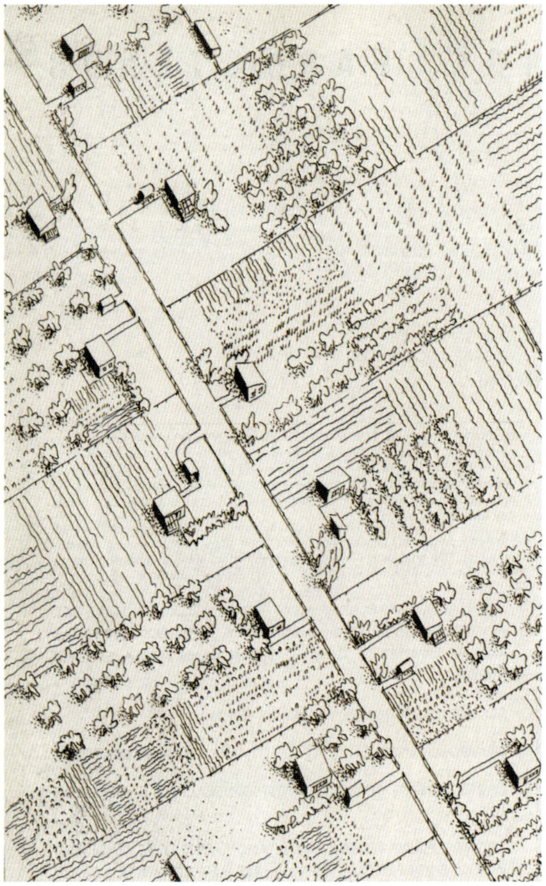

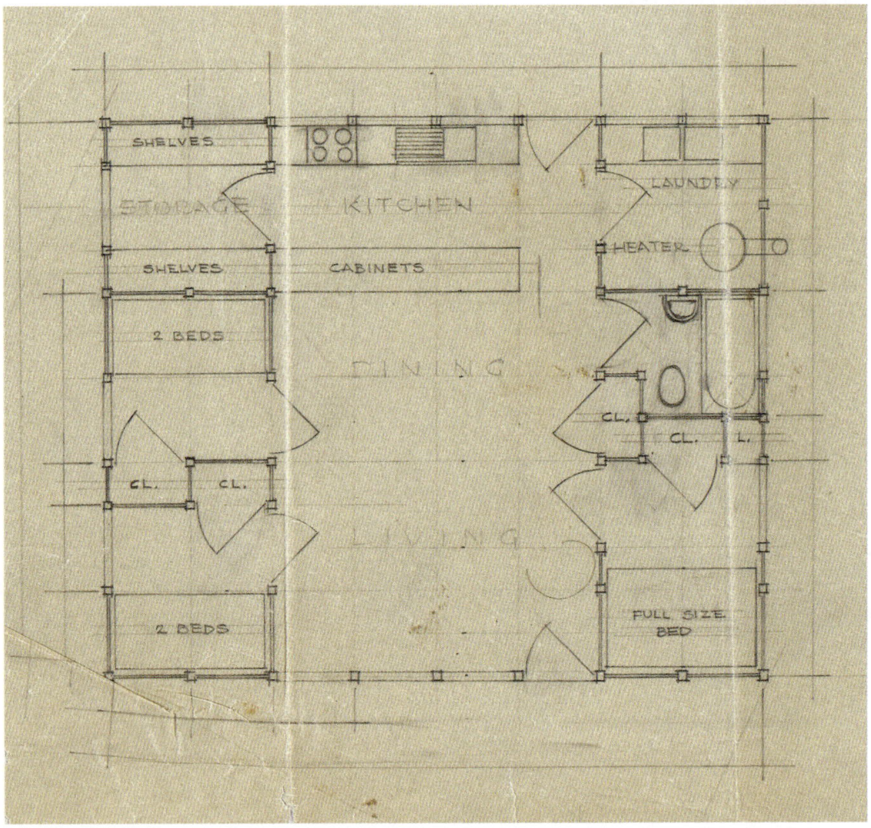

This page:

Figure 4.6. A. Lawrence Kocher and Albert Frey. 1934. Subsistence Farmsteads. Exterior perspective, interior view, and territorial layout of the farmsteads.

Figure 4.7. A. Lawrence Kocher and Albert Frey. 1934. Subsistence Farmsteads. Original pencil floor plan.

Next page:

Figure 4.8. A. Lawrence Kocher and Albert Frey. 1934. Subsistence Farmsteads. Published in *Architectural Record*, April 1934. Different construction methods, material options, and storage systems.

PREFABRICATED SYSTEM

(Fireproof)

Use is made of standard and available steel parts such as steel angles, channels, girders, floor deck and steel faced insulation board. This construction is cheap with quantity production. It is moderate in cost for 25 houses.

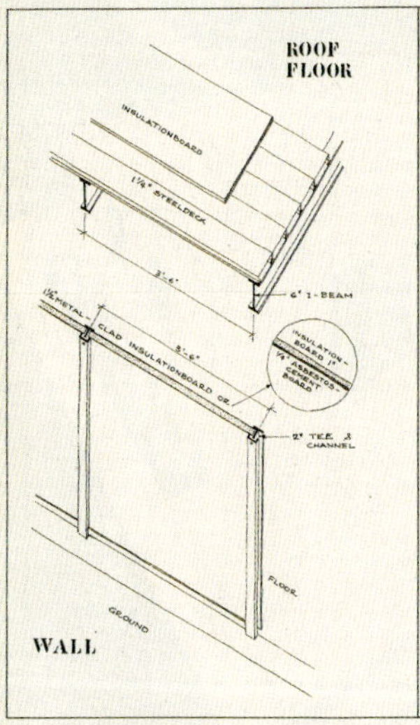

WOOD AND CANVAS

This construction method is cheapest of all. It has high insulation value and is very well suited to enlargement.

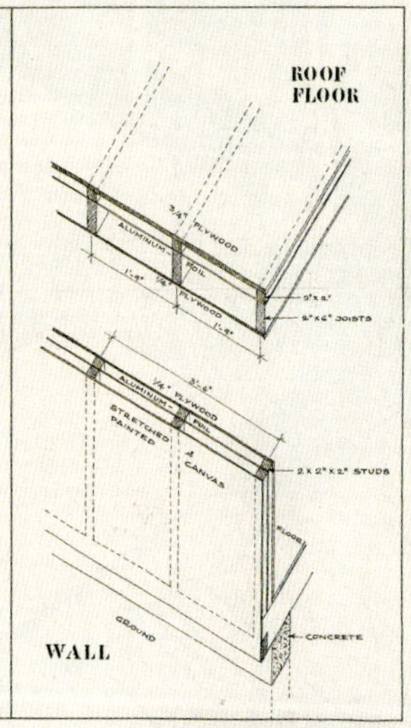

CINDER OR OTHER CONCRETE BLOCKS

(Fireproof)

This method is economical if blocks are cast in the field where building operation is carried on. This is especially so when sand or cinders are obtained locally.

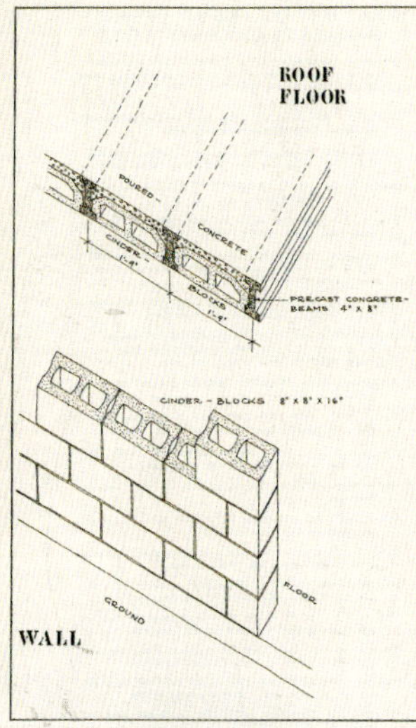

PRECAST CONCRETE (Post and Plank)

(Fireproof and termite-proof. Low maintenance)

It is not difficult for unskilled labor to erect the parts of this house. There would be supervision in the making of precast units of uniform size and in erection of posts and girders. A very economical system.

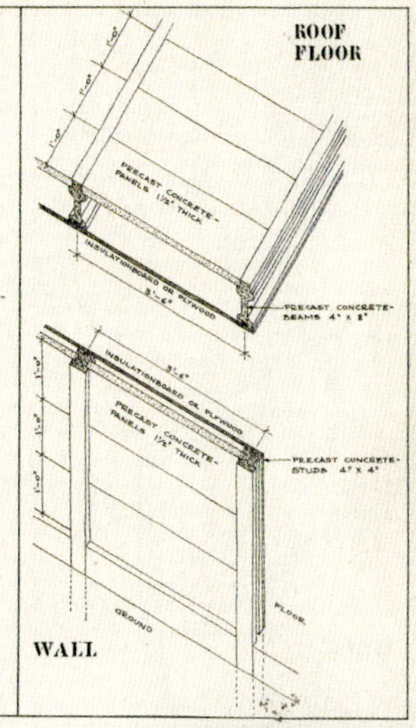

STRUCTURAL SYSTEMS ADAPTABLE FOR SUBSISTENCE FARMHOUSE CONSTRUCTION

KOCHER AND FREY
NEW YORK

CANVAS BEFORE PAINTING

CINDER BLOCKS WITH AND WITHOUT STUCCO COAT

TYPICAL CAST CONCRETE SURFACE

LIGHT STEEL MEMBERS

Connections by bolting and clips. Facing with light sheet steel or corrugated asbestos board. Inside walls faced with asbestos board. Ease of construction and reerection. High salvage value. Fireproof. Lightweight.

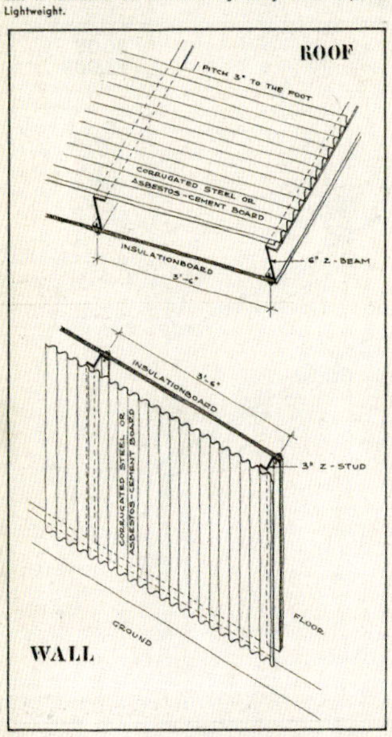

ACTUAL APPEARANCE OF CORRUGATED STEEL OR ASBESTOS-CEMENT BOARD

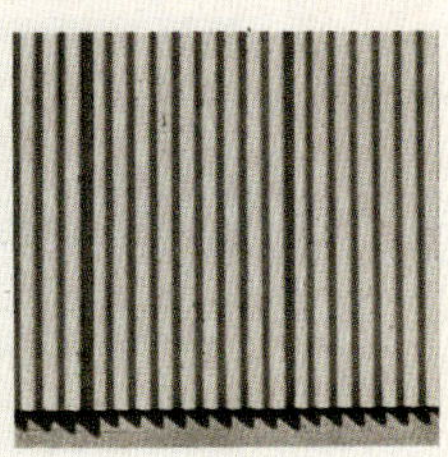

STATUS OF SUBSISTENCE HOMESTEAD PROJECTS

(Figures in parentheses for each project show approximate cash allocation and number of homesteads. Published by courtesy of U. S. Government, Subsistence Homesteads Division.)

Birmingham, Ala. ($750,000; 300)—Land acquired; plans well advanced; land improvement under way.

North Georgia Project (Jones & Putnam Counties)—($1,000,000; 500)—Acquiring land and doing survey work.

Pender County, N. C. ($1,000,000; 500)—Land acquired; land improvement under way.

Decatur, Ind. ($145,000; 48)—Land acquired; land improvement under way; about to start construction.

Westmoreland County, Pa. (stranded coal miners)—$200,000; 100)—Land acquired; land improvement under way; house plans nearly completed.

Tygart Valley (near Elkins) W. Va. ($250,000; 125)—Land being acquired; land improvement starting.

Monmouth County, N. J. (decentralization of industry involving Jewish needle workers)—($500,000; 200)—Land being acquired; plans almost complete.

Youngstown, Ohio. ($500,000; 160)—Land being acquired; organization set up.

Dayton, Ohio. ($359,000; 200)—Some houses complete in one unit; project being extended to four new units.

Reedsville, W. Va. (experimental village)—($500,000; 125)—50 houses nearly finished and rest ready to begin.

Austin, Minn. ($125,000; 50)—Land acquired; land improvement under way.

Wilmington, Del. ($200,000; 70)—Land being acquired; improvement and plans under way.

Crossville, Tenn. ($471,500; 250)—Land acquired; improvement under way; plans nearly complete.

Arlington, Tex. ($125,000; 50)—Land acquired; land improvement under way; plans nearly complete.

Wichita Falls, Tex. ($125,000; 50)—Land acquired; land improvement under way; plans nearly complete.

Three Rivers, Tex. ($125,000; 50)—Land acquired; land improvement under way; plans nearly complete.

Arlington, Tex. ($250,000; 100)—Land acquired; land improvement under way; plans nearly complete.

Houston, Tex. ($250,000; 100)—Land acquired; land improvement under way; plans nearly complete.

Wisconsin Forest Farms (Northern Wis.)—($450,000; 400)—Land acquisition beginning; surveys under way.

McComb, Miss. ($62,500; 25)—Land acquired; improvement under way; planning nearly done.

Laurel, Miss. ($62,500; 25)—Land acquired; improvement under way; planning nearly done.

Tupelo, Miss. ($62,500; 25)—Land acquired; improvement under way; planning nearly done.

Meridian, Miss. (62,500; 25)—Land acquired; improvement under way; jlanning nearly done.

Hattiesburg, Miss. ($62,500; 25)—Land acquired; improvement under way; planning nearly done.

Rochester, N. Y. ($100,000; 33)—Land being acquired and other plans being prepared.

Jasper, Ala. ($244,000; 100)—Land being acquired.

A two-unit project in Los Angeles, Calif., is to be announced.

Usually the planning and acquisition stage is longer than the actual construction on the above projects.

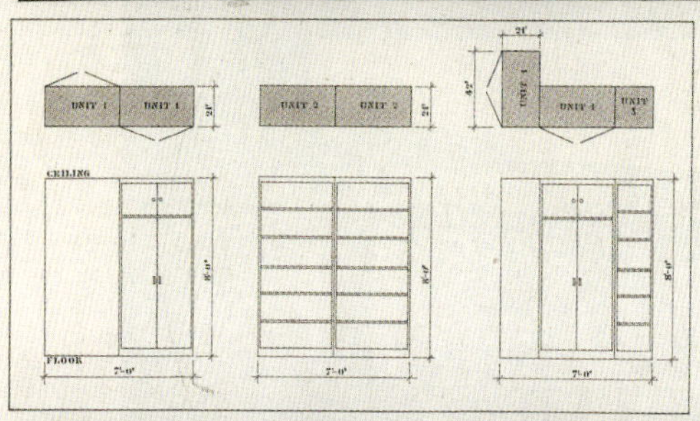

CLOSETS and CABINETS

for the subsistence farmhouse were designed so as to care for the usual storage for a farm. They are made of steel and in quantities of 200 are more economical than of wood construction. Closets extend from floor to ceiling. Cabinets are 56" high. See plan on page 350 for location of these steel units. These cabinets were detailed by Hamilton Manufacturing Company for A. Lawrence Kocher and Albert Frey; Arthur Barzaghi, consulting engineer.

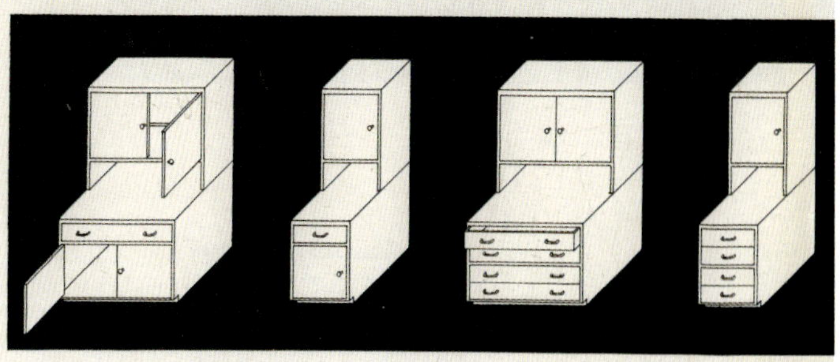

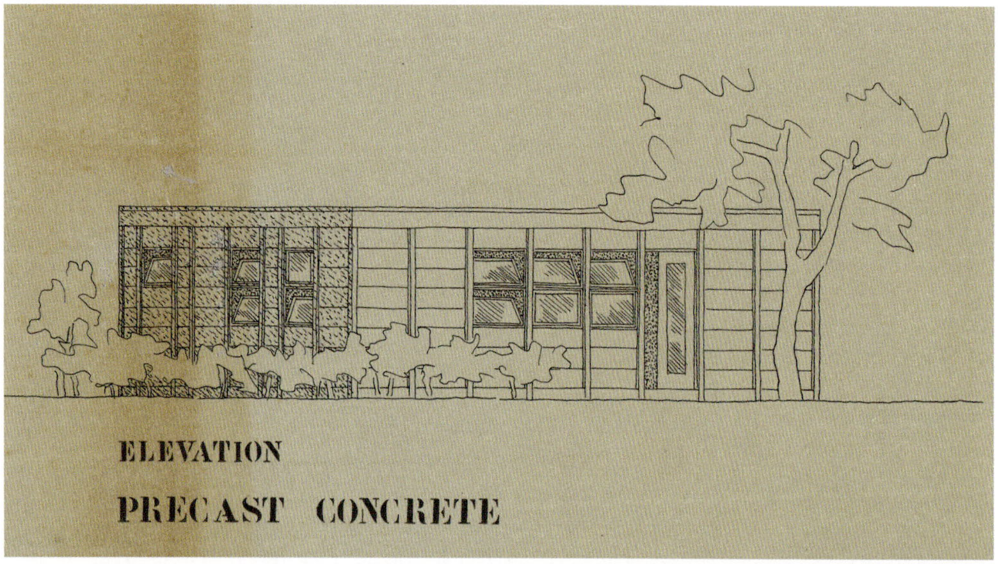

Figures 4.09 to 4.11.
A. Lawrence Kocher and Albert Frey. Subsistence Farmsteads. Original perspective views. Variations with different façade finishes: precast concrete, corrugated steel or asbestos-cement boards, and cinder blocks.

ture in Washington, D. C., from January through March 1934. There I designed minimal houses for farmers that they could build with the help of a carpenter—wood-frame buildings with flat roofs and corrugated metal siding.[24]

The work developed by Frey during these months was published in issue number 1738 (October 1934) of the *Farmer's Bulletin of the U.S. Department of Agriculture* alongside many other designs authored by the individual architects hired by the Bureau of Agricultural Engineering in the Department of Agriculture. Other design schemes were developed by the engineering and agriculture departments at various American universities, colleges, and institutes. All authors are credited in the drawing captions, unlike the anonymous designs in the Subsistence Homesteads Corporation bulletin.

Frey's designs included plan 6531 and, coauthored with R.G. Allen, plan 6532,[25] which stood out from the rest of the schemes as the only modern style with flat roofs and strictly modulated façades—all dimensions in the houses are multiples of three feet and six inches. Floor plan 6531 showed a layout in which bedrooms are set to one full length of the house— approximately one-third of the plan—and the remaining area is split in two for the living and service space. There are three porches in the house, one for each different area. The day-time area housed a living and dining room and a front porch; the night-time section includes three bedrooms with built-in closets, one complete bathroom, and a porch shared by two of the rooms. The service area has a kitchen, washroom, fuel and heater rooms, and a back porch that serves as a secondary entry through the washroom. Service and day-time areas are separated by a wall of storage that serves both sides, including a pass-through cupboard similar to the one in the Aluminaire House. The alignment of kitchen, heater, washroom, and bathroom reduces plumbing complexity and improves the efficiency of the water distribution. The heater is located two steps below the floor so plumbing can be easily assembled and accessed under the floor slab. Within the drawings, there were three perspectives of house 6531, each represented with a different façade finish. Moving from the top to the bottom of the page: the first façade uses a sheet-metal covering, the middle is composed with concrete blocks, and the last option applies a combination of lap siding and shingles or wide boards. With these options, the architect leaves open the option for the structure to be built using conventional methods or further simplified using pre-fabrication. In the second case, walls, partitions, windows, and doors can be prefabricated, therefore on-site construction would only involve bolting the prefab panels to the structure without need for skilled labor. **(Figures 4.1 to 4.3)**

If the previous 6531 house is compact and functional—in fact, quite conventional—house 6532 was even more experimental. This eagerness for innovation can be seen in the representational drawings for 6532: among all the designer schemes, it was the only house in the publication that included sections, a necessary means to explain its sophisticated spatial features. Experimentation follows two main directions in this design; first, the square footage of the house was increased while maintaining its footprint through the use of a complex sectional scheme. The partial B-B section through the bedrooms shows how the bunk beds and storage spaces stacked to take advantage of the clearance, creating a space for study desks near each window. Second, the design improved daylighting and ventilation inside the house by using clerestory windows over the central volume, including the living-dining room and bedroom hall, visible in partial section A-A. The U-shaped bedrooms and services wrapping around a central space was a scheme replicated in later projects, such as the Subsistence Farmsteads. Again, the heater is two steps below the ground floor level, eliminating the need for a basement, and construction could be done on site or prefabricated and assembled. **(Figure 4.4)**

Subsequent to these proposals for the U.S. Department of Agriculture, Frey returned to the office. Farm design had always been present in Kocher and Frey's office. For instance, during 1932, before Frey's European trip, he and Kocher had been developing different options to improve the flexibility of the 1931 Low-Cost Farmhouses. **(Figure 4.5)** Using this ever-expanding experience in low-cost farmhouse design, Kocher and Frey developed a new proposal for the Subsistence Farmsteads, published in the April 1934 issue of *Architectural Record.*[26] This monographic issue of the magazine was devoted to farm design and construction, and despite its generic title of "Better Homes as an Aid to Recovery," it featured a series of research articles by a diverse group of contributors. The article "Planning the Farm for Family Needs" by Maud Wilson from the Oregon State Agricultural College was especially compelling. It provided detailed drawings of storage units in bathrooms and kitchens, and measured sections and plans of auxiliary spaces like sewing rooms, walk-in closets, wardrobes, and dressers. There was also a survey of existing farm conditions and an extensive portfolio of farmhouses that included four houses developed by the Tennessee Valley Authority, and a selection of the U.S. Department of Agriculture low-cost farmsteads, including Frey's designs for 6531 and (collaborative) 6532. After this portfolio, Kocher and Frey cowrote an article, "Subsistence Farmsteads," where they outlined a detailed scheme—following the lead of the Subsistence Homesteads Program—for houses located on land owned by unemployed or underpaid urban workers wishing to grow their own produce. Ranging from the scale of a vegetable garden to a commercial farm, the farmsteads had to contain all the commodities of an urban apartment and accommodate light farming tasks. The exterior view suggested the presence of a greenhouse to help confront severe climates. Making it even more economical, the project was restricted to a single floor: rooms needed to be of a size that was perfectly adapted to the overall function within the building's limited footprint—small bedrooms were prescribed for spacious communal areas. The kitchen, storeroom, and laundry room formed a compact unit specifically suited to the uniquely contextual requirements of farm labor. As a programmatic and a technical requirement facilitating cross-ventilation, the warm zone of the kitchen had to be adjacent to the dining room, with its window to the vegetable garden. Under such strict requirements, the restroom was thoughtfully placed at the entrance for the workers returning from their vegetable gardens, and oriented so that the plumbing facilities could be grouped as closely as possible. Similarly, the house couldn't waste space in hallways or passages, so the rooms were adjacent and communicated directly through the living space. It had standardized closets from floor to ceiling, detailed in axonometric view in the publication. The closets were made of steel, because as stated by the

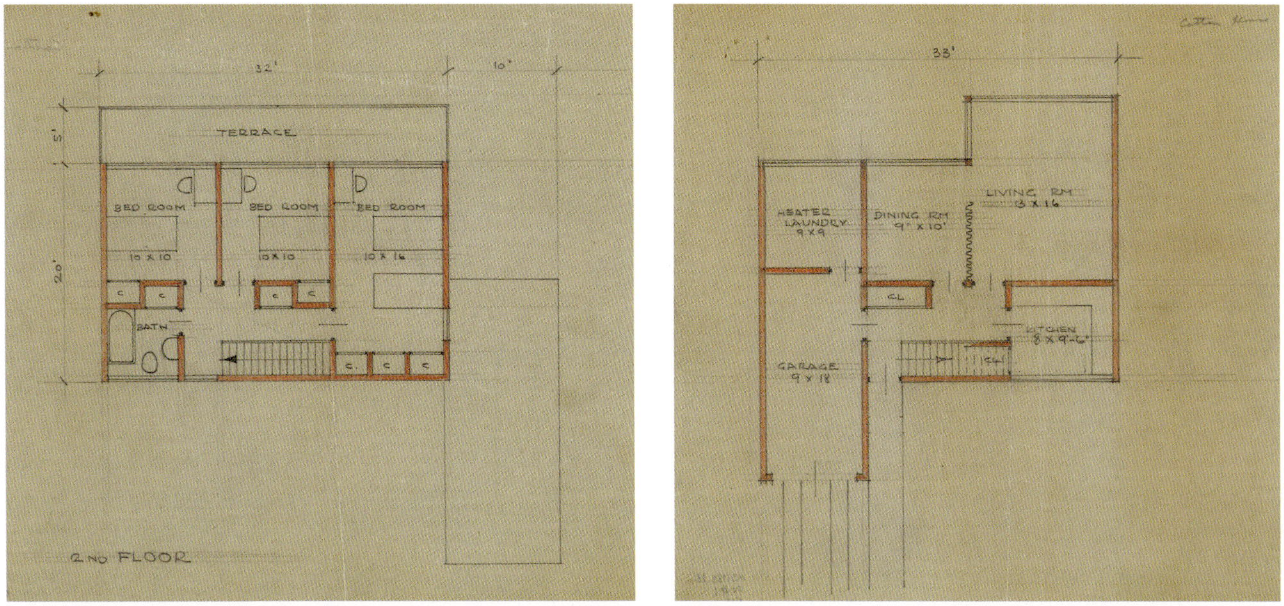

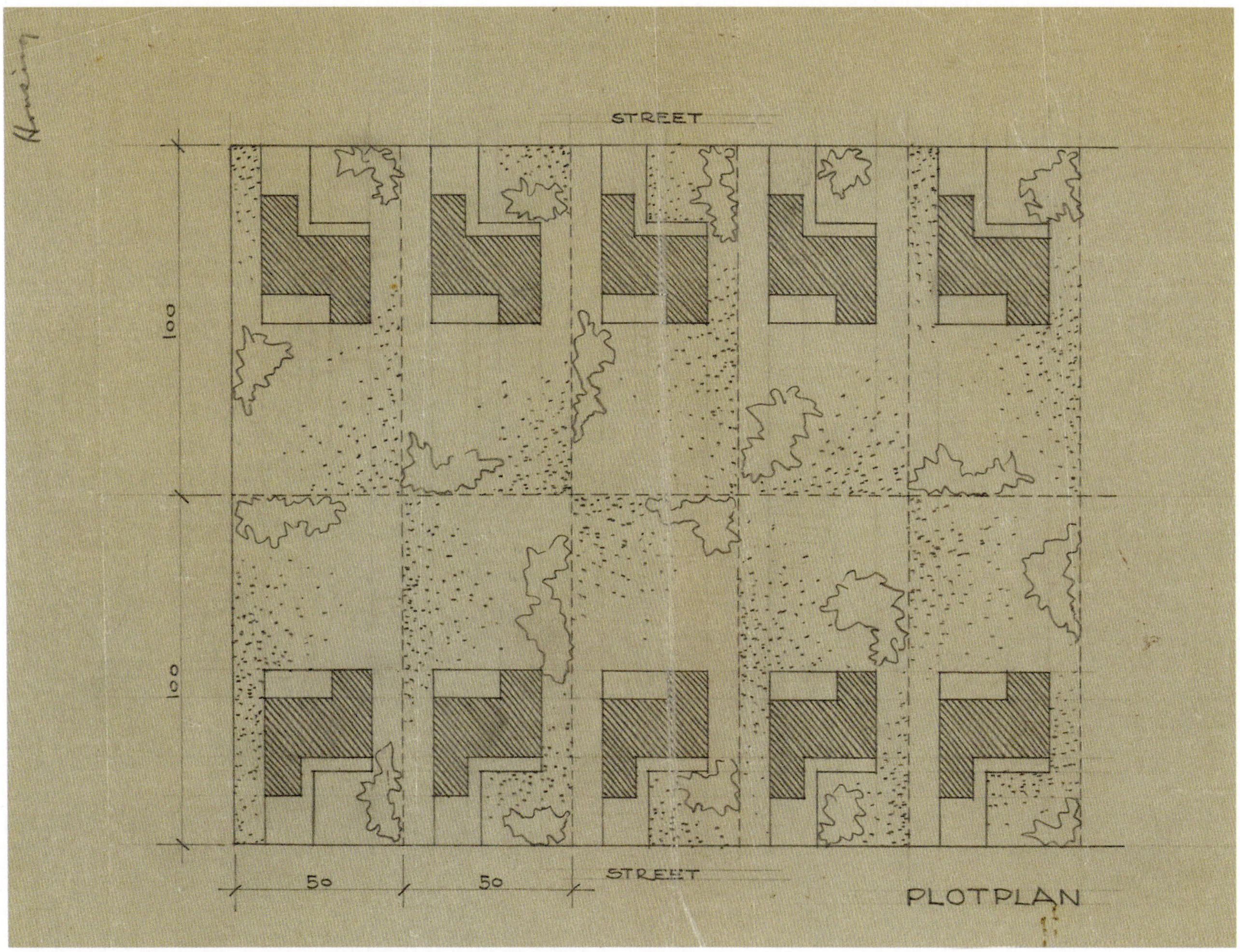

Figure 4.12. A. Lawrence Kocher and Albert Frey. 1934. Cotton Houses for the Cotton Textile Institute. Hybrid version beteen the Experimental Five-Room House (1932) and the Low-Cost Farmhouses (1931). Preliminary floor plans.
Figure 4.13. A. Lawrence Kocher and Albert Frey. 1934. Cotton Houses for the Cotton Textile Institute. Plot plan.

architects, in quantities over 200, it was more economical than wood construction. **(Figures 4.6 to 4.8)**

In the article, Kocher and Frey put forward proposals using five alternative systems of building technology for the farmsteads. The first proposal had similar cladding to that of the *Low-Cost Farmhouses* but replaced the structural system of steel bar trusses with six-inch rolled steel beams. In contrast, the second option featured a wood-framed structure and cotton cladding practically identical to the proposed systems for the Cotton-Steel Houses, later materialized in the Kocher Canvas Weekend House. There are two fire-proof options both with a precast concrete beam structure: one using concrete blocks as façade and roof material, the other built with inch-and-a-half-wide precast concrete panels. The last option used Z-shaped steel profiles for the structure and corrugated steel or asbestos boards for the decks and façades in a way that strongly resembled the constructive solutions developed one decade later during the Case Study House Program in California.[27] **(Figures 4.09 to 4.11)**

During the final months of 1934, the architects developed an unpublished two-story alternative version of the Experimental Five Room House. Capitalizing their findings from the farmhouses, they revamped the plan scheme of the precedent to design a Z-shaped plan with a central stair. The house included a garage, heater and laundry room, kitchen, and living-dining room on the first floor, with three bedrooms and one bathroom distributed on the second level. The plan's shape facilitated one terrace for each main façade. This version is allegedly a penultimate attempt to reactivate Kocher and Frey's proposals for the Cotton Textile Institute, directly linking them with the Subsistence Homestead Program.[28] **(Figures 4.12 to 4.19)**

Although it attracted a lot of attention among architects and was studied in several publications, the Subsistence Homestead Program was only a partial success.[29] Only 10,938 subsistence homes, of the targeted 25,000 families for relocation, were actually built in a handful of functional communities, such as Arthurdale and the African American community of Averdeen Gardens in Virginia, Westmoreland in Pennsylvania, Cumberland in Tennessee, and Tygert Valley in West Virginia.[30] Other projects were started but not completed, like Austin Acres in Minnesota; the subsistence homesteads near Birmingham, Alabama; El Monte in Los Angeles, California; Granger Homesteads in Iowa; Houston Gardens in Texas; Longview Homesteads in Washington; and Phoenix homesteads in Arizona. This also included the all-Jewish Jersey Homesteads in New Jersey, known today as the town of Roosevelt, designed by Alfred Kastner with the assistance of Louis Kahn.[31] After being transferred—first to the Resettlement Administration and then to the Farm Security Administration in the United States Department of Agriculture—the program officially ended in 1937. Following World War II, none of the Subsistence Homestead communities remained in public hands.

For Kocher and Frey's research-driven practice, the farmhouse designs were the vehicle to connect the dire needs dictated by their historical context with both modernity and vernacular American tradition. On the one hand, they pursued a close tie to the European modern movement exploring two essential aspects of their practice: functionalist design and rational construction using material and technological innovation. On the other hand, the connection to vernacular American architecture is achieved through the use of catalogs of prefabricated elements and systems, and the promotion of self-construction using mass-produced interchangeable parts, regarded by Kocher as a tradition in American practice.[32] This eagerness to connect with the American vernacular is evident in many other significant features of Kocher and Frey's farm-related domestic design. For instance, an unpublished drawing of Farmhouse type-A archived within the Kocher papers in Williamsburg shows a tentative color pattern in the façades that clearly link to Kocher's investigations about house painting in early American architecture.[33] Their experience with the Subsistence Homesteads Program helped the architects refine and redefine their design methodology, creating a cross-feed between publications, conference presentations, and constructed works. Conference papers and journal articles permitted them to explore and analyze different technological innovations and architectural configurations and establish a dialog with manufacturers, along with public and private research institutions. Building construction was, especially in Kocher's vision, not an end in itself, but a means for experimentation. The goal for construction was always to create prototypes to apply, test, assess, and disseminate the findings of their theoretical research, supported on the industry of building materials and construction technology. The farmhouses helped the architects to reinforce the concepts explored in the design of the Experimental Weekend House. After the Subsistence Farmsteads, Kocher and Frey's work was based on the idea of considering architecture as an *Ars Combinatoria*—an assemblage of ready-made pieces that form a coherent whole. These pieces could be chosen in an industry catalog, then transported and assembled by the owner with little or no intervention of external labor, resulting in complete design and budgetary control. This proposed architecture was formally akin to the custom prefabricated artifacts of Le Corbusier's modernism. It is also an architecture that now belongs as much to the tradition of American prefabricated housing as to the lineage of other alternative domestic solutions, like the motor cabin and the autocamp, where the thickness separating domesticity from nature is reduced to a minimum to achieve the fiction of mobility and the (then) idealized American notion of a transient way of life. This revolutionary vision of architecture was crystallized by Kocher and Frey in their 1935 Kocher Canvas Weekend House, thanks to the prototype efforts of the Experimental Weekend House and the farmstead designs. Built for Kocher as a holiday home on Long Island, Kocher Canvas Weekend House was the third house built by Kocher and Frey. The house serves as a key to understanding the evolution of North American modern architecture after the 1930s and the story of its design and construction is deeply related with the arrival in the U.S. of one of its main protagonists, Walter Gropius.

As previously indicated, Kocher benefited from notable prestige and influence in the early 1930s, when he was the managing editor of *Architectural Record.* He was recognized in academia and had already held the position of dean at the School of Architecture of Virginia University for two years. He was well known as a researcher with numerous prestigious publications about vernacular and modern architecture. This privileged position brought him into contact with Gropius. On their first visit to America in 1928, Ise and Walter Gropius met Kocher and his friend Robert L. Davison in the Plaza

This page:
Figure 4.14. A. Lawrence Kocher and Albert Frey. 1934. Cotton Houses for the Cotton Textile Institute. Final perspective view from the garden.
Figure 4.15. A. Lawrence Kocher and Albert Frey. 1934. Cotton Houses for the Cotton Textile Institute. Preliminary perspective view from the garden.

Next page:
Figure 4.16. A. Lawrence Kocher and Albert Frey. 1934. Cotton Houses for the Cotton Textile Institute. Street elevation.
Figure 4.17. A. Lawrence Kocher and Albert Frey. 1934. Cotton Houses for the Cotton Textile Institute. Garden elevation.

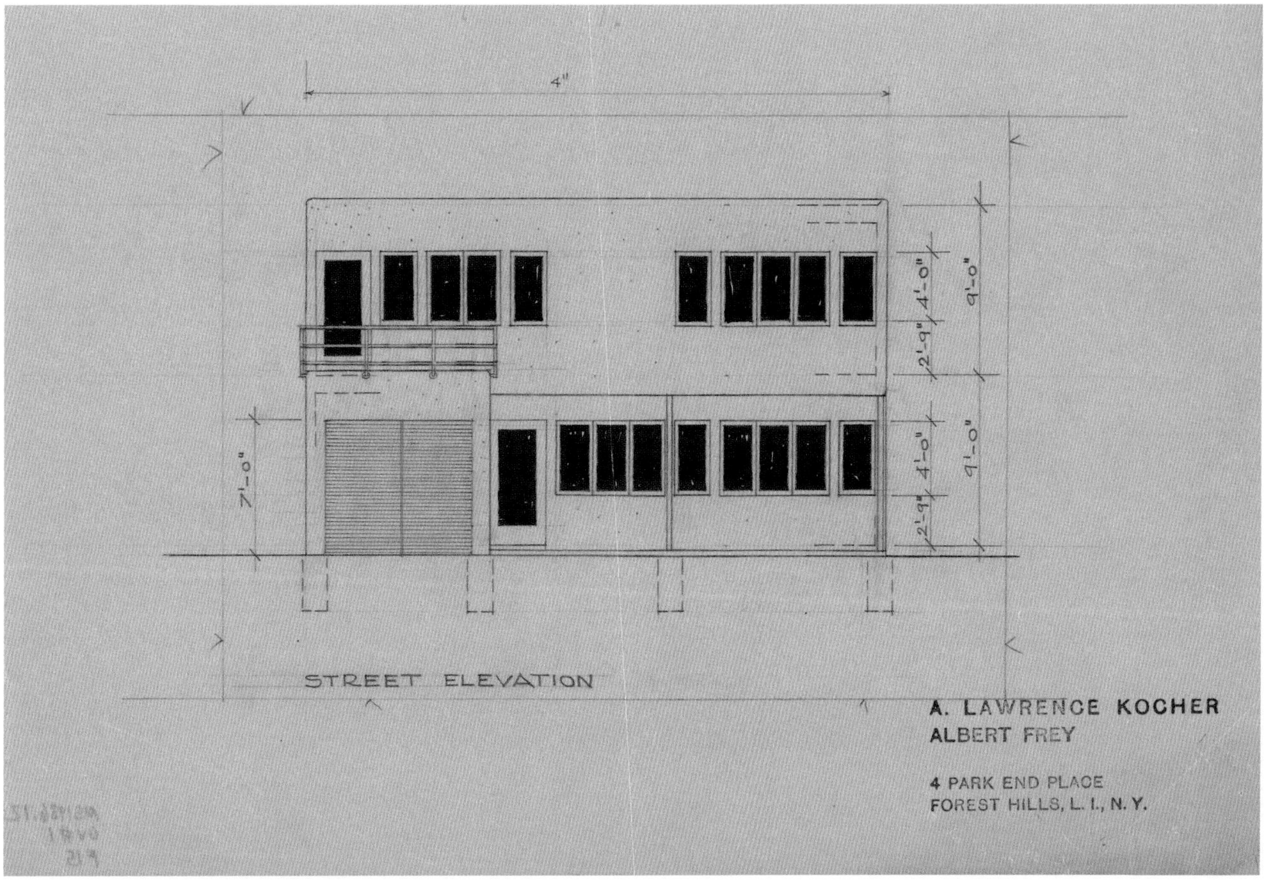
4"
2'-9"
4'-0"
9'-0"
7'-0"
STREET ELEVATION
A. LAWRENCE KOCHER
ALBERT FREY
4 PARK END PLACE
FOREST HILLS, L. I., N. Y.

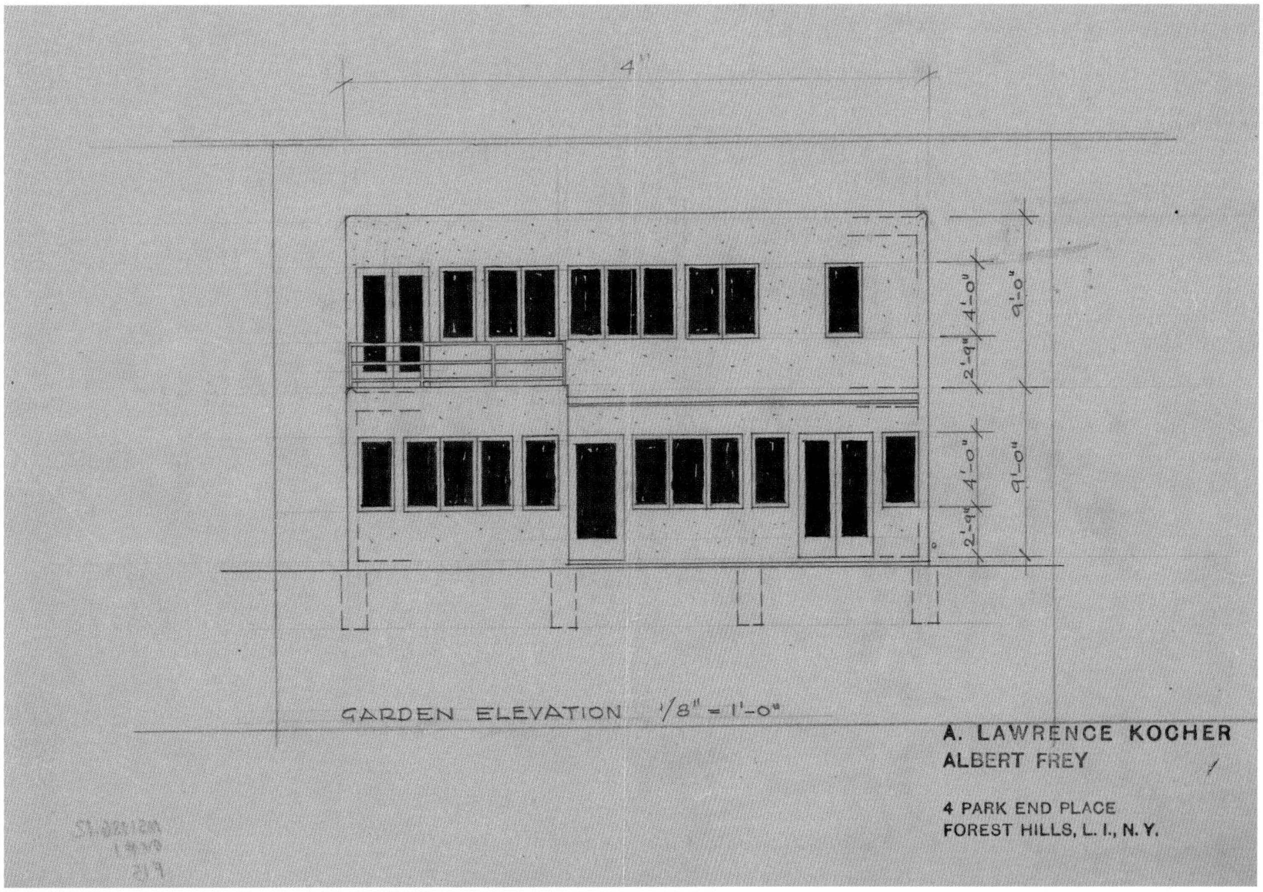
4"
2'-9"
4'-0"
9'-0"
GARDEN ELEVATION 1/8" = 1'-0"
A. LAWRENCE KOCHER
ALBERT FREY
4 PARK END PLACE
FOREST HILLS, L. I., N. Y.

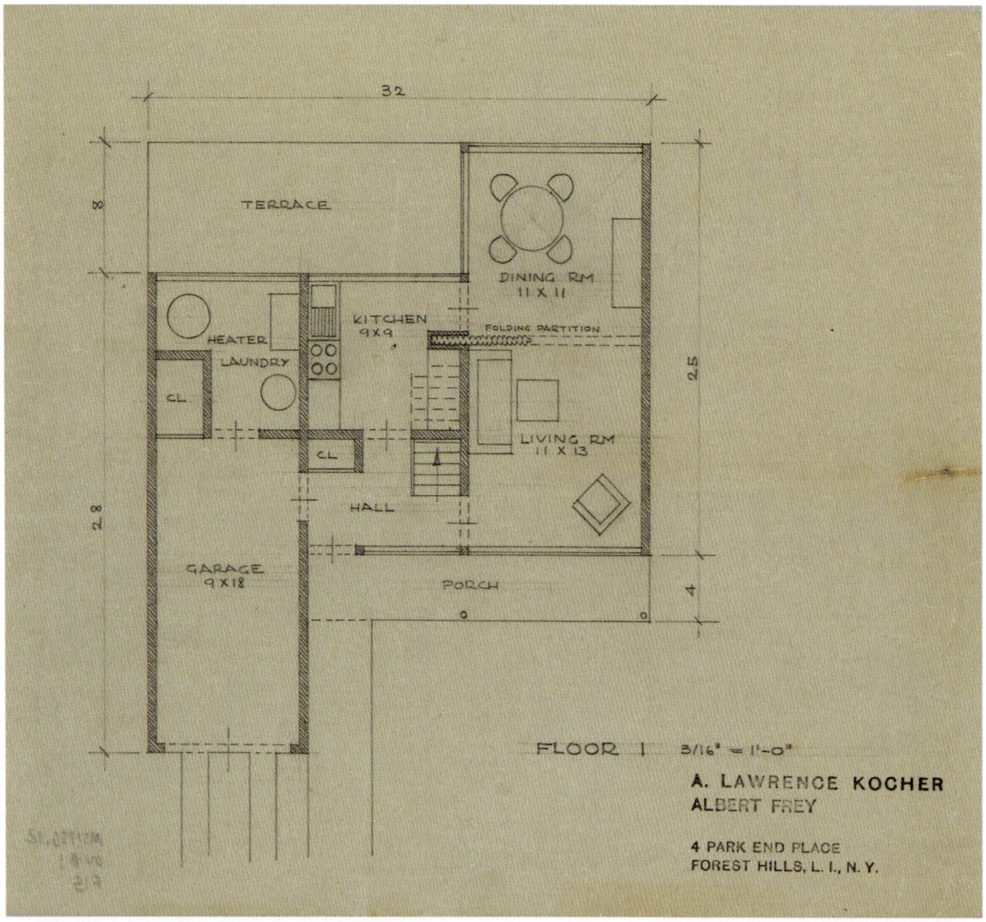

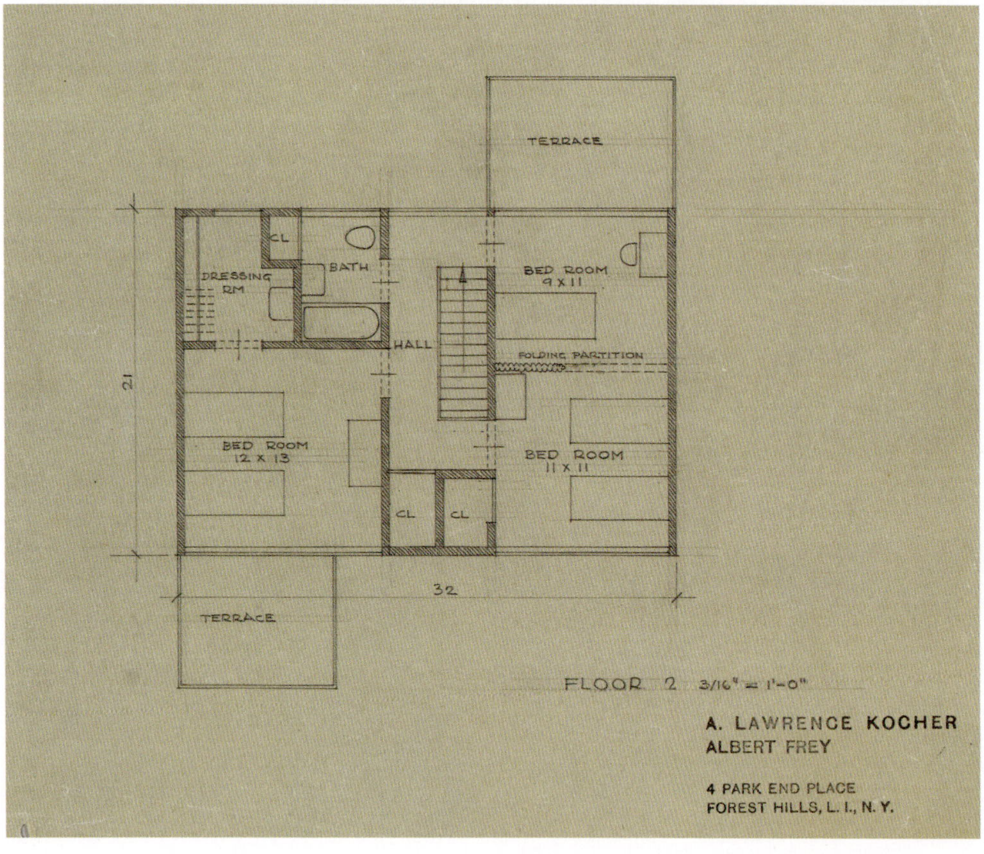

Figure 4.18. A. Lawrence Kocher and Albert Frey. 1934. Cotton Houses for the Cotton Textile Institute. First floor plan. Final version.

Figure 4.19. A. Lawrence Kocher and Albert Frey. 1934. Cotton Houses for the Cotton Textile Institute. Second floor plan. Final version.

Hotel in Manhattan at Gropius' request; their discussion continued via correspondence when Gropius returned to Europe. Eventually, Kocher left his position as dean to move to New York, where his first wife's severe illness could be treated. Nonetheless, he never gave up his academic interests and was maturing the idea of a new American architectural pedagogy that entailed a hands-on experience in construction and a closer relationship between industry, professional practice, and higher education. His building projects and the coming of the New Deal reactivated his plans around creating a new school of architecture that continued some of the pedagogical experiences of the Bauhaus. In Kocher's vision, Walter Gropius, founder and director of the Bauhaus until 1928, was the perfect candidate for this ambitious project.

In their epistolary exchanges in early 1934, Kocher actively encouraged Gropius to move to America, expressing the many opportunities that a life in the United States could offer the German architect. Initially, Gropius seemed willing to help bring the idea to fruition; he and Ise agreed to immigrate to the United States if Kocher would organize a series of conferences enabling Gropius to pay the cost of their stay.[34] Gropius also wrote to Kocher that it was necessary to do some teaching in an American school before starting his professional practice. In his own words:

> The circumstances for new architecture here are really not very advantageous and knowing all about the new building movement since more than twenty years I would incline to come over, trying to start an own atelier, but from the economical point of view I could do that only after having got a vocation for teaching, because I believe that one needs at least one year to get acquainted with the different professional conditions of the U.S.A. before starting a building job in a responsible manner.[35]

Thus, Kocher wrote to various deans of American architectural schools recommending Gropius. In a letter dated May 22, 1934, Kocher told Gropius that he was negotiating with Joseph Hudnut of Columbia University about bringing him on as a professor.[36] Kocher and Hudnut were close; Kocher was recommended by Fiske Kimball to succeed Hudnut at the University of Virginia, who resigned to become dean of the School of Architecture at Columbia University and later became the first dean of the Harvard Graduate School of Design (GSD).

Simultaneously, Kocher maintained updates with Gropius about his own plans for the new school. In a letter from April 16, Kocher gave an introduction to the topic saying that he was also willing to enroll Antonin Raymond, who was then practicing in Japan, as member of the faculty and invited Gropius to join the future endeavor. Raymond arrived in Japan in 1920 as Frank Lloyd Wright's assistant on the construction of the Imperial Hotel of Tokyo. Upon completion, Raymond remained in the country and was at the peak of his professional career in 1934. His works were published during that year in *Architectural Record*.[37] Kocher probably found that Raymond's integration of modernity and traditional crafts, and his reassessment of the highly standardized Japanese vernacular of detailing in timber, were very compatible with his own architectural ideals. Gropius responded with a letter on May 9, showing his approval for moving to the U.S. to develop his practice and his ideas about architectural education. Nevertheless, he wanted to hear more details before committing:

> But just because of my and rather far-reaching experience in this matter I know the great difficulty of a new foundation and that's why I should like to hear more details about Mr. A. Raymond and about your ideas concerning the new institute so that I get an impression about the whole atmosphere out of which you approach the problem.[38]

In the same letter, Gropius inquired about the financial details of the project and finished expressing his pre-eagerness to collaborate. Kocher's response was a very long letter on May 29, in which he explained many of the particulars of his plan: he had "already secured acreage about 40 miles from New York City where such school and work center could be located," and had plans to staff it with a small group of six to eight renowned architects that, "while working in group, would also possess, for each, an independence."[39]. Kocher's plan included the construction of a new building for the school. Raymond was even willing to invest in the construction of the school as Kocher states in his letter, "since [Raymond] has proposed coming to this country and he intends, if plans mature, to spend about $30,000 on the start of a building."[40] Kocher also expected the new school would work closely together with manufacturers and was confident that the industry would conversely assist with building construction. Actually, Kocher had purchased several plots of heavily wooded land in New York's Fort Salonga, Long Island, where he planned to establish the headquarters of the new school of architecture.

Kocher concluded the letter with the recommendation that Gropius consider lecturing at different architecture schools, instead of a more stable commitment to retain his freedom for pursuing a professional practice. This of course was a way of trying to avoid that other universities hired Gropius and therefore difficulted the inclusion of the German architect in Kocher's new school.

In the last letter of this series—dated July 7, 1934—Gropius communicated his willingness to relocate to the United States and participate in Kocher's academic project. The German architect offered one last and thoughtful piece of advice to Kocher.[41] In Gropius' own words:

> My long experiences in Germany, running the Bauhaus, taught me that it would be the best, to try to start workshops as laboratories which are paid directly by the industry, filled with the best skilled workmen, but headed by independent architects gifted both for design and Technik. So the students of Architecture could be taught in a creative sense as well in the offices for design as in the laboratory workshops of the school, always sticking to the very practice instead of a platonic curriculum. So the task of the institute ought to held two lines, as practical laboratory work for the industry and in teaching the rising generation in modern architecture, one supporting the other.[42]

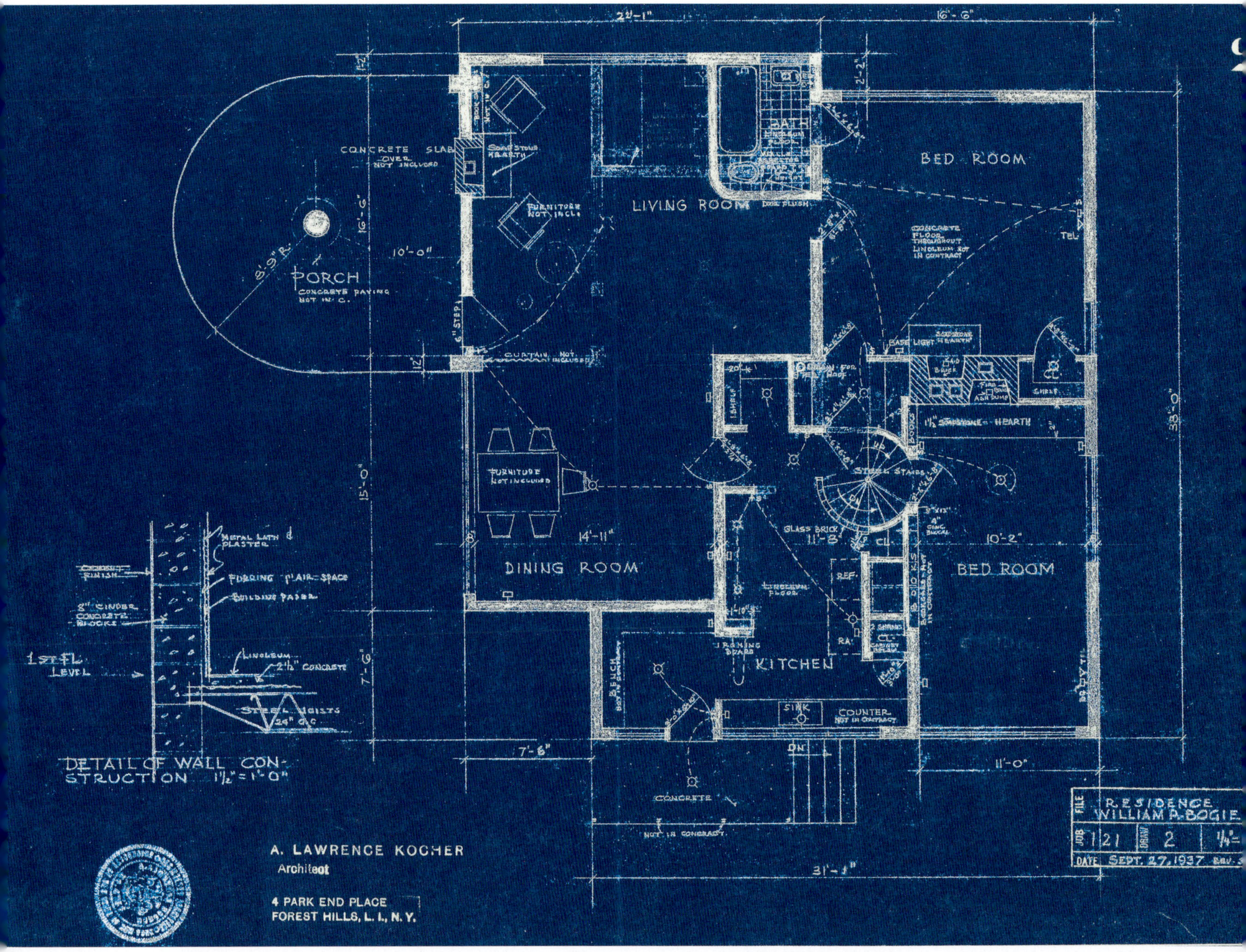

This page:
Figure 4.20. A. Lawrence Kocher. 1937. Bogie House. Dated 9-27-37. First floor plan.

Next page:
Figure 4.21. A. Lawrence Kocher. 1937. Bogie House. Dated 9-27-37. Section.
Figure 4.22. A. Lawrence Kocher. 1937. Bogie House. Dated 9-27-37. Elevations.

Gropius adds that this institute may be a key instrument to achieve an old dream of his: the mass fabrication of machine-made houses. For this end, he does not see a better-prepared country than the U.S., for "in no other country people seems prepared to accept houses from stock, as Sears Roebuck and Montgomery Ward ran that job for a long time for wooden country houses."[43] He ends the letter with a reference to the inauguration of an exhibition about his work in London that would soon change the course of events for Kocher and his dreamed American Bauhaus.

Gropius was invited to organize an exhibition of his work in the Royal Institute of British Architects, and to deliver lectures in London and Leeds. The exhibition was prepared in April 1934 and held from May 15th through 26th. During his visit to the United Kingdom (U.K.), Gropius received an invitation by Jack Pritchard and Maxwell Fry to start a practice, which included a commission to design an apartment building in Manchester associated with Fry. Gropius ultimately decided to leave an increasingly nazified Germany and establish a practice in the U.K., considering it a temporary haven closer to home and to his daughter Manon, who lived in Vienna while receiving aggressive treatment for polio. Despite the understanding that Gropius would not participate in his idea of a new American Bauhaus, Kocher kept working to secure him a position in the U.S. academia.[44] By the end of 1934, Kocher had contacted at least 12 American Universities to recommend an appointment for Gropius, among them, Harvard, Cornell, Yale, Princeton, the University of Minnesota, and the Massachusetts Institute of Technology (MIT).[45] Kocher was also very active promoting Gropius in *Architectural Record*; between 1928 and 1936, more than 10 illustrated articles referring to the architect appeared in the magazine, making the journal's readership very aware of his merits and of his most recent body of work. After Gropius' decision to remain in England, Kocher partially abandoned his plan to establish a new school, selling off several plots of the land purchased near Northport.

The situation in Germany worsened, and Manon died in April 1935, liberating Gropius from any remaining European ties. When Hudnut was appointed as the dean of the newly founded Harvard GSD in 1936, he hired Gropius as a professor for the following academic year, and subsequently promoted him to the role of Director of the Architecture Department. Gropius accepted the professorship appointment at Harvard in November of 1936 and left the U.K. to arrive in the U.S. on March 12th, 1937. Gropius' position at Harvard created a path precipitating the emigration of other renowned German architects, and definitively changed the practice of teaching architecture in America.[46] The relevance for the history of American architecture in this initial contact between Kocher and Walter Gropius has been underscored by scholars like Margaret Kentgens-Craig:

> Kocher's recommendation and persistence may be credited with Hudnut's appointment of Gropius at Harvard. Even if no other contacts established by the Bauhaus' founder had led to immediate results, Lawrence Kocher...was able to establish good relations with the various universities and to create opportunities for the dissemination of Bauhaus architecture.[47]

As the Bauhaus was more than a school—it also encompassed an experiment in living—Kocher focused on a second aim of his initial pedagogical plan: to establish a colony of experimental houses similar to the professors' houses at the Bauhaus of Dessau. His own contribution to this colony was the Kocher Canvas Weekend House. While the construction of the house was underway, Kocher convinced three families to buy lots in the colony and build modern houses on them, creating the Fort Salonga Colony of Experimental Houses. The buyers were Robert L. Davison, a former coworker at *Architectural Record*; Subhi Sadi, a bachelor friend of Davison; and William and Betty Bogie, neighbors and friends of the Kochers in Forest Hills Gardens.[48] Unfortunately, Kocher did not have the opportunity to build any of the colony houses. He did produce a set of preliminary drawings for the Bogie House; dated in September 1937 and reviewed in March of 1938, they show that the lot had a substantial change in grade. This fact allowed Kocher to design a small home distributed across three half levels. The entry happened through a circular porch situated in the upper grade, supported by a central circular concrete column, which connected directly to the intermediate level containing a living-dining room, kitchen, one bedroom, and one bathroom. The vertical circulation between the three levels was directed through a spiral stair situated in a small hall between the bedroom and the kitchen. The steps connected with a study-bedroom space situated a half-level upstairs and downstairs with the garage, a workroom, a dark room, and a small shop. The building technology was very straightforward: load-bearing concrete block walls with a cement exterior finish and plastered metal lath inside, supported by open-web steel joist floors and roofs. Although they were very fond of Kocher's ideas, the Bogies wanted something simpler and inexpensive, like a cabin in the woods, so they politely rejected Kocher's scheme and decided to design the house by themselves, acting as general contractors over the construction. **(Figures 4.20 to 4.22)**

The remaining two houses were designed by Davison's partner, the architect John Callender. The Davison and Sadi houses consisted of an assembly of two, four-room square test houses previously built for the Pierce Foundation and exhibited in Long Island City and the Grand Central Palace. The test houses were disassembled, trucked to the site, and stacked one on top of the other. The two levels of the house overlapped only in one quarter of the floor plan, leaving room for a porch and a garage underneath while also creating a terrace on the second floor. The original test houses were built with four-inch-thick Microporite boards and plywood made with non-waterproof glue, since it was constructed to be a study model and not meant to be exposed to the elements. To make the house watertight, cotton fabric was adhered to the façades and decks with a latex cement and then painted with Tornsite, a chlorinated rubber—a solution similar to that of the Kocher Canvas Weekend House.[49] Wanting to move back to America, Antonin Raymond and his wife, Noemi, also purchased a piece of land from Kocher in 1935, but they never built a house as they established their practice and a workshop on a farm in New Hope, Pennsylvania, in 1940.[50]

The only house designed entirely by Kocher and Frey that was built on the colony was the Kocher Canvas Weekend House. **(Figure 4.23)** Kocher supervised the construction of the house without Frey,

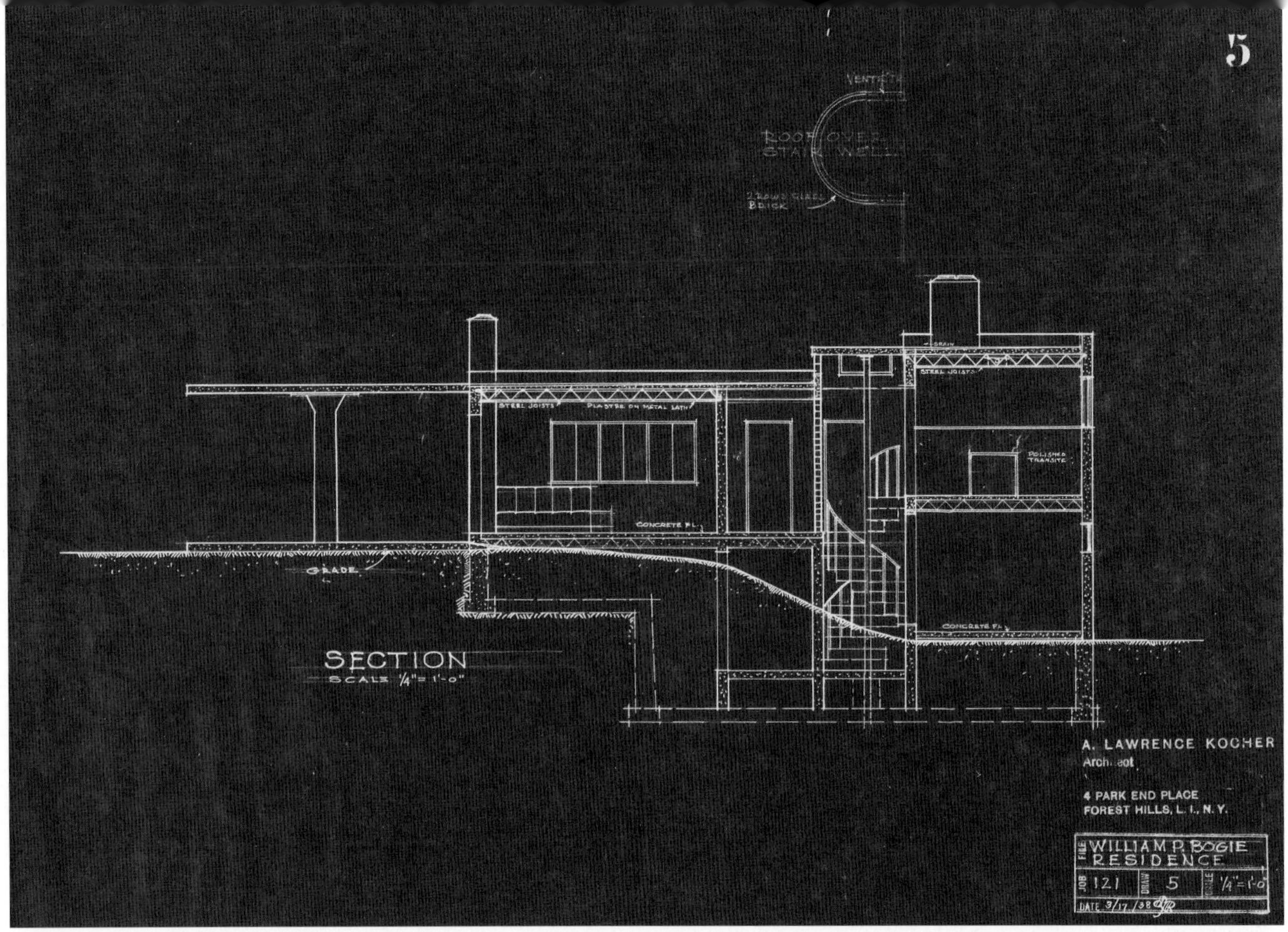
5
ROOF OVER STAIR WELL
STEEL JOISTS
CONCRETE FL.
GRADE
SECTION
SCALE 1/4" = 1'-0"
A. LAWRENCE KOCHER
Architect
4 PARK END PLACE
FOREST HILLS, L. I., N. Y.
WILLIAM P. BOGIE RESIDENCE
121
5
1/4" = 1'-0"

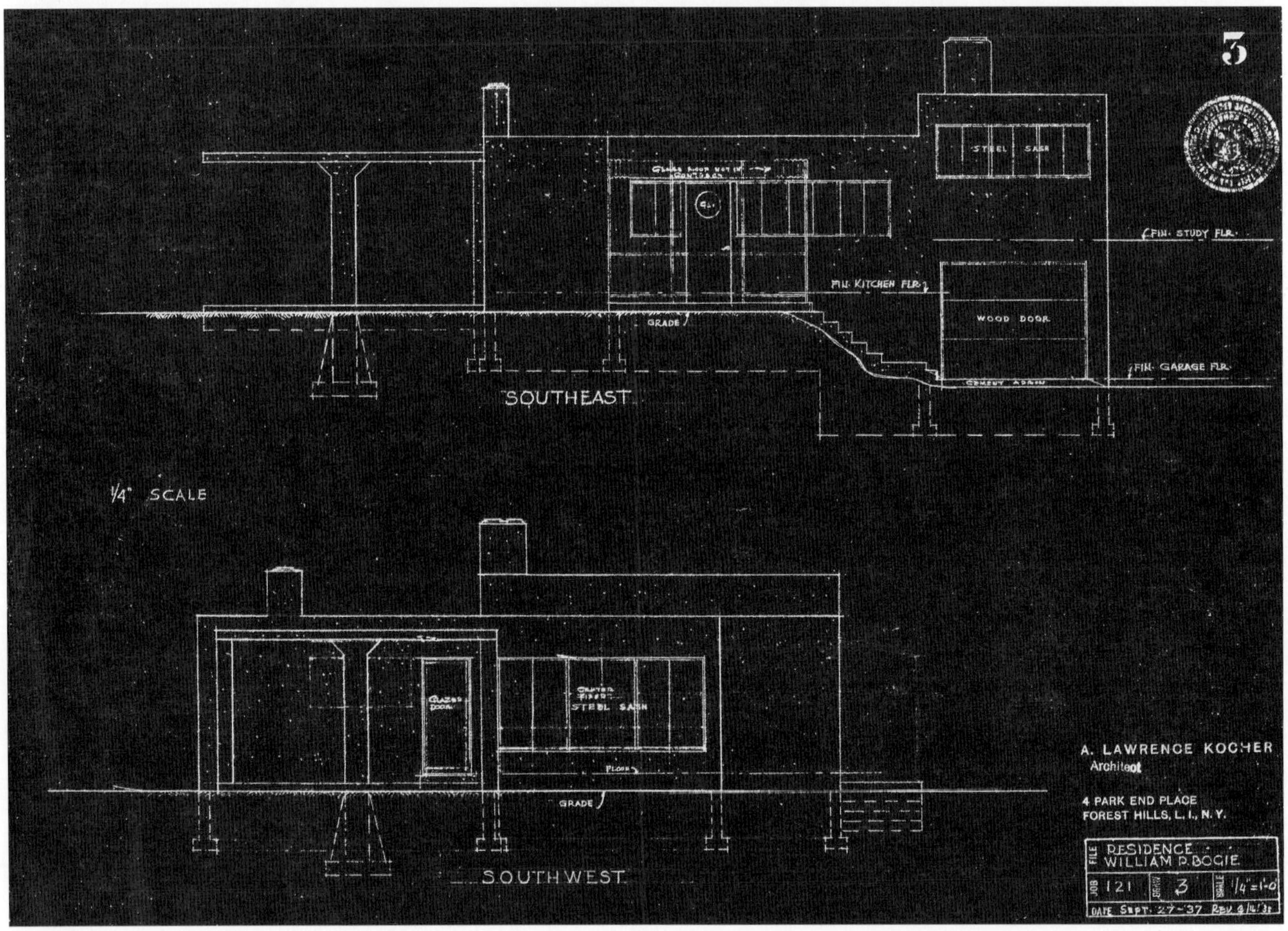
3
STEEL SASH
FIN. STUDY FLR.
FIN. KITCHEN FLR.
WOOD DOOR
FIN. GARAGE FLR.
GRADE
SOUTHEAST
1/4" SCALE
GLAZED DOOR
STEEL SASH
GRADE
SOUTHWEST
A. LAWRENCE KOCHER
Architect
4 PARK END PLACE
FOREST HILLS, L. I., N. Y.
RESIDENCE WILLIAM P. BOGIE
121
3
1/4" = 1'-0"

who was away overseeing the construction of a mixed-use building for Kocher's brother in Palm Springs, California. The Kocher Canvas Weekend House was the second built house in the collaborative series by Kocher and Frey designed for a specific location: a plot of land on the north of Long Island, one mile from the coast and 30 miles from the Kocher family's primary residence. The lot is described in publications as having been covered in cedar forest and slightly swampy.[51] The roughly square plan was oriented approximately 45 degrees, pointing its corners to the cardinal directions. A near replica of the Experimental Weekend House prototype, the house had slightly more generous dimensions, measuring 20 feet, six inches, by 23 feet, 10 inches, and featured the familiar prefabricated spiral staircase that provided access to all floors. **(Figures 4.24 and 4.25)** The structure used four-inch-diameter steel pillars embedded three feet into the ground through reinforced concrete foundations to support a primary structure of wooden double beams. The exterior face of the balloon frame was enclosed using wooden boards arranged on the diagonal, providing lateral bracing. At the fully glazed southern corner, its windows met a low wall and extended to the roof where they were protected by projecting, roll-up awnings, which were installed in 1936—after the published photos. On the façades, which joined to form the northern corner, there was only a door and a two small windows for the kitchen and bathroom. The majority of the home's windows, supplied again by the Truscon Steel Company, were fixed. Only the windows in the bathroom, kitchen and central south-west façade could be opened. Cross-ventilation could be achieved with only these minimal openings. Process images of the house, published in Alfred Roth's book *The New Architecture*, show that construction of the deck was extremely conventional, with the wooden joists braced using diagonal crosses—a typical feature of balloon frames.[52] **(Figures 4.26 to 4.32)**

Meanwhile, the exterior façades and roof were finished with lead paint, water- and fire-proofed cotton canvas applied horizontally from bottom to top and fixed with copper-headed nails every six inches. The walls were insulated with an intermediate layer of aluminum foil; rock-wool insulation was used in the ceiling and floor cavities of the main level. The interior walls were plywood boards finished with cotton canvas. Described in various publications, yet impossible to appreciate in the black-and-white photographs of the time, façades were painted with aluminum paint and used color in unique places.[53] The window frames were painted red to match the color of the awnings; the pillars, handrails, and rooftop solarium were painted green. In the case of the solarium, the color choice helped avoid any glare caused by the reflection of sunlight. In contrast, the materials on the interior were left in their natural state. This profusion of color was a completely distinctive trait of the house and contrasted with the sober monochrome palette of the Aluminaire House. **(Figures 4.33 to 4.37)**

Contrasting the spatial complexity of the Aluminaire House, the arrangement of the internal spaces of the Kocher Canvas Weekend House was very simple; like the Experimental Weekend House, the kitchen and bath were the only walled-off areas. Apart from the two walled zones, the rest of the house consisted of flexible space divided by furniture and curtains pulled from a central post along tracks on the ceiling. Program was contained in a reduced single volume without double-height rooms, a spatiality much closer to that of a log cabin, a box house, or even a camping tent or trailer than to the more intricate section of the Aluminaire House. **(Figure 4.38)** This simplicity in spatial distribution was perfectly adapted to the project's aim: to create a refuge among nature, a place to escape to on weekends and vacations, away from the hustle and bustle of city life. Kocher recalled the use of the house in a letter from the late '60s:

> In our age of pressures of city life (1930s-on) there has been a need for relief, such as is afforded by a close contact with the sea-shore, woods or mountains. The weekend house was conceived as an answer to such a need, and the site on Long Island (near Northport) was convenient for our family, then living in Forest Hills Gardens, a short distance from the Long Island parkways. We had a five-acre lot, which provided privacy and garden space for outdoor dining. The house being elevated ensured freedom from dampness and discouraged the pilferage and break-ins experienced by some of our neighbors during periods of absence.[54]

Although the house was designed as a weekend abode when the Kochers lived in Queens, this use changed almost immediately. The family moved first to Asheville, North Carolina, when Lawrence became a member of the teaching staff at Black Mountain College, and then to Williamsburg, Virginia, where Kocher worked on the restoration of the first state capital and taught at William and Mary University. As a result of these transitions, they converted the Kocher Canvas Weekend House into a summer residence. Kocher's wife would later insist on the fact that the house's elevated position on the pillars corresponded to the need for security in a building that was only occupied sporadically, as occurred in other classic, compact villas.[55]

In line with its precedents of mobile dwelling, the lived experience of the house was closer to camping than the typical American domestic life for Kocher; his wife, Margaret, and their two children, Larry and Sandra. In an interview with the researcher Caroline Rob Zaleski, Kocher's daughter gave an account of everyday life in the house, which lacked electricity, running water, and a telephone.[56] The Kochers would cook on a barbecue in the open air, and when it rained, they cooked inside over a kerosene burner. They drew their water from a nearby well using a hand pump, and lit the house using kerosene lamps. Parked in the shade of the house, the trunk of the car was at once the larder and the refrigerator. To operate the shower and toilet cisterns, they would haul buckets of water from the well. Thoughtfully designed, the house was transformed from day to night using the sliding curtains and moving furniture. During active hours, the beds were used as sofas and the aluminum-painted curtains were drawn inward to the central post. This post also contained the drain that collected rainwater from the roof terrace, creating a diaphanous living area for the entire family. At night, the beds were returned to their positions and curtains divided the space into three bedrooms. The exterior needed no curtains as privacy was ensured due to the raised position of the house, but red canvas awnings provided protection from the sun. The building, with its textile walls and roofs, wooden substructure, and semi-cylindrical white canvas roof

Figure 4.23. A. Lawrence Kocher and Albert Frey. 1934–1935. Kocher Canvas Weekend House. Long Island, New York. Photo of the original house. Exterior view.

Figure 4.24. A. Lawrence Kocher and Albert Frey. 1934–1935. Kocher Canvas Weekend House. Long Island, New York. Lateral elevation.

sunshades resembled a prairie schooner wagon amid the Long Island forests more than it appeared to be a conventional house. Despite its image of functionality, the house needed continuous maintenance. To get the house ready for the summer, the Kochers needed to erect a scaffolding every spring to replace or reinstall the red awnings and add a new layer of paint to both the façade and decks of the house.

Profusely disseminated both through national and international publications and exhibitions, the house was praised for its innovative use of cotton and its "severe rationalism, stringently utilitarian forms, rejection of tradition and traditional materials, and its uncompromising 'machine-age' aesthetics."[57] Nevertheless, the descriptions offered by the inhabitants of the house contradict the version offered in the various publications of the work. In these publications, it is explained that the house is equipped with electric power, water supply, hot water, electric stoves, and refrigerator.[58] The reality was more basic and even purposedly precarious. In fact, the house was later expanded by Kocher himself. In 1936, he added a ground-level volume, not fully connected to the original house, built from concrete blocks and glass-brick windows. The purpose of this volume is muddled in the various accounts offered by the house's inhabitants. Kocher's wife explained in a letter that the volume was occupied by the new "mechanical systems" of the house.[59] Meanwhile, the couple's daughter called it a "guest house" and said that it contained a basic ice chest.[60] It seems improbable that the volume could house guests, due to the arrangement and composition of the windows. In some photos a metallic chimney can be seen rising from the roof of the volume, causing speculation that it was, indeed, made to house mechanical systems. **(Figure 4.39)** The appearance of this addition is a sign of dysfunction and the difficulty of amending the design to provide the level of comfort required by its inhabitants. It is, therefore, a first indication of its imminent obsolescence as a technical object. **(Figures 4.40 to 4.43)** Probably the reason for these discrepancies—between the published idealization and the reality—was precisely the need to present the house as a modern machine for living with a built-in cutting-edge technology, when in fact it was no more than a basic shelter, much closer to a camping tent than to a modern Corbusian villa. The lot was later sold by the Kochers, and the house was demolished by a developer in the late 1950s.

Simultaneously with the construction of the Kocher Canvas Weekend House, Kocher and Frey were building their first project in California and their last as professional partners. Paradoxically, in keeping with the kind of loose partnership they always shared, the amicable dissolution of the professional practice of Kocher and Frey was not due to the scarcity of work, but on the contrary, to the receipt of this new commission in June 1934. John Jacob Kocher, M.D., Kocher's brother in Palm Springs, was the first and only physician practicing when the town was still a little desert village at the base of the San Jacinto mountains, a two-hour drive east of Los Angeles. Palm Springs was rapidly developing at that time, popularized by movie stars and their residences in the early 1930s. Dr. Kocher visited his brother during the summers in Forest Hills, and he commissioned the architectural duo to design a building to include an apartment on the upper floor, along with real estate and insurance offices for his company, Kocher and Samson Insurance Service, at street level. When the pair finished drawings for the Kocher-Samson Building, Kocher remained in New York and Frey drove west in October 1934 with the project drawings, stopping first in Pittsburgh, to finalize the layout of the structural steel decking material they were proposing for the second floor and roof of the building from the H. H. Robertson Company.[61] The plan was that while Kocher was building his own weekend house in Long Island, Frey would be in charge of supervising the Kocher-Samson Building in Palm Springs. **(Figures 4.44 to 4.48)**

The site was a typical narrow and deep business plot. Because of its narrow lot shape and because both sides of the building would be eventually built on, Kocher and Frey decided to arrange all the spaces to open internally to a series of enclosed gardens and covered terraces. The gardens and primary covered terrace had the exact size and proportion—12 by 12 feet—as the consultation offices, creating a solid-void checkerboard arrangement on the first floor based on a three-foot square modulation. **(Figures 4.49 to 4.53)** Probably overwhelmed by the desert nature of the land, the architects gave special attention to climatic considerations in the project, dividing the local weather into three main seasons. During the months of April, May, September, and October, the temperatures varied from warm to hot. In summer, the weather got extremely hot with temperatures as high as 115 degrees Fahrenheit. The remaining months of November through March had warm days and cool nights. Their complete analysis included the presence of scarce rain, complete absence of frost, possible sandstorms, and prevalent north and northwest cool winds happening almost daily with occasional gusts. According to these hydrothermal parameters, Kocher and Frey decided to use a passive environmental strategy, assisting air circulation by cross-ventilating all spaces. This was achieved through the use of windows and a complex system that combined ventilation—by both gravity and wind—through the airspace in the hollow concrete blocks of the walls and between the double-layered roofs. **(Figures 4.54 to 4.61)** Using the orientation and the vegetation of the gardens, the offices opened to the north and east, creating a maximum of shaded areas and protecting all windows from solar radiation. Each garden had a sprinkler at pavement level to produce humidity and coolness by evaporation. Containing a reception room that faced North Palm Canyon Drive, an extension of the highway to Los Angeles, the west front needed to be fully glazed for commercial purposes. Solar gain was mitigated with a front garden and the cantilever of the second floor, which also provided a gently shaded entrance. The connection between the office's various spaces always happened outdoors under the cover of the terrace, creating fluid interior–exterior relationships and a blurred perception of the building's internal boundaries that can be perceived in the published photographs. This environmental strategy also allowed the building to have limited waste in heating, which was solved by using mechanically produced and distributed warm air for the reception and apartment zones, and individually vented gas heaters for the private offices.

The Kocher-Samson Building's second floor was considered essential not only to insulate and shade the rooms below, but also because the vertical size of the building could be used as prime advertisement space, given its high-visibility adjacency to a major road. The architects strategically placed the company name in steel letters on the plain wall facing the street. Inside, the volume hosts

Figure 4.25. A. Lawrence Kocher and Albert Frey. 1934–1935. Kocher Canvas Weekend House. Long Island, New York. Photo of the original house. Spriral stair.

a single-bedroom apartment with two clearly differentiated areas: limiting the property, there is a narrow strip of service spaces adjacent to the south wall that includes the kitchen, dining room, and bathroom; the north area of the apartment has a vestibule, a living room, and a bedroom. The living room is separated from the bedroom by a sliding partition and from the dining room by an oiled silk curtain. The living room and the bedroom open to the north terrace though a large floor-to-ceiling window. A spiral stair connects the first-floor covered terrace with a second, smaller upper terrace to give access to the apartment. The materials inside the apartment are modern but luxurious looking. All partitions are faced with mahogany plywood and the kitchen has built-in flush-surface steel cabinets. The floors are finished in a neutral sand-colored linoleum. To avoid fine sand penetration during storms in the desert climate of Palm Springs, the joints of the building ought to be tight, with all sash weather-stripped with felt. Large fabric awnings had to be avoided because of the frequent wind gusts; the covering and shading devices are therefore sturdier, composed of a steel structure and a roof deck.

The construction of the building was twofold in nature: the first floor worked as an anti-seismic damper with load-bearing walls built using six-inch concrete blocks with vertical steel rods every six feet, tied to lintels and footings. All of the corners and wall ends are poured reinforced concrete. A continuous concrete bonding beam, eight to 12 inches in height and the same width of concrete blocks, runs over all walls, windows, and doors for a completely rigid frame to prevent any torquing during earthquakes. On the other hand, the second floor was built with a light, pressed-steel frame prefabricated into truck-transportable-size pieces, then electro-welded together on site.[62] All the roofs and floors in the Kocher-Samson Building are 18-gauge steel Robertson Keystone beams, left exposed in all ceilings. The floors are supported by bond beams over the walls and intermediate I-beams. Two steel pipe columns are necessary to supplement the walls in open corners, helping avoid any torsion in the upper beams. A steel tie-rod cross-bracing system was necessary for the street façade of the reception room. A small restroom enclosed with cement block walls in the southeast corner of this volume completes the bracing of the reception room's back façade. The roofs are insulated with one-and-a-half-inch waterproofed insulation board over the Robertson Keystone decks; the outside metal frame is faced with expanded metal lath. All of the exterior surfaces are finished in a cream-colored cement stucco and any metal trim is painted in Iron Oxide Red, named Indian Red in documentation. **(Figures 4.62 to 4.66)**

There is also a car shelter in the back lot that is not represented in the floor plans but can be seen in the scale models and pictures of the finished construction. It is a shed for three cars built with a welded framework of one-and-a-half-inch section steel pipes. The walls and side walls of 24-gauge corrugated steel panels were painted in a jade green for the interior and exterior aluminum. The construction was a combination between a traditional and easily executed building system on the first floor, dictated by the seismic requirements of the site, and a more sophisticated modern light prefabricated construction system on the second level, including all decks and roofs. Following Kocher's procedure for most of his designs, these prefabricated systems were first explored, and their performance assessed, in a lengthy article published in an *Architectural Record* article from August of 1935, entitled "Moderate-cost House Construction and Equipment." The Robertson Keystone Cellular Steel Units for floors and roofs, and the Bar Z Gunite Wall System developed by Soule Steel Co. of Los Angeles—both used in the construction of the Kocher-Samson building—were depicted on pages 128 and 129.[63]

The building was published in *Architectural Record* again, two months later in October, for an article that prioritized technical descriptions and graphic documents over theoretical explanations. It was very clear that the design intent of the project held objective requirements—like the climatic conditions, program necessities, and the morphology of the lot—over theoretical or aesthetic considerations. It was a building that, being completely modern in its overall aspects, incorporated several traits of a vernacular tradition previously unexplored by the architects. If their works on the East Coast included certain elements that could be related with the Colonial and Early-Republic architecture, the Kocher-Samson Building clearly linked to the Hispanic tradition of California with its stucco walls, the use of internal patios, the fragmented but coherent volume, the high thermal inertia of the construction, and the color palette.[64] **(Figures 4.67 to 4.96)**

Shifting in scale, the architects paid attention to the tiniest details of the building, including the design of modern chromium-plated steel-tube furniture. For many architectural historians, like David Gebhard, the Kocher-Samson Building is "probably the most pure and at the same time workable example of the International style in Southern California."[65] The building received immediate attention and was exhibited in the New York's Museum of Modern Art exhibition, "Modern Architecture in California," held from September 30 to October 24, 1935. As with the Aluminaire House, the exhibition placed the building and its architects yet again at the forefront of American modernism, selecting it alongside the works of architects like Richard Neutra and R. M. Schindler. The Kocher-Samson Building was described as being "typical of the restrained ingenuity of the eastern experimentalism which in contrast with that of California seems economical and chaste."[66] Kocher and Frey were the only architectural practice in the exhibition not based in California, and theirs was one of the first offices to build on both coasts. The Kocher-Samson Building was also included in many other publications, like *The Modern House in America*, published in 1940 to showcase examples of residential architecture built before 1940 in the American International Style, compiled by James Ford and Katherine Morrow Ford.[67] Even Gropius sent a letter praising Kocher and Frey's design after seeing the building in *Architectural Record*.[68] The Kocher-Samson Building was the largest and most ambitious work developed by the office so far, and Frey showed his satisfaction with the client, the completed building, and the process of construction in a text published years later, in the 1980s:

> In Palm Springs, I found Dr. Kocher most understanding and supportive of our innovative design, and it was a great pleasure to follow through with detailing, contracting, and supervising the construction. A nephew of the Kochers was an engineer with the Truscon Steel Company, which furnished the spiral stair, steel studs, and windows. I kept Lawrence informed of

Figures 4.26 to 4.28. A. Lawrence Kocher and Albert Frey. 1934–1935. Kocher Canvas Weekend House. Long Island, New York. Photos of the construction.

Figures 4.29 to 4.32. A. Lawrence Kocher and Albert Frey. 1934–1935. Kocher Canvas Weekend House. Long Island, New York. Photos of the construction.

This page:
Figure 4.33. A. Lawrence Kocher and Albert Frey. 1934–1935. Kocher Canvas Weekend House. Long Island, New York. Photo of the original house. Roof and tube railings.

Next page:
Figure 4.34. A. Lawrence Kocher and Albert Frey. 1934–1935. Kocher Canvas Weekend House. Long Island, New York. Photo of the original house. Exterior view.
Figure 4.35. A. Lawrence Kocher and Albert Frey. 1934–1935. Kocher Canvas Weekend House. Long Island, New York. Photo of the original house. Interior view.

the progress with snapshots as the building grew, and with professional photographs upon its successful completion.[69]

Fortunately, these were not the only gratifying traits of Frey's stay in Palm Springs. Having experienced the natural beauty, healthy life, and job prospects in California, he decided to move there to begin a new practice. Upon the completion of the Kocher-Samson Building in 1935, Frey settled in Palm Springs and established a new professional association with John Porter Clark.[70] It was in this prosaic manner that the years of collaboration between Kocher and Frey ended. Nevertheless, Frey never lost contact with Kocher, their friendship continued, and they even temporarily worked together once more in 1939, as Frey explains:

> My stay and architectural practice in Palm Springs continued with local architect John Porter Clark. I kept in touch with Lawrence Kocher, sending him documents on projects and finished buildings which he published in the *Architectural Record*. In 1937 I accepted the invitation of Philip Goodwin to join his firm, which with Edward D. Stone had been selected as architects for the new Museum of Modern Art building in New York City. Having enjoyed my years of living in Forest Hills with Lawrence Kocher, who still resided there with his wife Marge and daughter Sandra, I rented a nearby apartment. We continued our friendship and discussions on architecture and many other subjects, and we collaborated on some projects, including a design proposal for the Swiss Pavilion for the 1939 New York World's Fair. William Lescaze, originally from Geneva, was the successful competitor.[71]

One of these sporadic collaborations after Frey's move to California was the project for the Sherwin House of 1936. There are two consecutive versions of this unpublished and unbuilt project. In both versions, it is clear the design methodology used for the Sherwin House is close to that used for the Darien Guild Hall—an aggregation of individually designed pieces optimize the programs they host. Typologically, the Sherwin House is the heir of the Darien Guild Hall, but technologically speaking it is a precedent of Kocher's designs for Black Mountain College; the house was constructed by mixing concrete block with asbestos-board cladding. The directness and simplicity of the lineal volumetric aggregation of this house and the vertical prominence of the chimney as a counterpart of the horizontal scheme, also resembles some vernacular structures, like the aligned composition of volumes in the J. Priestley House (1796) in Northumberland, Pennsylvania, studied and drawn by Kocher in 1921 for his *Architectural Record* articles about vernacular American architecture.[72]

The first version of the Sherwin House, authored only by Kocher that April, is an aggregation of three elements. The living room is a rectangular parallelepiped, measuring 18 by 28 and a half feet, with a large window facing east, a glass-brick wall in the south, and higher ceilings than the rest of the house. The second element is a slender steel structure that forms a porch shading the windowpanes of the living room. The third piece contains the rest of the domestic program, distributed on the sides of a central passage. This area of the house contains the entry hall, kitchen, maid's room, two bathrooms on the west side of the corridor, and three bedrooms on the east side. **(Figures 4.97 and 4.98)** The second scheme, signed by both architects in May, is a slightly more sophisticated aggregation of four different elements. The service spaces—kitchen, heater room, maid's bedroom, and bathroom—are now completely segregated from the family's bedrooms. Both the service spaces and private family areas are attached to opposite sides of the large central living room, which opens to a terrace in the east through a series of folding glass panes, and to a screened porch attached to the west façade. Again, the volume of the living room is higher than the rest of the house; it features a large corner window and a glass-brick wall. The children's bedrooms have a similar configuration to those designed by Frey in his Farmhouse Number 6532 for the U.S. Department of Agriculture: two stacked bunkbeds, one set for each room in order to provide enough space for a closet and a study desk within a very limited floor area. This part of the house is completed with a bathroom and the parents' bedroom. **(Figures 4.99 to 4.102)**

The next stage of Frey's professional career in California is well-known and sufficiently documented in various monographs.[73] Yet the subsequently divergent career of Kocher has been less studied, and so we continue forward with a timeline of his later work demonstrating his evolution as an architect, his contributions to the architectural research community, and his role in shaping architectural pedagogy in the United States.[74]

Chapter endnotes

1 See: Brochure for "Sears Gallery Exhibition 1932," Box 5, A. Lawrence Kocher Collection, Colonial Williamsburg Foundation, John D. Rockefeller Jr. Library.

2 Brochure for "Sears Gallery Exhibition 1932."

3 Shepard Vogelgesang, "The New School for Social Research," *Architectural Record*, Vol. 69, No. 2 (February 1931): 138–150.

4 "Architectural Exhibition," New York Herald Tribune (January 22 1933), A. Lawrence Kocher Collection, Colonial Williamsburg Foundation, John D. Rockefeller Jr. Library.

5 A. Lawrence Kocher and Albert Frey, "New Materials and Improved Construction Methods," *Architectural Record*, Vol. 73 (April 1933): 281–289.

6 Kocher wrote an article about this topic in 1921: A. Lawrence Kocher, "Hand Books of Samuel Rhoads, Carpenter-Builder," *Architectural Record*, Vol. 50, No. 6 (December, 1921): 507–509.

7 Kocher owned a copy of Jefferson's Library catalog and purchased many books based on this collection, including nine different editions in Italian, French, and English of Palladio's *Four Books of Architecture*; a list of the books owned by Kocher can also be found in: Cynthia Zignego Stiverson, *Architecture and the Decorative Arts: The A. Lawrence Kocher Collection of Books at the Colonial Williamsburg Foundation* (West Cornwall, CT: Locust Hill Press, 1989), Preface, XXI.

8 The subtitle of the act indicated the RFC's purpose: "to provide emergency financing facilities for financial institutions, to aid in financing agriculture, commerce, and industry." Michael Gou, Gary Richardson, Alejandro Komai, Daniel Park, "Reconstruction Finance Corporation Act: January 22, 1932," *Federal Reserve History*, January 2022, https://www.federalreservehistory.org/essays/reconstruction-finance-corporation.

9 Robert McElvaine, *The Great Depression: America 1929-1941* (New York City: Times Books, 1993), 142.

10 A "Penny Auction" was a collective action taken by the neighbors of the farmer during the auction of a foreclosed property; physically threatening anyone who attempted to bid competitively, the farmers forced the bank to sell to them the property at an abnormally low price, usually at a few cents, with intent to return the property to its previous owner.

11 United States Division of Subsistence Homesteads; Federal Subsistence Homesteads Corporation, "National Advisory Committee on Subsistence Homesteads," *Bulletin 1: Information Concerning the Purposes and Policies of the Division of Subsistence Homesteads.* (Washington, D.C.: Federal Subsistence Homesteads Corporation, 1933): 9, https://archive.org/details/CAT31355382/mode/2up.

12 FDR quoted in: T. H. Watkins, *The Great Depression: America in the 1930s* (New York: Back Bay Books, 1995), 261.

13 "National Advisory Committee on Subsistence Homesteads," 2.

14 Ibid. 4.

15 Philip M. Glick, "The Federal Subsistence Homesteads Program," *Yale Law Journal*, Vol. 44 (June, 1935): 1,327.

16 L. O. Bercaw, A. M. Hannay, E. M. Colvin, *Bibliography on land settlement: with particular reference to small holdings and subsistence homesteads* (Washington, D.C.: U.S. Dept. of Agriculture, 1934).

17 The Subsistence Homestead Division itself was organized into three sections: the Planning Section, the Construction Section, and the Operations Section.

18 The Federal Subsistence Homesteads Corporation functioned as a parent corporation; subsidiary corporations would be created for each project to "take title to the land acquired, retain attorneys for preparation of title papers, contract for the construction of homestead, select the homesteaders and execute contracts with them to cover the sale of the homestead tracts, and operate and supervise the communities to be established." Glick, "The Federal Subsistence Homesteads Program": 1,335.

19 As examined in Chapter 3, Kocher and Frey had designed a proposal in November of 1931 for low-cost farmhouses built with prefabricated systems, presented at the President's Conference on Home Building and Home Ownership in Washington, D.C., and later published as "Model of Farmhouse of Low Cost," *Architectural Record*, Vol. 71, No. 5 (May 1932): 297. Held in Cleveland, The National Conference on Low-Cost Housing took place October 25th through 27th in 1933.

20 The National Housing Act of 1934 was enacted on June 27, 1934, creating two public agencies: the Federal Housing Administration (FHA) and the Federal Savings and Loan Insurance Corporation (FSLIC).

21 The conference took place on October 25–27, 1933 in Cleveland, Ohio. Eds. William M. Faber, Theodore Wolfe, *Proceedings of the National Conference on Low Cost Housing* (The Cleveland Engineering Society, 1933).

22 A. Lawrence Kocher and Albert Frey, "Low-Cost Farmhouse," *Architectural Record*, Vol. 75, No. 1 (January 1934): 30.

23 Publications like: Harvey Wiley Corbett, "The Gingerbread House Comes True," *The American Legion Monthly,* Vol. 12, No. 3 (March, 1932): 22–23.

24 Albert Frey, "Foreword," in Cynthia Zignego Stiverson, *Architecture and the Decorative Arts: The A. Lawrence Kocher Collection of Books at the Colonial Williamsburg Foundation* (West Cornwall, CT: Locust Hill Press, 1989).

25 Wallace Ashby, "Farmhouse Plans," *Farmers Bulletin*, No. 1738 (Washington, D.C.: U.S. Department of Agriculture, 1934): 40–43.

26 A. Lawrence Kocher and Albert Frey, Subsistence Farmsteads, *Architectural Record*, Vol. 75, No. 4 (April, 1934): 349–352.

27 This kind of steel construction is typical in many of the Case Study House Program's most iconic works, such as the Eames House (Case Study House #8, 1949) and Pierre Koenig's Stahl House (Case Study House #22, 1959). The lightness and ease of the construction elements and their transportation was very appropriate for the earthquake-affected and inaccessible lots on the hills of the Santa Monica Mountains in Los Angeles.

28 Documentation of this project in: Oversize, Series III: Project Files, Folder: Low-Cost Housing (1932–1936), A. Lawrence Kocher Collection, Colonial Williamsburg Foundation, John D. Rockefeller Jr. Library.

29 Another later example to support the relevance of the Subsistence Homesteads in the media is the monographic issue: "Unemployment and Subsistence Farming," *Architectural Record*, Vol. 77, No.1 (January 1935).

30 T. H. Watkins, *The Great Depression: America in the 1930s*, 262.

31 Russell Lord, Paul H. Johnstone, Eds., *A place on earth; a critical appraisal of subsistence homesteads* (Washington D.C.: United States Department of Agriculture, Bureau of Agricultural Economics, 1942).

32 In complete convergence with later researchers as David A. Hounshell. See: David A. Hounshell, *From the American System to Mass Production, 1800-1932: The Development of Manufacturing Technology in the United States* (Baltimore: Johns Hopkins University Press, 1985).

33 A. Lawrence Kocher, "Color in Early American Architecture, With Special References to the Origin and Development of House Painting," *Architectural Record*, Vol. 64, No. 4 (October, 1928): 278–290.

34 This letter was written months before Gropius' emigration to London, where he arrived in October of 1934. "Letter from Gropius to Kocher dated July 7, 1934," Box 1, A. Lawrence Kocher Collection, Colonial Williamsburg Foundation, John D. Rockefeller Jr. Library.

35 "Letter from Gropius to Kocher, dated March 25, 1934," Box 1, A. Lawrence Kocher Collection, Colonial Williamsburg Foundation, John D. Rockefeller Jr. Library.

36 "Letter from Kocher to Gropius. May 29th, 1934," Box 1, A. Lawrence Kocher Collection, Colonial Williamsburg Foundation, John D. Rockefeller Jr. Library.

37 In the March 1934 issue, it was published the Otis Elevators Factory Building, the French Embassy, and a Shell service station, all in Tokyo, and another Shell gas station built in Yokohama. The architect's summer quarters in Karuizawa and Morinojuke Kawasaki's residence in Tokyo appeared in the May 1934 issue. In later issues of the magazine, more works by Raymond were published like in the January 1936 Volume 79 number 1, that included two complete articles by Raymond. The first, in pages 9 to 36, fucuses on concrete architecture and is illustrated with Raymond's designs for the residence of Tetsuma Akaboshi, and the Church of Saint Paul in Karuizawa. The second in pages 49 to 51 shows Raymond's working drawings for a students' dormitory in Pondicherry; India, Akaboshi's House; and a town residence in Shanghai, China.

38 "Letter from Gropius to Kocher, dated May 9th, 1934," Box 1, A. Lawrence Kocher Collection, Colonial Williamsburg Foundation, John D. Rockefeller Jr. Library.

39 "Letter from Gropius to Kocher, dated May 9th, 1934," Box 1.

40 Ibid.

41 Gropius' words resonated in Kocher's future proposal for an "Architectural Center," published in Pencil Points in of 1943. Project by Kocher and Howard Dearstyne. A. Lawrence Kocher, Howard Dearstyne, "The Architectural Center: An Organization to Coordinate Building Research, Planning, Design, and Construction," *Pencil Points* (July 1943).

42 "Letter from Gropius to Kocher, dated July 7, 1934," Box 1, A. Lawrence Kocher Collection, Colonial Williamsburg Foundation, John D. Rockefeller Jr. Library.

43 "Letter from Gropius to Kocher, dated July 7, 1934," Box 1.

44 As he promises in a letter to Gropius dated June 6, 1935. Cited in: Reginald R. Isaacs, *Walter Gropius: Der Mensch Und Sein Werk* (Berlin: Mann. 1983): 746.

45 According to Kentgens in Isaacs, *Walter Gropius: Der Mensch Und Sein Werk*: 200.

46 Among the Bauhaus-related architects, only Joseph and Anni Albers preceded Gropius in their emigration to the United States.

47 Margaret Kentgens-Craig, *The Bauhaus and America: First Contacts 1919-1936* (Cambridge, Massachusetts: The MIT Press, 2001), 200.

48 A former student of James Ford, the Professor of Social Ethics at Harvard, Davison was one of the country's preeminent researchers in prefabricated construction for housing. From 1928 to 1931, Davison was in charge of the Technical News and Research at Architectural Record. After leaving the magazine, he created a Housing Division for the John B. Pierce Foundation, where he collaborated with John H. Callender on the development of new prefabrication systems for residential application. Although Davison did not hold an architectural degree, he and Callender designed, fabricated, and assembled a number of test houses; they experimented with concrete, plywood, composite boards, stabilized earth, and a hydro-calcium silicate composition known as Microporite. Davison also authored a series of technical articles for the Pierce Foundation, entitled "The Engineered Dwelling." Notably, James Ford later published two volumes of the most relevant and influential books from the 1930s; see: James Ford, *Slums and Housing. With a Special Reference to New York City. History, Conditions, Policy* (Cambridge, Massachusetts: Harvard University Press, 1936).

49 Robert L. Davison, John H. Callender, "House of Robert L. Davison. Northport, Long Island," *Architectural Record*, Vol. 80, No. 4 (October 1936): 277–278.

50 Caroline Rob Zaleski, *Long Island Modernism: 1930-1980* (New York: W.W Norton and Co. Inc., 2012), 36-51.

51 Rob Zaleski, *Long Island Modernism: 1930–1980*, 12.

52 Alfred Roth, *The New Architecture, Presented in 20 Examples* (Zurich: Verlag Dr. H. Girsberger, 1940), 11–16.

53 Roth, *The New Architecture, Presented in 20 Examples*, 12.

54 "Letter from Kocher to Mary Mix Foley, dated July 11th, 1968," Box 4, A. Lawrence Kocher Collection, Colonial Williamsburg Foundation, John D. Rockefeller Jr. Library.

55 "Letter from Kocher's wife, Margaret, to Bonny S. Radez (a first-year student in the Master of Architecture program at Columbia University), dated November 24th, 1975," Box 4, A. Lawrence Kocher Collection, Colonial Williamsburg Foundation, John D. Rockefeller Jr. Library.

56 Zaleski, *Long Island Modernism: 1930-1980*, 42.

57 John McAndrew, Ed., *Guide to Modern Architecture: Northeast States* (New York: Museum of Modern Art/MoMA, 1940), 54.

58 Roth, *The New Architecture, Presented in 20 Examples*, 12.
59 "Letter dated November 24th, 1975," Box 4, A. Lawrence Kocher Collection, Colonial Williamsburg Foundation, John D. Rockefeller Jr. Library.
60 Rob Zaleski, *Long Island Modernism: 1930–1980*, 36–51.
61 Frey had already visited California on a trip he took from July to August of 1932. On his cross-country journey, Frey experienced modern camping firsthand: he drove a Model T Ford and spent his nights in a small tent—acquainting him with the American industrial vernacular, which had a profound influence on his subsequent works.
62 A. Lawrence Kocher, Albert Frey, "Real Estate Office and Apartment Building at Palm Springs, California," *Architectural Record*, Vol. 78, No. 4 (October 1935): 267–275.
63 *Architectural Record*, Vol. 78, No. 2 (August 1935): 128–129.
64 Kocher and Frey were very impressed by the work of the Mexican architect Luis Barragán, who they had met in 1934 during one of the architect's visits to the United States. In his "Foreword" to a book on Kocher, Frey recalls meeting architect Luis Barragán: "The office was visited by many noted architects and photographers. I recall meeting Luis Barragán, the architect from Mexico City who was beginning to build outstanding houses and developments." Stiverson, *Architecture and the Decorative Arts: The A. Lawrence Kocher Collection of Books at the Colonial Williamsburg Foundation*. Kocher published several of Barragan's projects in the January and September issues of *Architectural Record* in 1935. *Architectural Record*, Vol. 77, No. 1 (January 1935): 33–46. *Architectural Record*, Vol. 78, No. 3 (September 1935): 165–169.
65 David Gebhard, *A Guide to Architecture in Southern California* (Los Angeles: Los Angeles County Museum of Art/LACMA, 1965), 140.
66 Extracted from the building's nomination application for Historic Site Class 1, prepared by Patrick McGrew in 2008 for the Palm Springs Preservation Foundation. http://www.pspreservationfoundation.org/pdf/kocher_samson_nomination.pdf.
67 James Ford, Katherine Morrow Ford, *The Modern House in America* (New York: Architectural Book Pub. Co., 1940).
68 "Letter from Gropius to Kocher, dated October 25th, 1935," Box 1, A. Lawrence Kocher Collection, Colonial Williamsburg Foundation, John D. Rockefeller Jr. Library.
69 Frey, "Foreword."
70 This association was only interrupted between 1937 and 1939 when Frey returned to New York to work in Philip Woodwin's office on the project of the new Museum of Modern Art of New York (MoMA). Joseph Rosa, *Albert Frey, Architect* (New York: Rizzoli International Publications, 1990), 36.
71 Frey, Albert. Foreword. In: Stiverson, *Architecture and the Decorative Arts: The A. Lawrence Kocher Collection of Books at the Colonial Williamsburg Foundation*. West Cornwall, CT: Locust Hill Press.
72 The plan layout resembles many other vernacular structures, for example the Brooking House in Virginia studied by Henry Glassie. Henry Glassie. *Folk Housing in Middle Virginia. A structural Analysis of Historic Artifacts*. (Knoxville: The University of Tennessee Press. 1975) 80–81. The plan is also very similar to the layout of the small Relic House at Jamestown, that Kocher will restore in the 1960's.
73 See bibliography. Joseph Rosa's book is, in our opinion, the most complete survey of Frey's trajectory. Other monographs, such as those by Jennifer Golub, Daniell Cornell, and Gloria Koenig, may be seen as complementary means of analysis.
74 This timeline follows the one published in: Lawrence Wodehouse, "Kocher at Black Mountain," *Journal of the Society of Architectural Historians*, Vol. 41, No. 4 (December 1982): 328–332.

This page:
Figures 4.36 and 4.37. A. Lawrence Kocher and Albert Frey. 1934–1935. Kocher Canvas Weekend House. Long Island, New York. Photo of the original house. Interior views of the glazed walls.

Next page:
Figure 4.38. A. Lawrence Kocher and Albert Frey. 1934–1935. Kocher Canvas Weekend House. Long Island, New York. Second floor plan and façade construction sections of the original house.

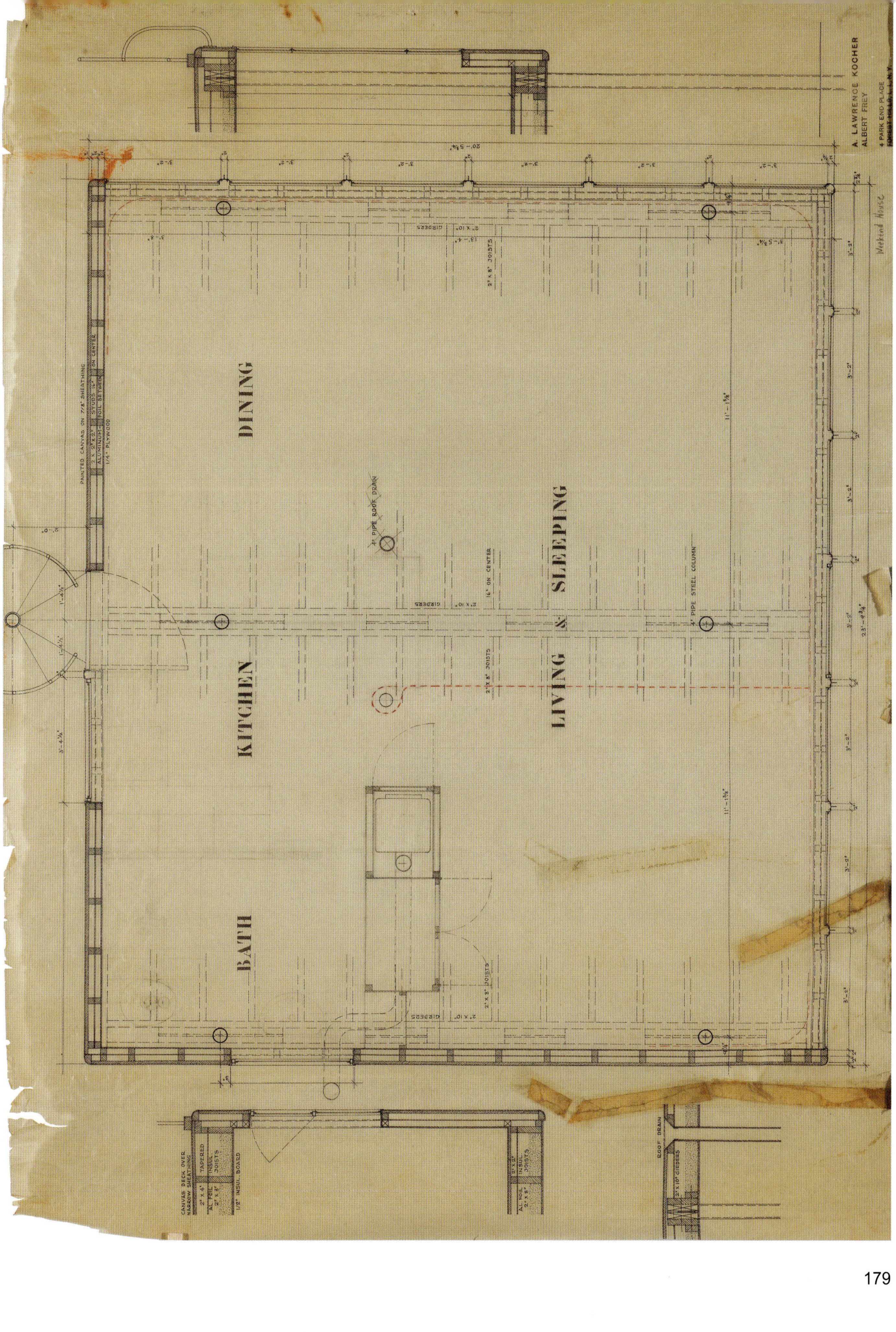

A. LAWRENCE KOCHER
ALBERT FREY
4 PARK END PLACE
DINING
KITCHEN
BATH
LIVING & SLEEPING
4" PIPE STEEL COLUMN
2" x 8" JOISTS
2" x 10" GIRDERS
14" ON CENTER
1/4" PLYWOOD
ROOF DRAIN
1/2" INSUL. BOARD

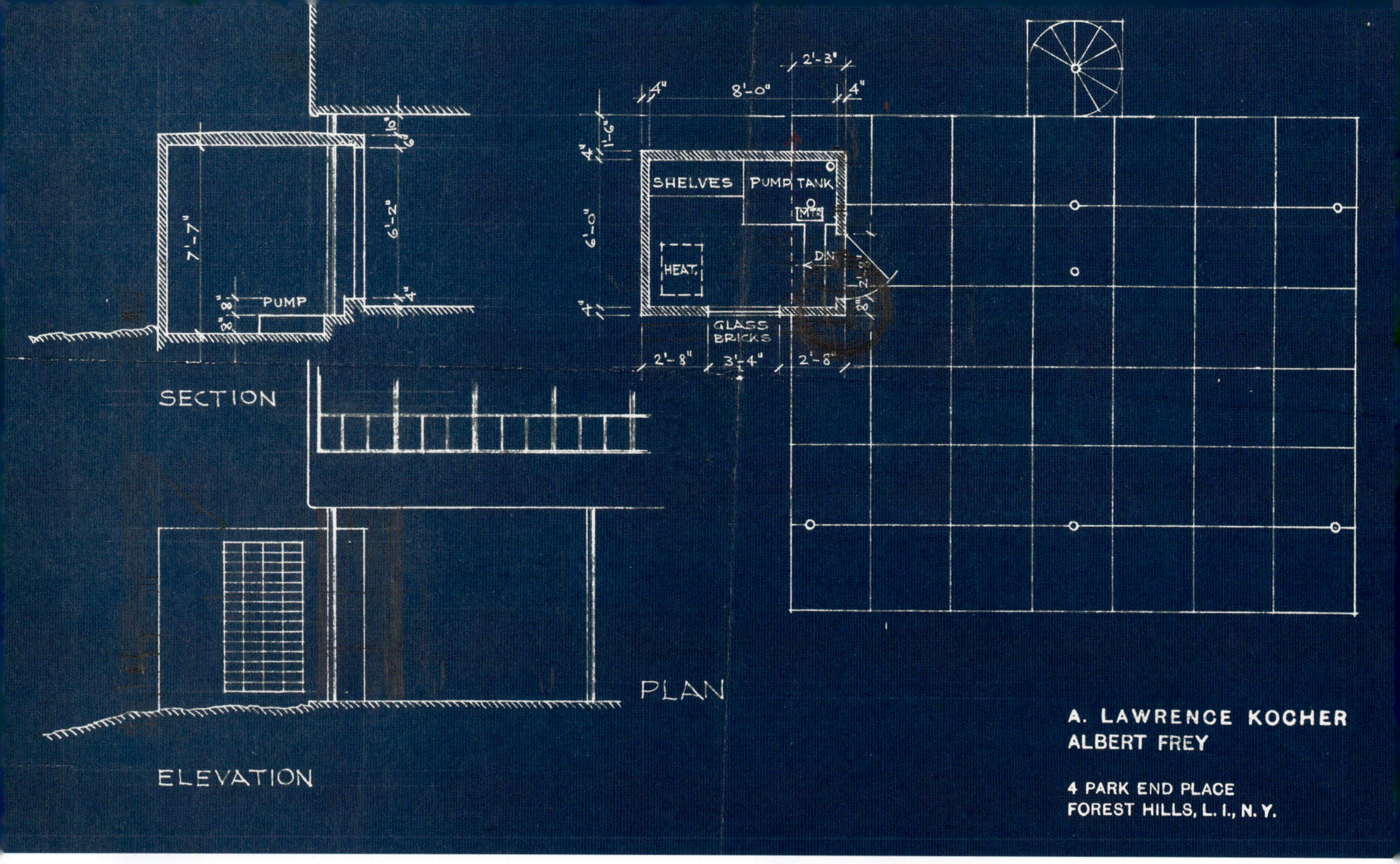

Figure 4.39. A. Lawrence Kocher. 1936. Kocher Canvas Weekend House. Long Island, New York. Floor plan and sections of the addition to the original house. Undated.
Figures 4.40 and 4.41. A. Lawrence Kocher and Albert Frey. 1936. Kocher Canvas Weekend House. Long Island, New York. Extended house. Photos of the exterior.

Figure 4.42. A. Lawrence Kocher and Albert Frey. 1936. Kocher Canvas Weekend House. Long Island, New York. Extended house. Photos of the exterior.

This page:
Figure 4.43. A. Lawrence Kocher and Albert Frey. 1936. Kocher Canvas Weekend House. Long Island, New York. Extended house. Photos of the exterior.

Next page:
Figure 4.44. A. Lawrence Kocher and Albert Frey. 1934–1935. Kocher-Samson Building in Palm Springs, California. Photo of internal patio by Willard.

This page:

Figure 4.45. A. Lawrence Kocher and Albert Frey. 1934–1935. Kocher-Samson Building in Palm Springs, California. Photo from parking area by Willard.

Figure 4.46. A. Lawrence Kocher and Albert Frey. 1934–1935. Kocher-Samson Building in Palm Springs, California. Photo of internal patio by Willard.

Next page:

Figure 4.47. A. Lawrence Kocher and Albert Frey. 1934–1935. Kocher-Samson Building in Palm Springs, California. Perspective of the final project. Undated.

Figure 4.48. A. Lawrence Kocher and Albert Frey. 1934–1935. Kocher-Samson Building in Palm Springs, California. Photo from the street by Willard.

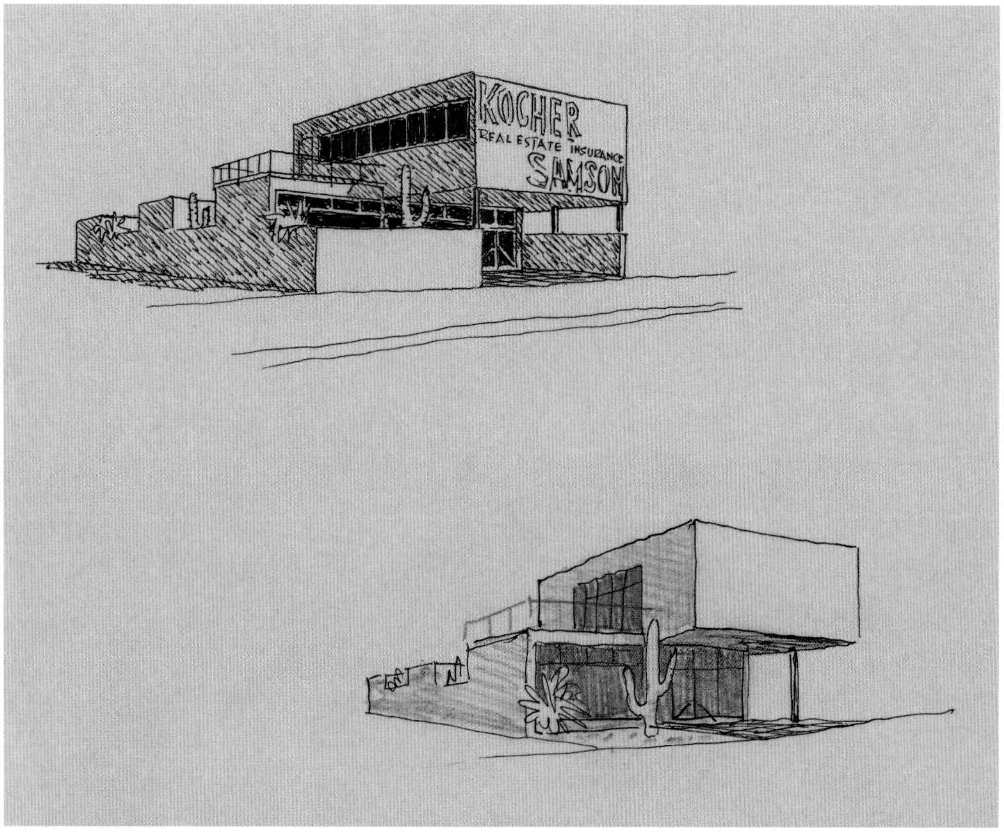

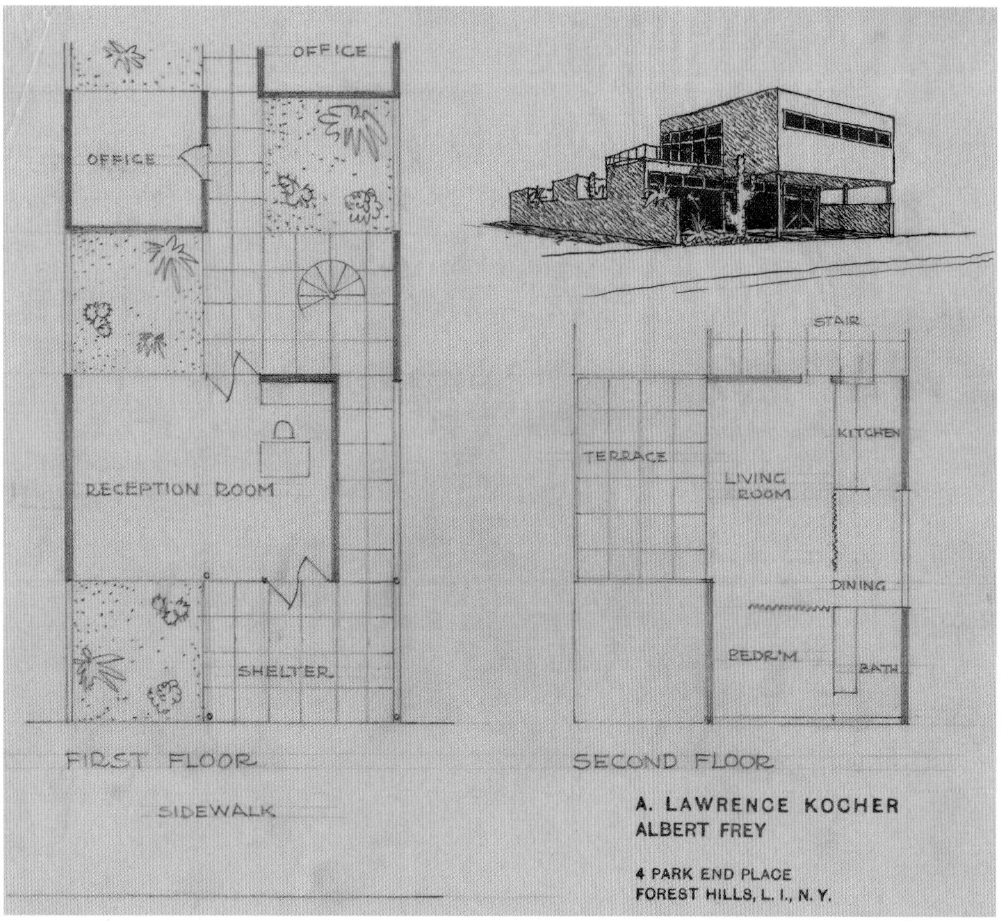

Figure 4.49. A. Lawrence Kocher and Albert Frey. 1934–1935. Kocher-Samson Building in Palm Springs, California. Perspective sketches. Views from the street. Top; preliminary option with front enclosed patio. Bottom; final option with open patio.
Figure 4.50. A. Lawrence Kocher and Albert Frey. 1934–1935. Kocher-Samson Building in Palm Springs, California. Perspective sketch and partial floor plans of the preliminary project. Undated.
Figure 4.51. A. Lawrence Kocher and Albert Frey. 1934–1935. Kocher-Samson Building in Palm Springs, California. Three photos of the model published in *The Architectural Record* in August 1935.

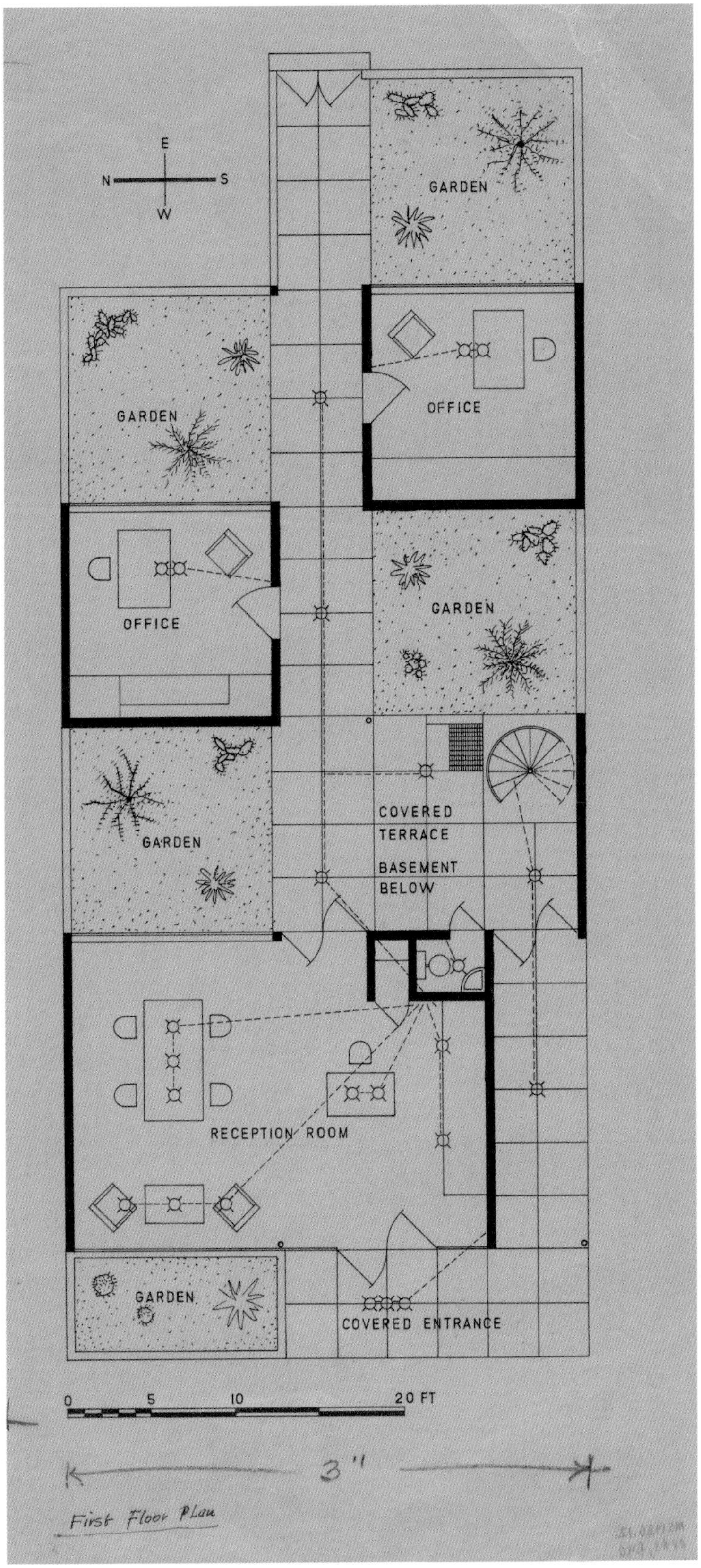

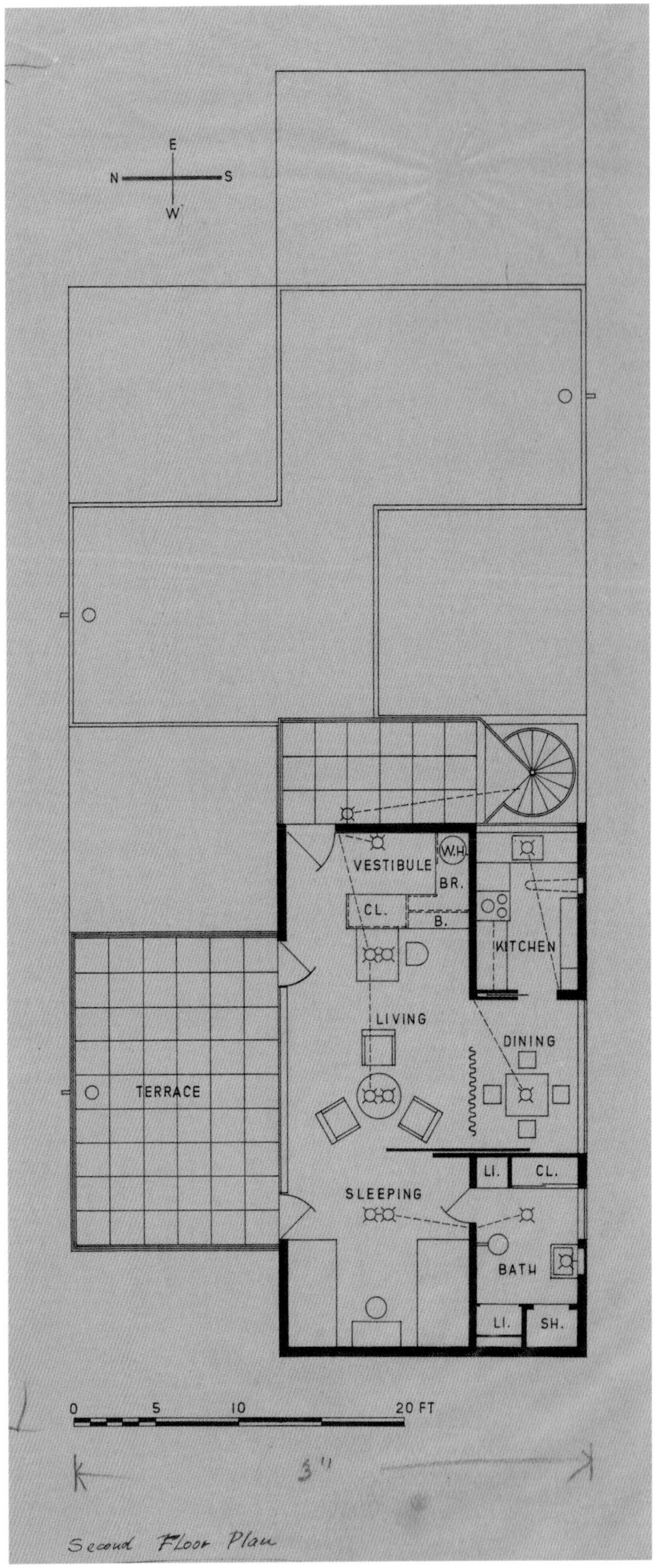

Figure 4.52. A. Lawrence Kocher and Albert Frey. 1934–1935. Kocher-Samson Building in Palm Springs, California. First floor plan as published in *The Architectural Record* in August 1935. Original drawing. Final project. Undated.

Figure 4.53. A. Lawrence Kocher and Albert Frey. 1934–1935. Kocher-Samson Building in Palm Springs, California. Second floor plan as published in *The Architectural Record* in August 1935. Original drawing. Final project. Undated.

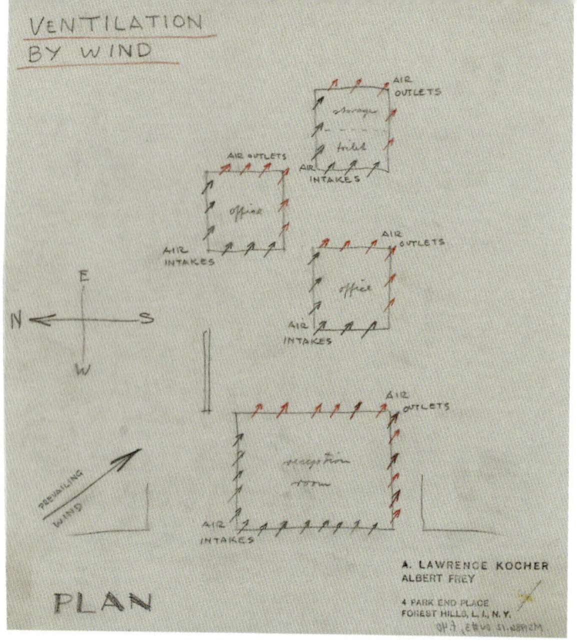
VENTILATION BY WIND
AIR OUTLETS
storage
toilet
AIR INTAKES
office
E
N
S
W
PREVAILING WIND
reception room
PLAN
A. LAWRENCE KOCHER
ALBERT FREY
4 PARK END PLACE
FOREST HILLS, L. I., N. Y.

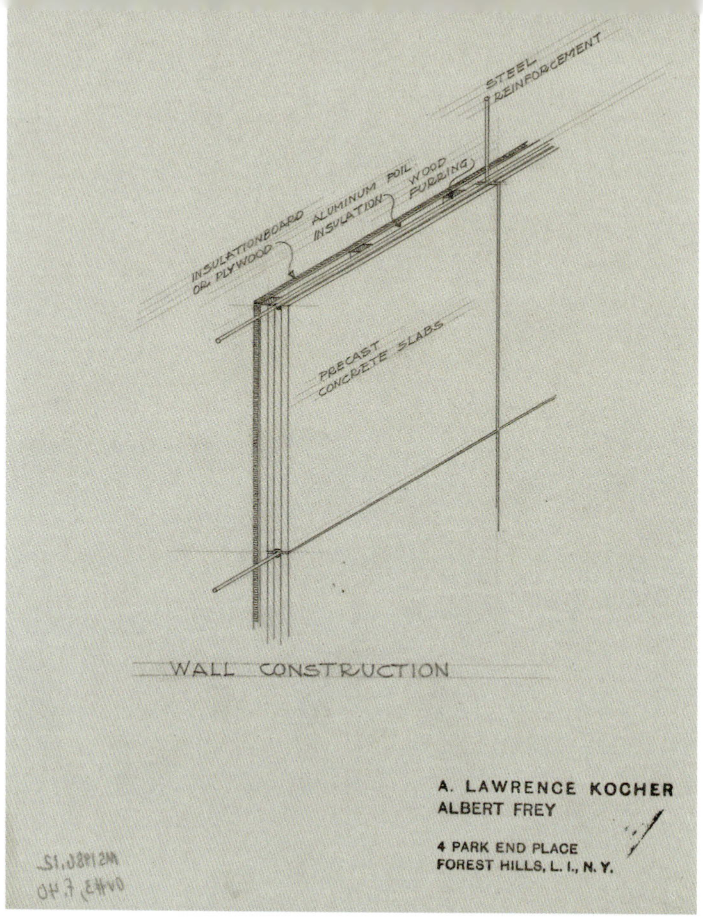
STEEL REINFORCEMENT
WOOD FURRING
ALUMINUM FOIL INSULATION
INSULATIONBOARD OR PLYWOOD
PRECAST CONCRETE SLABS
WALL CONSTRUCTION
A. LAWRENCE KOCHER
ALBERT FREY
4 PARK END PLACE
FOREST HILLS, L. I., N. Y.

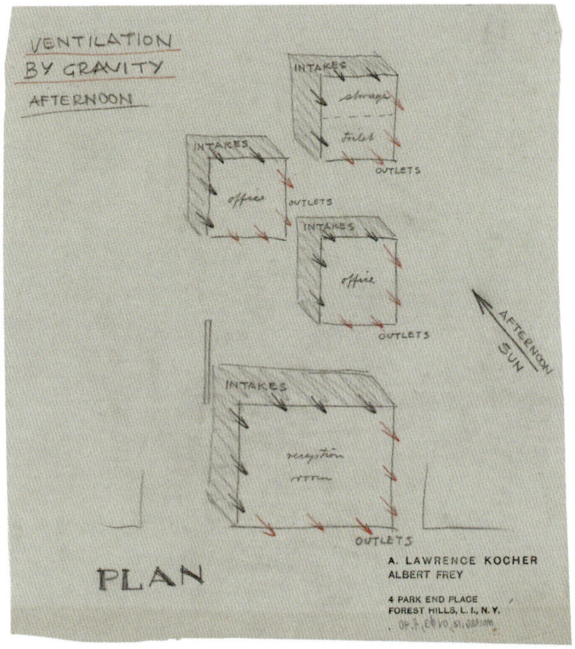
VENTILATION BY GRAVITY
AFTERNOON
INTAKES
storage
toilet
OUTLETS
office
AFTERNOON SUN
reception room
PLAN
A. LAWRENCE KOCHER
ALBERT FREY
4 PARK END PLACE
FOREST HILLS, L. I., N. Y.

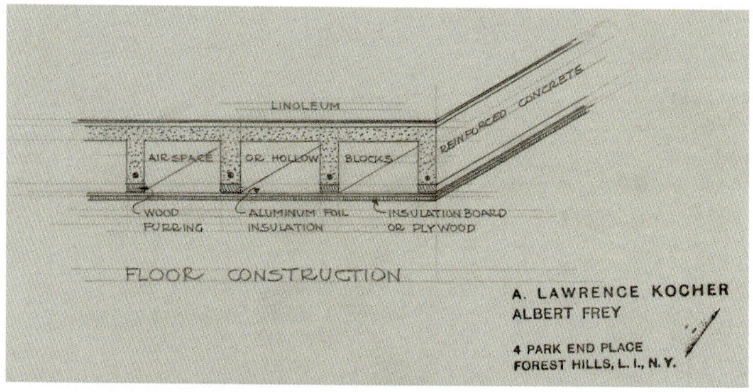
LINOLEUM
AIRSPACE OR HOLLOW BLOCKS
REINFORCED CONCRETE
WOOD FURRING
ALUMINUM FOIL INSULATION
INSULATION BOARD OR PLYWOOD
FLOOR CONSTRUCTION
A. LAWRENCE KOCHER
ALBERT FREY
4 PARK END PLACE
FOREST HILLS, L. I., N. Y.

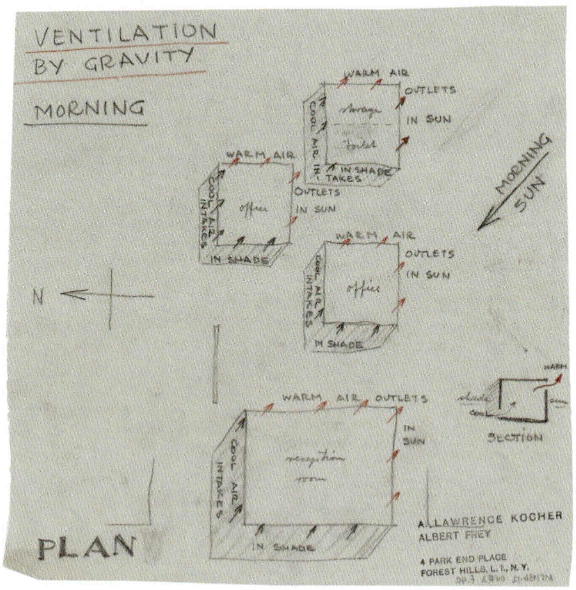
VENTILATION BY GRAVITY
MORNING
WARM AIR
OUTLETS
IN SUN
IN SHADE
COOL AIR INTAKES
office
MORNING SUN
N
WARM AIR OUTLETS
SECTION
reception room
PLAN
A. LAWRENCE KOCHER
ALBERT FREY
4 PARK END PLACE
FOREST HILLS, L. I., N. Y.

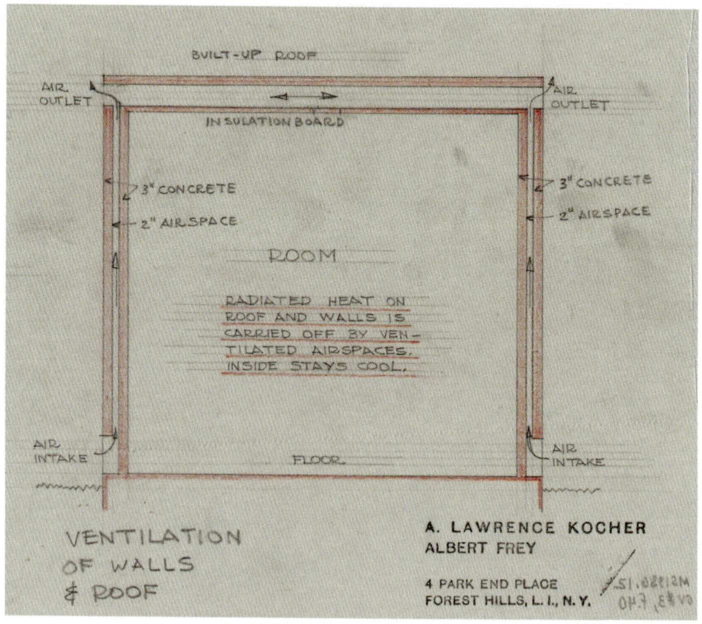
BUILT-UP ROOF
AIR OUTLET
INSULATION BOARD
3" CONCRETE
2" AIRSPACE
ROOM
RADIATED HEAT ON ROOF AND WALLS IS CARRIED OFF BY VENTILATED AIRSPACES. INSIDE STAYS COOL.
AIR INTAKE
FLOOR
VENTILATION OF WALLS & ROOF
A. LAWRENCE KOCHER
ALBERT FREY
4 PARK END PLACE
FOREST HILLS, L. I., N. Y.

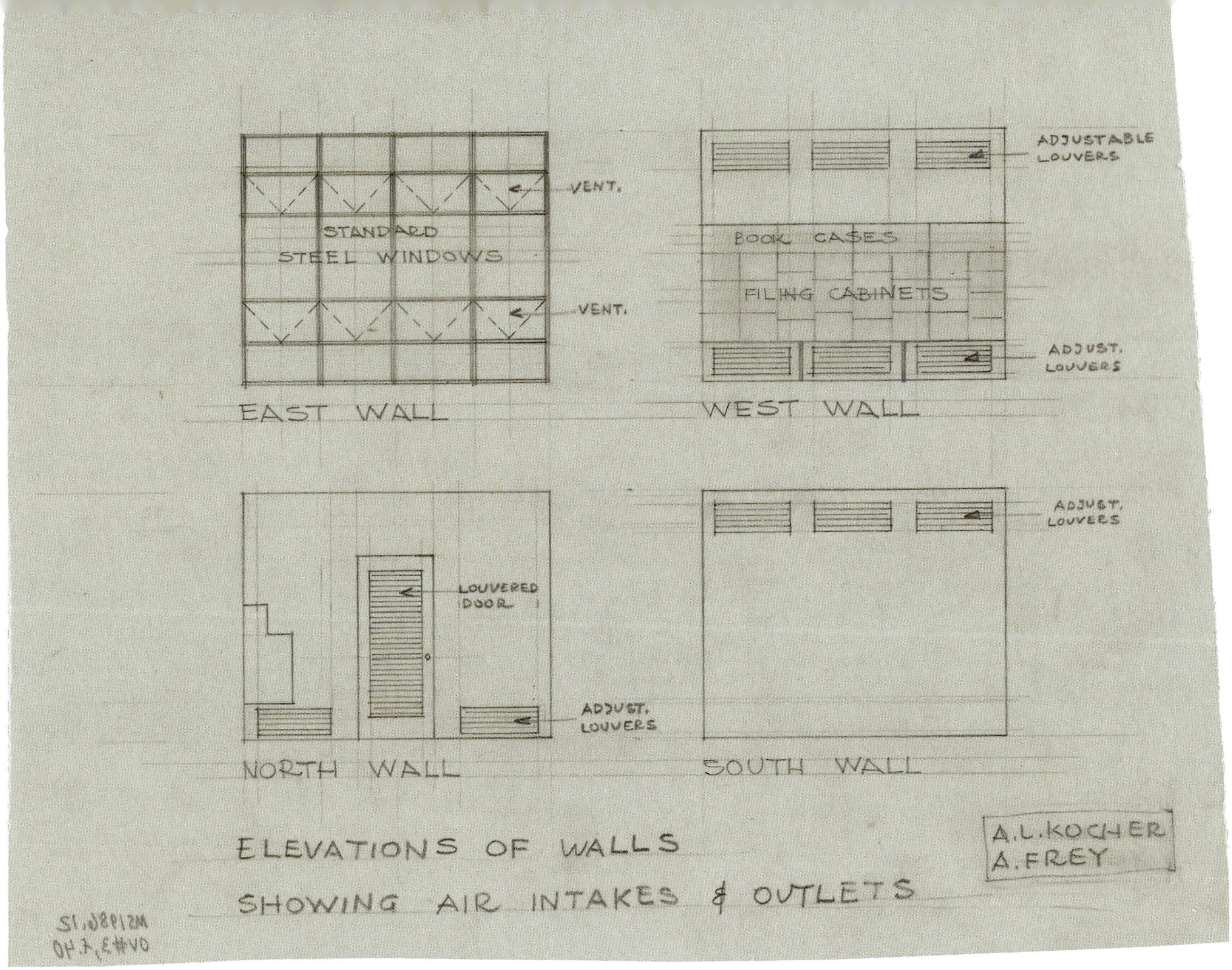

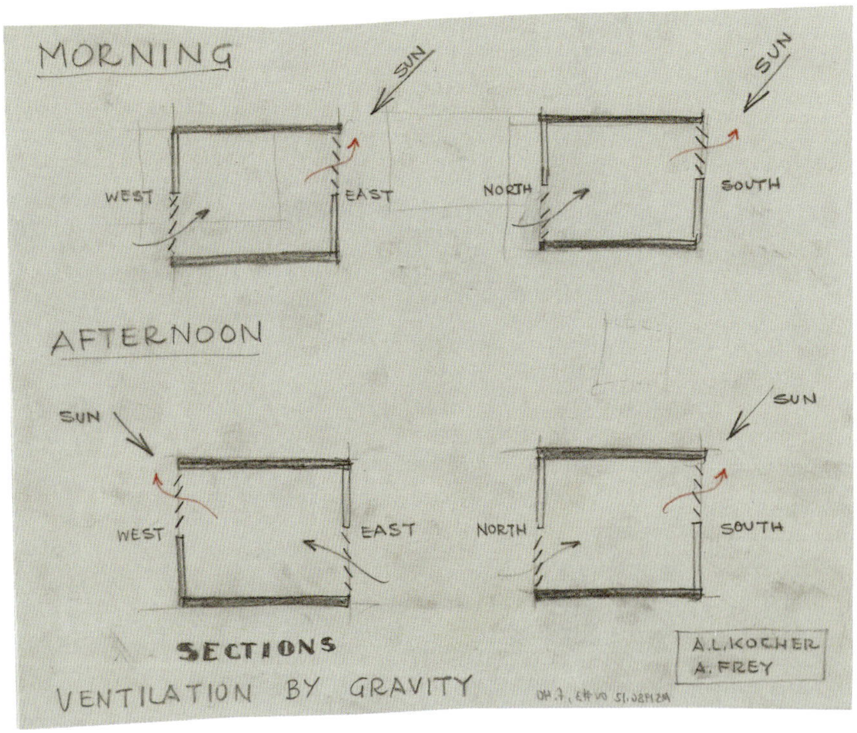

Previous page:
Figures 4.54 to 4.59. A. Lawrence Kocher and Albert Frey. 1934–1935. Kocher-Samson Building in Palm Springs, California. Diagrams. Construction of walls and floors and different natural ventilation systems of the building (Ventilation by gravity and ventilation by wind). Undated.

This page:
Figures 4.60 and 4.61. A. Lawrence Kocher and Albert Frey. 1934–1935. Kocher-Samson Building in Palm Springs, California. Diagrams. Situation of air intakes and outlets in elevations and diagram of ventilation by gravity during mornings and afternoons.

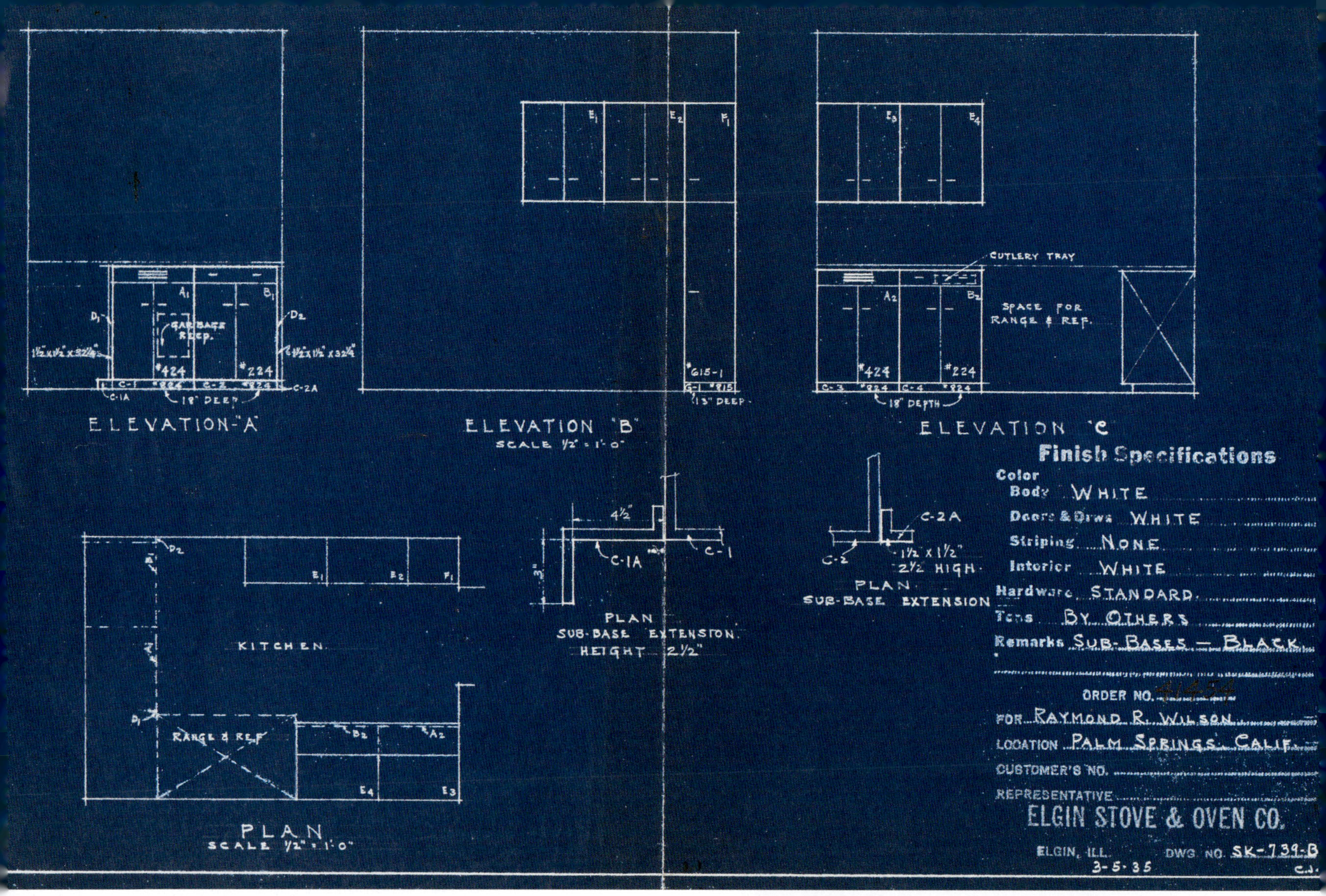
ELEVATION "A"
GARBAGE RECP.
ELEVATION "B"
SCALE 1/2" = 1'-0"
CUTLERY TRAY
SPACE FOR RANGE & REF.
ELEVATION "C"
PLAN
SUB-BASE EXTENSION
HEIGHT 2 1/2"
PLAN
SUB-BASE EXTENSION
KITCHEN
RANGE & REF
PLAN
SCALE 1/2" = 1'-0"
Finish Specifications
Color
Body WHITE
Doors & Drws WHITE
Striping NONE
Interior WHITE
Hardware STANDARD
Tops BY OTHERS
Remarks SUB-BASES — BLACK
ORDER NO.
FOR RAYMOND R. WILSON
LOCATION PALM SPRINGS, CALIF.
CUSTOMER'S NO.
REPRESENTATIVE
ELGIN STOVE & OVEN CO.
ELGIN, ILL.
DWG. NO. SK-739-B
3-5-35

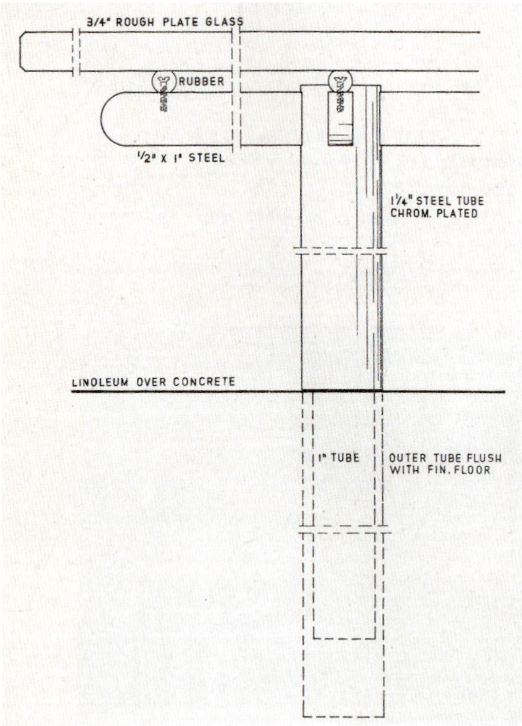
3/4" ROUGH PLATE GLASS
RUBBER
1/2" X 1" STEEL
1 1/4" STEEL TUBE CHROM. PLATED
LINOLEUM OVER CONCRETE
1" TUBE
OUTER TUBE FLUSH WITH FIN. FLOOR

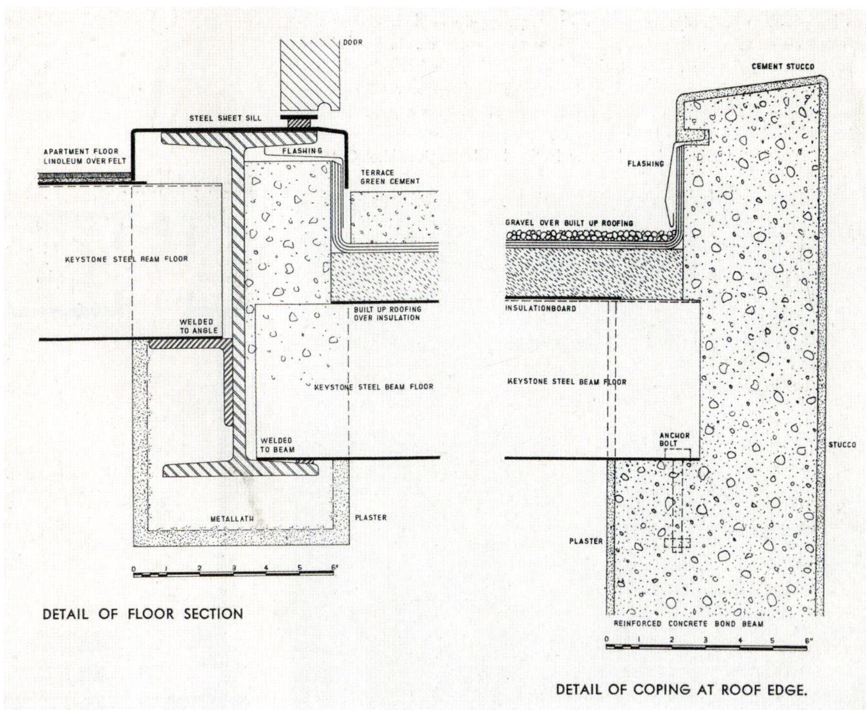

Previous page:
Figure 4.62. A. Lawrence Kocher and Albert Frey. 1934–1935. Kocher-Samson Building in Palm Springs, California. Details and specification of the kitchen. Blueprint dated 3-05-35.
Figures 4.63 and 4.64. A. Lawrence Kocher and Albert Frey. 1934–1935. Kocher-Samson Building in Palm Springs, California. Detail and phot of the kitchen as published in *The Architectural Record* in August 1935.

This page:
Figure 4.65. A. Lawrence Kocher and Albert Frey. 1934–1935. Kocher-Samson Building in Palm Springs, California. Board with construction photos.
Figure 4.66. A. Lawrence Kocher and Albert Frey. 1934–1935. Kocher-Samson Building in Palm Springs, California. Floor and roof details as published in *The Architectural Record* in August 1935.

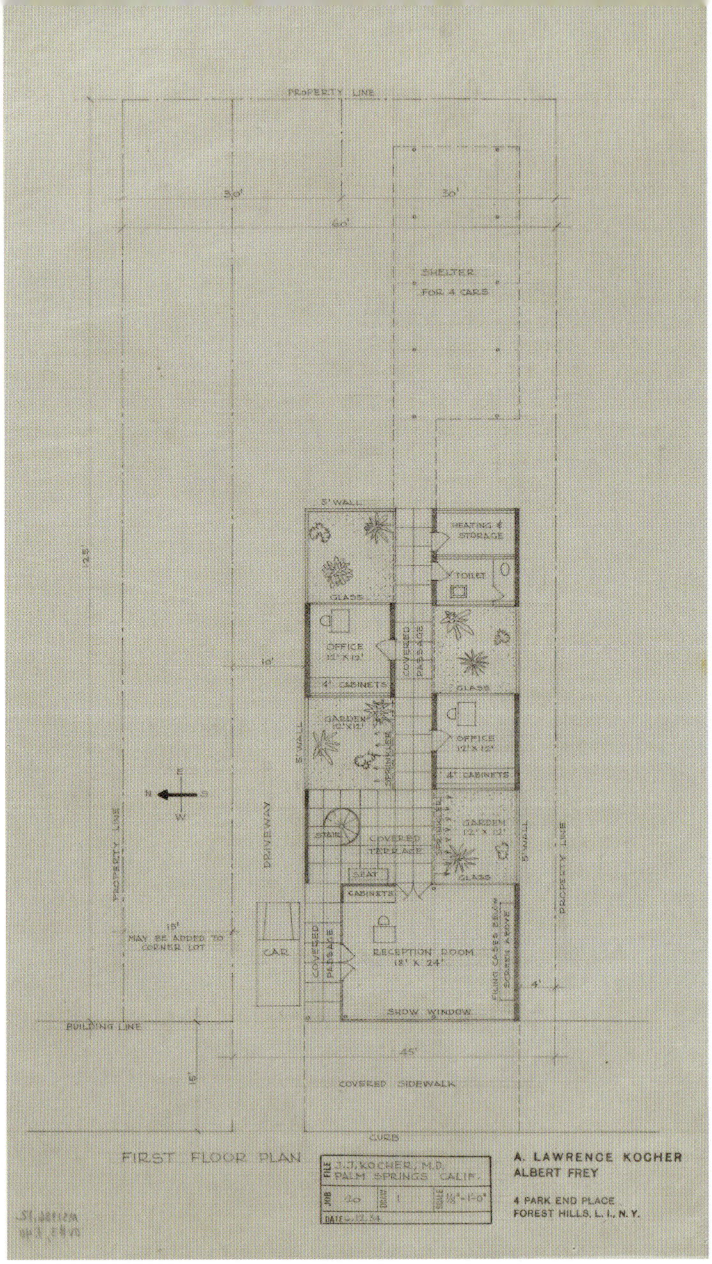
PROPERTY LINE
SHELTER FOR 4 CARS
HEATING & STORAGE
TOILET
OFFICE 12' X 12'
COVERED PASSAGE
GLASS
4' CABINETS
GARDEN 12' X 12'
OFFICE 12' X 12'
SPRINKLER
5' WALL
DRIVEWAY
STAIR
COVERED TERRACE
GARDEN 12' X 12'
SEAT
CABINETS
CAR
RECEPTION ROOM 18' X 24'
SHOW WINDOW
BUILDING LINE
COVERED SIDEWALK
CURB
15' MAY BE ADDED TO CORNER LOT
FIRST FLOOR PLAN
J.J. KOCHER, M.D.
PALM SPRINGS CALIF.
JOB 20
1
1/4"=1'-0"
DATE 6.12.34
A. LAWRENCE KOCHER
ALBERT FREY
4 PARK END PLACE
FOREST HILLS, L. I., N. Y.

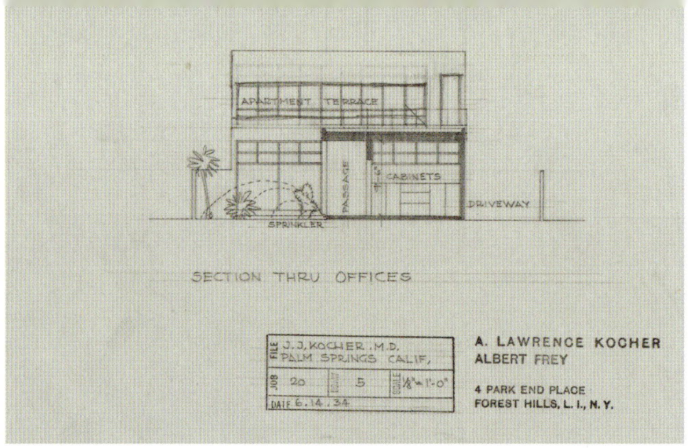
APARTMENT TERRACE
PASSAGE
CABINETS
DRIVEWAY
SPRINKLER
SECTION THRU OFFICES
J.J. KOCHER, M.D.
PALM SPRINGS CALIF.
JOB 20
5
1/8"=1'-0"
DATE 6.14.34
A. LAWRENCE KOCHER
ALBERT FREY
4 PARK END PLACE
FOREST HILLS, L. I., N. Y.

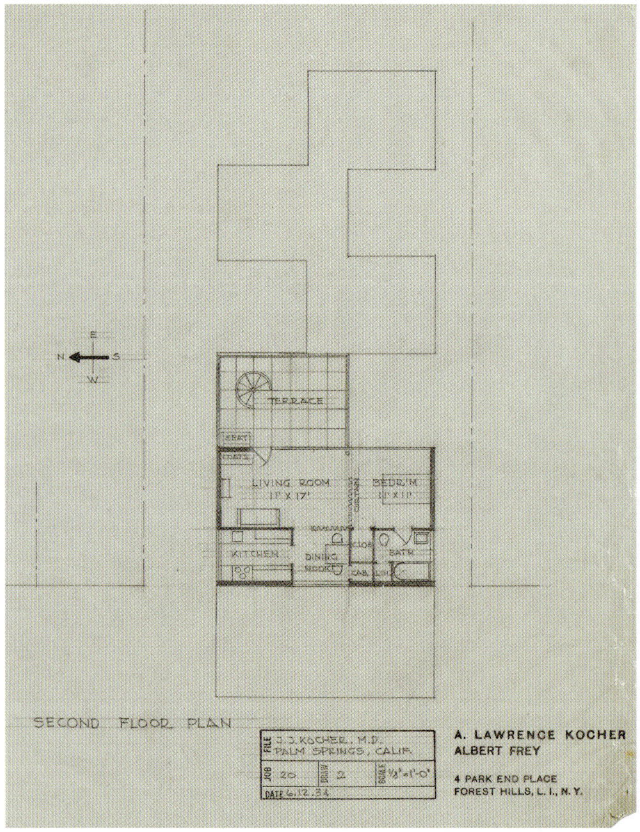
TERRACE
SEAT
LIVING ROOM 17' X 17'
BEDR'M
KITCHEN
DINING ROOM
BATH
SECOND FLOOR PLAN
J.J. KOCHER, M.D.
PALM SPRINGS, CALIF.
JOB 20
2
1/8"=1'-0"
DATE 6.12.34
A. LAWRENCE KOCHER
ALBERT FREY
4 PARK END PLACE
FOREST HILLS, L. I., N. Y.

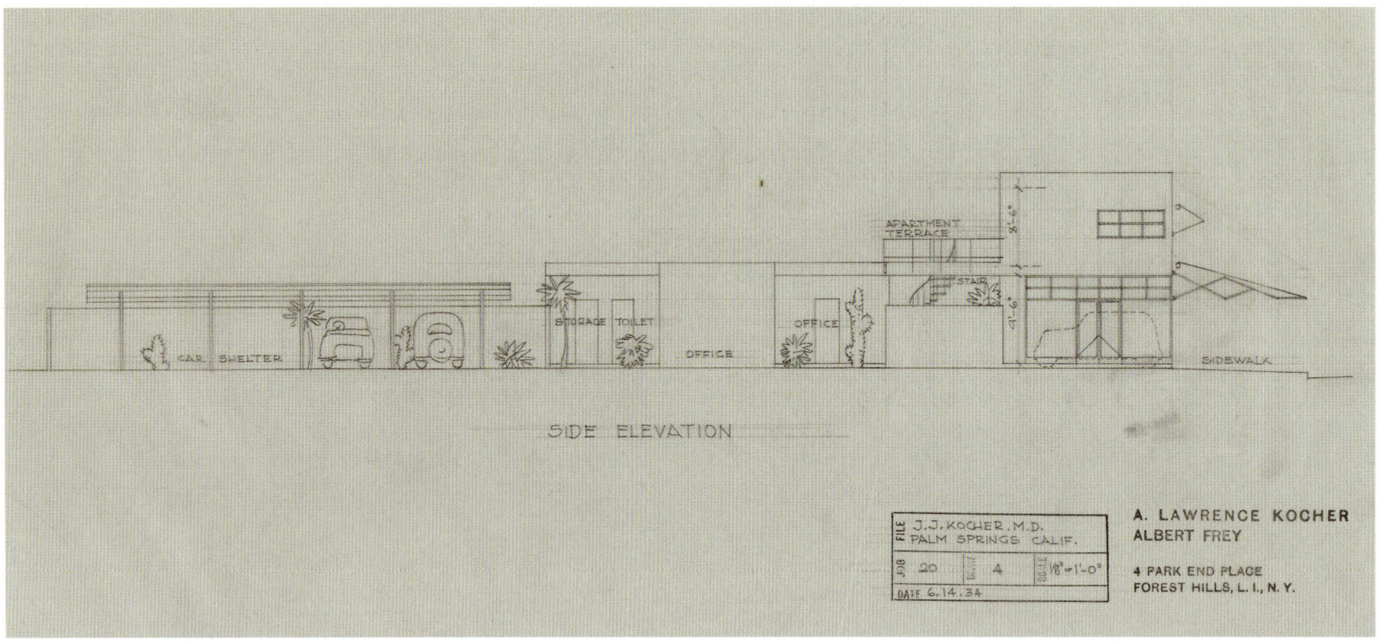
APARTMENT TERRACE
STAIR
CAR SHELTER
STORAGE
TOILET
OFFICE
OFFICE
SIDEWALK
SIDE ELEVATION
J.J. KOCHER, M.D.
PALM SPRINGS CALIF.
JOB 20
4
1/8"=1'-0"
DATE 6.14.34
A. LAWRENCE KOCHER
ALBERT FREY
4 PARK END PLACE
FOREST HILLS, L. I., N. Y.

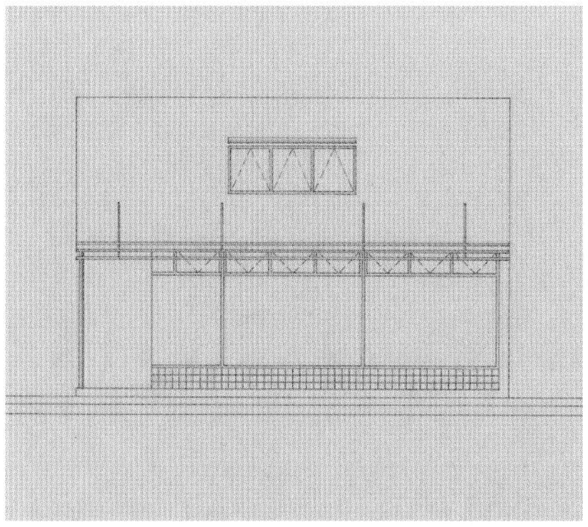

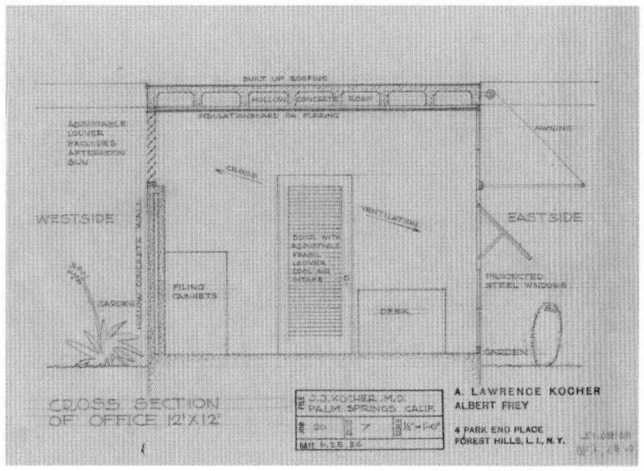

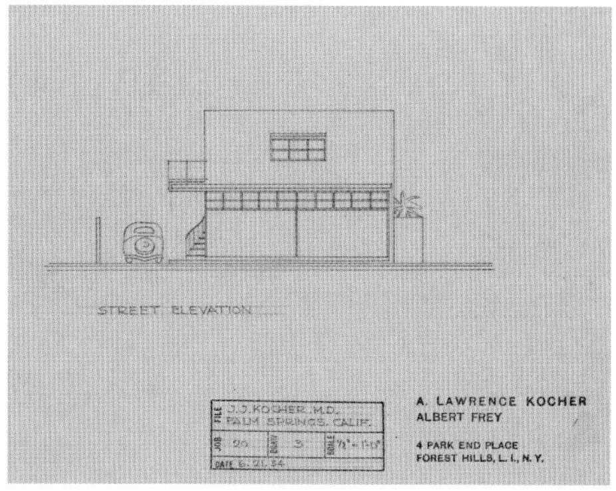

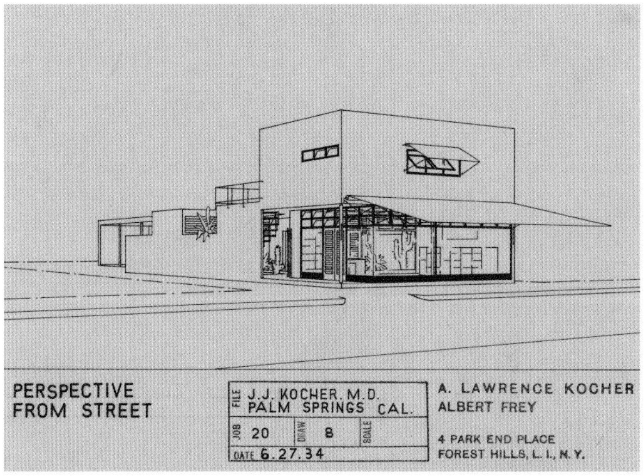

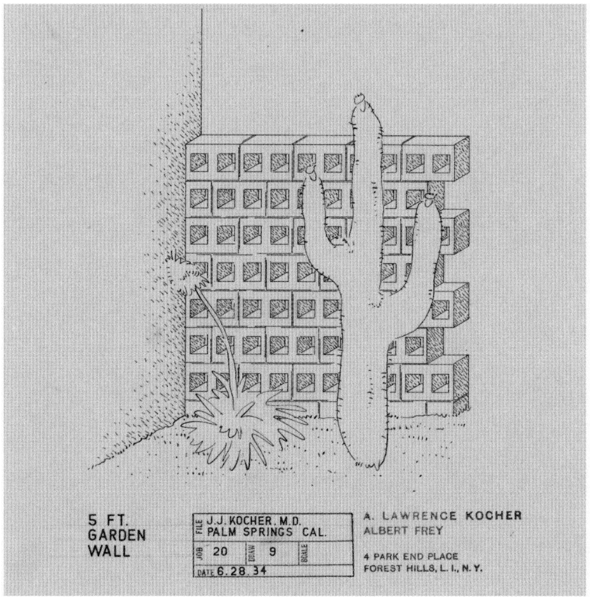

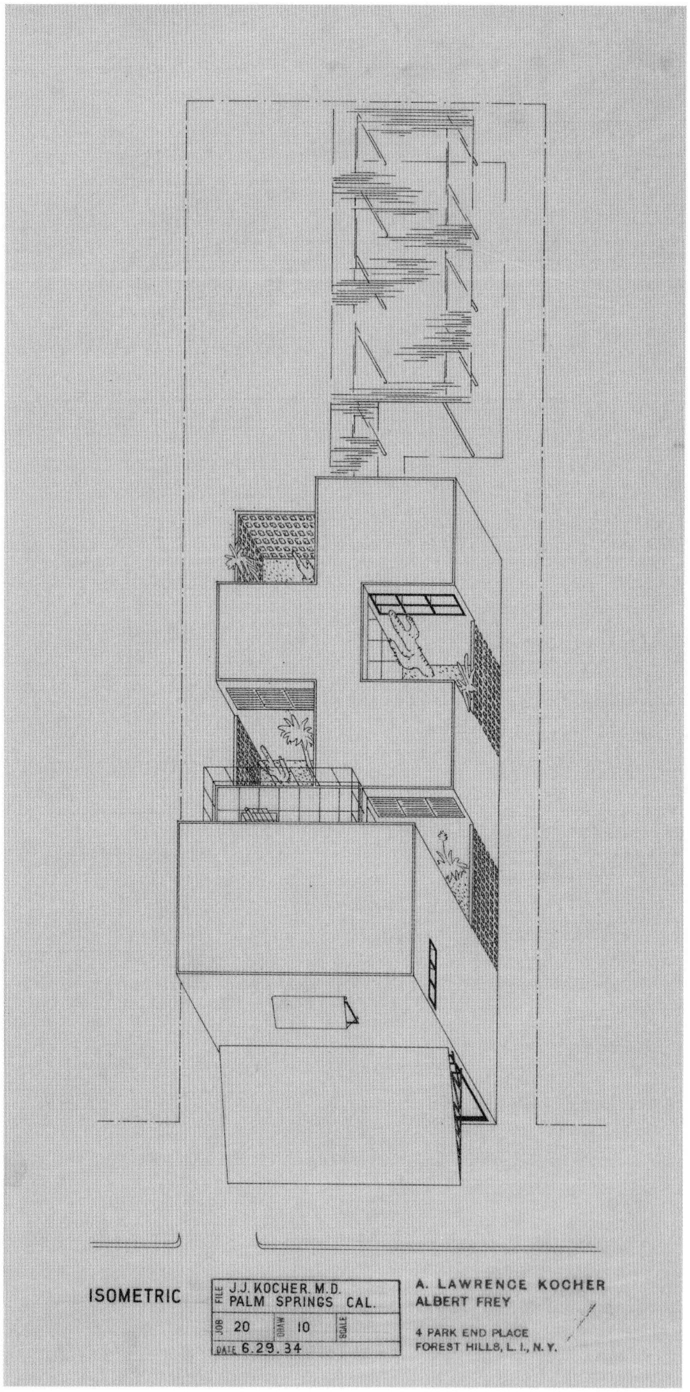

Previous page:
Figures 4.67 to 4.70. A. Lawrence Kocher and Albert Frey. 1934–1935. Kocher-Samson Building in Palm Springs, California. Diagrams. First preliminary project. June 1934. Different documents dated from June 12 and June 14.

This page:
Figures 4.71 to 4.76. A. Lawrence Kocher and Albert Frey. 1934–1935. Kocher-Samson Building in Palm Springs, California. Diagrams. First preliminary project. June 1934. Different documents dated from June 21 to June 29.

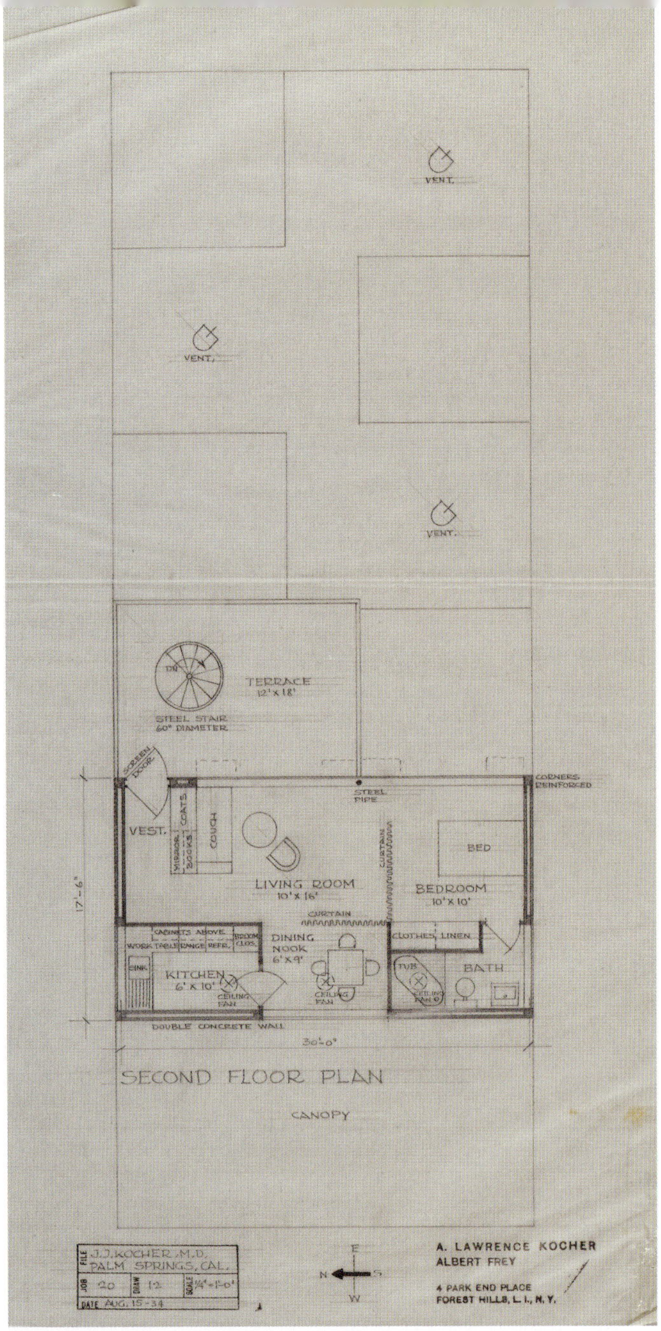

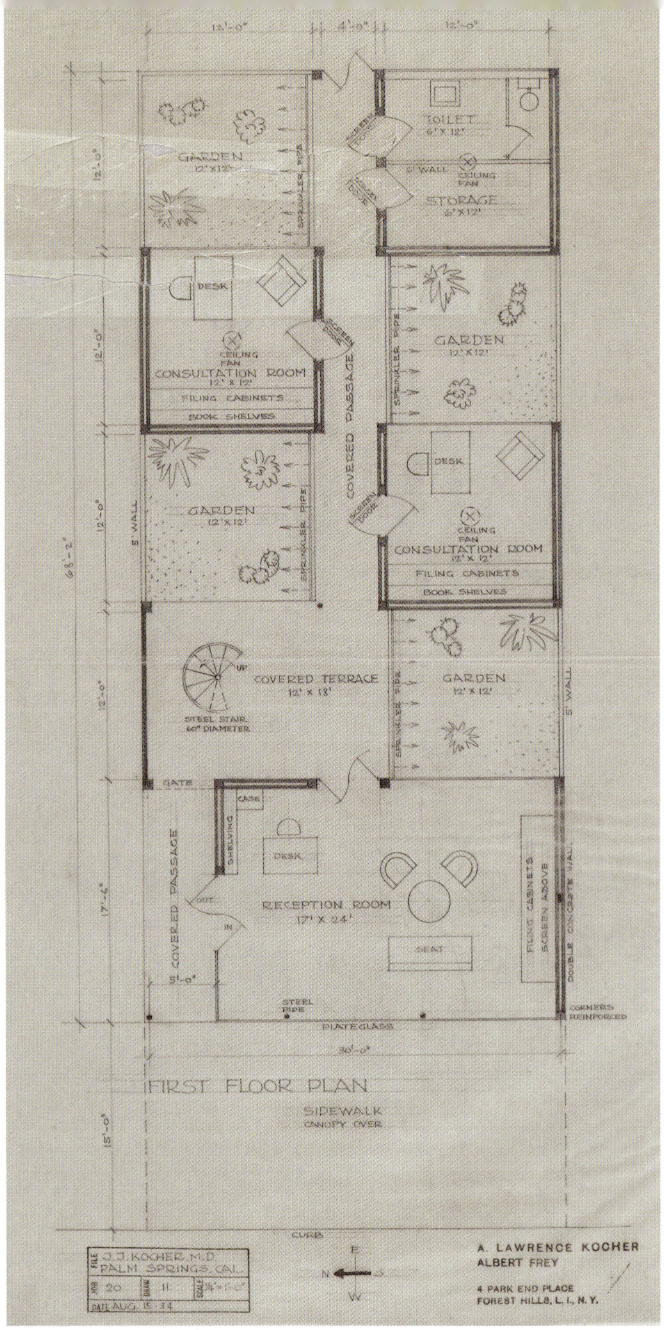

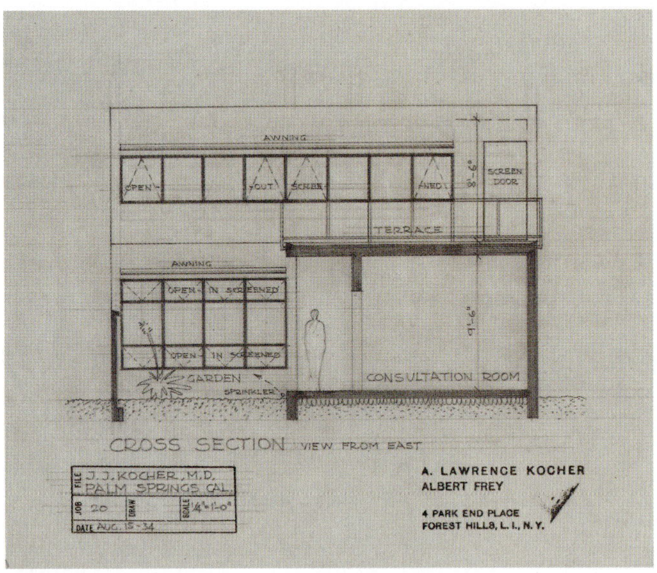

This page:
Figures 4.77 to 4.79. A. Lawrence Kocher and Albert Frey. 1934–1935. Kocher-Samson Building in Palm Springs, California. Diagrams. First preliminary project. Different documents dated in August, 1934.

Next page:
Figures 4.80 to 4.84. A. Lawrence Kocher and Albert Frey. 1934–1935. Kocher-Samson Building in Palm Springs, California. Diagrams. First preliminary project. Different documents dated in August, 1934.

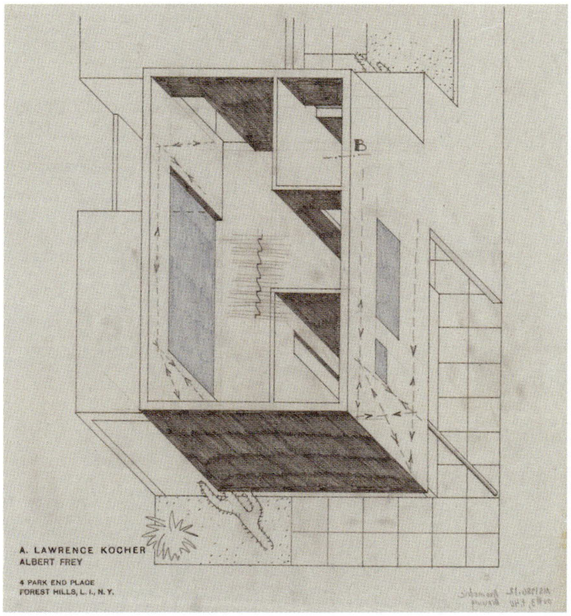
A. LAWRENCE KOCHER
ALBERT FREY
4 PARK END PLACE
FOREST HILLS, L. I., N. Y.

PERSPECTIVE FROM STREET
FILE J.J. KOCHER. M.D.
PALM SPRINGS. CAL.
JOB 20 DRAW 18 SCALE
DATE SEPT. 20 1934
A. LAWRENCE KOCHER
ALBERT FREY
4 PARK END PLACE
FOREST HILLS, L. I., N. Y.

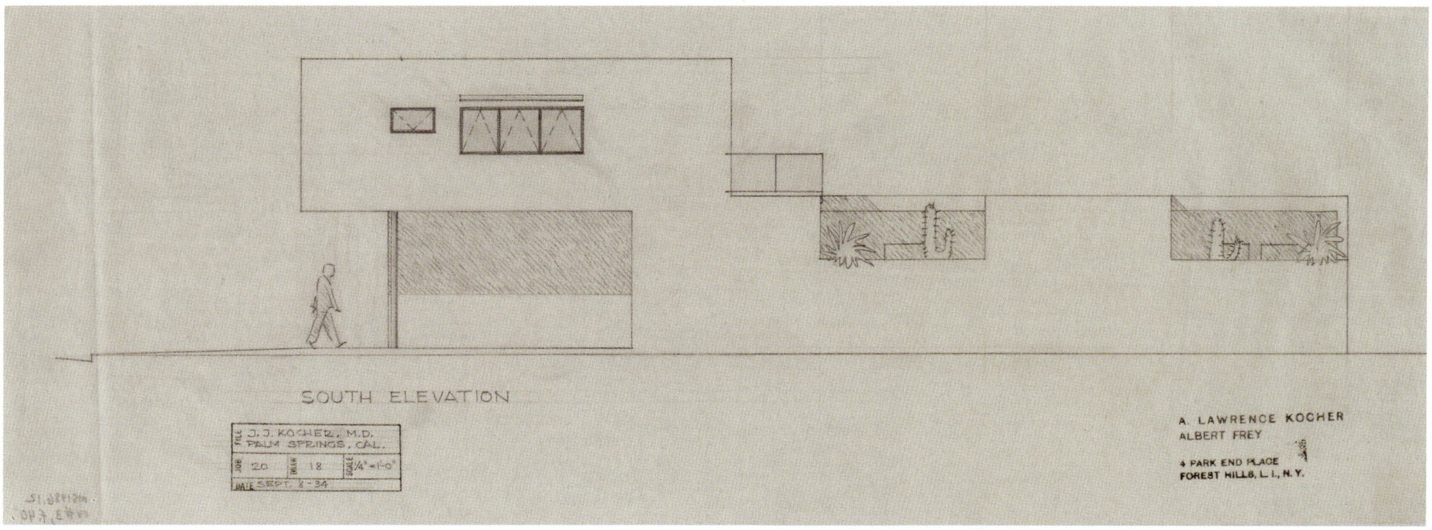
SOUTH ELEVATION
FILE J. J. KOCHER. M.D.
PALM SPRINGS. CAL.
JOB 20 DRAW 18 SCALE 1/4"=1'-0"
DATE SEPT. 8 - 34
A. LAWRENCE KOCHER
ALBERT FREY
4 PARK END PLACE
FOREST HILLS, L. I., N. Y.

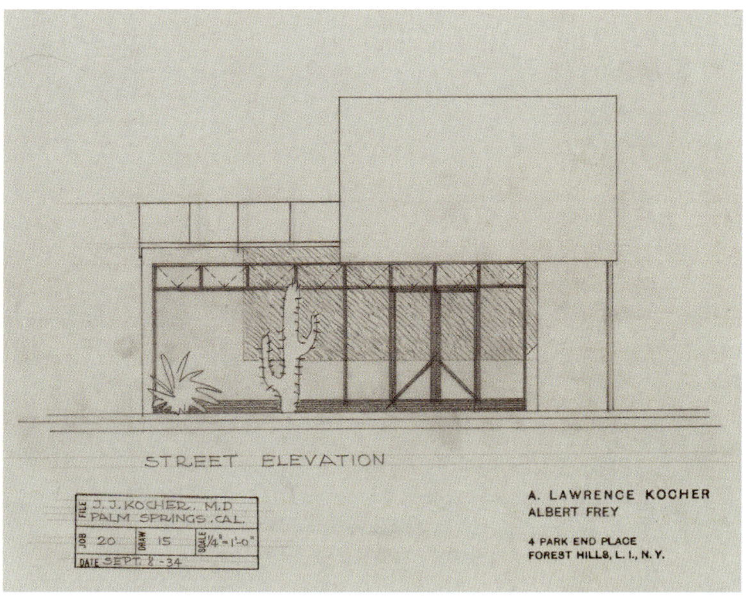
STREET ELEVATION
FILE J. J. KOCHER. M.D
PALM SPRINGS. CAL.
JOB 20 DRAW 15 SCALE 1/4"=1'-0"
DATE SEPT. 8 - 34
A. LAWRENCE KOCHER
ALBERT FREY
4 PARK END PLACE
FOREST HILLS, L. I., N. Y.

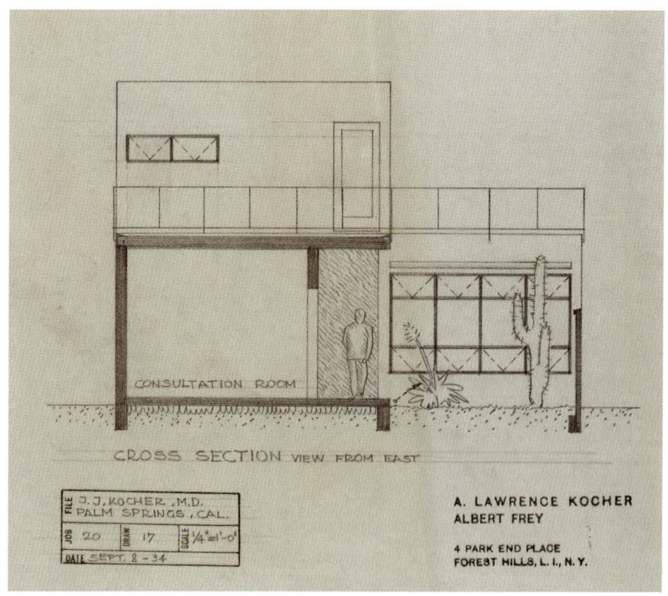
CONSULTATION ROOM
CROSS SECTION VIEW FROM EAST
FILE J. J. KOCHER. M.D.
PALM SPRINGS. CAL.
JOB 20 DRAW 17 SCALE 1/4"=1'-0"
DATE SEPT. 8 - 34
A. LAWRENCE KOCHER
ALBERT FREY
4 PARK END PLACE
FOREST HILLS, L. I., N. Y.

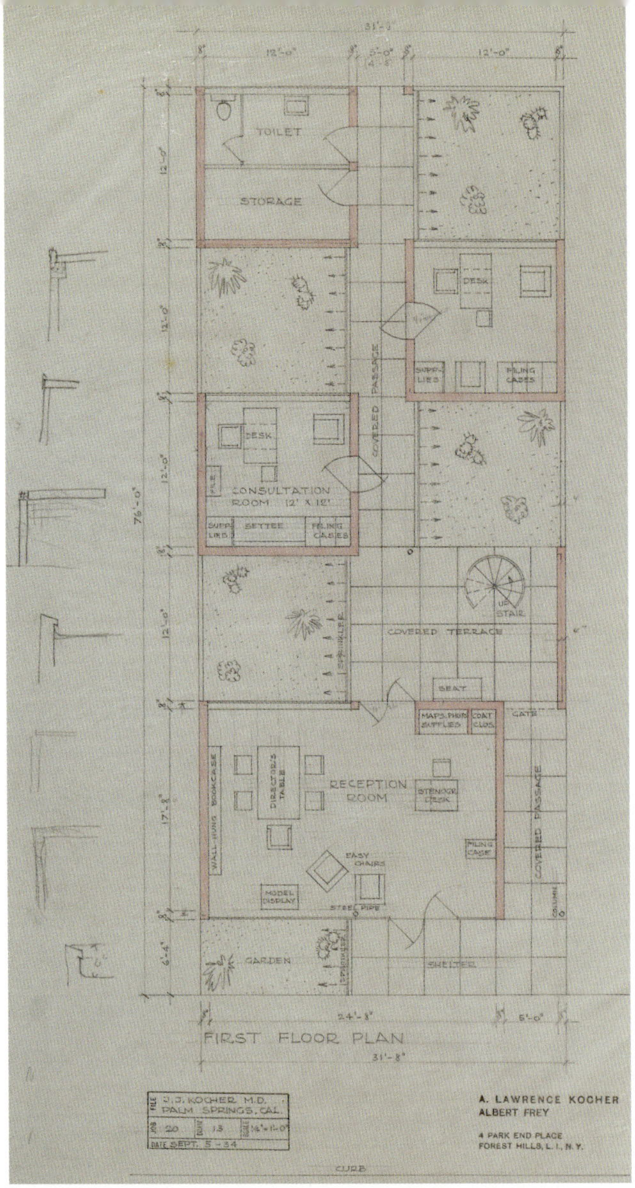

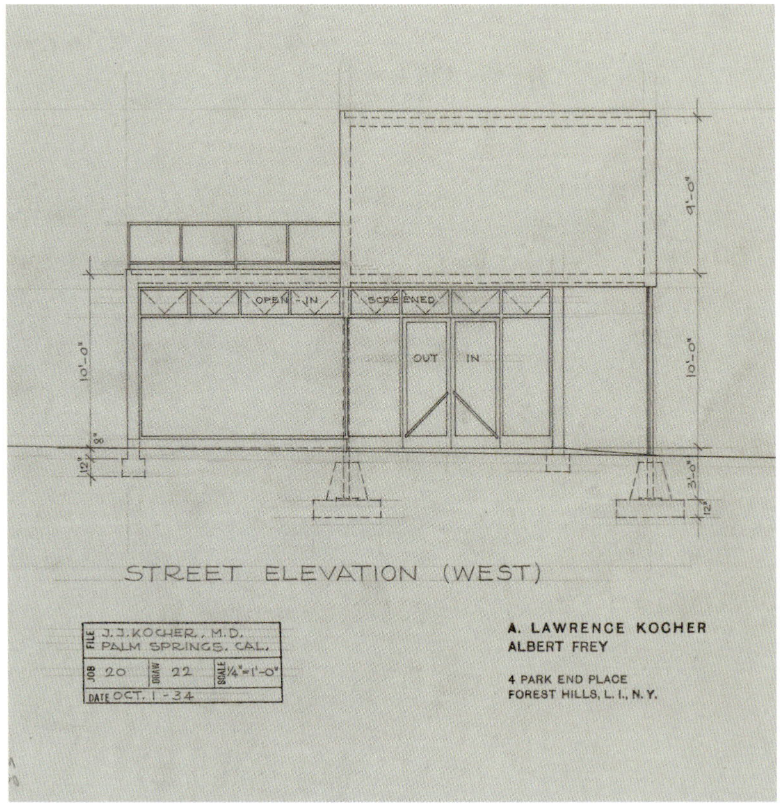

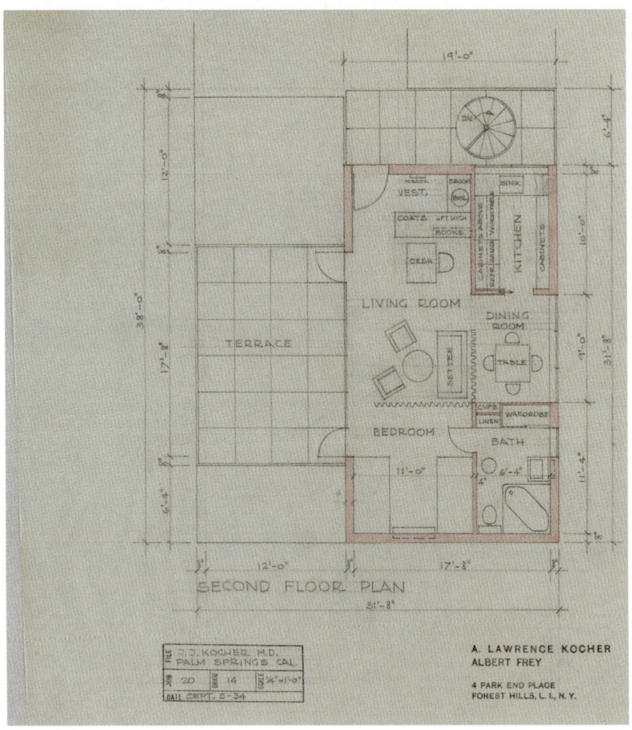

Figures 4.85 and 4.86. A. Lawrence Kocher and Albert Frey. 1934–1935. Kocher-Samson Building in Palm Springs, California. Final project. First and second floor plans. Dated September 1934.

Figure 4.87. A. Lawrence Kocher and Albert Frey. 1934–1935. Kocher-Samson Building in Palm Springs, California. Final project. Street elevation (west). Dated October 1934.

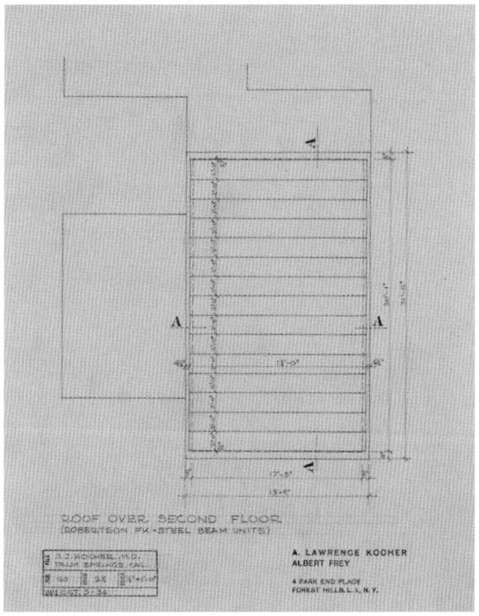

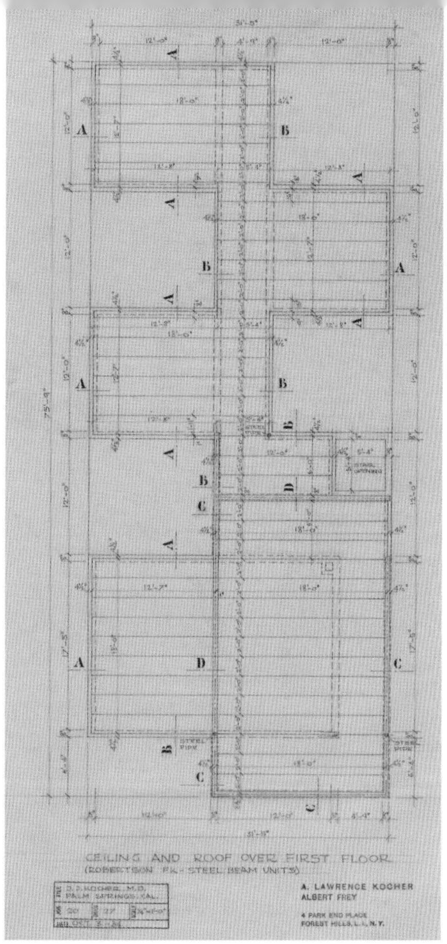

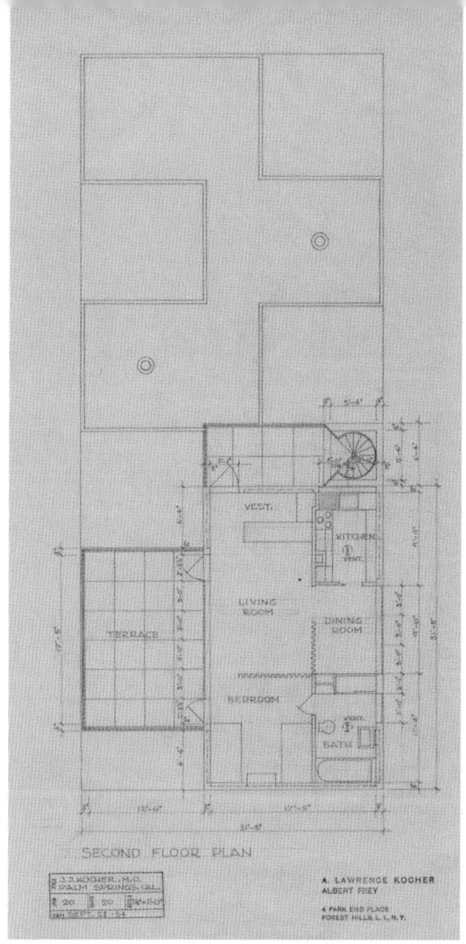

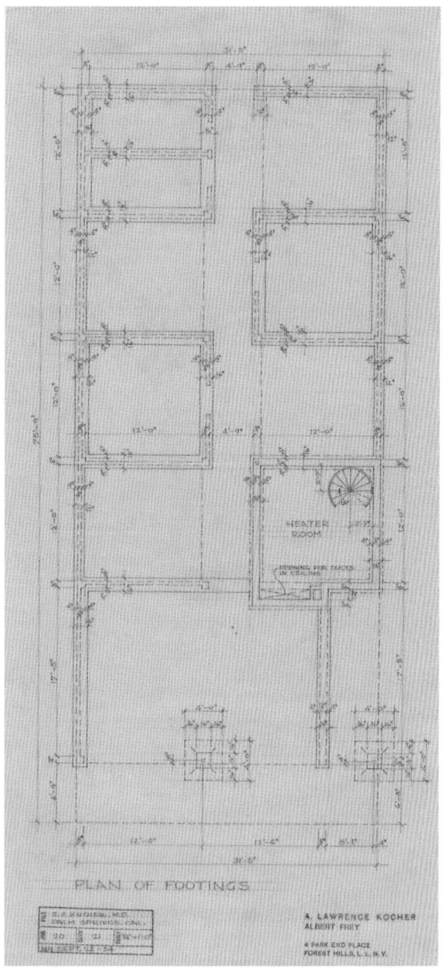

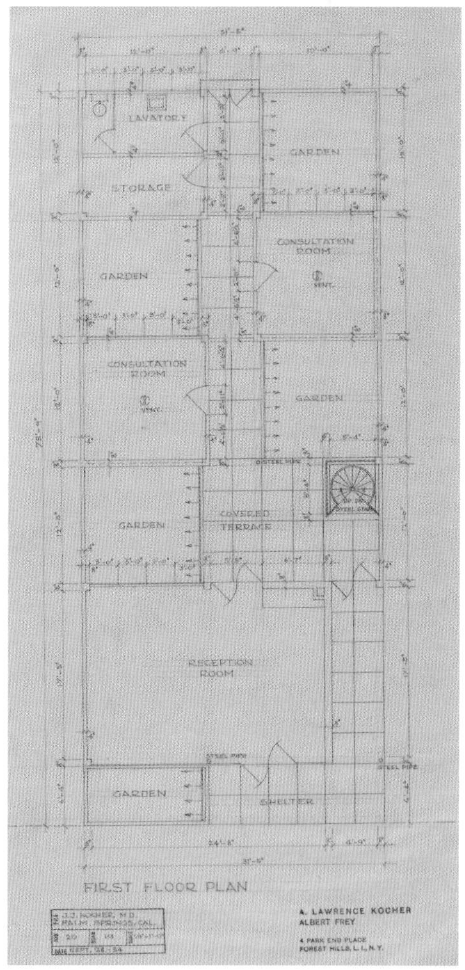

Figures 4.88 to 4.92. A. Lawrence Kocher and Albert Frey. 1934–1935. Kocher-Samson Building in Palm Springs, California. Final project. September–October 1934. Different documents dated from September 28 to October 3.

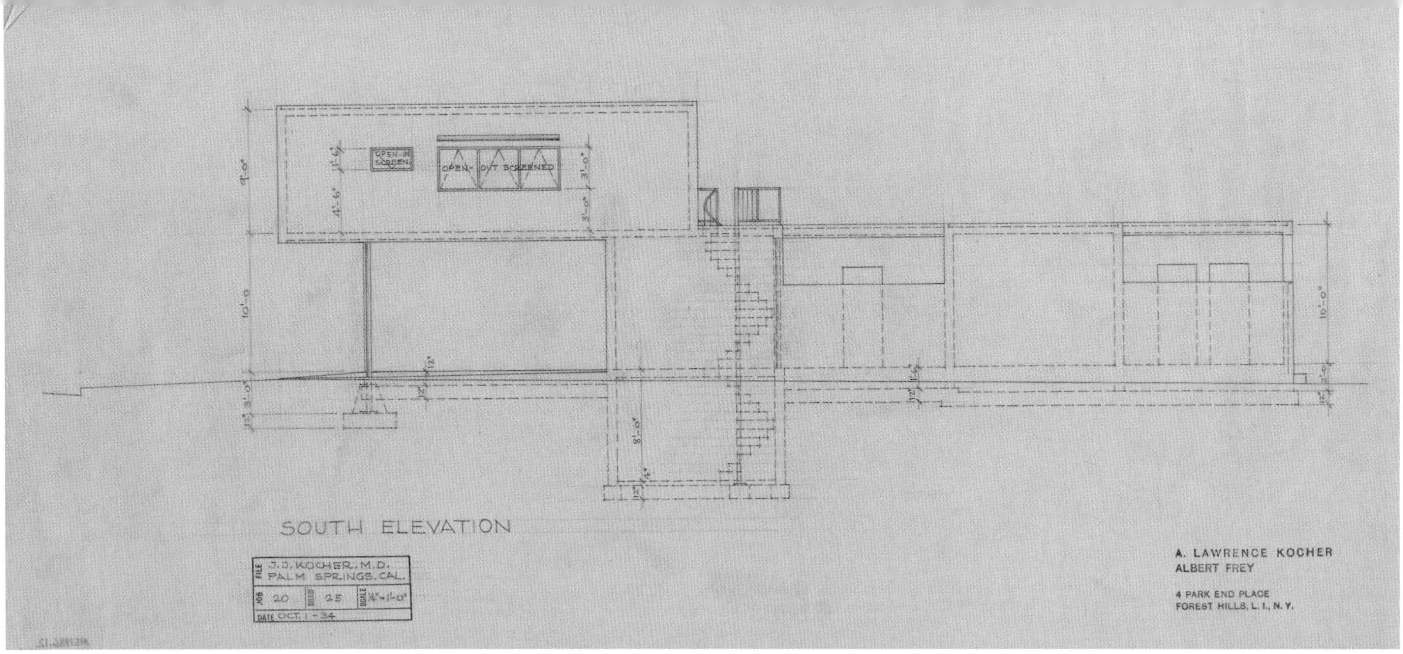
SOUTH ELEVATION
J.J. KOCHER, M.D.
PALM SPRINGS, CAL.
A. LAWRENCE KOCHER
ALBERT FREY
4 PARK END PLACE
FOREST HILLS, L. I., N.Y.

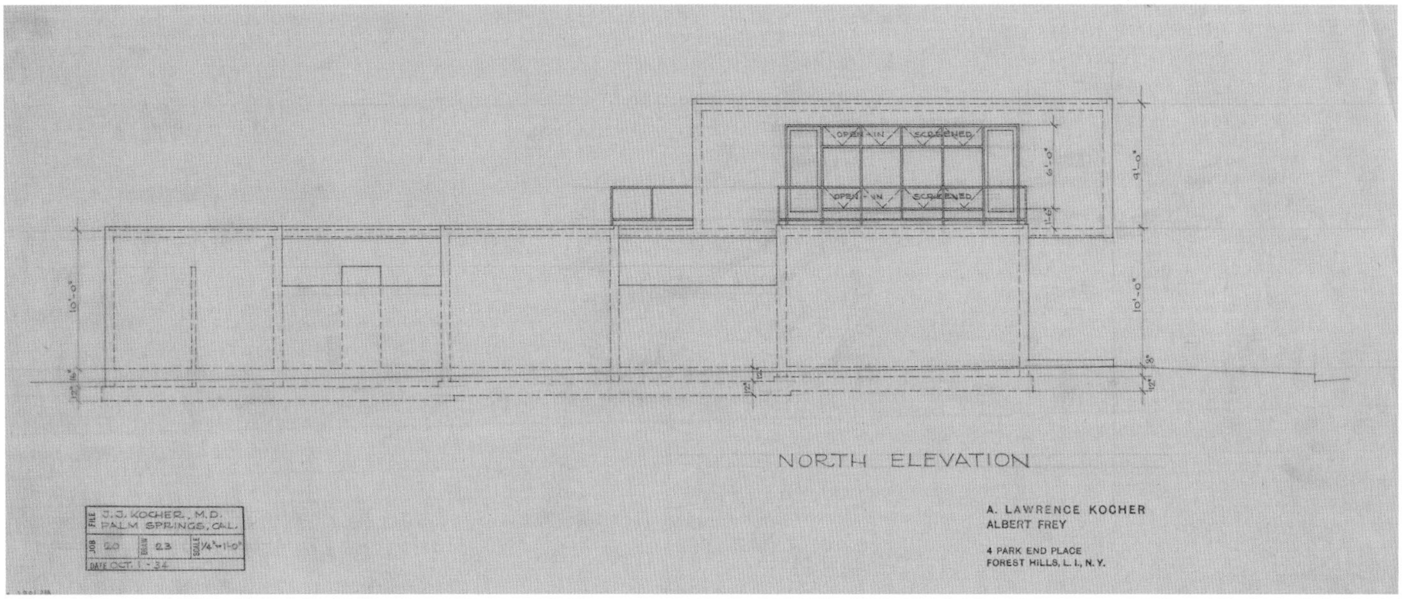
NORTH ELEVATION
J.J. KOCHER, M.D.
PALM SPRINGS, CAL.
A. LAWRENCE KOCHER
ALBERT FREY
4 PARK END PLACE
FOREST HILLS, L. I., N.Y.

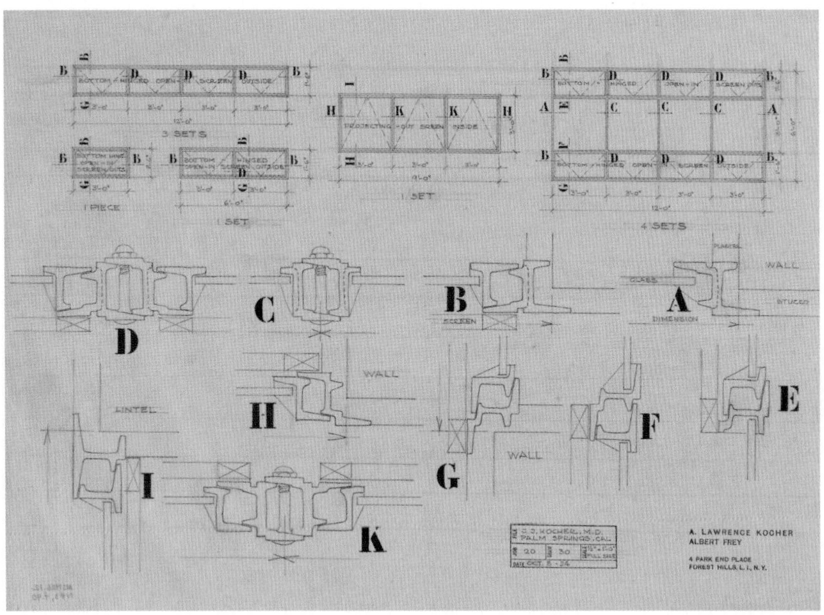
D
C
B
A
H
I
K
G
F
E
WALL
LINTEL
A. LAWRENCE KOCHER
ALBERT FREY
4 PARK END PLACE
FOREST HILLS, L. I., N.Y.

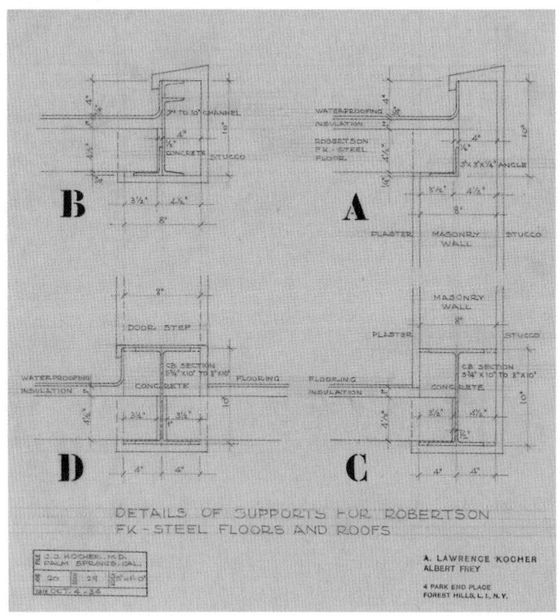
B
A
D
C
DETAILS OF SUPPORTS FOR ROBERTSON
FK-STEEL FLOORS AND ROOFS
A. LAWRENCE KOCHER
ALBERT FREY
4 PARK END PLACE
FOREST HILLS, L. I., N.Y.

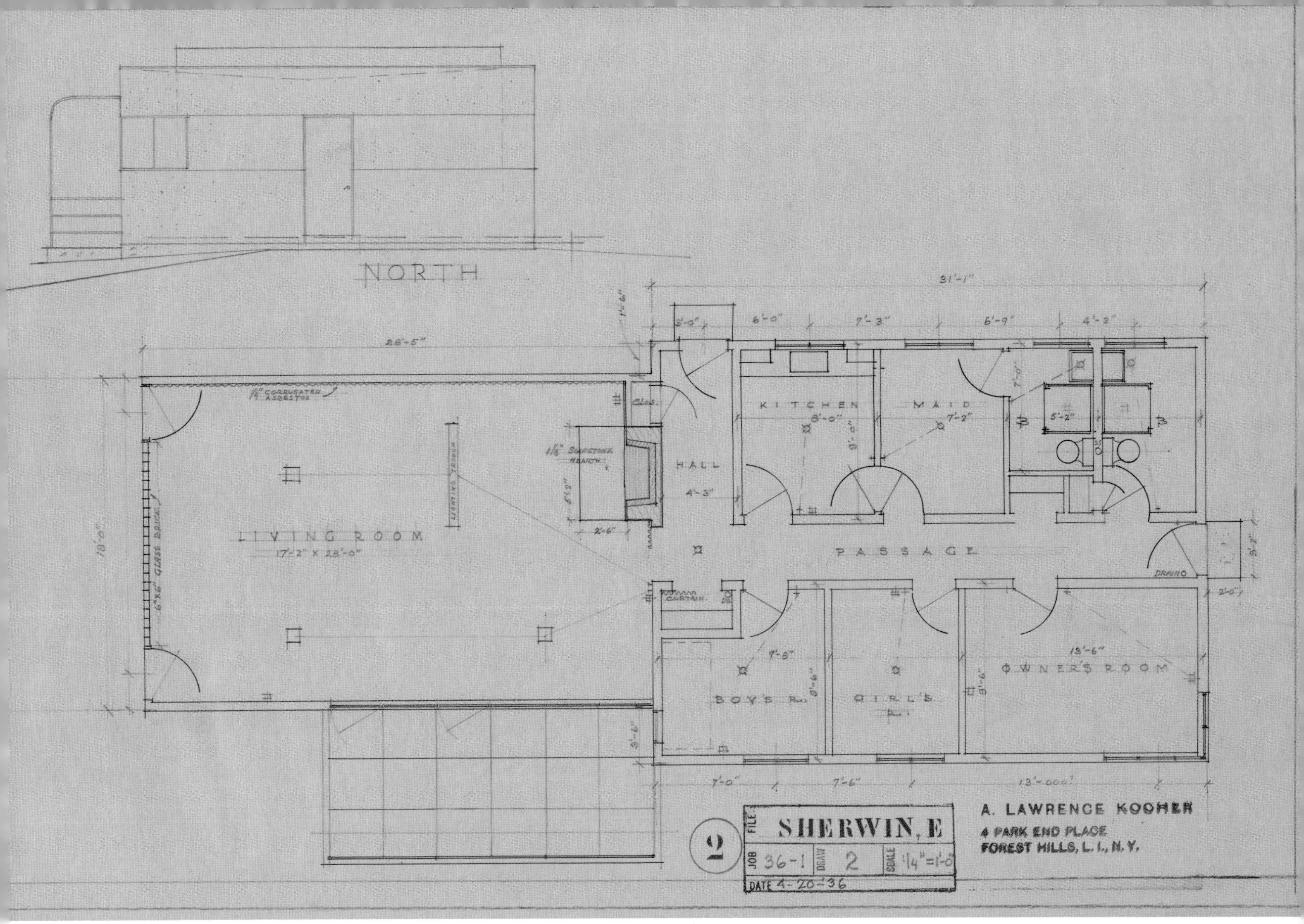

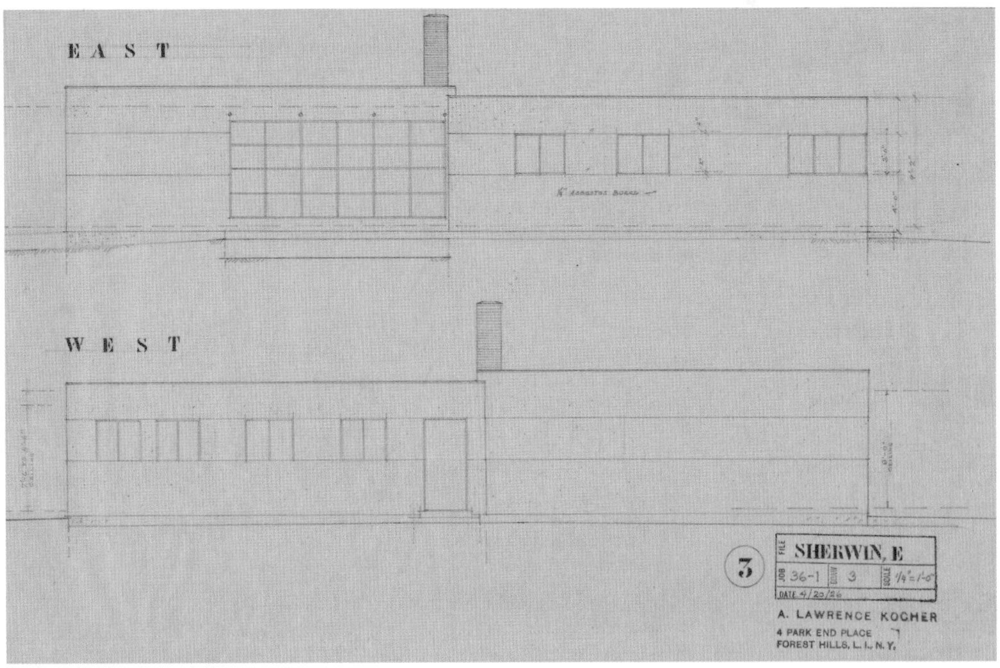

Previous page:

Figures 4.93 and 4.94. A. Lawrence Kocher and Albert Frey. 1934–1935. Kocher-Samson Building in Palm Springs, California. Diagrams. Final project. September-October 1934. Elevations dated 10-01-34.

Figures 4.95. A. Lawrence Kocher and Albert Frey. 1934–1935. Kocher-Samson Building in Palm Springs, California. Diagrams. Final project. September–October 1934. Window details dated 10-03-34.

Figures 4.96. A. Lawrence Kocher and Albert Frey. 1934–1935. Kocher-Samson Building in Palm Springs, California. Diagrams. Final project. September–October 1934. Floors and roofs details dated 10-04-34.

This page:

Figures 4.97 and 4.98. A. Lawrence Kocher. March–April, 1936. E. Sherwin House. First version. Floor plan and east and west elevations.

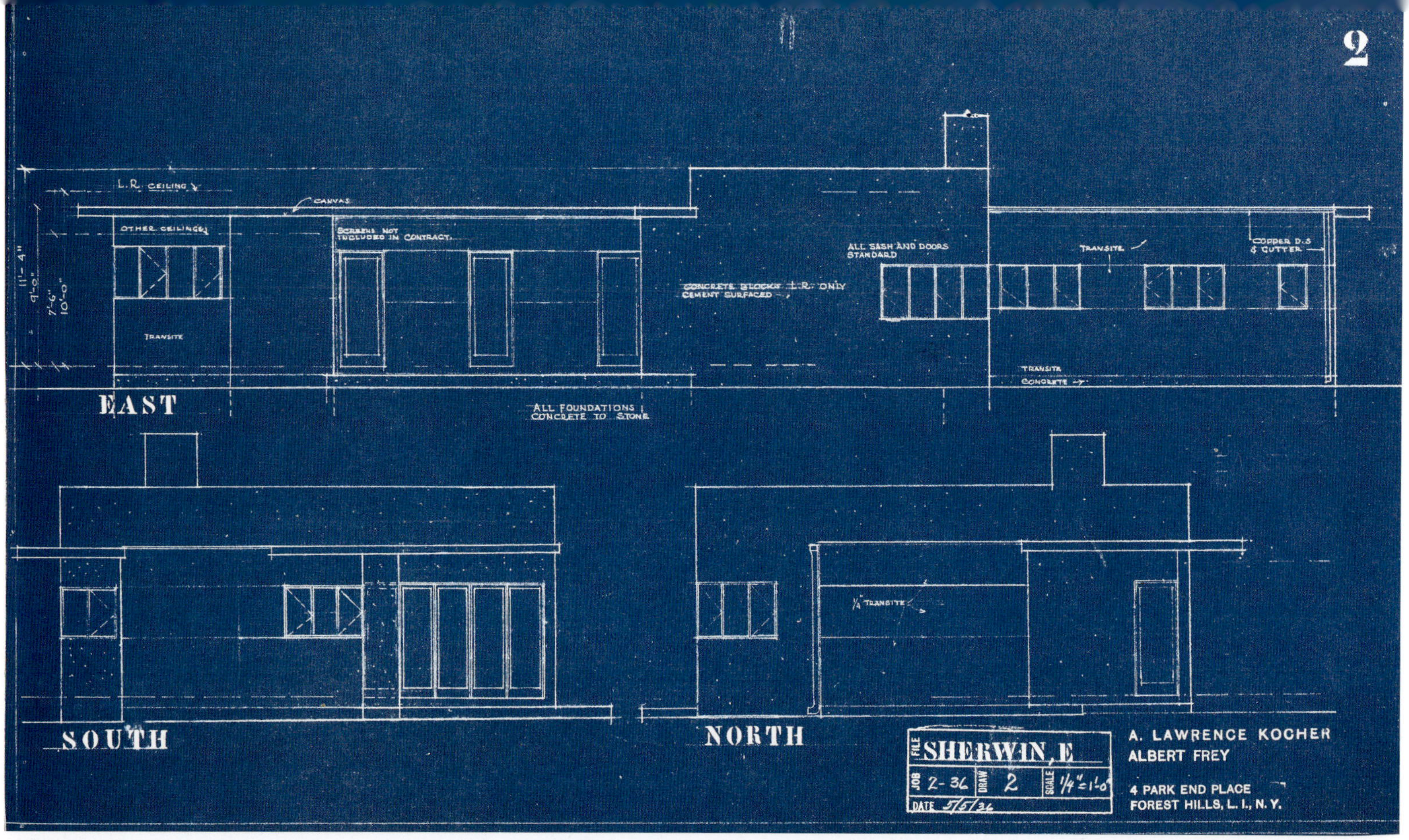
2
L.R. CEILING
CANVAS
OTHER CEILINGS
SCREENS NOT INCLUDED IN CONTRACT
TRANSITE
ALL SASH AND DOORS STANDARD
TRANSITE
COPPER D.S. & GUTTER
CONCRETE BLOCKS L.R. ONLY CEMENT SURFACED
TRANSITE
CONCRETE
EAST
ALL FOUNDATIONS CONCRETE TO STONE
SOUTH
NORTH
TRANSITE
SHERWIN, E
JOB 2-36
DRAW 2
SCALE 1/4"=1'-0"
DATE 5/5/36
A. LAWRENCE KOCHER
ALBERT FREY
4 PARK END PLACE
FOREST HILLS, L. I., N. Y.

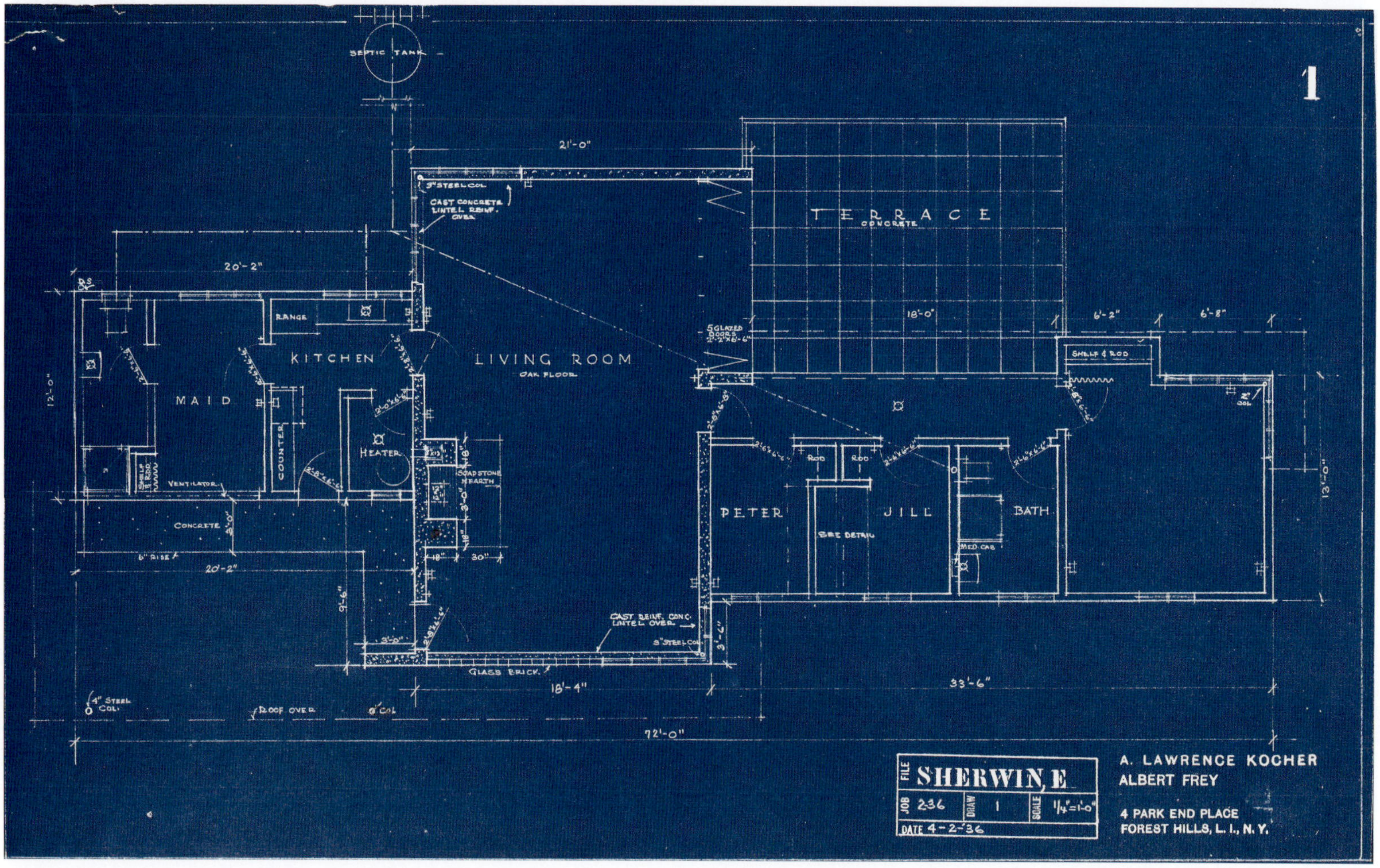
1
SEPTIC TANK
21'-0"
TERRACE
CONCRETE
20'-2"
RANGE
KITCHEN
LIVING ROOM
OAK FLOOR
MAID
COUNTER
HEATER
VENTILATOR
CONCRETE
20'-2"
18'-0"
6'-2"
6'-8"
SHELF & ROD
ROD
PETER
JILL
BATH
SEE DETAIL
MED. CAB.
13'-0"
12'-0"
9'-6"
GLASS BRICK
18'-4"
33'-6"
72'-0"
ROOF OVER
SHERWIN, E
JOB 2-36
DRAW 1
SCALE 1/4"=1'-0"
DATE 4-2-36
A. LAWRENCE KOCHER
ALBERT FREY
4 PARK END PLACE
FOREST HILLS, L. I., N. Y.

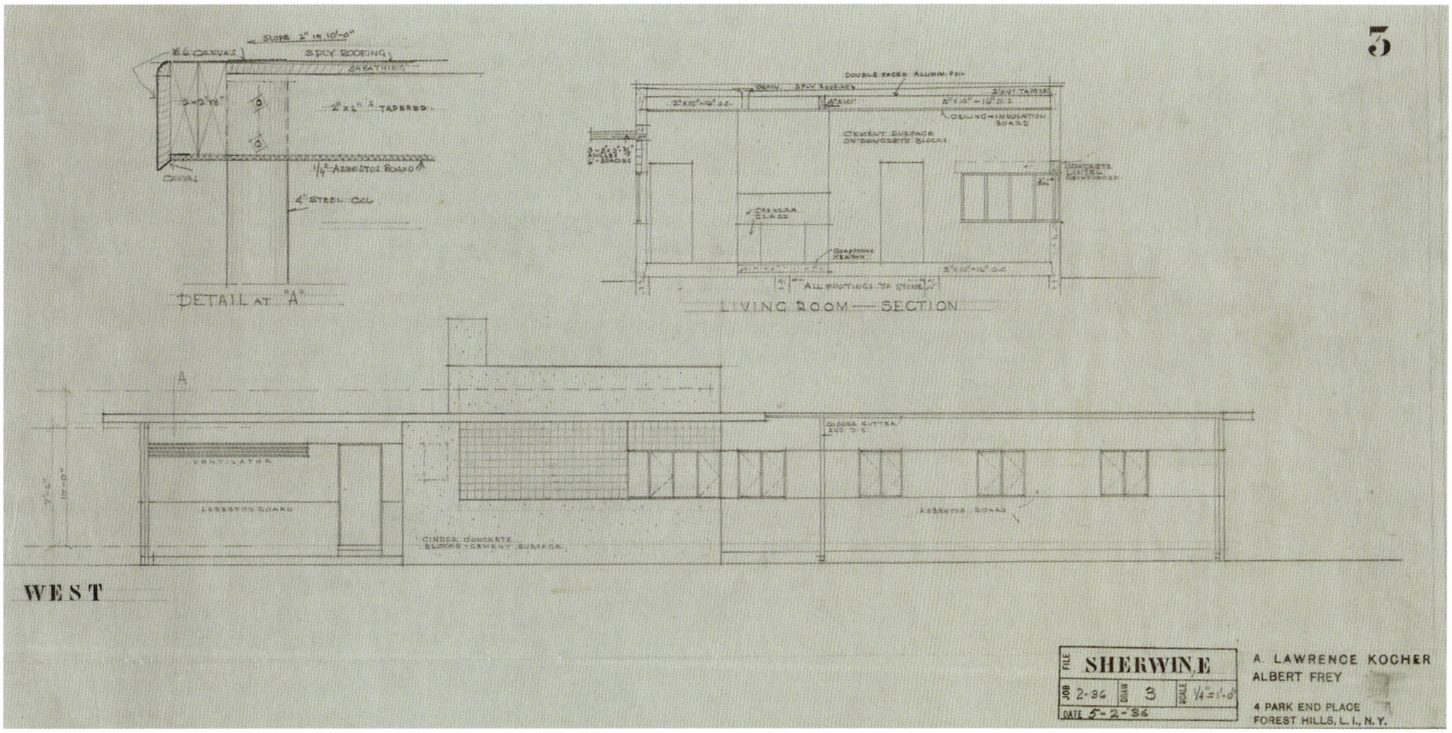

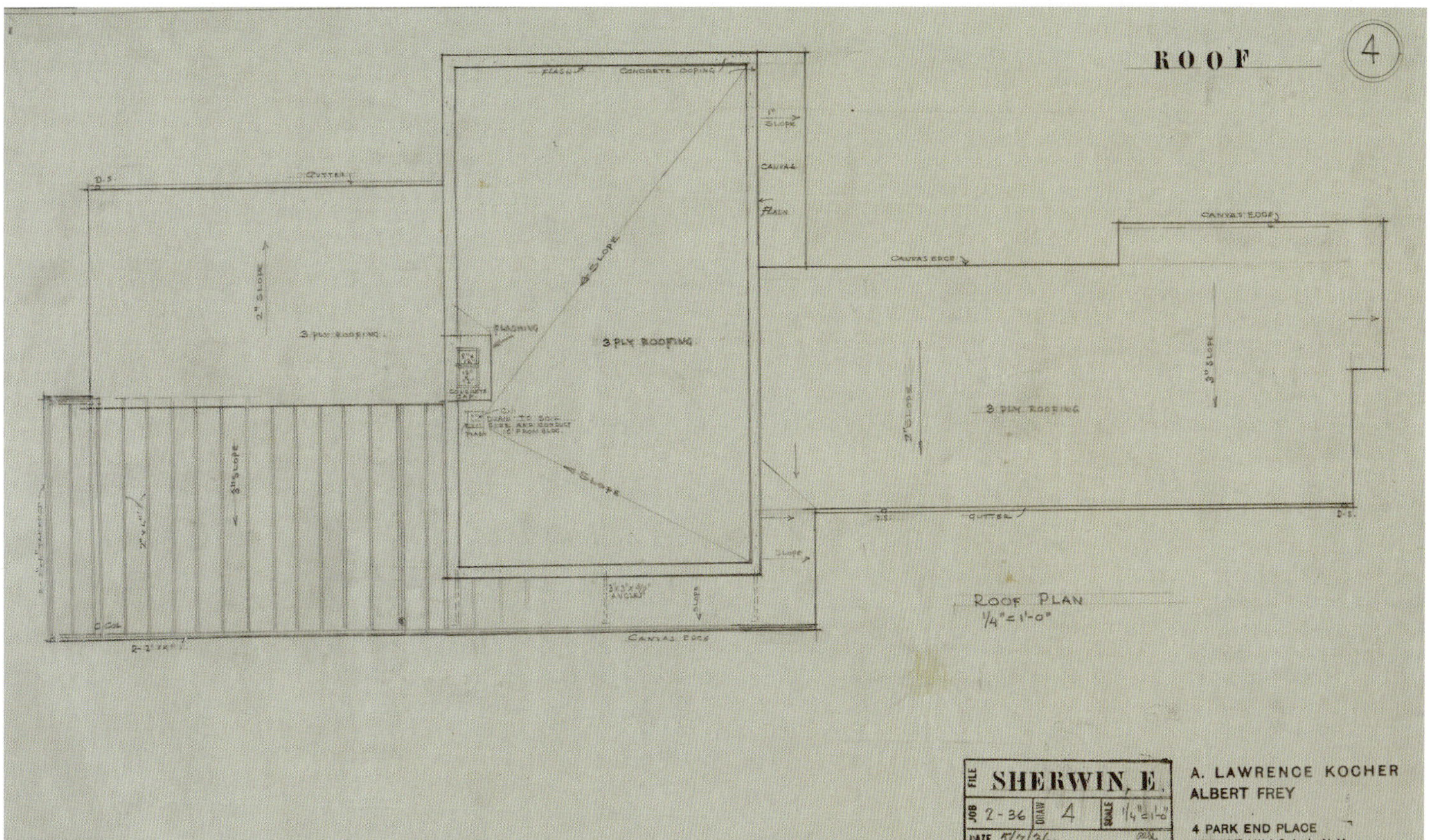

Previous page:
Figures 4.99 and 4.100. A. Lawrence Kocher and Albert Frey. May 1936. E. Sherwin House. Second version. Floor plan and east, south, and north elevations.

This page:
Figures 4.101 and 4.102. A. Lawrence Kocher and Albert Frey. May 1936. E. Sherwin House. Second version. West elevation and details, roof plan.

1935–1941

THE CARNEGIE TECH AND BLACK MOUNTAIN COLLEGE YEARS

By the end of 1935, the construction on the Kocher-Samson Building in Palm Springs and the Kocher Canvas Weekend House were nearing completion. A. Lawrence Kocher was at a crucial point of his professional life: between April and May of 1936, he produced the design of the Sherwin House alongside Albert Frey—their final collaboration as a team. The friendly dissolution of his association with Frey was added to Kocher's new family circumstances in a moment of deep economic uncertainty. He was now the father of two children Larry and Sandra, from his second marriage. The family still lived in the affluent neighborhood of Forest Hills Gardens in Queens, New York, and spent their weekends in the new Long Island house. Kocher was still the Managing Editor of *Architectural Record*, and still an Advisory Committee member of Architecture for the Restoration of Williamsburg, positions he had held since 1928. Nevertheless, his contract with *Architectural Record* would expire in 1938 and he looked for new challenges. In his own words:

> My leaving of the *Architectural Record* in 1938 had been planned in advance (1928). Having combined architectural practice with editing, 1928-1938, it was a wish to return to teaching and writing.[1]

It was a time of complete shift with regards to Kocher's job perspectives, and yet it was also a moment of sedimentation and maturation in his ideas about the relationship between architecture and technology. Kocher's architectural ideology still reflected his ongoing search for a national style that would be able to link the rationalism of the European modern movement with the American vernacular. After his published early writings on traditional architecture in the East Coast, and due both to Frey's influence and to the ethos of the New Deal, Kocher's categorical definition of "vernacular" transformed and now included anonymous artifacts of industrialization that plagued the American landscape; this also included a series of alternative dwelling solutions related to the automobile—like mobile homes, trailers, autocamp, and roadside cabins. The growing weight of anonymous architecture, in Kocher's conception of vernacular, is clearly illustrated both by his designs and by the number of articles devoted to the topic in *Architectural Record* during these years; in 1936 alone there were six articles addressing the challenge of domestic mobility in *Architectural Record*.[2] Nonetheless, the published article "Architecture on route U.S. 40 and 66" (May 1937) confirmed these mobile dwelling solutions—alongside industrial artifacts, like grain elevators and mills—as the new American vernacular by the magazine. Compiled by Douglas Haskell, the article includes pictures of a grain elevator in Kansas, a mobile house and cabins for nomads designed by the engineer William B. Stout, and several examples of roadside cabins and autocamps in the West and Midwest, all under the sub-title of "vernacular forms."[3] With Haskell and Kocher at the forefront of transient architecture and its benefits, the article summarizes the position of *Architectural Record*:

> The United States is the country of the automobile, one to every fourth inhabitant, and the main growth of many a Western city has occurred since the use of cars became widespread. This gives significance to the astonishing growth of such institutions as the trailer and the tourist camp. These are not to be understood as having any present structural or formal distinction. They are architecture in the vernacular (...) What may not yet have been fully realized is the importance of the trailer in the field as yet untouched by the tourist cabin, namely, as laboratory for scientific and economical shelter construction.[4]

The magazine's interest on mobile dwelling was a response to the historical moment, as the industry of the house trailer experienced an exponential growth. According to *Architectural Record*, from the beginning of the depression, the number of motorized nomads had increased to an estimated one million people, forming the base for the "fastest growing industry in America, trailers."[5] This success was attributed to the increased demand of these houses not as symbol of fun and freedom, but as the only kind of shelter affordable by the poor, evicted, or unemployed individuals and families who opted for trailers—often for the first time—as a permanent home during these depression years.

This new type of factory-made vernacular reinforced Kocher's methodological hierarchy and that the key concept to accomplish a coveted national style was still prefabrication. In the opening paragraph of a 1936 text, entitled "Prefabrication and Architecture," Kocher states, "the machine production of building materials and equipment is, in our modern age, the most powerful influence acting upon the character of the house. The dwelling is being unmistakably transformed by modern means of production, factories, machines, technology, and research."[6] This is a claim consistent with the most

CARNEGIE ARCHITECTS DO THEIR HOME WORK

IN THIS BUILDING in Pittsburgh Carnegie Institute of Technology is housed its Department of Architecture, which in its 33rd year is putting a new emphasis on American architecture's Depression child—housing. To help reorganize the department, Tech got Architect Alfred Lawrence Kocher to commute between Tech and his New York practice.

Top & bottom center, Bulletin Index Photos. Middle strip, Miller. Bottom left & right, Hay.

STUDENTS at Tech get plenty of practice along with their theory. To give architects the feel of materials, a muscular knowledge of how they are put together, students are learning to mortar bricks, lay them into a brick wall.

HERE Carnegie Tech students are learning to use plaster, one more of the hundreds of possible materials with which an architect can create. Architectural students this year are building a residential garden as a class project.

STUDENTS here learn to work with wood. Tech's faculty is distinguished in 1938-39 because Lawrence Kocher, former editor of *Architectural Record,* is a famed authority on small houses and their materials.

s house in-
four-room,
ging gently
h hopes to

HERE two students chat with Department Head William Frank Hitchens, who has taught at Tech since 1913. Besides Bachelor Hitchens, the faculty comprises 11 instructors for about 100 students who come from 14 states, three offshore areas.

THIS is the living room of the house Tech students built last year. Hitchens believes the house has been too long neglected in architectural schools, hopes Tech graduates will play a large part in the housing evolution of the U.S.

This page:
Figure 5.1. A. Lawrence Kocher and Carnegie Institute of Technology students. 1938. Design-build studio. Low-cost experimental house on the university campus. Pittsburgh. Publication.

Next page:
Figure 5.2 and 5.3. A. Lawrence Kocher and Carnegie Institute of Technology students. 1938. Design-build studio. Low-cost experimental house on the university campus. Pittsburgh. Pictures of the model.

Keep File – LADIES' HOME JOURNAL — May 1937 27

No. 394

For week ends, for summer, for year-round living, a minimum-cost house by A. Lawrence Kocher.

See Comment particularly P. 3

A House for the Two-Day Week

BY JOHN CUSHMAN FISTERE

The living-dining room, separated from the kitchen by a cabinet opening into both areas; and above, the compact but adequate plan.

LOG cabins used to be either what Presidents were born in, or what Old Black Joe and Uncle Tom grew old in. Except for vine, rose or honeysuckle covered cottages inhabited by honeymoon couples, they have probably been more celebrated in song and story than any other type of shelter. They are definitely romantic.

Nowadays, having lost none of their romance, cabins are becoming more and more an accepted part of the way we live, or at least the way we would like to live. Life hustles along at a pace that demands periodic braking, a change of scene or a new point of view. And a cabin in the pines—or its equivalent by the sea—is one of the best of all possible ways of getting it.

The new role of the cabin as a week-end "escape" has brought about refinements in planning, design, construction and equipment. I don't mean that they've become citified; simply that since they're being used more often, they're becoming more conveniently usable. Cabins still imply what we town dwellers like to call "roughing it"; but there's not much sense in spending all our time making up for (Continued on Page 92)

Prize-winning summer home in a California competition, designed by Samuel E. Lunden. Somewhat modern in feeling, the house is built of redwood.

No. 395

Complete plans and specifications for vacation homes are available for $1.00 each, from the LADIES' HOME JOURNAL Architectural Department, Philadelphia, Pennsylvania. An authoritative booklet on the planning and construction of log cabins is also available for 25 cents.

Figure 5.4. A. Lawrence Kocher. May 1937. "Two-day weekend Minimum Cost House." *Ladies' Home Journal.*

orthodox modernistic ideology, but it is not one that completely defines Kocher's position about prefabrication. He had always regarded prefabrication not only as a modernistic trait, but as the necessary link between modernity and traditional American architecture, denying the modernist claims of "originality," as prefabrication is an inherent vernacular feature of American architecture since colonial times. In an undated and unpublished text, archived among his papers in Williamsburg, he elaborates his ideas about prefabrication as a vernacular attribute:

> The claim of modernists as having devised 'something new' in proposing the technique of prefabrication as a novel construction method with economy of design and savings 'no end' because of mass production of the easily fitting parts, is being challenged.[7]

After citing Leonardo Da Vinci, and even a passage from the Book of Kings, as historic precedents for modern prefabrication, Kocher focuses on portable cottages for emigrants. These structures were designed by H. John Manning in 1832, and published in *An Encyclopedia of Cottage, Farm, and Villa Architecture and Furniture* by John. C. Loudon in 1846.[8] Kocher then offers John Havilland's 1830 prefabricated bank, published in a later edition of Owen Biddle's *Young Carpenter's Assistant* as the first example of American prefabrication.[9] He ends the article with a vindication of tradition that challenges every principle used by his European modernist counterparts and their rejection of historical heritage (such as Gropius):

> The application of knowledge is fundamental to the idea of a scientific and artistic profession such as that of the architect. It is tradition from past and knowledge today what makes the world as it was, as it is now, and is making the world of tomorrow.[10]

The notion of prefabrication as part of the American vernacular would be complemented by the conception of architectural design as the art of combining industrially produced elements, selected in a catalog, and assembled by the architect into a coherent whole. This position contrasted the customized construction of European modernist pioneers, such as Gropius or Le Corbusier, and was reinforced in Kocher's ideology with every addition to his ever-growing collection of American construction handbooks from the 18th and 19th centuries. As a result, prefabricated construction became one of the main axes of Kocher's research during the second half of the decade, with the other axis of his investigations being architectural pedagogy.

According to Frey's recollections, in 1936 Kocher was already making plans for his professional future after stepping down from *Architectural Record*.[11] The magazine had been the laboratory in which Kocher researched and promoted innovative methods of prefabricated construction and new building materials. The magazine was the primary medium for broadcasting his designs either before or after being actually built. Despite shifting his publication to the academic milieu, his idea of using the built project as a prototype to test the performance of his research findings remained unchanged. As was always the case in Kocher's professional development, this shift was propelled by economic and social context.

In 1935, the economic situation of the United States worsened again, requiring a new plan of action from the Roosevelt administration. Between January and September, Roosevelt set in place several of the most durable and relevant social programs in what it became known as the Second New Deal. The Social Security Act was presented at the beginning of the year and approved on August 14, ensuring retirement benefits, unemployment insurance, and aid for disabled workers based on lifetime payroll tax contributions. This piece of legislation was, in the opinion of prestigious historians like Kenneth S. Davis, "one of the major turning points in American History."[12] The Emergency Relief Appropriations Act of April 1935 provided a legislation suitable for the foundation of the Work Progress Administration (WPA), which during the following years employed more than 8.5 million workers to build highways and thousands of public facilities. Most importantly, for Kocher's new plans on education, the WPA provided funds for the development of art through a group of programs known collectively as "Federal Project Number One." An executive order in June 1935 established the National Youth Administration (NYA). The NYA operated on two levels: the first, which never worked properly, was the Out of School Program that concentrated on creating work opportunities for unemployed youth in local communities; the second and more successful program was the Student Work Program, which provided universities funds for work assignments to students, so they could economically support their time in college. These funds were granted by the federal government but administered by the schools and colleges themselves.[13] This circumstance was swiftly and wisely capitalized by Kocher in his subsequent involvement of student construction work and design-build as part of a pedagogical experience. As an anticipatory rumination about his future plans, Kocher wrote in 1936 that "the architectural schools should, by their instruction, interpret and translate the results of research in terms of applied design."[14]

Kocher's renewed interest in architectural education was immediately reflected in *Architectural Record.* The September 1936 issue published an extensive portfolio of innovative pedagogical experiences carried out in a number of schools of architecture. The article—unattributed yet likely the teamwork of the magazine's editorial staff, comprised of architects and led by Kocher—was based on many findings from a pioneer study prepared by F. H. Bosworth and R. C. Jones and commissioned by the Association of Collegiate Schools of Architecture (ACSA), published in 1932. The study started with a survey of 49 architecture schools during the fall and spring of 1930 to 1931 and evaluated North America's architecture education by analyzing all aspects of the architectural curriculum and its interdisciplinary relations.[15] The published portfolio of "Education of the Architect" in *Architectural Record* was the departure point for Kocher's second period of intense activity as an educator. It gave Kocher the possibility to reactivate or establish a network of contacts in several higher education institutions and serve as a compendium of the latest pedagogical trends in these schools. The conclusions of the article insist on the disconnect

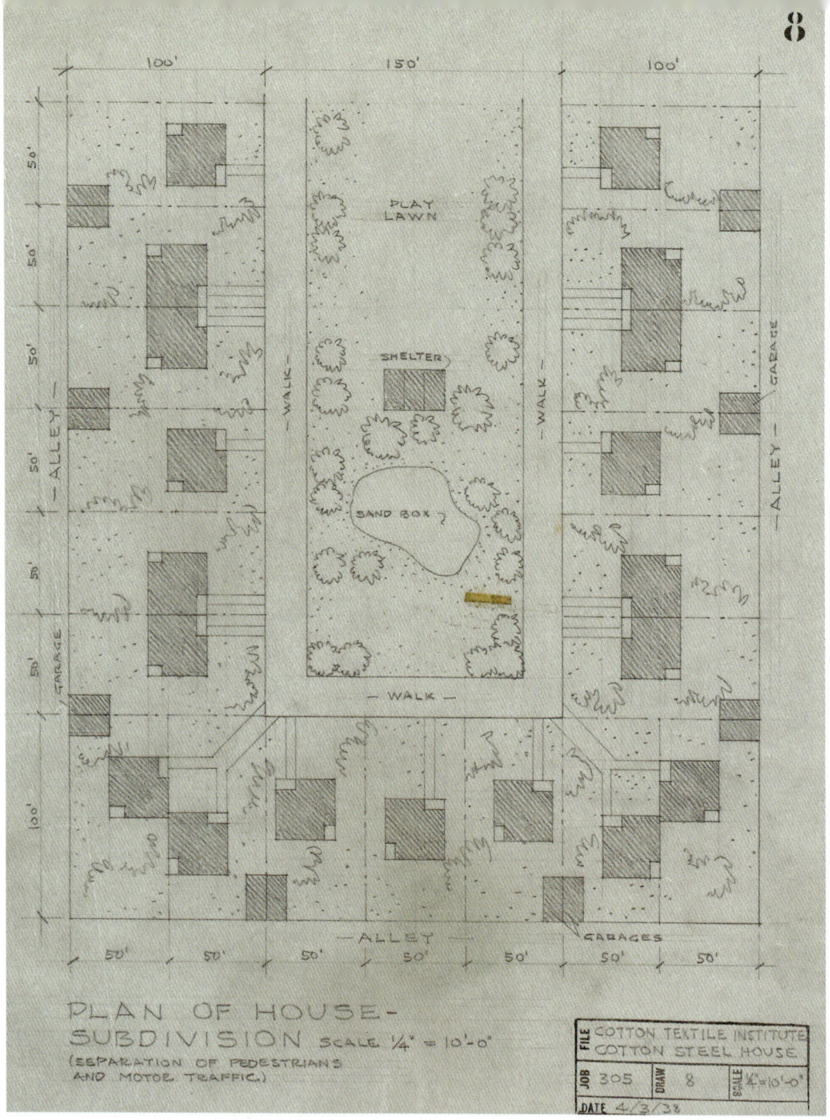

Figure 5.5. A. Lawrence Kocher. 1938. Cotton Steel House. Low Cost House for the Cotton Steel Institute. Plan of House Subdivision. Dated 4-3-38.
Figure 5.6. A. Lawrence Kocher. 1938. Cotton Steel House. Low Cost House for the Cotton Steel Institute. Front page of the brochure. External rendering of the house.

between schools and social demands—already detected in Bosworth and Jones' book—and ends with a summary of recommendations to rebuild that connection, a testament to *Architectural Record*'s position on architectural education. The summary contains nine recommendations:

> First, the appointment as professors or leaders of architects of outstanding experience and technical ability. Second, increasing the specialization of planning requirements. Third, the establishment of the school of architecture as the source from which is disseminated a well-defined and applied knowledge of construction materials, processes, and construction methods. Fourth, include the knowledge of pertinent facts about economics, living conditions, building management, building codes, and financing within the general education of the architect. Fifth, provide practical experience in construction in the nature of field work. Sixth, include town planning in the curriculum. Seventh, abolish any teaching of design that places emphasis on "fine form" or "fine appearing." Eighth, train the architect for reality. And ninth, abolish competitions which place award on presentation of building appearance.[16]

Points three and five are especially significant due to their close alignment with Kocher's own pedagogical positions. The promotion of construction knowledge is followed by a paragraph advocating for a tighter relationship between schools and industry: a relationship based on the need for new materials and the application of new standards by schools, followed by a technical response from the industry, producing innovative solutions for the needs established by scholarly research. Point five encourages hands-on experience in construction for students in their college years, aligning both with the Bauhaus tradition and the new possibilities for federally-funded student work opened by the National Youth Administration programs. Therefore, this recommendation honors a modern tradition beloved by Kocher and additionally has the very practical goal of attracting federal funds to the schools.

The portfolio in *Architectural Record* is complemented at the beginning of the magazine with a list of contributors to the research, entitled "The Architect in the Modern World."[17] The listed institutions, selected as case studies or as contributors, showed a combination of Kocher's old acquaintances, like MIT, Harvard, and New York University, and schools relevant to his near-future educational trajectory, such as Black Mountain College and Carnegie Institute of Technology. The shift in Kocher's design methodology from journal-based research to academic research was set up. Kocher maintained a sustained series of contacts with these universities during that year, one of which resulted in a teaching opportunity exciting enough to be accepted following Kocher's tenure at *Architectural Record.* William F. Hitchens, professor and head of the department of architecture at the Carnegie Institute of Technology, invited Kocher to join the faculty in Pittsburgh. Hitchens was a University of Pennsylvania graduate and had been teaching at Carnegie Tech since 1913. He was appointed head of the department of architecture in 1936, and immediately proposed a notable shift in emphasis for the curriculum that encompassed two major changes:

> [the first] new approach to the study of design tends toward broadening the viewpoint of the student in three-dimensioned design and in giving greater realism to his work by a closer correlation of design, construction, and materials. The second change intends giving a student a clearer understanding of the significance of buildings as related to the community through city planning and research into the programs of single structures.[18]

Hitchens saw housing design as the perfect research field to achieve both of these goals. The interest in affordable housing was an urgent social demand in the Depression years, and the construction of houses was a perfect laboratory to conduct building technology research. Hitchens scanned Europe and the United States to find a housing expert who could teach at Carnegie Tech and found Kocher available and eager to start again his academic career. Kocher was always interested in the problem of housing, but now, imbued with the civic ethos of the New Deal, he saw in prefabricated construction the solution to home precarity caused by the depression. He was the perfect match for a school that wanted to place a "new emphasis on American architecture's Depression child-housing."[19] Kocher planned a new curriculum for Carnegie Tech in which he would be able to continue his prefabrication experiments and simultaneously pursue a new model of architectural education. As Kocher explained in a later letter to Henry Chang, the appointment included more than just teaching loads: "Carnegie Institute of Technology, Pittsburgh, induced me to reshape their course of study in architectural design, which I endeavored to do."[20]

As any American educator influenced by John Dewey's pragmatist theories, Kocher had always placed experience and production at the center of his pedagogical methodology.[21] This preoccupation is evident even in his earliest pedagogical endeavors, like the 1921 article series he organized for *Architectural Record,* entitled "Library of the Architect," while he was still at Pennsylvania State University, and published in 1925. With the goal of collecting a basic list of books on aesthetics and theory of architecture, and on general interests for architecture students, Kocher began a letter-writing campaign asking several national and international architects and artists to recommend readings for young architects. Kocher always treasured the handwritten letter of George Bernard Shaw as one of his favorites for his radical positioning:

> I should say that architects are made by building, not by books. An architect may read Vitruvius, Piranesi, Adam, Ruskin and Morris to add culture to his professionalism; but a comparison of 12th-century architecture with 16th-century, or Greek with Latin, will suggest strongly that the more an architect knows academically the worse he builds. Reading, picture gazing, and globe-trotting all tend to shift an architect's eyes to the back of his head. In England, we have so many eminent 14th-century faker-experts that the 19th century never had a dog's chance architecturally.[22]

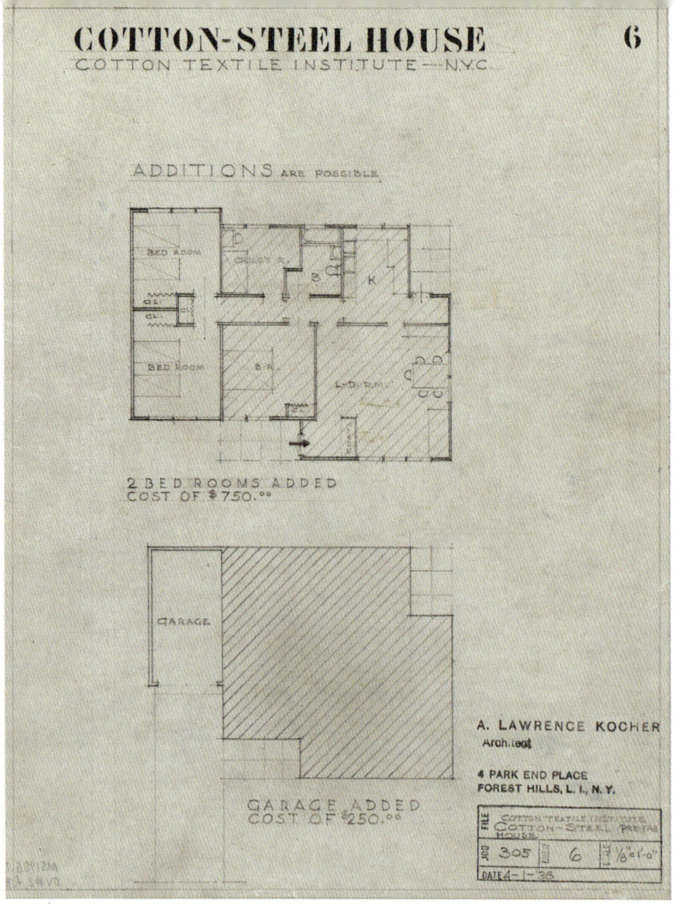

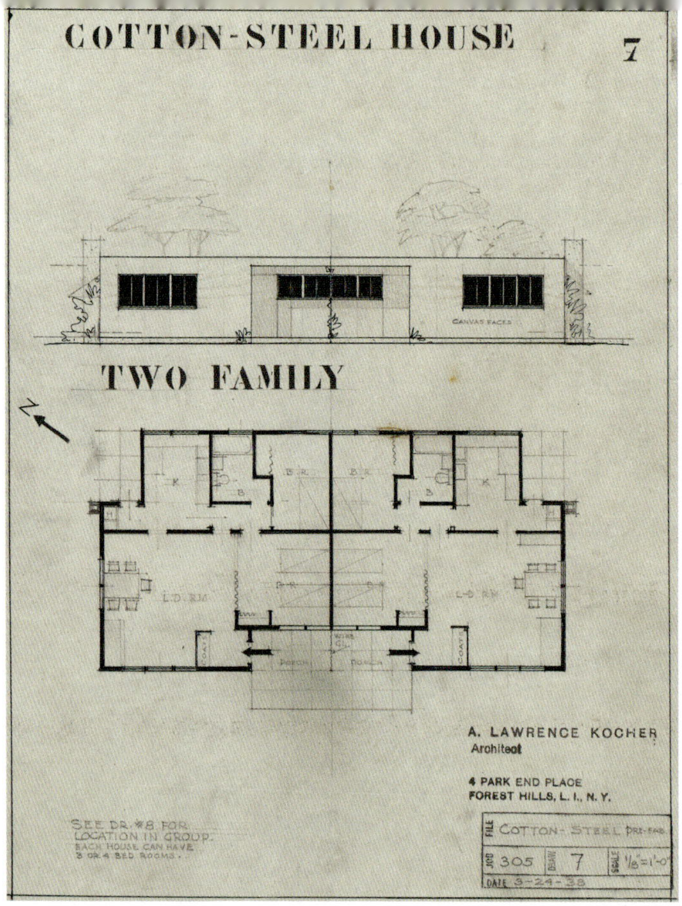

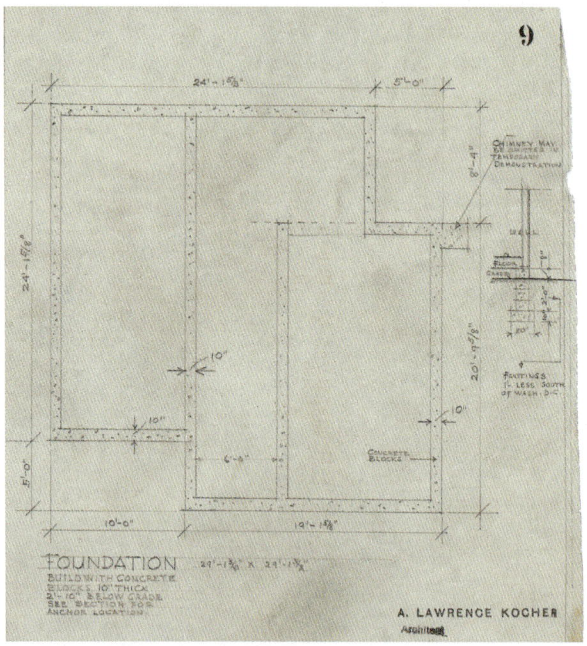

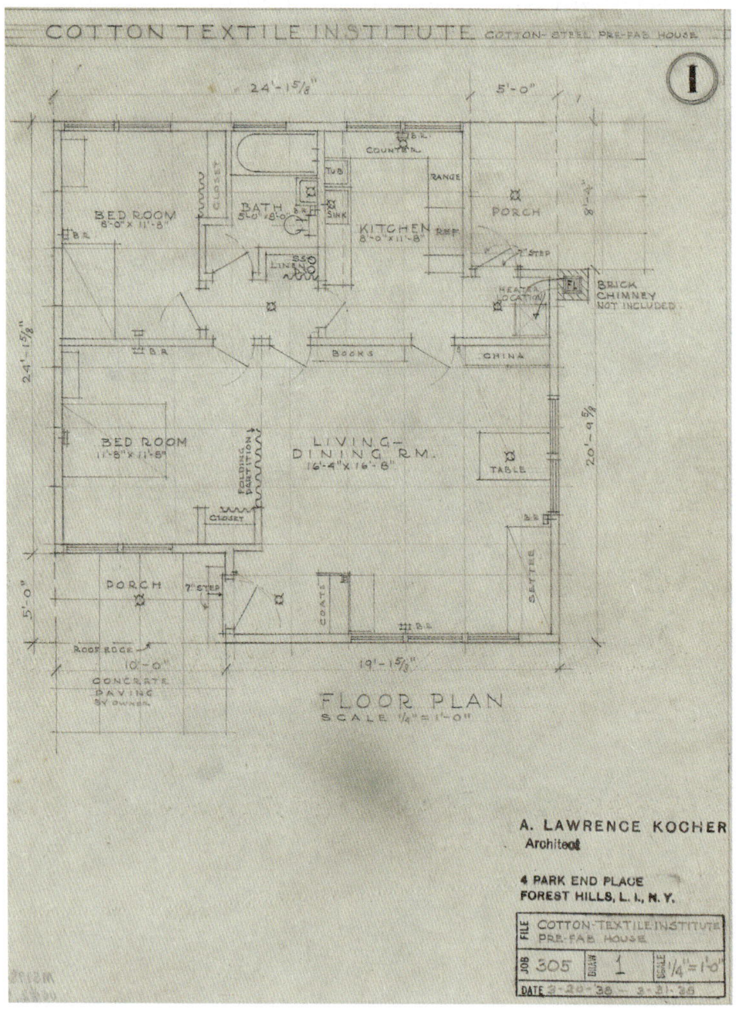

Figure 5.7. A. Lawrence Kocher. 1938. Cotton Steel House. Low Cost House for the Cotton Steel Institute. Possible additions to the house. Dated 4-1-38.
Figure 5.8. A. Lawrence Kocher. 1938. Cotton Steel House. Low Cost House for the Cotton Steel Institute. Aggregation of two houses. Dated 3-24-38.
Figure 5.9. A. Lawrence Kocher. 1938. Cotton Steel House. Low Cost House for the Cotton Steel Institute. Floor plan. Dated 3-31-38.
Figure 5.10. A. Lawrence Kocher. 1938. Cotton Steel House. Low Cost House for the Cotton Steel Institute. Foundation plan. Dated 3-12-38.

Since the beginning of the Fall semester in 1938, Kocher commuted between the Carnegie Institute of Technology campus in Pittsburgh and his home in New York for alternating three-week periods. He organized the first pedagogical experience in the U.S. that can be properly categorized as a design-build studio, setting up the construction of a low-cost experimental house on the university campus at the intersection of Forbes Street and Morewood Street. The house was expected to be erected in a three-year period by the students and host a family of three members in a first phase, later to be expanded to spatially accommodate a family of six during subsequent stages of the program.[23] **(Figures 5.1 to 5.3)**

In his contribution to Joan Ockman's book, *Architecture School*, historian Richard W. Hayes lists a series of precedents to the American design-build studios that include John Ruskin, who organized a team of Oxford undergraduates to build a road in a rural slum in the outskirts of the town in 1874, aligning with the manual labor and social engagement prescribed by his arts and crafts ideology. Some American antecedents may be identified of this pedagogical trend. For instance, around 1900, the African American educator, writer, and politician Booker T. Washington organized and supervised the construction of up to 36 buildings on the campus of the Tuskegee Normal and Industrial Institute in Alabama, which he directed using student labor with a focus on the pedagogical value these activities would have for students. A similar implementation of student work in construction can be found in the Hampton Institute of Virginia, also around the turn of the century. The closest precedents to Kocher's experience can be found in the apprentice-oriented experiences of Frank Lloyd Wright, both at Taliesin East—with a student work force carrying out the construction of the architect's summer house in Wisconsin—and in Taliesin West, where students performed several tasks for the construction of Wright's headquarters and the private school in Scottsdale, Arizona.[24] Kocher was perfectly aware of and undoubtedly built on previous design-build experiences, like Wright's Taliesin West construction that *Architectural Record* published in the September 1936 issue. Nevertheless, there were very substantial differences between these experiences and Carnegie Tech's pioneer design-build course. On the one hand, Kocher's course was based on the remuneration of student work partially through NYA funds, and therefore not only served as a pedagogical experience, but also to economically support the students in a scenario of social distress.[25] On the other hand, all precedents set up a building campaign using student labor for a specific purpose established in advance: the construction of buildings for the university, a summer residence, or a road to improve the living conditions of the economically disfavored. In Kocher's pedagogical experiment, research on the construction process is an end in itself, not just a means to reach a predetermined objective. The house built by Kocher's students was, therefore, a purely experimental construction with the aim of testing and assessing different construction systems and materials in order to ask manufacturers for new and improved solutions.[26]

In this sense, the closest precedent may be the Bauhaus, which advocated for a workshop-based curriculum with the goal of connecting the university with industry. The Bauhaus produced several demonstration houses—such as the Sommerfeld House (1920–1921) and the *Haus am Horn*—built for the Bauhaus *Werkschau* (1923), which featured the work of the students and instructors on the interior furnishings and fittings.[27] Likewise, the Carnegie Tech campus house can be considered a demonstration house in which to show customers and companies the novel advantages of prefabricated construction systems. It was not a demonstration of the school's design capacities, but rather an exhibition of industrial systems and materials assembled using a building process designed by the students. This third trait of Carnegie Tech's design-build discloses a shift from the Bauhaus precedent and a profound connection with Kocher's vernacular imaginary. The aim of the studio was not only building a demonstration object, but also to devise a construction method with materials that could be replicated by unskilled laborers using a simple set of instructions. The owners of the houses could, therefore, skip any cost derived from external labor except for the supply of the prefabricated systems, and independently build or expand their houses. This goal aligns with that of the carpenters and builders of the American 18th century, when writing their handbooks. One of these handbooks, Batty and T. Langley's *The builder's jewel, or, The Youth's remembrancer: explaining short and easy rules, made familiar to the meanest capacity*, was studied by Kocher in an article and set a similar objective to that of the design-build studio:

> I have therefore at the Request of many good Workmen, and for the Sake of young Students, compiled this Work; wherein I have reduced the whole to such short and easy Rules that the Workmen may, not only at the first View renew his Memory, as Occasions may require, but Apprentices, who may be absolutely unacquainted with this noble Art, and are so unfortunate as many have been, and are to be bound to Jobbing Masters, who know but little; may without the Help of any, by assiduous Application at their leisure Hours, in Evenings when the Business of Days is over, make themselves such Masters herein, that few Masters are able or willing to make them.[28]

The August 1938 issue of *Architectural Record* was the last to credit Kocher as Editor, though he had already been diversifying his professional activity since the prior year. For example, he was appointed American delegate to the international congress of art and applied arts that took place in Paris. Also in 1937, Kocher submitted a middle-class version of the Subsistence Farmsteads of 1934 to be published in the *Ladies' Home Journal*. As an optimistic sign of the country's evolving economic situation, he transformed the agrarian working-class design—developed to assure domestic alimentary needs amid the worst of the depression years—into a suburban weekend house.[29] **(Figure 5.4)** He even carried out the idea of exchanging issues of the *Architectural Record* and the *Architectural Review* in March 1937. This idea occurred to Kocher because he was offered an exchange professorship at the University of Liverpool, declaring, "If we exchange professorships, why can't we exchange editors?"[30]

His imminent departure from *Architectural Record* and his new teaching responsibilities reactivated Kocher's practice as well. Between March and April of 1938, Kocher produced a last attempt to build demonstration houses for the Cotton Textile Institute. The new scheme was signed by Kocher alone, although he names

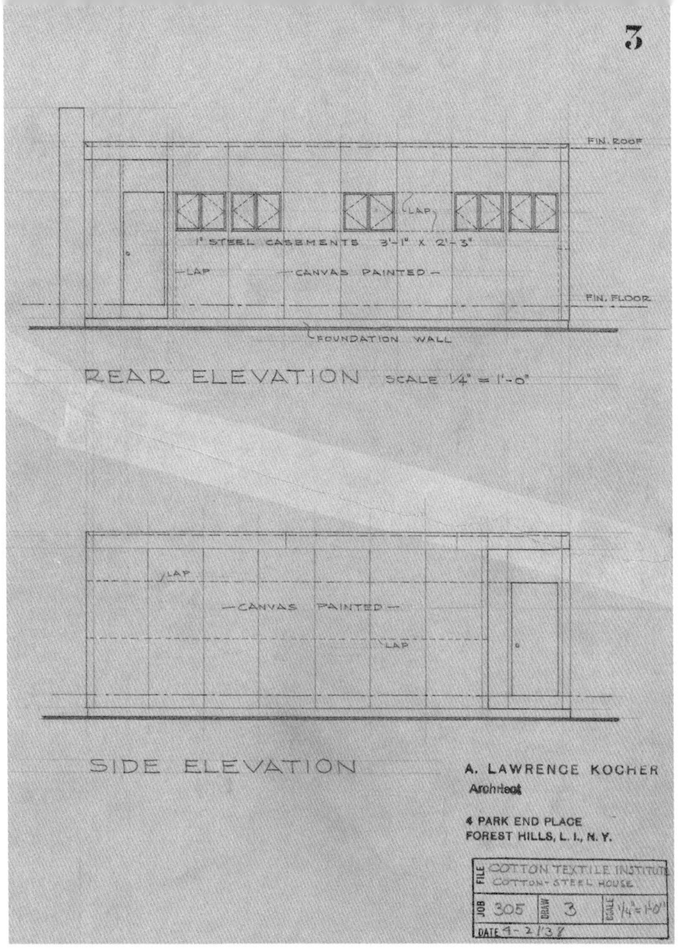

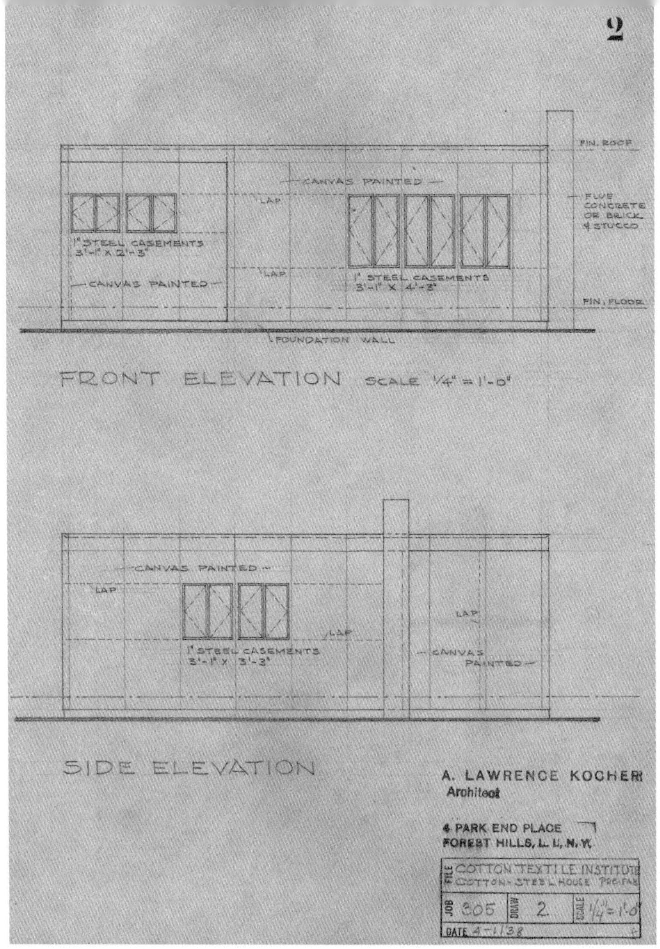

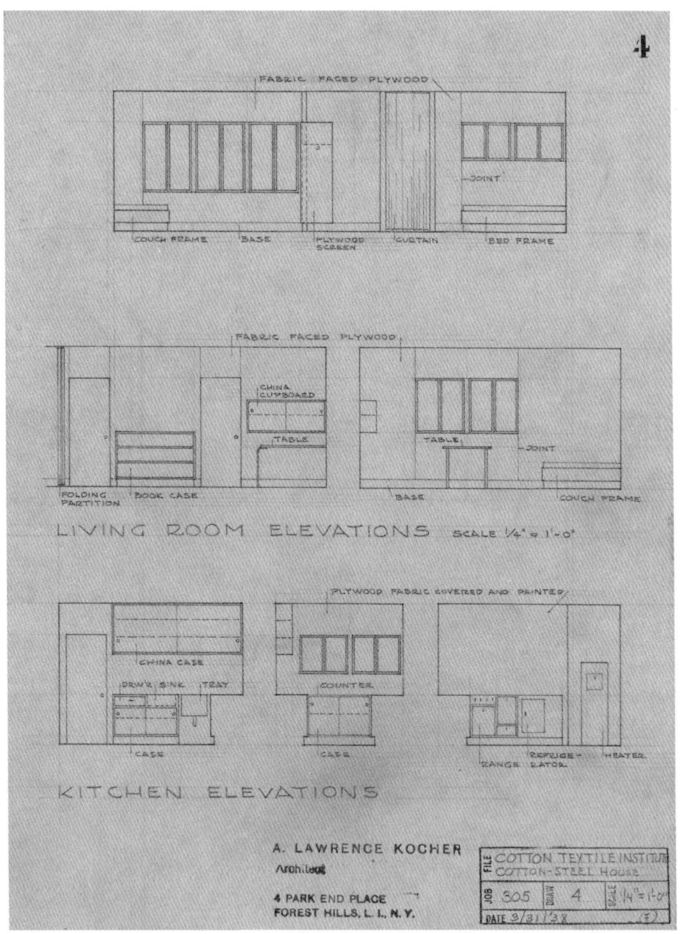

Figure 5.11. A. Lawrence Kocher. 1938. Cotton Steel House. Low Cost House for the Cotton Steel Institute. Elevations. Dated 4-21-38.
Figure 5.12. A. Lawrence Kocher. 1938. Cotton Steel House. Low Cost House for the Cotton Steel Institute. Elevations. Dated 4-11-38.
Figure 5.13. A. Lawrence Kocher. 1938. Cotton Steel House. Low Cost House for the Cotton Steel Institute. Internal elevations of kitchen and living room. Dated 3-31-38.
Figure 5.14. A. Lawrence Kocher. 1938. Cotton Steel House. Low Cost House for the Cotton Steel Institute. Exterior perspective sketch. Undated.

Frey in the acknowledgments section at the end of the project specifications alongside Robert L. Davison, Charles Everett, and other individuals, and institutions.[31] This Low-Cost House was a more compact version of the Experimental Five-Room House and reconsidered the possibilities of attachment and enlargement to the units unexplored in the original 1932 design. The 1932 house did not have a garage and was neither elevated from the terrain, nor did it have the roof terrace of its precedent; whereas the 1938 house was developed with a precise, modulated construction system, which Kocher planned as a 19-house subdivision. The advantages of this modular solution over the original scheme were complemented with the possibility of aggregation in pairs, along with the addition of an attached garage or extra two bedrooms at an estimated cost of $250 and $750 respectively; the garages are independent sheds adjacent to the pedestrian circulation and sidewalks and kept the motor traffic strictly segregated. The constructive system is based on three-inch pressed-steel channels spaced 20 inches on center. The wall units are prefabricated in 40-inch modules, consisting of an exterior layer of one-and-a-half-inch insulation board, and an interior finish of a one-and-a-half-inch plywood board. While all the windows and doors are installed into wall units with one-inch steel casement in the factory, the glazing and application of the six-ounce cotton fabric exterior finish over the façade boards is done on site. The assembly of the house—not including plumbing and wiring, painting, and surfacing with fabric—is designed to require less than 70 hours of labor. Therefore, a team of six workers can accomplish the construction of the complete house in nine days: two days for the erection of the frame, and seven to finalize the assembly of the façade and prefabricated partition units. The design capitalized Kocher's accumulated experience during the Depression; it was a cost-efficient and highly functional minimal house, free of all constraints derived from the rigid application of the Modern movement's precepts. **(Figures 5.5 to 5.15)**

On July 16, 1938, Kocher was also appointed consultant in the Works Progress Administration (WPA) at a salary of $25 per day. This insight into public administration informed his next design endeavor.[32] In November of 1938, he produced a proposal for a Community Art Center in the Appalachian village of Big Stone Gap, at the south-west end of Virginia. The project was part of the WPA Federal Art Project, which devised the program in collaboration with the local community. The project site was located in a municipal park and had a drop of 18 feet from the upper to the lower grade. Taking advantage of the topography, Kocher designed a two-floor scheme with public access located on the upper level. Following certain findings of the Darien cultural center, he created a central lobby that could extend to the auditorium using folding walls to host large events. Illuminated by overhead skylights, the lobby provided surveillance and access to the museum containing a permanent collection of paintings and colonial art objects, a gallery for temporary exhibits, a special room for the display of prints, and a library. The lower level included the community center program with studios, workshops, toilets, locker rooms, mechanical service rooms, and the required storage for the museum and the library. All deliveries happened in this lower level, including a shipping and packaging room adjacent to the museum storage. The design of the building is neatly modern, with large horizontal windows and abstract cubic forms. Despite the clearly Modernist style of the overall design, the materiality of the building is heavy and unprecedented in any of Kocher's projects. With façades built using a local stone described as "common random ashlar" and floors featuring Robertson-stamped steel keystone decks, Kocher's material selection was in the hope that the WPA would be able to provide the construction workforce using the local, unemployed population.[33] **(Figures 5.16 to 5.25)**

During that same year, Frey came back to New York for a short period of time and, in collaboration with Kocher, produced an entry for the Swiss pavilion competition to be built in 1939's New York World's Fair. **(Figure 5.26)** The proposal was a structurally daring scheme that featured four parabolic arches to suspend, using steel cables, a flat roof over the exhibition and cafeteria areas that encompassed the entire building program. Completely free of any structural support, the interior space organized visitor circulation around a central courtyard. The structure and the façades were stepped diagonally in plan to create glazed surfaces in the direction of the circulation on the south façade, and a staggered glass wall on the north. The scheme was a free plan with the kitchen, restrooms, and a cheese cellar as the only enclosed spaces. Although the competition winner was William Lescaze, and Albert Frey returned to Palm Springs after the competition submittal, Kocher remained engaged with the New York World's Fair. Kocher was appointed Associate Designer of the Domestic Utilities Building and produced several pieces of expanded metal furniture that were exhibited in the "Design for Industry" section. Furthermore, while Kocher was still teaching at the Carnegie Institute of Technology and following the pattern of collaboration between industry and architecture established by the architect's previous works, he designed the "House of Plywood" for an exhibition entitled *The Town of Tomorrow* at the World's Fair. The design was commissioned by the Douglas Fir Plywood Association and investigated the use of plywood as an architectural material. **(Figure 5.27)** The construction was financed similarly to the Aluminaire House: materials were donated by various companies and listed in a promotional brochure. Although this house was not formally related to the previous projects developed by Kocher, it shares a common interest in prefabrication and material experimentation. During his tenure as managing editor at *Architectural Record*, Kocher had fostered many technical developments of American plywood construction and its booming industry. Since 1935, at least seven articles featured the products and systems developed by the Forest Products Laboratory of the Forest Service, a division of the U.S. Department of Agriculture in cooperation with the University of Wisconsin. The first of these articles showed a completely prefabricated, all-wood demonstration house erected in Madison, Wisconsin, in 21 hours by seven workers.[34] The use of plywood has parallel histories in Europe and in the United States. The first European patents were those of Otto Hetzer in 1901 for straight beams and in 1906 for curved parts. The use of plywood became widespread in central Europe after the Universal Exhibition in Brussels in 1910. The patent reached the United States in 1923 yet had little success. The first building to use the patented material—a gym in Peshtigo, Wisconsin—was built in 1934. Meanwhile, in the United States, the Portland Manufacturing Company had been

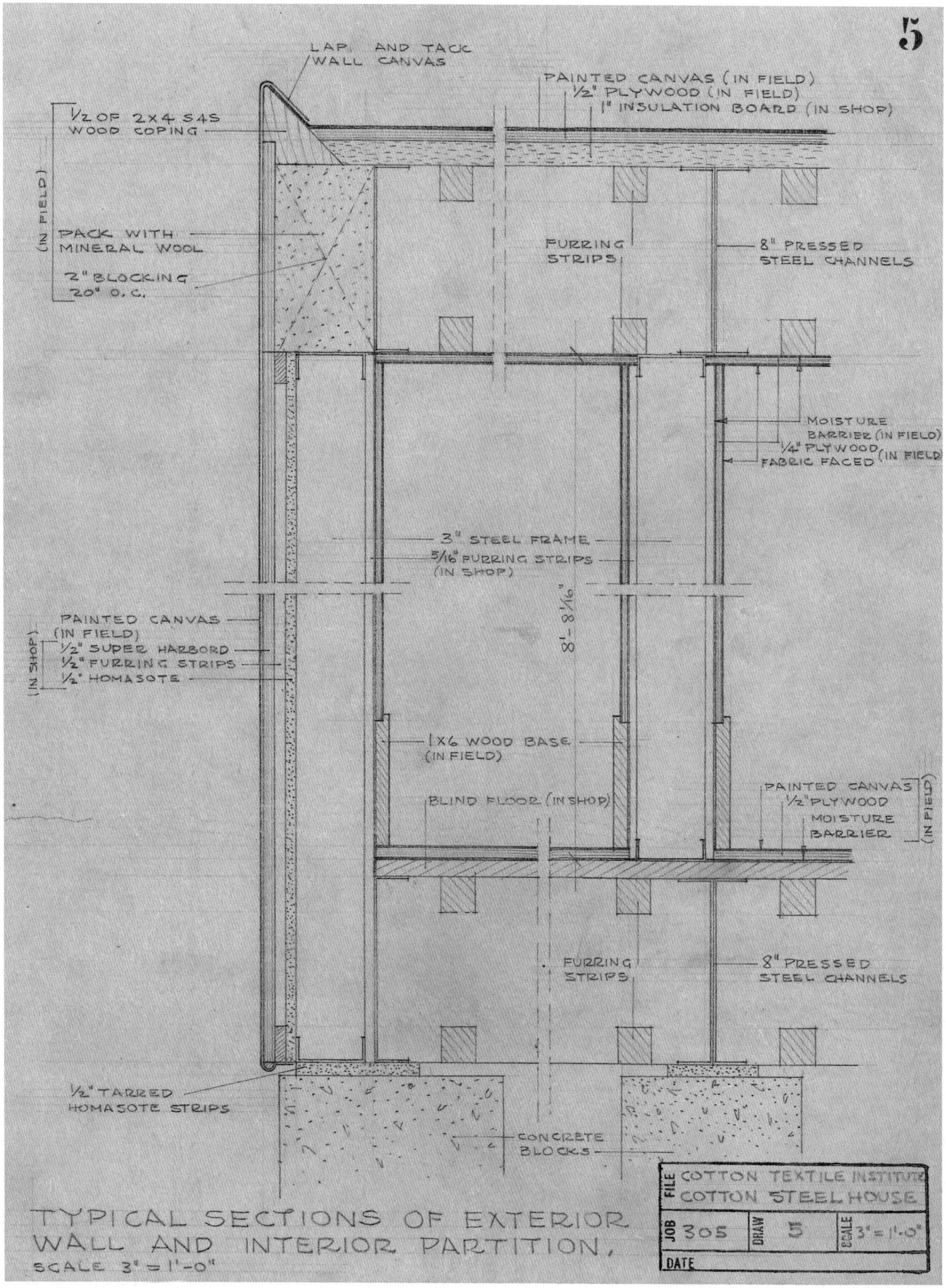

Figure 5.15. A. Lawrence Kocher. 1938. Cotton Steel House. Low Cost House for the Cotton Steel Institute. Typical construction section. Undated.

manufacturing plywood doors and boards since 1905.[35] The market expanded into the automobile industry, then grew into 17 plywood factories in the American Northwest, producing approximately 33 million square meters of board annually. These manufacturers became associated in 1933, forming the Douglas Fir Plywood Association, which struggled to survive until 1938, when they managed to market plywood as a standardized commodity rather than a collection of individually branded products. Additionally, a new waterproof adhesive—invented by chemist James Nevin, who worked for Washington's Harbor Plywood Corporation of Aberdeen—was approved for outdoor use. The advancements in waterproof plywood using synthetic resinous bonding agents, previous to the final patents, and the procedures to avoid plywood's shrinking and swelling were published in *Architectural Record*'s 1937 article, "Technical News and Research."[36]

It was precisely in 1938 that the Douglas Fir Plywood Association commissioned Kocher to design the first of many demonstration houses for their products. In fact, the technological innovations demonstrated in the Plywood House had notable relevance for the future construction trends in the United States. Since the 1939 New York World's Fair, in which the Plywood House was exhibited, over a million houses have been built with dry-mount plywood systems.[37] This trend accelerated with the advent of World War II and the restrictions on the use of other construction materials such as steel. The Plywood House modeled the use of sub-base for flooring and finishes (PlyScor), ceilings and walls (PlyWall), furniture panels (PlyPanel), and façade finishes (PlyShield). The list of companies that donated other materials for the Plywood House included the Truscon Steel Company, which supplied the steel sashes, as they had done in the Aluminaire House and the Canvas Weekend House. Another 10 companies, including General Electric, donated materials and supplies. The most innovative systems were applied to the roof that used a 3/8-inch plywood sheathing and a waterproof canvas finish, varnished, and painted in aluminum paint. This roofing system was termed "Con-Ser-Tex," manufactured by William L. Barrell Company, and was applied with copper or galvanized nails over a heavy bedding paint.[38] The house was organized on one level and, although modern, it was less radical than its predecessors. It had an L-shape plan in which separate sides were devoted to day and night activities, leaving access areas in between. The taller living area had a clerestory and was capped by the kitchen and a semicircular dining room. Designed to be the home of a couple with one child, the program was more ambitious than in the previous houses, including: two bedrooms, one bathroom, a living room, a dining alcove, kitchen, a screened porch, and a mechanical room in the basement directly accessible from the rear entrance hall. Following a common practice in his work, Kocher provided the furniture and fixture designs for the house, such as cabinets, built-in closets and bookcases, chairs, tables, and even a china cupboard with a sliding door made out of white birch half-rounds glued on a canvas. The estimated budget for the construction was between $4,000 and $5,000. The Plywood House was praised by Lewis Mumford in the July 1939 issue of *The New Yorker*, where he heralded "the best house in the lot…done with the real inventiveness that has been conspicuously lacking in house design."[39] **(Figures 5.28 to 5.37)**

Kocher's practice during these years was not restricted to his work on the World's Fair. The Florida Weekend House, which Kocher designed for Dr. George R. Norton in May 1939, was the final member in the typological family that emerged from the Aluminaire House. Despite never being built, the Florida Weekend House was raised with a footprint similar to that of the Canvas Weekend House—including a flexible interior divided into two parts of identical size by sliding curtains—but it featured a covered porch accessible by a spiral stair. The bright-yellow space-dividing curtains and the yellow and brown striped awnings were detailed in the project's written documentation and specifications. The bathroom and kitchen were grouped in the northwest corner, and access to the bath was through the kitchen; two built-in cupboards divide the restroom from the bedroom. This grouping of closed spaces liberates the northeast corner of the house, which becomes a gallery and dining area, mediating the zone between the kitchen and the terrace occupying the entire east side of the house. The east façade had a large, floor-to-ceiling window that was shielded from the sun by the terrace's overhanging roof. Manufactured by the Truscon Steel Co., the windows wrapped around the northeast corner and narrowed along the north façade. Where the windows turned the corner in the area of the dining room, they met at a low sill and reached the ceiling, but they tapered toward the kitchen area meeting a higher wide lintel. The windows of Florida Weekend House are asymmetrical due to both the solar orientation and the views, as specified on the plan drawings. These are noteworthy observations as the position of these windows is not consistent in the various project documents; in fact, the plans feature a façade wall between the dining room and kitchen that is not drawn on the elevations. **(Figures 5.38 to 5.40)**

The house did not have a roof garden, and, from the exterior it appears to be slightly streamlined with a single-slope roof that had rounded corners and was higher over the porch. It is possible to deduce the building's primary structural composition from the project's construction report.[40] The structure had six round steel columns, each measuring four inches in diameter and supporting wooden beams. At their meeting point with the beams, the columns met eight-by-36-inch rectangular steel brackets of 3/4-inch thickness on the first floor and six-by-36-by-3/4-inch brackets at the ceiling. These brackets were attached with screws to the main wooden beams running in an east–west direction and forming two cantilevers at their ends. One cantilever coincided with the width of the terrace; the other (western) end was much shorter. The total height of the columns was 20 feet on the east side and 19.5 feet on the west side of the house. The façade construction involved a wood frame and 3/8-inch PlyScord plywood panels, supplied by the Douglas Fir Plywood Association, attached with nails. A base layer of bedding paint from L. Barrell and Co. was applied to this plywood sheeting; the cotton canvas finish, which had a width of 36 inches, was then adhered to this layer while it was still wet and had to be pulled taut as it was applied. The stretched canvas covered all the house's façades and roofs. **(Figures 5.41 to 5.45)** Interestingly, the design of the Florida Weekend House is similar to that of motor homes manufactured after the Second World War and to the proposals for portable homes that were transported in two parts, like the one developed by the Tennessee Valley Authority in 1942.[41] **(Figure 5.46)** In terms of composition, the house is arranged

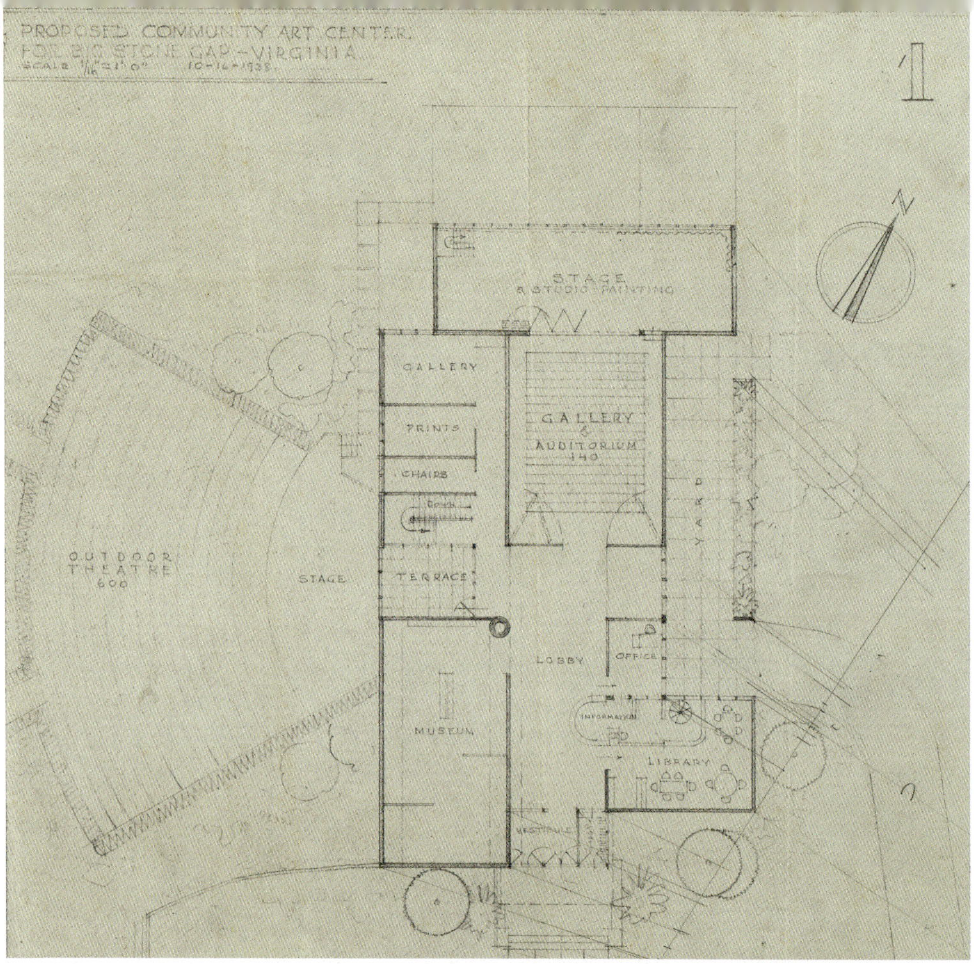

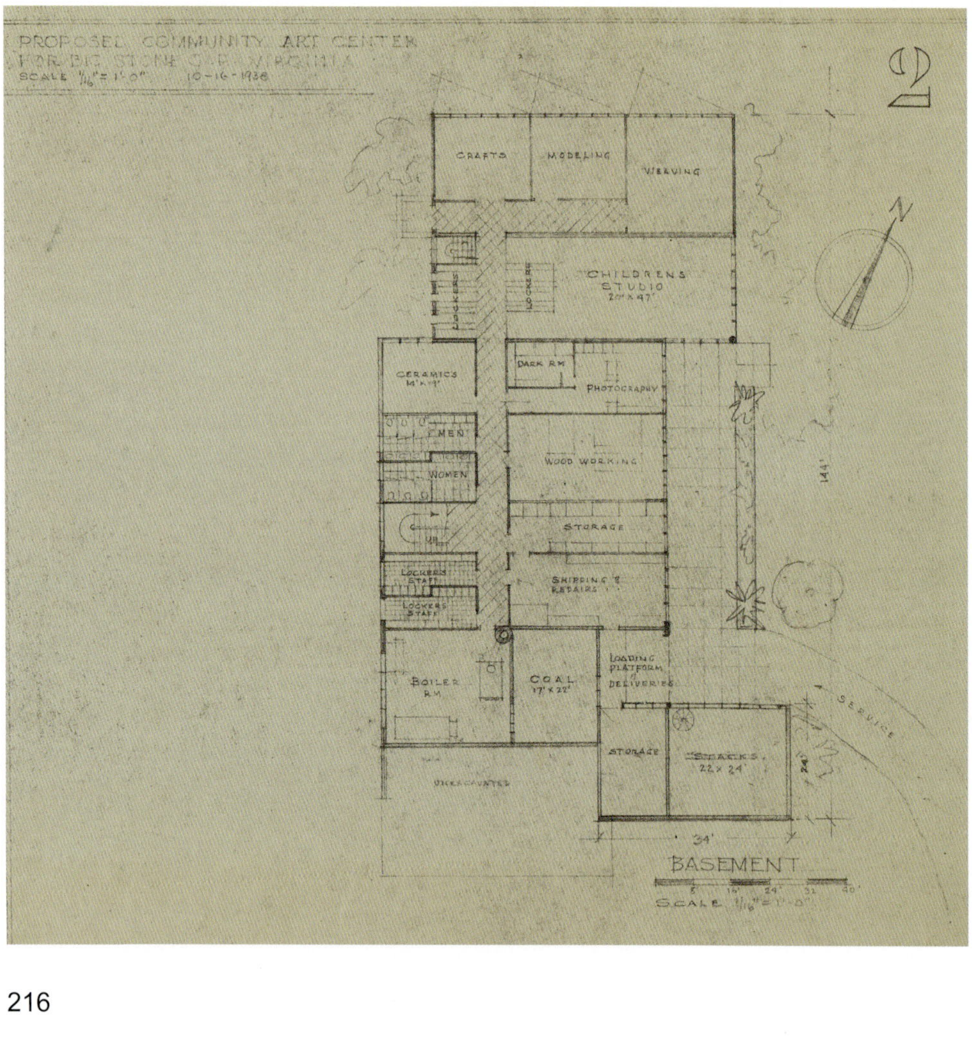

Figure 5.16. A. Lawrence Kocher. 1938. Community Art Center in Big Stone Gap, Virginia, for the Works Progress Administration. First floor plan.

Figure 5.17. A. Lawrence Kocher. 1938. Community Art Center in Big Stone Gap, Virginia, for the Works Progress Administration. Basement plan.

like a typical double trailer-home, but its rootedness in a specific place means that it can forgo the typical symmetry of mobile objects, designed with an implied direction yet lack specificity with regards to their orientation.

The last houses designed by Kocher and Frey enable the integration of family life into the natural landscape. They break the box of the Aluminaire House and no longer share its desire to create an artificial bubble exporting an urban lifestyle into a totally alien environment. Though their sites may be remote, they are opposed to the isolation and "site-less" space typified by the Aluminaire House.[42] In the form and function of the Florida Weekend House and the Kocher Canvas Weekend House, Kocher proposed a lifestyle truly different from the urban, one more closely connected to the covered wagon or campsite. The domestic program made notable usage of exterior spaces and the surrounding natural spaces; the formal and spatial simplification required to achieve this proposed lifestyle meant shedding the typified qualities of architectural objects. These experiments emerged from the Aluminaire House, which in contrast, like the classical villa, was intended to be a satellite of urban life, transporting urban comfort and amenities to a rural environment. On the contrary, the variety and quality of the Aluminaire House's interior spaces is undeniable to the spatial simplicity of the weekend house typology. The fascination architects have for this house can be explained in the same way Reyner Banham explains the intense adoration professed by architects for the Airstream trailer. This admiration lies in the Airstream's proximity to the ideal, as postulated by Le Corbusier, of the house as a mass-produced habitation machine, a dwelling designed like a plane and produced like a car.[43] Of course, the same can be said of the Experimental Weekend House, the Kocher Canvas Weekend House, and the Florida Weekend House. The same ironic criticism that Banham makes of the Airstream could also be applied to these three houses:

> A recent cartoon showed a man unloading tables, chairs, a standard lamp and a television from a trailer home in the middle of some wild forest glade, at what time his wife says: 'I thought we came here to get away from it all, but you've brought it all with you!' Within the Airstream's perfect technological shell lies the promise that, after all, you can take it with you.[44]

Besides his professional practice and innovative architectural pedagogies, the center of Kocher's preoccupations during these years focused on the creation of new academic institutions that could host and promote the necessary changes in architectural education and its reconnection with industry. Despite his previously unfruitful attempt to create an architecture school with Gropius, Raymond, and Frey during 1934, Kocher never completely gave up his idea of a new American Bauhaus. After the arrival of Gropius in America to teach at Harvard in March of 1937, Kocher started correspondence with Laszlo Moholy-Nagy, director of the newly minted American School of Design (now known as The Institute of Design at the Illinois Institute of Technology, or IIT Institute of Design).[45] This exchange of letters began when Kocher was compiling information about the possible influence of the Bauhaus over Alvar Aalto's furniture designs while writing his catalog contribution for the Museum of Modern Art's (MoMA) exhibition, *Aalto, Architecture and Furniture*.[46] The topics in the letters soon turned to prefabrication and design-build pedagogy, although Moholy-Nagy's lack of architectural education prevented them from further deepening this specific dialogue.[47]

In addition to acquiring this new acquaintance, Kocher never lost contact with the old ones. He had always seen Gropius as a potential leader for the future development of modern architecture in America and was eager to help smooth his landing in the country. In May of 1937, two months after Gropius's arrival at Harvard, *Architectural Record* published an article in its opening pages authored by the German architect explaining his plans for architectural education and his future contributions to American modern architecture. In the text, copy-edited personally by Kocher as it aligned with his own ideas, Gropius states his "general intentions" including his wish to "teach Americans what American architecture should be like" and not to "introduce a so to speak cut and dried 'Modern Style' from Europe."[48] This article situates Gropius as a new and powerful ally in Kocher's search of an American architecture.[49] Furthermore, Hélène de Mandrot—the Swiss patron of modern art and architecture famous for sponsoring and hosting the first CIAM congress in 1928 at her castle in La Sarraz—visited the United States and ignited Kocher's expectations in creating an American Bauhaus. The "La Sarraz Declaration," in which 26 European modern architects proposed a new architecture based on their Taylorist ideas, it called for radical separation from the Beaux Arts schools tradition and responded to the rationalization demanded by the general economic system.[50] The elected executive body of CIAM was known by the acronymous CIRPAC *Comité international pour la résolution des problèmes de l'architecture contemporaine* (International Committee for the Resolution of Problems in Contemporary Architecture). Kocher sent a memorandum to Gropius proposing him to lead a selected group of 10 to 12 American architects to find "solutions for a new and normal architecture in America" and to:

> develop a program of endeavor with the intention of sending a representative to the New Congress of New Architects in Europe, transmitting the result of their combined investigations on architectural and social problems of concern to the architect.[51]

Kocher suggested that the topic of architectural education should also be considered; Gropius expressed his wish to help in the endeavor, but politely declined the invitation to lead it. He recommended the creation of an American CIRPAC and nominated Neutra and Lonberg-Holm to join the committee.[52] Once more, Kocher failed to engage Gropius in one of his initiatives.

Kocher's networking efforts before leaving *Architectural Record* were not restricted to Gropius and Moholy-Nagy. Since he included Black Mountain College in the *Architectural Record*'s article on new pedagogies in the September 1936 issue, Kocher had been very attentive to the school development of a pedagogical methodology very consistent with his own ideas about architectural education. Founded by John Andrew Rice, Theodore Dreier, and several other former professors of the Rollins College—a private college in Winter

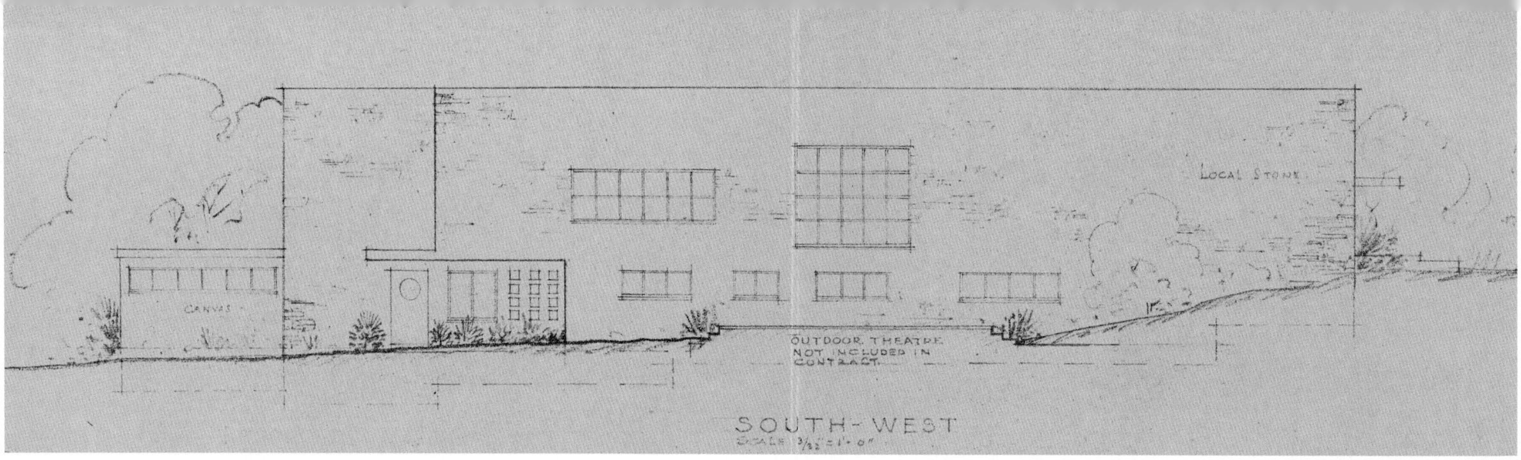
LOCAL STONE
CANVAS
OUTDOOR THEATRE
NOT INCLUDED IN
CONTRACT.
SOUTH-WEST
SCALE 3/32" = 1'-0"

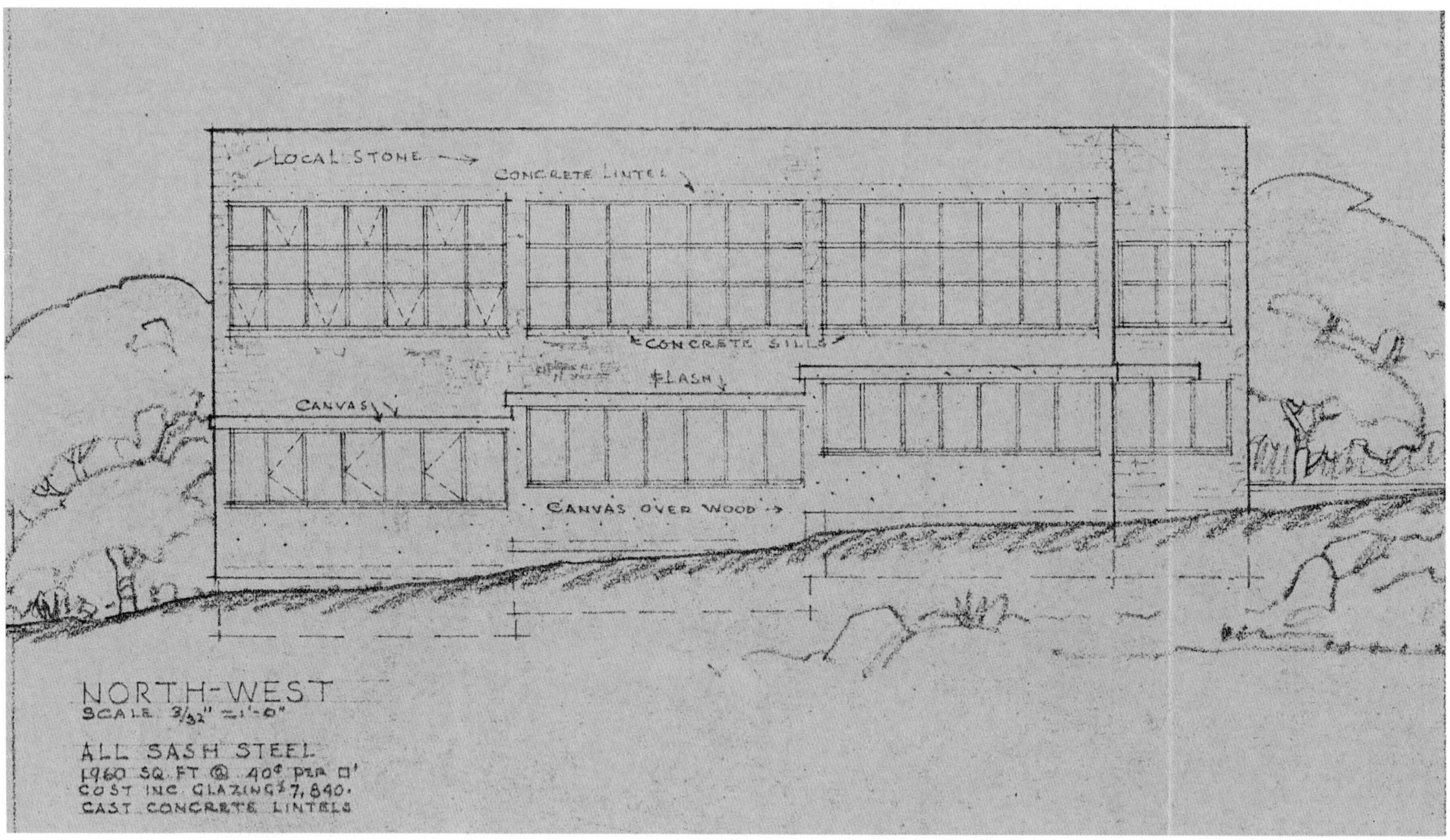
LOCAL STONE
CONCRETE LINTEL
CONCRETE SILLS
FLASH
CANVAS
CANVAS OVER WOOD
NORTH-WEST
SCALE 3/32" = 1'-0"
ALL SASH STEEL
1960 SQ FT @ 40¢ PER □'
COST INC GLAZING $7,840.
CAST CONCRETE LINTELS

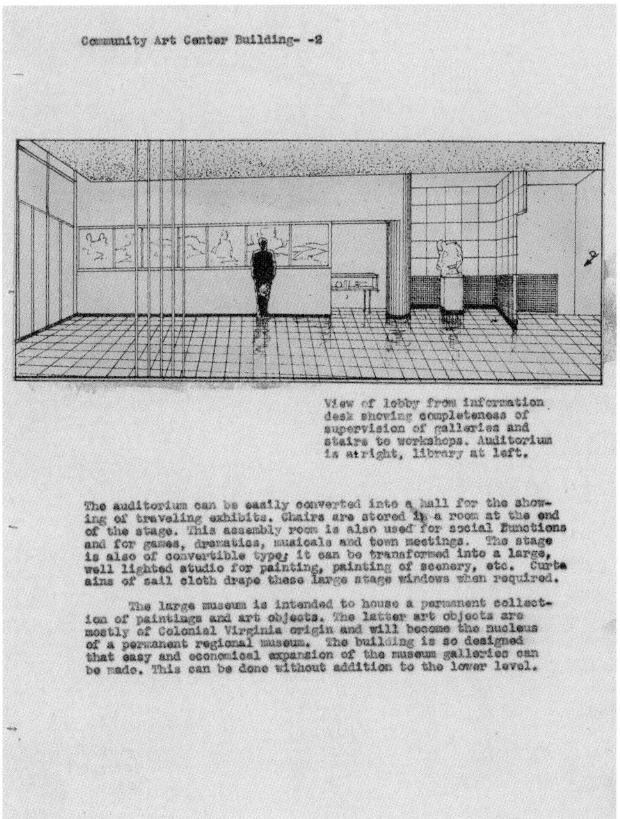

Community Art Center Building- -2

View of lobby from information desk showing completeness of supervision of galleries and stairs to workshops. Auditorium is at right, library at left.

The auditorium can be easily converted into a hall for the showing of traveling exhibits. Chairs are stored in a room at the end of the stage. This assembly room is also used for social functions and for games, dramatics, musicals and town meetings. The stage is also of convertible type; it can be transformed into a large, well lighted studio for painting, painting of scenery, etc. Curtains of sail cloth drape these large stage windows when required.

The large museum is intended to house a permanent collection of paintings and art objects. The latter art objects are mostly of Colonial Virginia origin and will become the nucleus of a permanent regional museum. The building is so designed that easy and economical expansion of the museum galleries can be made. This can be done without addition to the lower level.

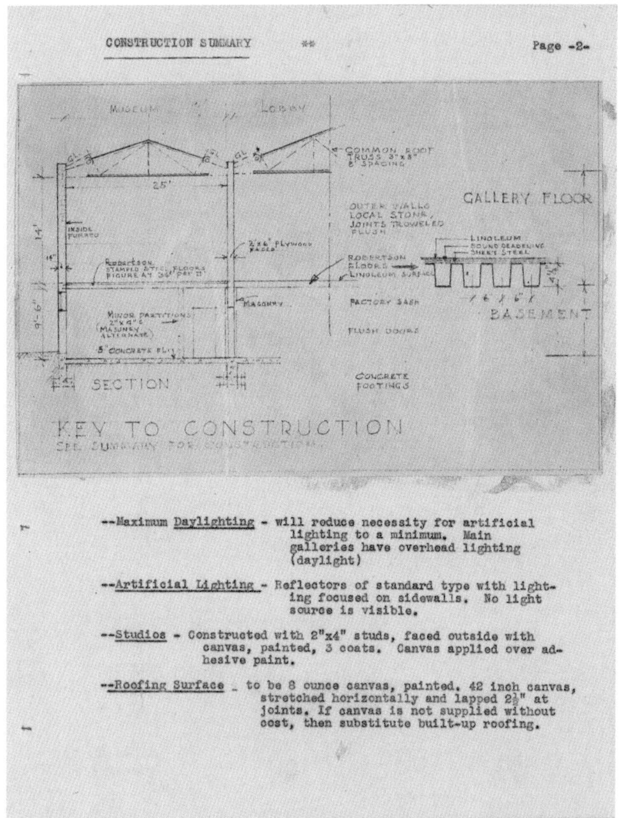

CONSTRUCTION SUMMARY -- Page -2-

KEY TO CONSTRUCTION

--Maximum <u>Daylighting</u> - will reduce necessity for artificial lighting to a minimum. Main galleries have overhead lighting (daylight)

--<u>Artificial Lighting</u> - Reflectors of standard type with lighting focused on sidewalls. No light source is visible.

--<u>Studios</u> - Constructed with 2"x4" studs, faced outside with canvas, painted, 3 coats. Canvas applied over adhesive paint.

--<u>Roofing Surface</u> - to be 8 ounce canvas, painted. 42 inch canvas, stretched horizontally and lapped 2½" at joints. If canvas is not supplied without cost, then substitute built-up roofing.

Previous page:
Figures 5.18 to 5.20. A. Lawrence Kocher. 1938. Community Art Center in Big Stone Gap, Virginia, for the Works Progress Administration. Elevations.

This page:
Figure 5.21. A. Lawrence Kocher. 1938. Community Art Center in Big Stone Gap, Virginia, for the Works Progress Administration. Front elevation.
Figure 5.22 and 5.23. A. Lawrence Kocher. 1938. Community Art Center in Big Stone Gap, Virginia, for the Works Progress Administration. Pages of the brochure. View of the lobby and construction section.

This page:
Figure 5.24. A. Lawrence Kocher. 1938. Community Art Center in Big Stone Gap, Virginia, for the Works Progress Administration. Final rendering of the north-east façade.
Figure 5.25. A. Lawrence Kocher. 1938. Community Art Center in Big Stone Gap, Virginia, for the Works Progress Administration. Preliminary rendering of the north-east façade.

Next page:
Figure 5.26. A. Lawrence Kocher and Albert Frey. 1938. Swiss Pavilion competition for the 1939's New York World's Fair. Sketch.

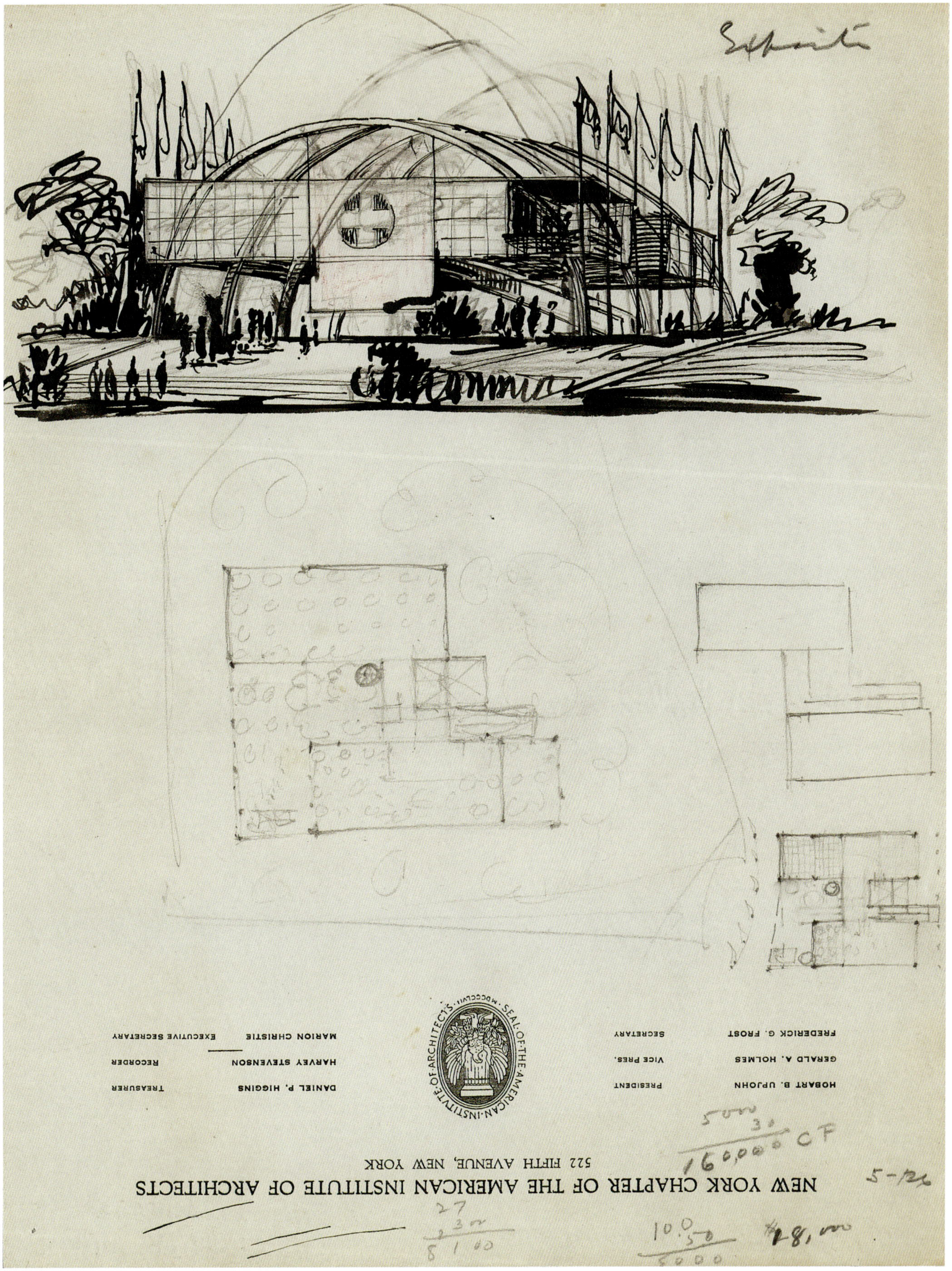
NEW YORK CHAPTER OF THE AMERICAN INSTITUTE OF ARCHITECTS
522 FIFTH AVENUE, NEW YORK
HOBART B. UPJOHN PRESIDENT
GERALD A. HOLMES VICE PRES.
FREDERICK G. FROST SECRETARY
SEAL OF THE AMERICAN INSTITUTE OF ARCHITECTS
DANIEL P. HIGGINS TREASURER
HARVEY STEVENSON RECORDER
MARION CHRISTIE EXECUTIVE SECRETARY
160,000 CF

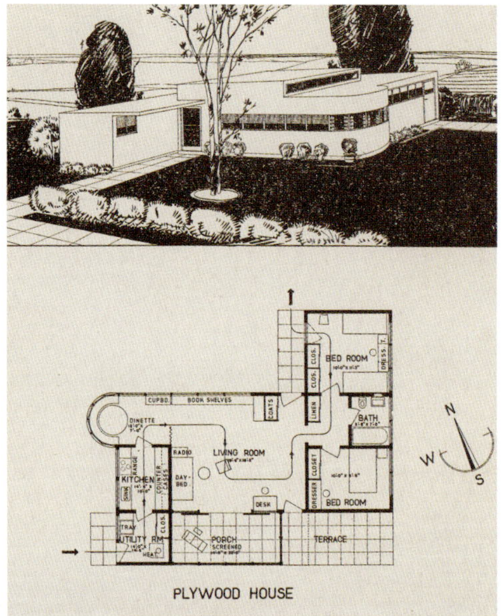

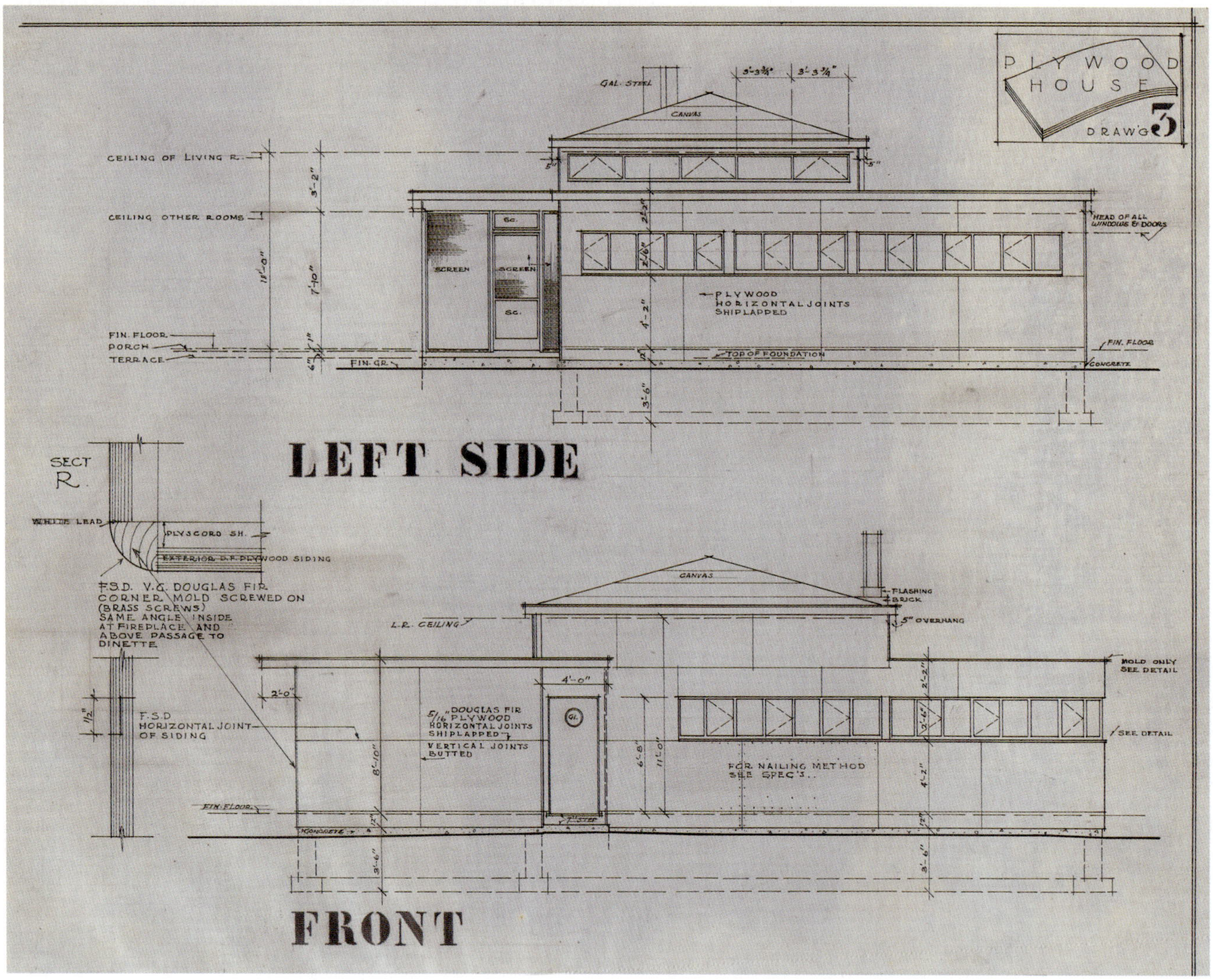

Figure 5.27. A. Lawrence Kocher. 1939. House of Plywood. New York World's Fair. Demonstration house. Board for publication.
Figure 5.28. A. Lawrence Kocher. 1939. House of Plywood. New York World's Fair. Demonstration house. Elevations.

Park, Florida—Black Mountain College started operations in 1933. They rented several buildings during the winter off-season at the Blue Ridge Assembly YMCA at Black Mountain, in the Appalachian area of North Carolina. The college used only a few cottages, the dining hall, the gymnasium, and the Robert E. Lee Hall as living headquarters on a regular basis. The initial 19 students and 10 faculty and their families, lived, worked, and had meals together. The founders of Black Mountain College envisioned "an intimate educational community that would learn, live, and work together," including activities like farming and forest management, along with building renovation and construction.[53] Manual work was always an essential part of Black Mountain College's pedagogy. Shared work was seen as a way of tightening the relationship between faculty and students, as a means of personal development, and also played an important role in securing the institution's economic survival. Soon after the college's founding, students and faculty agreed in starting a farm as a way of saving money and creating a stronger community. From one to four in the afternoons, everybody, including faculty spouses, were supposed to work on the farm or perform other maintenance duties for the community. By 1936, this physical labor was formalized as the Work Program.

Following John Dewey's ideas on education, holistic personal development was achieved at Black Mountain College through a multi-disciplined experimental curriculum including but not restricted to: music, weaving, pottery, painting, sculpture, architecture, mathematics, scenography, photography, furniture design, acting, dance, product design, and poetry. The college offered an egualitarian and democratic model of governance shared among students and faculty without the interference of administrators or a board of trustees. Their ideals incorporated a complete academic freedom: there were no grades, nor required courses or set curriculum. No teaching methods were prescribed, hence faculty set up their courses according to their pedagogical ideas. Students held the responsibility of choosing their own education in a radical exercise of intellectual autonomy and independence. Dewey visited the college at Lake Eden many times, was invited to join the advisory board, and praised the institution's work as "imperative in the long run interests of democracy. The college exists at the very 'grass-roots' of democratic way of life."[54]

In 1937, the economic depression and its structurally meager income forced the school to insure security against the possibility of being suddenly evicted by the YMCA. To this end, the college purchased a summer camp and resort surrounding the man-made Lake Eden, two miles northwest of the village of Black Mountain.[55] The property consisted of 726 heavily wooded acres with 15 buildings including two large lodges, a dining hall with kitchen, a farmhouse, and several cottages. After the purchase, the college worked as a dual-campus, operating an inn and a faculty residence on the new property during the summer, cultivating its farmland all-year-round as part of the Work Program, all the while keeping the classes mainly at Blue Ridge Assembly. Nevertheless, the original idea of the purchase was always to completely move to Lake Eden, and they soon realized that the existing buildings were insufficient, and a newly built campus was needed. With this goal in mind, the institution's founders sought external advice from Kocher.

In a letter dated July 9, 1937, Kocher replied to Theodore Dreier discouraging the organization of an open architectural competition for the design of the new campus. Instead, he recommended the project commission be given to Walter Gropius, who had arrived two months prior at Harvard University. The correspondence that followed reveals how Kocher insisted on the necessity and convenience of a modern functional design that only Gropius could provide. In another letter, dated September 24, 1937, he wrote to Dreier that, "the setting up of space and activity requirements...would be an inspiring example to other schools, all of whom were too strongly influenced at the outset by a desired appearance."[56] Once the Black Mountain College founders were convinced by Kocher's arguments, the commission went to Gropius, who then shared it with Marcel Breuer—who had followed Groupius, his mentor, first to London and now to Cambridge. Gropius and Breuer worked together with Black Mountain College faculty and students to develop an architectural scheme adapted to the needs of the clients and the specificities of the site.

Aside from their own houses, this was the second architectural job they undertook since their arrival in the United States; the first had been a design proposal entry for the Wheaton College Art Center competition in Norton, Massachusetts, which was awarded second place in 1938. In 1939, Gropius and Breuer produced a proposal for Black Mountain College consisting of a ribbon of bent buildings tightly following the lake's southern shoreline. The project prescribed the demolition of several existing structures and occupied an amphibious situation with several buildings situated partially over the water, making inevitable the partial drainage of the lake and the construction of expensive yet necessary retaining walls and foundations. **(Figure 5.47)** These two decisions made the budget increase prohibitive for the school. Furthermore, in May of 1940, President Roosevelt addressed Congress asking for over two billion dollars to develop American defenses, given the country's inevitable involvement in World War II.[57] Confronting an unaffordable budget—due to the purchase of the land and the immediate lack of funds thereafter, along with the foreseen wartime restrictions on labor and building materials—Dreier raised the need to desist, at least temporarily, from building the Gropius-Breuer designs for the campus at a community meeting.

In the summer of 1940, Rice and Dreier approached Kocher again with a petition to make an alternative, less costly design for the Black Mountain College campus. After traveling to Cambridge to speak with Gropius, Kocher accepted the commission.[58] His decision to accept the job proposal was influenced by the appeal of Black Mountain College not only for its experimental education model, but also for its ties with the Bauhaus. This Bauhaus influence over Black Mountain College began with the appointment of Joseph Albers in 1933—the very same year the Bauhaus closed—who introduced pedagogical methodologies comparable with those employed at the German school. Many Bauhaus faculty and former students joined Black Mountain College during Albers' tenure, with the first being his spouse, Anni Albers, who taught weaving and textile design. Others followed in the years thereafter, like Xanti Schawinsky, Howard Dearstyne, Marli Ehrmen, and Lyonel Feininger.[59] At the time, Black Mountain College and the American Institute of Design

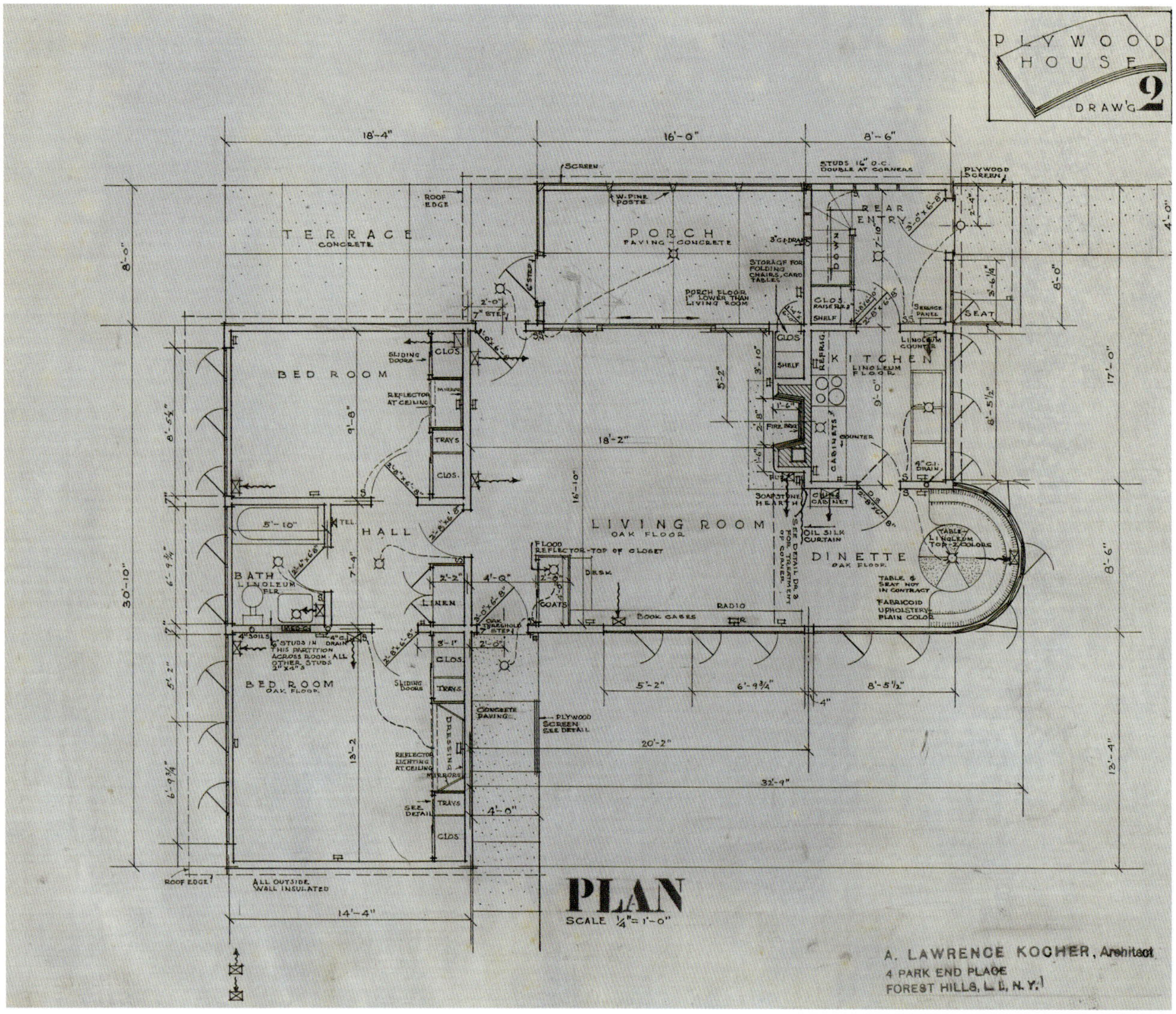

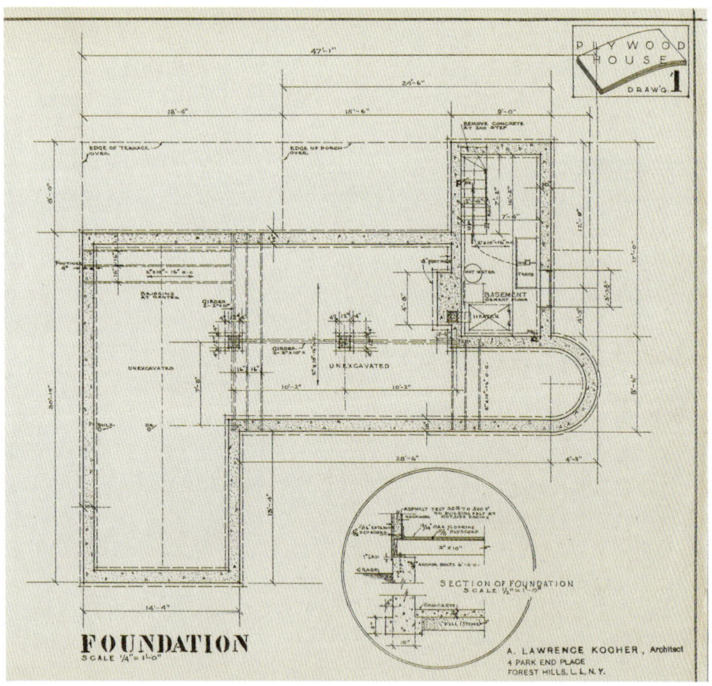

Figure 5.29. A. Lawrence Kocher. 1939. House of Plywood. New York World's Fair. Demonstration house. Floor plan.
Figure 5.30. A. Lawrence Kocher. 1939. House of Plywood. New York World's Fair. Demonstration house. Foundation plan.

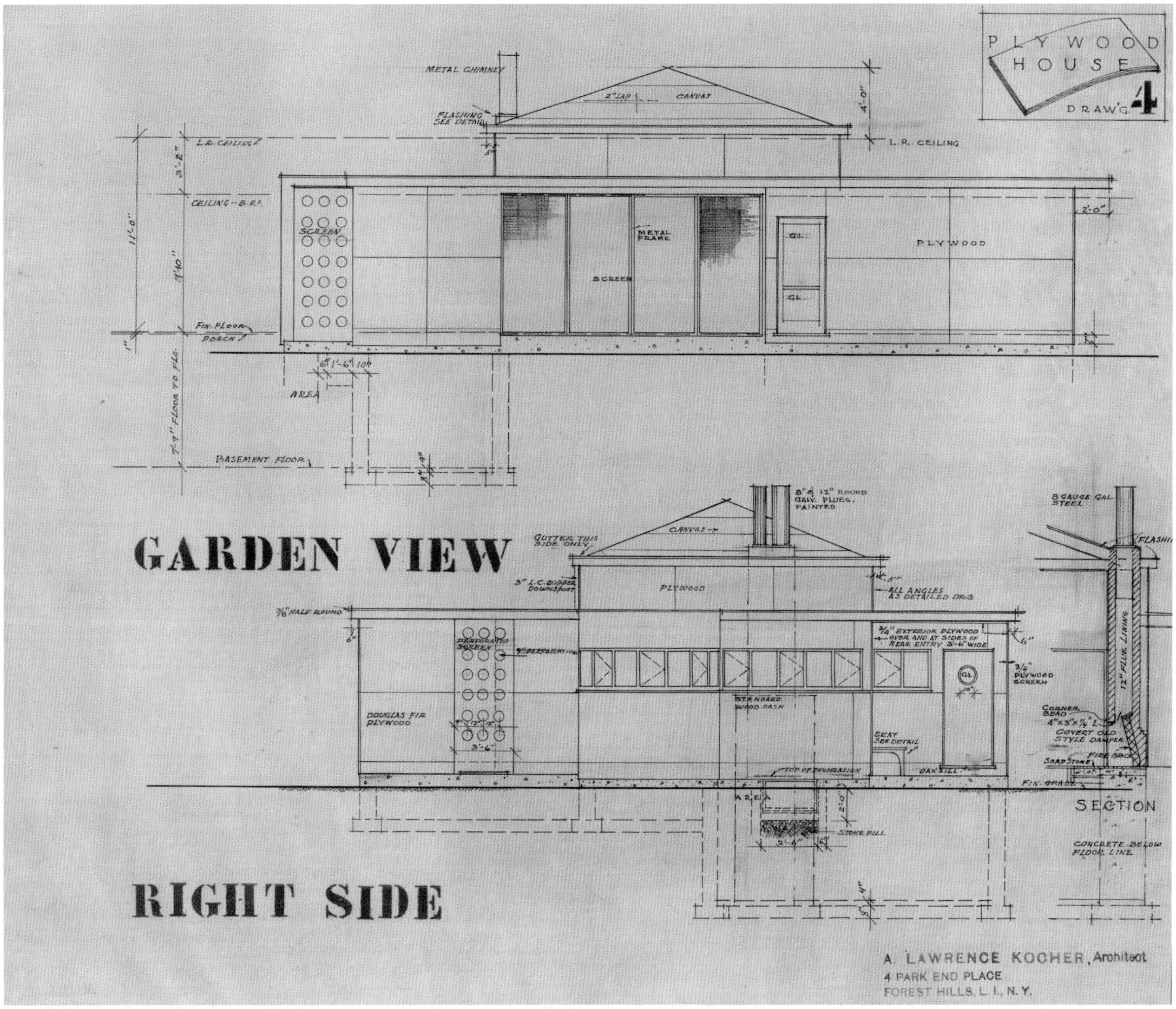

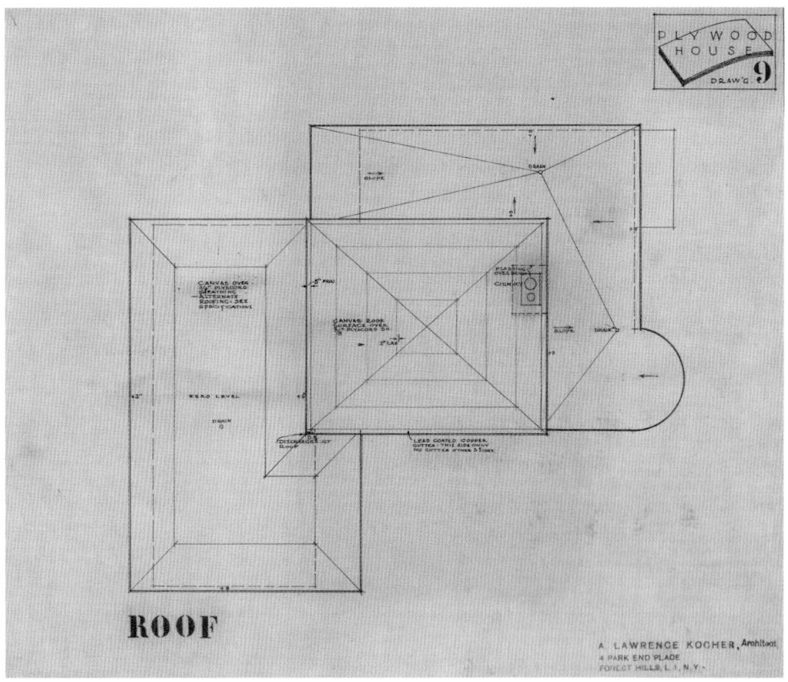

Figure 5.31. A. Lawrence Kocher. 1939. House of Plywood. New York World's Fair. Demonstration house. Elevations.

Figure 5.32. A. Lawrence Kocher. 1939. House of Plywood. New York World's Fair. Demonstration house. Roof plan.

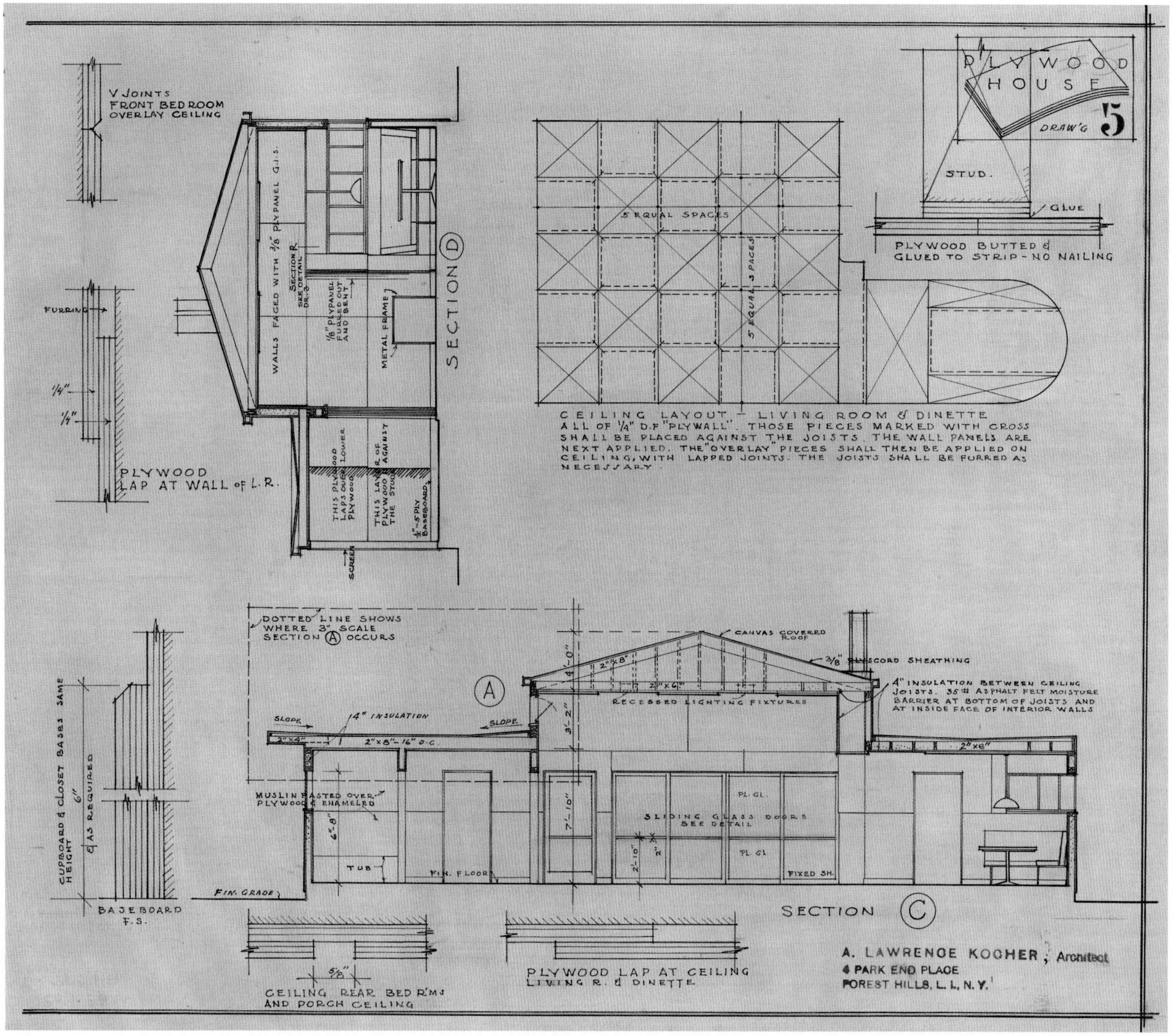

This page:
Figure 5.33. A. Lawrence Kocher. 1939. House of Plywood. New York World's Fair. Demonstration house. Sections and ceiling layout.

Next page:
Figure 5.34. A. Lawrence Kocher. 1939. House of Plywood. New York World's Fair. Demonstration house. Roof and façade details.
Figure 5.35. A. Lawrence Kocher 1939. House of Plywood. New York World's Fair. Demonstration house. Doors and furniture details.

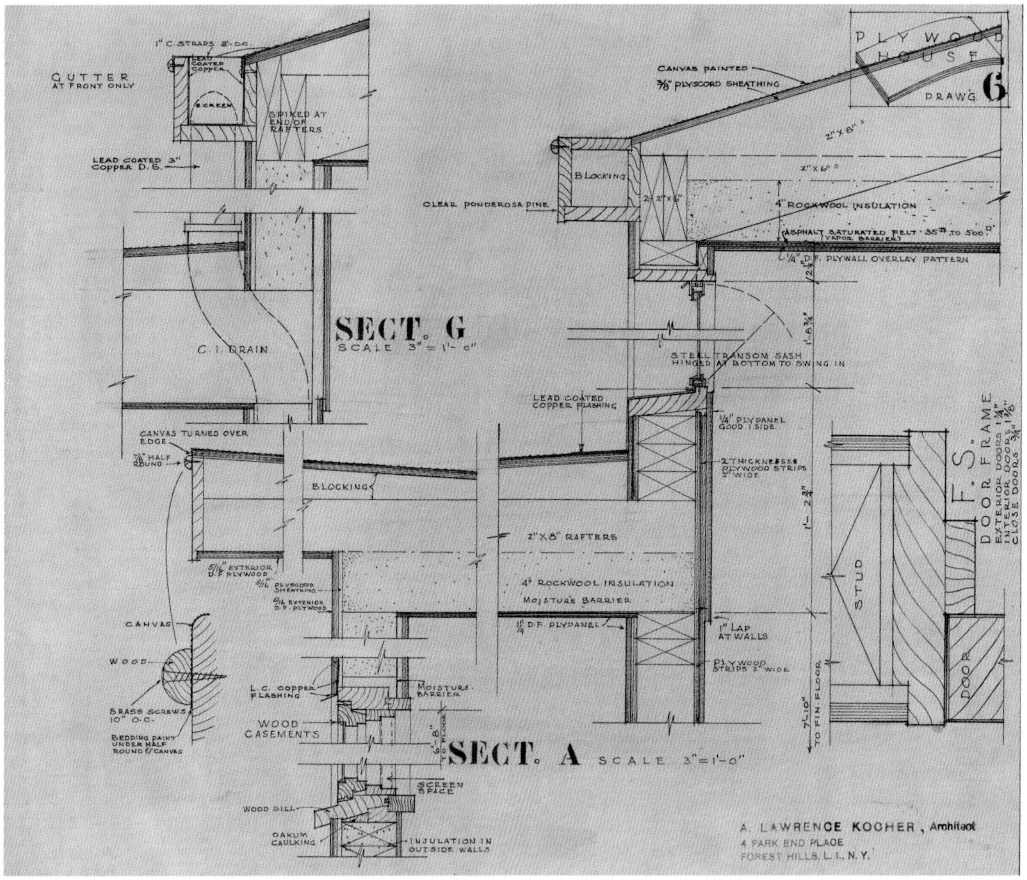
PLYWOOD HOUSE
DRAW'G 6
GUTTER AT FRONT ONLY
SECT. G SCALE 3" = 1'-0"
C. I. DRAIN
CANVAS PAINTED
3/8" PLYSCORD SHEATHING
CLEAR PONDEROSA PINE
BLOCKING
4" ROCKWOOL INSULATION
STEEL TRANSOM SASH HINGED AT BOTTOM TO SWING IN
LEAD COATED COPPER FLASHING
2" X 8" RAFTERS
4" ROCKWOOL INSULATION
MOISTURE BARRIER
CANVAS
WOOD
BRASS SCREWS 10" O.C.
WOOD CASEMENTS
SECT. A SCALE 3" = 1'-0"
WOOD SILL
OAKUM CAULKING
INSULATION IN OUTSIDE WALLS
F.S. DOOR FRAME
STUD
DOOR
A. LAWRENCE KOCHER, Architect
4 PARK END PLACE
FOREST HILLS, L. I., N. Y.

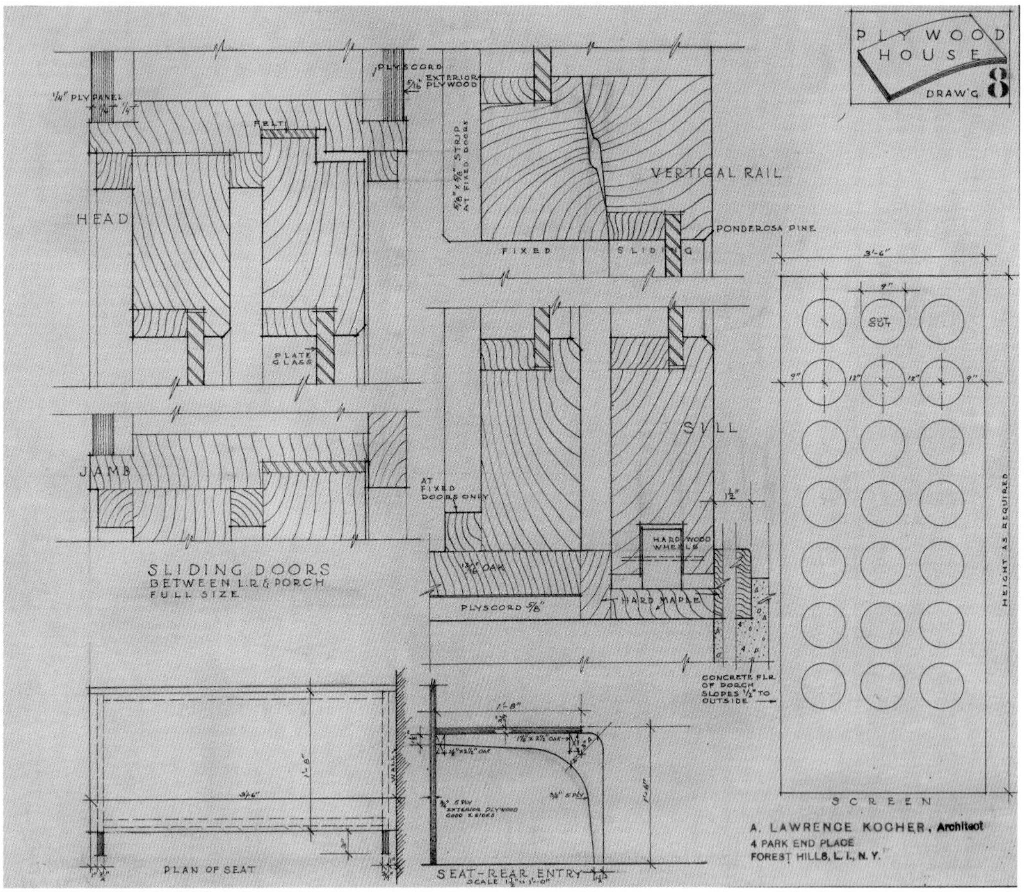
PLYWOOD HOUSE
DRAW'G 8
HEAD
JAMB
PLATE GLASS
VERTICAL RAIL
PONDEROSA PINE
FIXED
SLIDING
SILL
HARD WOOD WHEELS
HARD MAPLE
PLYSCORD 5/8"
CONCRETE FLR. OF PORCH SLOPES 1/2" TO OUTSIDE
SLIDING DOORS
BETWEEN L.R. & PORCH
FULL SIZE
SCREEN
HEIGHT AS REQUIRED
PLAN OF SEAT
SEAT-REAR ENTRY
A. LAWRENCE KOCHER, Architect
4 PARK END PLACE
FOREST HILLS, L. I., N. Y.

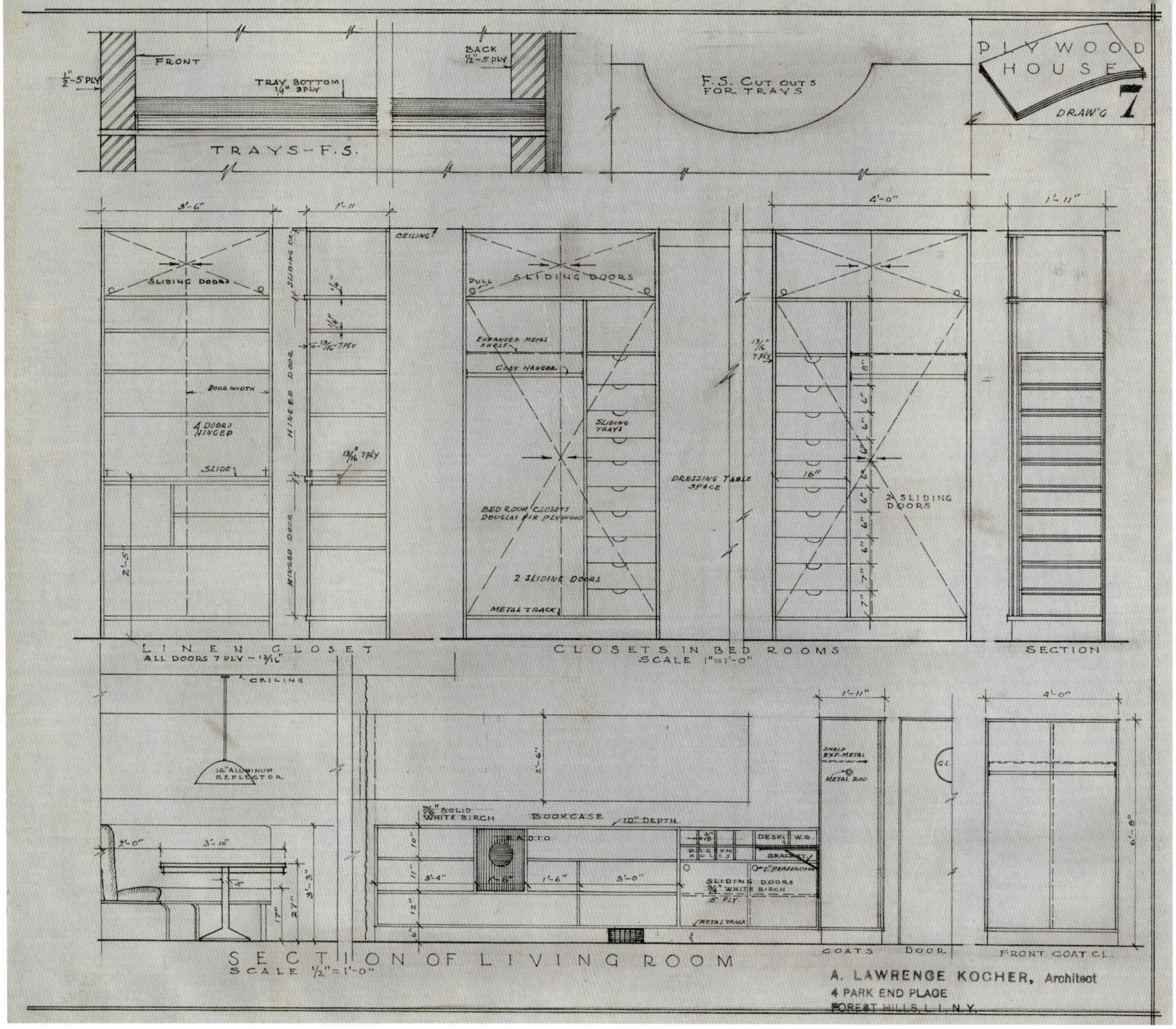

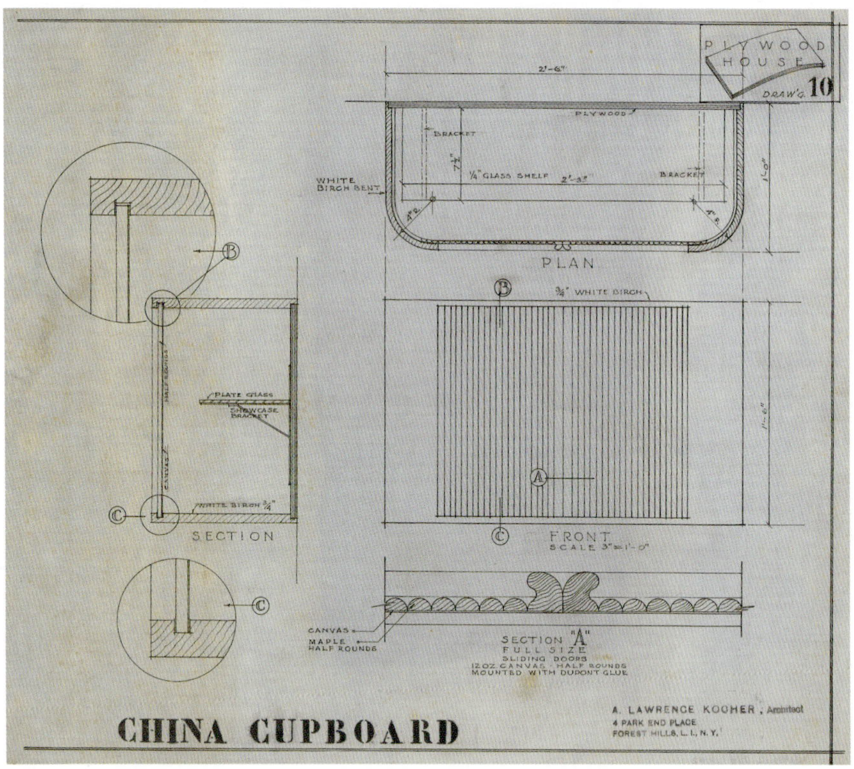

Figure 5.36. A. Lawrence Kocher. 1939. House of Plywood. New York World's Fair. Demonstration house. Closets details.

Figure 5.37. A. Lawrence Kocher. 1939. House of Plywood. New York World's Fair. Demonstration house. China cupboard details.

at Chicago were justly considered as the only heirs of the Bauhaus on American soil.

Kocher visited the site during July of 1940 and, within one month, produced a modern design that would use a construction method and material conventional enough to be inexpensive and executed by unskilled and semi-skilled student labor. Furthermore, he made the decision of placing the building on the north shore of the lake, avoiding the demolition of existing buildings and its associated cost. The design consisted of four radial buildings converging in a central irregular hexagonal entry hall. Taking advantage of the level drop in the hillside site, the entrance to the building happened on the upper floor of this hexagonal element. The buildings radiating from this center had a variety of specific programs. The smallest, at the left of the entrance, was dedicated to the reception and administration offices. Moving clockwise, the next building was the library, connected to the lobby through a bridge-like piece used as exhibition space. The next wing was the Studies Building—the only constructed piece of the set. This 200-feet-long and 28-feet-wide wing had two enclosed stories, main and intermediate floor levels (corresponding to third and second floors), which provided 50 student studies; 14 faculty studies and classrooms; one common terrace; two faculty apartments; and the main stairwell for the complex. The last wing, Studies Building number 2, to the right of the entrance, included 29 extra student studies, two faculty apartments, two conversation rooms, two shared studios, a club room, and an exhibition space. The ground floor of these buildings was completely open and executed with concrete and stone walls; only the ground floor under the Studies Building had an enclosed portion dedicated to workshop. In 1940, after heavy rains resulting in the flooding of the area where the Studies Building would be constructed, the open spaces on the ground floor—with its stone and concrete construction—were used to minimize future circumstantial damages. **(Figures 5.48 to 5.52)**

Kocher planned the construction to be carried on by students, but was also supported and advised by Charles Godfrey, a local contractor. Both agreed on using only materials available on site: the stone for the footings and walls, and the wood for the second and third floors of the building were obtained on the Lake Eden property. The building technology of Studies Building number 1 was straightforward. On the ground floor, concrete pylons and stone walls provided lateral stability while three rows of slender steel columns supported the second-floor deck. The columns did not have vertical continuity beyond ground level except in an apartment under the terrace. An eight-foot modulated load-bearing wood frame provided floors, roof, façades, and inner partitions in these upper levels. The façades had steel horizontal window sashes for the entire length and an exterior facing of Transite, a cement-asbestos fiber corrugated board. Internally, all studies were faced with eight-by-four-foot plywood sheets, and were furnished with plywood book stacks under the windows along with a desk hung from the ceiling by a steel tube—a kind of device previously tested by Kocher in several designs of the Aluminaire House. Kocher justified the material adaptations and technological decisions he made in the design of the first Studies Building not only from an economic and architectural perspective, but also in pedagogic terms, adding another chapter to his previous experiences in design-build teaching. **(Figures 5.52 to 5.54)** Described in the *Black Mountain College Bulletin*, the Studies building construction:

> Not only assists in the solution of an economic problem, but also constitutes, through the Work Program, an extension of one of the College's educational ideas...Voluntary practical activities, on different levels, have been always regarded as part of general education and as indispensable for the full development of the student. The participation by students in the present building project is, then, the fruition of a fundamental idea rather than an innovation or a change in ideology.[60]

According to the construction schedule, construction began with the clearing and draining of the site on September 9, 1940. **(Figure 5.55)** Kocher created a second Work Program in Black Mountain College, specifically named the Building Program. As a demonstration of his own pedagogical theories on design-build, Kocher formed a group of 25 to 30 students who would be responsible for constructing the Studies Building under his supervision. The students worked on the construction of the shop, faculty studios, and student dormitories four afternoons per week for a year. **(Figures 5.56 to 5.59)**

The Studies Building perfectly represented Kocher's ideal of an architecture based on building technology, construction methodology, and experiential learning—his most outstanding achievement as a tenacious advocate of the design-build pedagogy. The building enacts the concluding stage of a long-standing historic era: the material and labor restrictions, the design sobriety, and the modest, even anonymous, look of the building are the result of the New Deal ethos and war-time economy. It is a design produced to efficiently and inexpensively solve an urgently present problem. The building also explores the possibility and implementation of a fully American modernism. Far from being a mere transplant of European ideas, the design grafted a rationalist branch onto the trunk of the local vernacular, including prefabrication and industrialization, which Kocher considered the two main components and essence of American architectural culture. In this project, Kocher also made extensive use of standardized catalog elements, following the American tradition on the use of building treatises and architectural handbooks. With its communal construction method, along with its individual study rooms for faculty and students, the Studies Building reflected the client's scale of values, aligning completely both with Black Mountain College's radically egalitarian and democratic values in the community relations, and its encouragement of autonomous thinking and intellectual self-development.

Concurrent with the construction of the Studies Building, and consistent with Kocher's interest in vernacular architecture, he also directed the rehabilitation and winterization of many existing structures on the campus.[61] The priority of allocating the students to a private study space dictated the need for the studies wing as the first construction. When the college moved to Lake Eden in September of 1940, construction of the Studies Building had yet to start, and students were alternatively accommodated in the lodges, using pulleys

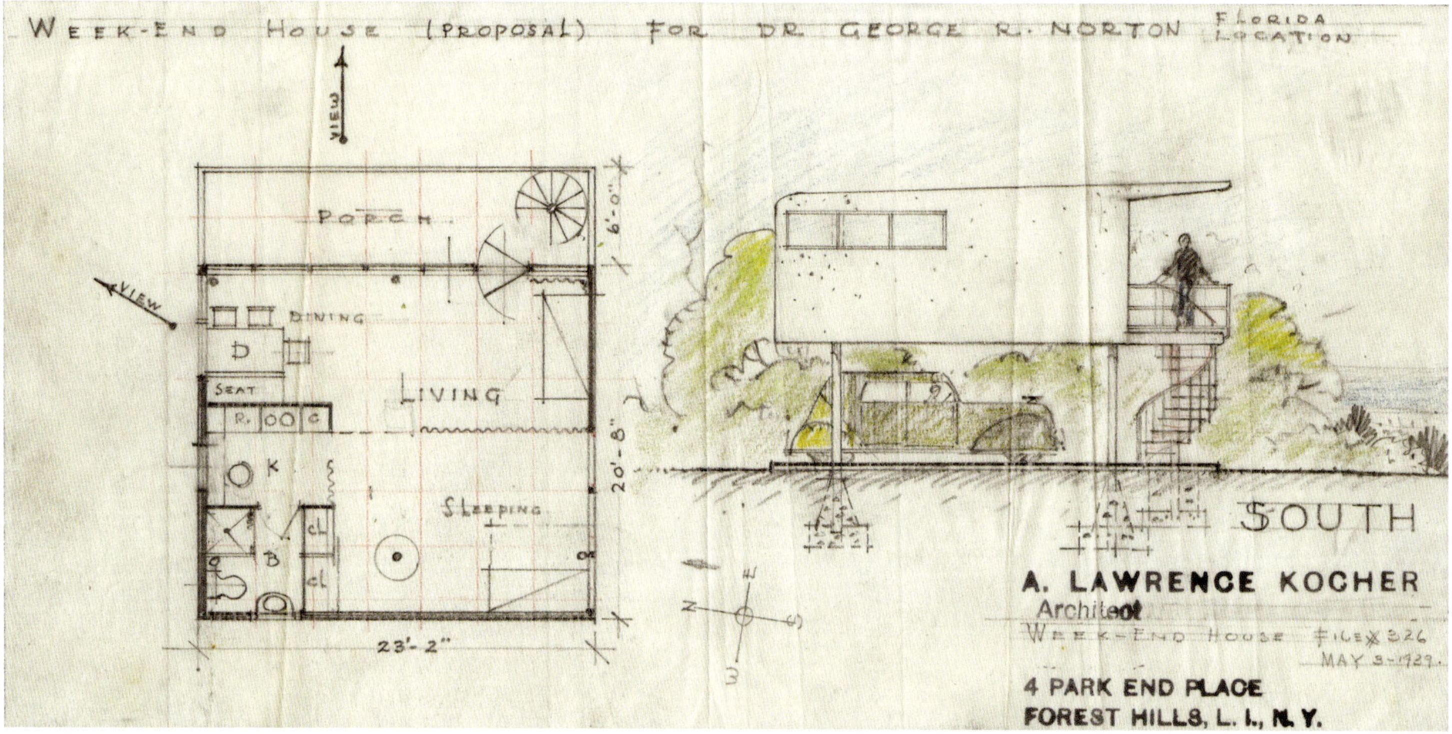

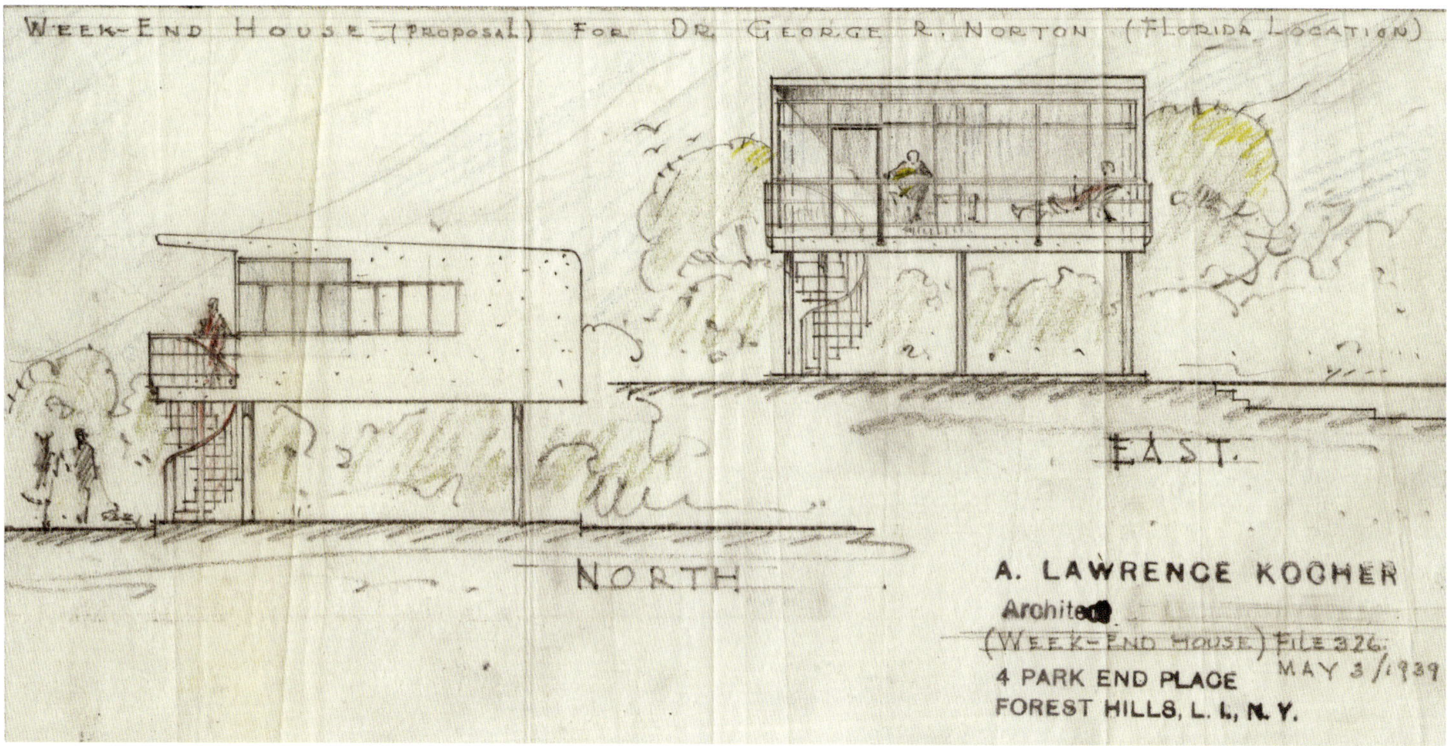

This page:

Figure 5.38. A. Lawrence Kocher. 1939. Florida Weekend House. Preliminary drawings. Floor plan and south elevation. Dated 5-3-39.

Figure 5.39. A. Lawrence Kocher. 1939. Florida Weekend House. Preliminary drawings. North and east elevations. Dated 5-3-39.

Next page:

Figure 5.40. A. Lawrence Kocher. 1939. Florida Weekend House. Preliminary drawings. Floor plans, elevations, and situation on the lot. Dated 5-20-39.

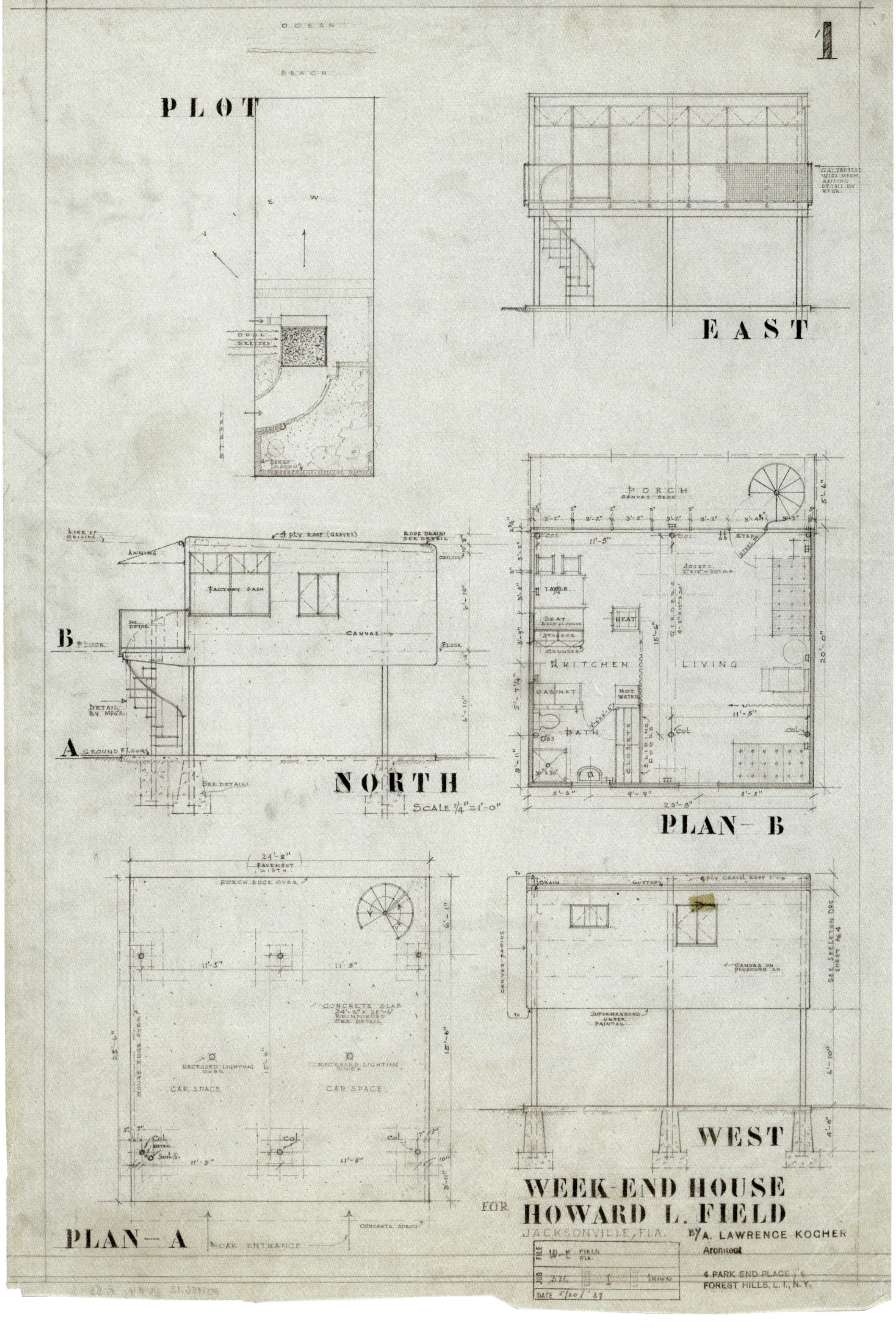

OCEAN
BEACH
PLOT
EAST
NORTH
SCALE 1/4" = 1'-0"
PLAN-B
PORCH
KITCHEN
LIVING
BATH
CLOSETS
PLAN-A
CAR SPACE
CAR SPACE
CAR ENTRANCE
WEST
WEEK-END HOUSE
FOR HOWARD L. FIELD
JACKSONVILLE, FLA.
BY A. LAWRENCE KOCHER
Architect
4 PARK END PLACE
FOREST HILLS, L. I., N. Y.

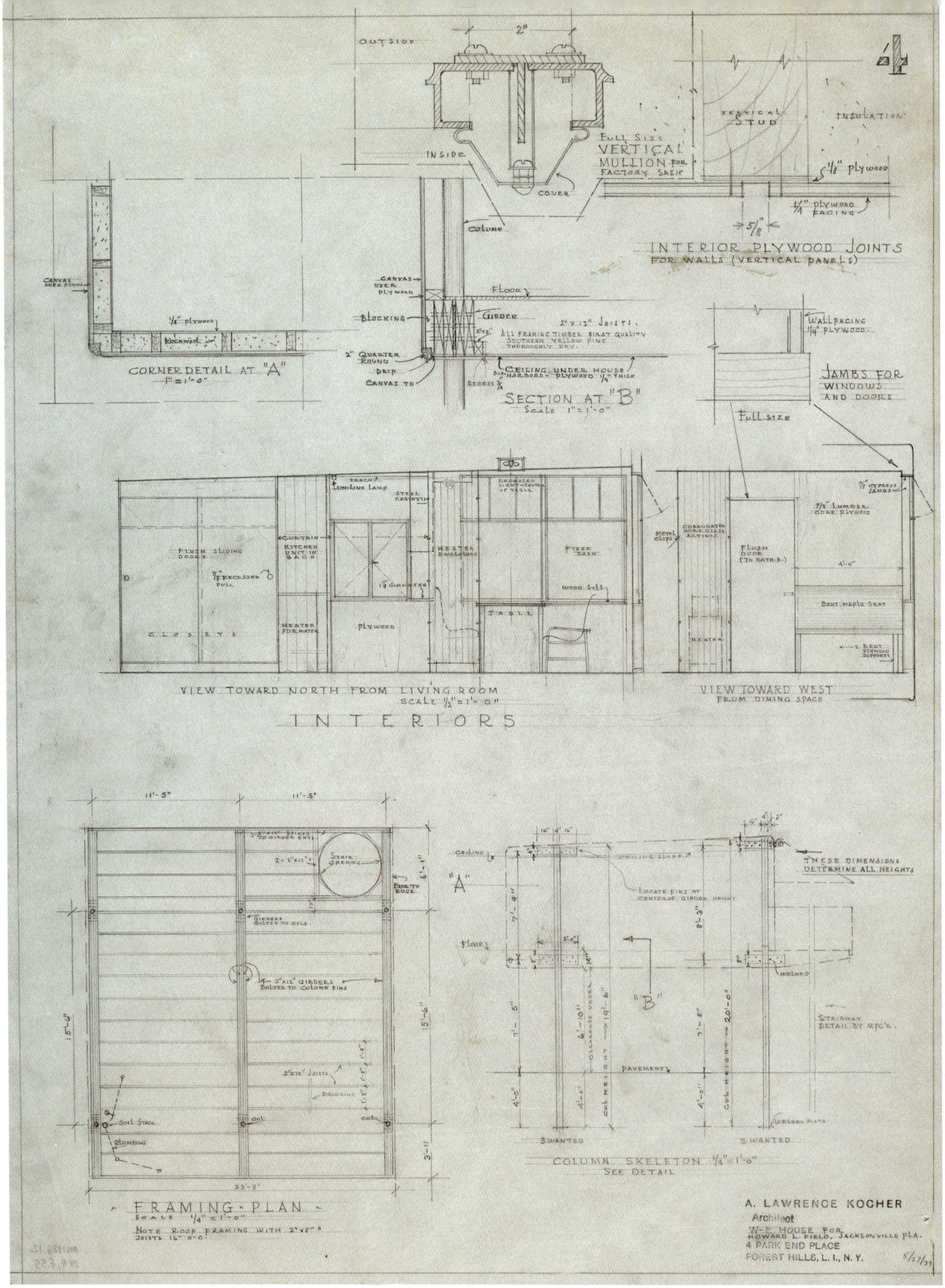

Figure 5.41. A. Lawrence Kocher. 1939. Florida Weekend House. Preliminary drawings. Interior elevations, framing plan, and structure details. Dated 5-27-39.

to lift beds to the ceiling to facilitate space for daytime study. In December of 1940, the *Black Mountain College Newsletter* described construction status as:

> Every effort is being made to complete the shell of the building before Christmas in order to save the framework from damage by rain and snow. At the beginning of the year the Work Committee planned a weekly schedule which has been closely followed.[62]

After this first construction effort, Black Mountain College also established a four-week summer work camp, leading to the completion of the Studies Building in the fall of 1941. Nonetheless, Kocher's responsibilities at the College were not limited to the construction of the building; he was also hired as an instructor and started teaching in the fall of 1940. By that time, he was still a visiting professor at Carnegie Tech, and the first two years of his Black Mountain College salary was paid by the Carnegie Foundation of New York. In his third year of teaching, Kocher's salary was covered by a donation of $1,000 from Philip L. Goodwin, architect of the MoMA building, a good friend and a sporadic employer of Albert Frey.

In his first year, Kocher taught a course on contemporary architecture that tried to cover the full spectrum of architectural design: from the general organization of a neighborhood to the individual building, with a special emphasis on materials and their application in building structures, finishes, and furniture. During 1941, this class was making a study on wall types and floor materials, designing furniture for production to be used in the new building, and producing designs for small low-cost houses.[63] In a letter dated July 17, 1940, to Theodore Dreier, A. Lawrence Kocher explained the intent of the course:

> I would be interested in conducting some student instruction in design partly related to what may be termed 'shelter and furnishings.' I would be anxious that this instruction be in the nature of training in thinking with respect to forms and requirements of the setting for living and working. In other words, design should relate to reality; the reality of the life for today; the houses for improved living, improved community planning; and a richer life which presupposes the philosophy of surroundings that are attractive, sanitary and efficient.[64]

In the 1941 to 1942 academic year, the courses offered by Kocher were Architectural Elements, Intermediate Design, Advanced Design, Mechanics, Structural Design 1 and 2, History of Architecture, and Field Work. In addition to the Studies Building on the Black Mountain College campus, Kocher designed a barn, music practice cubicles, and an undated—and unbuilt—design for a medium-sized community theater on campus. **(Figure 5.60)** He also worked on a small house for resident music teacher Heinrich Jalowetz and his wife Johanna, who taught voice and bookbinding. The Jalowetz House was designed for prefabrication, using means and materials appropriate for student labor—both for instruction and experimentation purposes. The job captain, student Claude Stoller, who later became a prominent architect in California, was advised during construction by Kocher and a local carpenter. The plan was modulated using eight-by-four-foot plywood sheets as a base, with an intention to experiment with the structural possibilities of plywood without studs, as Kocher had explored previously in his 1939 World's Fair Demonstration House. The house was also an experiment on acoustics as the living room also served as a music classroom; the ceiling was covered with vermiculite plaster and the walls finished in perforated plywood boards to deaden sound. The distribution of the two-bedroom, one-bathroom house, the disposition of windows and porches, and the section of the shed roof are designed to cool the house with prevailing winds and to protect from excessive sun exposure. **(Figures 5.61 to 5.64)** As was customary in Kocher's architectural works, he designed all the furniture of the house, including the closets, storage, and kitchen cabinets. Likely as a means of using leftover materials from the Studies Building construction, the façades of the house and the front of the chimney are partially cladded in cement-asbestos corrugated panels.[65] **(Figures 5.65 to 5.72)**

A. Lawrence Kocher's years at Black Mountain College were always remembered as fruitful and happy times for both him and his family. They were highly appreciated members of the academic community, and the academic freedom granted by the institution allowed Kocher to develop his teaching and his practice simultaneously, inside and outside the college, along with his ongoing research on prefabrication and low-cost housing. However, once again, far-reaching historical circumstances were about to profoundly modify his professional plans. On Sunday, December 7, 1941, Japan began a series of coordinated attacks on the British Commonwealth territories of Malaya, Singapore, and Hong Kong. The U.S.-held Philippines, Guam, Wake Island, and the naval base at Pearl Harbor in Honolulu, Hawaii, were also attacked. The United States was a neutral country at the time, but the attack led President Roosevelt to declare its formal entry into World War II the next day, radically changing the economic and political picture of the country. In 1942, a year after the completion of the Studies Building, the draft began to impact the school's enrollment. The drop-off in male student applications and the restrictions of the war economy made it impossible to undertake another design-build project. In lieu of teaching, Kocher took a leave of absence to write during the spring of 1943 but returned to Black Mountain College that summer. He eventually presented his official resignation in 1946, while continuing to conduct his professional practice and research projects outside the institution. Kocher kept in contact with Black Mountain College and its endeavors until the closure of the school in 1957. The school never lost hope of reinstating him in its faculty, as is evident in a 1948 letter from Dreier:

> We are all looking forward to a time when you may return here. Although the adjustment of living in the North must certainly be not an easy one for you to make, I think it may still pay dividends in the long run specially because of the additional contacts and experience that you may gain. When you return here, I should think these could all be made to count a great deal.[66]

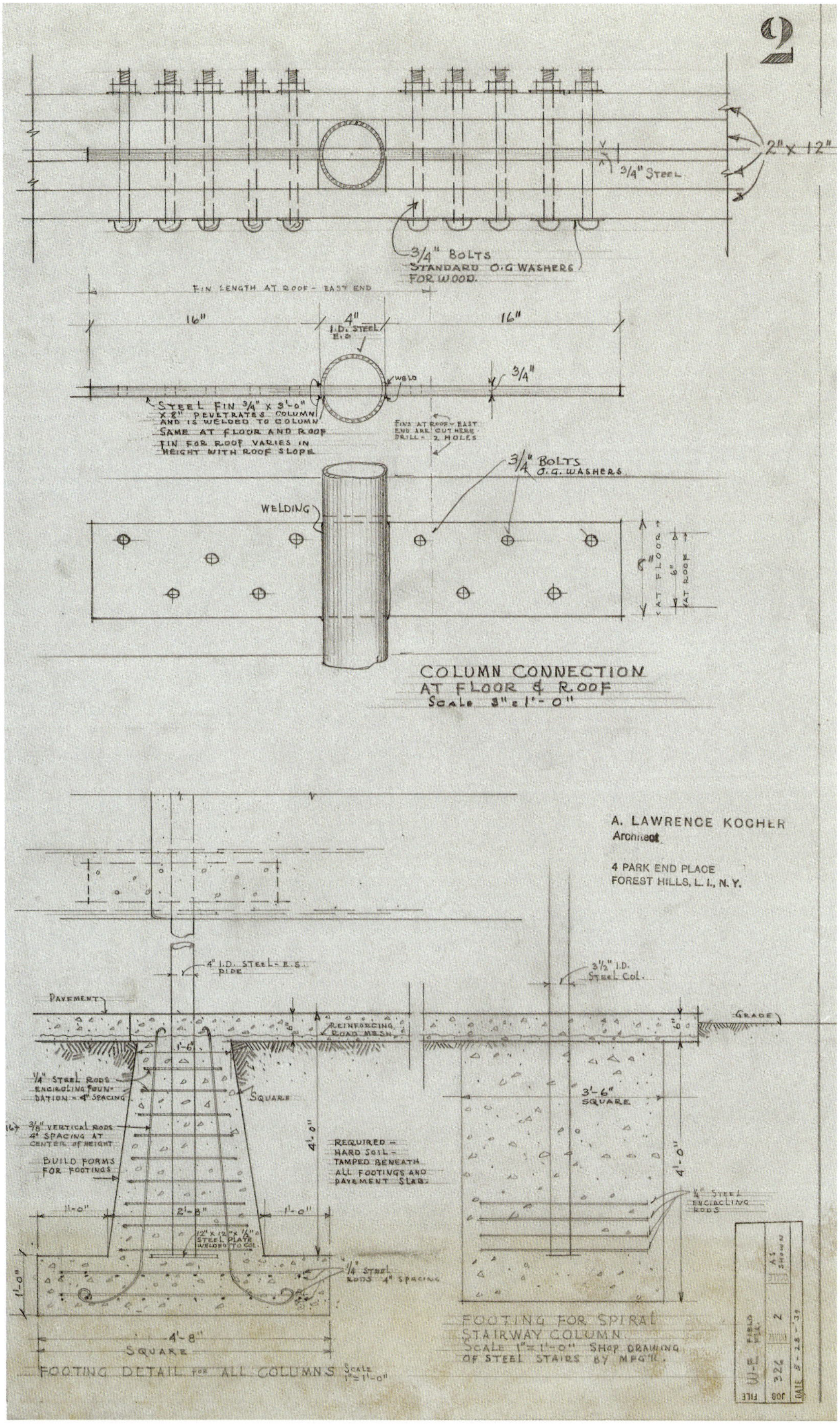

Figure 5.42.
A. Lawrence Kocher. 1939. Florida Weekend House. Preliminary drawings. Foundation and structure details. Dated 5-28-39.

This return to Black Mountain College never happened, as Kocher was already reinventing himself in several simultaneous new professional endeavors. Black Mountain College would not be Kocher's last teaching experience, but it was undoubtedly his farewell to Bauhaus-derived pedagogy and to "design-build" as a teaching methodology.

Chapter endnotes

1 "Letter from Kocher to Henry Chang, dated May 19, 1964," Box 1. A. Lawrence Kocher Collection, Colonial Williamsburg Foundation, John D. Rockefeller Jr. Library.

2 The six articles (in chronological order): National Lumber Manufacturer's Association, "Portable House: Plan no 5," *Architectural Record*, vol. 79, No. 2 (February 1936): 170. National Lumber Manufacturer's Association, "Structural Mobility," *Architectural Record*, vol. 79, no. 4 (April 1936): 332. National Lumber Manufacturer's Association, "Prefabricated Units," *Architectural Record*, vol. 79, no. 4 (April 1936): 333. National Lumber Manufacturer's Association, "Structural Mobility: Two Story Mobile House," *Architectural Record*, vol. 80, no. 1 (July 1936): 64–65. Ernestine Evans, "Trailers in the World's Fair," *Architectural Record*, vol. 80, no. 2 (August 1936) 160–164. Ernestine Evans, "Housing" Convention in Sandusky," *Architectural Record*, vol. 80, no. 3 (September 1936): 175.

3 Douglas Haskell, "Architecture on Routes U.S. 40 and 66," *Architectural Record*, vol. 81, no 5 (May 1937): 15–22.

4 Haskell, "Architecture on Routes U.S. 40 and 66," 18–19.

5 "'Housing' Convention in Sandusky," *Architectural Record*, vol. 80, no. 3 (September 1936): 175.

6 See the book introduction by A. Lawrence Kocher, "Prefabrication and Architecture," in Albert F. Bemis, *The Evolving House, Volume III: Rational Design* (Cambridge, Massachusetts: The MIT Press, 1936), XXXIII–XXXV.

7 A. Lawrence Kocher, "Prefabrication by Our Forefathers and Others" (unpublished manuscript, undated), box 8, folder: Architecture, Pre-fabrication, A. Lawrence Kocher Collection, Colonial Williamsburg Foundation, John D. Rockefeller Jr. Library.

8 John C. Loudon, *An Encyclopedia of Cottage, Farm, and Villa Architecture and Furniture* (London: Longman, Brown, Green, & Longmans, 1846), 256–257. https://archive.org/details/encyclopdiaofc00loud.

9 Owen Biddle, John Haviland, *An improved and enlarged edition of Biddle's young carpenter's assistant: being a complete system of architecture for carpenters, joiners, and workmen in general, adapted to the style of building in the United States; revised and corrected, with several additional articles, and forty-eight new designs, chiefly of full size, working drawings of modern finish, in detail; particularly adapted for country use* (Philadelphia: M'Carty & Davis, 171 Market Street, 1833).

10 A. Lawrence Kocher, "Prefabrication by Our Forefathers and Others."

11 "Having experienced the natural beauty and healthy life in California, and with Lawrence Kocher planning to leave the Architectural Record and New York, I returned to Palm Springs in the fall of 1939." Albert Frey, "Foreword," in Cynthia Zignego Stiverson, *Architecture and the Decorative Arts: The A. Lawrence Kocher Collection of Books at the Colonial Williamsburg Foundation* (West Cornwall, CT: Locust Hill Press, 1989).

12 Davis quoted in T. H. Watkins, The Great Depression: America in the 1930s (New York: Back Bay Books, 1995), 269.

13 After the approval of the Reorganization Act of 1939, the NYA was transferred from the WPA to the Federal Security Agency (FSA). In 1942, the NYA was transferred to the War Manpower Commission (WMC); the NYA was then discontinued in 1943. Ernest K. Lindley, Betty Lindley, *A New Deal for Youth: The Story of the National Youth Administration* (New York: The Viking Press, 1938). Also see: *United States, National Youth Administration, Final report of the National youth administration, fiscal years 1936-1943* (Washington D. C.: Federal Security Agency, War Manpower Commission, 1944).

14 Kocher, "Prefabrication and Architecture." XXXIV.

15 F. H. Bosworth, R.C. Jones, *A Study of Architectural Schools* (New York: Charles Scribner's Sons, 1932).

16 "Education of the Architect," *Architectural Record*, vol. 80, no. 3 (September 1936): 201–214.

17 "Architects and Educators," *Architectural Record*, vol. 80, no. 3 (September 1936): 178–179.

18 Hitchens cited in: R. L. Duffus, "The Architect in the Modern World," *Architectural Record*, vol. 80, no. 3 (September 1936): 181–192. Also see: "The Architect and Engineer," *Architectural Record*, vol. 80, no. 4, (October 1936): 47.

19 "Carnegie Architects Do Their Home Work," *Pittsburgh's Bulletin Index*, vol. 114 (March 2, 1939): 8.

20 "Letter from Kocher to Henry Chang, dated May 19, 1964," Box 1, A. Lawrence Kocher Collection, Colonial Williamsburg Foundation, John D. Rockefeller Jr. Library.

21 See: John Dewey, *The School and Society and The Child and the Curriculum* (Chicago: The University of Chicago Press, 1902).

22 "Letter from G. B. Shaw to Kocher, dated March 27, 1923," box 2, folder series II: Literary Materials-Correspondence resulting in "The Library of an Architect" series, A. Lawrence Kocher Collection, Colonial Williamsburg Foundation, John D. Rockefeller Jr. Library.

23 "The Bulletin Index: Education," *Pittsburgh Weekly Magazine* (March 2, 1939): 9, box 5, folder: Carnegie Tech-Experimental House, A. Lawrence Kocher Collection, Colonial Williamsburg Foundation, John D. Rockefeller Jr. Library.

24 Richard H. Hayes, "Design-Build" in Joan Ockman (Ed.), *Architecture School: Three Centuries of Educating Architects in North America* (Cambridge, Massachusetts: The MIT Press, 2012), 286–290.

25 By 1938, graduate college youth were paid an average of $17.93 a month for "work study" projects at their schools. By 1939, the wage increased to $21.14. Source: *United States National Youth Administration, Final report of the National youth administration, fiscal years 1936-1943* (Washington D. C.: Federal Security Agency, War Manpower Commission, 1944), 57.

26 "Experimental" as defined by the *Cambridge English Dictionary*: "(Adjective) Using new methods, ideas, substances, etc. that have not been tried before, usually in order to find out what effect they have."

27 The Sommerfeld House was built for the industrialist and building entrepreneur Adolf Sommerfeld, who specialized in timber structures.

28 A. Lawrence Kocher, "Hand Books of Samuel Rhoads, Carpenter-Builder," *Architectural Record*, vol. 50, no. 6 (December 1921): 507–509.

29 John Cushman Fistere, "A House for the Two-Day Weekend," *Ladies' Home Journal* (May 1937): 27, 92, 93.

30 "U.S. and British Magazines Swap Editors," *New York Herald Tribune* (January 16, 1937), box 12, folder: Career portfolio, A. Lawrence Kocher Collection, Colonial Williamsburg Foundation, John D. Rockefeller Jr. Library.

31 Specifications of the project found in: Oversize Series 3, Project Files, folder: Low-Cost Housing, A. Lawrence Kocher Collection, Colonial Williamsburg Foundation, John D. Rockefeller Jr. Library.

32 "Letter from France Kelley, Director of Personnel at WPA to Kocher, dated July 16, 1938," box 1, series 1: Correspondence General, folder: Works Progress Administration, A. Lawrence Kocher Collection, Colonial Williamsburg Foundation, John D. Rockefeller Jr. Library.

33 A. Lawrence Kocher, "Community Art Center. A proposal for Big Stone Gap, VA" (unpublished manuscript, undated), box 4, folder: Big Stone Gap Community Center (Proposed 1938), A. Lawrence Kocher Collection, Colonial Williamsburg Foundation, John D. Rockefeller Jr. Library.

34 George W. Trayer and Hamilton Beatty (Forest Products Laboratory, Forest Service U. S. Department of Agriculture), "Moderate-cost House Construction and Equipment: Prefabrication with Wood," *Architectural Record*, vol. 78, no. 2 (August 1935): 102–107.

35 Previously, plywood patents already existed in the United States—such as John K. Mayo's 1886 patent for a series of bridge structures—though they had had no commercial success.

36 Technical News and Research, "Building in Plywood, *Architectural Record*, vol. 81, no. 2 (February 1937): 41–47.

37 For more on Dri-Bilt with plywood, see: "History of APA, Plywood, and Engineered Wood," *APA – The Engineered Wood Association*, accessed January 22, 2020, https://www.apawood.org/apas-history.

38 Specifications of the project found in: Oversize Series 3, Project Files, folder: Plywood House, A. Lawrence Kocher Collection, Colonial Williamsburg Foundation, John D. Rockefeller Jr. Library.

39 Mumford quoted by Kocher in: box 12, subseries C: Career Portfolio, folder: Personal career portfolio 1963, A. Lawrence Kocher Collection, Colonial Williamsburg Foundation, John D. Rockefeller Jr. Library.

40 Box 5, folder: Cotton and metal house 1938, A. Lawrence Kocher Collection, Colonial Williamsburg Foundation, John D. Rockefeller Jr. Library.

41 F. R. S. Yorke, *The Modern House* (London: The Architectural Press, 1951), 207.

42 A roughly contemporaneous exaggeration of this mobile bubble from which Kocher and Frey diverged may be found in Raymond Roussel's Roulotte—a project built in 1926,

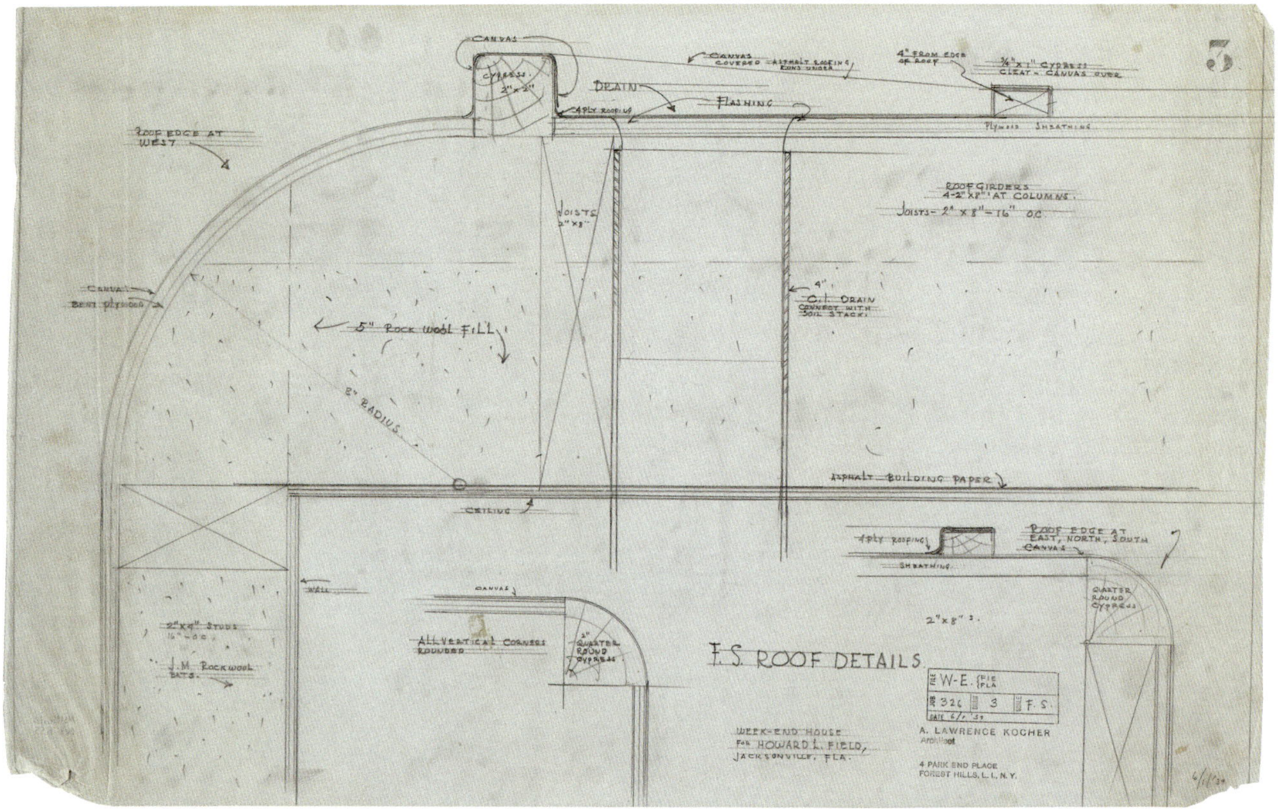
F.S. ROOF DETAILS
WEEK-END HOUSE
FOR HOWARD L. FIELD,
JACKSONVILLE, FLA.
A. LAWRENCE KOCHER
Architect
4 PARK END PLACE
FOREST HILLS, L. I., N. Y.
5" ROCK WOOL FILL
ROOF EDGE AT WEST
DRAIN
FLASHING
ROOF GIRDERS
JOISTS
C.I. DRAIN
ASPHALT BUILDING PAPER
CEILING
ROOF EDGE AT EAST, NORTH, SOUTH
ALL VERTICAL CORNERS ROUNDED

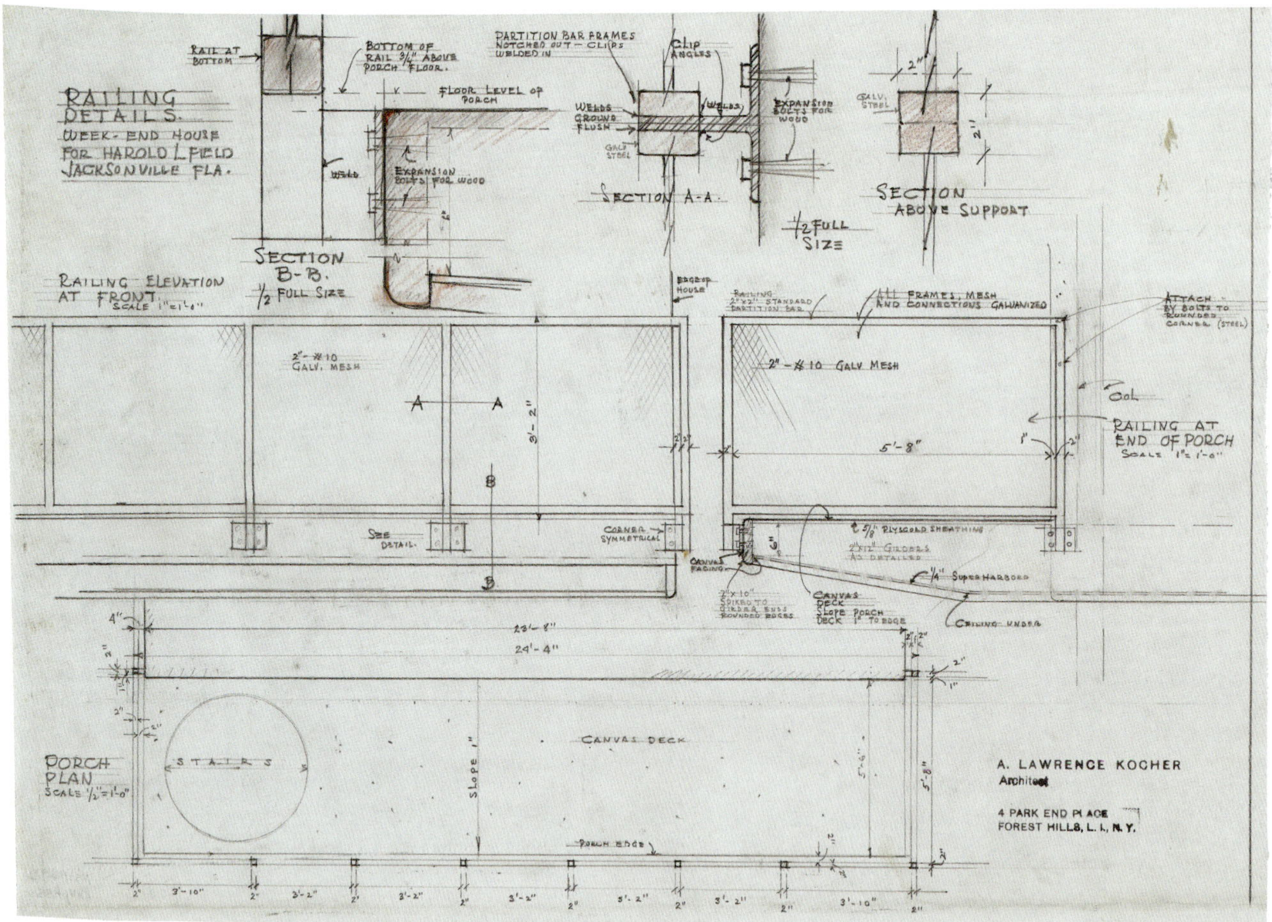
RAILING DETAILS.
WEEK-END HOUSE
FOR HAROLD L FIELD
JACKSONVILLE FLA.
SECTION B-B.
1/2 FULL SIZE
SECTION A-A.
SECTION ABOVE SUPPORT
1/2 FULL SIZE
RAILING ELEVATION AT FRONT
2"-#10 GALV. MESH
2"-#10 GALV MESH
ALL FRAMES, MESH AND CONNECTIONS GALVANIZED
RAILING AT END OF PORCH
PORCH PLAN
STAIRS
CANVAS DECK
PORCH EDGE
A. LAWRENCE KOCHER
Architect
4 PARK END PLACE
FOREST HILLS, L. I., N. Y.

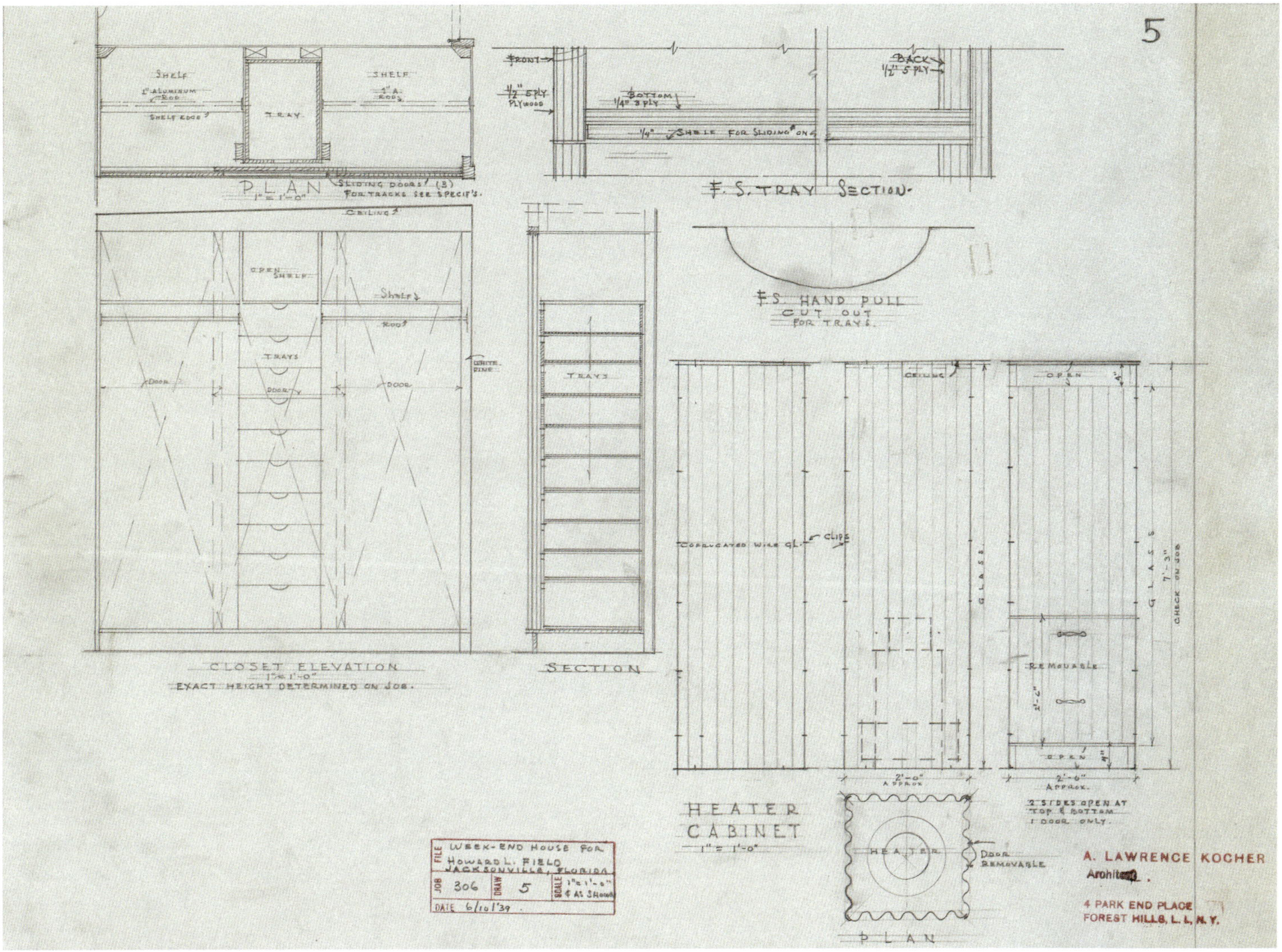

Previous page:
Figure 5.43. A. Lawrence Kocher. 1939. Florida Weekend House. Preliminary drawings. Roof details. Dated 6-1-39.
Figure 5.44. A. Lawrence Kocher. 1939. Florida Weekend House. Preliminary drawings. Railing and porch details. Undated.

This page:
Figure 5.45. A. Lawrence Kocher. 1939. Florida Weekend House. Preliminary drawings. Closet and cabinet details. Dated 6-10-39.
Figure 5.46. Tennessee Valley Authority motor homes. 1942. Advertisement brochure.

designed to isolate the French writer from the outside world during his travels so that he would not be distracted from his literary activity. Roussel's mobile home was furnished like an authentic French chateau and created a complete fiction of permanence and stability for its occupant.

43 Reyner Banham, "Taking It with You," *New Society* 45, no. 826 (August 1978): 252–253. Also reprinted in Reyner Banham, *A Critic Writes: Selected Essays by Reyner Banham*, (Berkeley: University of California Press, 1996), 223–226.

44 Reyner Banham, "Taking It with You," 226.

45 Founded by the Association of Arts and Industries in Chicago, the school started classes on October 18, 1937, bearing the auto-imposed title of the New Bauhaus. At Gropius's recommendation, they hired Moholy-Nagy as director and several other former Bauhaus teachers, such as lighting- and furniture-designer Hin (Heinrich) Bredendieck, and Hungarian artist Gyorgy Kepes. The faculty also included other avant-garde artists, like American photographer Henry Holmes Smith, Russian sculptor Alexander Archipenko, along with R. Buckminster Fuller, and American architect George Fred Keck. Under Moholy-Nagy's direction, the school set up a curriculum based on the Bauhaus.

46 Kocher not only contributed a chapter in the catalog, but also lent some of his own Aalto furniture pieces for the exhibition, held at MoMA New York from March 15 to April 18, 1938. A. Lawrence Kocher, "Furniture" in John Mc Andrew, *Aalto: Architecture and Furniture* (New York City: MoMA, 1937), 13–23.

47 Box 1, series 1: Correspondence General, folder: American School of Design, 1938-1939, A. Lawrence Kocher Collection, Colonial Williamsburg Foundation, John D. Rockefeller Jr. Library.

48 Walter Gropius, "Architecture at Harvard University," *Architectural Record*, vol. 81, no. 5, (May 1937): 9–11.

49 Found alongside the typewritten text—copy-edited by hand by Kocher—Gropius asked Kocher in a letter to "check the wording of my article and improve it if it should not be correct. I should like to see the improved copy before you publish it." "Letter from Gropius to Kocher, dated March 22, 1937," box 1, series 1: Correspondence General, folder: Gropius, Walter, A. Lawrence Kocher Collection, Colonial Williamsburg Foundation, John D. Rockefeller Jr. Library.

50 Eric Paul Mumford, *The CIAM Discourse on Urbanism, 1928-1960* (Cambridge, Massachusetts: The MIT Press, 2000).

51 "Letter from Kocher to Gropius, dated December 24, 1937," box 1, series 1: Correspondence General, folder: Gropius, Walter, A. Lawrence Kocher Collection, Colonial Williamsburg Foundation, John D. Rockefeller Jr. Library.

52 "Letter from Gropius to Kocher, dated December 31, 1937," box 1, series 1: Correspondence General, folder: Gropius, Walter, A. Lawrence Kocher Collection, Colonial Williamsburg Foundation, John D. Rockefeller Jr. Library.

53 "Abstract," PC.1956, The Theodore and Barbara Loines Dreier, Black Mountain College Collection (Dreier BMC Collection, 1925-1988), Western Regional Archives, State Archives of North Carolina. https://axaem.archives.ncdcr.gov/findingaids/PC_1956_Theodore_and_Barbara_Lo_.html.

54 John Dewey quoted in Ruth Erickson's essay, "A Progressive Education" in Helen Molesworth, *Leap Before you Look: Black Mountain College 1933-1957* (New Haven: Yale University Press, 2015), 79.

55 "The purchase price was $35,000 of which $17,500 was paid in cash, with the balance due in four equal installments of $4,375 on or before 2, 3, 4 and 5 years at 6% interest. The purchase was made possible by a gift of $12,500 by Stephen Forbes, a former student, and $800 of the $2,000 in underwriting which Edward and Ethel Dreier, parents of Theodore Dreier, pledged at the college's founding and of which they made a gift." https://blackmountaincollegeproject.org, accessed December 15, 2021.

56 "Letter from A. Lawrence Kocher to Theodore Dreier, dated September 24, 1937," Theodore Dreier and Barbara Loines Dreier Papers, North Carolina State Archives.

57 May 16 and 30, Roosevelt: "On May 16, in a message to the Congress, I pointed out that the swift and shocking developments of that time forced every neutral nation to look to its defenses in the light of new factors loosed by the brutal force of modern offensive war...I asked at that time for a sum totaling $1,182,000,000 for the national defense. On May 31, 1940, I again sent a message to the Congress, to say that the almost incredible events of the then past two weeks in the European conflict had necessitated another enlargement of our military program, and at that time I asked for $1,277,741,170 for the acceleration and development of our military and naval needs as measured in both machines and men." F. D. Roosevelt, "Message to Congress on Appropriations for National Defense, July 10, 1940," *The American Presidency Project online* by Gerhard Peters and John T. Woolley, https://www.presidency.ucsb.edu/documents/message-congress-appropriations-for-national-defense-0.

58 Lawrence Wodehouse, "Kocher at Black Mountain," *Journal of the Society of Architectural Historians*, vol. 41, no. 4 (December 1982): 328–332.

59 Howard Dearstyne, who will play an important future role in Kocher's professional life, was one of the few Americans that studied at the Bauhaus. He studied with Mies van der Rohe, Wassily Kandinsky, and Josef Albers, among others, and graduated in 1932.

60 *Black Mountain College Bulletin*, Number 6 (December, 1940), box 4, series 3: Project Files, folder: Black Mountain College, Bulletins, Newsletters, Publications. A. Lawrence Kocher Collection, Colonial Williamsburg Foundation, John D. Rockefeller Jr. Library.

61 When considering the architectural articulation of the Studies Building, Lawrence Wodehouse has pointed out the possible influence of William Lescaze's designs for three student dormitories (Blacklers, Chimmels, and Orchard) built in 1935 at Dartington Hall, Devonshire. Although there are many formal similarities between these two projects, and Kocher likely knew them due to his familiarity with Lescaze's work, it was more plausible that the façades of the Black Mountain building adapted to the specific program and site conditions through an evolution of Kocher's previous designs. The Canvas Weekend House, the Experimental Weekend House, and even the Aluminaire House had similar façade configurations, window sash details, and identical relationships with the terrain as the Studies Building.

62 *Black Mountain College Newsletter*, Number 10 (December 1940), box 4, series 3: Project Files, folder: Black Mountain College, Bulletins, Newsletters, Publications, A. Lawrence Kocher Collection, Colonial Williamsburg Foundation, John D. Rockefeller Jr. Library.

63 *Black Mountain College Bulletin*, Number 11 (January 1941), box 4, series 3: Project Files, folder: Black Mountain College, Bulletins, Newsletters, Publications, A. Lawrence Kocher Collection, Colonial Williamsburg Foundation, John D. Rockefeller Jr. Library.

64 "Letter from A. Lawrence Kocher to Theodore Dreier, dated July 17, 1940," Theodore Dreier Papers, North Carolina State Archive.

65 The house was published in: A. Lawrence Kocher, "House in Black Mountain NC," *The Architectural Forum* (July 1944): 108–109.

66 "Letter from Dreier to Kocher, dated September 17, 1948," box 4, series 3: Project Files, folder: Black Mountain College, Correspondence general, A. Lawrence Kocher Collection, Colonial Williamsburg Foundation, John D. Rockefeller Jr. Library.

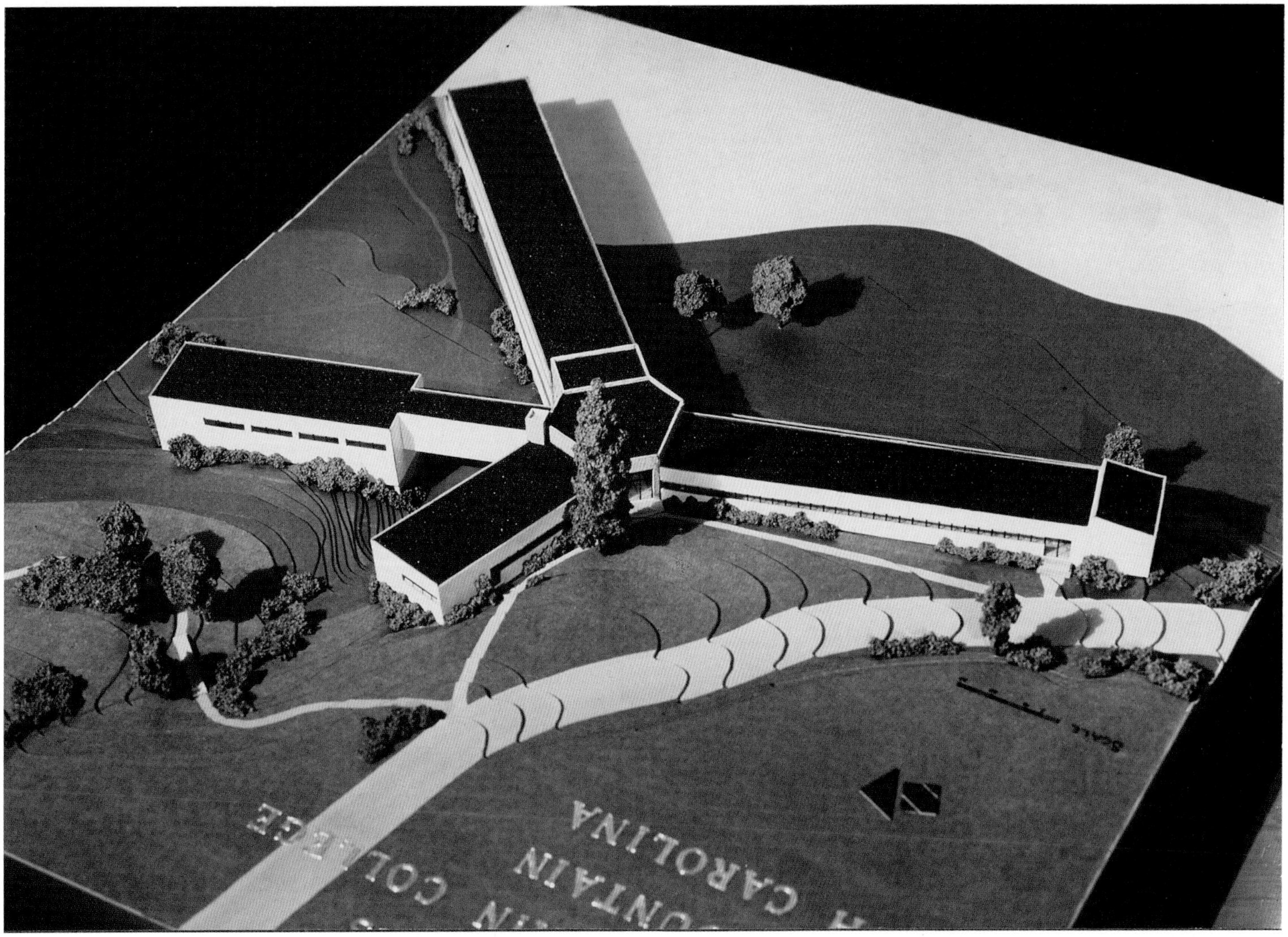

Figure 5.47. (Bottom). Walter Gropius and Marcel Breuer. 1939. Proposal for Black Mountain College. Sketch of the massing. BMC postal card.
Figure 5.48. (Top). A. Lawrence Kocher. 1940. Black Mountain College Building. Model of the complete proposal.

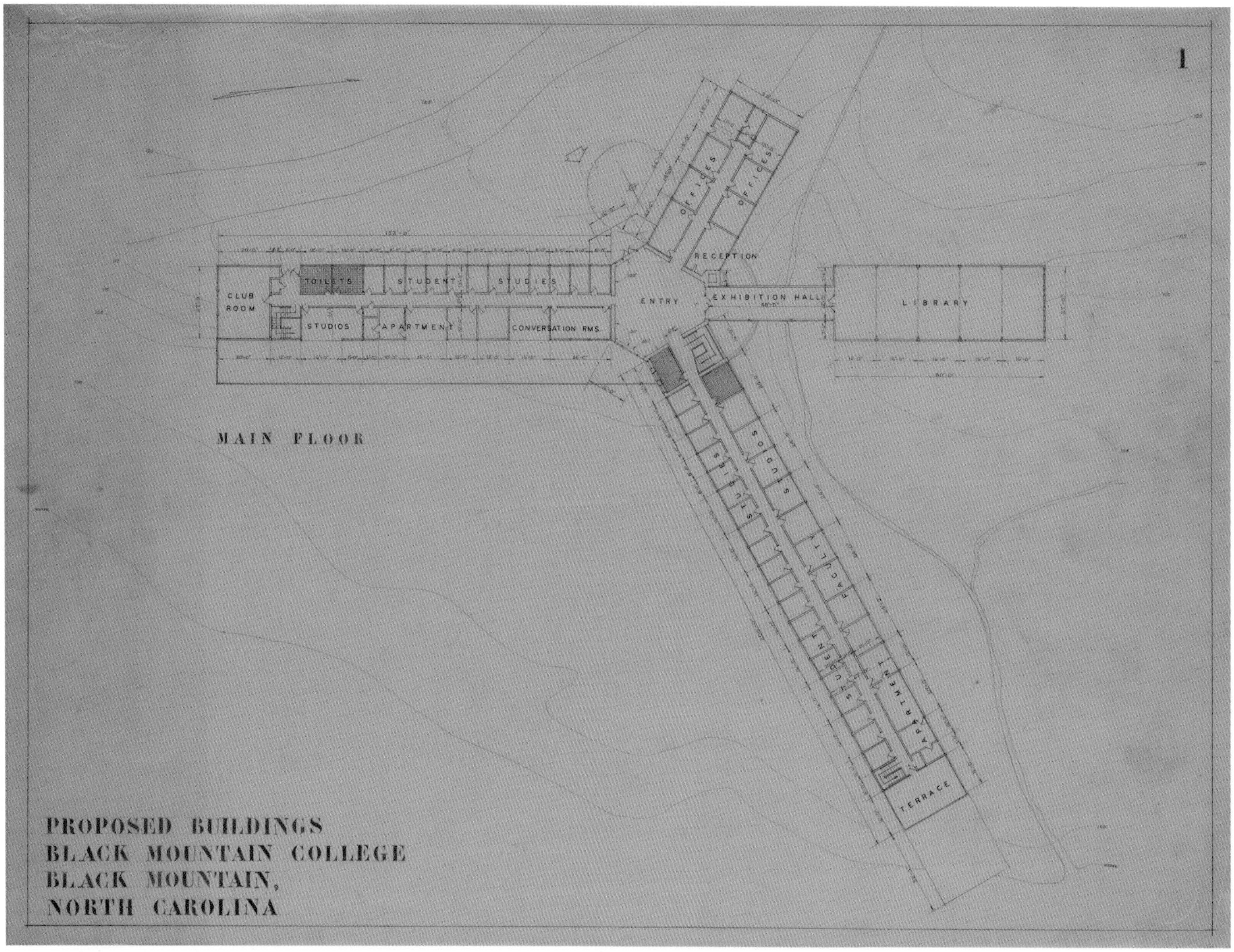

This page:
Figure 5.49. A. Lawrence Kocher. 1940. Black Mountain College Building. Complete proposal. Second floor plan.
Figure 5.50. A. Lawrence Kocher. 1940. Black Mountain College Building. Picture of the constructed wing. Studies Building.

Next page:
Figure 5.51. A. Lawrence Kocher. 1940. Black Mountain College Building. Complete proposal. First floor plan.
Figure 5.52. A. Lawrence Kocher. 1940. Black Mountain College Building. Complete proposal. Exterior view from the lake.

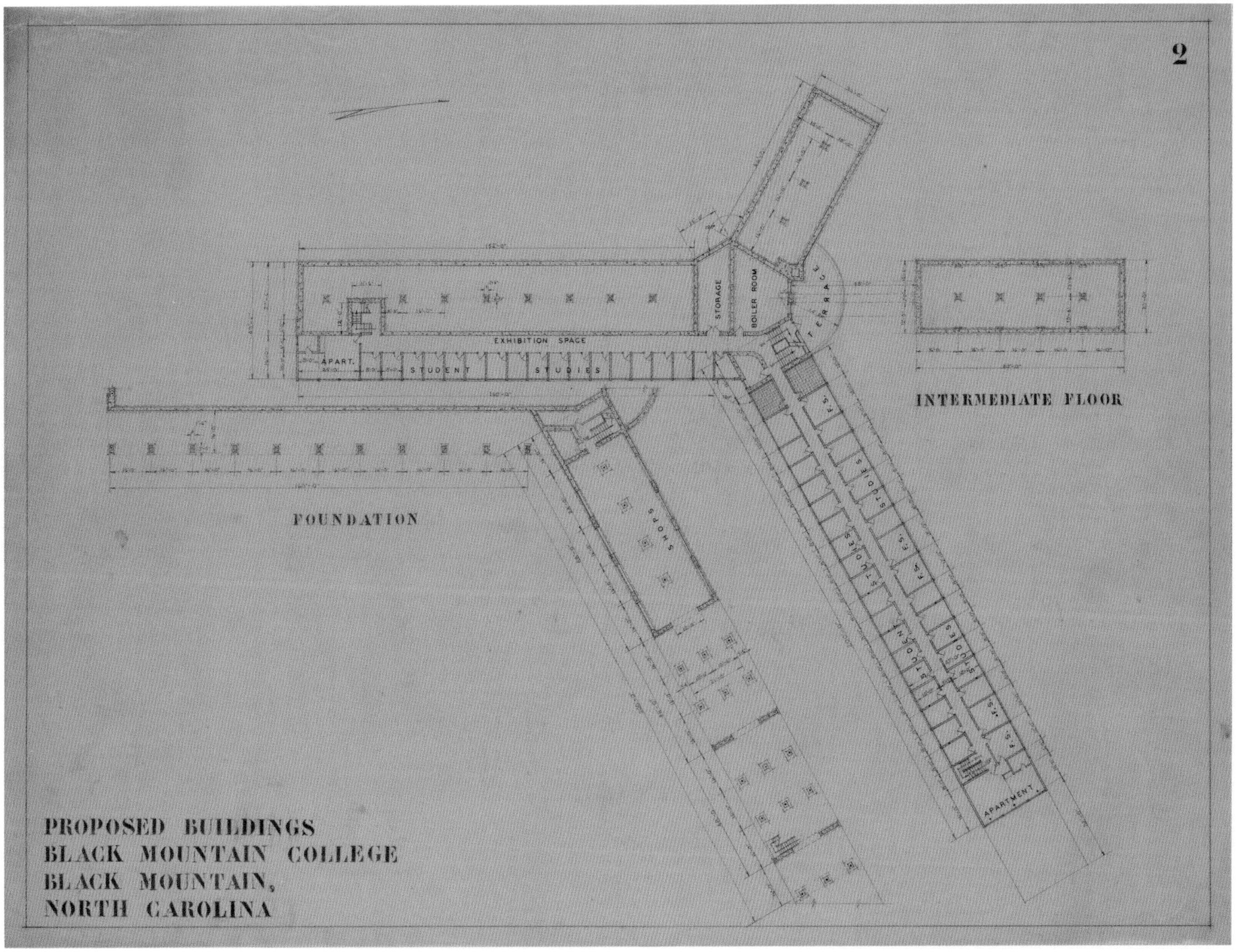
2
EXHIBITION SPACE
APART.
STUDENT STUDIES
STORAGE
BOILER ROOM
TERRACE
INTERMEDIATE FLOOR
FOUNDATION
SHOPS
APARTMENT
PROPOSED BUILDINGS
BLACK MOUNTAIN COLLEGE
BLACK MOUNTAIN,
NORTH CAROLINA

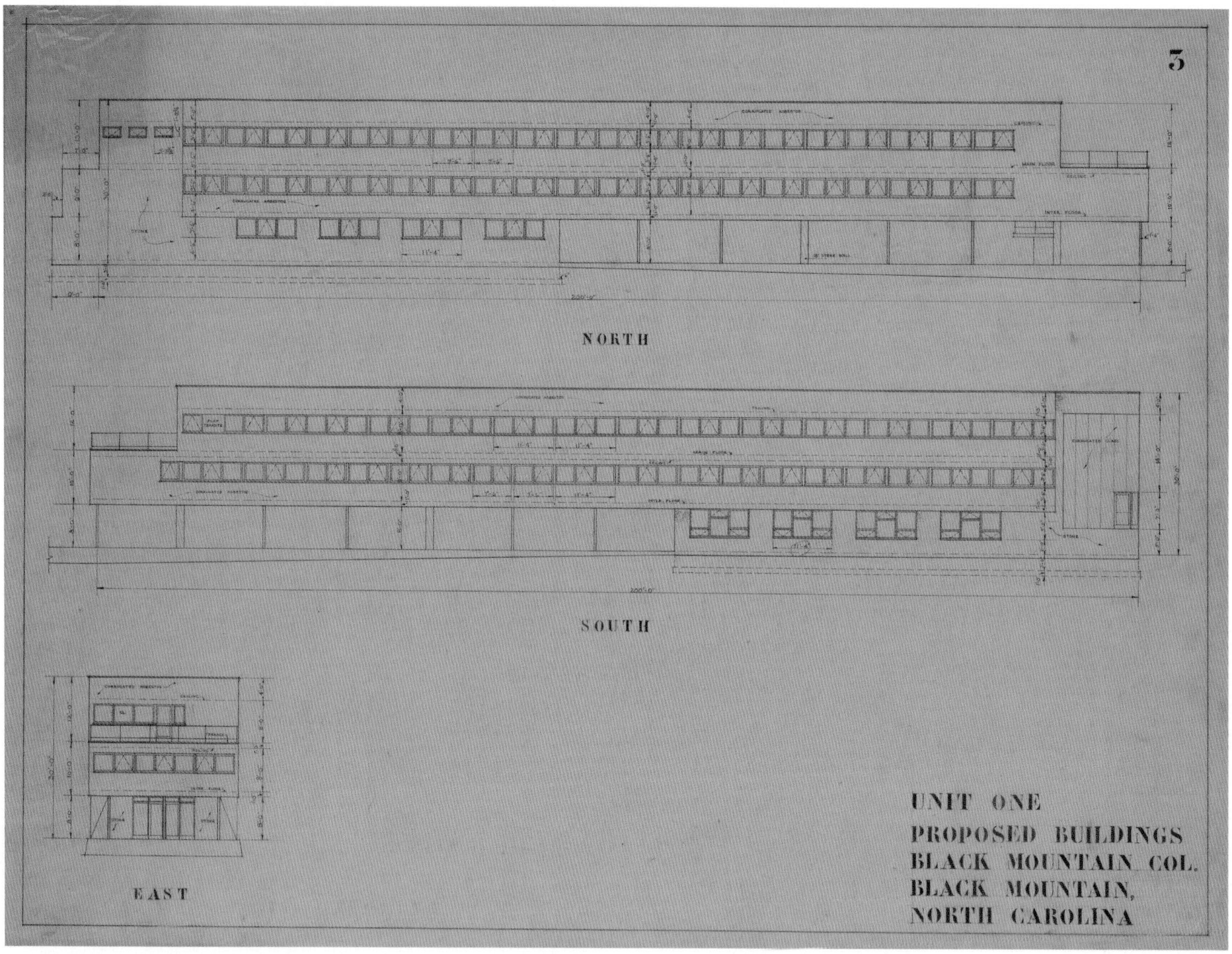

Figure 5.53. A. Lawrence Kocher. 1940–1941. Black Mountain College. Elevations of the Studies Building.
Figure 5.54. 1941. Black Mountain College. Brochure including the construction of the Studies Building.

'OR THE DURATION America

vants soldiers of its men and

vomen.

'hen, why college?

'his is one answer. It was con-

eived long ago in a time of

eace as a challenge to an

ge of comfort.

)f a sudden, on a certain day

n December, we were no lon-

er in a time of peace and this

nswer was no longer heret-

cal.

The basic function of a college is still the same, for the duration and beyond the duration, in war and in peace: to teach men **to understand and to act.**

Not to act is cowardice. Not to understand is suicide.

The war will not be won by a knowledge of Latin. The problems of a devastated world will not be solved, nor the values of a people determined, by a knowledge of arc-welding.

But the learning of a skill may be the implement by which one comes to general understanding. And this is reciprocal, for the greater the understanding the greater the mastery over new skills.

Accordingly, **the skills** — listed opposite — **are brought into the classroom,** not as substitutes for education, but as part of the knowledge which will be both immediately useful in military life and at the same time contribute to the understanding.

The skill leads to the general principle. Both are necessary.

ART & ARCHITECTURE
- maps
- drafting & lettering
- photography

AGRICULTURE
- farm machinery
- general principles

BIOLOGY & PHYSIOLOGY
- first aid
- public health
- hygiene & sanitation
- weather

CHEMISTRY
- explosives
- fuels & gases
- munitions

DRAMATICS

GOVERNMENT & ECONOMICS
- economics of war
- martial law
- governmental agencies
- military organization

HISTORY

LANGUAGES

LITERATURE

MATHEMATICS
- trajectories
- surveying & compass
- map-making

MUSIC

PHILOSOPHY

PHYSICS
- gasoline engines
- photography
- electricity
- telescopes & lenses
- aircraft principles

PSYCHOLOGY
- propaganda analysis

THE WORK PROGRAM began with the college. It was conceived originally as a necessary addition to bookish education. Now, suddenly, a work program has become an imperative demand for all colleges — and rightly.

The work is voluntary, by both men and women, regardless of whether they pay a full-maintenance fee of $1200 or $450 to the college. It is run by the student work committee.

Three large college buildings have already been constructed and a 100-acre farm begun. The work is not artificially fabricated; it is of practical value to the community.

The coming work program anticipates:

- an extension of the mountain pasturage for beef and dairy cattle;
- planting and harvesting of feed for cattle, hogs, dairy cows, and poultry;
- four 'war acres' of vegetable gardens;
- quarrying and lumbering, carpentry and wiring and plumbing for completion of the college buildings.

In conformity with the principle that time and age, like credits and hours, are no adequate measurement of the maturity and understanding of the individual, BMC will accept as freshmen certain **younger students** who have not completed high school.

To qualify for such admission a younger student needs:

> **a genuine desire for higher education** for its own sake (not the superficial trappings of a paid football team, luxurious surroundings, or sorority life);
>
> **evidence of real ability** (not necessarily high marks but a demonstrated competence for knowing and understanding himself and the world about him).

Because secondary schools may be justifiably skeptical of any acceleration of the educational program, BMC extends this offer only in co-operation with high school and preparatory school principals, in the belief that in most cases they are best able to judge which students are mature enough to go to college at an earlier age. Write for special application.

Beginning in June 1942 BMC will offer four quarters of eleven weeks each, in order that students who so desire **may finish college in three years.** As heretofore, students will continue to graduate when they are prepared to do so, since there is no fixed residence requirement.

For further information: Registrar
Black Mountain College
Black Mountain, N. C.

The war will end. There will be a 'beyond' to the duration. It may come while high school students are still in college. It may come long afterwards.

One thing is certain. In and beyond the duration we will require all the knowledge, skill, and strength that can be mustered.

And in and beyond the duration one of the particular problems is the study of

> **Pan-American Affairs,** particularly the cultural achievement, so frequently overlooked by callous "yanquis."
>
> **The Language, the Literature, the Politics, and the Art of the 21 Republics,** to be the basis of a concentrated study, integrated with the regular Liberal Arts program.

You, the generation now in the schools of our country, are asked by history to be heroic and wise at an age when you would ordinarily be still preparing for a comfortable existence.

You will have to wage and to win a war and you will have to create the world order of the future.

It is no light task; there is no easy answer. Yet the problem of deciding is inescapably yours. This pamphlet, like others, merely suggests. Look to it.

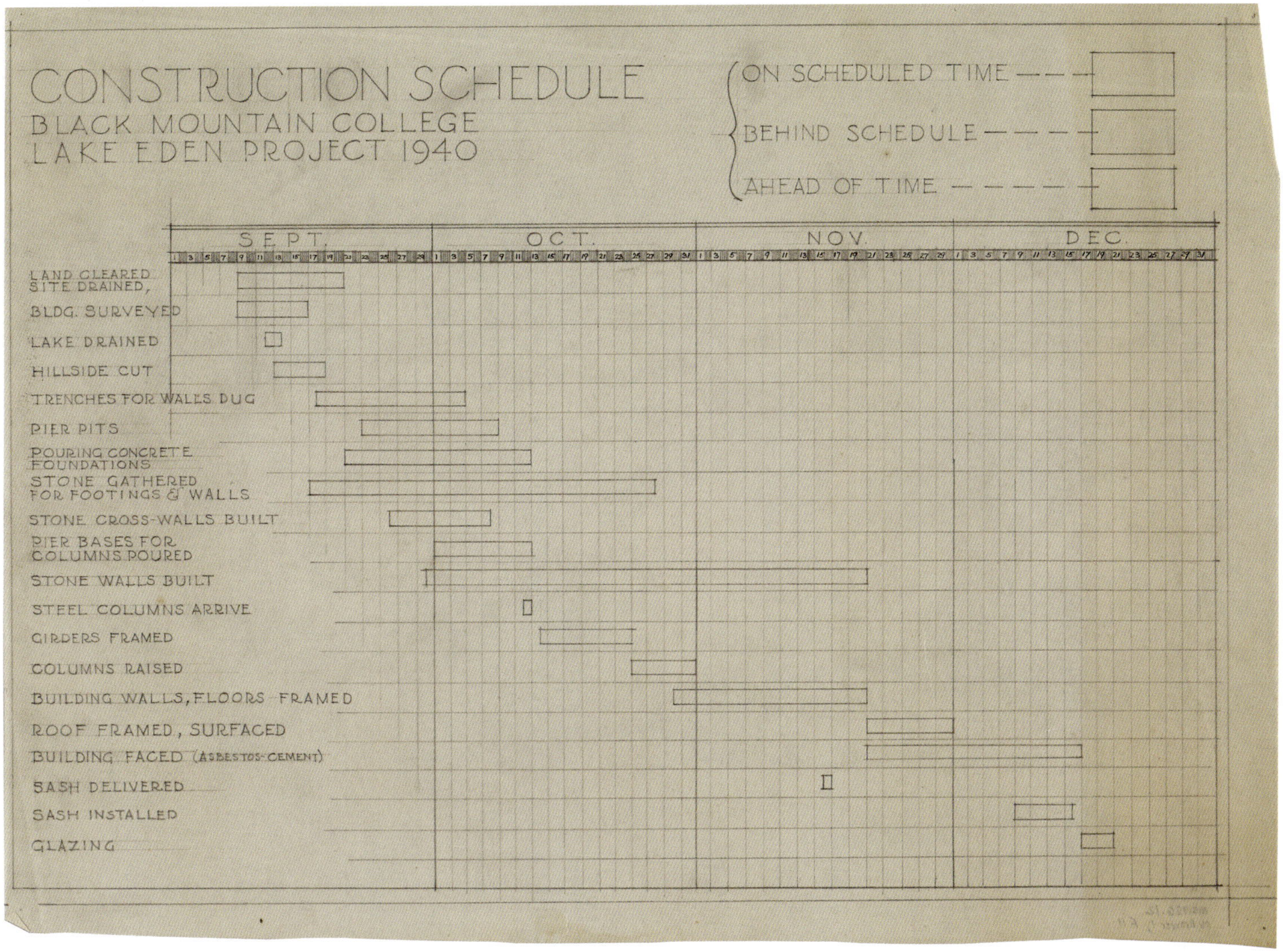

Figure 5.55. A. Lawrence Kocher. 1940–1941. Black Mountain College. Studies Building. Construction schedule from September to December 1940.
Figure 5.56. 1941. Black Mountain College. Brochure including the Student Work Program.

This page:

Figure 5.57. A. Lawrence Kocher. 1940. Black Mountain College. Studies Building. Picture from the lake.

Figure 5.58. A. Lawrence Kocher. 1940. Black Mountain College. Studies Building. Interior view of one of the student's rooms.

Next page:

Figure 5.59. A. Lawrence Kocher. 1940. Black Mountain College. Studies Building near completion. Photo by F.S. Lincoln.

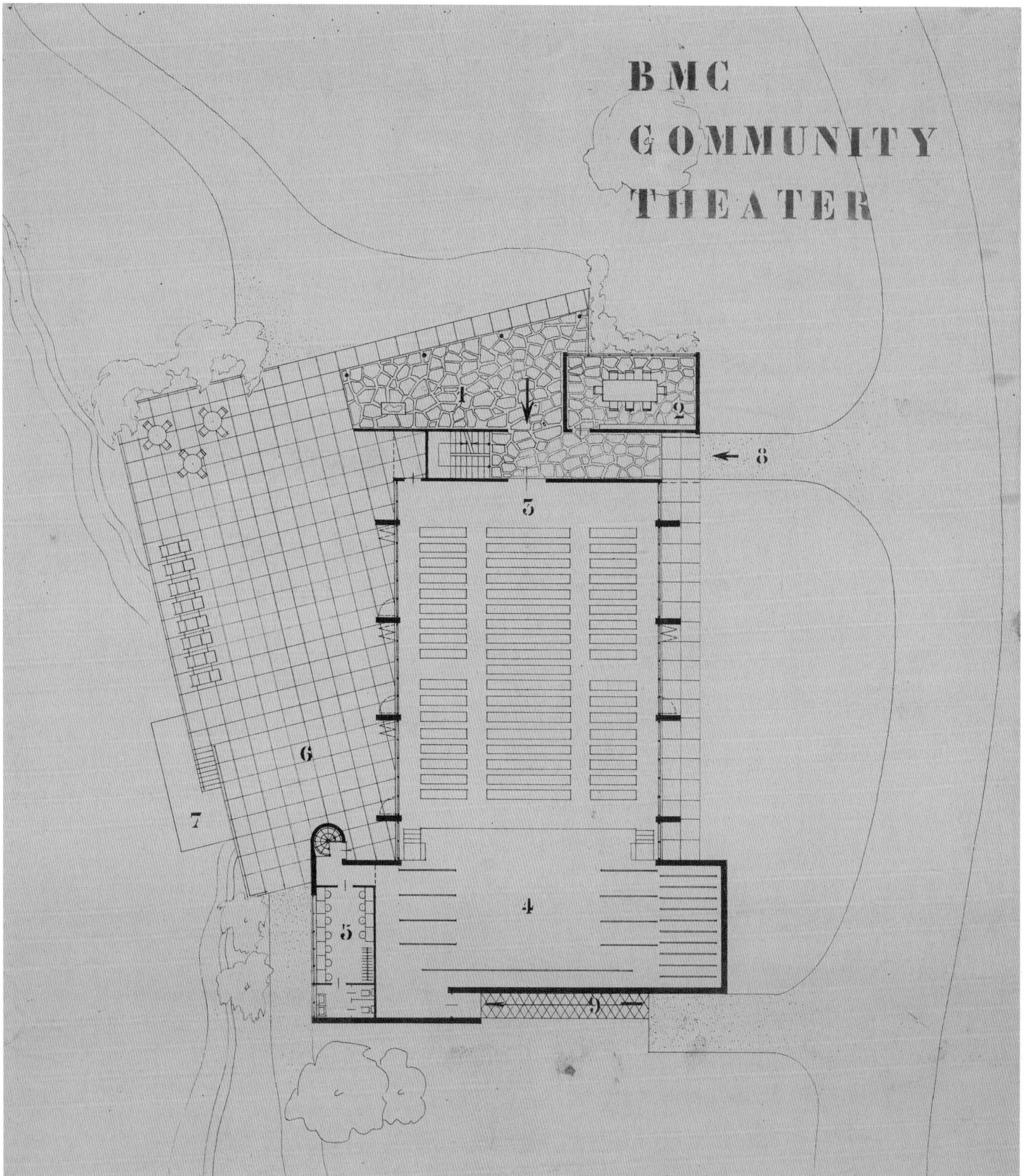

Figure 5.60. A. Lawrence Kocher. 1941–1942. Community Theater. Floor plan.

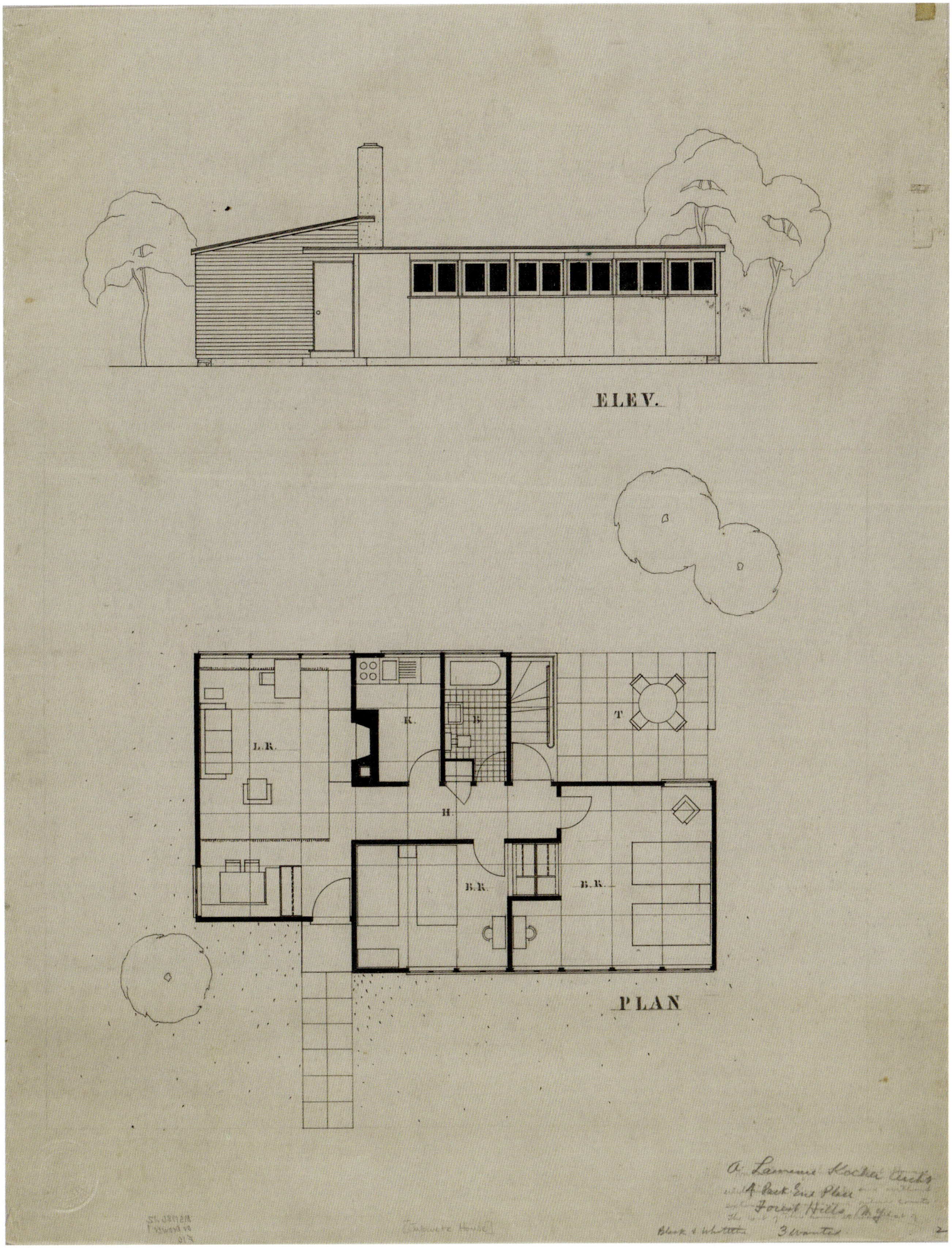

Figure 5.61. A. Lawrence Kocher and Black Mountain College Students. 1941–1942. Jalowetz House. Elevation and floor plan.

Figure 5.62. A. Lawrence Kocher and Black Mountain College Students. 1941–1942. Jalowetz House. Main façade photo.
Figure 5.63. A. Lawrence Kocher and Black Mountain College Students. 1941–1942. Jalowetz House. Photo of the prefabricated panels.

Figure 5.64. A. Lawrence Kocher and Black Mountain College Students. 1941–1942. Jalowetz House. Terrace photo.

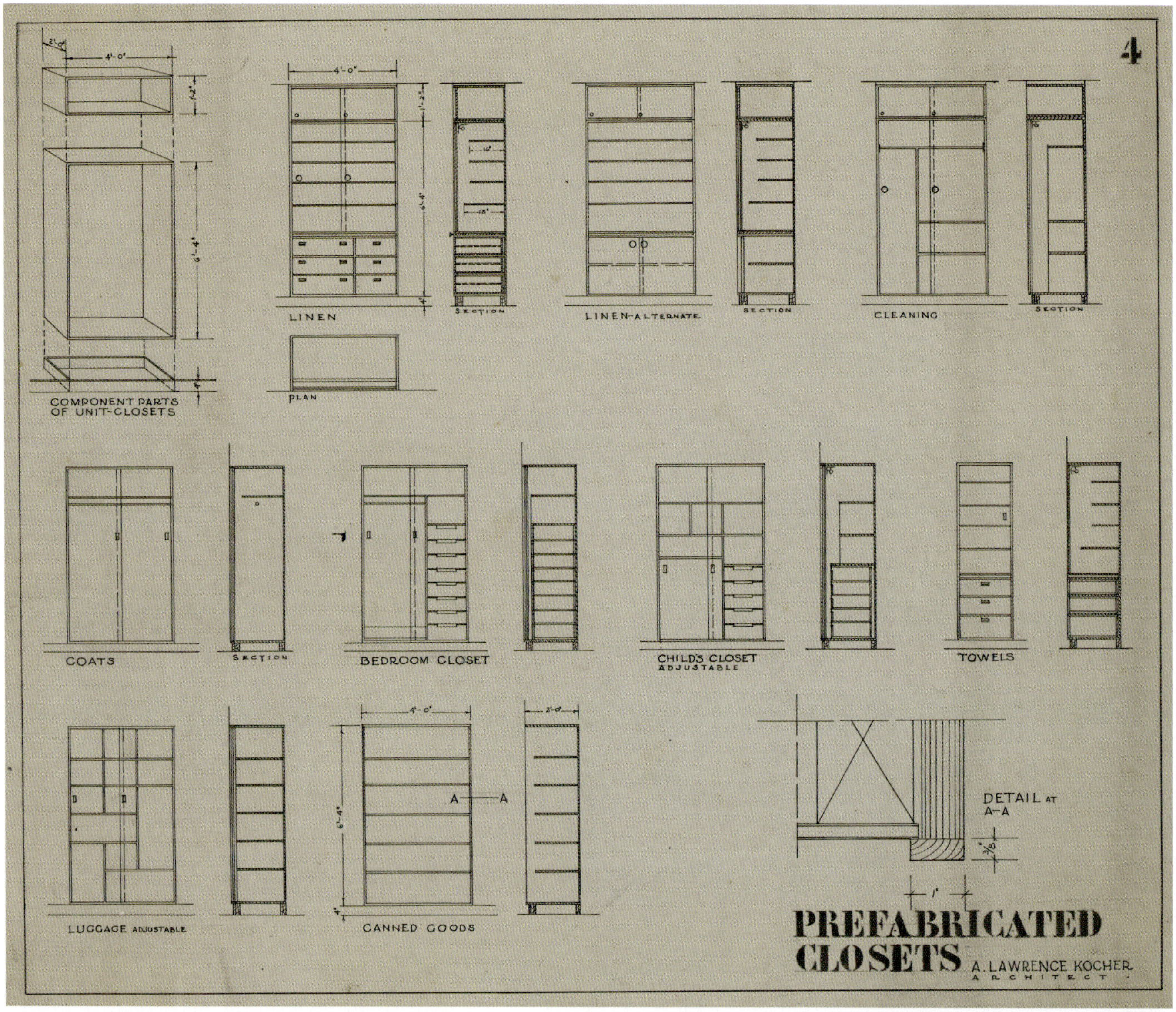
4
COMPONENT PARTS OF UNIT-CLOSETS
LINEN
SECTION
PLAN
LINEN-ALTERNATE
SECTION
CLEANING
SECTION
COATS
SECTION
BEDROOM CLOSET
CHILD'S CLOSET ADJUSTABLE
TOWELS
LUGGAGE ADJUSTABLE
CANNED GOODS
DETAIL AT A-A
PREFABRICATED CLOSETS
A. LAWRENCE KOCHER ARCHITECT

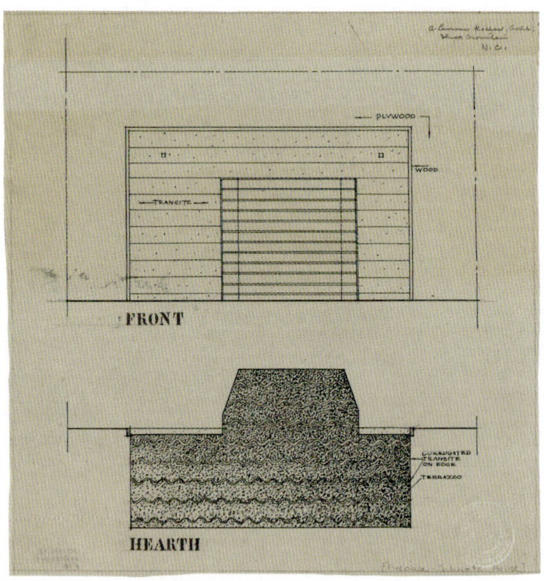
PLYWOOD
WOOD
TRANSITE
FRONT
HEARTH

Previous page:
Figure 5.65. A. Lawrence Kocher and Black Mountain College Students. 1941–1942. Jalowetz House. Prefabricated closets schedule.
Figure 5.66. A. Lawrence Kocher and Black Mountain College Students. 1941–1942. Jalowetz House. Hearth detail.
Figure 5.67. A. Lawrence Kocher and Black Mountain College Students. 1941–1942. Jalowetz House. Hearth photo.

This page:
Figure 5.68. A. Lawrence Kocher. 1941–1942. Plywood and fabric arm chair.
Figure 5.69. A. Lawrence Kocher. 1941–1942. Steel mesh and steel tube storable stools.
Figure 5.70. A. Lawrence Kocher. 1941–1942. Plywood chair.
Figure 5.71. A. Lawrence Kocher. 1941–1942. Steel and leather foldable stool.
Figure 5.72. A. Lawrence Kocher. 1941–1942. Wood stool and table.

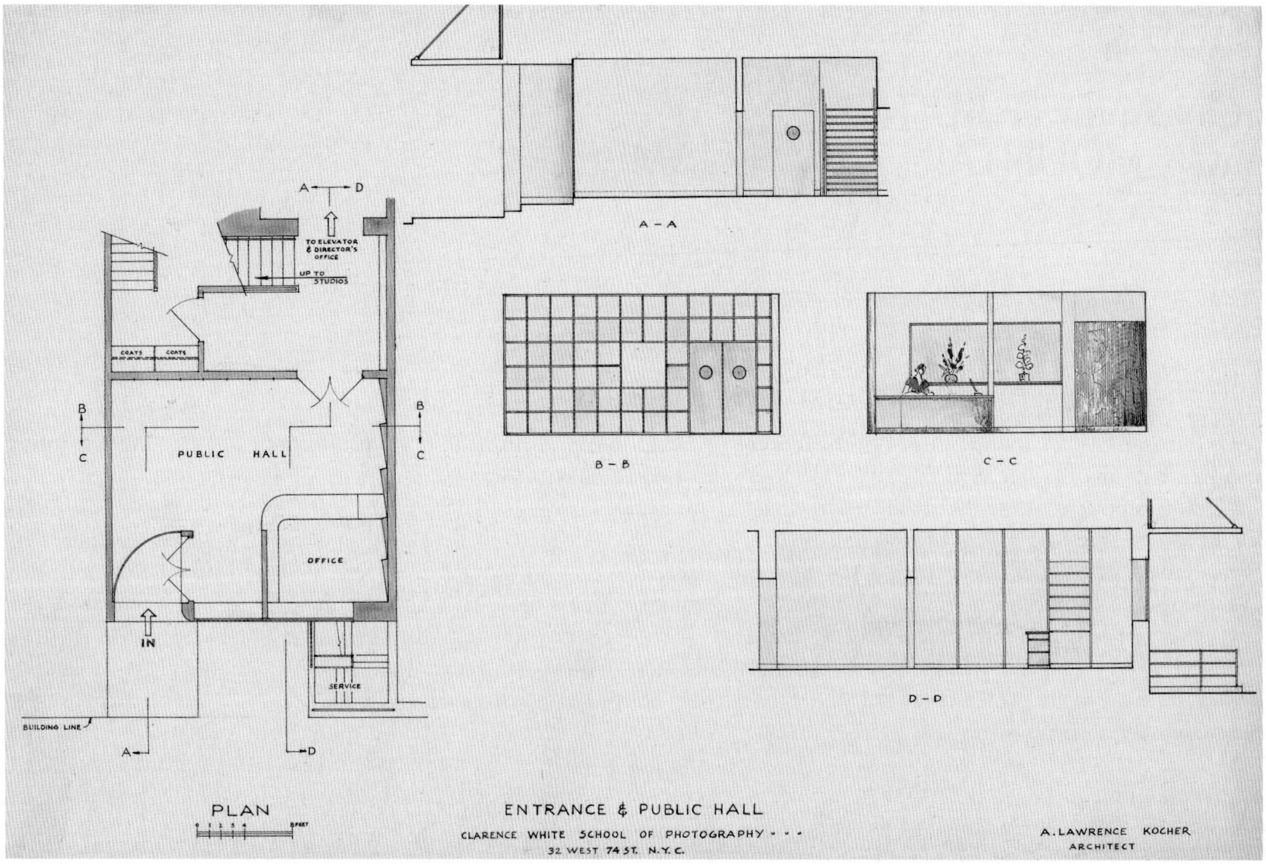

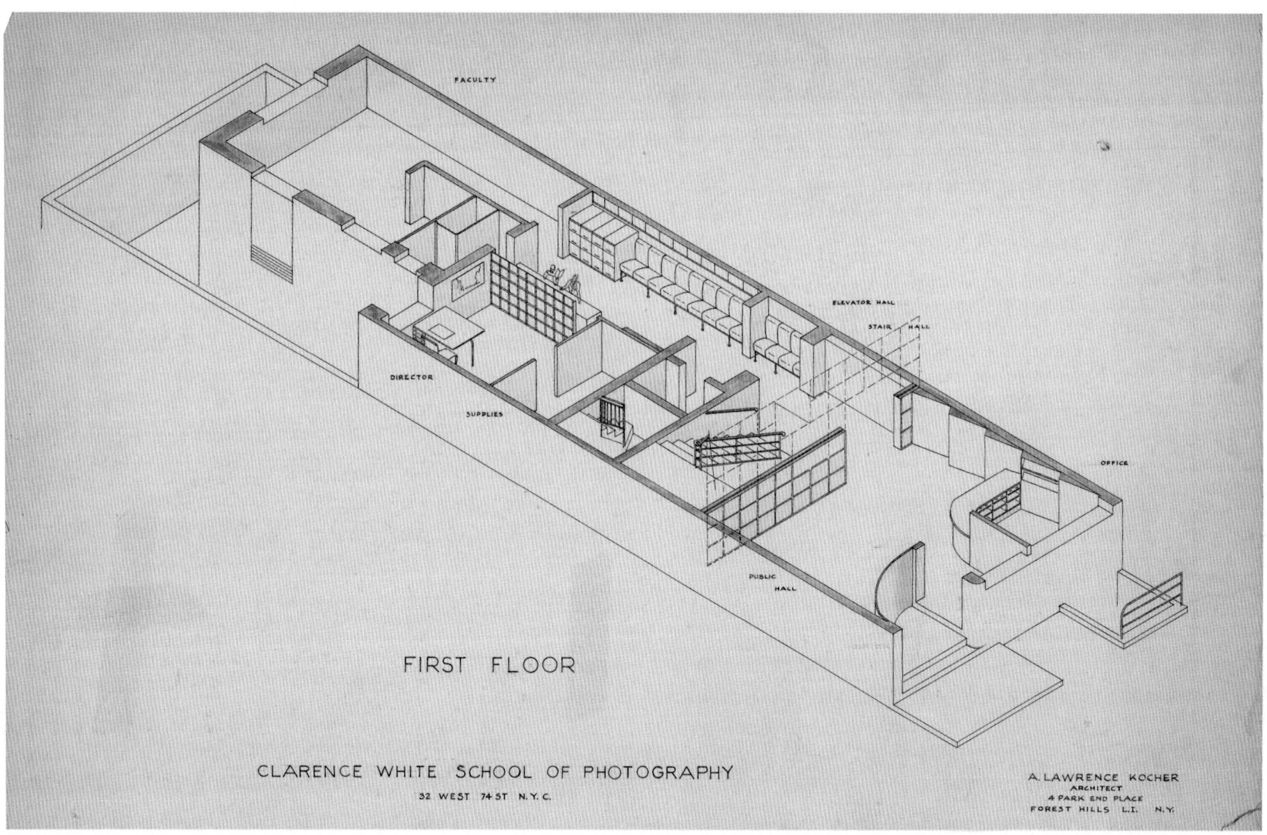

Figure 6.1. A. Lawrence Kocher. 1939–1943. Clarence White School of Photography. Unbuilt. Floor plan of the public hall.
Figure 6.2. A. Lawrence Kocher. 1939–1943. Clarence White School of Photography. Unbuilt. First-floor axonometric view.

came as a direct result of his work there. Edgar Kaufmann Jr. was formerly Frank Lloyd Wright's apprentice at Taliesin. His father was the owner of the Kaufmann's Department Store in Pittsburgh and of the Fallingwater House in Bear Run, Pennsylvania (1938).[3] In 1941, Kaufmann Jr. visited Black Mountain College during a car trip to Mexico and was deeply impressed by the ongoing construction of the Studies Building. Kaufmann owned property on a ridge of the many hills that overlooked downtown Pittsburgh. He commissioned Kocher to design a four-floor building containing five one-room rental apartments, one primary apartment for his personal use, common services, a garage for six automobiles, and an upper terrace with a common solarium. The high visibility of the construction site and the social prominence of the commissioner resulted in a project with a design approach that Kocher had scarcely explored before. Though architecture historically deals with symbolism, iconography, and meaning, the Kaufmann Apartment Building is the first and only project where a public representation of Kocher's patron takes a leading role in the process of architectural design.[4] Curiously enough, this peculiarity also makes this project the most site-specific design in Kocher's professional career, otherwise consistently detached from the physical context. These two facts explain the extraordinary emphasis observed in the building's elevation designs, which work as a public statement of the patron's status and civic responsibility.

The lot was surrounded by wooded cliffs and had excellent views on its north and west sides. The access was only possible through the ridge of the hill that extended to the south. With all these constraints, Kocher—along with the Hungarian emigree László Gábor—drew a variety of building options, paying special attention to the volume, composition, and shadow effects of the more publicly exposed north and west façades, along with the south-access sequence. All these diverse versions can be grouped in three main iterations of the project. The first and least-developed version is a variation of the 1934 plan for the Cotton Textile Institute House, which follows a Z-shape scheme that serves to project and open the building to the views on the north side. The staircase, lobby, common services, and the covered parking garage are simply attached to the south side of this original Z-form. **(Figure 6.9)** Building on this first scheme, the second iteration of the project has a more compact floor plan, composed of three similarly sized rectangles attached in a clockwise spiral shape, with the stair situated in the middle of the south rectangle. The typical floor contains two one-bedroom, one-bathroom apartments; the ground floor includes common services and a two-bedroom apartment occupying the north side with an enlarged living room that protrudes from the northwest corner and creates a volumetric discontinuity in the public-facing façades.[5] **(Figures 6.10 to 6.12)** There are a large number of drawings focusing on the design of this protruding volume and its discontinuity with tentative solutions that range from a very rational and strict disposition of the windows to an expressionist S-shape created through the dislocation of first- and second-floor plans. These options were only explored in elevation drawings and were never reflected on the floor plans. **(Figures 6.13 to 6.26)**

After these formal experimentations, Kocher withdrew to a more familiar design methodology. Without renouncing the public representation requirements of the project, Kocher and Gabor produced a much more serene, austere, and classically modern solution, consistent with his body of work. This definitive variation of the project is contained within a simple rectangular parallelepiped; the only discontinuities in this geometry happen on the first floor and in the primary apartment level, again, in search of a more complex articulation of the building's north-west corner. In this option, all of the service spaces in the apartments accumulate in the south façade alongside a protruding, partially glazed staircase that conforms to a T-shape plan on all levels. The windows of this south façade are narrow, longitudinal sashes that allow for the privacy of kitchens and bathrooms—a contrast to the north façade's floor-to-ceiling windows, which enable the desired views from the living rooms. Since the project seems to have been abandoned in its preliminary design stage, the materiality and building technology are difficult to guess. Nonetheless, there is a drawing with a plan scheme of the façade's corner that suggests Kocher's intention was to use a Transite cement-asbestos corrugated board similar to those used in the Black Mountain Studies Building. **(Figure 6.27)** The reason for abandoning the project in this early stage is, however, easier to guess, as Edgar Kaufmann Jr. was mobilized in 1942 and served with the US Air Force until 1946, during World War II. **(Figures 6.28 to 6.33)**

Kocher's final years at Black Mountain were not only a time of grand historic events, but a moment of complete transformation for the American economy and, most importantly, a period of profound change in the underlying sensibility and common imaginary affecting all levels of American social organization. Even before the official and active involvement of the country in World War II, President Roosevelt committed to the transformation of the United States in the "Arsenal of Democracy" and to the adaptation of American industry to a war-production mode.[6] Ford and other automobile producers started fabricating military aircraft and tanks, as shipyards turned out entire fleets of war vessels. This wartime production was the logical continuation of mechanisms put in place during the New Deal, with the state assuming the role as the only purchaser and consumer of industrial production. As wartime production boomed, the increasing demand for jobs, coupled with the mobilization of a large share of the population, dropped unemployment to a historic minimum of 1.2 percent in 1944 from 14.6 percent in 1940. Sixteen million men and women marched to war, while 24 million were employed in defense jobs, often for a higher wage than they previously had ever earned.[7] By the time the atomic bombs detonated in Hiroshima and Nagasaki on August 6th and 9th of 1945, Americans had been living under wartime rationing for over three years. There were limits on strategic materials like concrete, steel, aluminum, rubber, plastic, and petroleum, along with common goods such as shoes, sugar, coffee, meat, butter, milk, and soap; there was also limited vehicle usage and purchase of luxury items. The Office of Price Administration (OPA) encouraged the population to save their money for a more economically comfortable future.[8] Americans started purchasing financial products, like war bonds, to help the war effort, and were saving a still-unequaled record average of 21 percent of their disposable income.[9] The unprecedented mobilization of workforce and resources, the acceleration of industrial production, and the subsequent rise of employment opportunities and family savings created a relevant impact on the attitudes of the American social body. The Depression-era ethos of austerity and the immediate

This page:
Figure 6.3. A. Lawrence Kocher. 1939–1943. Clarence White School of Photography. Unbuilt. Main façade preliminary sketch.
Figure 6.4. A. Lawrence Kocher. 1939–1943. Clarence White School of Photography. Unbuilt. Third-floor axonometric view.

Opposite page:
Figure 6.5. A. Lawrence Kocher. 1939–1943. Clarence White School of Photography. Unbuilt. Movable furniture.
Figure 6.6. A. Lawrence Kocher. 1939–1943. Clarence White School of Photography. Unbuilt. Fixed furniture.

Next two pages:
Figure 6.7. A. Lawrence Kocher. 1939–1943. Clarence White School of Photography. Unbuilt. Basement plan.
Figure 6.8. A. Lawrence Kocher. 1939–1943. Clarence White School of Photography. Unbuilt. Fourth- and fifth-floor plans.

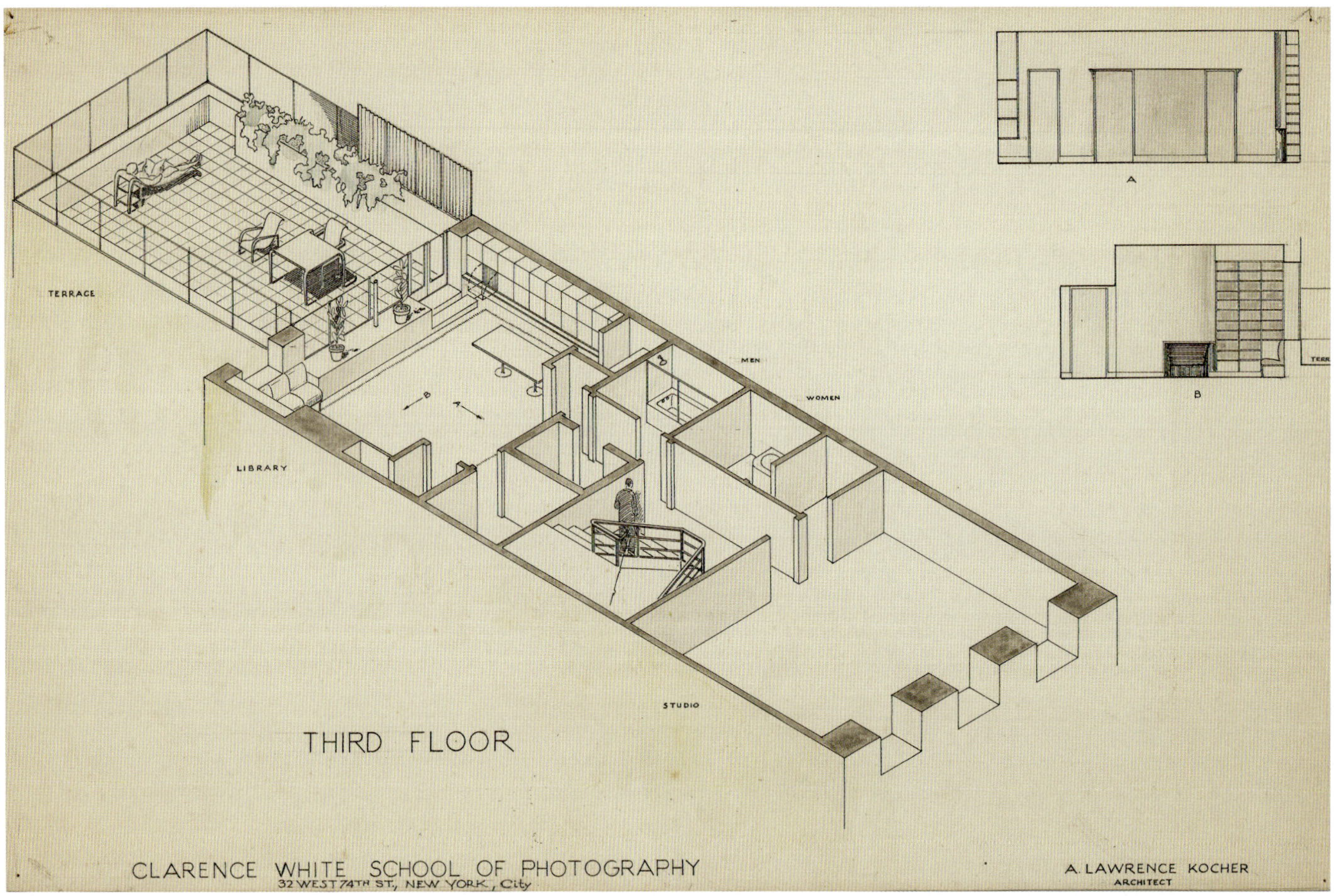

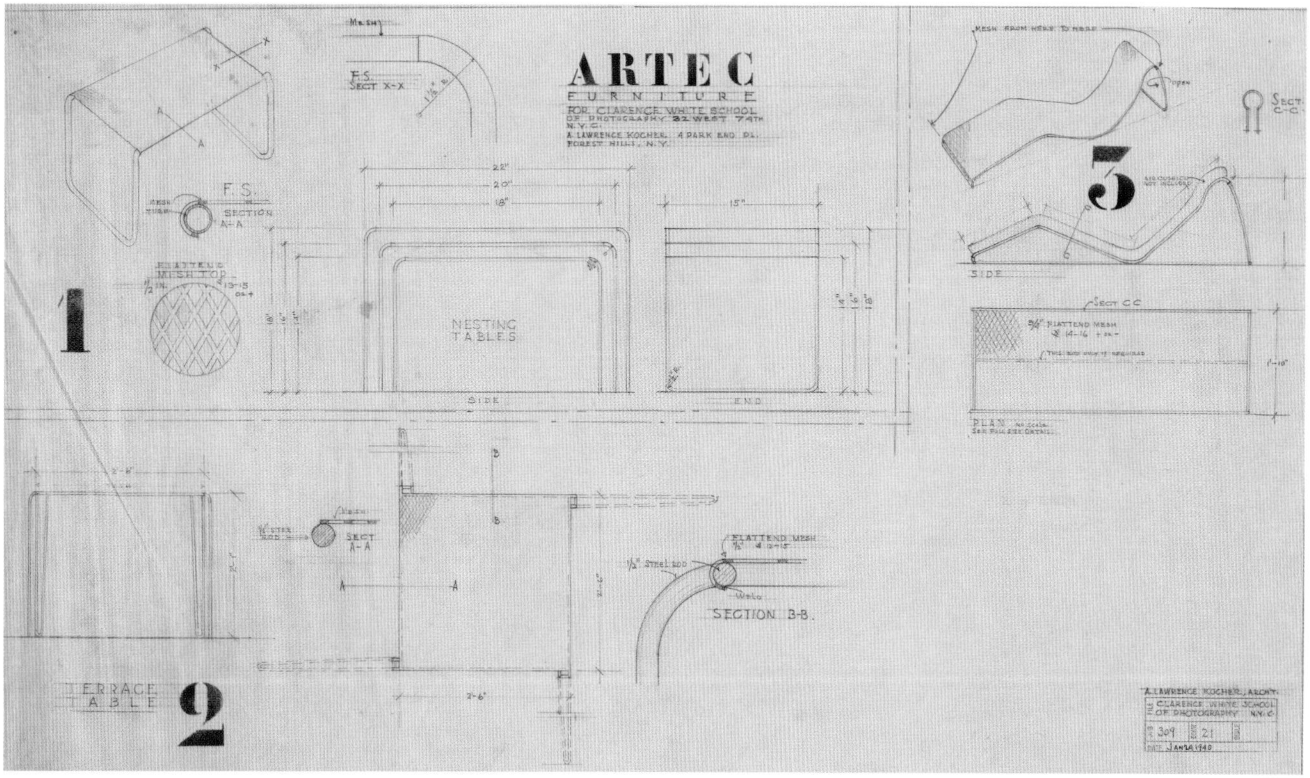

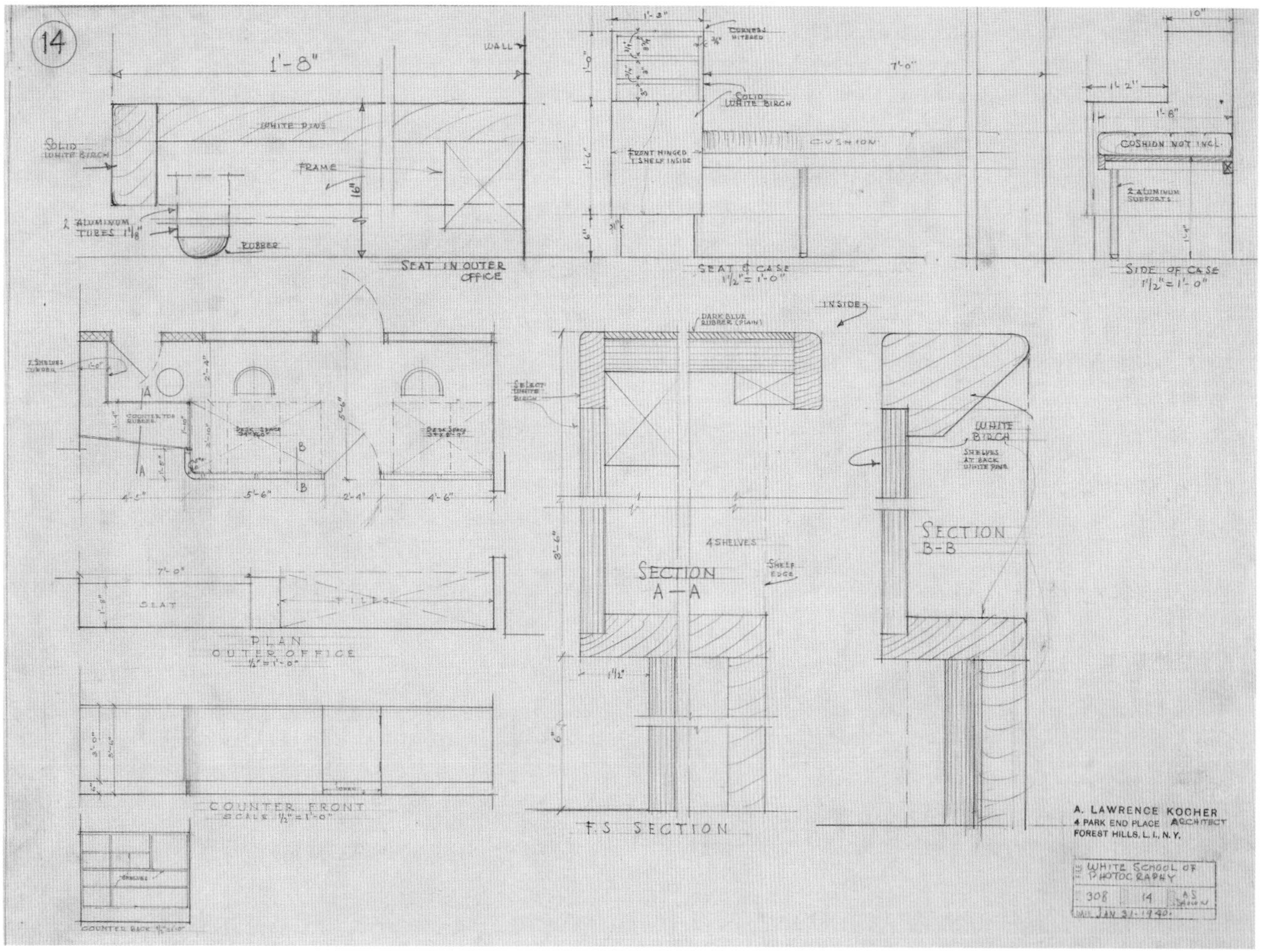

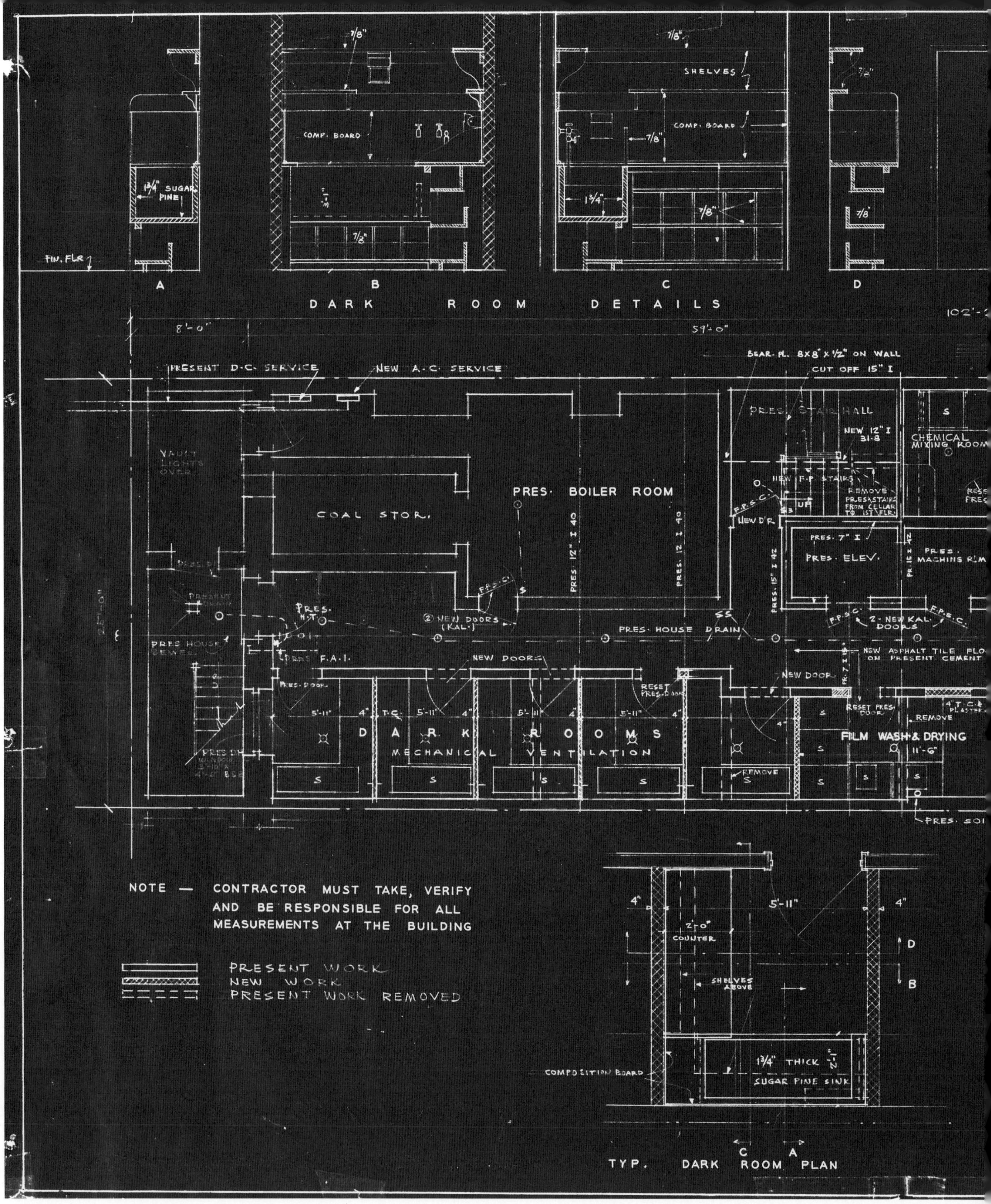
DARK ROOM DETAILS
A
B
C
D
COMP. BOARD
SHELVES
1¾" SUGAR PINE
FIN. FLR
PRESENT D-C- SERVICE
NEW A-C- SERVICE
BEAR. PL. 8X8" X ½" ON WALL
CUT OFF 15" I
PRES. STAIR HALL
CHEMICAL MIXING ROOM
NEW 12" I
NEW F.P. STAIRS
REMOVE PRES. STAIRS FROM CELLAR TO 1ST FLR.
VAULT LIGHTS OVER
PRES. BOILER ROOM
COAL STOR.
PRES. ELEV.
PRES. MACHINE R.M.
PRES. 12" I 40
PRES. 15" I 42
② NEW DOORS (KAL.)
PRES. HOUSE DRAIN
PRES. HOUSE SEWER
2 - NEW KAL. DOORS
NEW ASPHALT TILE FLO ON PRESENT CEMENT
NEW DOORS
NEW DOOR
RESET PRES. DOOR
DARK ROOMS
MECHANICAL VENTILATION
FILM WASH & DRYING
REMOVE
PRES. SOI
NOTE — CONTRACTOR MUST TAKE, VERIFY AND BE RESPONSIBLE FOR ALL MEASUREMENTS AT THE BUILDING
PRESENT WORK
NEW WORK
PRESENT WORK REMOVED
2'-0" COUNTER
SHELVES ABOVE
1¾" THICK SUGAR PINE SINK
COMPOSITION BOARD
TYP. DARK ROOM PLAN

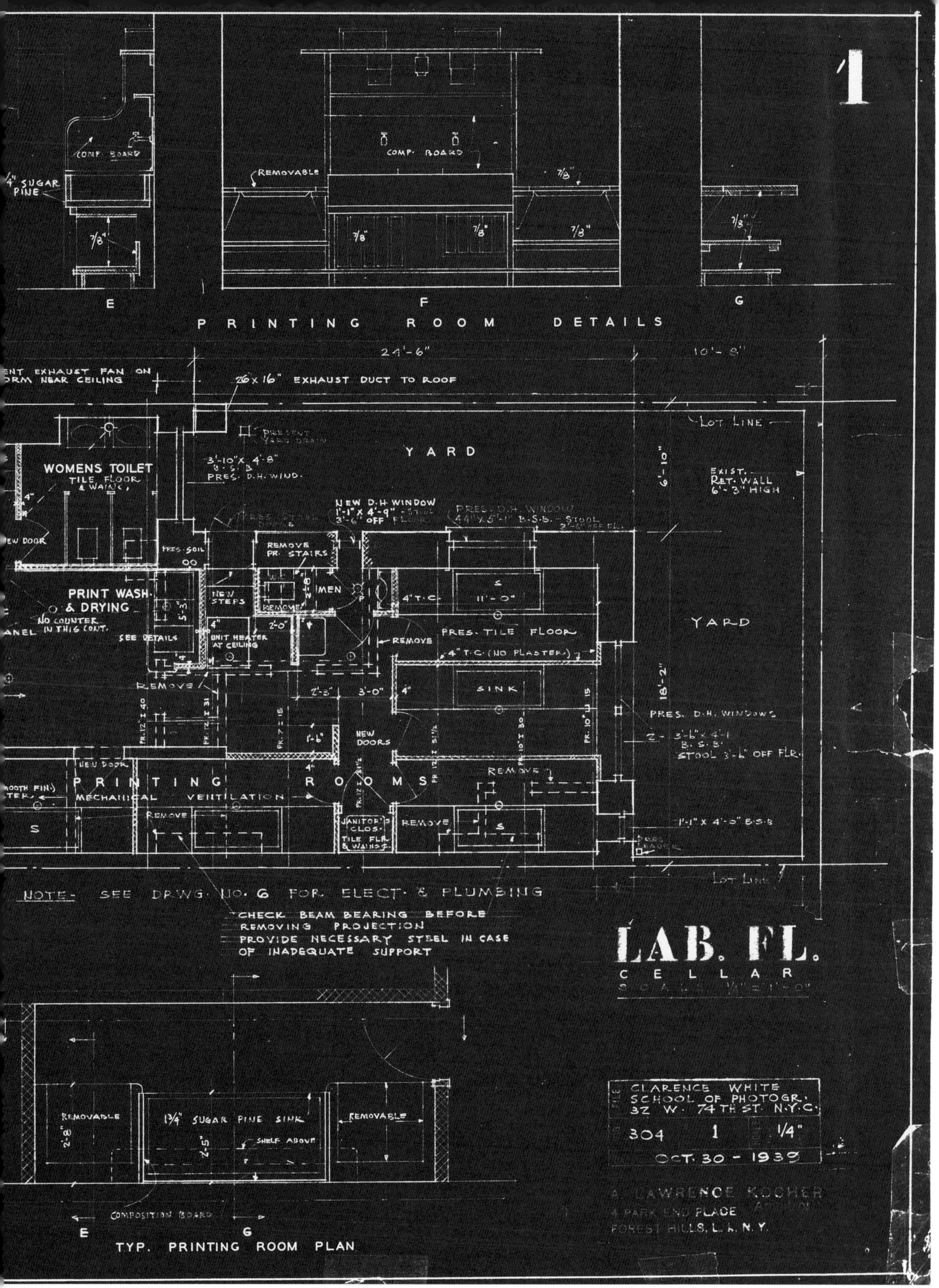
1
COMP. BOARD
3/4" SUGAR PINE
7/8"
REMOVABLE
E
F
G
PRINTING ROOM DETAILS
24'-6"
10'-8"
26"x16" EXHAUST DUCT TO ROOF
YARD
LOT LINE
WOMENS TOILET
TILE FLOOR & WAINS.
3'-10" X 4'-8" B.S.B. PRES. D.H. WIND.
NEW D.H. WINDOW 1'-1" X 4'-9" 3'-6" OFF FLOOR
EXIST. RET. WALL 6'-3" HIGH
NEW DOOR
PRES. SOIL
REMOVE PR. STAIRS
MEN
PRINT WASH & DRYING
NO COUNTER IN THIS CONT.
SEE DETAILS
NEW STEPS
UNIT HEATER AT CEILING
REMOVE
PRES. TILE FLOOR
4" T.C. (NO PLASTER)
SINK
PRES. D.H. WINDOWS
STOOL 3'-1" OFF FLR.
NEW DOORS
PRINTING ROOMS
MECHANICAL VENTILATION
JANITOR'S CLOS. TILE FLR. & WAINS.
1'-1" X 4'-0" B.S.B.
NOTE - SEE DRWG. NO. 6 FOR ELECT. & PLUMBING
CHECK BEAM BEARING BEFORE REMOVING PROJECTION
PROVIDE NECESSARY STEEL IN CASE OF INADEQUATE SUPPORT
LAB. FL.
CELLAR
CLARENCE WHITE SCHOOL OF PHOTOGR. 32 W. 74TH ST. N.Y.C.
304 1 1/4"
OCT. 30 - 1939
A. LAWRENCE KOCHER
4 PARK END PLACE
FOREST HILLS, L. I., N.Y.
REMOVABLE
1 3/4" SUGAR PINE SINK
SHELF ABOVE
COMPOSITION BOARD
TYP. PRINTING ROOM PLAN

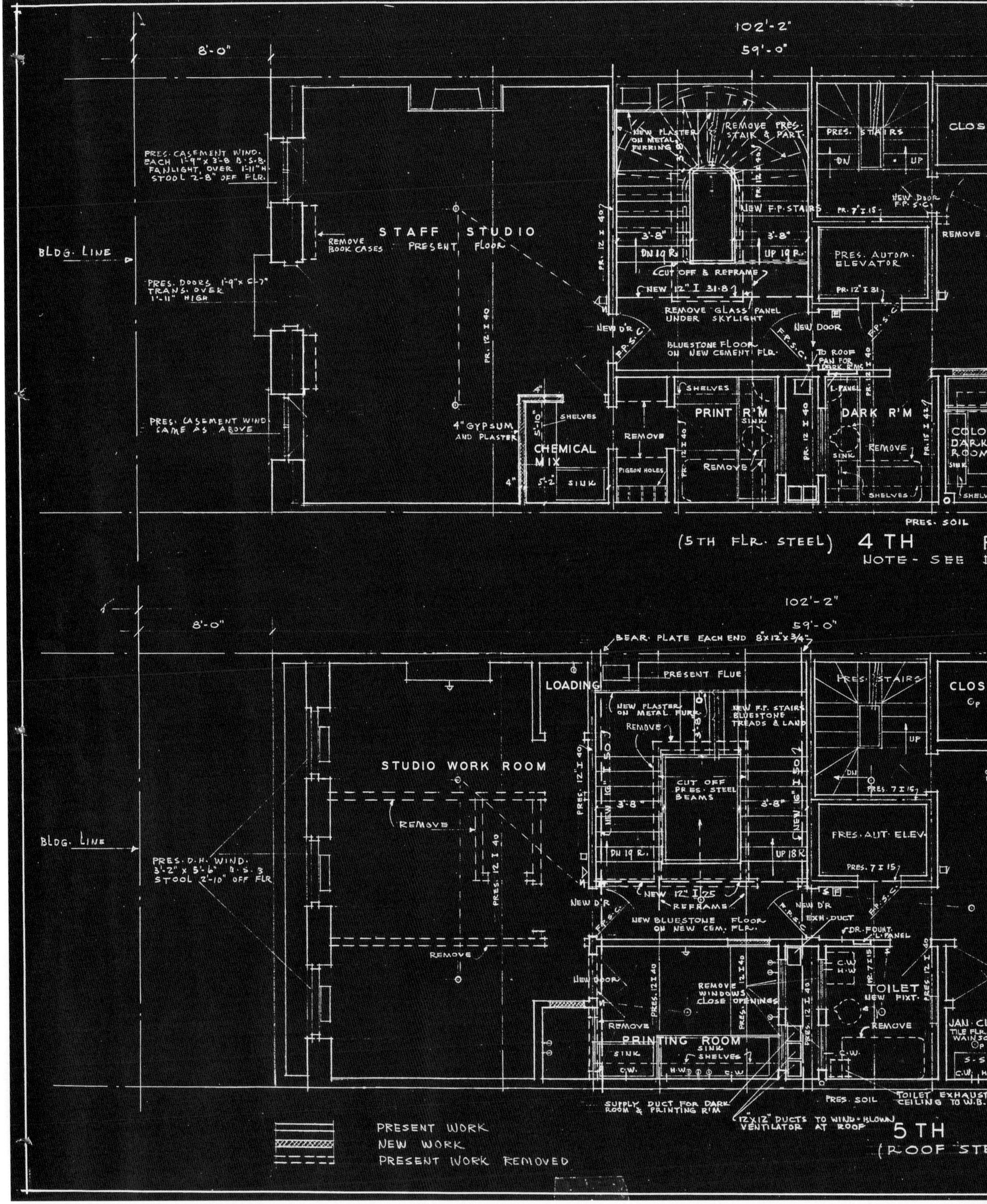

102'-2"
59'-0"
8'-0"
STAFF STUDIO
PRESENT FLOOR
REMOVE BOOK CASES
BLDG. LINE
PRES. CASEMENT WIND. EACH 1'-9" x 3'-8 B.S.B. FANLIGHT, OVER 1'-11" H. STOOL 2'-8" OFF FLR.
PRES. DOORS 1'-9" x 6'-7" TRANS. OVER 1'-11" HIGH
PRES. CASEMENT WIND. SAME AS ABOVE
4" GYPSUM AND PLASTER
CHEMICAL MIX
SHELVES
SINK
REMOVE
PIGEON HOLES
PRINT R'M
DARK R'M
COLOR DARK ROOM
NEW PLASTER ON METAL FURRING
REMOVE PRES. STAIR & PART.
NEW F.P. STAIRS
DN 19 R.
UP 19 R.
CUT OFF & REFRAME
NEW 12" I 31.8
REMOVE GLASS PANEL UNDER SKYLIGHT
BLUESTONE FLOOR ON NEW CEMENT FLR.
NEW D'R
NEW DOOR
TO ROOF FAN FOR DARK RMS
PRES. STAIRS
CLOS.
PRES. AUTOM. ELEVATOR
PRES. SOIL
(5TH FLR. STEEL) 4TH F
NOTE - SEE D
102'-2"
59'-0"
8'-0"
BEAR. PLATE EACH END 8"x12"x3/4"
PRESENT FLUE
LOADING
NEW PLASTER ON METAL FURR.
NEW F.P. STAIRS BLUESTONE TREADS & LAND
STUDIO WORK ROOM
REMOVE
CUT OFF PRES. STEEL BEAMS
DN 19 R.
UP 18 R.
PRES. AUT. ELEV.
BLDG. LINE
PRES. D.H. WIND. 3'-2" x 5'-6" B.S.B. STOOL 2'-10" OFF FLR.
NEW 12" I 25
REFRAME
NEW BLUESTONE FLOOR ON NEW CEM. FLR.
EXH. DUCT
DR. FOUNT.
REMOVE WINDOWS CLOSE OPENINGS
PRINTING ROOM
TOILET
NEW FIXT.
JAN. CLO
SUPPLY DUCT FOR DARK ROOM & PRINTING R'M
12"x12" DUCTS TO WIND-BLOWN VENTILATOR AT ROOF
PRES. SOIL
TOILET EXHAUST CEILING TO W.B.
5TH
(ROOF STE
PRESENT WORK
NEW WORK
PRESENT WORK REMOVED

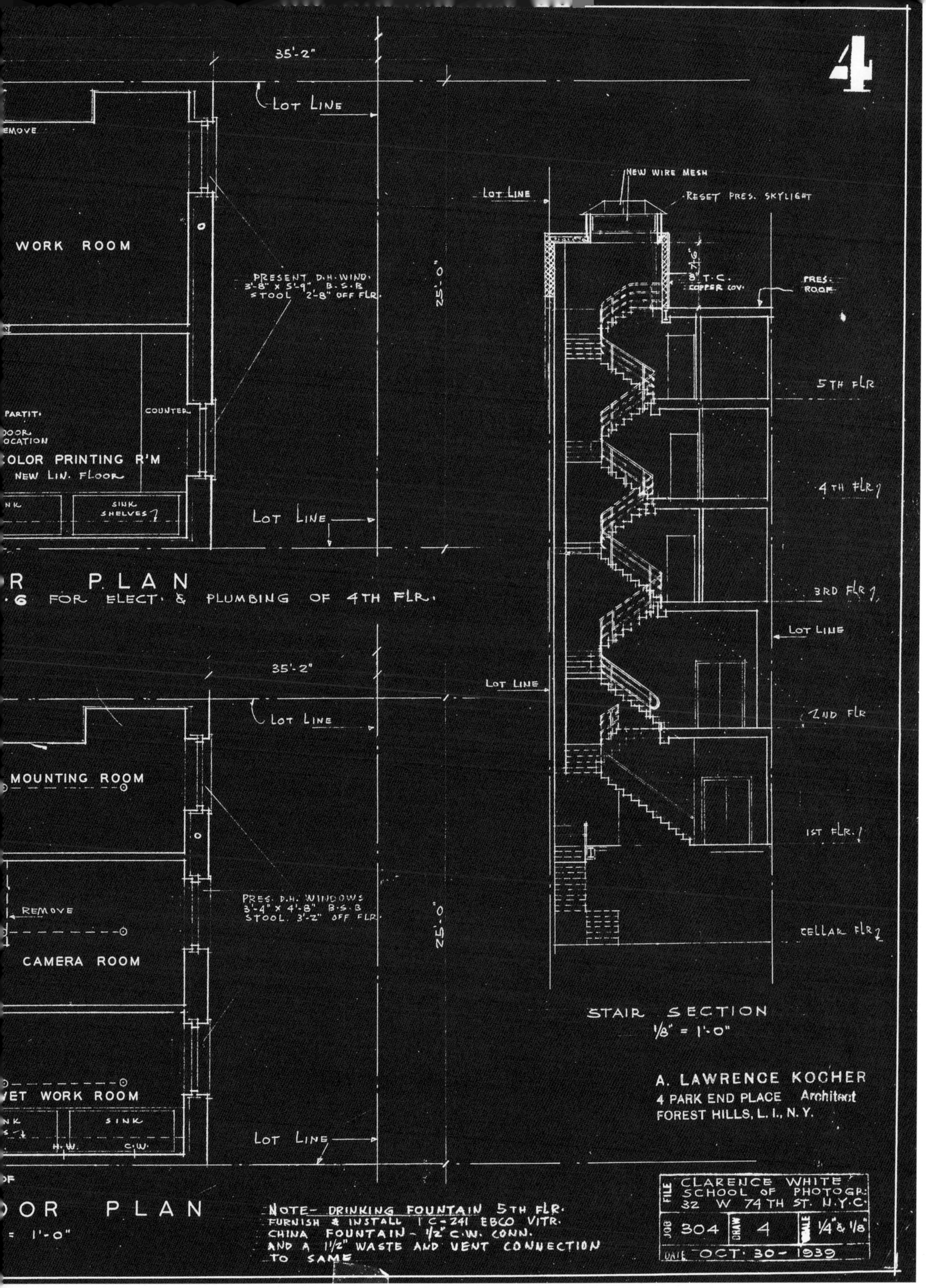
4
35'-2"
LOT LINE
WORK ROOM
PRESENT D.H. WIND. 3'-8" x 5'-9" B.S.B STOOL 2'-8" OFF FLR.
25'-0"
COLOR PRINTING R'M
NEW LIN. FLOOR
LOT LINE
PLAN
FOR ELECT. & PLUMBING OF 4TH FLR.
MOUNTING ROOM
REMOVE
CAMERA ROOM
PRES. D.H. WINDOWS 3'-4" x 4'-8" B.S.B STOOL 3'-2" OFF FLR.
WET WORK ROOM
SINK
LOT LINE
OOR PLAN
= 1'-0"
NOTE- DRINKING FOUNTAIN 5TH FLR. FURNISH & INSTALL 1 C-241 EBCO VITR. CHINA FOUNTAIN - 1/2" C.W. CONN. AND A 1 1/2" WASTE AND VENT CONNECTION TO SAME
NEW WIRE MESH
RESET PRES. SKYLIGHT
8" T.C. COPPER COV.
PRES. ROOF
5TH FLR
4TH FLR
3RD FLR
LOT LINE
2ND FLR
1ST FLR.
CELLAR FLR
STAIR SECTION
1/8" = 1'-0"
A. LAWRENCE KOCHER
4 PARK END PLACE Architect
FOREST HILLS, L. I., N. Y.
FILE CLARENCE WHITE SCHOOL OF PHOTOGR. 32 W 74TH ST. N.Y.C.
JOB 304 DRAW 4 SCALE 1/4" & 1/8"
DATE OCT. 30 - 1939

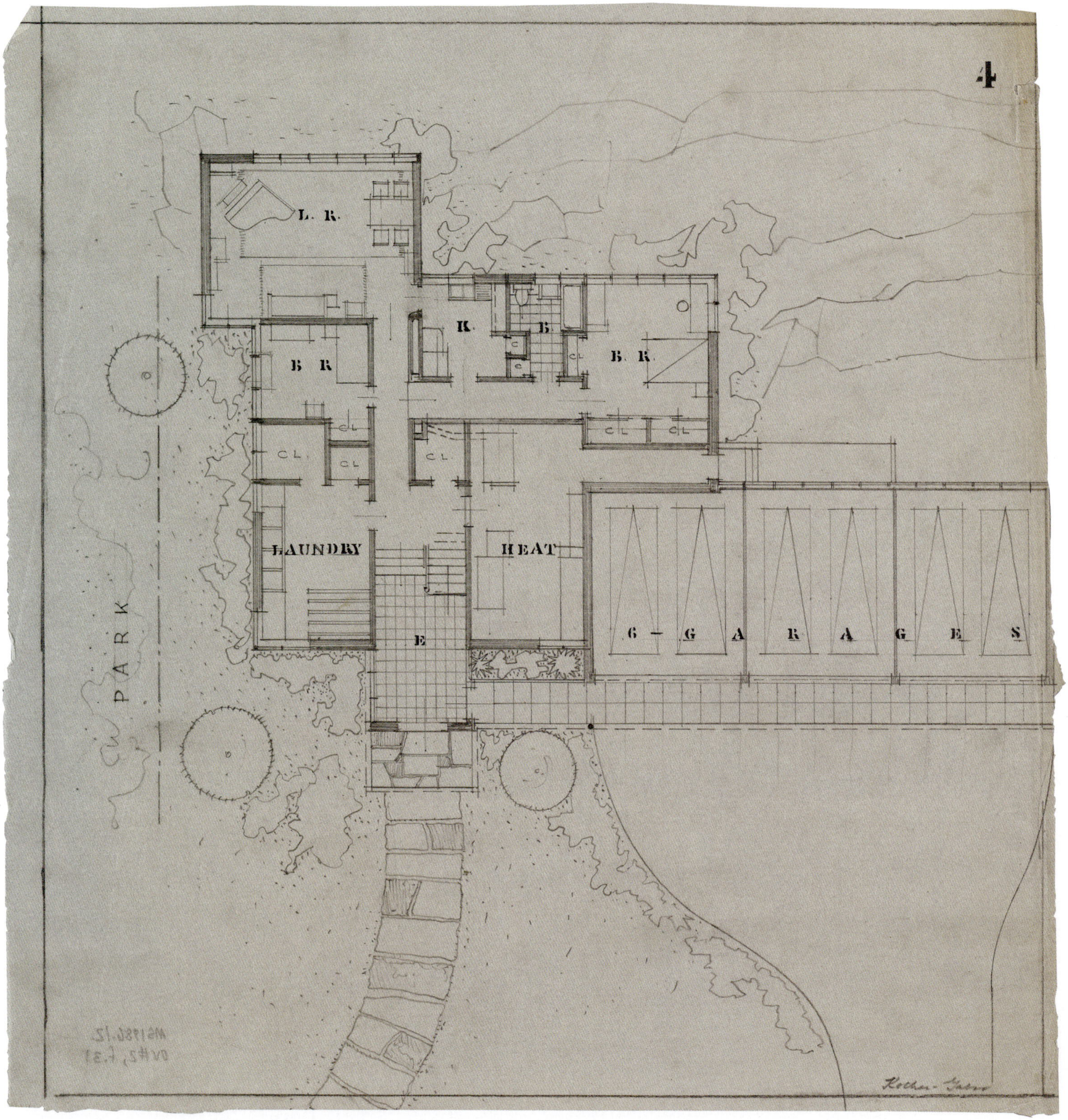

Figure 6.09. A. Lawrence Kocher. 1941. Kaufmann Apartment Building in Pittsburgh. First version. First floor plan.

remediation of everyday hardships was gradually substituted by an optimism in the fact that a wealthier and easier life was possible—compensation for hard work and responsible planning. Meanwhile, in the same line of thought, the U.S. government tried to avoid a new possible crisis—mass unemployment and inflation, caused by the returning men and women in uniform—and began planning for the reconversion of industry, from military to civilian production, after the war. One of the best-positioned industries at this time was residential development and construction.

In the 1940s, the Federal Housing Administration (FHA) and the Servicemen's Readjustment Act (G.I. Bill) gave many returning veterans the opportunity to buy a home. Companies like Levitt & Son capitalized on the residential boom by applying the mass-production techniques of the auto industry to home building.[10] Many industrial companies, however, were still developing a more prospective and experimental approach to the topic of mass production in housing. One of the most relevant examples of this wide-scope research was developed under the patronage of the Revere Cooper Company, which started fabricating rolled copper sheets in Canton, Massachusetts, in 1801. In the late 1920s, the company became Revere Copper and Brass Inc. and moved its headquarters to Rome, New York. During World War II, they supplied kitchenware and ranked among the top-100 companies with more military-related contracts. At the end of the war, the company, like many others, raced to meet the housing demands of those returning from the service. It was a time of material experimentation in housing construction as wartime restrictions were lifted; many production efficiencies and re-engineered materials by the military industry were now available for consumer building technologies. By the late-1940s, and with the aim to promote their products in this newly booming market, Revere Copper and Brass Inc. joined with the Southwest Research Institute, part of the Housing Research Institute, and created the Revere Quality Institute. The institute teamed with *Architectural Forum* magazine to create a national program soliciting proposals that featured quality, modern house design—marking peak public recognition of the institute's architectural patronage. One of the eight demonstration homes commissioned and built by the institute was the famous Revere Quality House in Siesta Key, Sarasota, Florida, designed by the architects Paul Rudolph and Ralph Twitchell in 1948.

Since 1941, Revere Cooper and Brass Inc. published a series of brochures, most of them around 10 to 12 pages, that explored the future possibilities of neighborhood planning and housing construction—two topics that became critical in the post-war architectural discourse and real estate market. As the promoter of cutting-edge architectural research, these investigation fields were encompassed by Revere's promise of "Better Living," a phrase heavily abused during that period by many companies in advertisements. The phrase's origin can be traced back to the famous 1935 DuPont slogan, "Better Things for Better Living…Through Chemistry," which was used to whitewash DuPont's image after being exposed as one of the American corporations profiteering during World War I.[11] The complete title of the series of Revere's publications is a very clear statement of its goals and vision: "Revere's Part in Better Living...: A Series Bringing to the American Public the Concepts of Noted Architects and Engineers for Better Homes and Better Living in Years Ahead."[12]

Other companies, like Celotex, Bohn Aluminum, Stran-Steel Corporation, Douglas Fir Plywood, Allied Chemical and Dye Corporation, Pittsburgh Plate Glass, and United States Gypsum, produced similar advertisements related to architectural design during these years, but Revere was the first to include the architectural avant-garde as part of the equation for "Better Living."[13] Revere was also unequaled in their extensive range and diffusion of these investigations—their advertisements ran monthly in the *Saturday Evening Post*, the most widely disseminated magazine of the day, and in the *Architectural Forum*, the most prestigious magazine specialized in architecture alongside *The Architectural Record*. **(Figure 6.34)** In addition, the Revere pamphlets were widely distributed, expanding advertisement information and designs by leading progressive American architects. Some of the booklets focused on neighborhood scale, which happened to coincide with the architectural interests and professional associations that merged architectural design with urban planning at this time.[14] Two such pamphlets were designed by Oscar Stonorov and a young Louis I. Kahn entitled, "Why city planning is your responsibility," and "You and Your Neighborhood: A Primer for Neighborhood Planning," published in 1942 and 1944. Stonorov and Kahn's booklets advocated for modern architecture and aligned with an emergent social interest for the design of communal leisure and recreational facilities.[15] Both works encouraged grassroots citizen collaboration with designers, city planning agents, and social institutions as the essential element for a successful and democratic replanning of neighborhoods.

Stonorov and Kahn's booklets for Revere advocate for modern architecture and align with an emergent social interest for the design of communal leisure and recreational facilities. Some other Revere brochures precisely explored the design of these kinds of communal facilities. Good examples of this trend include "A citizens country club or leisure center," by William Lescaze; "Your Children Could Romp Here While You Shop," by George Nelson; and Serge Chermayeff's "A children's center or nursery school."[16] Nonetheless, the bulk of the Revere publications were dedicated to the problem of housing approached from very different and contrasting standpoints. These approaches to post-war housing ranged from the utopian fantasy of 1943 Carl F. Boester's "Home...for a nation on wings," in which modernistic suburban homesteads condensed water from the air, created energy by burning trash, produced electricity from aero-generators, and connected residents to work in the city by personal aircrafts; this also included the down-to-earth social and technical focus of Richard Buckminster Fuller's "Better homes for lower incomes."[17] Kocher's work for Revere can be classified within this second category.[18] Revere Copper and Brass Inc. ads were one of the most influential forms of cultural anticipation of the post-war era. These ads provided an alternate future than the one fostered by the specialized architectural press; and their message was disseminated among a wider and more varied audience of potential customers. The campaigns soon established a consistent standard format: a portrait of the architect, a brief declaration of intent, a graphic rendering of the design, and an explicit show of support for the war.

The house scheme developed for Revere's campaign was the third work undertaken by Kocher during his stay at Black Mountain. For Kocher, it is the second design opportunity (after the Kaufmann

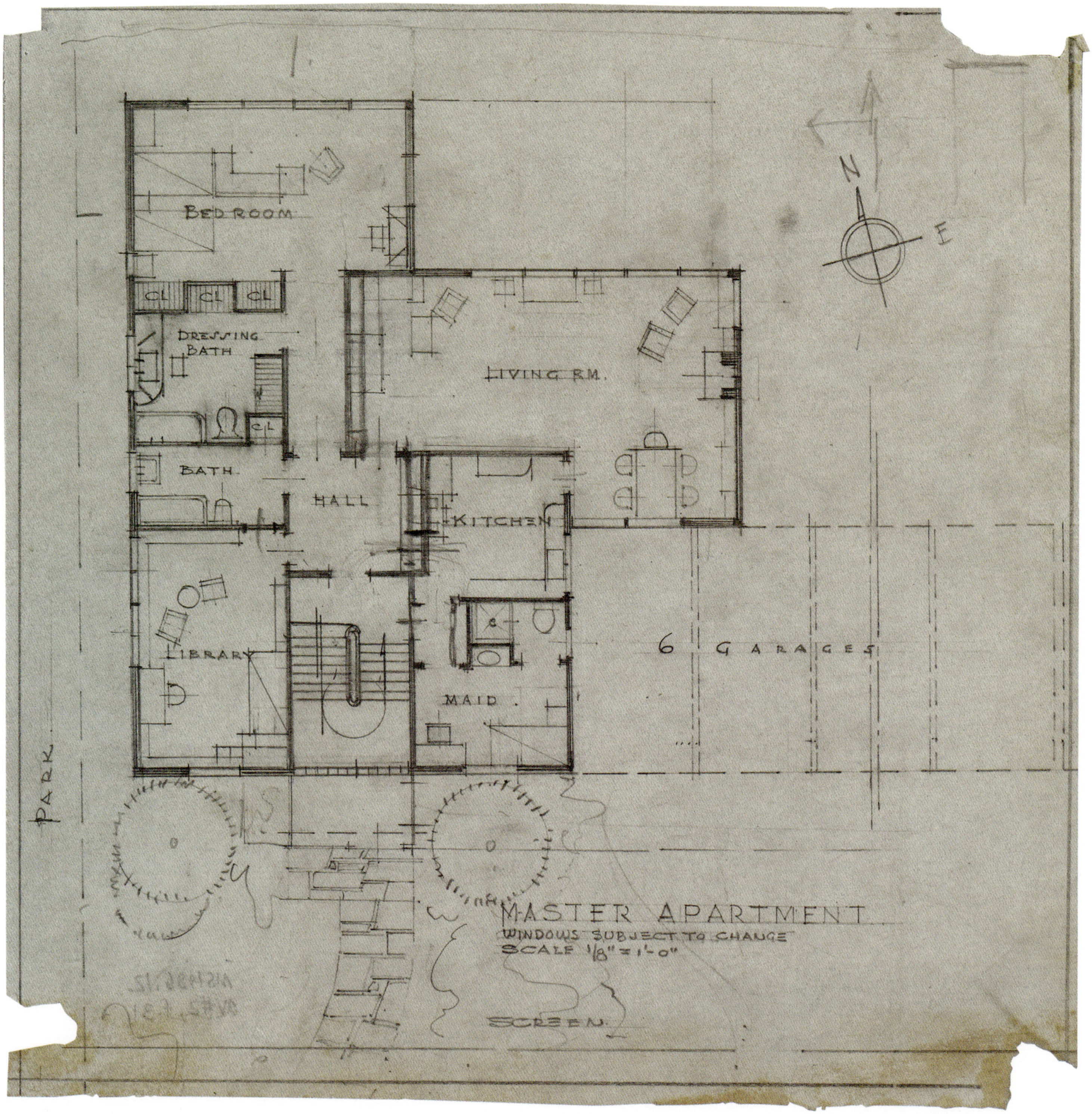

This page:
Figure 6.10. A. Lawrence Kocher. 1941. Kaufmann Apartment Building in Pittsburgh. Second version. Master apartment plan.

Next page:
Figure 6.11. A. Lawrence Kocher. 1941. Kaufmann Apartment Building in Pittsburgh. Second version. Typical upper-floor plan.
Figure 6.12. A. Lawrence Kocher. 1941. Kaufmann Apartment Building in Pittsburgh. Second version. Roof-sun deck floor plan.

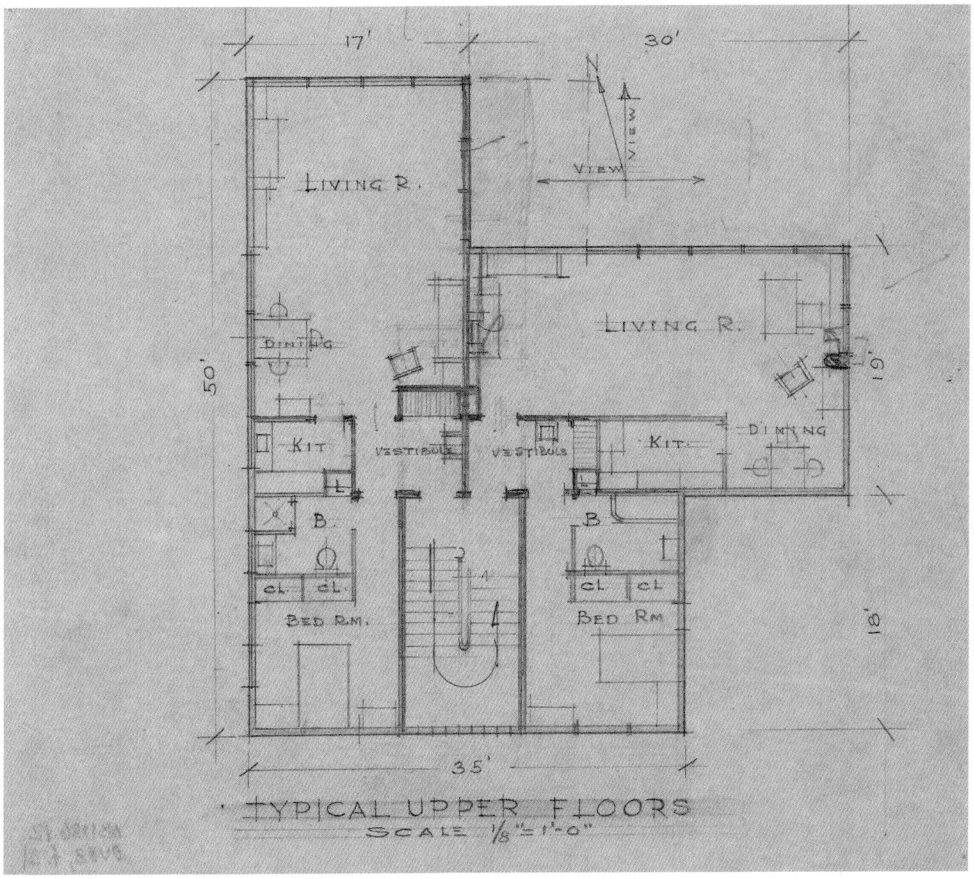

17'
30'
VIEW
VIEW
LIVING R.
LIVING R.
DINING
50'
19'
KIT
VESTIBULE
VESTIBULE
KIT
DINING
B.
B.
CL
CL
CL
CL
BED RM.
BED RM
18'
35'
TYPICAL UPPER FLOORS
SCALE 1/8"=1'-0"

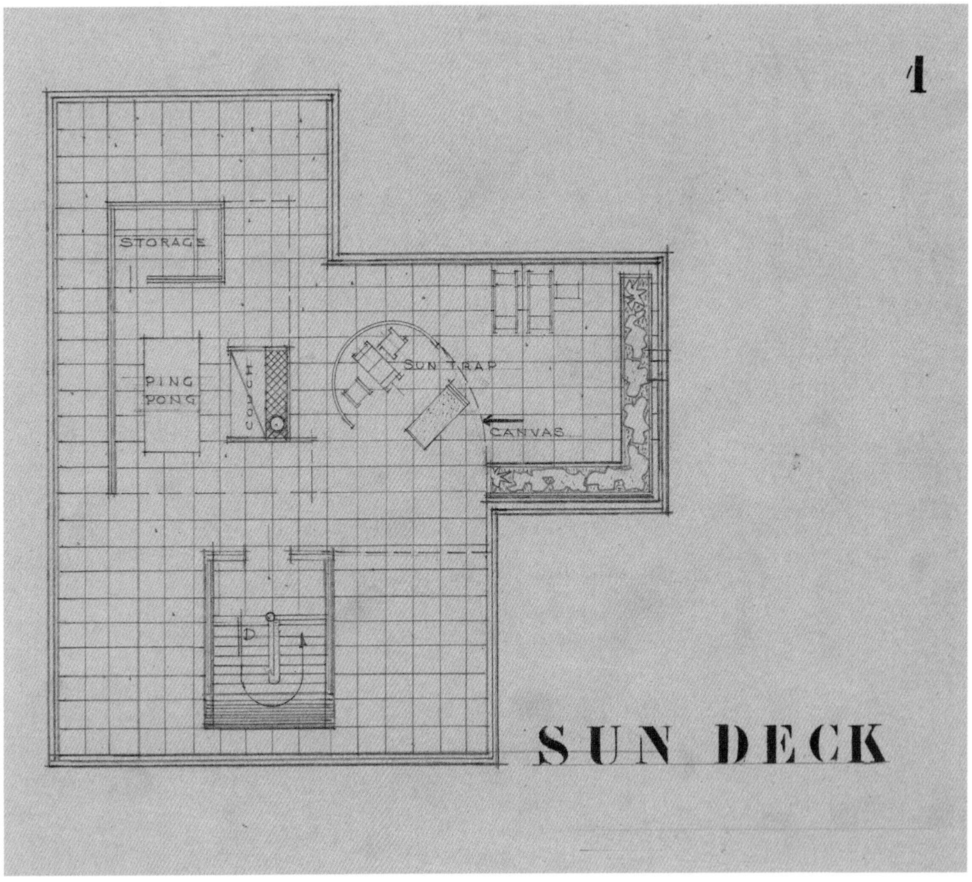

1
STORAGE
PING PONG
COUCH
SUN TRAP
CANVAS
SUN DECK

Figures 6.13 to 6.17. A. Lawrence Kocher. 1941. Kaufmann Apartment Building in Pittsburgh. Second version. Different iterations of façade design.

Figure 6.18 to 6.22. A. Lawrence Kocher. 1941. Kaufmann Apartment Building in Pittsburgh. Second version. Different iterations of façade design.

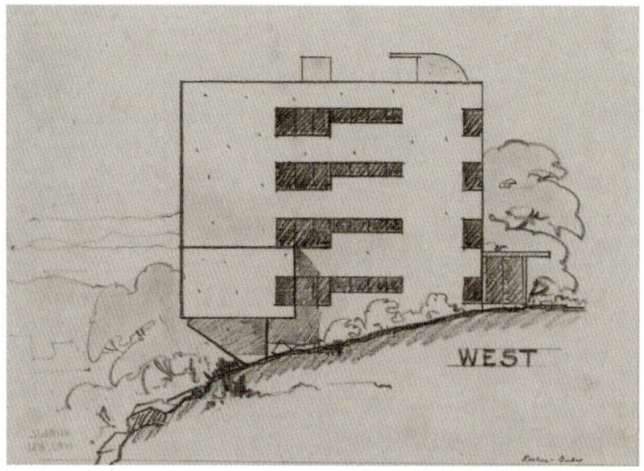

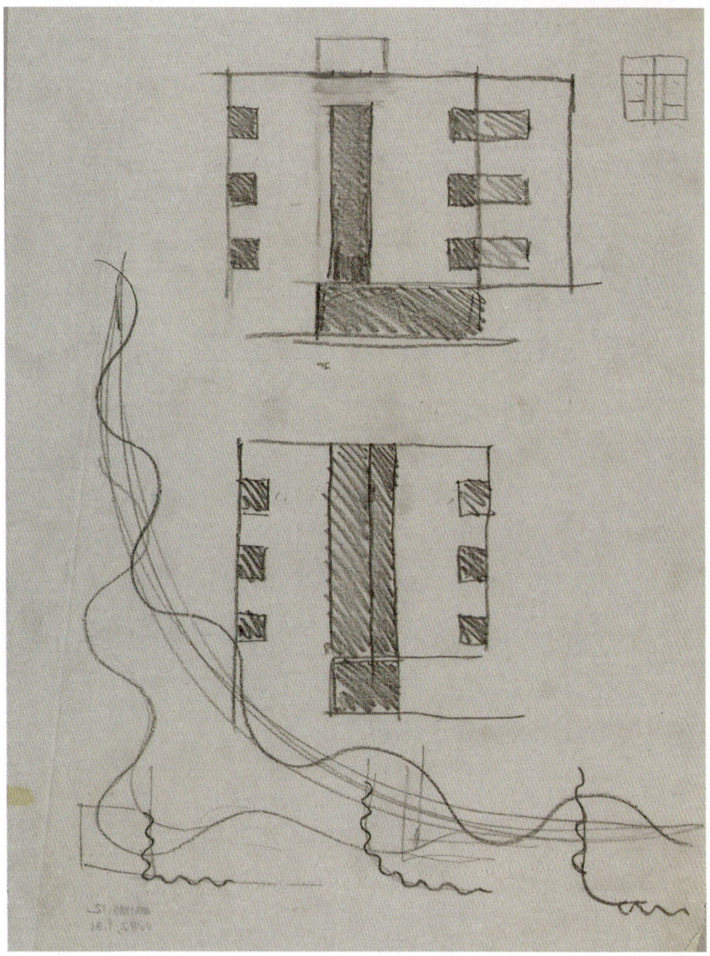

This page:

Figures 6.23 to 6.26. A. Lawrence Kocher. 1941. Kaufmann Apartment Building in Pittsburgh. Second version. Iterations of the elevations and interior render.

Figure 6.27. (Left-bottom) A. Lawrence Kocher. 1941. Kaufmann Apartment Building in Pittsburgh. Second version. Elevations with diagram of the material quality of the corner in plan.

Next page:

Figure 6.28. A. Lawrence Kocher. 1941. Kaufmann Apartment Building in Pittsburgh. Final version. Front elevation.

Figure 6.29. A. Lawrence Kocher. 1941. Kaufmann Apartment Building in Pittsburgh. Final version. Master apartment floor plan.

Figure 6.30. A. Lawrence Kocher. 1941. Kaufmann Apartment Building in Pittsburgh. Final version. Typical floor plan.

Figure 6.31. A. Lawrence Kocher. 1941. Kaufmann Apartment Building in Pittsburgh. Final version. Back elevation.

Figure 6.32. A. Lawrence Kocher. 1941. Kaufmann Apartment Building in Pittsburgh. Final version. Sundeck floor plan.

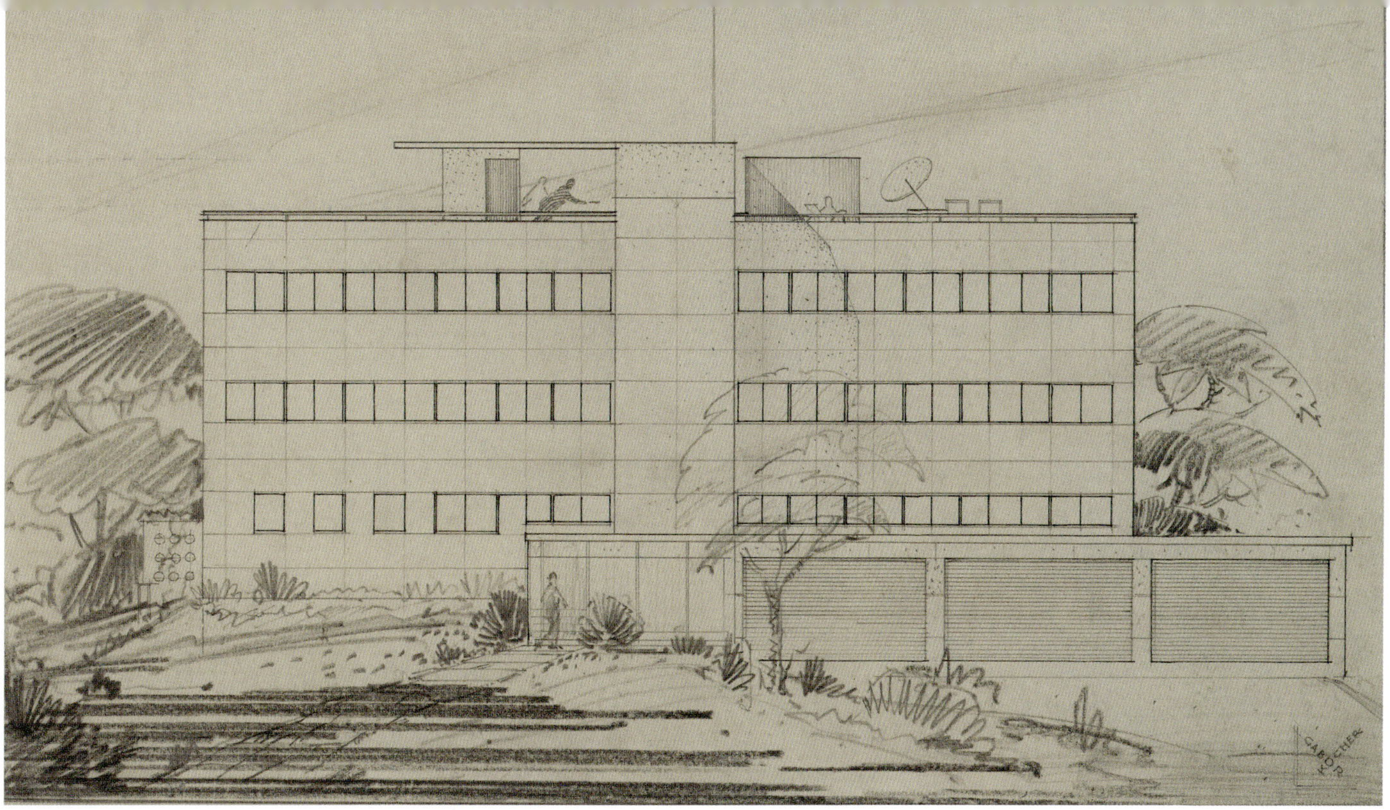

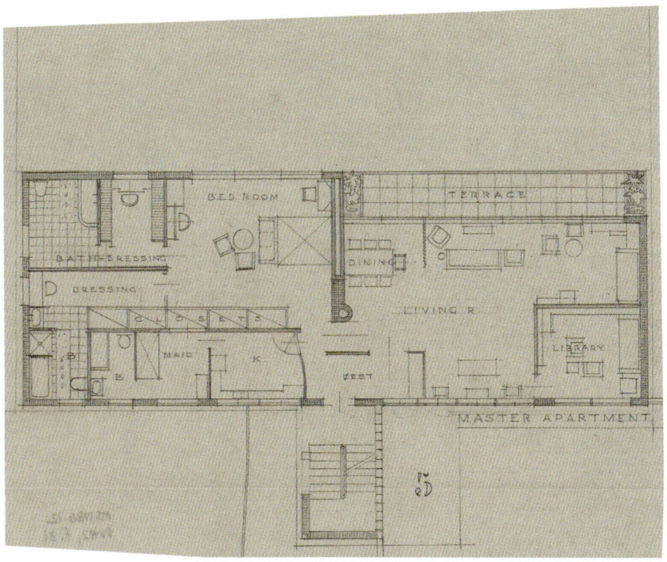

BED ROOM
TERRACE
BATH DRESSING
DRESSING
DINING
CLOSETS
LIVING R
MAID
K
VEST
LIBRARY
MASTER APARTMENT
5

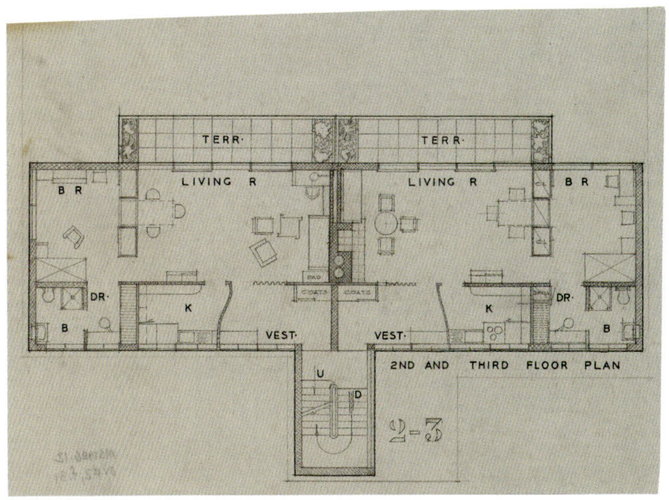

TERR·
TERR·
B R
LIVING R
LIVING R
B R
DR·
K
K
DR·
B
VEST·
VEST·
B
U
D
2ND AND THIRD FLOOR PLAN
2-3

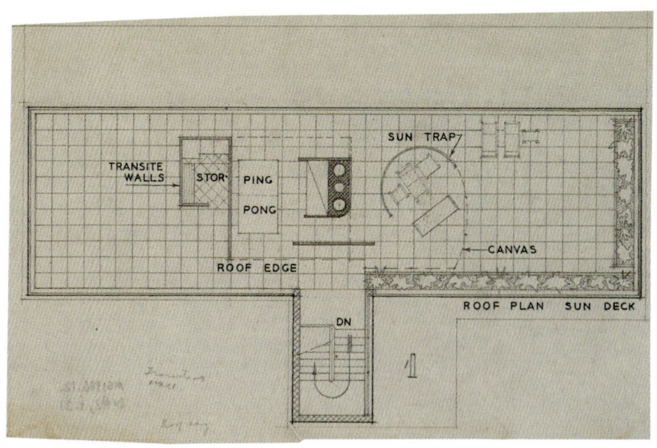

SUN TRAP
TRANSITE WALLS
STOR
PING
PONG
CANVAS
ROOF EDGE
ROOF PLAN SUN DECK
DN
1

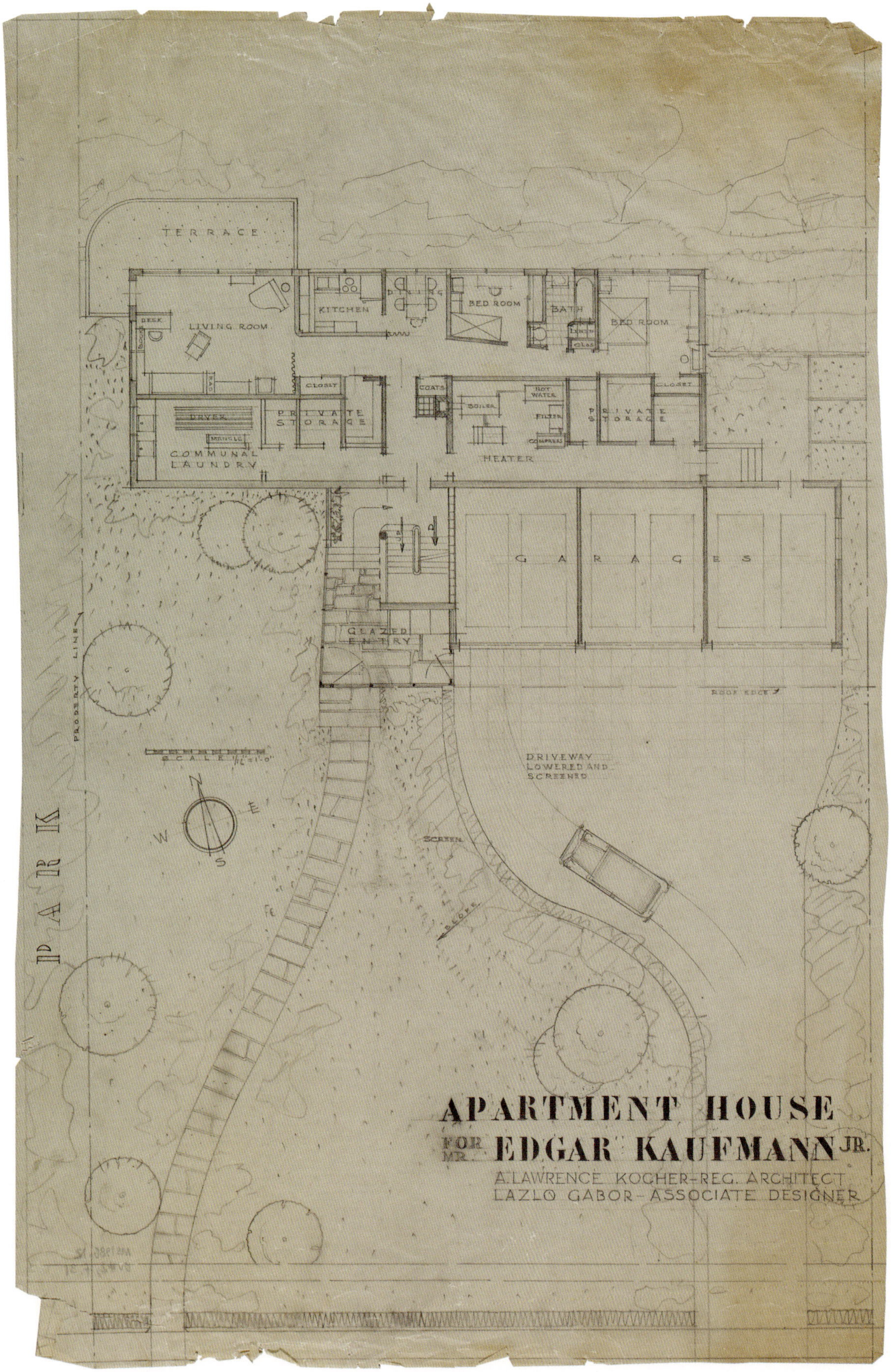

Figure 6.33. A. Lawrence Kocher. 1941. Kaufmann Apartment Building in Pittsburgh. Final version. First floor plan.

Apartments) to use a completely different architectural approach and mindset than his work during The New Deal years. If the change in design methodology in the first case stemmed from the client's necessity for public representation, this second scenario derives from the more profound social and cultural change in the United States during the war. Kocher's Revere advertisement, "Beyond the War Waits Happiness," was one of the first in the campaign series published.[19] His title instills an optimistic feeling—one that is distant from the austerity and crude realism of the Depression-era ethos, and entails a solid trust in progress and the anticipation of a wealthier future for families, a concept that needed recovery after the hardships and basic-survival spirit stemming from the Depression. The advertisement text follows up and introduced the term "Planning" as one of the era's main slogans:

> After the war youth has a new world to look forward to. For today's young men and women can plan instead of dream, can be sure that the homes their parents merely wished for can become a reality for them...It is a house to be lived in for a lifetime. If your family grows so more rooms are needed, you can add them. They have been already provided for in the original plan. Even the closet and storage space have been carefully worked out to hold the many possessions which all families accumulate through the years.[20]

After almost a decade of government-organized economy, along with the new context of war, "planning" became a central term for all economic activities in the U.S.—a notable contrast to its previous, common usage in the urban and regional design fields. The culture of planning permeated Kocher's project, providing the advanced solution to any eventuality that the family may have in the future. Additionally, the project was also concurrently embedded in the culture of consumerism. Revere Copper and Brass Inc. required architects to frame their work in terms of consumer culture—considered not as an individual self-gratification, but as a patriotic duty.

After World War II, architecture culture would be indivisible from an institutionally encouraged consumer culture, as American Studies historian Lizabeth Cohen brilliantly explains:

> If encouraging a mass consumer economy seemed to make good economic sense for the nation, it still required extensive efforts to get Americans to cooperate...Hence, beginning during the war and with great fervor after it, business leaders, labor unions, government agencies, the mass media, advertisers, and many other purveyors of the new postwar order conveyed the message that mass consumption was not a personal indulgence. Rather, it was a civic responsibility designed to improve the living standards of all Americans, a critical part of a prosperity-producing cycle of expanded consumer demand fueling greater production, thereby creating more well-paying jobs and in turn more affluent consumers capable of stoking the economy with their purchases.[21]

Due to the weight of the building industry's role over post-war recovery and the symbolic importance of the house as the bearer of American ideals of democracy, independence, and individuality, homes became the main objects of desire for consumers after 1945. Kocher stressed the suitability for accumulating appliances in the Revere booklet, noting the "new inventions and conveniences which copper has brought to modern living," in a house "made available through mass production, for not more than $2,000." The required individuality is achieved through the design of 36 different modular parts that "can be assembled in diversified arrangements, so it never need look or be just like your neighbor's."[22] Kocher's design offered an incremental house in which the design focused on the final version of the family's dream house, which could be implemented according to their life circumstances and economic growth through a series of attachable modular elements. **(Figures 6.35 to 6.39)** Each prefabricated part was completed in factory with its connection devices, insulation, installed fixtures, and surface finishes, along with wiring and copper tubing for plumbing and panel heating. Stressed by the sponsor of the publication, the use of copper was extended to the roof, gutters, downspouts, and even some of the interior walls, which were finished in woven copper stripes. Instead of designing for scarcity, as he did for his Depression-era houses, Kocher designed for future abundance. This intention is clearly defined in the booklet, adding a slight criticism to his own previous architectural production:

> Having pioneered and worked for twelve years on the idea of low-cost houses for millions of Americans, I have come to believe that mere cheapness can never make a house acceptable to the public. Such box-like structures would be a drug on the building market. Nor could they attempt to meet the real living needs of American people...The house that is wanted and needed must have eye appeal in addition to reasonable cost. It must open new vistas to improved living, to more comfort, to new and surprising attractiveness.[23]

To achieve this "eye appeal," the houses are stylistically fully modern: abstract with a one-story flat roof. The relation between exterior and interior spaces was extremely sophisticated and the garden seemed to be considered an element of familiar enjoyment, far from the production and subsistence role played by gardens in Kocher's previous body of work. This objective was clearly stated in the advertisement when it described a "home where every window can frame a garden view, where there is space for all the pleasures and purposes of living, where doors can move aside to enlarge favorite rooms or to include garden and terrace as part of the living area."[24] Through this feature, Kocher's design conveyed the ideals of a new era, one interested in leisure, sports, healthy life, and free time.

The Revere design was used as a base for another project later developed by Kocher, deemed the House of Moderate Cost, which had a very similar floor plan configuration to that of the Revere Copper and Brass Inc. booklet and advertisement.[25] **(Figures 6.40 and 6.41)** Both the Revere scheme and the House of Moderate Cost were completely modern designs, with similar square footage and distribution including three bedrooms and two bathrooms. They shared many other traits, like a strict two-by-two-foot modulation and a car shelter that served as a threshold from the public sidewalk. Both houses have a flat roof extending over the terraces and gardens

Figure 6.34. A. Lawrence Kocher. Revere House. Advertisement in the Saturday Evening Post. July 11, 1942.

to help shade the windows and to integrate exterior and interior spaces. The roof edge was angled in the House of Moderate Cost, and parallel to the façade in the Revere House. The advertised version seemed to have been optimized in terms of cost, suppressing the hearth, and packing the main bathroom and kitchen back-to-back to share plumbing infrastructure; in terms of privacy, it extended all the walls beyond the roof edge to more clearly define the different uses of the gardens and terraces. These extended walls also served as a support for the possibility of future expansions, while also controlling the exterior-to-interior views. The rotation of the child's room in the Revere version produced an airier and more nuanced Z-shaped entry hall, providing complete privacy for the living spaces. The existing documentation of the House of Moderate Cost does not include any construction detail or building technology specifications. On the contrary, the specifications of the Revere brochure were very comprehensive and prescribed radiating panes in floors, ceiling, and walls for the house's heating system. There is also an explicit intention to avoid monotony but keep consistency in the neighborhood planning expressed in the Revere booklet:

> The house illustrated is built with 36 units that are to be factory produced. Their size is as large as present-day trucks can transport to the site...By the use of these large units the planning of the house is at once made free, flexible, and irregular in contour, thus avoiding standardization and monotony. This is the result of architectural juggling with spacious walls rather than with constricted units only three or four feet in width...The variety of the exterior can be unlimited, but always with sufficient uniformity of elements to relate all of the houses of this kind harmoniously in a community.[26]

Since civil construction was completely banned in the early 1940s, Kocher and many other architects used the Revere Copper and Brass Inc. advertisements and booklets as an instrument to prefigure and disseminate architectural ideas that would later develop in the professional realm during the post-war construction boom. One such idea was that the house in this post-war scenario was not a primary human necessity that should grant the subsistence of American families. From now on, houses would be considered the most relevant asset within the family investment portfolio. As any other investment, this asset is supposed to grow and steadily increase its value. Typically, families of the post-war era would periodically move to a larger house, taking advantage of their ever-growing wealth and fulfilling their patriotic duty as citizen-consumers. Challenging this domestic nomadism, Kocher's proposal rooted families in place with a house that grows and adapts to their needs at every stage of their economic development. The design reinforced the identification of its inhabitants with a determinate territory and the sense of belonging to a stable community. In addition, all the neighborhood houses would grow according to a premediated design strategy, which further enhanced the possibilities of successful planning.

With the design of the Revere House, Kocher demonstrated the growing significance of planning as a social tool and aligned with current preoccupations that architects collectively held about the scope of their own disciplinary field. According to a survey report commissioned by the American Institute of Architects (AIA) to examine the contribution and situation of a career architect during the post-war years, 30 percent of architects served in the armed forces, with only 36 percent of them having performed some duty related to architecture. Within the remaining 70 percent of architects left on the home front, only 29 percent found work in architecture.[27] With this disciplinary struggle in mind, Joseph Hudnut, dean of Harvard's Graduate School of Design (GSD), expressed his conviction that America should not "return after the war to that form of individualism which characterized the era of expansion and exploitation," and that the emphasis on architecture's social responsibility should be key during the post-war years.[28] In 1944, Hudnut summoned (what he called) the progressive members of the architectural profession to confront the conservative, Beaux-Arts-oriented American Institute of Architects (AIA), and created a new professional organization for architects deemed the American Society of Planners and Architects (ASPA). As its name clearly indicates, ASPA aimed to unify the disciplines of planning, landscape architecture, and architecture, taking advantage of the City Planning Institute's weakness (a planning counterpart to the AIA), which suspended the publication of *The Planners' Journal* during wartime and was about to cease operations.

As previously highlighted, one of Kocher's endeavors was to establish a branch of CIAM in the United States. Many of his letters to Walter Gropius, dated in the late 1930s, focus on convincing the German architect to lead the initiative. Gropius always expressed his willingness to join any initiative, yet his refusal to lead CIAM because, "as a newcomer" he "must be careful not to take the initiative which must come from Americans."[29] Although Kocher was unsuccessful on this front, he continued to develop his ideas in ASPA, which absorbed all members of the still-underdeveloped CIAM New York chapter. With a focus on neighborhood planning, both via the CIAM chapter and in his Revere House, Kocher was again one of the field's pioneers—pointing the direction to follow. ASPA's interest in community planning and housing was exemplified by several theoretical proposals by its members—meant to compete with speculative builders in a post-war construction-boom scenario—such as the "American Village," designed by Kahn (the association's second president) and used as a token of modern architecture's social engagement.

Initially, membership in the ASPA was only accessible by invitation, specifically for those who had "taken a stand on behalf of modern architecture and have given some proof of accomplishment in this field," either building or writing.[30] In the first membership list, there were prominent names, like Kahn, George Howe, Eero Saarinen, Paul Rudolph, Philip Johnson, Richard Neutra, Pietro Belluschi, Walter Gropius, Marcel Breuer, Serge Chermayeff, Jose Luis Sert, Sigfried Giedion, and of course, A. Lawrence Kocher. The reticence of Gropius taking a leading role in any American association proved wise with regards to the second aim of the ASPA: to promote the creation of a fully American version of the modern movement. Hudnut elaborated,

> I think it would be greatly to the advantage of our cause if our organization could have from the beginning an American

Figure 6.35. A. Lawrence Kocher. 1942. Revere House. Revere Copper and Bass Inc. Booklet entitled "Homes to Enrich Our National Standard of Living." Front page.

those living in the house. Straight lines, smooth surfaces, right use of materials, simple proportions and pure colors are all applicable to the house we require.

The designer of this improved house for better living will work more and more with the manufacturer using machines. His materials are no longer largely restricted to the "natural" ones, but now include many with specific fitness for modern building such as plastics, glass, plywood, asbestos-cement, copper, and metal alloys.

More Diversification in Tomorrow's Homes

The curse of monotony has been the dread of many who think of building or buying a house. But the form of a mass produced house need not have the rigidity of a mold. The form can vary with the requirements, with the size of the family to be accommodated, with the variation in the use and the diversity of arrangement of the parts of the house. The dull monotony of row upon row of similar shaped dwellings is avoided by the adoption of a few house types placed, not in straight-line rows, but with intermediate setbacks from the property line and with groupings in accordance with a developed and landscaped community plan.

The construction system shown in this booklet has, by virtue of its large panels, the inherent advantage of producing exteriors that vary in contour. Flat surfaces such as cards, when set up at right angles to each other, can produce radiating planes; in the same way, walls can be made to continue the extent of space from the interior to the outside of the house. By this method a house can be designed that gives the effect of "unlimited space."

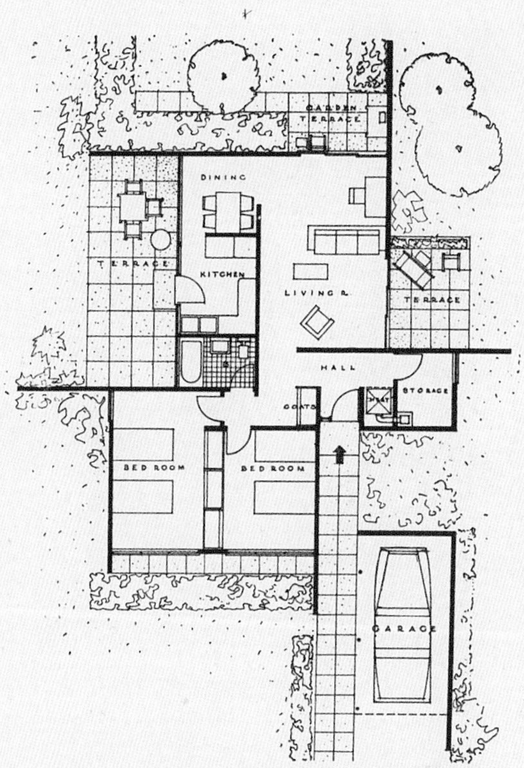

The room arrangement, showing how the living and sleeping parts of the house are separated from each other. There is access to terraces and garden spaces on all sides. The living room can be expanded to include sitting or garden terraces. A separate dining alcove is provided, usable also as part of the living room. The dining terrace is accessible directly from the kitchen.

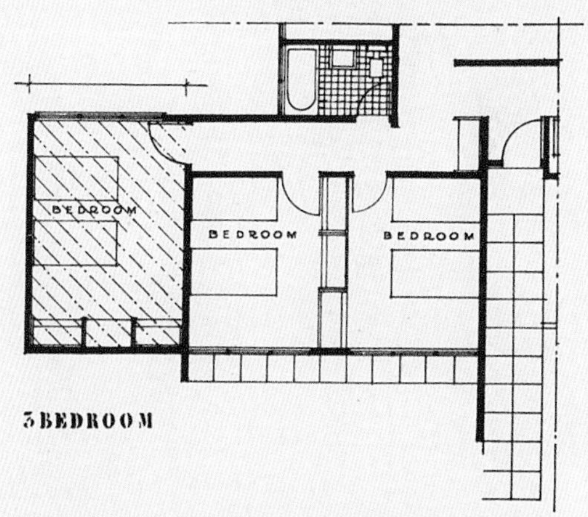

Additions to the house are possible, as shown in this 3-bedroom plan. A fourth room can be produced by extending the length of the storage room from the front hall.

6

Figure 6.36. A. Lawrence Kocher. 1942. Revere House. Revere Copper and Bass Inc. Booklet entitled "Homes to Enrich Our National Standard of Living." Initial standard-size floor plan and additions.

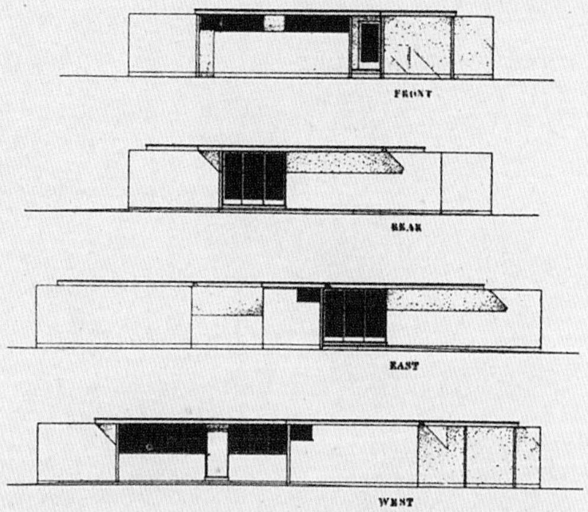

Exterior views or elevations. Exterior appearance can be varied by interchanging the wall elements, depending upon the requirements of the room arrangement.

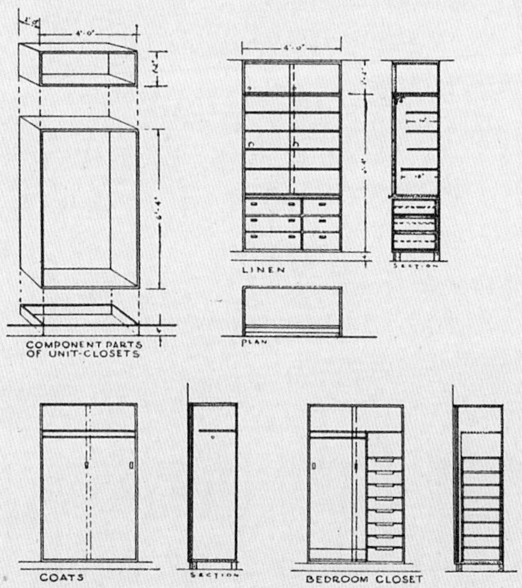

"Essential" storage reduced to standard-size units. These closets for specific purposes would be factory produced and would serve as partitions as well as structural elements for the house.

The house illustrated is built with 36 units that are to be factory produced. Their size is as large as present-day trucks can transport to the site. Each part is complete with its connecting devices, insulation, installed fixtures, surface finishes, its wiring and copper tubing for plumbing and panel heating. Panel heating is an improved method whereby entire walls or floors or ceilings supply a room with heat.

Because of their large expanse they need be kept only gently warm. Drafts are avoided and there is never any feeling of "chilliness," yet the air temperature in the room need never be raised to a point unhealthfully high.

Panels for walls are of two or three standard sizes up to the truck maximum of twenty feet. The same window unit is repeated singly or in multiples throughout the house. The windows are installed also as large solid panel units, complete with their surrounding frames and walls.

By the use of these large units, the planning of the house is at once made free, flexible, and irregular in contour, thus avoiding standardization and monotony. This is a result of architectural juggling with spacious walls rather than with constricted units only three or four feet in width. Garden courts at two, three, or four sides of the house occur naturally. And these courts can become terraces for sitting and dining. The interior rooms can all have access to the garden, the yard, or the terraces.

The variety of the exterior can be unlimited, but always with sufficient uniformity of elements to relate all of the houses of this kind harmoniously in a community. Entrance is by a paved walk from the street or garage. Sleeping rooms

7

Figure 6.37. A. Lawrence Kocher. 1942. Revere House. Revere Copper and Bass Inc. Booklet entitled "Homes to Enrich Our National Standard of Living." Modular furniture.

are segregated from the living areas for quiet and convenience. The living room and dining space are at the rear, with access to the garden by sliding doors. Kitchen and bathroom adjoin one another and are prefabricated as complete units. There is a storage room off the hall which can be enlarged as required to fulfill a multitude of uses, such as a work room, office, child's room or sewing room. There are spacious and organized closets.

Storage for Everything

The 19th Century writer, Thoreau, listed 32 articles as ample for his manner of living at Walden Pond. Today, the homeowner with 20th Century habits surrounds himself with paraphernalia and possessions which overflow the storage and closet space provided even by the medium-size house.

For many years I have collected listings of the articles owned and used (many of them useless) by the average American family. These lists have been obtained from Government surveys, from farm

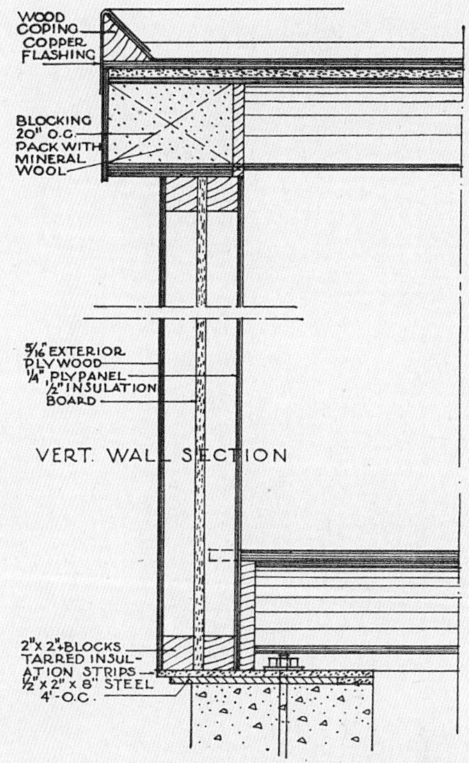

The house structure. Walls are composed of undulating plypanels with rigid insulation at their core and under the roof level. No studs. Floors of plypanels in compression support finish flooring consisting of large size plywood panels with hardwood surface.

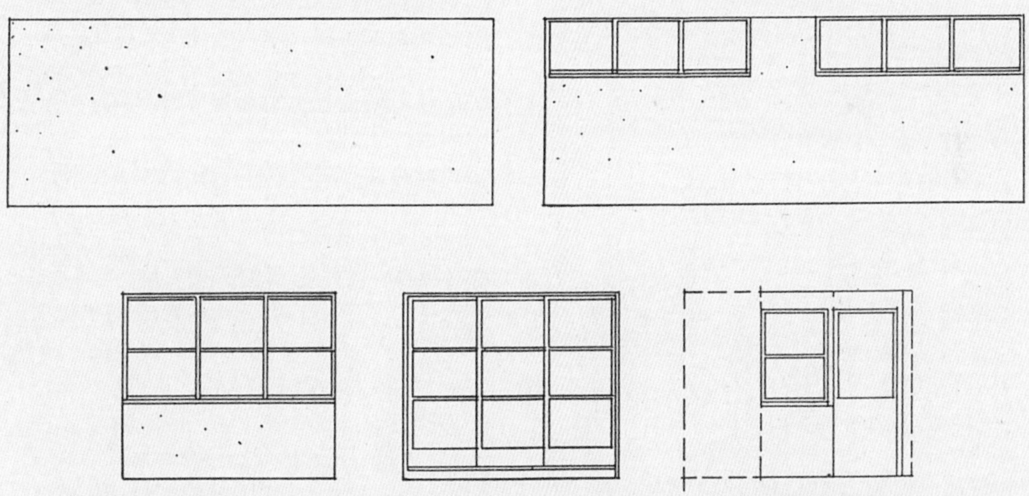

The size of the house elements is the maximum for truck transportation. Two trucks could deliver the entire house structure. Trucking zones would serve a radial distance of approximately 200 miles from the regional factory.

8

Figure 6.38. A. Lawrence Kocher. 1942. Revere House. Revere Copper and Bass Inc. Booklet entitled "Homes to Enrich Our National Standard of Living." Modular façade and construction details.

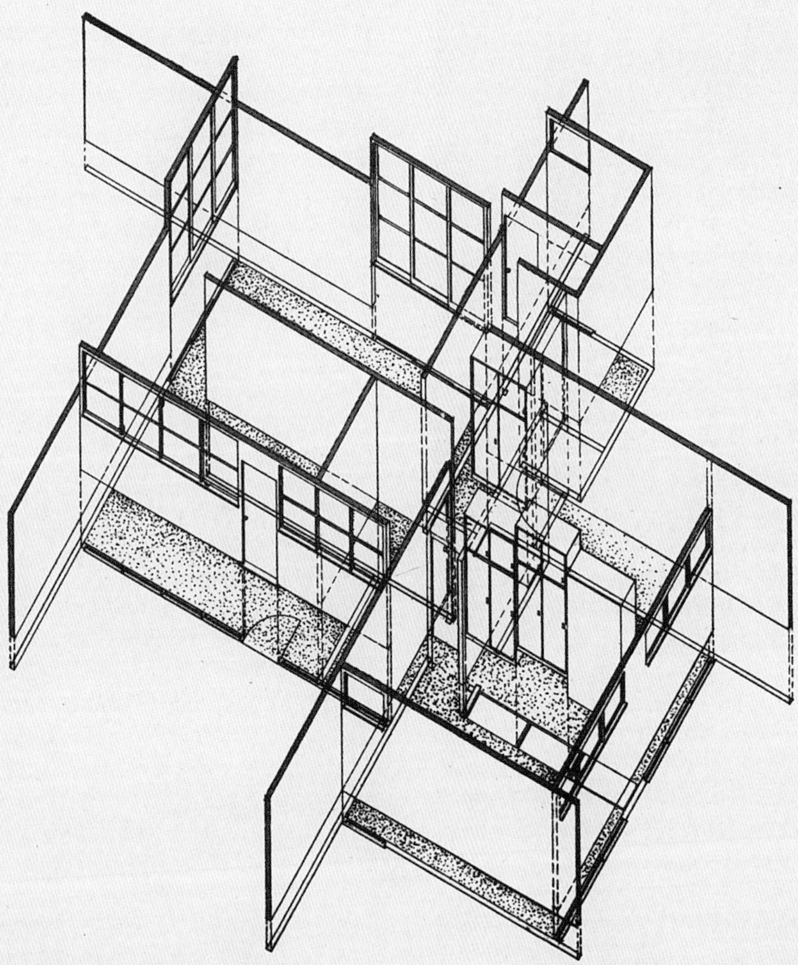

The "large unit" principle on which the house is based includes complete wall and cabinet units which are hoisted in place with the aid of a derrick mounted on a truck. Walls are joined to adjacent walls at right angles to one another. There are no end-to-end connections. This method permits erection speed, as well as variation in the location of walls.

titions. And the same closets would become the internal supporting structure of the house, thereby eliminating closets as so much dead weight.

Such a house as this could bring you the advantages of fresh air, sunlight and the maximum of outdoor living without sacrifice of privacy. It could have the natural charm of a country cottage with its garden and flowers and vines, and at the same time provide you with every new convenience and comfort that modern developments make possible. Through the use of desirable materials such as copper, it would protect you against high upkeep expense for a lifetime. It is a house that in a very real sense could be a home of happiness for you and for your children.

10

Figure 6.39. A. Lawrence Kocher. 1942. Revere House. Revere Copper and Bass Inc. Booklet entitled "Homes to Enrich Our National Standard of Living." Axonometric view of the construction system.

> flavor and look less like something imported. In my judgement, the word 'International Style' has done infinite damage to the cause of modern architecture, and the sooner the word 'international' is forgotten, the better.[31]

Both the ASPA's objectives—the incorporation of planning to the architectural discipline and the development of an American version of the European modern movement—were among Kocher's longstanding aspirations. Neighborhood planning was a latent feature in many of Kocher's projects, as in the Aluminaire House, and a very evident goal in many others like the "Real Estate Subdivisions for Low-Cost Housing," or the numerous designs for the Cotton Textile Institute.[32] The search of an American modern style was explored in Kocher's research and in his designs through the consideration of prefabrication, catalog construction, industrialized building technologies, and transient dwelling forms related to the automobile as essential elements of a renovated American vernacular architecture. The search for the fulfillment of these two objectives finds its best expression within the Architectural Center, Kocher's last project developed while at Black Mountain College.

In Kocher's mind, neither of these objectives would be achieved without a deep change in architectural education methodology. In 1943, Kocher was granted a leave of absence at Black Mountain College that meant his effective detachment from the institution. Along with his family, Kocher moved back to their house in Forest Hills in Queens, New York. He teamed up with Howard Dearstyne, another Black Mountain College faculty member, to investigate how architectural education could be reframed through the creation of a new institution, the Architectural Center. This was the starting point for a new and durable partnership with Dearstyne, one that lasted until Kocher's retirement.[33] The drawings and texts of the Architectural Center proposal were developed in a space lent to them by the photographer F. S. Lincoln within his New York City studio.[34] Using the experimental pamphlet format—as in the Revere House—the project was published in the magazine *New Pencil Points* and was developed in two analytical schemes.[35] The organizational management of the institution was defined by a graphic diagram drawn by Herbert Matter. The Architectural Center would serve as a national clearing house for four groups of activities, represented as branches connected to a central institution: industry, architecture and engineering private practices, architecture and engineering schools, and research laboratories. There was a fifth branch devoted to the dissemination of the institution's work in the media and to its public relations. At the core of Matter's diagram was the Architectural Center's mission statement of "uniting research with planning and design; design with experimental construction; and experiment with the 'trial-by-use' of model buildings."[36] **(Figure 6.42)** In the connections between the diagram's center and the different branches, are descriptions outlining several ways in which each branch cooperates; the authors considered the center's final aim to (once again) be summarized by one of those omnipresent mottos of the era: "better living."[37] The pamphlet explained its scope by comparing it to a medical center:

> The Architectural Center will have a significance to building similar to that which a medical center has to medicine. It will be an institution for the investigation and study of human, social, economic, and technical aspects of building, for the working out of sound and basic solutions to the diverse and complex problems confronting planning and architecture, and for the actual execution of construction projects.[38]

In its physical arrangement, the Architectural Center project encompassed the construction of three buildings, each with clearly differentiated programs, meticulously depicted in the booklet. **(Figure 6.43)** The Administrative and Design Building was at the core of the complex and hosted the main program. A public lobby connected the administrative office, the cafeteria, and spaces related to the dissemination of knowledge—a lecture room and exhibition spaces. In addition, a majority of the first floor was devoted to research and design, including a large drafting room, a research library, and prescription-writing offices. The basement contained the general storage and shipping room, the model shop, a blue-print room, press room, bindery, photographic studio, and a large recreational area for staff. The second floor housed the business administration offices, conference rooms, and entertainment rooms, along with special work ateliers and lodging for visiting designers and staff. **(Figures 6.44 to 6.49)** The second structure was the Human Environmental Laboratories Building, composed of two perpendicular wings. One wing included classrooms and an experimental theater to investigate the use of audiovisuals, while the other was a greenhouse-like structure with an aural-visual-tactile studies lab (to study human reactions when interacting with full scale-models), a solar laboratory, and workshops. **(Figures 6.50 to 6.53)** The third component of the complex was the Shop and Assembly Building. It was meant to serve as an interface between industry and creative design. Its programmatic focus was the production of mock-ups and models to test the functionality of new construction systems and components. The building included engineering offices; a shop drafting room; a woodworking shop; metal works, including fabrication, die casting, and stamp shops; and space for trial assembly and final testing, preparing final deliverable prototypes to industry. It is a lineal factory-like structure supported with a prefabricated steel frame and naturally lit by roof monitors. Adjacent to this building, there is a large yard for a building plant and material storage. **(Figures 6.54 and 6.55)**

The Architecture Center is laid out on a hypothetical site, its buildings connected by a triangular path. In addition to the main building, the project foresaw the construction of an experimental settlement, similar to that of the Bauhaus, to test the prototyped houses under actual living conditions. They would host visiting and permanent researchers and their families. The main goal of the project—the tight connection between architectural education, practice, and industry—proved revelatory of a trend soon extended to the many American schools that established their research laboratories, sometimes directly funded by industrial companies, during the following years. Kocher reinforced,

> the fundamental purpose of the Center is to relate design with industry. Far from competing with industry, it is the intention of the Center to work closely with manufacturers, to the mutual advantage of both.[39]

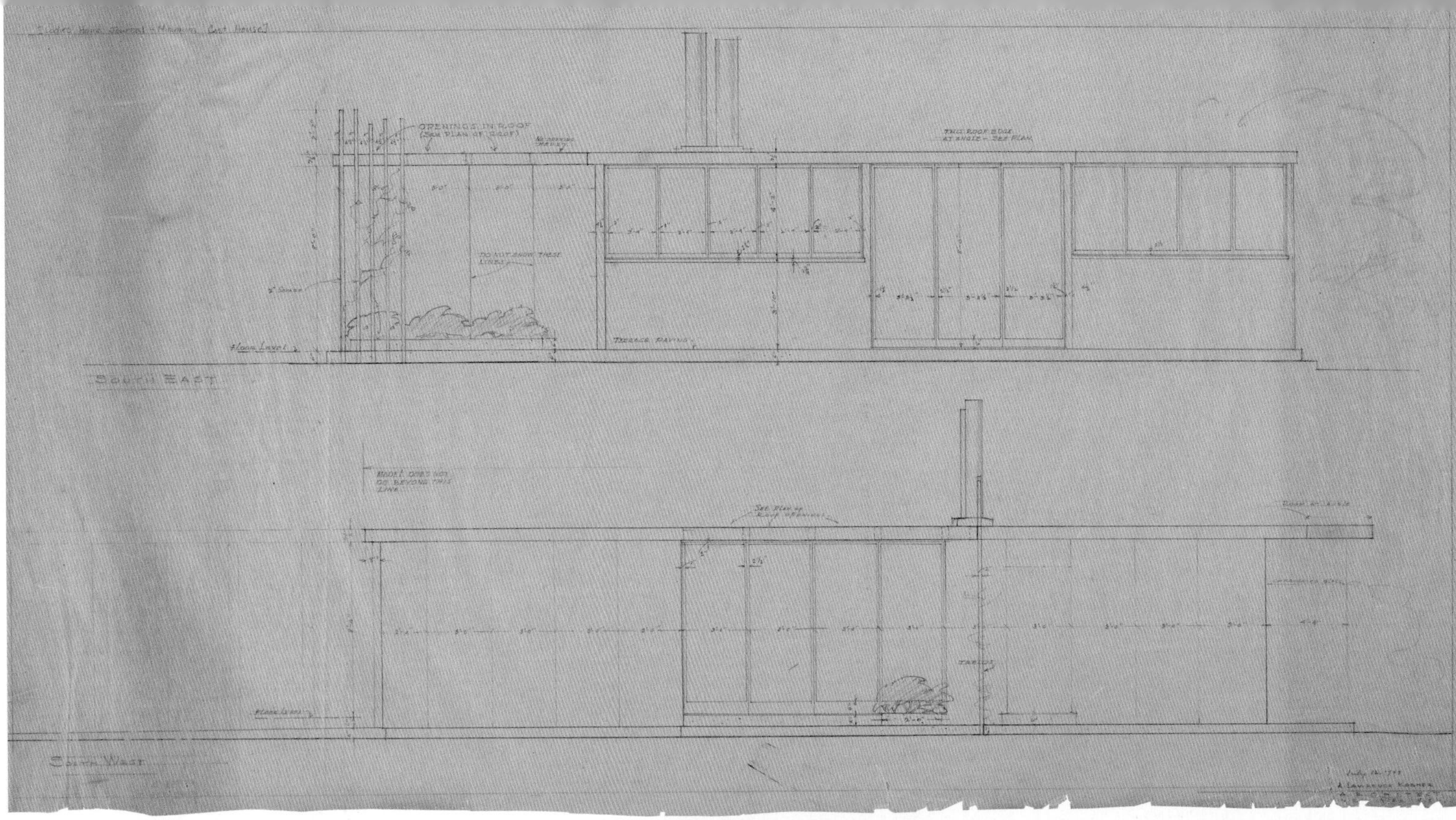

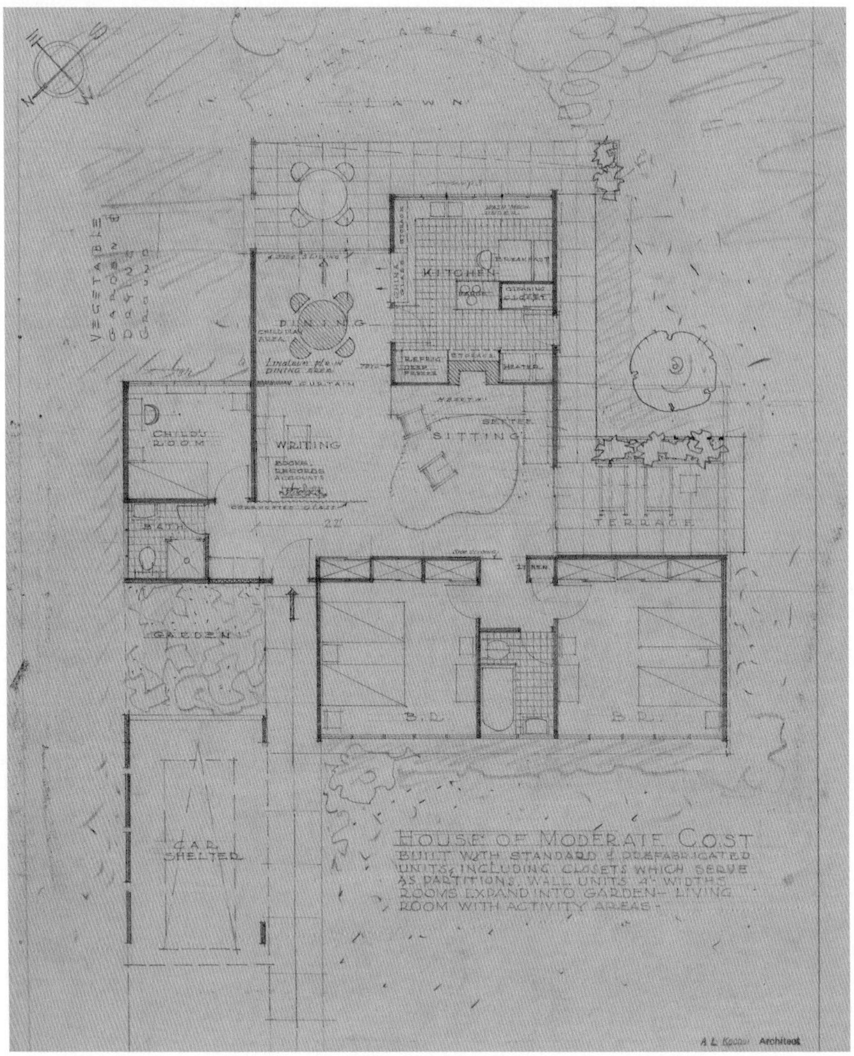

Figure 6.40. A. Lawrence Kocher. 1945. House of Moderate Cost. Elevations.
Figure 6.41. A. Lawrence Kocher. 1945. House of Moderate Cost. Floor plan.

The Center was supposed to offer a comprehensive training in architecture, engineering, planning, factory practice, construction superintendence, and other professions related to building construction. Students would effectively participate in conducting experiments, fabrication, and building operations on the field. **(Figure 6.56)** Therefore, from a pedagogical standpoint, the design was also firmly aligned to Kocher's design-build ideology and to his previous attempts of changing American architectural education in the 1930s; the Bauhaus and his correspondences with Walter Gropius were his main inspirational sources.[40] The Architectural Center can be understood as a criticism of architectural education in the early 1940s, as Kocher and Dearstyne revealed,

> the most efficacious teaching combines theoretical training with practical experience. Our architectural schools have for generations concentrated upon theory and neglected, almost altogether, actual participation in building operations.[41]

As the *New Pencil Points* magazine highlights, a relevant trait of the *Architectural Center* pamphlet is its iconography. It includes a series of images ranging from animal nests and hives to anonymous traditional structures, and from technical objects to modern buildings. **(Figures 6.57 and 6.58)** This catalog of images has a twofold purpose: it simultaneously tried to define an extended field of vernacular architecture that would include animal dwellings, industrial artifacts, and the work of anonymous builders, while also establishing continuity between this expanded vernacular and modern architecture. This interest in the expanded vernacular aligned with Kocher's prior research on early American architecture, his work at Colonial Williamsburg, and with the findings and iconography of Albert Frey's book *In Search of a Living Architecture* (1939), and Sigfried Giedion's *Building in France. Building in Iron. Building in Ferro-Concrete* (1928).[42]

The *Architectural Center* pamphlet can also be regarded as a precedent of a postwar shift towards anonymous design and vernacular culture which informed seminal publications, such as Sigfried Giedion's *Mechanization Takes Command: A Contribution to Anonymous History* (1948), Sybil Moholy-Nagy's *Native Genius in Anonymous Architecture* (1957), and the later works of practitioners like ATBAT-Afrique and Team 10, along with cultural researchers, like Bernard Rudofsky and Karl von Frisch in the 1970s.[43] It also preceded, by more than 40 years, the direct connection between modern European architecture and the American industrial vernacular revealed in Reyner Banham's *Concrete Atlantis*.[44]

Once the *Architectural Center* pamphlet was published in *New Pencil Points*, Kocher started a promotional campaign that included the mass-mailing of reproductions of the work to numerous private and public institutions, universities, research institutes, museums, libraries, popular and specialized magazines, and prominent individuals in the field of architecture, including the U.S. Senate, the Office of the Vice President, the *Reader's Digest*, and Revere Copper and Brass Inc. Kocher additionally wrote to the *Architectural Review*, inquiring about the possibilities of publishing *Architectural Center* in future issues. They diverted Kocher to the *Architectural Journal*, where a simplified version was published in 1945. The responses to his letters clearly show that the design of the Architectural Center was received with sympathy yet did not raise much direct support or additional enthusiasm. This lack of interest was likely ignited by two main factors. First, its harsh criticism of the American architectural education system and its possible interference with the future interests of private construction companies could be interpreted as un-American activities in a wartime homefront context. Second, the project could be perceived as still anchored to the New Deal ethos, which would soon be overcome in the post-war period. The pamphlet could even be likened with totalitarian positions; a token of *Architectural Center's* critical reception by the architectural profession as a whole can be found in a note published in the *Illinois Society of Architects Monthly Bulletin,* stating that "the whole scheme reads like a New Deal Plan, inspired by Soviet Russia."[45]

The cold reception of *Architectural Center* did not present very promising prospects for Kocher and Dearstyne, and Kocher's return to Black Mountain was unthinkable due to the economic hardships that the institution suffered during the war. Kocher and Dearstyne devoted nearly one year to research and production for the *Architectural Center* pamphlet. To economically support his family during this time, Kocher worked part-time for Donald Deskey's industrial design office at the International Building of the Rockefeller Center in New York City.[46] From the early fall of 1943 through the summer of 1944, Kocher was in charge of the architectural research section of Deskey's firm, where he produced a memorandum describing a standardized mechanical core for mass-produced houses based on the recommendations of a 1938 Federal Housing Administration report on home standardization. By 1944, Kocher was 59 years old and decided to move to Williamsburg, Virginia, to gain a more solid position that would allow him to carry on his practice and research. He accepted a position as Editor of Architectural Records at the Colonial Williamsburg Foundation.[47] Concurrently, to maintain his involvement with academia, he also agreed to serve as lecturer in Fine Arts and Architecture at Thomas Jefferson's alma mater, the College of William and Mary in Williamsburg.

As the Editor of Architectural Records at Colonial Williamsburg, Kocher's first endeavor was to compile a glossary of 18th-century architectural terms, translating them into contemporary language. He would continue this compilation until his death, which is now archived in the A. Lawrence Kocher Papers at Colonial Williamsburg. Besides this more personal endeavor, Kocher's primary work at the institution was to produce reports about the different buildings in the reconstructed colonial capital. Kocher soon incorporated his associate Dearstyne with the institution and together they produced 45 new reports and five addenda to previous reports from 1944 to 1954.[48] The reports focused on both reconstructed or in-the-process-of-reconstruction Williamsburg buildings: from the most prominent Governor's Palace to the smaller works of the George Wythe Kitchen and outbuildings. Typically, these reports included a narrative stating the phases of previous reconstructions and describing the current state of original and new architectural elements. The narrative is usually supplemented with a very comprehensive graphic documentation, including measured floor plans, elevations, sections, details, and many times illustrations from 18th-century architecture handbooks to establish the criteria for future interventions. Many

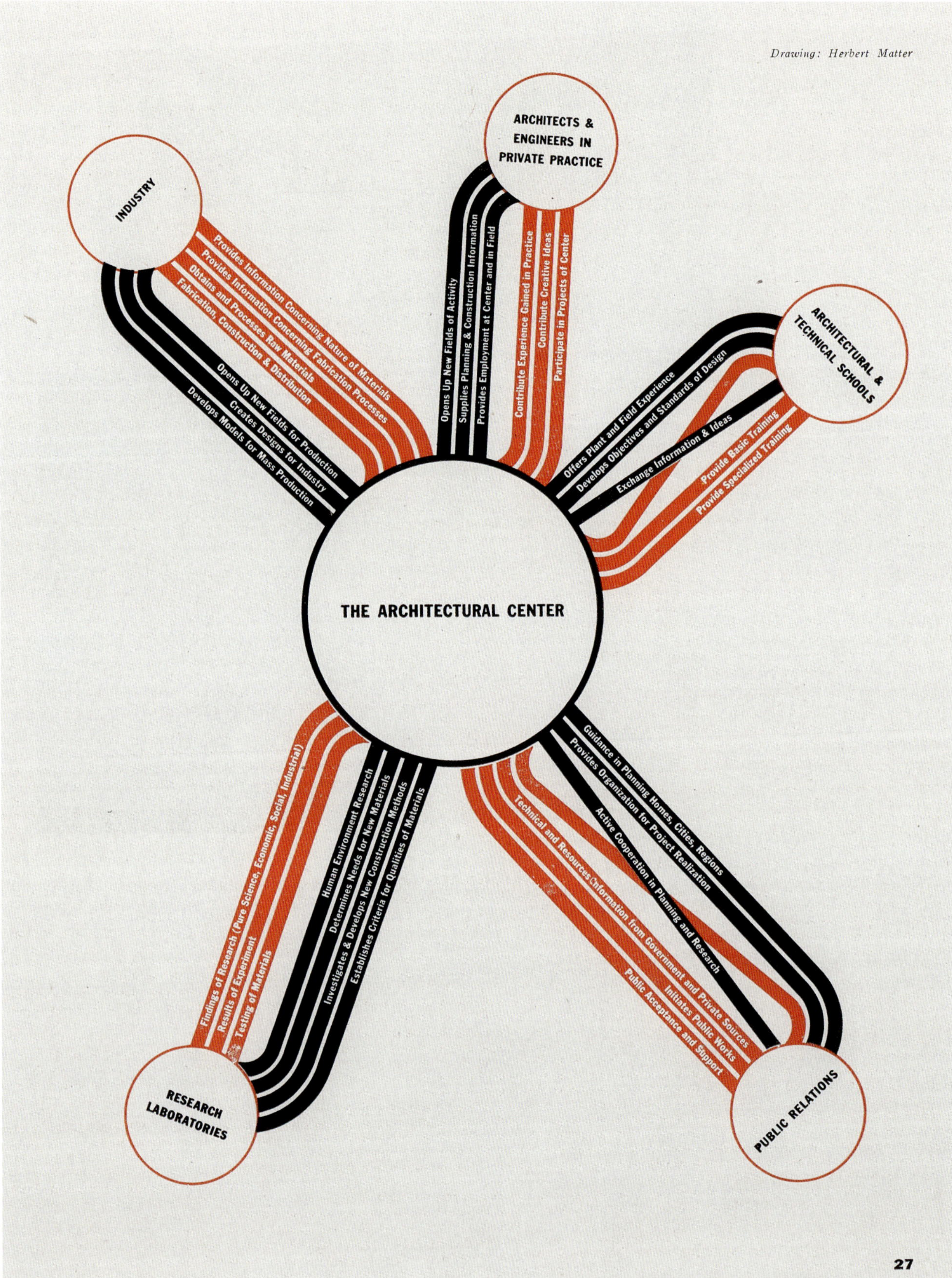

Figure 6.42. A. Lawrence Kocher. 1943. The Architectural Center. Organizational management of the institution. Graphic diagram drawn by Herbert Matter.

reports incorporated a color study, photos of previous works, a hardware schedule, an archeological report, and an annotated bibliography. The purpose of these reports was to create an archival record inventorying each building's current status, and to produce guidelines for future interventions, which were still supposed to align with the 1928 decalogue created by the advisory board of the Williamsburg restoration chaired by Kocher.[49]

Not all of the building reports follow the same pattern. In fact, the most interesting of these documents was the one that Kocher and Dearstyne produced in 1950 about the proposal of establishing a new cultural center at the College of William and Mary, and of the construction of an extension to the Wren Building to house its activities.[50] The authors praise the "intention of expanding, in the near future, the facilities for the study of the fine arts" as an "indication of a desire on the part of the College to provide at William and Mary a soil friendly to the growth of cultural things."[51] They also supported the idea to expand the Wren Building, as long as it was executed "in accordance with a plan originally conceived by its late-17th-century builders and later given definite form in a proposal of Thomas Jefferson."[52]

This report was followed by a very comprehensive and detailed paper about the Wren Building, authored by Kocher and Dearstyne and published in the American Notes section of the *Journal of the Society of Architectural Historians* in 1951.[53] The paper provided three documentary evidences that "the original builders never intended the building to remain U-shaped."[54] The first evidence is a letter from the trustees appointed to supervise the construction of the college to the governor, Sir Edmund Andros, on April 22, 1697, reporting the end of the construction—"two sides of the designed square of the colledge [sic]."[55] The second was a statement by Robert Beverley on his History & Present State of Virginia (1705) with the intention of the college leadership to finish the existing construction in the form of a quadrangle. The third and most irrefutable proof was a plan of the building drafted by Theodorick Bland in his Map of Williamsburg where the Wren building is depicted with the already constructed part drawn in a continuous black line, and the future addition drawn in a dotted line, forming an almost square shape with a court at the center. Despite all this evidence, the building was never completed due to a lack of funds, although the idea of the quadrangle was never abandoned.

At the request of Lord Dunmore, Governor of the Colony of Virginia at that time, Jefferson drew a plan for the completion of the quadrangle between 1771 and 1772.[56] In this obscure and little-known document, lacking in many monographs about Jeffersonian architecture, the future president planned an almost symmetrical addition to the existing wings and intended to continue the arcade of the old building's west façade and around the court. The drawing also showed the idea of opening passages to allow the building to be crossed both in north–south and in east–west directions in the typical fashion of English quadrangles. Kocher and Dearstyne provided evidence that the college administrators had started executing Jefferson's plans, quoting a note in the Virginia Gazette on September 3, 1772, announcing the appointment of a committee to procure an expense estimate and to "study proposal from those who want to undertake the construction works." Kocher and Dearstyne also found entries in the Bursar's Book of the College for November of 1774 to pay for the materials stored on site to build the addition. According to Kocher and Dearstyne's hypothesis, the foundations of the building were laid but the construction was interrupted in April of 1775 due to the start of the Revolutionary War.[57]

The most important point of the Wren Building paper was the credit given to Jefferson's project. The foundation remains were unearthed during excavations conducted immediately west of the Wren Building by Colonial Williamsburg archeologist James K. Knight. The excavations were executed during September and October of 1950, three months after the original Kocher and Dearstyne report (dated on June 9, 1950) and completely proved the assumptions made in the document, based on previously very partial evidence discovered accidentally in 1940 when planting a new row of trees.[58] As the 1951 paper demonstrates, the foundations matched almost exactly with an inverted version of Jefferson's drawing. **(Figures 6.59 to 6.61)** The Wren Building report and subsequent research article were proof of Kocher's persistent interest in and close familiarity with Jefferson's body of work—from his professional beginnings in Charlottesville to his final stages at Williamsburg. Furthermore, Kocher's interest in American vernacular architecture was reignited by all the reconstruction work of the historic structures at Williamsburg and the research on architectural history topics.

This reinvigorated interest in American vernacular architecture can also be perceived in Kocher's lectures for his new teaching appointment at the College of William and Mary, where he abandoned his previous experimental pedagogies and embraced the more traditional format of master classes. Kocher's process of preparing the lectures during this period helped him to reconsider and refine many of his long-standing research topics. A good example of these recapitulations included his lecture about the architectural handbooks archived in the John D. Rockefeller Jr. Library in Williamsburg.[59] The lecture's delivery date was not stated anywhere in the draft document, but its references to "the Wren Building of the College" suggest that his audience was acquainted with William and Mary's campus and, therefore, it was primarily aimed at the students at this institution. The lecture starts with the reminder that the use of handbooks did not become common until 1700, and no building erected before that date can claim the aid of such publications. Kocher explains that in the early 18th century, a self-defined architect and carpenter called William Halfpenny was the most prolific popular author of these kind of books to be imported into the American colonies, most of them published as small-format pattern books aimed primarily to workmen.[60] The most influential author in the colonies was nevertheless Batty Langley, who also produced small-format pattern books. [61] These modest publications coexisted with more luxurious folio-size publications as James Gibbs' *Book of Architecture* (1728) and the neo-Palladian *Vitruvius Britannicus* by Colen Campbell, which, in lieu of depicting the construction of architectural elements, showed complete designs for different kinds of buildings and interior spaces.[62] Many of these books were specifically aimed to the American colonies; as Gibbs suggested in his introduction, the solutions offered by the book "might be useful to gentlemen building in remote parts where little assistance in design is to be secured."[63] Other authors, like Abraham Swan—in his 1757 book, *Designs in Architecture*—, provided plans

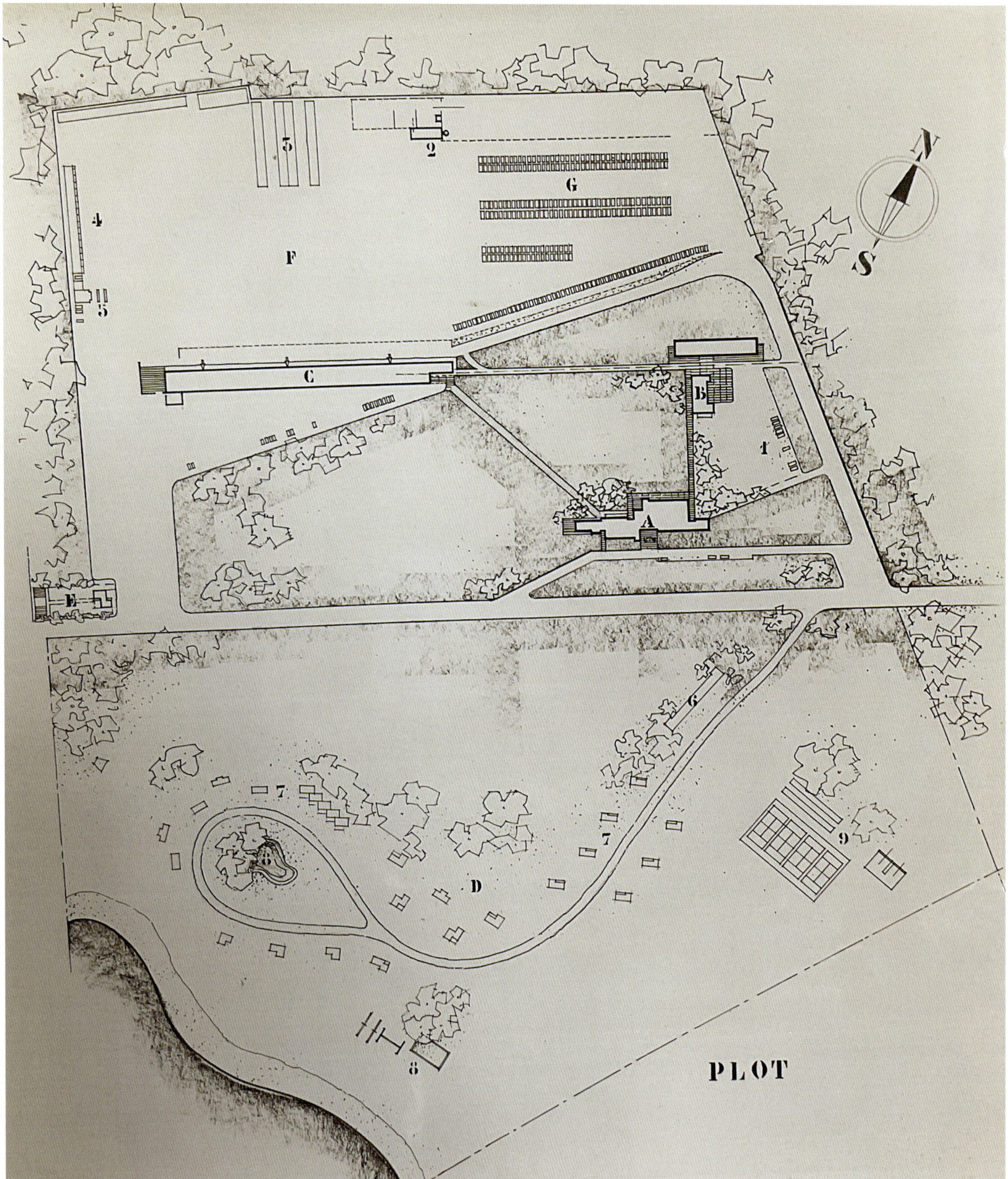

Figure 6.43. A. Lawrence Kocher. 1943. The Architectural Center. Physical layout of the buildings on the plot.

and elevations of less expensive examples that could be closely reproduced by colonial builders.

After enumerating the titles of the most influential books and their authors, Kocher offered evidence of their deployment in the Virginia colony using documentary sources, such as records of construction, where the purchase of these books is listed. Furthermore, the advertisement in the colonial newspapers, like *The Virginia Gazette*, of over 36 architectural handbooks between 1736 and 1775 offered confirmation that these publications were quite popular among the local builders. Kocher also provided material proof of several buildings, or elements of buildings, that closely followed models included in the handbooks.[64] The last paragraphs of the lecture draft praised the ingenuity of those colonial builders who transcended the acritical copy and produced a new architecture, blending the European treatises with local crafts and material procedures. Kocher had always considered the use of handbooks and the standardized building elements contained in them as the local ingredient to be added to the European functionalism for the creation of an American national modern architecture based on the updated concepts of standardization and prefabrication.

Kocher's new life in Williamsburg was financially supported by his work at the Colonial Williamsburg Foundation and supplemented by his part-time teaching and research, leaving some room for his architectural practice. His new commissions were predominantly local: neighbors wanting to enlarge, restore, or renovate their houses, private and governmental organizations that invited Kocher to submit theoretical housing projects or reconstruction plans for historic structures, and institutional commissions related to the Colonial Williamsburg Foundation. In late summer of 1945, after just arriving in Williamsburg and still finalizing the design of the House of Moderate Cost, Kocher received a local residential commission. It was a modest addition to the house of a Williamsburg neighbor, Mrs. M. Miller. Although there is no indication in the existing documentation of the addition's site placement in reference to the house, it seemed to be a small backyard pavilion comprised of two overlapping squares. One of these squares was a double-height painting studio with a large window likely facing south.[65] The other square was divided into an intermediate open porch and an enclosed L-shape containing a washroom and storage for the studio, a guest bedroom and bathroom, a kitchen with access only from the garden, and a stair to a future rental apartment on the upper floor. The architecture is very abstract and functional, using a similar material palette to other Kocher's projects, like plywood façades; industrial steel sashes; and cement, wood, and stone floors. **(Figures 6.62 and 6.63)**

In this last stage of his professional life, Kocher started the first of many works as an architectural advisor for the reconstruction and renovation of historic buildings. In December of 1945, he received the request of J. D. Rockefeller Jr. to assist Dr. Hugh. G. Rowell on the architectural research of Washington Irving's house, known as Sunnyside, in Tarrytown, New York.[66] Kocher spent one day taking notes on drawings and other documentary materials related to the house in several libraries of New York City and visited the house on March 16th and 17th of 1946.[67] By the end of the month, he had already produced his first nine-page report providing general advice and an evaluation of the building's current state. This first report stated that despite a very comprehensive record of the house—including photos from all periods of its lifetime and records of all changes and additions—it was advisable to keep the original van Tassel farmhouse along with all renovations carried out during Washington Irving's life, and discard all additions executed after 1859. Kocher advised all restoration of architectural elements to follow the exact details of a list of handbooks on the Gothic revival from 1830 to 1845, which he appended to the report. He also recommended not to level the irregularities of walls and roofs, to keep the natural effect of time and not to "replace age by adding newness."[68] Kocher closely followed the restoration's execution and submitted many other supplementary reports, some more technical—about foundations, water tightness, and even the preservation of the existing vines on the façades—others advising about paint, furniture, carpets, and general ornamentation in the house.[69] The work was finished by October of 1947 and the house immediately opened to the public.[70]

Kocher's historic heritage restoration works are extremely relevant as part of a strategy of building a common national identity in a country composed of immigrants with very different cultural backgrounds. Specifically, Kocher's work on Sunnyside at Tarrytown was one of many restorations for the "American Shrines"—houses of prominent national figures like George Washington, Thomas Jefferson, James Madison, Alexander Hamilton, and Paul Revere; these were preserved memorials where new generations could worship the American heroes and places where "present may learn from the past."[71] This collective effort, involving private and public institutions and individuals, was applied to various sites at that time: including fields, battlegrounds, forts, bridges, churches, and cemeteries. This reconstruction effort was one of the key tasks for many American architects who, like Kocher, were interested in traditional construction as the foundation for a new American architecture. Kocher contributed to this effort in Colonial Williamsburg beginning with his tenure as chairman for the 1928 advisory board of the colonial capital's restoration and culminating with his work as the Editor of Architectural Records, including the collaborative publication, alongside Dearstyne, of *Colonial Williamsburg: Its Buildings and Gardens* (1949). During the last stage of his professional life, his implication on the restoration of national historic heritage increased notably with various works, like the Airslie Farm's main residence in Keswick, Virginia (1951); Warner Hall Court House in Gloucester County, Virginia (1955–1960); Joseph Priestley House in Northumberland, Pennsylvania (including its relocation in 1955 to 1959); and the Isle of Wright Courthouse and The Groove House in Smithfield, Virginia (1960). Especially relevant was the reconstruction of multiple buildings in Historic Jamestowne (part of Virginia's Colonial National Historic Park), including row-housing (1956) and the Relic House (1962 to 1963).[72] **(Figures 6.64 and 6.65)**

Along with the ongoing historic restoration projects, Kocher's main endeavor during the 1950s was his and Dearstyne's book recording the material culture of Virginia between 1850 and 1900, specifically through the study of two photographers, George and Huestis Cook, and their work.[73] Entitled *Shadows in Silver*, the book was published in 1954, and although there are chapters illustrating

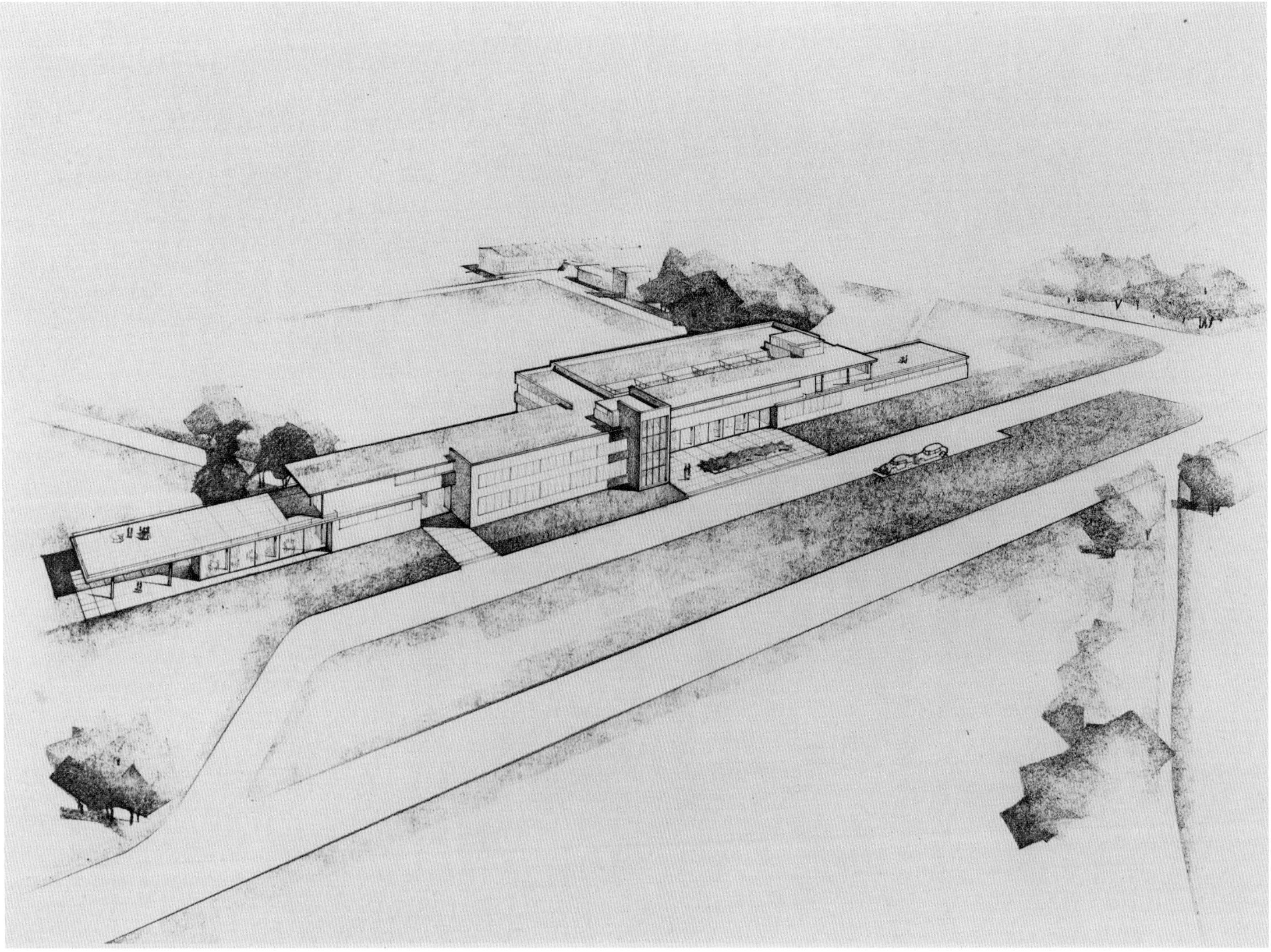

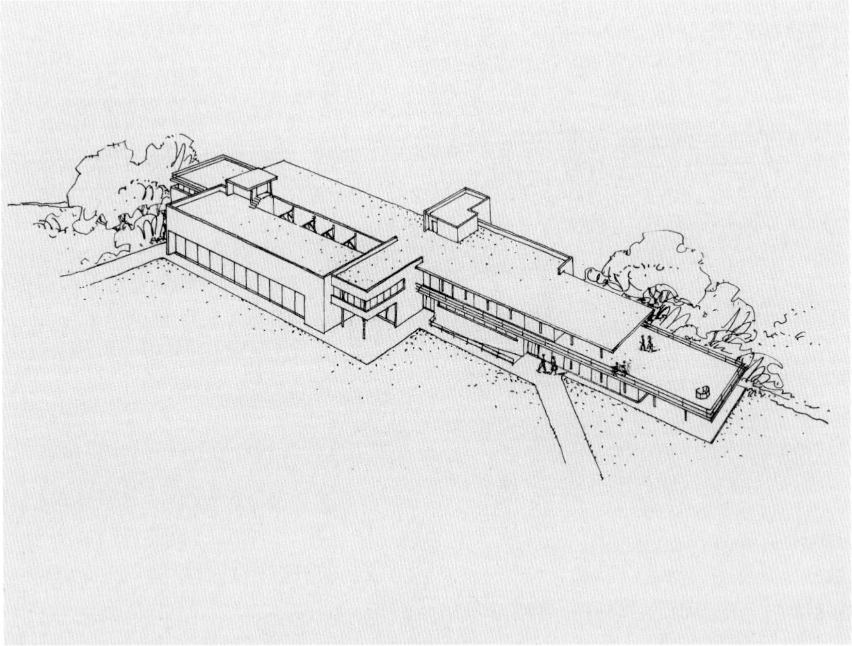

This page:

Figure 6.44. A. Lawrence Kocher. 1943. The Architectural Center. Administrative and Design Building. Perspective bird's-eye view from the south.

Figure 6.45. A. Lawrence Kocher. 1943. The Architectural Center. Administrative and Design Building. Perspective bird's-eye view from the north.

Next page:

Figure 6.46. A. Lawrence Kocher. 1943. The Architectural Center. Administrative and Design Building. Ground floor plan.

Figure 6.47. A. Lawrence Kocher. 1943. The Architectural Center. Administrative and Design Building. Basement and second floor plans.

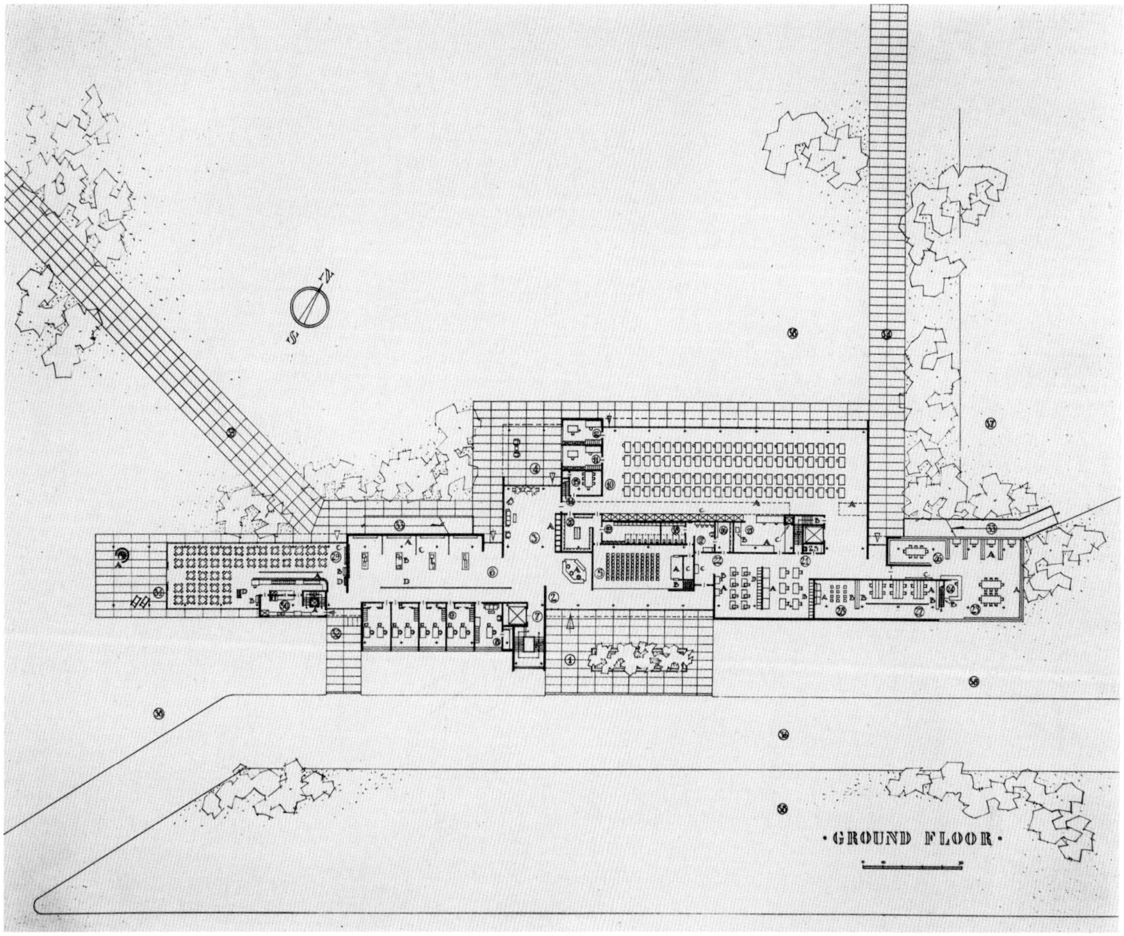
·GROUND FLOOR·

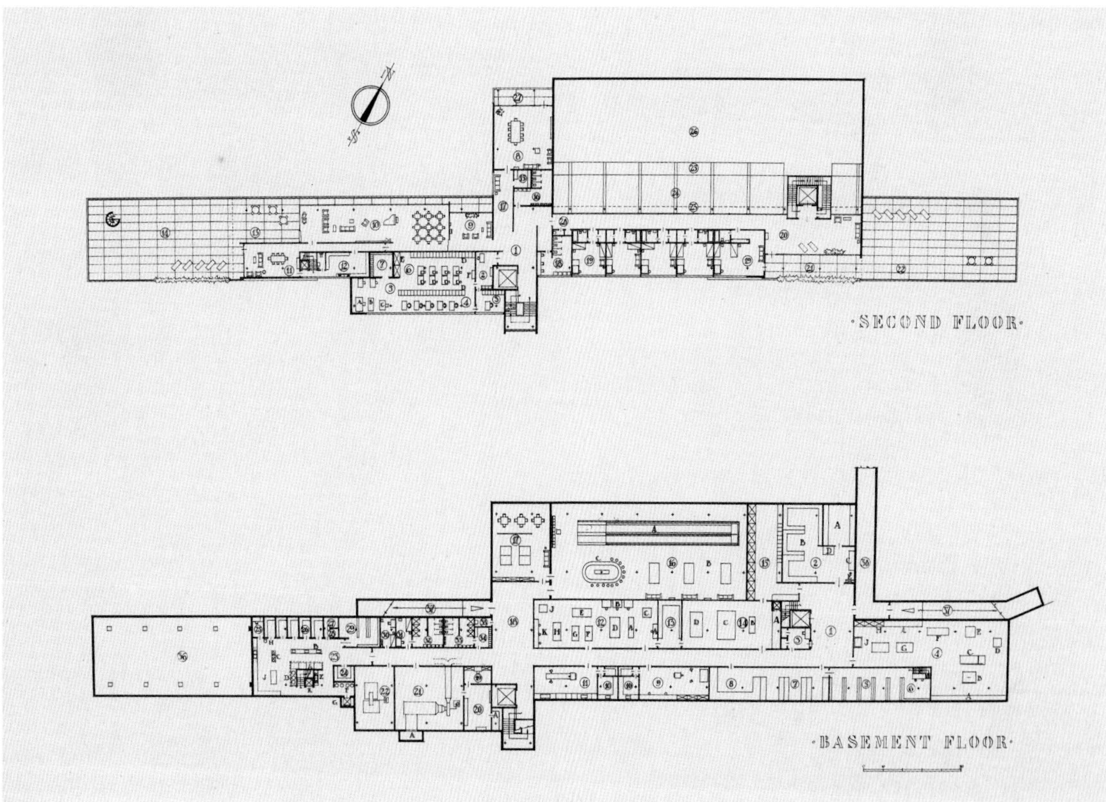
·SECOND FLOOR·
·BASEMENT FLOOR·

Figure 6.48. A. Lawrence Kocher. 1943. The Architectural Center. Administrative and Design Building. Rendering of the south façade entrance.
Figure 6.49. A. Lawrence Kocher. 1943. The Architectural Center. Administrative and Design Building. Rendering of the drafting room.

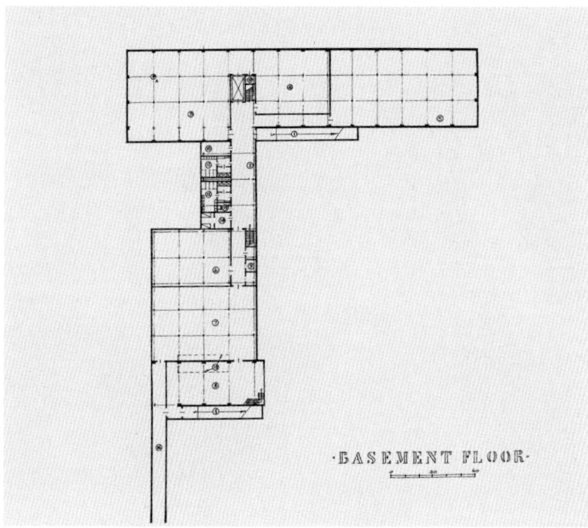

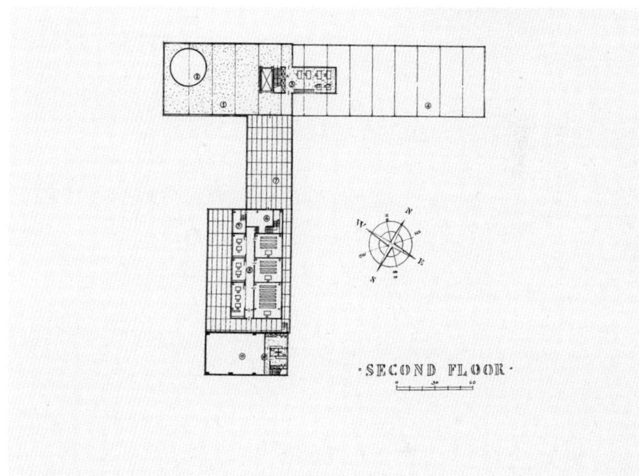

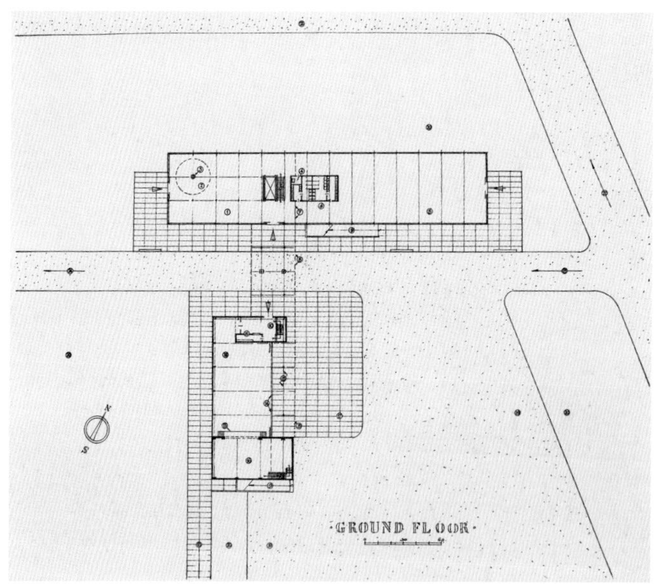

Figure 6.50. A. Lawrence Kocher. 1943. The Architectural Center. Human Environmental Laboratories Building. Perspective bird's-eye view from the south.
Figure 6.51. A. Lawrence Kocher. 1943. The Architectural Center. Human Environmental Laboratories Building. Basement floor plan.
Figure 6.52. A. Lawrence Kocher. 1943. The Architectural Center. Human Environmental Laboratories Building. Second floor plan.
Figure 6.53. A. Lawrence Kocher. 1943. The Architectural Center. Human Environmental Laboratories Building. Ground floor plan.

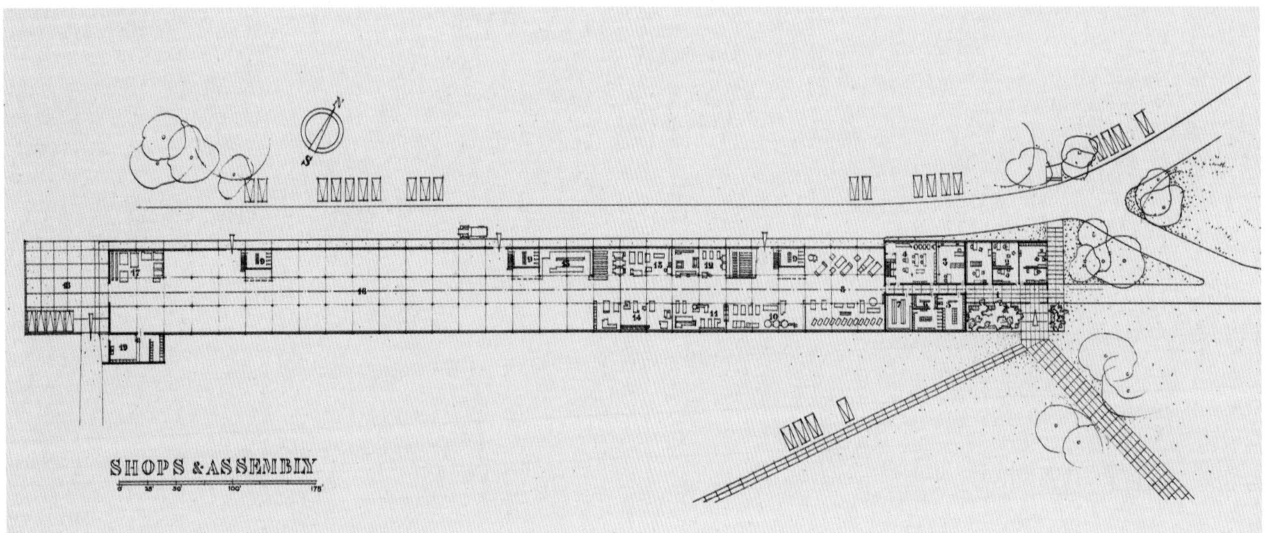

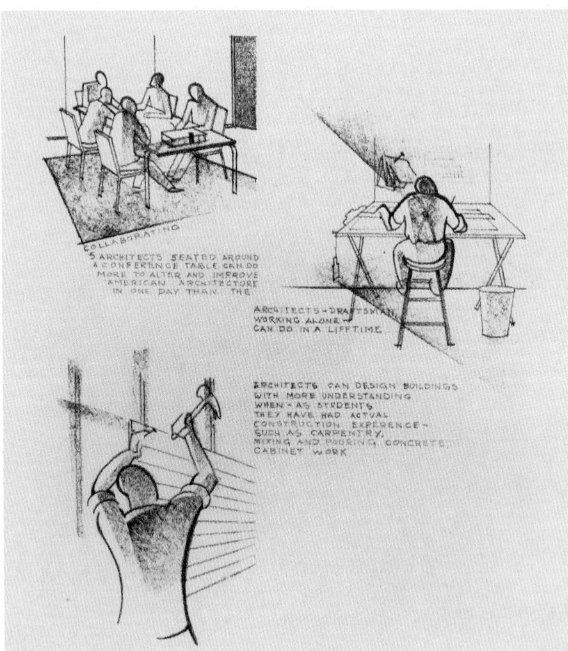

Figure 6.54. A. Lawrence Kocher. 1943. The Architectural Center. Shop and Assembly Building. Perspective bird's-eye view from the south.

Figure 6.55. A. Lawrence Kocher. 1943. The Architectural Center. Human Environmental Laboratories Building. Ground floor plan.

Figure 6.56. A. Lawrence Kocher. 1943. The Architectural Center.

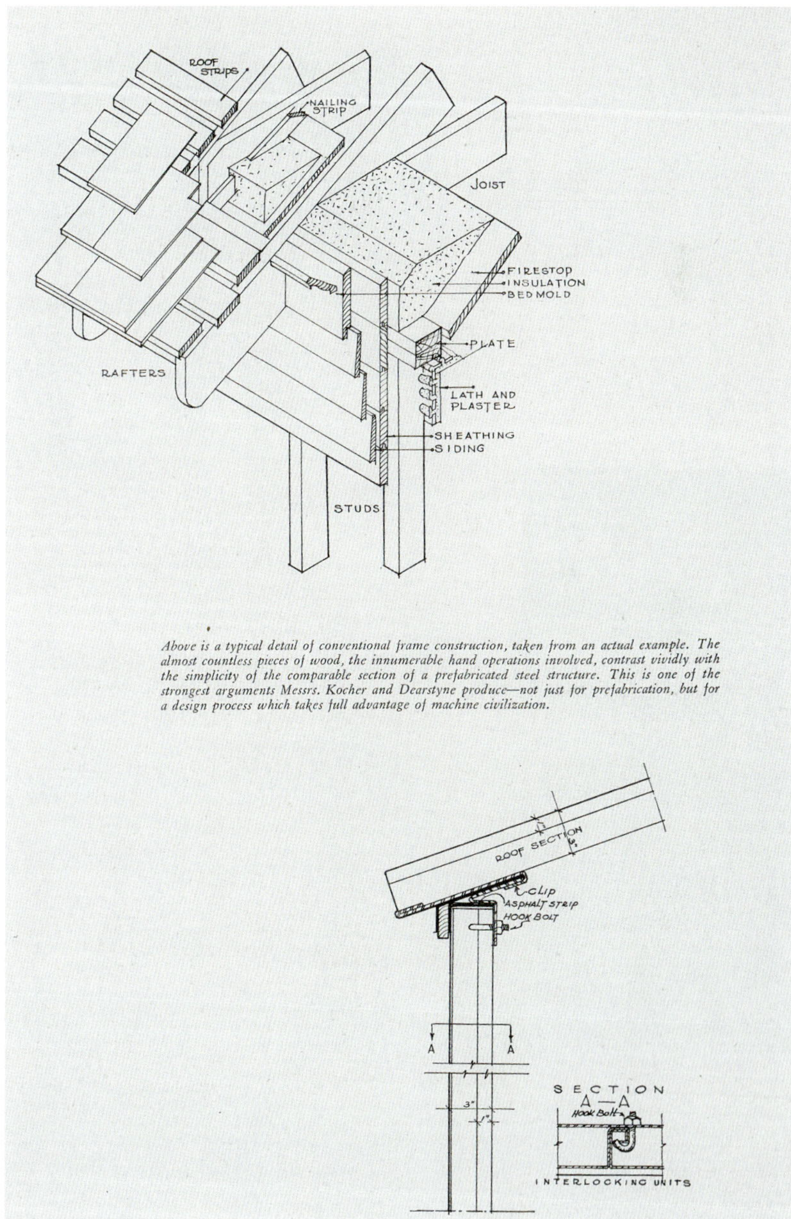

Figure 6.57. A. Lawrence Kocher. 1943. The Architectural Center. Shop and Assembly Building. Iconography.
Figure 6.58. A. Lawrence Kocher. 1943. The Architectural Center. Construction details.

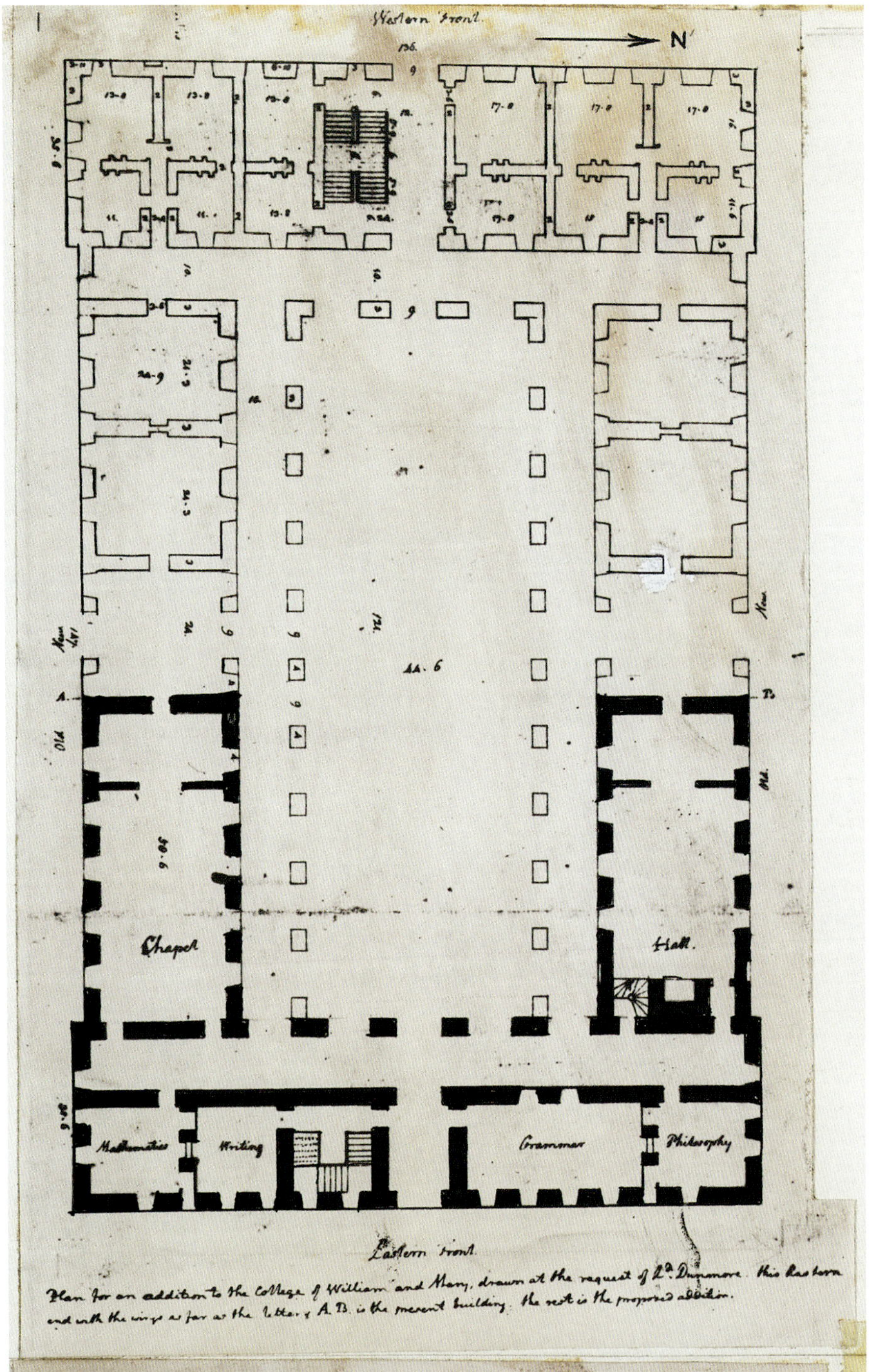

Plan by Thomas Jefferson, showing the Wren Building (blacked-in) and his proposal for an extension to it (all walls not blacked-in). The plan was drawn at the request of Lord Dunmore, royal governor of Virginia , between 1771-1772. The foundations for the west most portion of the addition had actually been laid when the Revolutionary War put a stop to building operations. (Note: In order to make it easier to distinguish between the building which existed in Jefferson's time and the addition he proposed, the writers have taken the liberty of blacking-in the walls of the existing building. Except for this and the addition of the direction arrow, no changes have been made in Jefferson's drawing.) ✓

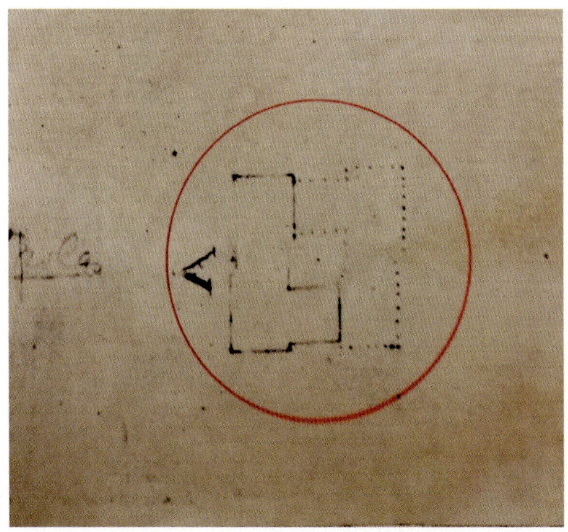

Figure 6.59. A. Lawrence Kocher and Howard Dearstyne, "Discovery of Foundations for Jefferson's Addition to The Wren Building," Journal of the Society of Architectural Historians, vol. X, no. 3 (October 1951).

Figure 6.60. A. Lawrence Kocher and Howard Dearstyne, "Discovery of Foundations for Jefferson's Addition to The Wren Building," Journal of the Society of Architectural Historians, vol. X, no. 3 (October 1951). Diagram of the planned extension of the Wren Building.

other manifestations of material culture, architecture was predominant and received special attention throughout. The descriptions and evaluations of the historic artifacts made by Kocher and Dearstyne were considered relevant by the historical preservation expert of the time and were the base for many nominations of buildings to be added to the National Register of Historic Places after the establishment of this institution in 1966.

Probably, this increasing dedication to vernacular architecture was one of the main the reasons behind Kocher's progressive abandonment of modern precepts, which is evident in this phase of his architectural practice. Nevertheless, his designs of the late 1940s were still completely modernist, as in the Solar House, an unbuilt project designed in 1947. The design was the result of the Libbey-Owens-Ford Glass Company initiative and response to the growing interest of many social groups—builders, real estate developers, architects, engineers, journalists, bankers, and governmental and civic planning groups—on the concept of a solar house.[74] The company started the Solar House Program in 1944 with the publication of a 23-page booklet, which was the first standalone publication on the topic. The booklet included a fairly general definition of a solar house and the application of three fundamental principles—orientation, large windows, and sun control—for houses able "to take advantage of sun radiation as an auxiliary source of heat."[75] In a 1947 press release, G. F. MacNichol, vice president of the company, specified that the solar houses "should be oriented to take advantage of the sun through extensive windows, or even walls of glass, not only to enlist solar energy as an auxiliary heating plant, but also to unite interiors with out-of-doors in a spacious, cheer-filled atmosphere."[76] By 1945, Libbey-Owens-Ford Glass Company saw the program as a tool to increase their new and technologically innovative products, especially their insulated double glass, Thermopane. Following the first booklet publication, the company invited a jury of 30 individuals—affiliated in one way or another with architectural design, architectural pedagogy, and the building industry. This jury nominated 49 architectural offices to design one solar house in each of the contiguous United States, including the District of Columbia. The list of nominees included very prominent names like Oscar Stonorov and Louis Kahn for Pennsylvania, George Fred Keck for Illinois, Pietro Belluschi for Oregon, among others; of course, A. Lawrence Kocher was nominated for Virginia. The invitation letter arrived at Kocher's office at Colonial Williamsburg in August of 1945 and likely caught his attention as it aligned completely with his previous ideas and work methodologies. The letter expressed the intention of building one demonstration home in each state "under different climate conditions."[77]

Kocher teamed up with the Richmond architects Louis W. Ballou and Charles C. Justice to design the house. They produced comprehensive documentation for the Solar House, including floor plans—for both the foundations and first floor—elevations, construction details, furniture details, several renderings, and 11 pages of specifications, all submitted to the Libbey-Owens-Ford Glass Company in 1947. Although a book including the 49 solar houses was published that same year, none of the houses were ever built. Some scholars rightly note that while most of the designs followed the three fundamental principles of solar houses, none of them addressed the issues of solar heating and its influence over architectural form, nor the objective of saving energy through the reduction of mechanized environmental systems.[78] Nevertheless, the book constituted a valuable first collective step towards contemporary research on sustainability and passive means of environmental control in housing.

Upon further examination, Kocher's collaboratively designed Solar House is a compact version of the House of Moderate Cost and, by extension, part of the typological progeny of the Revere House. Aside from the arrangement of the kitchen and child's room, the main difference between the House of Moderate Cost and the Solar House was the 12-foot double-height living room lit through large windows and an additional clerestory. Kocher explains the uniformity of typical American dwellings in his introductory paragraph:

> [The] American house is the same whether North, East, South, or West…A Virginia house of today differs only from a characteristic New England dwelling only in some few special provisions for shade and coolness, requisite in the South, and possibly more accommodations for outdoor living.[79]

Accordingly, there are only a few native Virginian features in the Solar House, like the painted brick of the walls, the walled vegetable garden, and the extensive use of screened porches and covered terraces that protect windows from excessive sun exposure, taking advantage of the state's mostly mild climate. **(Figures 6.66 to 6.71)** Due to space restrictions, the published book includes a limited portion of the documents developed by the architects: only one plan and three rendered views—from the street, the garden, and a bird's-eye view of the house on the site. **(Figures 6.72 and 6.73)**

The remaining architectural work during Kocher's time in Williamsburg cannot be considered as fully modernist designs. All of them increasingly contained features inspired by American vernacular architecture. An exception from this trend is the design for a Community Center in Williamsburg, developed in various stages from 1954 to 1958. There were three variants of the preliminary 1954 study adapted to different lots archived at Williamsburg, but the definitive design is dated November of 1958, and is the last of Kocher's built projects. **(Figures 6.74 to 6.76)** The Community Center had two wings connected at a 135-degree angle with the main entrance situated at their intersection. The entrance was articulated through a round steel canopy, like that of the Bogie House. The larger wing contained a club room with a stage, a big chimney, a snack bar, lobby, and public restrooms; there was an apartment on the second floor over the lobby. Situated at a lower level, due to the steep topography, the smaller wing hosts the youth center. Both wings are covered with a pitched roof supported by light, open-web steel joists. The combination of this pitched roof, the modern prefabricated steel-and-glass façade of the clubroom, and the bare, concrete-block walls resulted in a stylistically hybrid design—an epilogue to Kocher's search of a modern American architecture based on the translation of vernacular construction and design methodologies to contemporary material culture. **(Figures 6.77 to 6.82)** Additional examples of this phase in Kocher's career show a further disconnection with modernism, and instead use

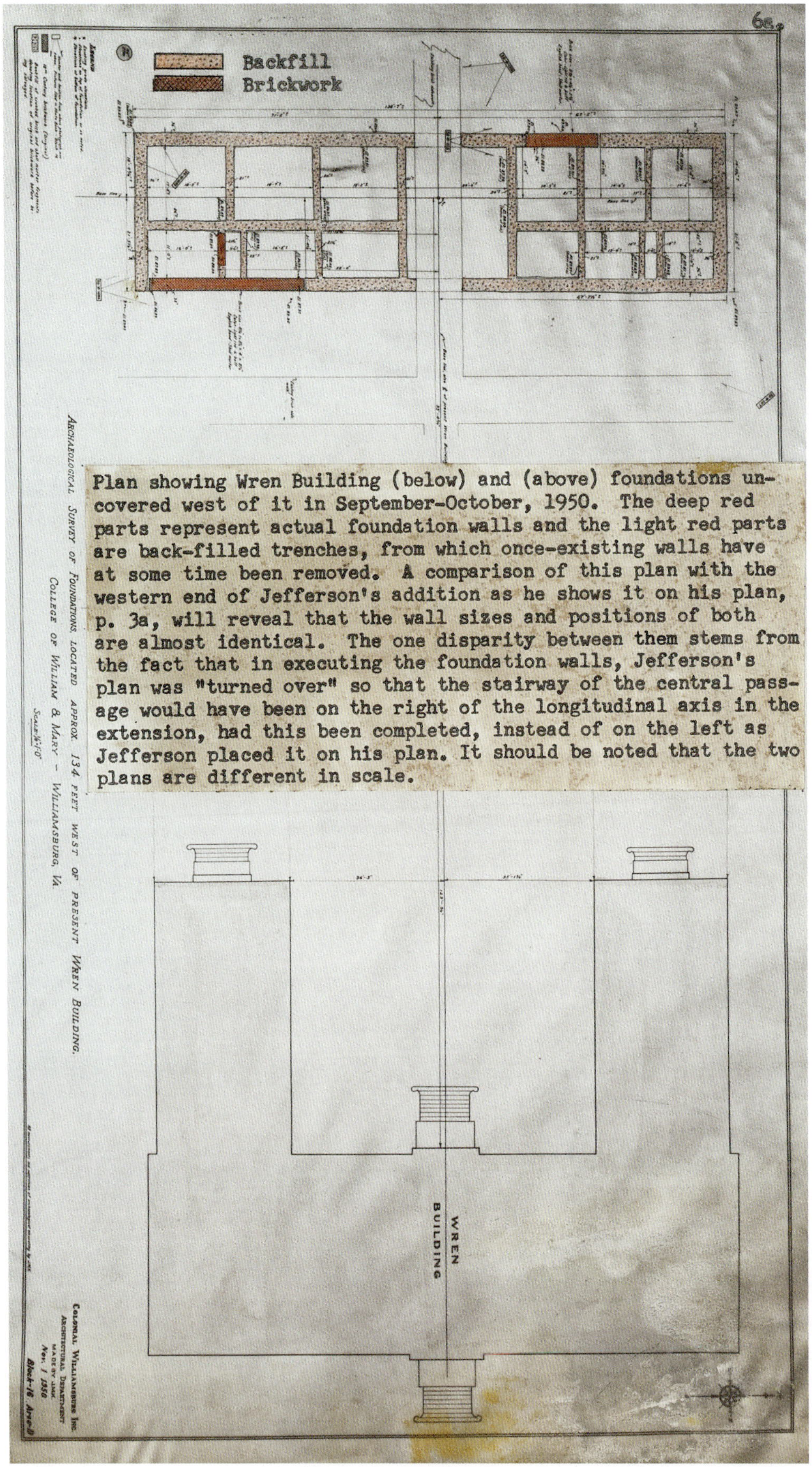

Figure 6.61. A. Lawrence Kocher and Howard Dearstyne, "Discovery of Foundations for Jefferson's Addition to The Wren Building," Journal of the Society of Architectural Historians, vol. X, no. 3 (October 1951).

vernacular forms and elements in a more literal fashion; some even divulge in a completely uninhibited traditionalism. Many of these projects demonstrate a high level of accuracy in the use of traditional architectural elements and techniques and are closer to historic recreations than to original designs. This is the case in the Barnett and the Calkins Houses (Williamsburg, both designed in 1955), the Morton House (Williamsburg, 1956), the John D. Wallace Country House in Oyster Bay (New York, 1962), and the small addition to the Ritchie House (Williamsburg, 1963). **(Figures 6.83 and 6.84)**

After his retirement from the Colonial Williamsburg Foundation in 1958 and the College of William and Mary in 1959, Kocher still found time to join the utopian and pop spirit of the 1960s. On July 15, 1960, Kocher sent a letter with an idea for the 1964 New York World's Fair to his old friend Wallace K. Harrison, who was the chair of the World's Fair Committee. The letter elaborated a plan for "a gigantic sphere to be erected, 250 feet in diameter, to be placed in the principal lagoon of the fair site. The lower third of the sphere would be submerged."[80] Kocher's vision for the sphere included an external "geographical representation of the world." Internally, the sphere would host a planetarium in the upper portion of the space, and an oceanographic center in the lower portion. Kocher proposed a design team that included Hugh Ferris, charged with the task of visualization; David B. Steinman and Holton D. Robinson, as the main engineers; and himself as the architect. Harrison forwarded the letter to the Fair's Board of Design on July 18th, and succeeded in convincing them about the feasibility and impact of the proposal, but not about the composition of the design team. Maybe because of Kocher's age—he was 75 by July of 1960—or because of other unknown circumstances, the New York City Department of Parks and Recreation commissioner Robert Moses rejected Kocher's team and announced the construction of the so-called "Unisphere" as the main symbol of the fair in February of 1961, following the design of the engineer Gilmore D. Clarke.[81] The built design was 120 feet in diameter, barely half the size of Kocher's proposal, and retained only the exterior geographical representation of the world, removing all interior programs. It was constructed by the American Bridge Company, a division of U.S. Steel, beginning in March through August of 1963. Although there is no evidence of Kocher submitting any preliminary design to the Board of Design, the letters archived at the A. Lawrence Kocher Collection in Williamsburg contain very detailed descriptions of the project that suffice to attribute him with the initial idea of the "Unisphere." His contribution to the project remains uncredited so far in the existing literature about the 1964 World's Fair. **(Figure 6.85)**

No doubt frustrated by the outcome of his last architectural endeavor, Kocher onboarded two other projects—each a singular token of his evergreen enthusiasm for utopian design, even in his last days. In November of 1960, he submitted a letter to real estate investor, developer, Broadway producer, and philanthropist Robert W. Dowling (1895–1973). Dowling was the owner of one of the largest investment companies of the country, the City Investing Group of New York, and Kocher thought he was the right man for his ambitious vision for the future of Manhattan Island. The letter explains Kocher's grand scheme of diverting "half of the waters that flow through the East River, into the Hudson by way of a widened Harlem River and contract the East River to a deepened channel."[82] The final aim of this engineering operation was to create a vast lineal park on the riverbed—including some housing, green and recreational areas—and link Manhattan to Brooklyn and Queens with a system of bridges from alternate streets. Kocher explains to Dowling that this idea had been harbored in his mind since the 1930s and was previously rejected by the U.S. Department of Defense. The second project was Kocher's last attempt to participate in the 1964 World's Fair, after the disappointment of the Unisphere. It was a proposal for a planetarium and oceanography center derived from the original program of the Unisphere and designed in 1961. The only graphic information available for this proposal are two floor plans depicting a spherical building half submerged in what seems to be a river, with the planetarium and the oceanography center respectively occupying the upper and lower halves of the sphere. A system of bridges and spiral ramps on opposite sides of the sphere allows the arrival and departure of visitors. **(Figures 6.86 and 6.87)** This final futurist project demonstrates Kocher's intellectual consistency and his deep engagement with the social imaginaries of the various historic moments he participated in as an architect, educator, and researcher. His lifelong interest in the future of modernist architecture and on the development of an American style was the center of all of Kocher's professional activity since his first designs, until his death on June 6, 1969. As eloquently expressed in his 1926 article on the country house:

> Are we any nearer a realization of the old yearning for an 'American style?' Perhaps no nearer than our novelists to the 'great American novel.' But if such a style is to be achieved it will be, not by the general adoption of any group of historic shapes and details, but by the free selection and development of styles to meet the newer and more diverse needs of modern life. Regional differences, the variety of local materials, and above all the fundamental American characteristic of looking toward the future rather than toward the past make the outlook decidedly a hopeful one.[83]

Chapter endnotes

1 Still-life photography is based on the display of the photographed object. It does not give clues about other topics, like the context or include any narrative. Kocher's design aligns to this concept hiding any hint of administrative or technical task carried out in the spaces and showcasing only the school's output.

2 These advertisement commissions were continuous for the school faculty and students thanks to White's connections with magazine editors and art directors. Bonnie Yochelson, "The Clarence H. White School of Photography," *Object:Photo, Modern Photographs: The Thomas Walther Collection 1909–1949, An Online Project of The Museum of Modern Art*, Eds. Mitra Abbaspour, Lee Ann Daffner, and Maria Morris Hambourg (New York: The Museum of Modern Art, 2014). http://www.moma.org/interactives/objectphoto/assets/essays/Yochelson.pdf.

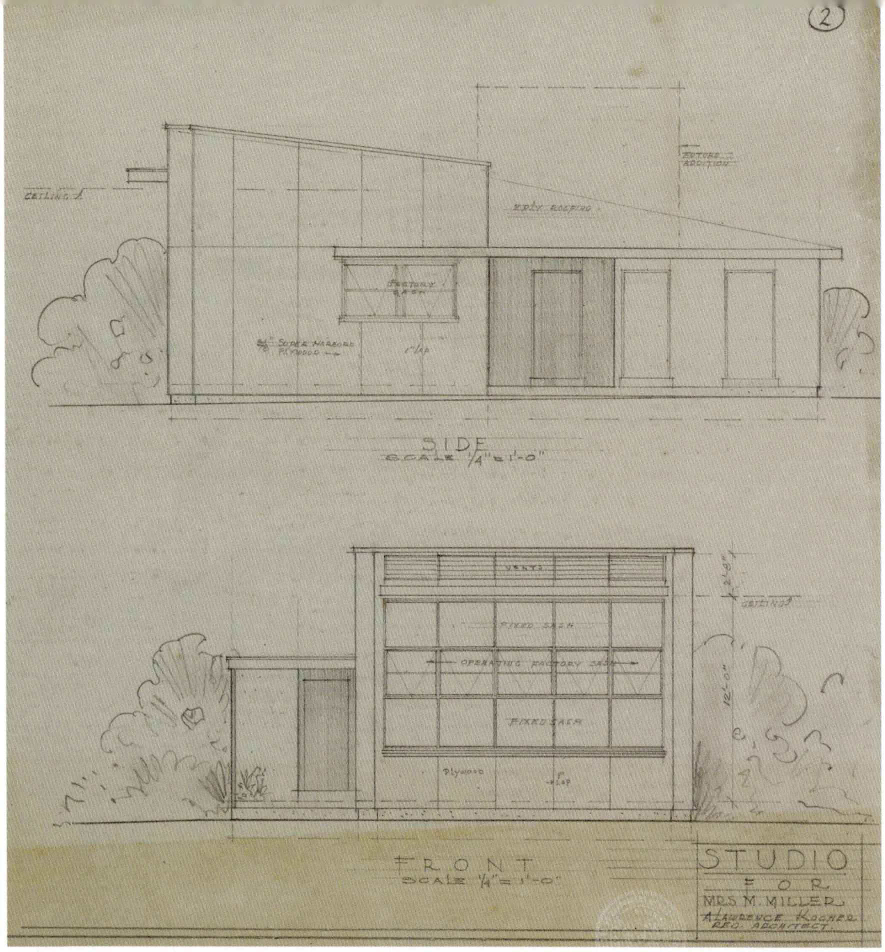

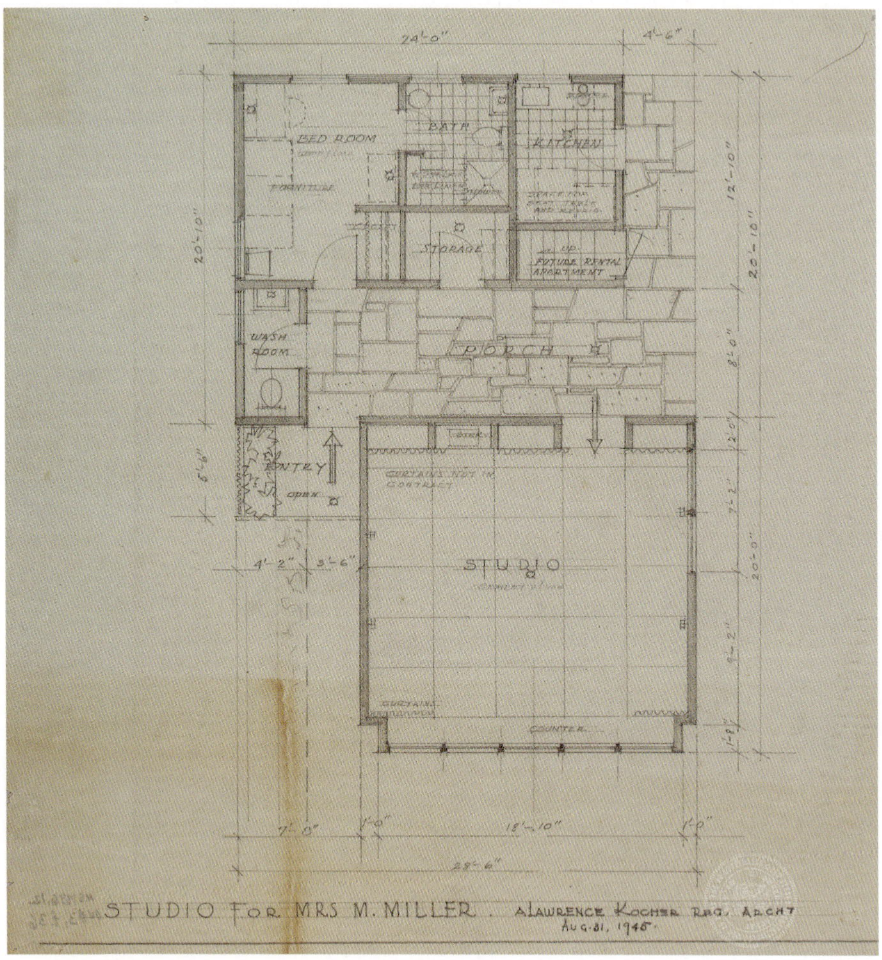

Figure 6.62. A. Lawrence Kocher. 1945. Studio for Mrs. M. Miller. Williamsburg, Virginia. Elevations.
Figure 6.63. A. Lawrence Kocher. 1945. Studio for Mrs. M. Miller. Williamsburg, Virginia. First floor plan.

3 In 1946, the Kaufmanns commissioned Richard Neutra to design their iconic Desert House as their winter retreat in Palm Springs, California.

4 The Kaufmanns approached their civic duties as seriously as their commercial affairs. Aside from their patronage of many architects and artists, the Kaufmanns had a philanthropic agenda that included the Young Men and Women's Hebrew Association, the Emma Kaufmann Clinic, the Liliane S. Kaufmann School of Nursing, and many more foundations related with community development and social well-being. See: Marylynne Pitz and Laura Malt Schneiderman, *Kaufmann's: The Family That Built Pittsburgh's Famed Department Store* (Pittsburgh: University of Pittsburgh Press, 2022).

5 This apartment was planned as the Pittsburg home of Edgar Kaufmann Jr. and his life partner, the architect and industrial designer Paul Mayen.

6 "Arsenal of Democracy" was the central concept used by President Roosevelt in a radio broadcast delivered on December 29, 1940. The phrase refers to the collective efforts of American industry in supporting the Allies—enrolling private companies as Ford Motor Company, General Motors, Westinghouse Electric Company, and others in the war effort—and transforming many industrial centers in cities (such as Detroit, Cleveland, Philadelphia, and Buffalo) into armament manufacturing facilities.

7 Christopher J. Tassava, "The American Economy during World War II," *EH. Net Encyclopedia*, Ed. Robert Whaples, February 10, 2008. https://eh.net/encyclopedia/the-american-economy-during-world-war-ii/.

8 The OPA's main responsibility was to limit the prices of most goods and to control consumption by rationing.

9 Lizabeth Cohen, *A Consumer's Republic: The Politics of Mass Consumption in Postwar America* (New York: Alfred A. Knopf, 2003).

10 The 1944 G.I. Bill's long title was very explicative of its purpose: "An act to provide Federal Government aid for the readjustment in civilian life of returning World War II veterans."

11 Andrew M. Shanken, "Better Living: Toward a Cultural History of a Business Slogan," *Enterprise & Society*, vol. 7, no. 3 (Cambridge University Press, 2006): 485–519.

12 Motto repeated in all brochures.

13 Andrew M. Shanken, *194X: Architecture, Planning, and Consumer Culture on the American Home Front* (Minneapolis: University of Minnesota Press, 2009), 199–207.

14 As in, for example, the newly founded ASPA.

15 Gaia Caramellino, "You and Your Neighborhood: Neighborhood, Community, and Democracy as New Paradigms in Wartime American Architecture," *Urban Planning*, vol. 7, no. 1 (2022): 369–384. Oscar Stonorov and Louis Kahn, *Why city planning is your responsibility* (Revere Copper & Brass, 1942). Oscar Stonorov and Louis Kahn, *You and your neighborhood: A primer for neighborhood planning* (Revere Copper & Brass, 1944).

16 William Lescaze, *A citizens country club or leisure center* (Revere Copper & Brass, Inc., 1942). Serge Chermayeff, *A children's center or nursery school* (Revere Copper & Brass, Inc., 1944). George Nelson, *Your Children Could Romp Here While You Shop* (Revere Copper & Brass, Inc., 1943).

17 Carl F. Boester, *Home … for a nation on wings* (Revere Copper & Brass, Inc., 1943). R. Buckminster Fuller, *Better homes for lower incomes* (Revere Copper & Brass, 1943).

18 The work of many other relevant architects, engineers, and designers of the moment can also be included within this last category; such brochures include: "Homes for tomorrow's happy living" by George Fred Keck, "New homes for better living!" by Walter Dorwin Teague, "A hillside built this house" by Antonin Raymond, "A flexible house for happier living" by William Wilson Wurster, "A house with a future" by Harwell Hamilton Harris, "Uplifting the downtrodden" by William Lescaze, "After Total War Can Come Total Living" by Lawrence Bradford Perkins, "Tomorrow's Homes for the Many" by Norman Bel Geddes, and "Apartment homes for tomorrow's better living" by Walter B. Sanders.

19 A. Lawrence Kocher, "Beyond the War Waits Happiness," *Saturday Evening Post* (July 11, 1942): 37.

20 Kocher, "Beyond the War Waits Happiness," 37.

21 Lizabeth Cohen, "A Consumers' Republic: The Politics of Mass Consumption in Postwar America," *Journal of Consumer Research*, vol. 31 (June): 236.

22 Kocher, "Beyond the War Waits Happiness," 37.

23 A. Lawrence Kocher, *Homes to Enrich Our National Standard of Living* (New York: Revere Copper and Bass Inc., 1942), 4.

24 Kocher, *Homes to Enrich Our National Standard of Living*, 4.

25 There is only one floor plan and two elevations of the project, dated July 12, 1945, A. Lawrence Kocher Collection, Colonial Williamsburg Foundation, John D. Rockefeller Jr. Library.

26 Kocher, *Homes to enrich our national standard of living*, 7.

27 These statistics can be found in the first of the AIA report's two volumes; Ed. Turpin C. Bannister, *The Architect at Mid-Century: Evolution and Achievement. report of the Commission for the Survey of Education and Registration of the American Institute of Architects* (New York: Reinhold, 1954), 78–79.

28 Joseph Hudnut, Architecture after the Peace, *Magazine of Art*, no. 36 (April, 1943): 122–27.

29 Letter from Gropius to Kocher, dated December 21, 1937, Box 1, Series I, Correspondence General, Folder: Walter Gropius, A. Lawrence Kocher Collection, Colonial Williamsburg Foundation, John D. Rockefeller Jr. Library.

30 ASPA, Minutes of the meeting, April 1, 1944, UAV 322.7, subseries X, HUA, GSD Papers, Records of External Offices and Organizations. Quoted in: Jill Pearlman, *Inventing American Modernism: Joseph Hudnut, Walter Gropius, and the Bauhaus Legacy at Harvard* (Charlottesville: University of Virginia Press, 2007), 149.

31 Letter from Hudnut to George Fred Keck, June 28, 1944, GSD Papers, HUA. Quoted in: Pearlman, *Inventing American Modernism*, 148.

32 A. Lawrence Kocher and Albert Frey, "Real Estate Subdivisions for Low-Cost Housing," *Architectural Record*, vol .69, (April, 1931).

33 Howard Dearstyne was born in 1903, in Albany, New York. His professional biography is closely related to A. Lawrence Kocher. After graduating with an A.B. at Columbia College in 1925, he studied for three years at Columbia's School of Architecture and, in 1928, moved to Germany to attend to the Bauhaus, first in Dessau and then in Berlin during 1932–1933. After the Gestapo raided the school and forced its closure in 1933, Dearstyne studied privately under Ludwig Mies van der Rohe until 1934. Dearstyne was the first American to graduate at the Bauhaus. After Dearstyne returned to the U.S.A, he worked for the architects Wallace K. Harrison and J. A. Fouilhoux (1935–1939), for the industrial designer Raymond Loewy (1940), and for Antonin Raymond in Pennsylvania (1941). During 1941 and 1942, he was an instructor in architecture and structural design at Black Mountain College. After this moment, his professional life links with Kocher as a partner in many of his architectural designs, books, and, since 1946, as a coworker both at William and Mary College and as the assistant architectural records editor at Colonial Williamsburg. Dearstyne was also a prestigious photographer. Biographical Note, Howard Dearstyne Papers, 1911–1988, Library of the Congress, Washington, D.C.

34 F. S. Lincoln (1894–1975) was an old acquaintance of Kocher. He produced the photographic works covering the various building projects and renovations at Williamsburg Colonial. He was also the photographer of many of Kocher's works during the 1930s and the 1940s.

35 A. Lawrence Kocher and Howard Dearstyne, "The Architectural Center: An Organization to Coordinate Building Research, Planning, Design, and Construction," *New Pencil Points* (July, 1943): 26–49.

36 Kocher and Dearstyne, "The Architectural Center," 26.

37 Ibid, 43.

38 Ibid, 33.

39 Ibid, 40.

40 At this point, it becomes prescient the 1934 letter from Gropius to Kocher recommending an architectural education based on "workshops as laboratories which are paid directly by the industry." Letter from Gropius to Kocher dated July 7th, 1934. John D. Rockefeller Jr. Library. Williamsburg. A. Lawrence Kocher Collection. Box 1.

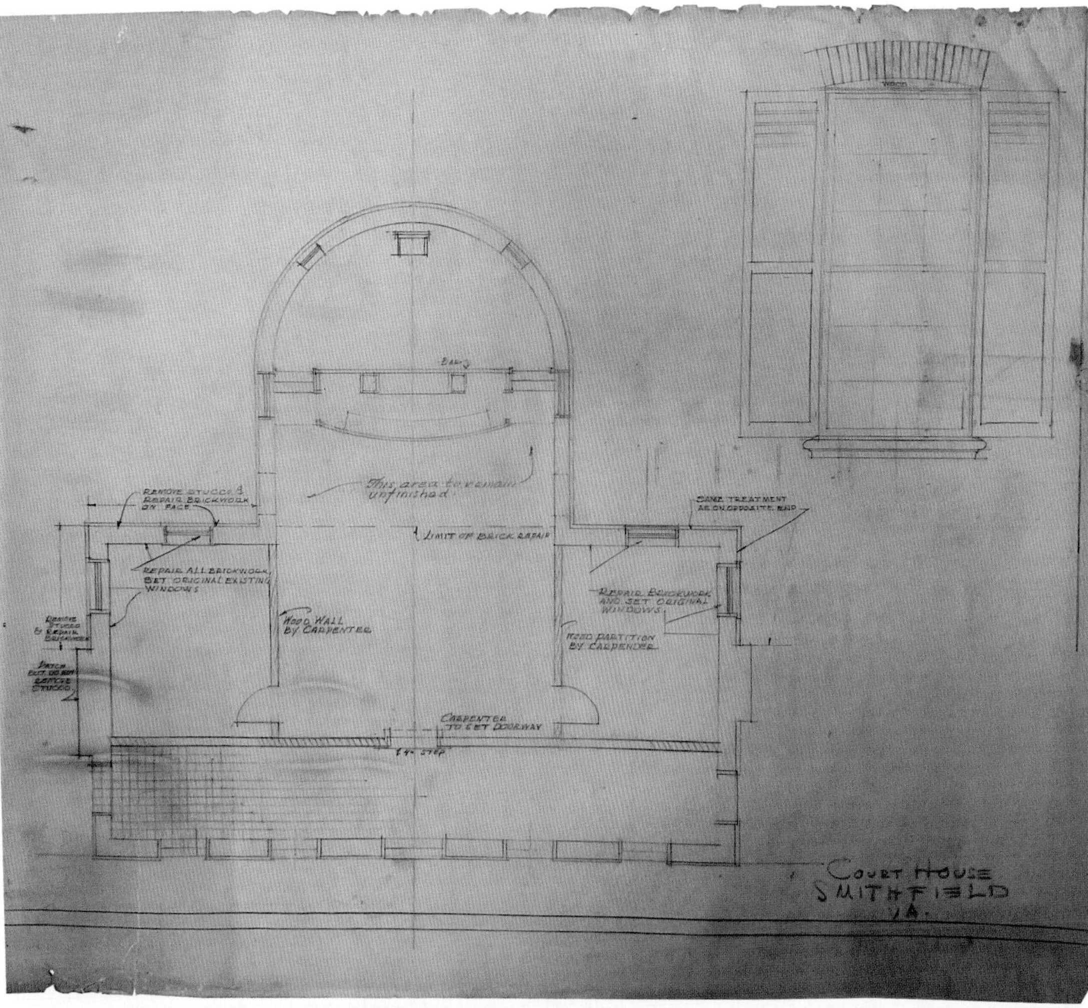

Figure 6.64. A. Lawrence Kocher. 1955–1960. Smithfield, Virginia, Old Isle of Wight Court House. Restoration project.

Figure 6.65. A. Lawrence Kocher. 1956. Jamestown, Virginia. Row Housing. Conjectural elevation using actual foundations.

41 Kocher and Dearstyne, "The Architectural Center," 42.

42 Albert Frey, *In Search of a Living Architecture.* (New York City: Architectural Book Publishing Company, Inc., 1939). Sigfried Giedion, *Bauen in FrankReich, Bauen in Eisen, Bauen in Eisenbeton* (Leipzig: Klinkhardt & Biermann, 1928).

43 Sigfried Giedion, *Mechanization Takes Command: A Contribution to Anonymous History* (Oxford: Oxford University Press, 1948). Sibyl Moholy-Nagy, *Native Genius in Anonymous Architecture* (New York City: Horizon Press Inc., 1948). Bernard Rudofsky, *Architecture Without Architects: A Short Introduction to Non-pedigreed Architecture* (New York City: The Museum of Modern Art – Doubleday, 1964). Karl von Frisch, *Tiere als Baumeister* (Frankfurt: Ullstein, 1974). Bernard Rudofsky, *The Prodigious Builders* (New York City: Harcourt Brace Jovanovich, 1948).

44 Reyner Banham, *A Concrete Atlantis. U.S. Industrial Building and European Modern Architecture* (Cambridge: The MIT Press, 1986).

45 *Illinois Society of Architects Monthly Bulletin* (January, 1945): 5.

46 Donald Deskey (1894–1989) was a prominent industrial and interior designer who trained as an architect at the University of California. He was well known for his furniture, lighting, and textile designs, as well as for the interior design of the Radio City Music Hall, and his colorful packaging designs (Crest and Gleem toothpastes, Jif peanut butter, and Tide dishwasher soap, among others).

47 Kocher was already a very active member of the Colonial Williamsburg's Advisory Committee of Architects since 1928.

48 In the Colonial Williamsburg Digital Library, there are 53 reports authored by Kocher, many of them alongside Dearstyne: two reports in 1945, one report in 1947, four reports in 1948, 12 reports in 1949, 11 reports in 1950, five reports in 1951, four reports in 1952, four reports in 1953, and two reports in 1954. There are also five addenda to previous reports distributed during the years of 1950, 1951, and 1952.

49 The 1928 decalogue was later compiled in: A. Lawrence Kocher and Howard Dearstyne, *Colonial Williamsburg: Its Buildings and Gardens, A Descriptive Tour of the Restored Capital of the British Colony of Virginia* (Williamsburg, VA: Colonial Williamsburg, 1961), 48–49.

50 The original Sir Christopher Wren Building was erected between 1695 and 1700, before Williamsburg was founded and Jamestown was still the capital of the Virginia colony. It is the oldest college building still standing in the United States and the oldest of the restored public buildings in Williamsburg. The building was gutted by fire in 1705, 1859, and 1862, and rebuilt three times. The last reconstruction in 1928, was based on the 1716 re-erection after the 1705 fire and used the existing foundations and walls but also introduced many changes to the original structure.

51 A. Lawrence Kocher and Howard Dearstyne, "Wren Building Architectural Report, Block 16 Building 3" (Originally entitled, "Proposal for the Establishment of a Cultural Center at the College of William and Mary"), 1950. Colonial Williamsburg Foundation Library Research Report Series 1319, Williamsburg, Virginia, 1.

52 Kocher and Dearstyne, "Wren Building Architectural Report, Block 16 Building 3."

53 A. Lawrence Kocher and Howard Dearstyne, "Discovery of Foundations for Jefferson's Addition to The Wren Building," *Journal of the Society of Architectural Historians*, vol. X, no. 3 (October, 1951): 28–34.

54 Kocher and Dearstyne, "Discovery of Foundations for Jefferson's Addition to The Wren Building," 28.

55 Letter archived in the Public Records Office, London, C.O.S.-1309.

56 Archived at the Huntington Library in San Marino, California.

57 Consequently, Lord Dunmore retired his support to the project; the materials assembled for the construction were sold through an advertisement published in the September 13th and September 20th issues of The Virginia Gazette.

58 These findings consisted of a fragment of two 18th-century brick foundation walls and filled-in trenches. A record drawing was made but no further archaeological explorations were executed at that time.

59 A. Lawrence Kocher, Lecture: "Use of Architectural Handbooks in the Colonies," Box 2, Literary Materials, A. Lawrence Kocher Collection, Colonial Williamsburg Foundation, John D. Rockefeller Jr. Library.

60 Halfpenny published the very popular *Art of Sound Building* in 1725 and a dozen more titles in the following years.

61 Batty Langley authored several books that were enormously influential in the American colonies, such as *A Sure Guide to Builders* in 1729, *Builder's Complete Assistant* in 1738, *The Builder's Jewell* in 1741, and *The Workman's Golden Rule* in 1750.

62 The *Vitruvius Britannicus* was published in three volumes between 1715 and 1725 in England.

63 A. Lawrence Kocher, Lecture: "Use of Architectural Handbooks in the Colonies."

64 Among others: Mount Airy Plantation's Mansion in Richmond County, Virginia (1764), derived directly from Plate LVIII of Gibbs' book, and the large Venetian Window of Mount Vernon built in the 1770's followed the model of plate 51 in Batty Langley's *The City and Country Builder's and Workman's Treasury of Designs* (1740).

65 There is no indication of the north orientation in the drawings; our guess is derived from the fact that the large studio window is protected from sun incidence with just a narrow horizontal overhang that would be needless if it faced north, or useless if it faced east or west. In addition, there is another smaller window for the studio in the façade that corresponds to the east orientation, which would not make any sense if oriented west.

66 In 1945, Rockefeller purchased Sunnyside and about 20 adjacent acres from Irving's collateral descendants as part of his efforts in historic preservation. Rowell was the President of The Historical Society of The Tarrytowns, the organization in charge of the restoration and of lending Irving domestic objects from their collections to add to the furnishings bought with the house. The house was restored using Kocher's advice and opened to the public in 1947 under the management of the Historical Society. "Irving Home To Be Restored," *State and Local History News* 3, no. 1/2 (1945): 7.

67 According to his own notes, Kocher visited the Avery Library at Columbia, the New York Historical Society, the New York Public Library, and the Metropolitan Museum Collection. Sunnyside (Tarrytown. N.Y), Box 7, Correspondence, A. Lawrence Kocher Collection, Colonial Williamsburg Foundation, John D. Rockefeller Jr. Library.

68 Report on "Sunnyside," visited March 16 and 17, 1946, Box 7, Correspondence, A. Lawrence Kocher Collection, Colonial Williamsburg Foundation, John D. Rockefeller Jr. Library.

69 Kocher mailed a second report on May 21, 1946, after an earlier visit on May 8th through 10th; subsequent reports are dated on September 27th and 30th, and October 5, 1946.

70 A special issue of the *American Collector* journal was published for the occasion, explaining all the restoration works and outcomes. *American Collector,* vol. XVI, no. 9 (October, 1947). A second phase of the Sunnyside restoration, again with Kocher in charge as the supervising architect, happened in 1958. This phase included the demolition of an 1896 wing, the restoration of the north façade, the reconstruction of the kitchen yard—including outbuildings, greenhouse, and fences—and the construction of a new pavilion for events. It also entailed the restoration of the surrounding landscape to the era of Washington Irving.

71 Charles Messer Stow, "The Restoration: Latest Link of a Chain," *American Collector*, vol. XVI, no. 9 (October, 1947): 36.

72 Kocher's contributions to the projects ranked from advisory and supervisory appointments to the interpretative work developed in Jamestown, delivering drawings of reconstructed houses compatible with the excavated foundations. Kocher was also an advisor to the Historic Richmond Foundation on the salvaging of 19th-century buildings threatened with demolition in 1955.

73 A. Lawrence Kocher and Howard Dearstyne, *Shadows in Silver: A Record of Virginia 1850-1900 in Contemporary Photographs taken by George and Huestis Cook with Additions from the Cook Collection* (New York: Charles Scribsner's Sons, 1954).

74 This interest in solar houses was preceded by several pioneering experiences by Fred and William Keck and Frank Lloyd Wright, and a by a series of topical articles published in the early 1940s in very popular magazines, such as *Newsweek* (September 1943), *Reader's Digest* (January 1944), and the *New York Times* (April 1945). Additionally, more specialized magazines, like *House Beautiful* published Keck's Duncan House in September 1943, explaining the basic principles of its solar strategy. Anthony Denzer, *The Solar House: Pioneering Sustainable Design* (New York: Rizzoli, 2013), 74.

75 Maron J. Simon, *Solar Houses: An Architectural Lift of Living* (Toledo: Libbey-Owens-Ford, 1945), 6.

76 Undated press release, Box 7, Solar House 1945-47, Correspondence, Published in *The Virginia Gazette* (October 10, 1947), A. Lawrence Kocher Collection, Colonial Williamsburg Foundation, John D. Rockefeller Jr. Library.

77 Letter dated August 25, 1945, Box 7, Solar House 1945-47, Correspondence, A. Lawrence Kocher Collection, Colonial Williamsburg Foundation, John D. Rockefeller Jr. Library.

78 Denzer, *The Solar House: Pioneering Sustainable Design,* 79.

79 Maron J. Simon, *Your Solar House: A Book of Practical Homes for All Parts of the Country* (New York: Simon and Schuster, 1947), 53.

80 Letter dated July 30, 1960, Box 8, Folder: World's Fair 1964, A. Lawrence Kocher Collection, Colonial Williamsburg Foundation, John D. Rockefeller Jr. Library.

81 "A 120-Foot Steel 'Unisphere' Will Be Symbol of the '64 Fair," *The New York Times* (February 15, 1961): 37. "'Unisphere' Is Fair's Symbol," *Newsday* (February 14, 1961): 4.

82 Letter dated November 12, 1960, Box 1, Series 1, Correspondence, Folder: Colonial National Historical Park, A. Lawrence Kocher Collection, Colonial Williamsburg Foundation, John D. Rockefeller Jr. Library.

83 A. Lawrence Kocher, "The Country House: Are We Developing an American Style?" *Architectural Record*, vol. 60, no. 5 (November 1926): 395.

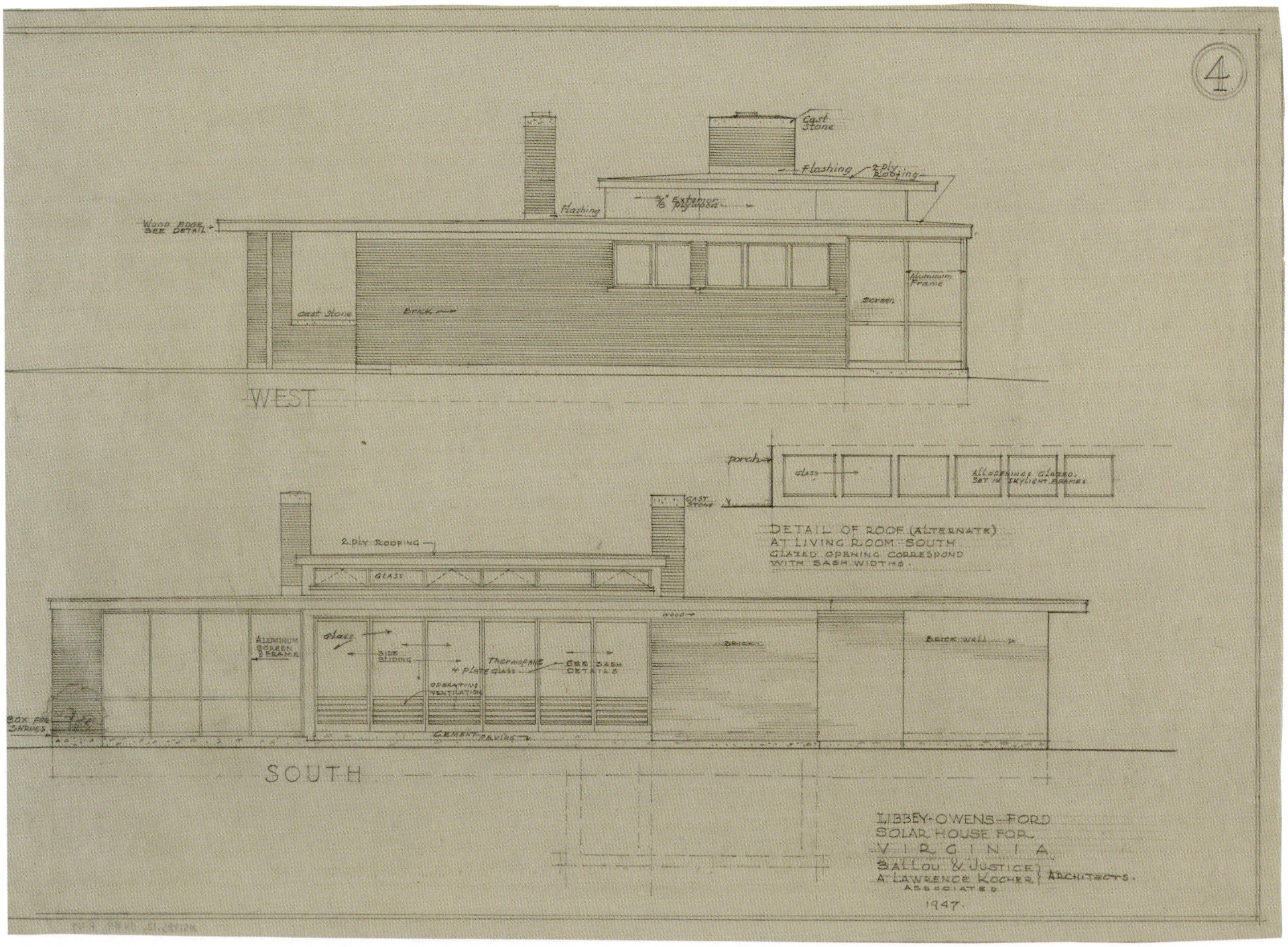

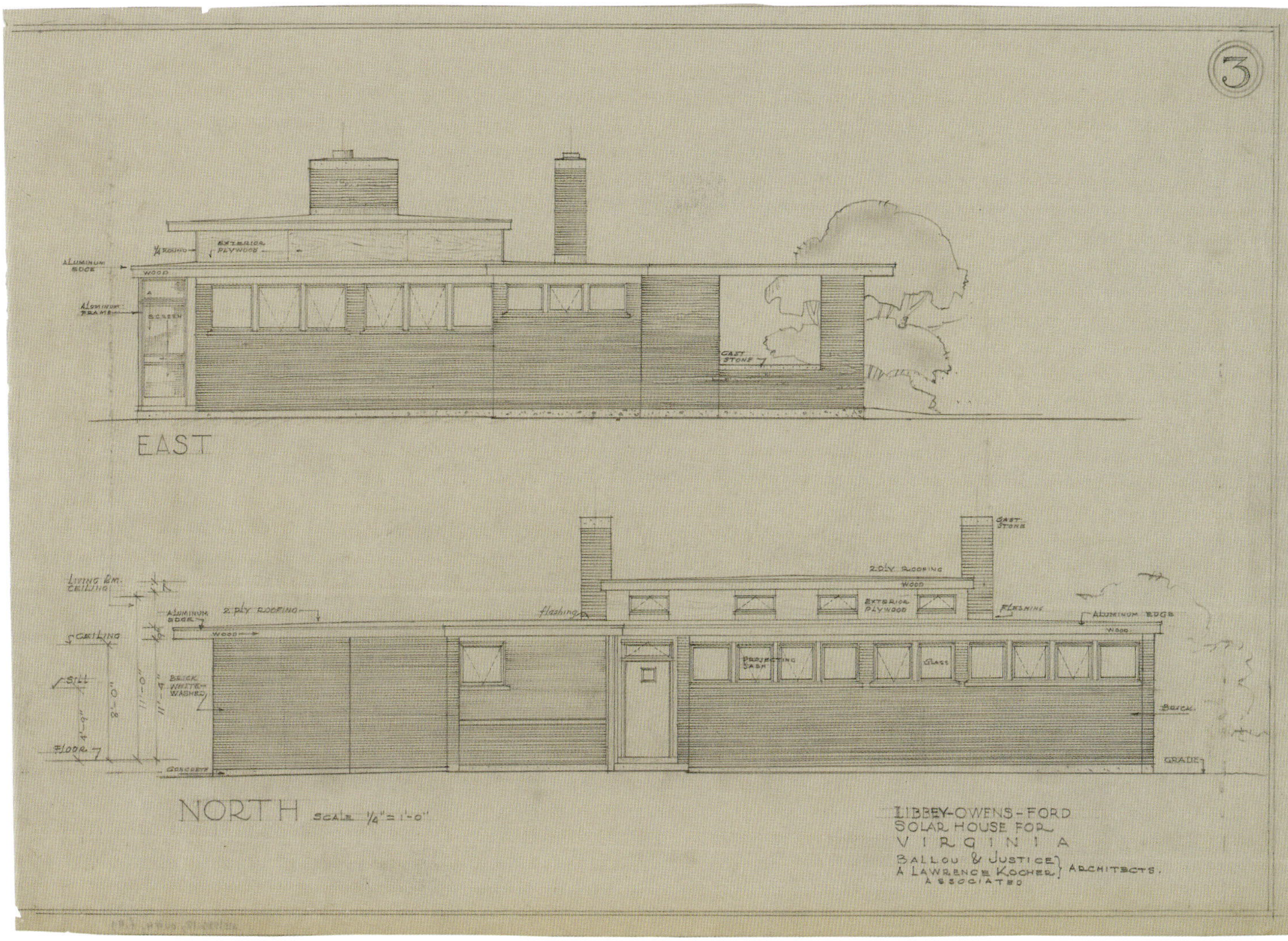

Previous page:
Figure 6.66. A. Lawrence Kocher, Louis W. Ballou, and Charles C. Justice. 1947. Solar House for Virginia. Original project. Elevations.

This page:
Figure 6.67. A. Lawrence Kocher, Louis W. Ballou, and Charles C. Justice. 1947. Solar House for Virginia. Original project. Elevations.

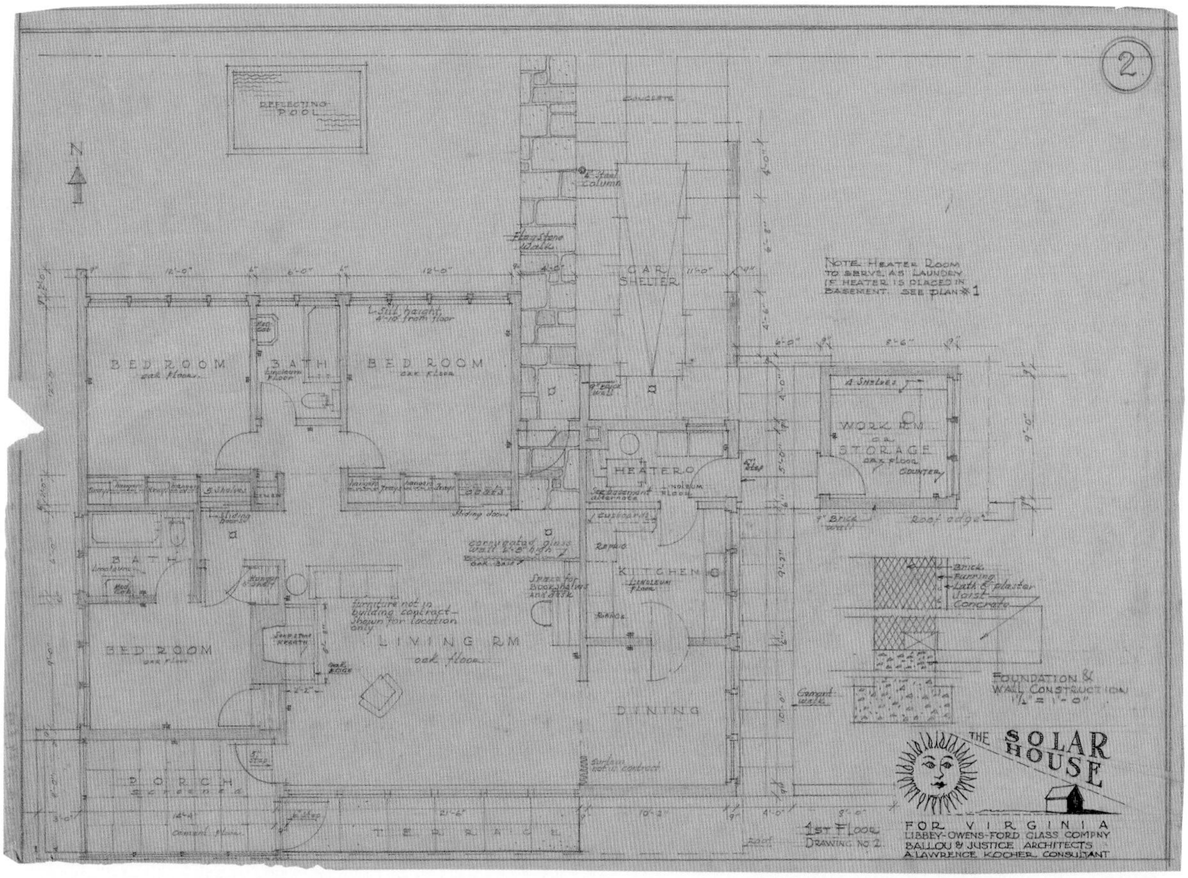

REFLECTING POOL
CAR SHELTER
NOTE: HEATER ROOM TO SERVE AS LAUNDRY IF HEATER IS PLACED IN BASEMENT. SEE PLAN #1
BED ROOM
BATH
BED ROOM
WORK RM
STORAGE
HEATER
KITCHEN
BATH
BED ROOM
LIVING RM
oak floor
DINING
PORCH
TERRACE
FOUNDATION & WALL CONSTRUCTION
THE SOLAR HOUSE
FOR VIRGINIA
LIBBEY-OWENS-FORD GLASS COMPANY
BALLOU & JUSTICE ARCHITECTS
A. LAWRENCE KOCHER CONSULTANT
1st FLOOR
DRAWING NO. 2

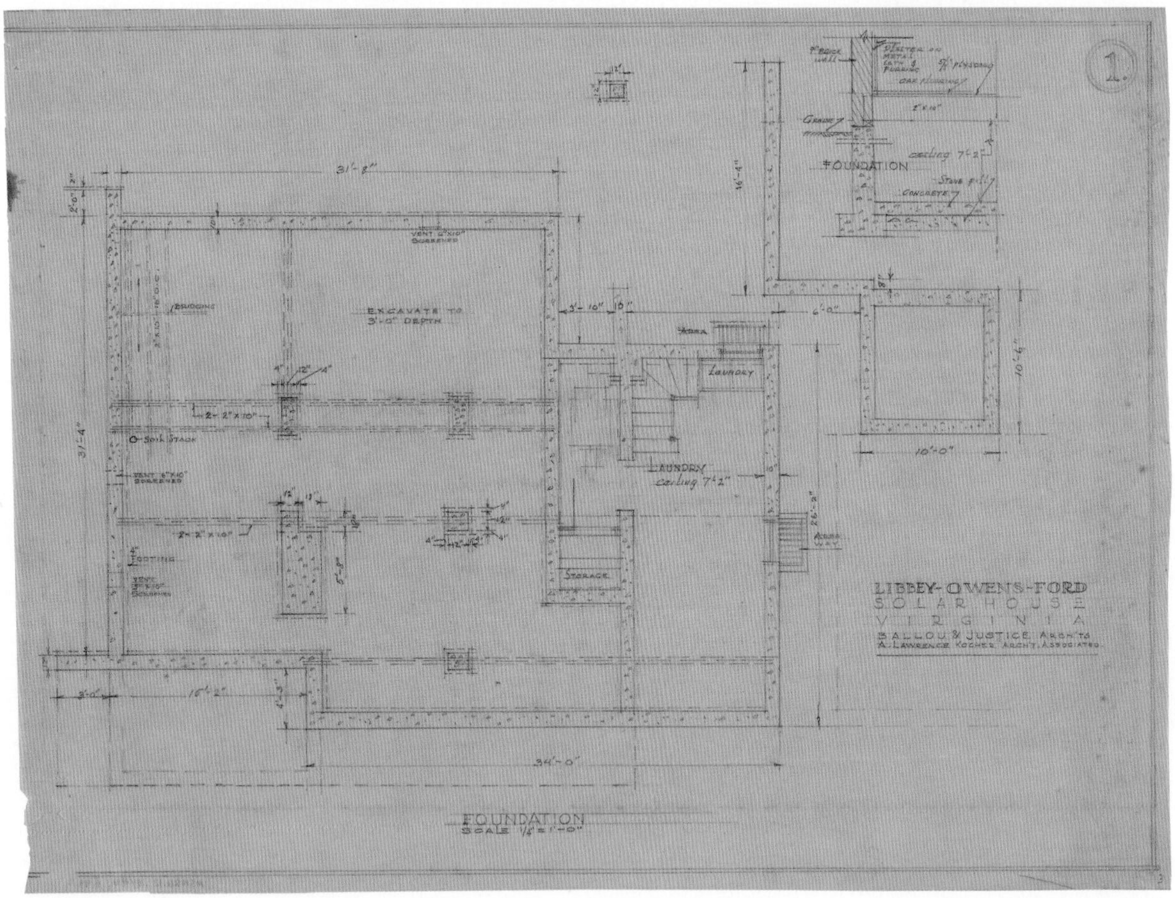

EXCAVATE TO 3'-0" DEPTH
LAUNDRY
STORAGE
FOUNDATION
LIBBEY-OWENS-FORD
SOLAR HOUSE
VIRGINIA
BALLOU & JUSTICE ARCHITECTS
A. LAWRENCE KOCHER ARCHT. ASSOCIATED
FOUNDATION
SCALE 1/8" = 1'-0"

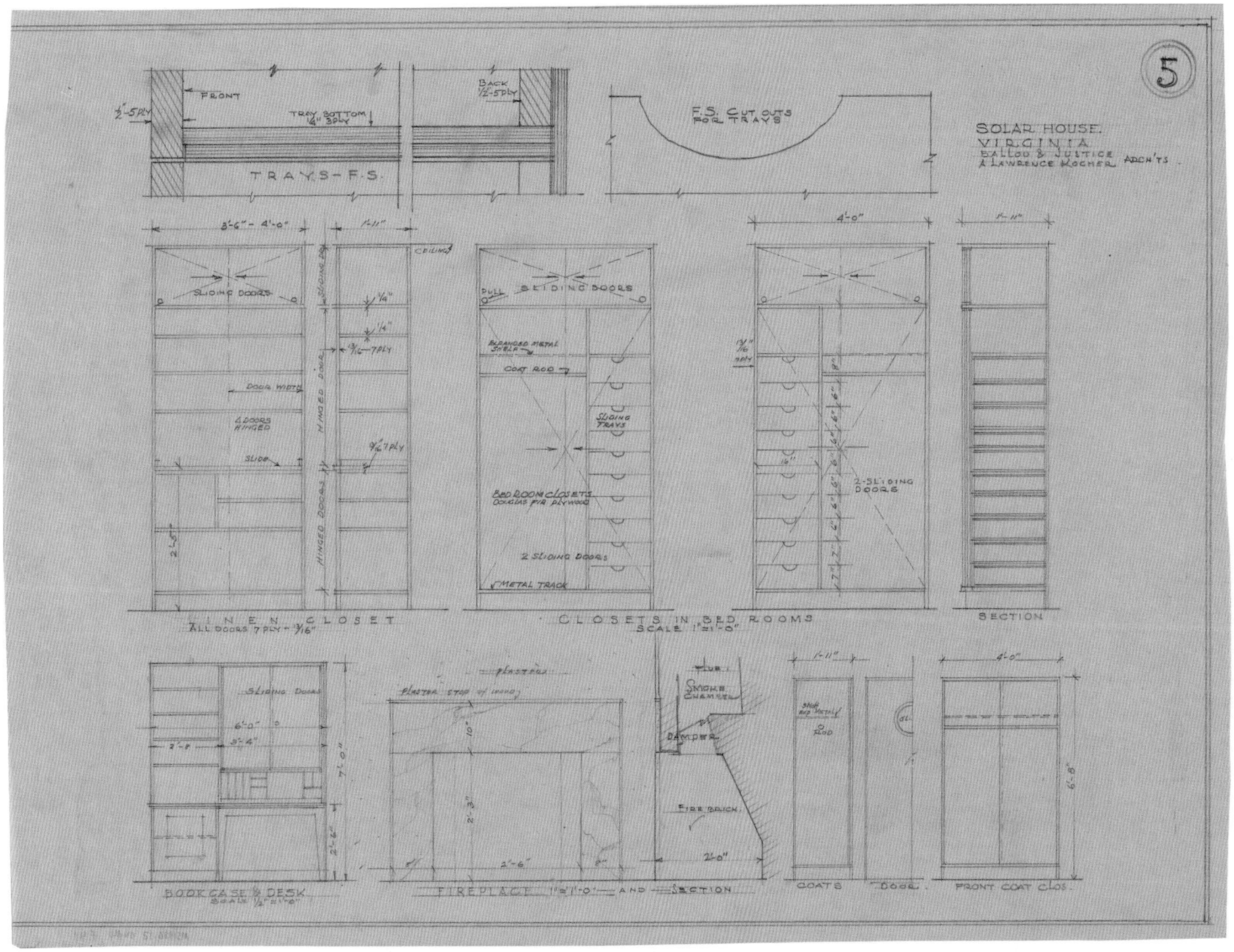

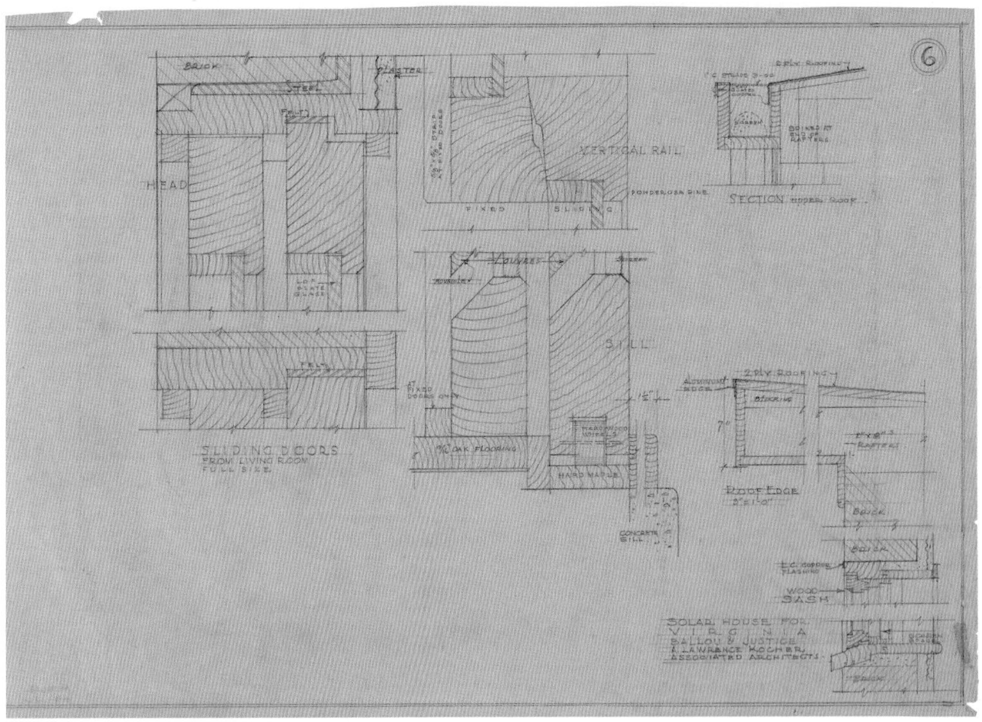

Previous page:
Figure 6.68. A. Lawrence Kocher, Louis W. Ballou, and Charles C. Justice. 1947. Solar House for Virginia. Original project. First floor plan.
Figure 6.69. A. Lawrence Kocher, Louis W. Ballou, and Charles C. Justice. 1947. Solar House for Virginia. Original project. Foundation floor plan.

This page:
Figure 6.70. A. Lawrence Kocher, Louis W. Ballou, and Charles C. Justice. 1947. Solar House for Virginia. Original project. Construction details.
Figure 6.71. A. Lawrence Kocher, Louis W. Ballou, and Charles C. Justice. 1947. Solar House for Virginia. Original project. Furniture and cabinet details.

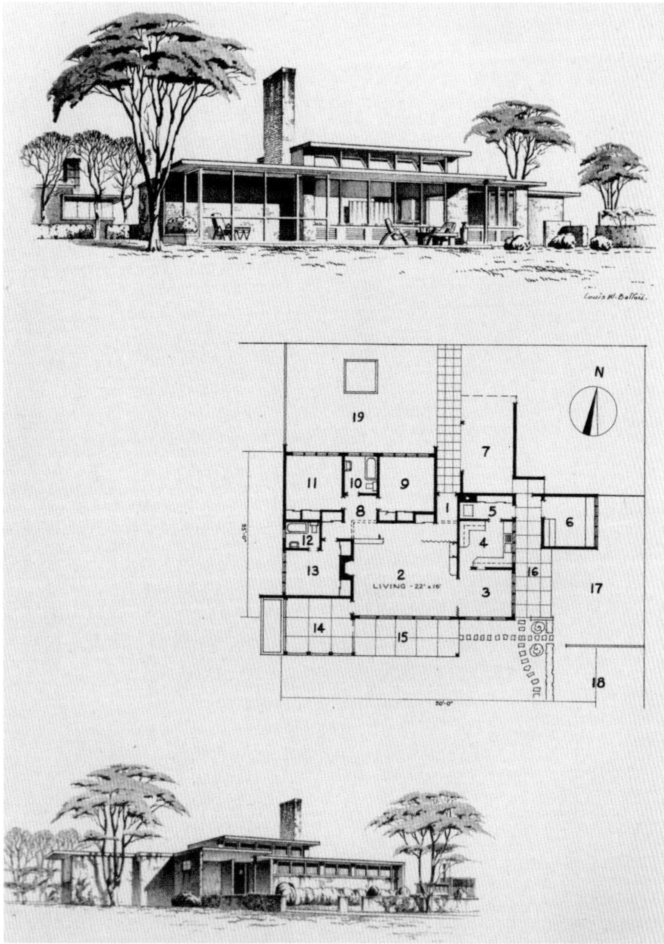

Figure 6.72. A. Lawrence Kocher, Louis W. Ballou, and Charles C. Justice. 1947. Solar House for Virginia. Published documentation. Floor plan and perspective views from the garden and from the street.

Figure 6.73. A. Lawrence Kocher, Louis W. Ballou, and Charles C. Justice. 1947. Solar House for Virginia. Published documentation. Bird's-eye view of the house.

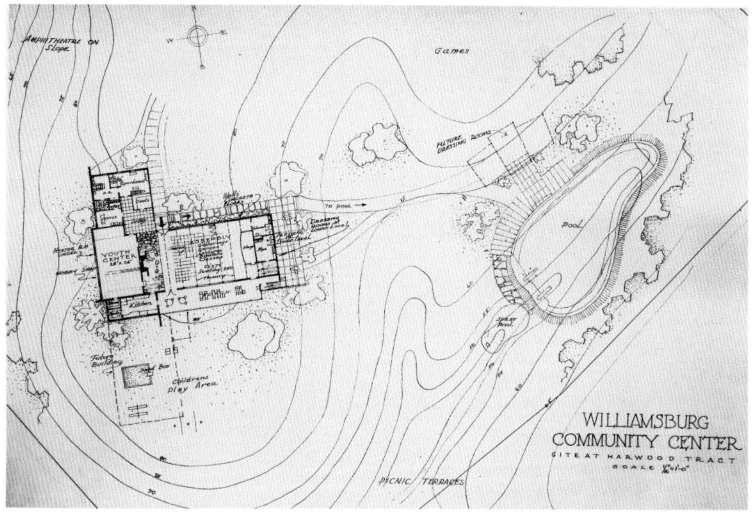

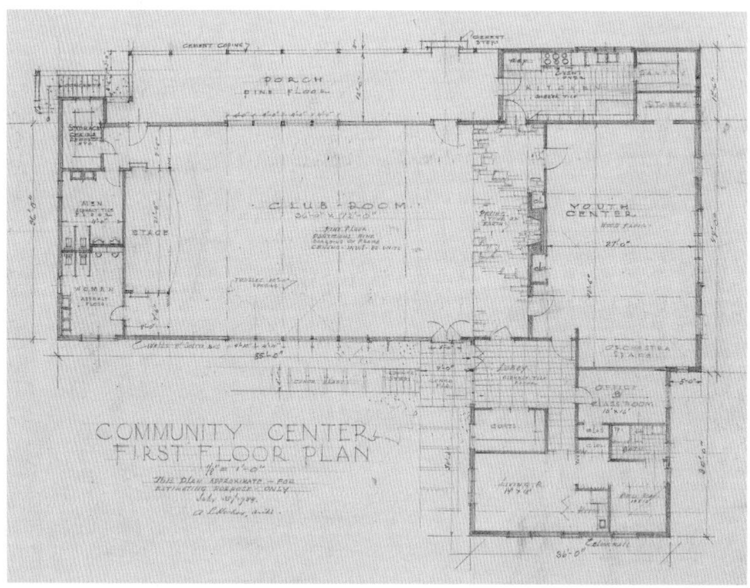

Figure 6.74. A. Lawrence Kocher. Williamsburg Community Center. 1954. Preliminary project. Site plan.

Figure 6.75. A. Lawrence Kocher. Williamsburg Community Center. 1954. Preliminary project. Elevation.

Figure 6.76. A. Lawrence Kocher. Williamsburg Community Center. 1954. Preliminary project. First floor plan.

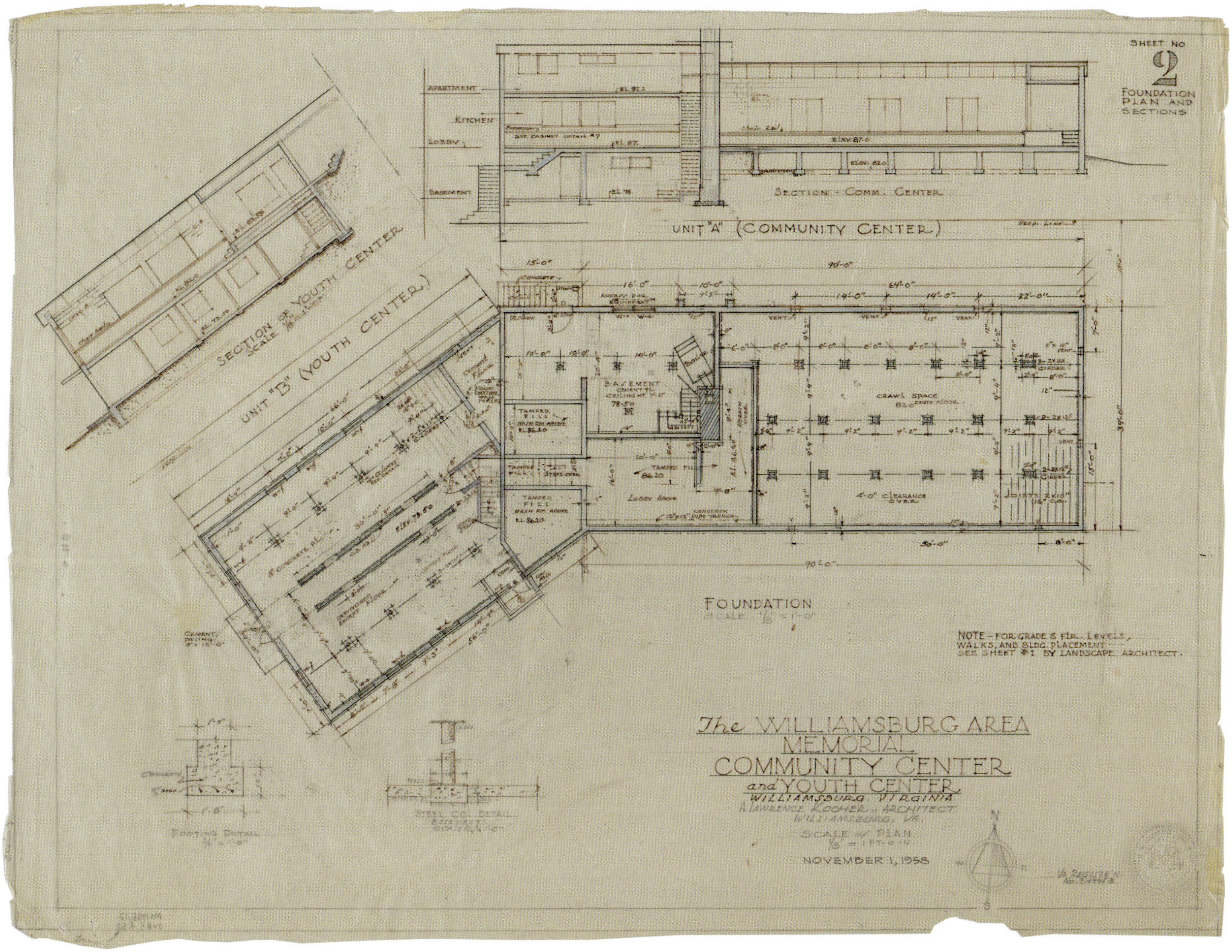

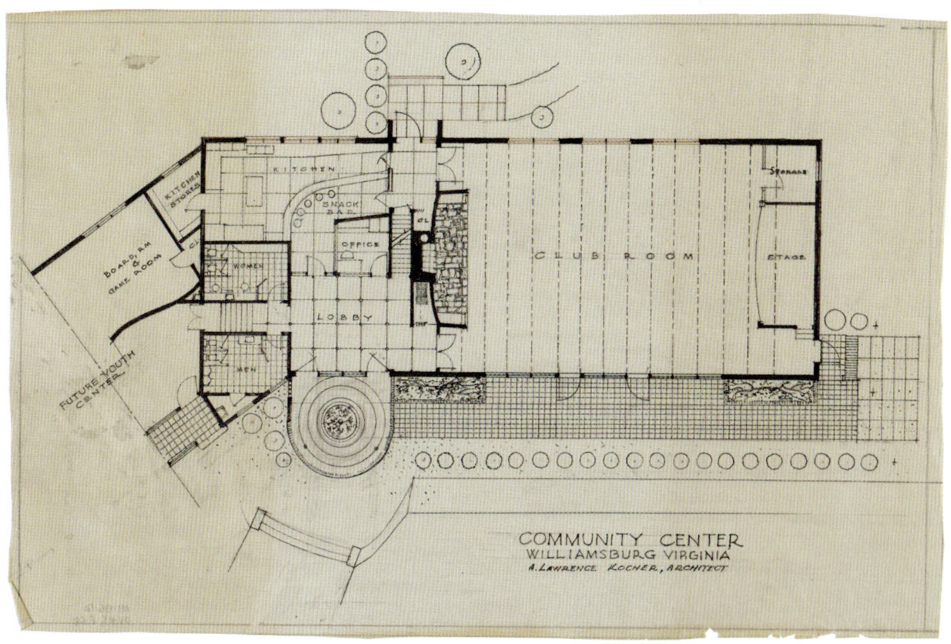

Figure 6.77. A. Lawrence Kocher. Williamsburg Area Memorial Community Center. 1958. Final project. Foundation.
Figure 6.78. A. Lawrence Kocher. Williamsburg Area Memorial Community Center. 1958. Final project. Second floor plan.

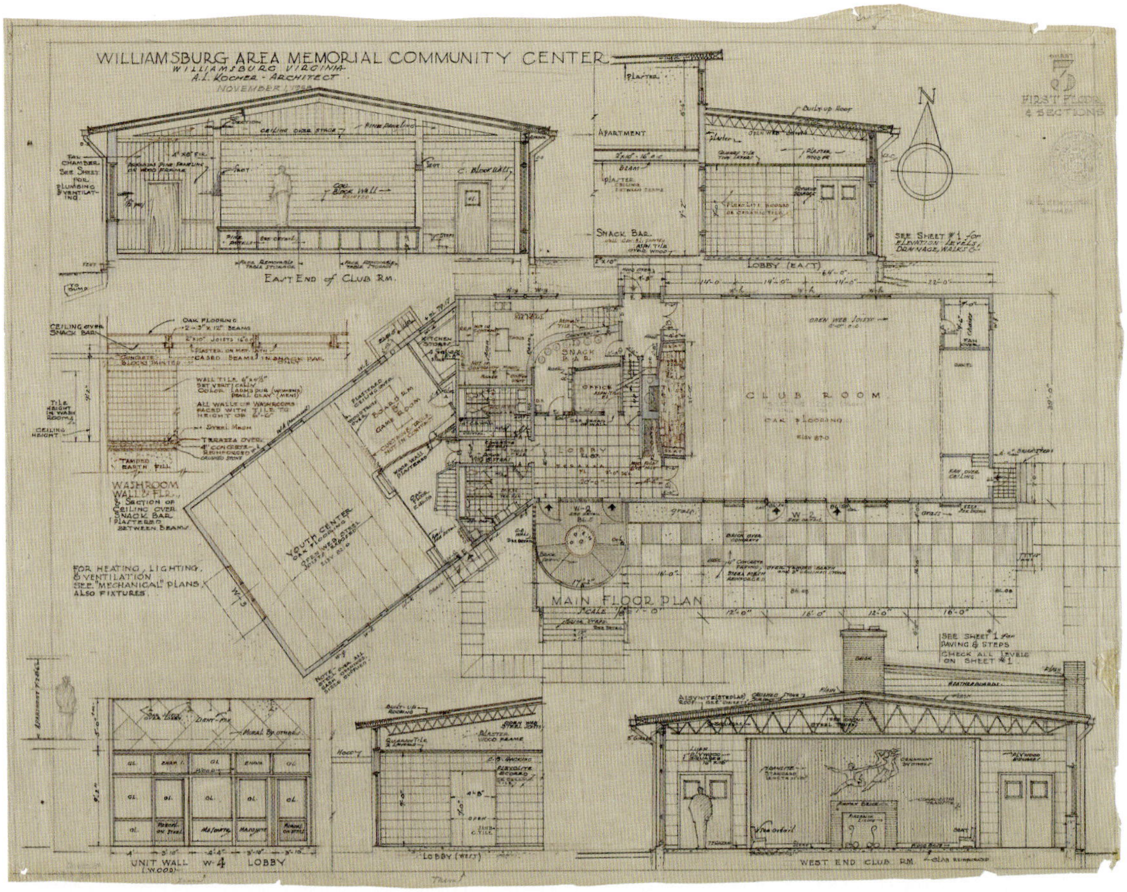
WILLIAMSBURG AREA MEMORIAL COMMUNITY CENTER
WILLIAMSBURG VIRGINIA
A.L. KOCHER - ARCHITECT
EAST END of CLUB RM.
LOBBY (EAST)
CLUB ROOM
MAIN FLOOR PLAN
YOUTH CENTER
WASHROOM
UNIT WALL W-4 LOBBY
WEST END CLUB RM.

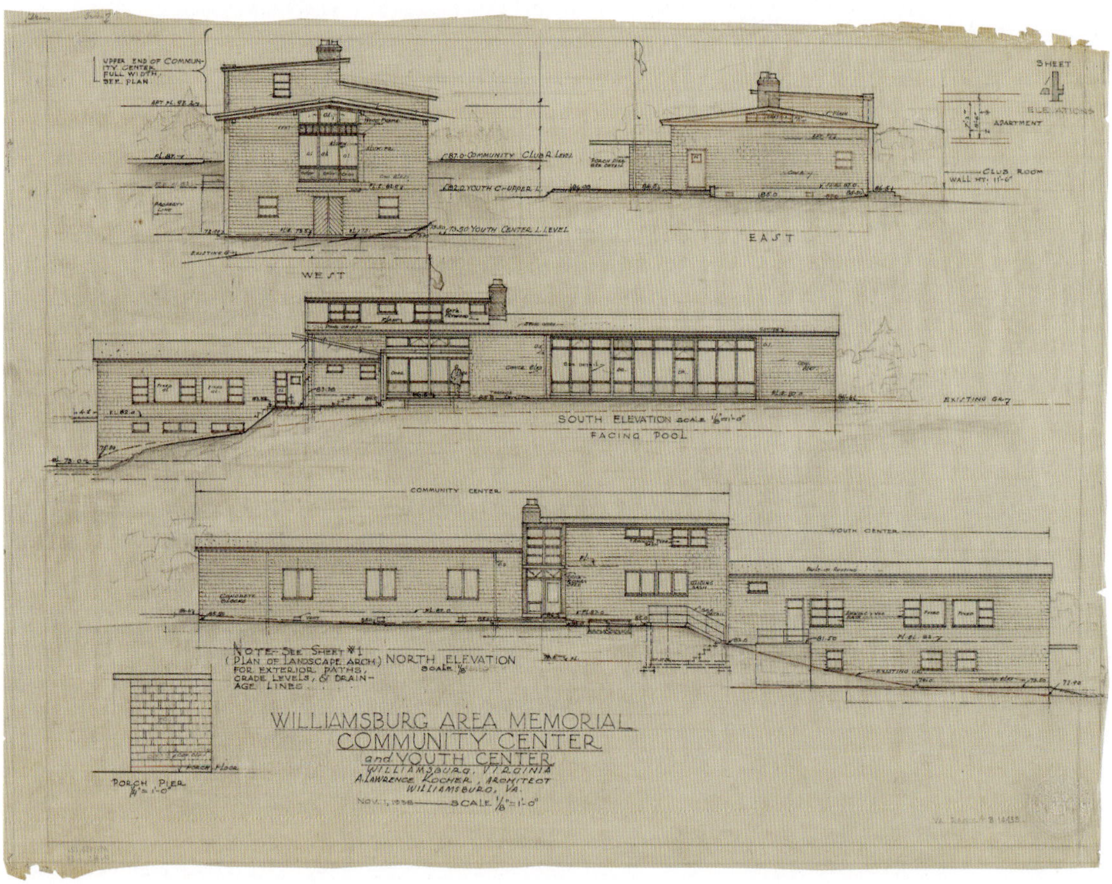
WEST
EAST
SOUTH ELEVATION
FACING POOL
NORTH ELEVATION
PORCH PIER
WILLIAMSBURG AREA MEMORIAL
COMMUNITY CENTER
and YOUTH CENTER
WILLIAMSBURG, VIRGINIA
A. LAWRENCE KOCHER, ARCHITECT
WILLIAMSBURG, VA.

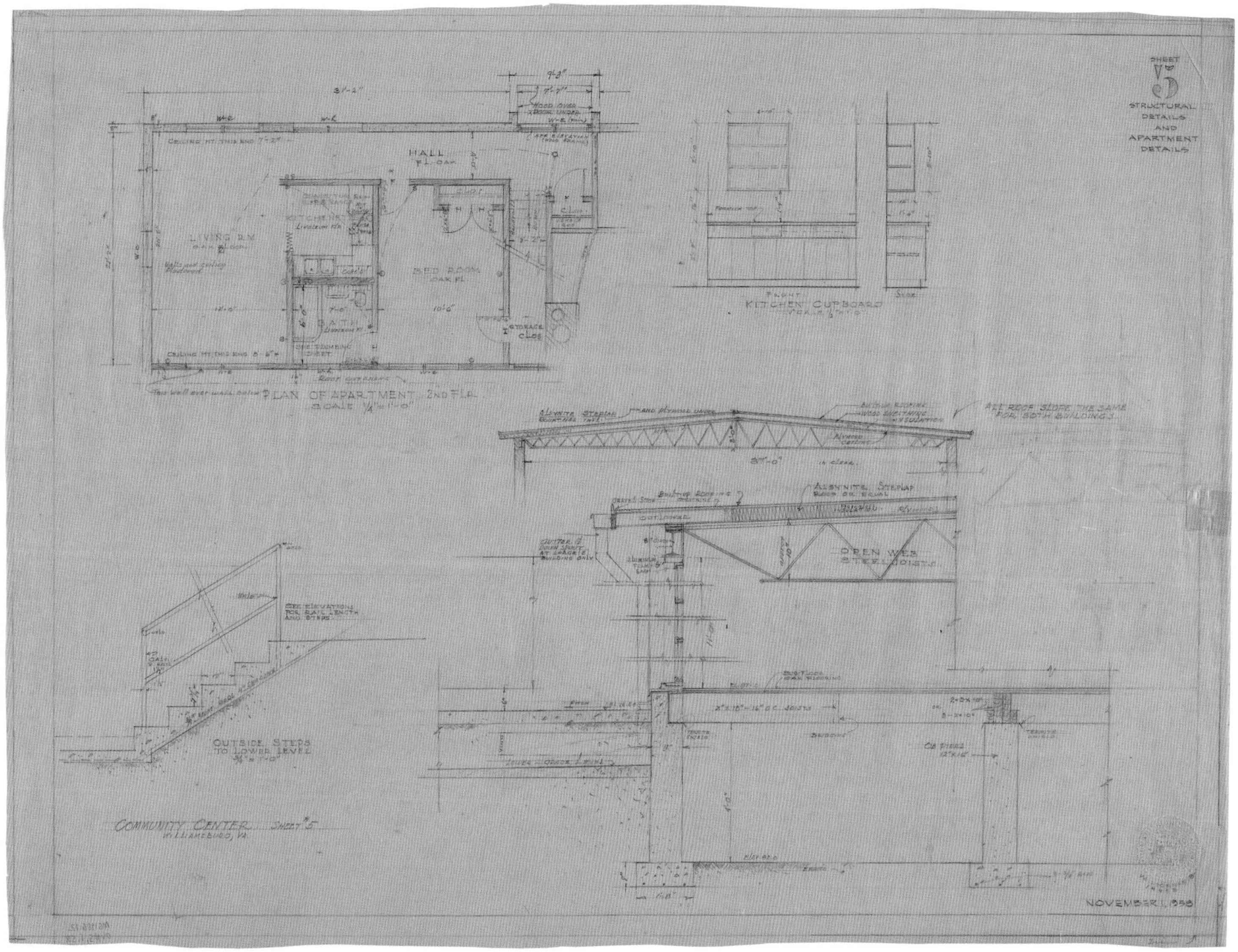

Previous page:
Figure 6.79. A. Lawrence Kocher. Williamsburg Area Memorial Community Center. 1958. Final project. First floor plan and sections.
Figure 6.80. A. Lawrence Kocher. Williamsburg Area Memorial Community Center. 1958. Final project. Elevations.

This page:
Figure 6.81. A. Lawrence Kocher. Williamsburg Area Memorial Community Center. 1958. Photo of the entrance.
Figure 6.82. A. Lawrence Kocher. Williamsburg Area Memorial Community Center. 1958. Final project. Details.

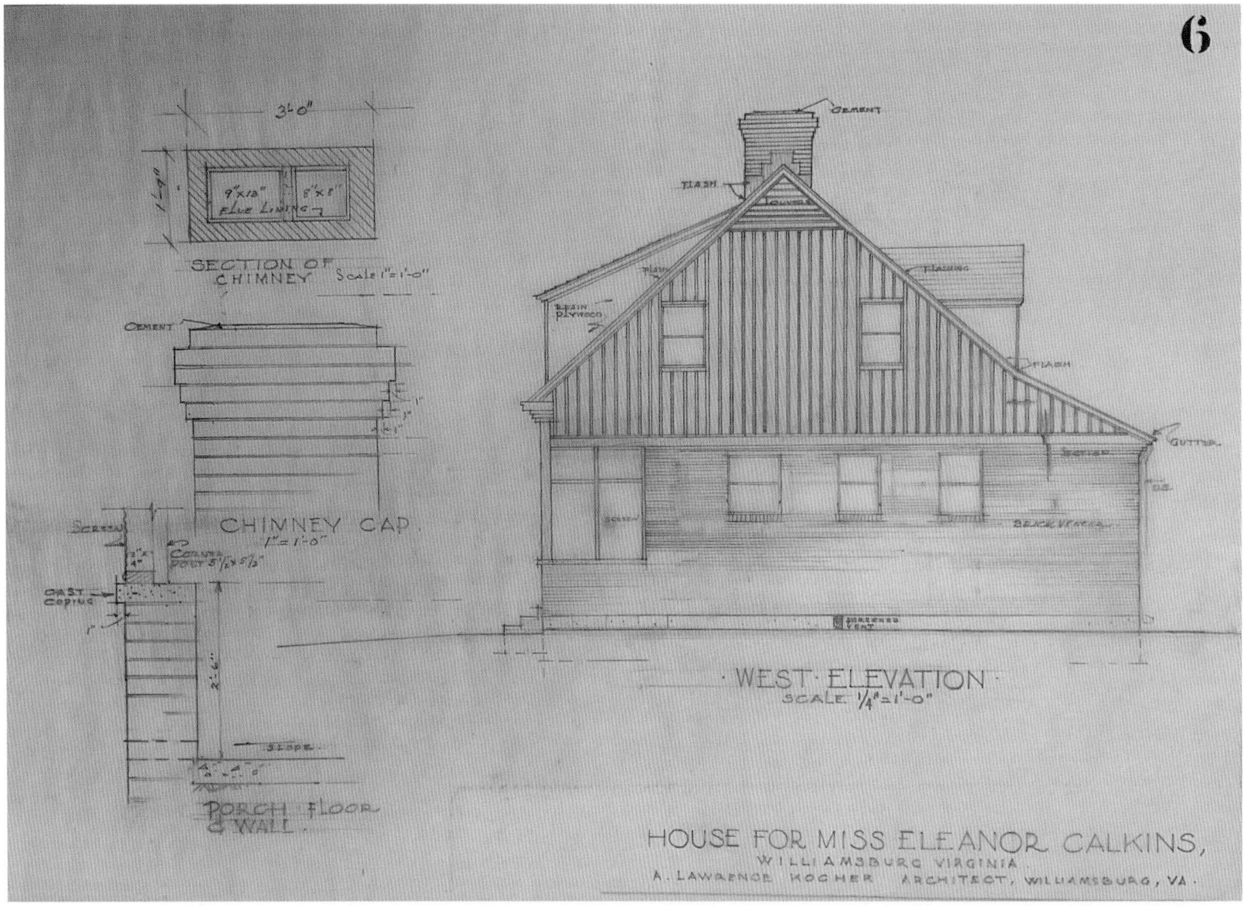
6
SECTION OF CHIMNEY Scale 1"=1'-0"
CHIMNEY CAP 1"=1'-0"
PORCH FLOOR & WALL
WEST ELEVATION
SCALE 1/4"=1'-0"
HOUSE FOR MISS ELEANOR CALKINS,
WILLIAMSBURG VIRGINIA
A. LAWRENCE KOCHER ARCHITECT, WILLIAMSBURG, VA.

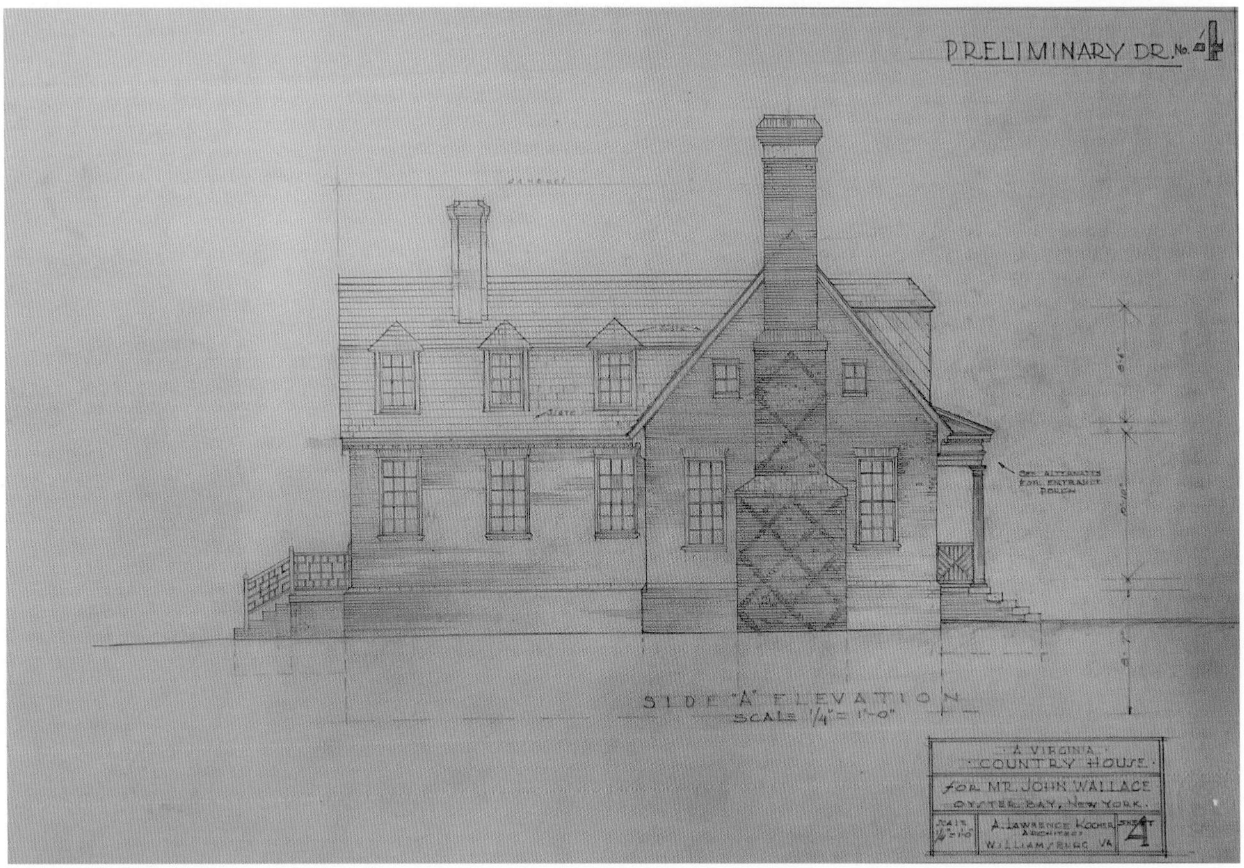
PRELIMINARY DR. No. 4
SIDE "A" ELEVATION
SCALE 1/4"=1'-0"
A VIRGINIA COUNTRY HOUSE
FOR MR. JOHN WALLACE
OYSTER BAY, NEW YORK.
A. LAWRENCE KOCHER ARCHITECT WILLIAMSBURG VA.
4

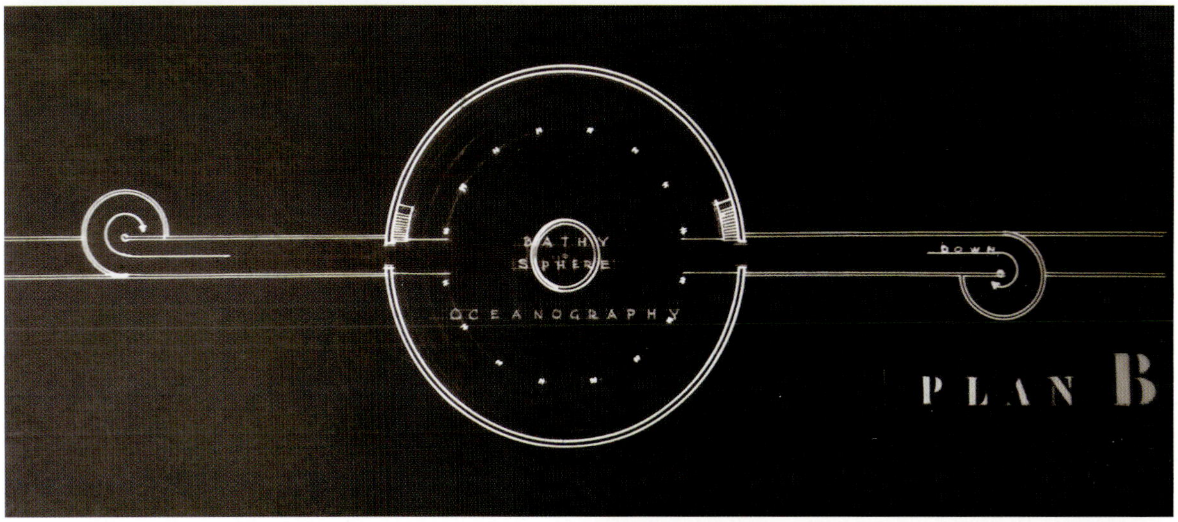

WORLD'S FAIR SYMBOL
This is artist's rendering of the Unisphere which will be theme symbol of New York's 1964-65 World's Fair, President Robert Moses of the Fair Corporation said Tuesday. Unisphere will represent the earth, with continents in raised outline and with three surrounding orbits. A light, representing a satellite, will move along each orbit. Unisphere, built of stainless steel, will be 120 feet in diameter, tilted on an elevated base, embedded in a pool. Overall height of structure, including its pedestal, will exceed 135 feet. (AP)

Previous page:
Figure 6.83. A. Lawrence Kocher. 1955. Calkins House. Williamsburg, Virginia. Elevation.
Figure 6.84. A. Lawrence Kocher. 1962. Country house for Mr. John Wallace. Oyster Bay, New York.

This page:
Figure 6.85. (Right-bottom) Unisphere. Final project by 1964 World's Fair. Gilmore D. Clarke.
Figure 6.86. (Below) A. Lawrence Kocher. 1960. Planetarium and Oceanography Center proposal for the 1964 World's Fair. Upper floor plan.
Figure 6.87. (Above) A. Lawrence Kocher. 1960. Planetarium and Oceanography Center proposal for the 1964 World's Fair. Lower floor plan.

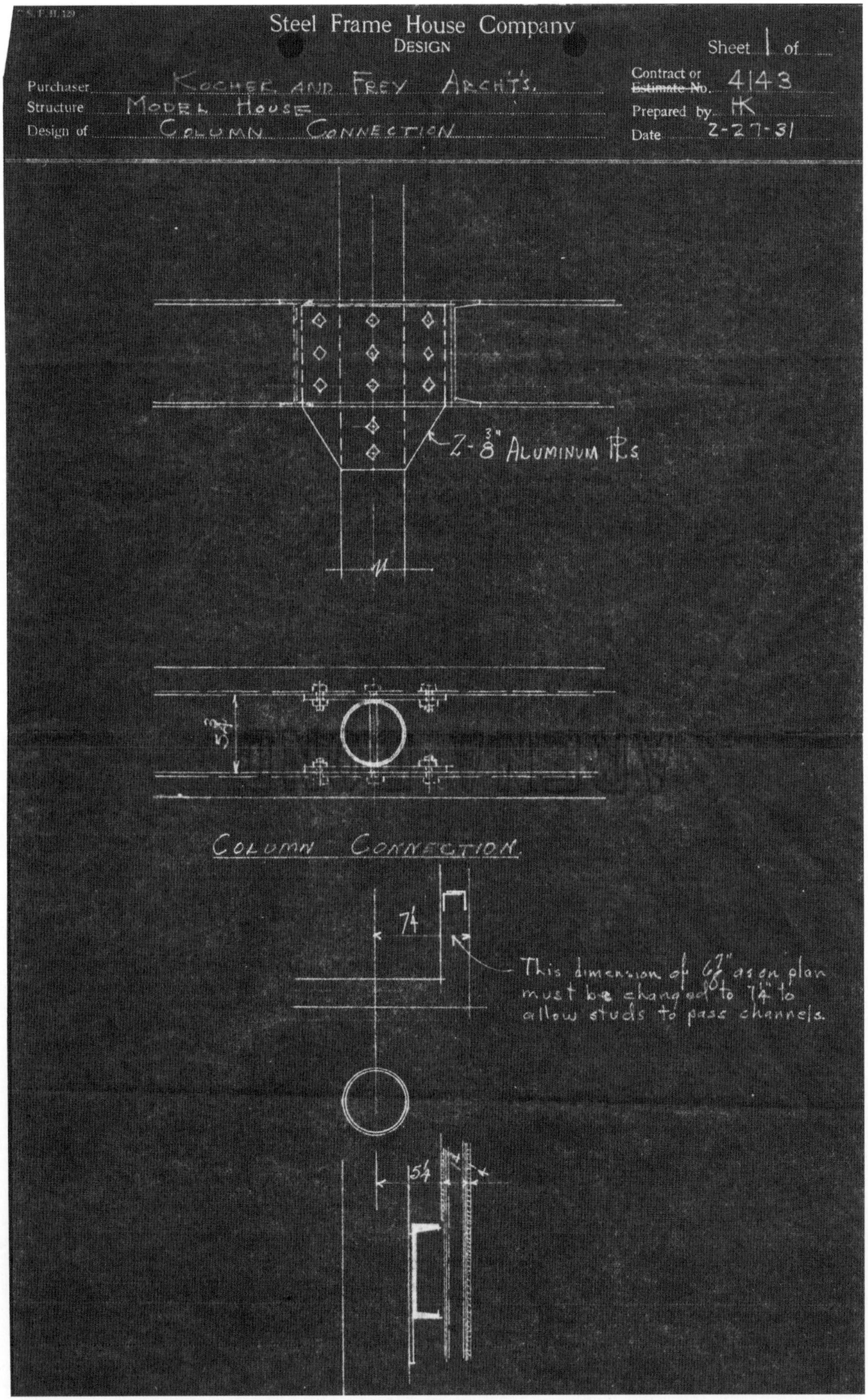
S.F.H. 129
Steel Frame House Company
DESIGN
Sheet 1 of
Purchaser Kocher and Frey Archt's.
Structure Model House
Design of Column Connection
Contract or Estimate No. 4143
Prepared by K
Date 2-27-31
2-3/8" Aluminum Pl.s
Column Connection.
7¼
This dimension of 6⅞" as on plan must be changed to 7¼ to allow studs to pass channels.
5¼

CONCLUSIONS

AND NOTES ON THE GRAPHIC RECONSTRUCTION

A. Lawrence Kocher, American Architect

> When the *International Style* exhibition opened at the Museum of Modern Art in New York, Alfred Barr, the museum's director, announced: 'The present exhibition is an assertion that the confusion of the past 40 years, or rather of the past century, may shortly come to an end.' As important as the London 1851 or the Chicago 1893 exhibitions, the Museum of Modern Art exhibit named and legitimatized a brand of Modernism that came to dominate American and international developments…In 1932 there also occurred another important opening: the public viewing of the first buildings of Colonial Williamsburg. Somewhere between the two openings in Virginia and New York, most American architecture existed.[1]

Architectural historian Richard Guy Willson defines the spectral limits in which American architecture operated in 1932, the year of Hitchcock and Johnson's exhibition at MoMA. Marked on one end by the *International Style* exhibition and by the inauguration of Colonial Williamsburg's reconstructed buildings on the other end, the architectural range at this time held opposing directions and conflicting views for the future of American architecture. One moved toward the past and the nostalgia for the traditional and vernacular American styles, the other pointed toward the future through an architectural ideology imported from Europe. These conflicting views about architecture—that the MoMA exhibition aimed to favor the European Modern Movement—caused an initial confusion among American architects. When modern architecture was first published in American magazines, almost every architect in the country took a quite dogmatic position against or in favor of the new architecture. There was division among traditionalists and advocates of the Modern Movement alike, even among those defending alternate versions of modernism and the new champions of strict functionalism.[2] There were few recorded exceptions of architects taking a more balanced position, A. Lawrence Kocher being the most relevant among them.

A. Lawrence Kocher was the only architect who was a main protagonist in both of these defining cornerstones in the architectural debate during those years; Kocher's work was included in the MoMA exhibition and in the subsequent book by Hitchcock and Johnson, as one of the few American representatives in these two cultural productions.[3] Simultaneously, Kocher was a very influential member of the advisory board for the Williamsburg restoration, which pioneered collaboration between different disciplines on restoration with a methodology based on local fieldwork.[4] This duality in Kocher's architectural ideology was a constant from the beginning of his professional life. Kocher gained scholarly reputation investigating the formal manifestations of east-coast American vernacular architecture while concurrently acting as the main advocate of the European Modern Movement through his leadership role at *Architectural Record* starting in 1928. Even more relevant than Kocher's protagonist role in this duality was the content and particular focus of his participation, which can be summarized in two aspects. First, although the search for a new expression for a national American architecture was a general preoccupation of the era, Kocher was one of the few architects who envisioned the need for a synthesis between the European modern movement and American vernacular as the way to achieve the goal of creating a national style. Secondly, to this end, Kocher had to also produce an interpretative change of the two ends of the spectrum—modern European and vernacular American architecture—to accommodate his objective.[5]

Kocher's architectural ideology and its resulting designs were based on a redefinition of what is encompassed within the term "American vernacular." Kocher not only considered vernacular artifacts the architectural objects produced during the colonial period and the early years of the American independent republic; he also categorized the most recent non-authored devices related to the American tradition of transitional dwelling. These unconventional architectures range from all kinds of mobile dwellings—like trailers, wagons, and camping tents—to all habitational solutions related to the automobile like autocamps, roadside cabins, and motels. Kocher also regarded all types of prefabricated houses as vernacular, from the most modern to classical styles. One of the singularities of this new vernacular was the makeshift and minimalistic use of materials not produced to be used in the construction industry. Textiles, aluminum sheets, plywood boards, and improvised assemblies of scrap reclaimed materials were frequently used in both designed and anonymous constructions. The lack of aesthetic concerns in the design and the eagerness for experimenting cheaper and more efficient materials and building systems created a field of informal research promptly adopted and capitalized by Kocher in his own designs. All artifacts included in this expanded vernacular also shared an imper-

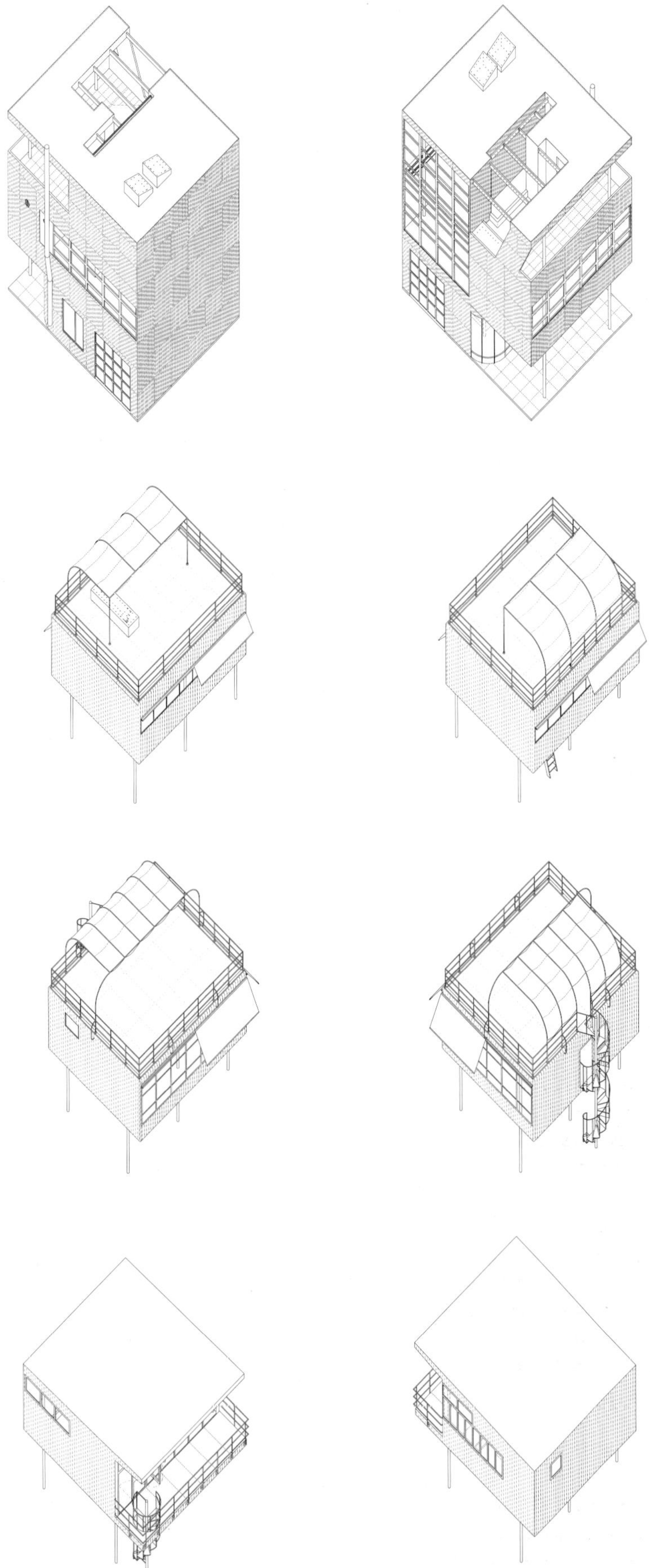

Figure 7.1. A. Lawrence Kocher and Albert Frey. Axonometric view of all the case studies. From top to bottom: Aluminaire House 1930 (Built), Experimental Weekend House 1932 (Unbuilt), Kocher Canvas Weekend House 1934–1935 (Built), and Florida Weekend House 1937 (Unbuilt).

manence and transportability—their light materiality permitted a minimally invasive and temporary occupation of the territory, along with a more fluid and permeable relation between the domestic and the natural environments. This extension of the vernacular realm, which Kocher elaborated upon in many of his articles and lectures, was precisely due to his consideration of prefabrication and standardization, not as modern inventions, but as a strategy already used by anonymous builders.

A secondary (re)interpretation of the latter is that Kocher shifted the special principles of modern architecture from formal, spatial, and stylistic traits—like those used by Hitchcock and Johnson in their seminal book—to the material culture, methods, and processes of production.[6] Modern architecture, in Kocher's view, was not solely about a modern style, but rather an architecture designed to incorporate the modern forms of production and the new materials selected for their improved functional performance. The call for the inclusion of prefabrication and standardization within the vernacular was supported by Kocher's research on the documented use of handbooks on standard architectural elements and details for the construction of traditional American architecture. The idea is explicitly explained by Kocher in his writings and lectures and served as a powerful tool for his theoretical and practical endeavors, favoring the use of a catalog of mass-produced industrial products over customized designs. This is illustrated by his consistent use of the same constructive solutions in many of his built and unbuilt projects spanning different times and locations. Characteristic of Kocher's practice, such solutions allowed him to explore a new field of research developed in close collaboration with industry. Kocher's research followed a two-directional path: he not only used his building as a testing laboratory for industrial products, but also reported back and demanded further development of new constructive solutions from industry to satisfy the novel functional requirements required by new social uses. Experimental intent was always present in Kocher's buildings, whether it focused on material use and performance, construction methodology, on-site construction labor management, or all of the above. In his buildings, details were treated as an assembly of standard parts and the whole building was considered as a coordinated aggregation of diverse prefabricated systems. This shift from form to production was the way in which Kocher was able to close the circle and establish his criteria for a new American architecture.

Kocher's ideological position and his continuous eagerness for experimentation transformed him into an atypical practitioner. While many of his contemporaries were purely design focused, he established a very avant-garde symbiosis among his three main endeavors: his work as an educator, as a scholar, and as a practitioner. His articles published in *Architectural Record* and other journals, his books, teaching methodology, and built and speculative designs composed an extremely consistent and intertwined whole. Some of his architectural works can be seen as manifestos that would later further develop in the articles of *Architectural Record*. Some others are the direct and material demonstrations of industrial systems, materials, and principles previously explored in his articles. Even other works are conceived and executed as part of a pedagogical activity. It is rare to find an architectural design in Kocher's body of work that does not demonstrate a multitude of interconnections among his pedagogy, his editorial work, and his scholarship.

Keenness for technological innovation in the field of construction systems, processes, and materials also pervaded his work as an educator. Kocher can arguably be considered the pioneer of design-build pedagogy in American academia. He is the first educator who considered the act of the students designing and constructing a building not only to meet a practical need—of the school or the adjacent social context—but also as a pedagogical activity. It tested advancements produced by industry and created feedback about the results relating to social needs that would shape future innovations. The experiences in design-build studios—first at the Carnegie Institute and later at Black Mountain College—were innovative in the implementation of federal policies as the Work-Study program which furnished students with hands-on acquired knowledge and the means to partially cover, especially during periods of crisis, the financial requirements of an increasingly costly architectural education. In a different form, and with several modifications, both the design-build pedagogy and the Work-Study Program are still in use within the American university.

Alongside his pedagogical experiments, Kocher's efforts as the editorial head of *Architectural Record* and his work as an independent scholar can be considered the main complements for his experimental practice. He authored a series of articles with Albert Frey, published in the magazine between 1931 and 1932, versing on standard dimensions and performance of various industrialized elements. The articles were entitled either with the name of the group of elements studied—stairs, clothes closets, windows—or grouped under the generic titles of "Dimensions" first and of "Design and Drafting Problems" later.[7] This catalog of elements was developed by Kocher and Frey using data supplied by different manufacturers. It was derived from Kocher's study of American colonial builders and their work methodology, and built on the experience of a sister magazine at the F.W. Dodge Corporation, *Sweet's Indexed Catalog of Building Construction*.[8] The articles are the first of their kind in the United States and predate (by four years) the publication of the most reputed and widely circulated book on the topic: Ernst Neufert's *Bauentwurfslehre*, released in 1936.[9]

Kocher's work as managing editor of *Architectural Record* coincided with the most successful stage of the magazine and the peak of its influence over the coeval architectural debates. He turned the magazine from a portfolio-based venue into a forum for ideological discussion especially focused on the role of technology within architectural design and its transformative effect over society. Kocher, alongside chief editor Michael Mikkelson, recruited a completely new team that renovated the magazine's focus and content. They started publishing articles by prominent modern architects like Le Corbusier and Walter Gropius, and Henry Russel Hitchcock became a regular contributor to the magazine. Knud Lonberg-Holm, Theodore Larson, Douglas Haskell, and Robert L. Davison were hired to create and develop new sections devoted to different topics, like the "Series of Early American Architecture" and "Technical News and Research," and rework others, like a more typologically focused version of the existing "Portfolio of Current Architecture," now packed with examples of modern architecture in

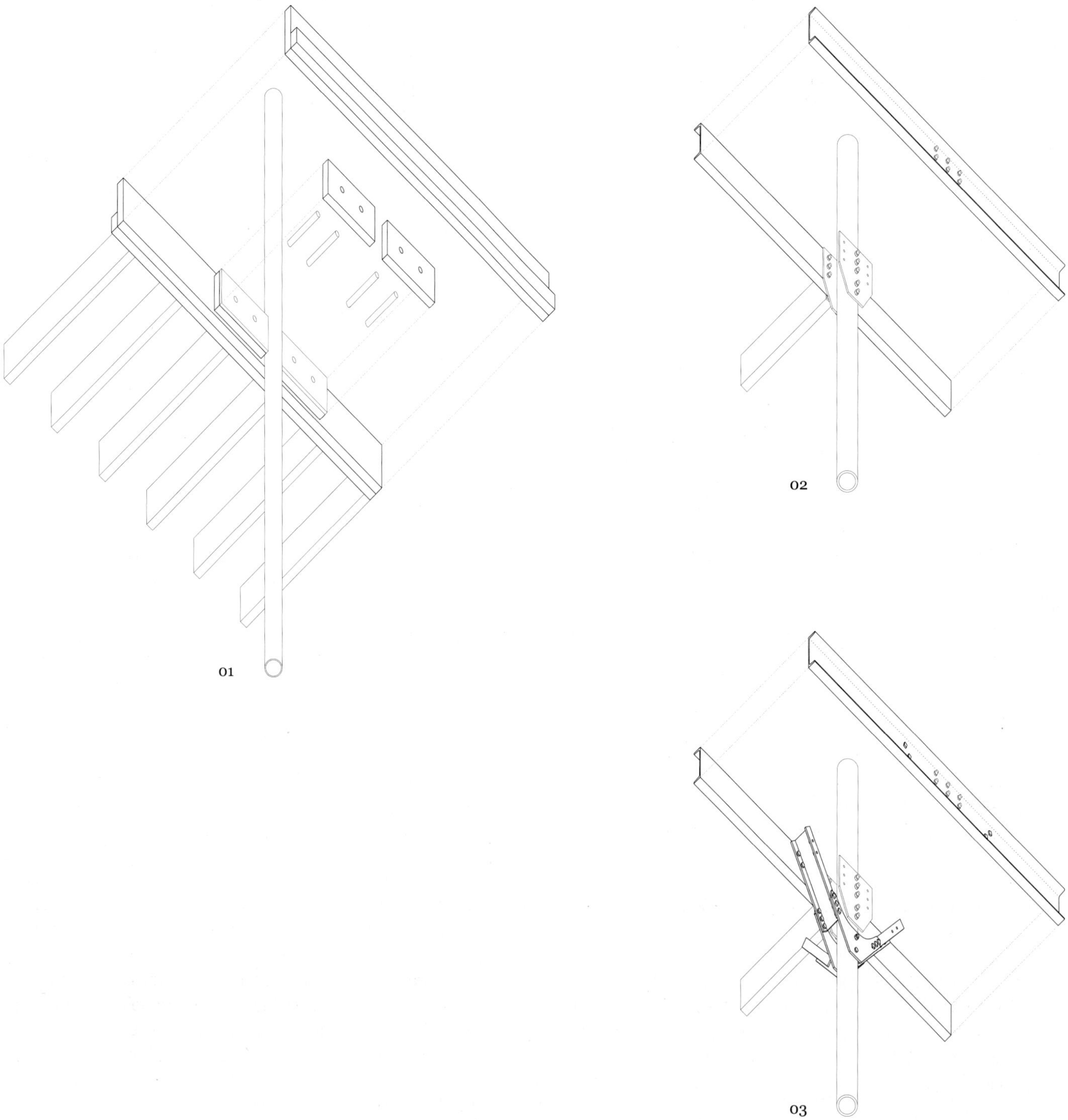

Figure 7.2. A. Lawrence Kocher and Albert Frey. Exploded axonometric view of the typical column-beam connections. Scale 3/8"=1'-0". Aluminaire House 1930 (Built), Experimental Weekend House 1932 (Unbuilt), Kocher Canvas Weekend House 1934–35 (built), and Florida Weekend House 1937 (Unbuilt).
01. Experimental Weekend House, Kocher Canvas Weekend House, Florida Weekend House. Standard detail.
02. Aluminaire House. Original detail.
03. Aluminaire House. Modified detail.

both Europe and the United States. As the names of the new sections evidence, Kocher, although strongly advocating for new modern architecture, always kept the magazine's support for historical heritage preservation and to the study of vernacular architecture alive as a possible way to "Americanize" the findings of the new trend imported from Europe.

During his years at the magazine there was always a very fluid cross-pollination between the sections and articles of *Architectural Record* and Kocher's professional practice. Many of the construction materials, elements, and systems studied in "Technical News and Research," and in Kocher's articles about dimensions in architecture, were later tested and evaluated in his built projects. Closing the loop, these projects were then often published in the magazine to illustrate the use of materials and tectonic principles consistent with the magazine's new technological focus. An excellent example of this fertile interaction between the magazine and Kocher's built work was the series of designs for the weekend houses. Kocher and Frey designed the first member of this typological family in early 1932, the unbuilt Experimental Weekend House, a speculative project developed with Frey for an exhibition in Washington, D.C., sponsored by the Cotton-Textile Institute. The Experimental Weekend House was profoundly intertwined with the development of the legislation that established the two-day weekend as a social right and with the popularization of the automobile in the United States. This house was the physical incarnation of the ideas expressed by Knud Lonberg-Holm in his 1930 *Architectural Record* article on the topic.[10] A 1934 issue of *Architectural Record* published the hypothetical design, which was instrumental for the development and construction of the Kocher Canvas Weekend House, along with the design of the Florida Weekend House.[11] The magazine reinforced this line of research with several publications focused on alternate dwellings, the kind facilitated by the 1920s and 1930s automobile mass production boom, like roadside cabins, autocamps, tourist homes, cabin camps, cottage courts, motor courts, motor inns, and highway motels.[12]

The weekend houses, and their relationship with the five-day workweek, illustrate the profound involvement of Kocher's work with the socio-economic and political context at the time.[13] This trend was exacerbated during the Great Depression due to the extreme hardships to be overcome in the field of architecture, but it has been present in Kocher's work since his early involvement in the public and private efforts to create the first American historical heritage preservation institutions. During the Great Depression, Kocher was one of the leading voices in the field of housing and prefabricated construction. He extended his influence as a member of the White House Conference on Home Building and Home Ownership, as an American delegate to the International Congress of Art and Applied Arts of Paris in 1937, a consultant in the Works Progress Administration in 1938, and as the 1939's New York World's Fair Associate Designer of the Domestic Utilities Building. His academic leadership appointments as Head of the Department of Art and Architecture at the McIntire School of Architecture and Fine Arts of the University of Virginia, Head of the Department of Architecture at the Carnegie Institute of Technology, and his time as architecture instructor at Black Mountain College, gave him a deep understanding of the importance of architectural education as a means of reinforcing the social commitment of the discipline. His work left a durable footprint in American academia. Kocher's numerous infructuous attempts of creating a new school of architecture to more closely engage industry, production, and technical aspects of architecture finally came together in his unbuilt 1943 proposal for the Architectural Center. Although this project may paradoxically be considered the only project in which Kocher was not perfectly attuned to the spirit of his time, it still rendered important lessons for the future of architecture schools. Kocher's influence over the dissemination of the modern movement and shaping of American architecture while in charge of *Architectural Record* was enormous, but it was enhanced by his facilitation of the arrival of many European architects to America. His generosity and vision, sharing his commissions with immigrant architects, such as Ziegler and Frey, and looking for economic support to convince Gropius to teach and practice on American soil marked the proliferation of modernity in the United States.

In many cases, Kocher's work bears a dual or even collective—in the case of the works at Black Mountain College—authorship in which Kocher, although sole recipient of the commission, intentionally reserved himself as *primus inter pares*. Alongside this unconventional authorship, Kocher's transdisciplinary exuberance might have been the other main reason for his secondary position within the modern American canon. The stylistic diversity of Kocher's body of work derived from the complexity of his multifaceted design process. Kocher was an architect of ideas more than he was an architect of forms. His body of work ranged from the most comprehensive and historically accurate architectural reconstructions to the radical modernity of works like the Aluminaire House and the Kocher Canvas Weekend House. This stylistic diversity and his relative lack of aesthetic preoccupation made Kocher very difficult to be catalogued, classified, and therefore situated within the American modern architecture history, notwithstanding his deep influence over its development and evolution. The most homogeneous part of Kocher's body of work regarding its stylistic adherence to modernity starts with the Sunlight Towers (1929) and ends with the Solar House (1947); it can be understood as a series of research paths in which writings, theoretical proposals, pedagogical experiences, and constructed buildings blended. When these theoretical research paths took architectural form, whether on paper or on the construction site, they were resolved by Kocher in the form of a typological sequence with an experimental intention. These lineages evolved from an ideological and formal core, operating as a laboratory, resolving between inquiries for advancement and technological reality to respond to new, and changing social requirements. As a result, the produced architectural artifacts, stand in an intermediate point between the modern architecture and that new mobile vernacular imagined by Kocher. His artifacts exhibited a threshold between natural and domestic spaces, reduced to a minimum thickness to exhibit the fiction of mobility—a transient way of living that Kocher thought was embedded in the essence of American dwellings. Kocher deemed necessary to create an architecture not founded on the solidity of modern examples imported from Europe, but on what—in Professor Peter Waldman's words—"is the essence of American architecture: the proneness towards a potential (or real)

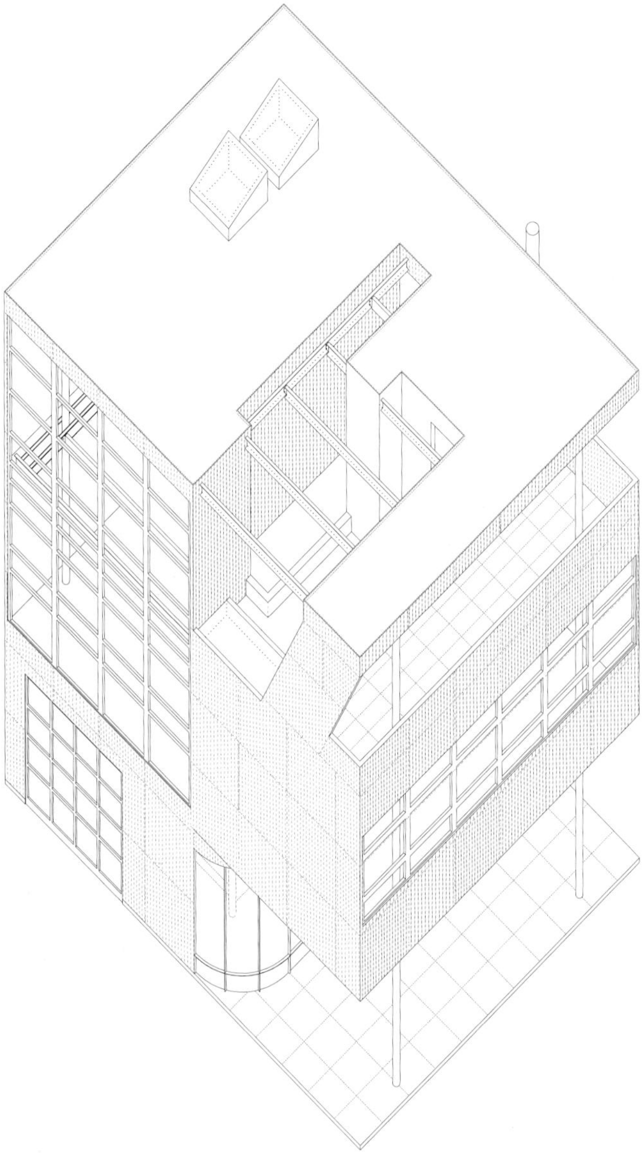

01

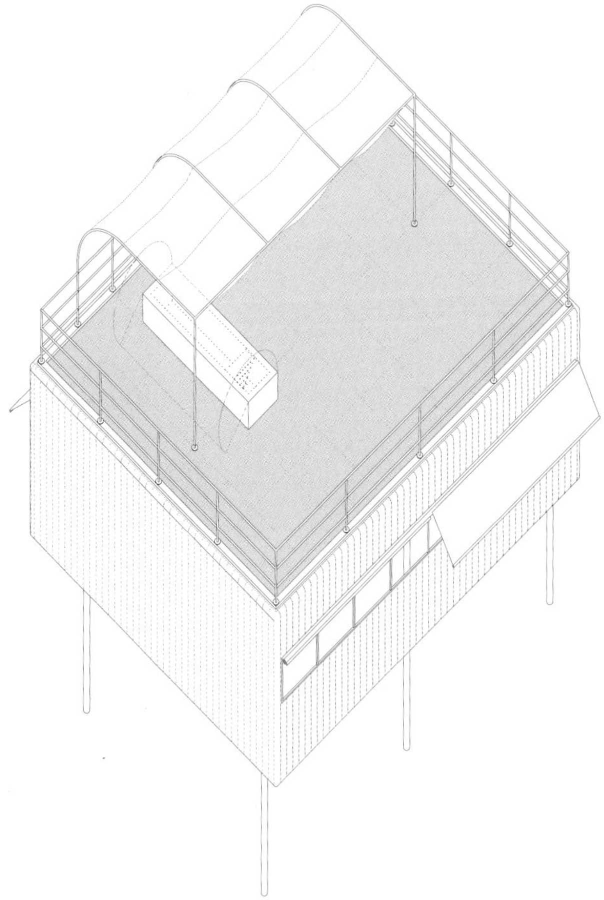

02

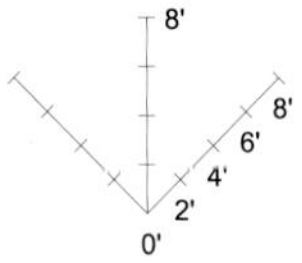

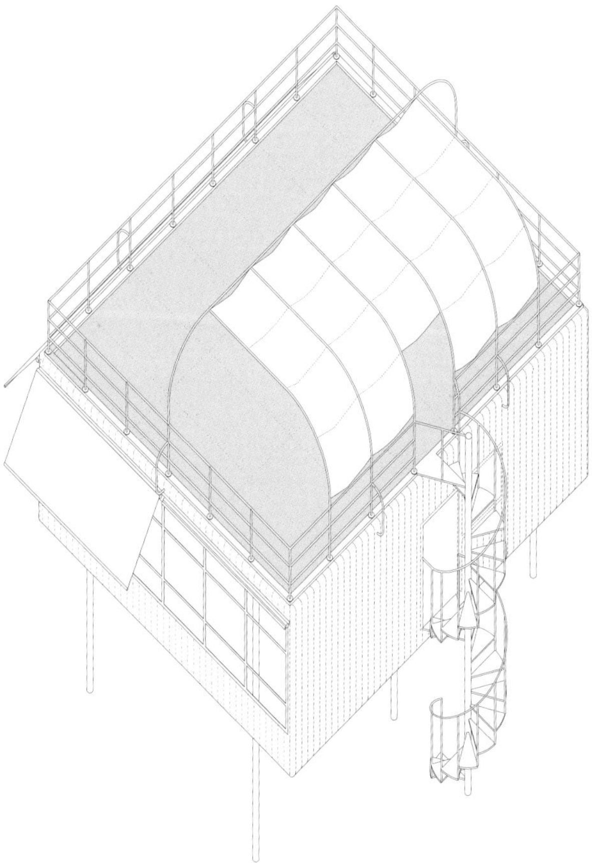

03

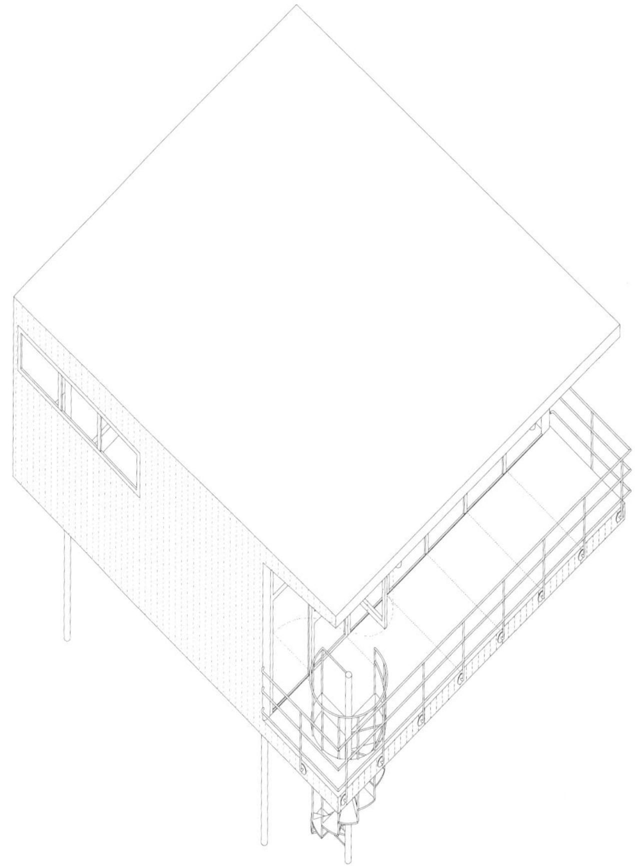

04

Figure 7.3. A. Lawrence Kocher and Albert Frey. Axonometric view of all the case studies. Exterior envelopes.
01. Aluminaire House 1930 (Built).
02. Weekend Experimental House 1932 (Unbuilt).
03. Kocher Canvas Weekend House 1934–35 (Built).
04. Florida Weekend House 1937 (Unbuilt).

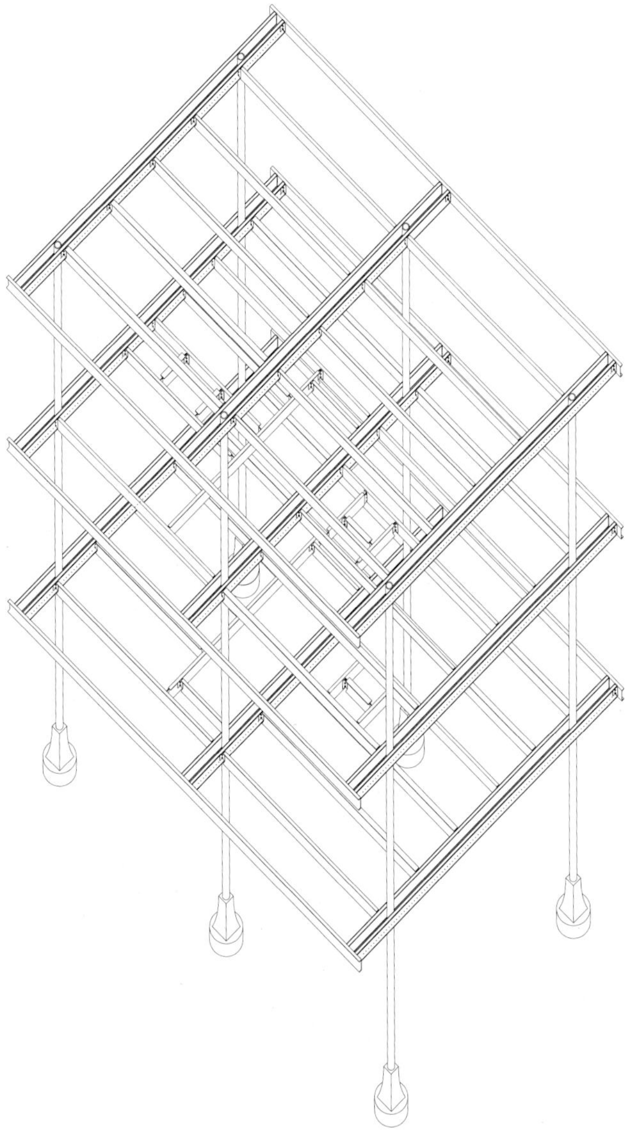

01

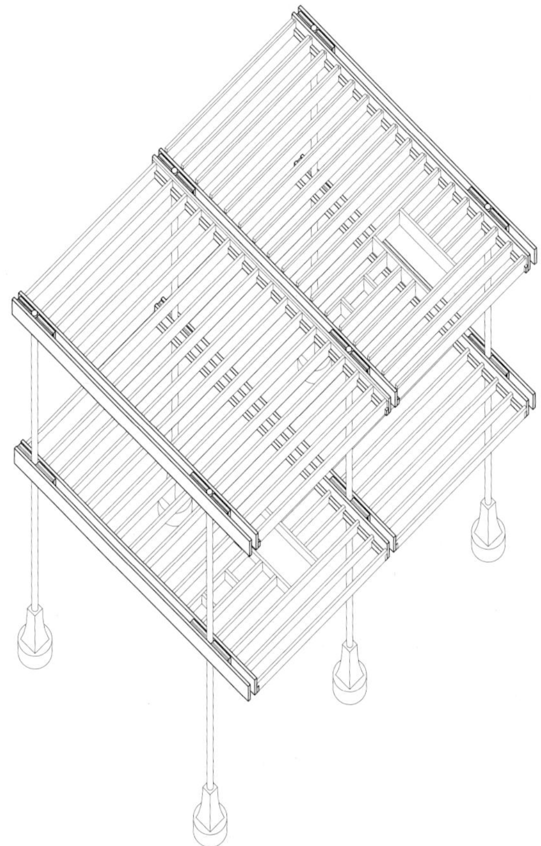

02

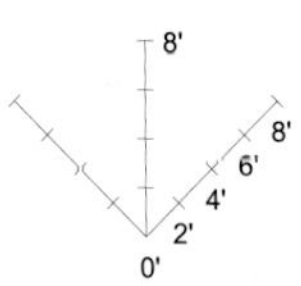

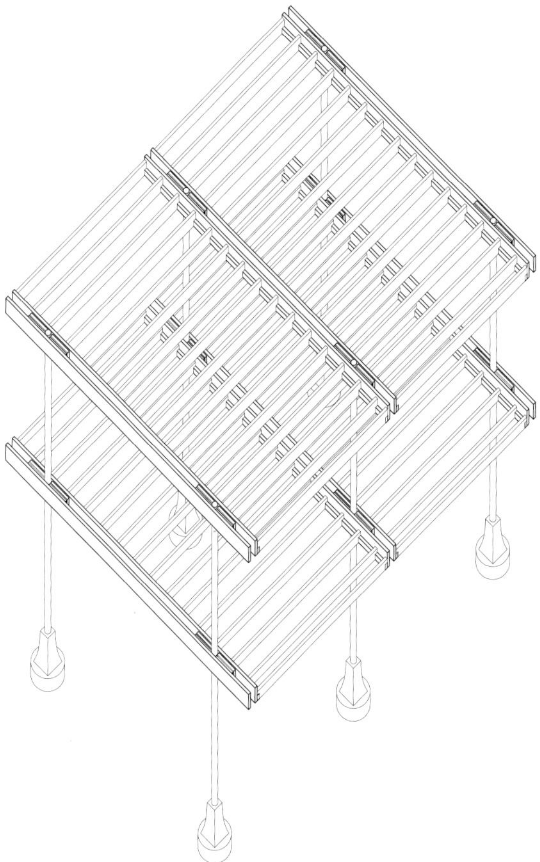

03

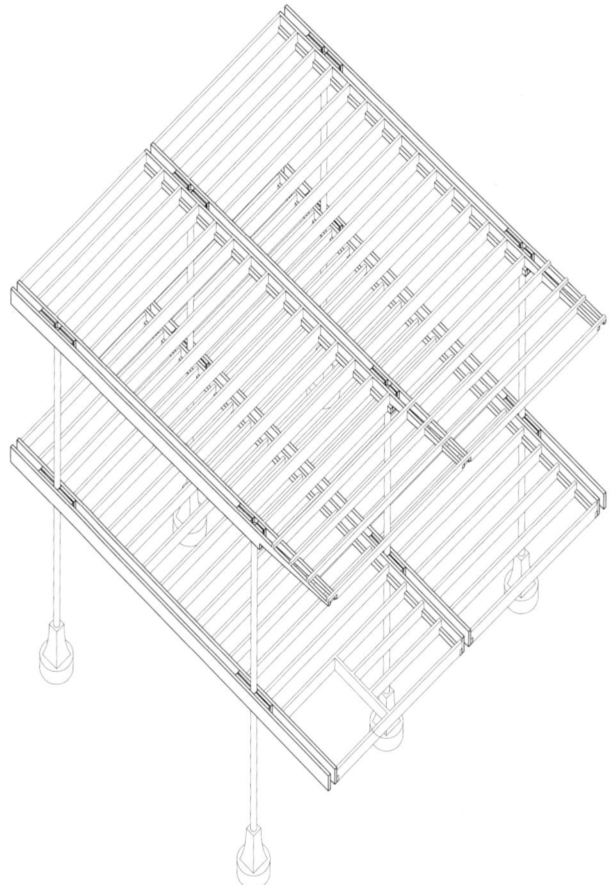

04

Figure 7.4. A. Lawrence Kocher and Albert Frey. Axonometric view of all the case studies. Structural systems.
01. Aluminaire House 1930 (Built).
02. Weekend Experimental House 1932 (Unbuilt).
03. Kocher Canvas Weekend House 1934–35 (Built).
04. Florida Weekend House 1937 (Unbuilt).

state of movement."[14] These series of extremely light and provisory constructions predated and foreshadow the insightful observations about American architecture by British critic Reyner Banham:

> Left to their own devices, Americans do not monumentalize or make architecture. From the Cape Cod cottage, through the balloon frame to the perfection of permanently pleated aluminum siding with embossed wood-graining, they have tended to build a brick chimney and lean a collection of shacks against it…And it hit me then, that if dirty old Nature could be kept under the proper degree of control (sex left in, streptococci taken out) by other means, the United States would be happy to dispense with architecture and buildings altogether…This suspicion is inarticulately shared by the untold thousands of Americans who have already shed the deadweight of domestic architecture and live in mobile homes which, though they may never be moved, still deliver rather better performance as shelter than do ground-anchored structures costing at least three times as much and weighing ten times more.[15]

Notes on the Graphic Reconstruction: Rhopography of American Modernity

The documental reconstruction carried out in this book has the main objective of graphically supporting the typological evolution of Kocher's houses, starting with the Aluminaire House (1931) and ending with the Florida Weekend House (1937). The typological lineage inaugurated by the Aluminaire House had its origin in the Renaissance villa transformed by Le Corbusier into a "machine for living." Corbusian influence over the Aluminaire House was then progressively diluted in the next member of the typological series, substituted instead by traits closer to a new American vernacular. This novel style was redefined by Kocher to include not only the different residential types of Colonial and Early Republican America, but most importantly, other kinds of transitional dwelling artifacts, such as roadside cabins, autocamps, mobile houses, and trailers. Kocher's intention was to use these vernacular artifacts, alongside the concepts of prefabrication and industrialization inherent to them as a base to construct a new national architecture. According to Kocher's vision, this vernacular foundation would be grafted with the attention to contemporary social needs and new materials, derived from the modern rationalist architecture of the International Style, to give way to a new American style adapted to the new ways of living of each era.

The selected case studies were specifically reduced to focus on houses; this narrowing allowed for a more precise comparison of solutions regarding the internal flexibility of domestic space. While this selection process would have otherwise been challenged by the inclusion of a multipurpose building, such as the Studies Building, it is possible to identify many other typological threads in Kocher's body of work. For example, one thread is based on the aggregation of different programmatic volumes and includes the Rex Stout House (1930), the Darien Guild Hall (1930), the Kocher-Samson Building (1935), the Sherwin House (1936), and the Big Stone Gap Community Center (1938). The Sunlight Towers (1929), the Revere Copper and Brass House (1942), the House of Moderate Cost (1944), and the Solar House (1945–1947) thread together projects with an aggregation of open-air and closed volumes that articulate a complexly layered façade to deal with thermal efficiency and sustainability. The single-family houses were selected as graphic reconstruction case studies because of this architectural type's quick response to social changes and their close connection to the evolution of domestic lifestyles. Due to their small budget and restricted impact on the site context, this kind of building is more open to experimentation, the perfect laboratory for material and building technology innovations to test within the field of architecture. It can also be argued that the case studies selected leave out other possible members of the same typological family, such as the Studies Building at Black Mountain College (1940), very similar regarding its elevated situation, simple volume, and the lay out of the façades.

In this final section of the book, we carry out a detailed graphic reconstruction of only four architectural objects: Aluminaire House (1931), Experimental Weekend House (1932), Kocher Canvas House (1934–1935), and Florida Weekend House (1937). We define the term "reconstruction" in two complementary ways: as an interpretation and as a graphic recovery of construction documents for each project. In the case of unbuilt projects, we understand the word "reconstruction" to mean the interpretation and redefinition of the original documents in pursuit of two objectives: the guarantee of the geometric consistency and assurance of each work's constructability. In the case of unbuilt projects—comprised of the Experimental Weekend House and the Florida Weekend House—, the available graphic documentation was understandably more limited and less precise than in other realized projects, containing inconsistencies due to the unresolved nature of the projects. Nonetheless, these inconsistencies have the power to produce insight about the expected living conditions within the homes. The existing inconsistencies between the various project documents have been resolved using functional logic. Following this principle, hypotheses were made where project details are missing or are contradictory to prioritize typical activities of a domestic environment. Where the means of construction were not defined, inferences have also been made about the most likely construction technology. To this end, we utilized detailed descriptions, when available, provided in project reports. When such documents were not available, we resorted to partial descriptions, both graphical and textual, from contemporary publications. Where possible, we always relied upon the original documents as the basis for our reconstructions.

A second interpretation of "reconstruction" reflects our focus on construction and building technology. It is our intention that the reconstruction of the houses should not be restricted to the visual aspects of each project. We avoid the type of graphic reconstruction commonly used in architectural monographs, which very often focus only on the spatial aspects of the discipline yet overlook the technological and material aspects we believe to be vital to the understanding of the case studies in question. Instead, our objective is to redraw their technological conditions as well. We have endeavored to precisely reproduce the construction technology detailed in the project documents so that the houses may regain a key aspect of their original character and intent, which is their role as buildable and reproducible technical objects.

Our methodology of reconstruction is also an attempt to pay homage to the development evinced in the theories of Kocher and Frey architects, especially those of Kocher. His insistence on prefabrication practices and the use of appropriate technology placed him at the architectural forefront and connected modern architecture with American vernacular. We trust that the meticulous technological reconstruction of these objects will highlight their transitory nature. By dissecting their dismountable mobile components and systems, we attempt to reveal how the functional issues present in the designs, as well the difficulty involved in their extension or modification, did not stem from existing construction technology, but rather from spatial plans still rooted in the traditional European villa.

In short, through these reconstructions, we have attempted to focus our research on a key understanding architecture typically overlooked: construction syntax. We consider this syntax to be crucial in the studied houses since Kocher looked to technology as the primary vector for the formal evolution of architecture. We therefore analyze what has been made trivial: the obvious, the ordinary, the background noise, that which is very often obscured by the music of spatiality. These reconstructions represent an unearthing of what is hidden behind the fundamental principles of *Volume, Regularity,* and *Suppression of Ornament,* touted by Hitchcock and Johnson as the essential features of modern architecture. Our effort is a form of architectural rhopography, of depicting the unseen and often messy elements, which are essential to modernity.

In his book, *Looking at the Overlooked: Four Essays on Still Life Painting,* art historian Norman Bryson uses the term "rhopography" in opposition to "megalography," which he defines as:

> The depiction of those things in the world which are great—the legends of the gods, the battles of heroes, the crises of history. Rhopography, from rhopos, trivial objects, small wares, trifles, is the depiction of those things which lack importance, the unassuming material base of life that 'importance' constantly overlooks.[16]

Bryson explains the way in which these two categories are interlinked: since mankind always seeks relevance, they cannot be separated. There is always a humble sub-product that "can arise only by separating itself from what it declares to be trivial and insignificant."[17] With this focus on humility in mind, we concentrate on the architectural object through its internal syntax. Using this form of still life as a reference, we work to delve deeper, leaving behind the supposedly "relevant," in the way that Bryson describes:

> Still life's potential for isolating a purely aesthetic space is undoubtedly one of the factors which made the genre so central to the development of modernism (…) In its quality of attention, still life possessed a delicate and ambiguous instrument. Its whole project forces the subject, both painter and viewer, to attend closely to the preterit objects in the world which, exactly because they are so familiar, elude normal attention. Since still life needs to look at the overlooked, it has to bring into view objects which perception normally screens out. The difficulty is that by bringing into consciousness and into visibility things that perception normally overlooks, the visual field can come to appear radically unfamiliar and estranged.[18]

The selected case studies offer a transversal vision of Kocher's design interests during his professional practice. They can be considered as iterations in lighter materiality, improved constructability, and decreased overall cost. All selected examples adhere to the modern movement's rules but simultaneously refer to another set of vernacular influences, informing a typological lineage within Kocher's body of work. The four houses share a number of morphological traits: the use of terraces, porches, fabrics, and movable parts tie back to the open air and flexibility of alternate living styles, such as camping, trailers, and road-side temporary dwellings. The separation from the ground, compactness of volumetry, and especially the lightness and simplicity of the building technology fosters an ease of assemble-disassemble-reassemble, demonstrating how these architectural objects evolved into such alternate American vernacular forms of movable and transportable dwelling. Having explained the rationale and inspiration for our methodology, we will describe the specific criteria for the reconstruction of each case in chronological order.

Aluminaire House, 1930 (Built)

With regards to existing archival documentation, the Aluminaire House presented a particularly interesting series of challenges when we considered its technological reconstruction. Though the documentation of the original project is complete, enabling us to recreate even the very smallest details of the house as it was exhibited in the Grand Central Palace of New York in 1931, a challenge arose from subsequent adaptations of the Aluminaire House to its later sites and real domestic use.

When the house was moved and reconstructed on the land of Wallace K. Harrison, it underwent a series of modifications integrating it to its new site, further establishing the difference between the exhibited original and how it translated into its new site(s). The primary modifications made to adapt it to this location were structural; the joints between the beams and pillars had to be redesigned. In the existing photos of the house at this site, the column has a new flat steel capital overlapping the corbels, arranged parallel to the main beams. The new capital bracketed the previous one, formed of three metallic cross braces that gave rigidity to the joint, resulting in greater strength both parallel and perpendicular to the beams. We hypothesize that this addition corrected a lack of bracing against lateral forces, generally caused by the wind, pushing perpendicular to the main structure; these forces may have been unaccounted for when originally installed at the exhibition hall. Other real-world concerns resulted in further changes to the project upon its first reconstruction outside. In the photos of the first reconstruction, we note the incorporation of new elements, like drainpipes for the evacuation of rainwater from the roof, which were not detailed in the original plans. The new features include new foundations embedded three feet into the ground and connected to the structure's pillars. However, where the home's original condition served to illustrate the logic of future modifications, we faithfully reconstructed the first detail; hence, the capitals of the pillars were reconstructed in their original form.

We observed further modifications or discrepancies in the reassembly of the house by the professors and students at the New York Institute of Technology. In the assembly process photos, the distance between the façade uprights corresponded with the position of the vertical profiles of the windows; the distance between these uprights measured three feet, eight inches (112 centimeters). Yet in most other sources—including the project description, details published in *Architectural Review*, and *The Modern House* by F. R. S. Yorke—the given distance between the uprights is closer to that of a balloon frame at 16 inches (41 centimeters).

In our graphic reconstruction we opted for the three feet, eight inch interval—this configuration is simpler to construct, as the points of contact between the façade and the structure are reduced to a minimum. The connections use profiles that are screwed at both ends, reducing the number of parts necessary to make a connection and resulting in a substantial decrease in required labor and construction costs. Furthermore, the alignment of this interval with the window mullions means that construction is extremely rational and simple, and the interval is compatible with the standard dimensions of the finishing panels (usually four by eight feet, 122 by 244 centimeters).

The structure was reconstructed using building plans drawn by the Steel Frame House Co. of Pittsburgh, Pennsylvania. These plans detailed each of the structural dimensions and all of the profiles used. Through these documents, we understand that the architects placed an emphasis on industrialization, standardization, and prefabrication. The structure used all standard components and was composed of two basic profile types: seven-inch-by-three-feet-by-5/8-inch I-beams, and seven-inch-by-two-feet-by-1/8-inch C-beams, both with a seven-inch thickness. The joints used screws and three-by-three-inch angle brackets of various thicknesses (mainly 5/16 inch and 3/8 inch). As the basis for the graphic reconstruction of the rolled-steel profiles, we used the first edition (sixth print run) of the *American Institute of Steel Construction* (A.I.S.C.) manual, published in 1930.

We have given full dimensions to both the constructed furniture and the designs that remained on the page. Our aim is to realize not only the practical and technological features of the design, but to give a fuller picture of the dwelling as integral to a flexible and impermanent domestic lifestyle proposed by the architects. In some instances, the designs were atypical for domestic standards, but where this occurred, we opted to follow original project documentation. For example, the front door opens outwards, as the building was originally designed to be visited by a large number of people, whereas an inward swing would have been standard for residential construction. The decision to uphold this feature undermines the house's idealized domesticity and instead preserves the character of the house as an abstract object designed to exhibit the technological advancements of its own construction.

Experimental Weekend House, 1932 (Unbuilt)

The surviving drawings of the Experimental Weekend House are only a small set available in various publications where the project was featured. We found a schematic plan, a few photos of the model, and a series of rough descriptions. Since the Experimental Weekend House served as a prototype of the Kocher Canvas Weekend House, we drew inferences from the construction technology of the later house in the reconstruction of the first.

The *Bessler* fold-away stairs, which connected the home at both the second and roof-terrace levels, were described in publications of the work and have been reconstructed using the documentation of U.S. Patent No. 1,811,709, awarded to Frank E. Bessler on June 23, 1931—just months before the design of the Experimental Weekend House. This type of staircase, which is still a common feature in the attics of American homes, folds and pivots so that it is stored in the upper floor. As a feature of the second-floor living space, the folding stair secured the house from the outside when raised to its closed position, but there it would also have presented a significant obstacle on the floor of the house. Since it is not shown in the published plans, we have tried to resolve this detail through addition. In our reconstruction, the folded stair is housed in a box, which could be used as a chair or low table. This staircase storage box is repeated on the roof, where it plays an even more vital role ensuring that the house remains watertight.

In the published depictions of the house, the structure is also unresolved; neither the floor nor the roof has a defined structure, and no vertical support is shown. We used photos of the model to complete the hypothesis for the floor's construction. We also made inferences relating to rainwater drainage from the upper terrace as well as wastewater drains for the bathroom and kitchen; these inferences increase the feasibility of the graphic reconstruction and maintain the operability of domestic functions.

Kocher Canvas Weekend House, 1934–1935 (Built)

The original project documentation for this house consists of a floor plan, two construction cross-sections, and a roof drainage detail. The documentation is additionally supplemented by numerous photos of the house pulled from various publications, including those located in Alfred Roth's *The New Architecture,* which were especially useful.[19] In addition to a description of the project's building technology, Roth's publication featured numerous construction photos, pictures of the completed first and second floors, a construction cross-section, and details of both the structural connections and window framing. The foundation is three-feet deep in order to make a moment-frame connection, embedding the columns within it. This foundation system is consistent in the project documents and the existing construction photos.

Our reconstruction relied on all these graphic materials; where there were gaps in the available documents, we relied on standard balloon-frame details. In some instances, the actual construction seen in published photos contrasts with as-drawn plans; in these circumstances, we drew things as-built. For example, the details of the vertical profile of the windows do not match those shown in the project plans. The windows appear to have been built using a closed profile instead of the T-profile that was drawn.

Florida Weekend House, 1937 (Unbuilt)

The existing documentation for the Florida Weekend House is more complete than that of the Experimental Weekend House. In the A. Lawrence Kocher Collection at the John D. Rockefeller Jr. Library, a plan, three elevations, and several construction details have been preserved, giving full definition to the house's exterior. Even so, there are inconsistencies between the elevations and plan. For the purpose of reconstruction, these discrepancies were coordinated to safeguard both the exterior design intent and interior functionality. The technological reconstruction was carried out using construction documents and a meticulous description of the project—written by Kocher for his client, found in the same archive—and by relying on the Kocher Canvas Weekend House as a model where archival material lacked definition or detail.

In the reconstruction of furniture and domestic facilities, we relied upon dimensions specified in the plans. In cases that lacked specificity, we relied upon the series catalogue of dimensions for household elements published by Kocher and Frey in *Architectural Record* between 1931 and 1934.

Through each of these reconstructions, the necessity of not only applying consistent criteria, but also adhering to a flexible set of rules—dependent upon the status of development and availability of technical documentation in each project—has been carefully considered. The single goal unites the reconstruction criteria in each project, bringing all of the houses to the same level of technical graphic depiction. In this way, we may establish a more comparative chart of their typological confluences and divergences.

Chapter endnotes

1 Richard Guy Wilson, "International Style: The MoMA Exhibition," *Progressive Architecture*, (February 1982): 92–105.

2 Richard Guy Willson gives examples of these alternative modern styles: Neo-Traditional-Modern, Functional, Decorative, Stripped Classical, Streamlined, Wrightian, and Expressionist.

3 The other America-born architects in the book were George Daub, McKendree Tucker, Albert Howell, and Raymond Hood.

4 The board defined the basic rules to be applied in the reconstruction of the colonial capital; this decalogue of precepts deeply influenced future preservation work in the country that remains in place today. The board was created in 1928 and consisted of Sidney Fiske Kimball, Thomas Tallmadge, Edmund Campbell, Finlay Ferguson, Milton Medary, Robert E. Lee Taylor, Robert Bellows, and A. Lawrence Kocher.

5 This text adheres to the concept of influence considered not as a passive reception but as a reinterpretation of a tradition coming from an active agent in the present, defended by authors like Harold Bloom, Michael Baxandall, and Kenneth K. Ruthven.

6 Hitchcock and Johnson's principles for modernity—architecture as volume, regularity, and avoidance of applied decoration—were all explained from an aesthetic and perceptive point of view disregarding building technology and material use. Building technology is studied only in Chapter VIII of *Architecture and Building*, a book title that very well illustrates this disconnection between architectural design and technological preoccupations sought by the authors. In this chapter, the use of different materials is evaluated only regarding their aesthetic result and their possible effect over the stylistic principles of the International Style.

7 Some of the articles were later compiled in: "Check List for New Construction and Modernization of Houses including Dimensions of Essential Equipment and Furniture," *Architectural Record*, vol. 76 (October, 1934): 257–286.

8 *Sweet's Catalog* was founded by Clinton. W. Sweet and Frederick Warren in 1906, with the intention to be a comprehensive compilation of all trade catalogues published by American manufacturers yearly. Sweet and Dodge also owned *Architectural Record*. Andrew M. Shanken, "From the Gospel of Efficiency to Modernism: A History of Sweet's Catalogue, 1906-1947, "*Design Issues*, vol. 21, no. 2 (2005): 28–47.

9 Published in English with the title *Architect's Data*.

10 Knud Lonberg-Holm, "The Week-End House," *Architectural Record*, vol. 68, no. 2 (August, 1930): 177–179.

11 A. Lawrence Kocher and Albert Frey, "Weekend House," *Architectural Record*, vol. 75, no. 1 (January, 1934): 34.

12 Being the most relevant of these: "Roadside Cabins for Tourists," *Architectural Record*, vol. 74, no. 6 (December, 1933): 457–462.

13 For example, the 30-hour workweek bill passed by senator Hugo Lafayette Black in 1932 and backed by the American Federation and President Roosevelt.

14 Peter Waldman is the William R. Kenan, Jr, Professor of Architecture at the University of Virginia School of Architecture. Quoted in: Jaime Sanz Haro, "Objetos de la Posguerra," unpublished doctoral dissertation (ETSAM-UPM, School of Architecture, Polytechnic University of Madrid, 2021), 205.

15 Reyner Banham, "A Home is Not a House," *Art in America*, vol. 2 (1965): 70–79.

16 Norman Bryson, *Looking at the Overlooked: Four Essays on Still Life Painting* (Cambridge: Harvard University Press, 1990), 61.

17 Bryson, *Looking at the Overlooked*, 61.

18 Ibid.

19 Alfred Roth, *The New Architecture: Examined on 20 examples* (Zurich: Verlag Dr. H. Girsberger, 1940), 11–16.

ALUMINAIRE HOUSE 1930 (BUILT).

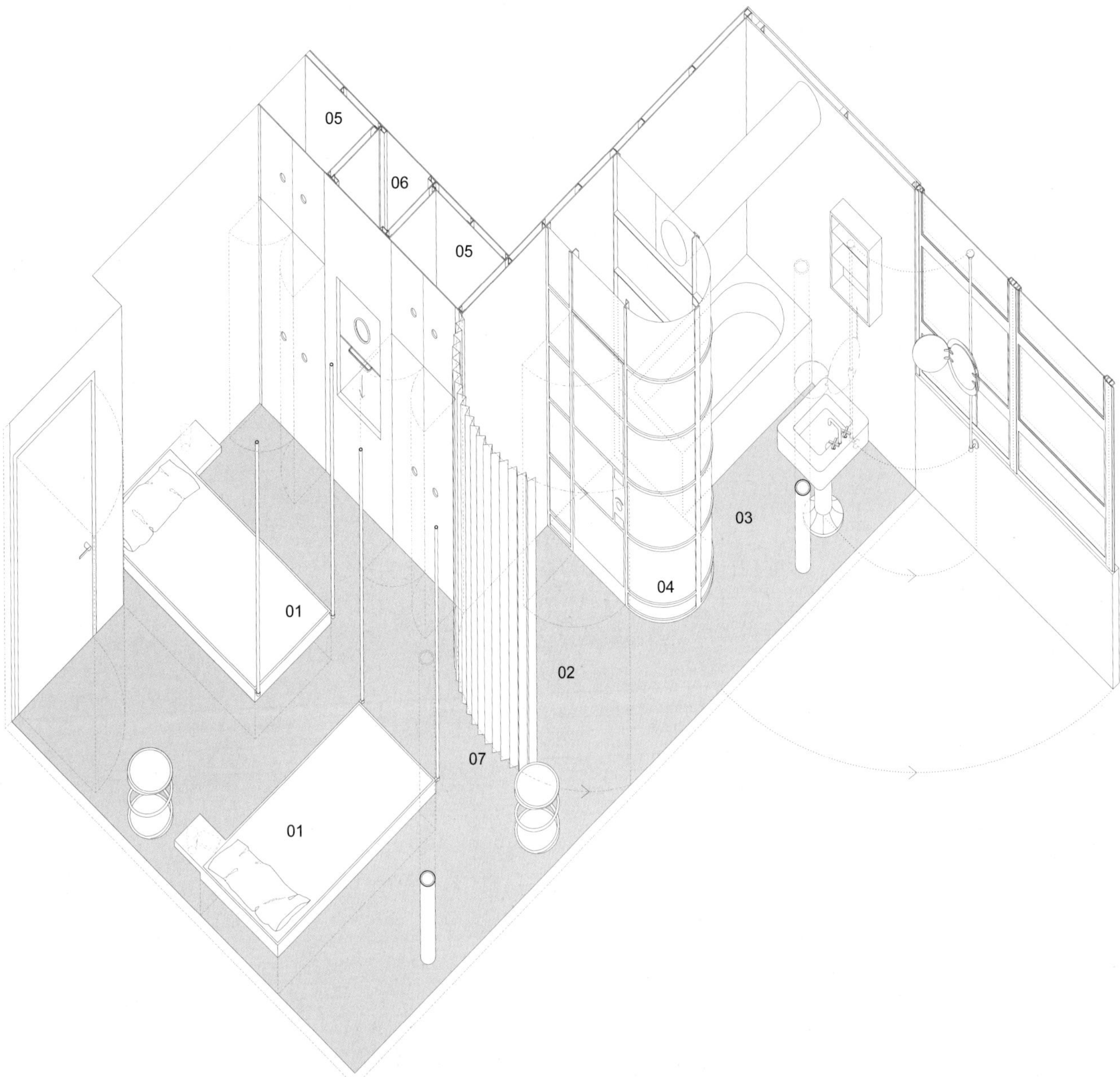

01. Hanging furniture. Beds.
02. Exercise room.
03. Bathroom.
04. Toilet.
05. Storage closets.
06. Dumbwaiter.
07. Folded-curtain removable partition.

Figure 7.5. A. Lawrence Kocher and Albert Frey. Aluminaire House 1930 (Built). Axonometric view of the bed room, bath room, and exercise room.

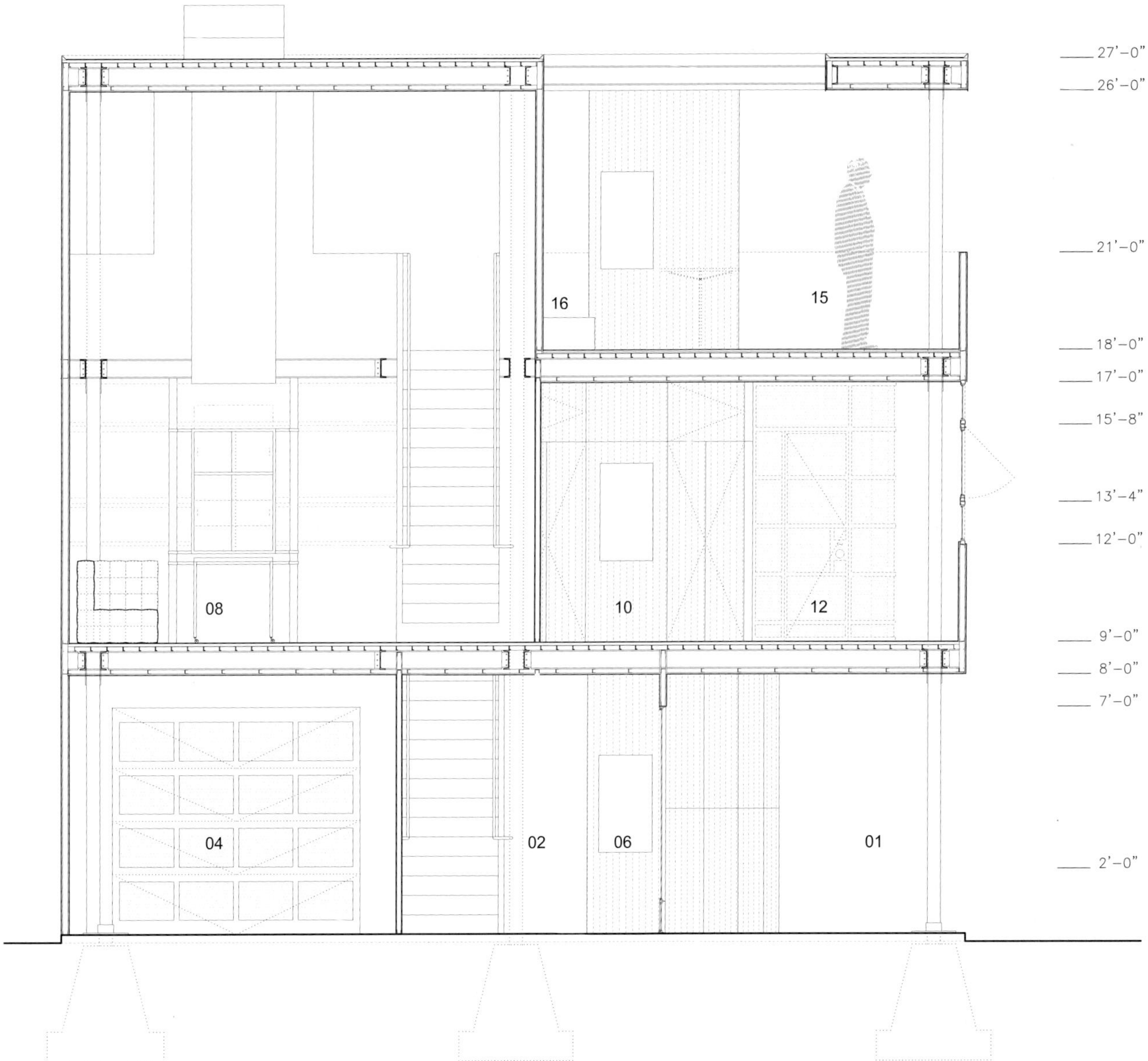

01. Access porch.
02. Vestibule.
03. Boiler room.
04. Garage.
05. Storage under the stair.
06. Dumbwaiter.
07. Dining room.
08. Living room.
09. Kitchen.
10. Bedroom.
11. Bathroom.
12. Exercise room.
13. Library-auxiliary bed room.
14. Bathroom.
15. Terrace.
16. Terrace gardens.

Figure 7.6. A. Lawrence Kocher and Albert Frey. Aluminaire House 1930 (Built). Section. Scale 3/16"=1'-0".

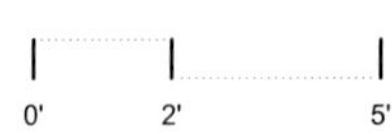

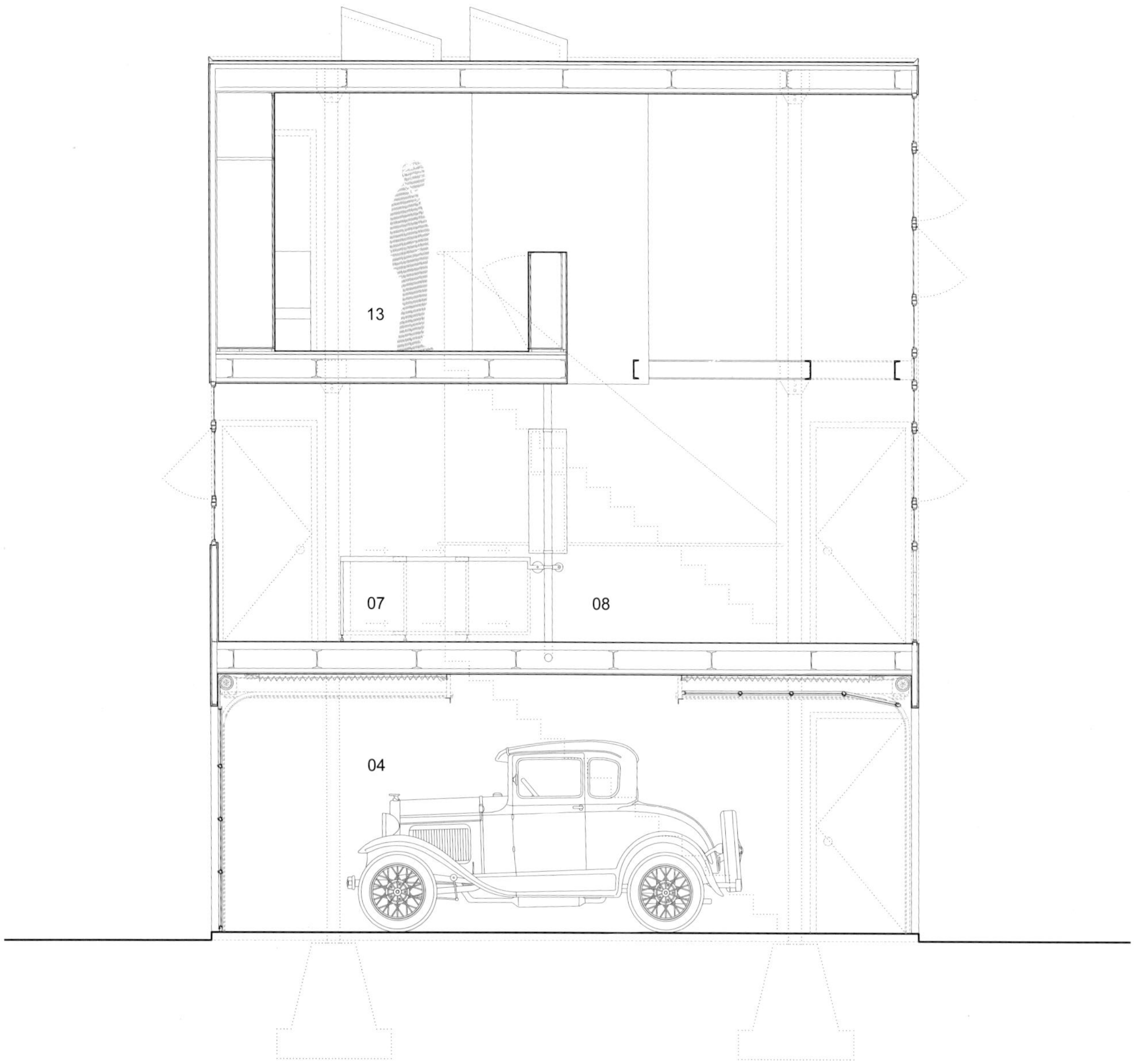

01. Access porch.
02. Vestibule.
03. Boiler room.
04. Garage.
05. Storage under the stair.
06. Dumbwaiter.
07. Dining room.
08. Living room.
09. Kitchen.
10. Bedroom.
11. Bathroom.
12. Exercise room.
13. Library-auxiliary bed room.
14. Bathroom.
15. Terrace.
16. Terrace gardens.

Figure 7.7. A. Lawrence Kocher and Albert Frey. Aluminaire House 1930 (Built). Section. Scale 3/16"=1'-0".

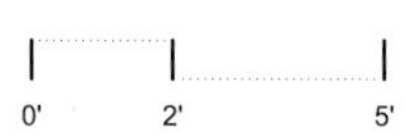

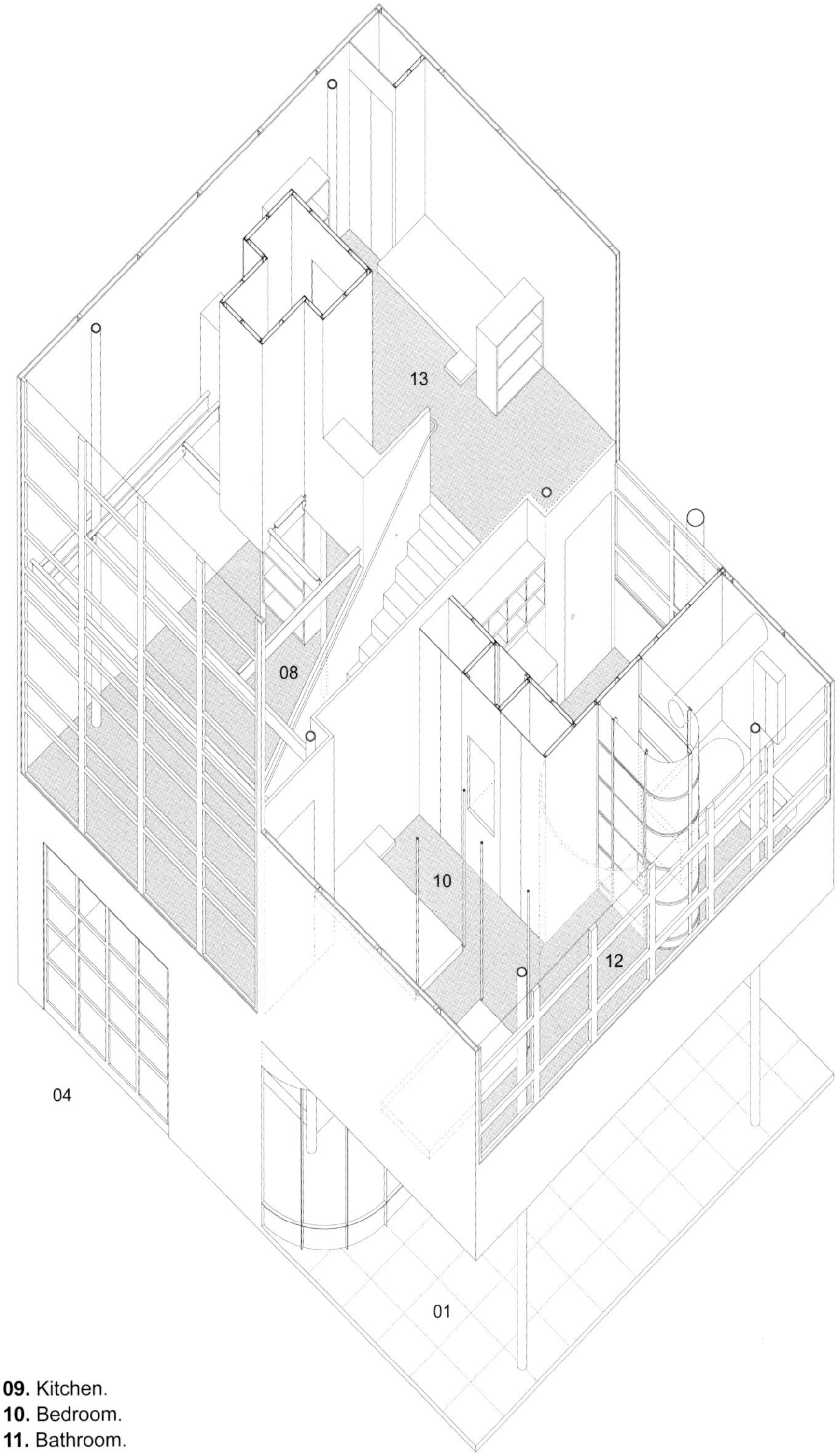

01. Access porch.
02. Vestibule.
03. Boiler room.
04. Garage.
05. Storage under the stair.
06. Dumbwaiter.
07. Dining room.
08. Living room.
09. Kitchen.
10. Bedroom.
11. Bathroom.
12. Exercise room.
13. Library-auxiliary bed room.
14. Bathroom.
15. Terrace.
16. Terrace gardens.

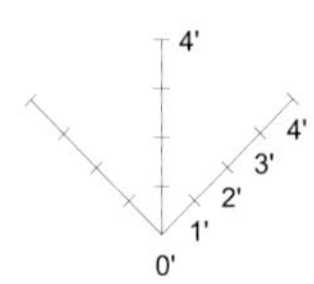

Figure 7.8. A. Lawrence Kocher and Albert Frey. Aluminaire House 1930 (Built). Cut-away axonometric view showing the living room, reading room, kitchen, and bedroom areas. Scale 3/8"=1'-0".

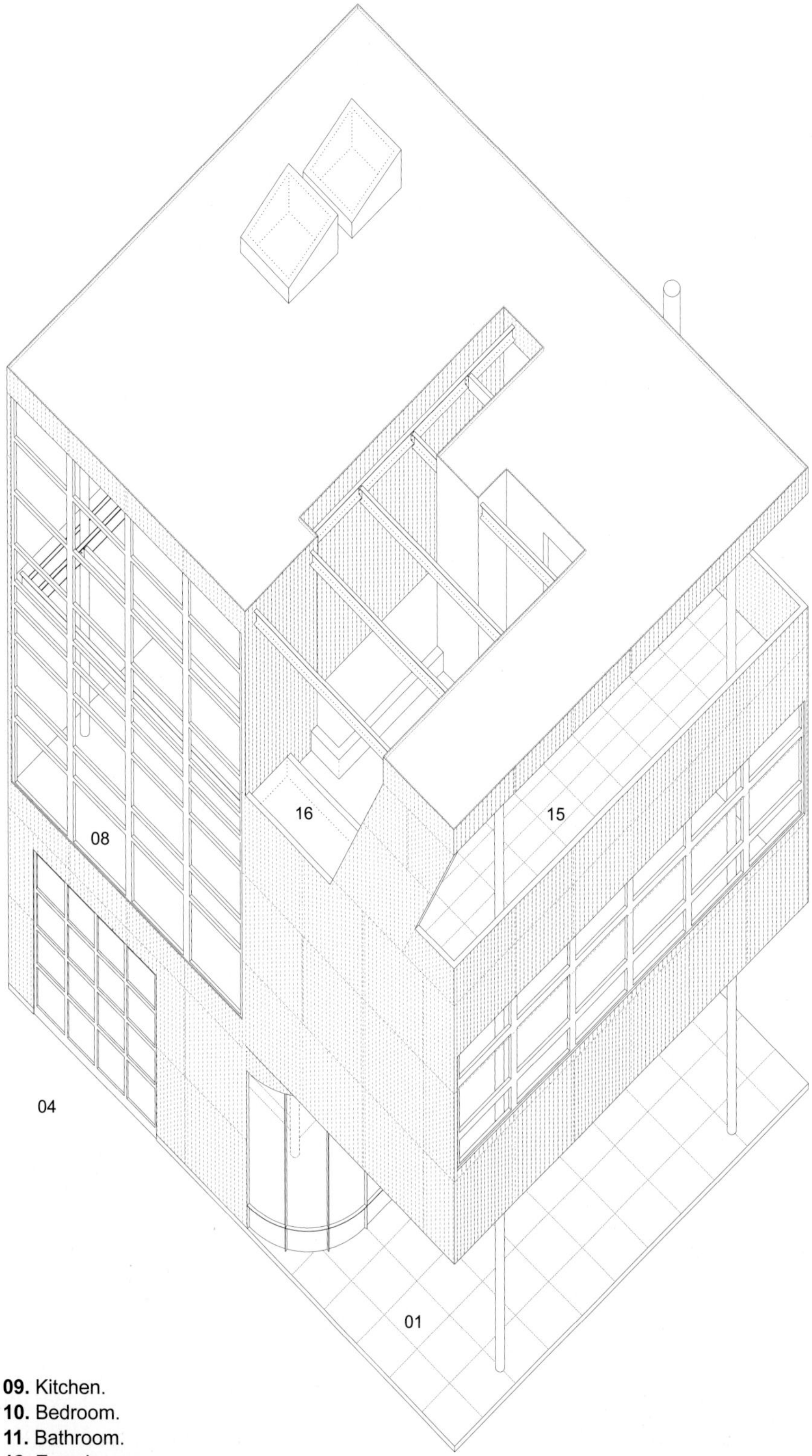

01. Access porch.
02. Vestibule.
03. Boiler room.
04. Garage.
05. Storage under the stair.
06. Dumbwaiter.
07. Dining room.
08. Living room.
09. Kitchen.
10. Bedroom.
11. Bathroom.
12. Exercise room.
13. Library-auxiliary bed room.
14. Bathroom.
15. Terrace.
16. Terrace gardens.

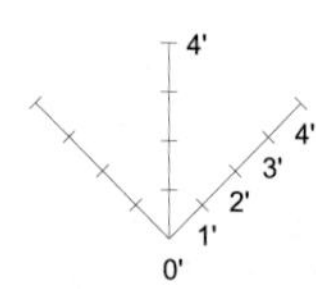

Figure 7.9. A. Lawrence Kocher and Albert Frey. Aluminaire House 1930 (Built). Axonometric view showing the exterior envelope. Scale 3/8"=1'-0".

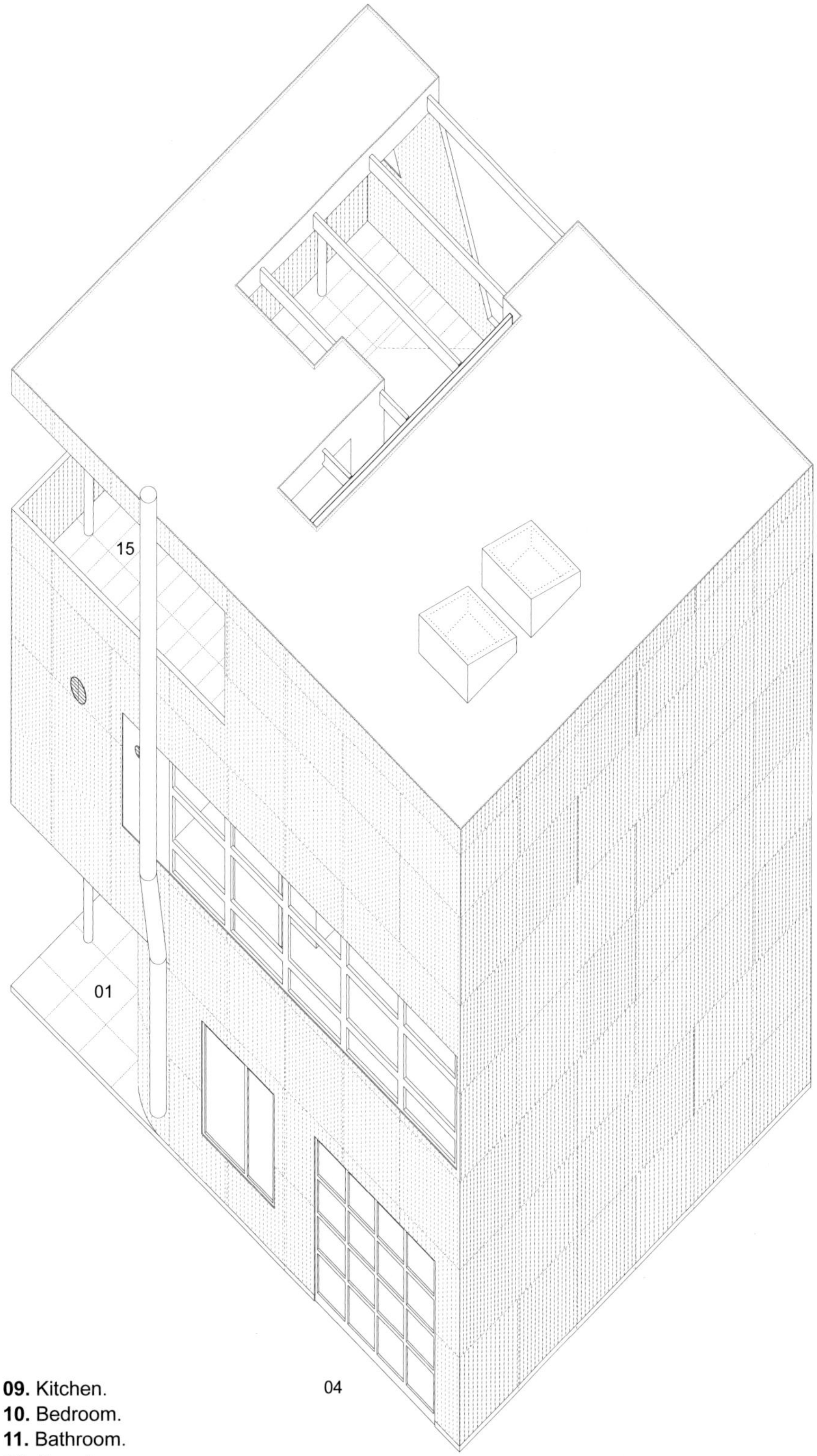

01. Access porch.
02. Vestibule.
03. Boiler room.
04. Garage.
05. Storage under the stair.
06. Dumbwaiter.
07. Dining room.
08. Living room.
09. Kitchen.
10. Bedroom.
11. Bathroom.
12. Exercise room.
13. Library-auxiliary bed room.
14. Bathroom.
15. Terrace.
16. Terrace gardens.

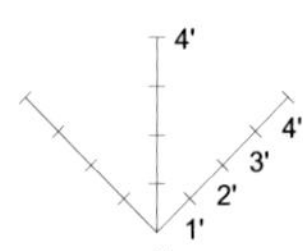

Figure 7.10. A. Lawrence Kocher and Albert Frey. Aluminaire House 1930 (Built). Axonometric view showing the exterior envelope. Scale 3/8"=1'-0".

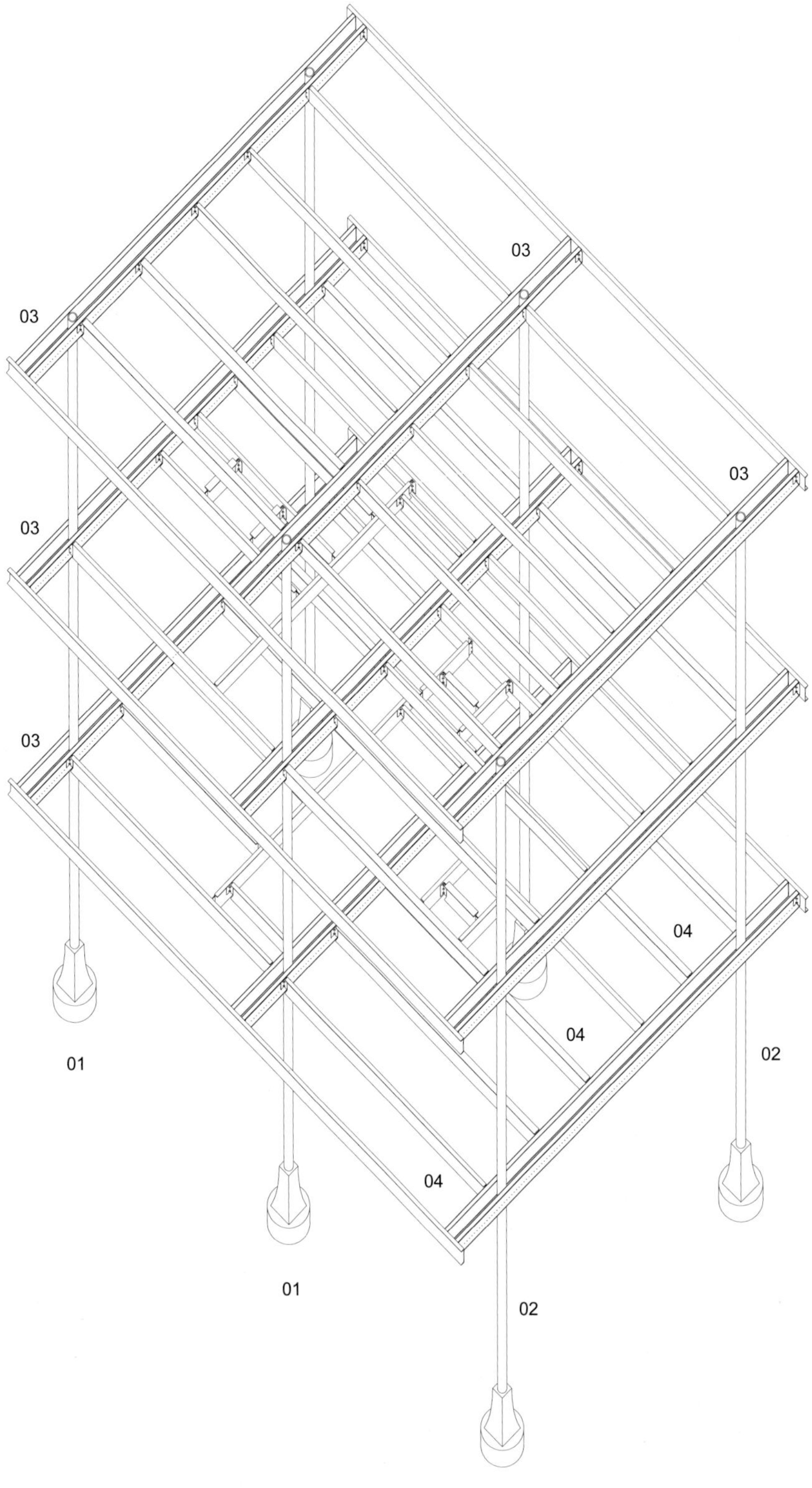

01. Reinforced concrete footings.
02. Round steel columns.
03. Main girders. Double-channel steel profiles.
04. Floor joists. Channels and I-beams.

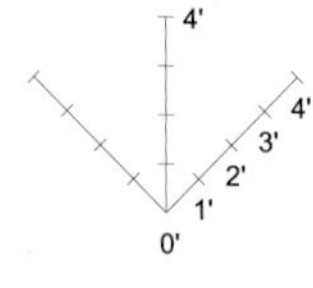

Figure 7.11. A. Lawrence Kocher and Albert Frey. Aluminaire House 1930 (Built). Axonometric view of the structural system. Scale 3/8"=1'-0".

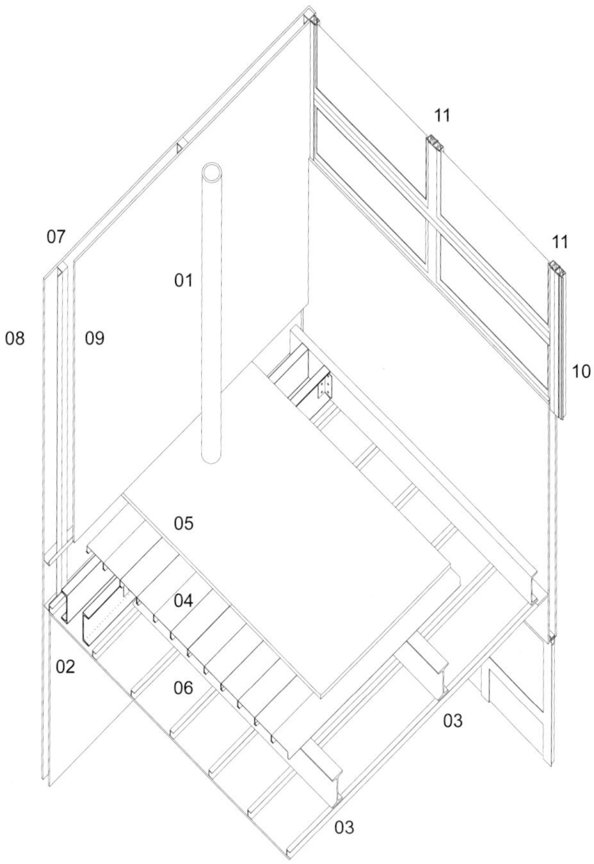

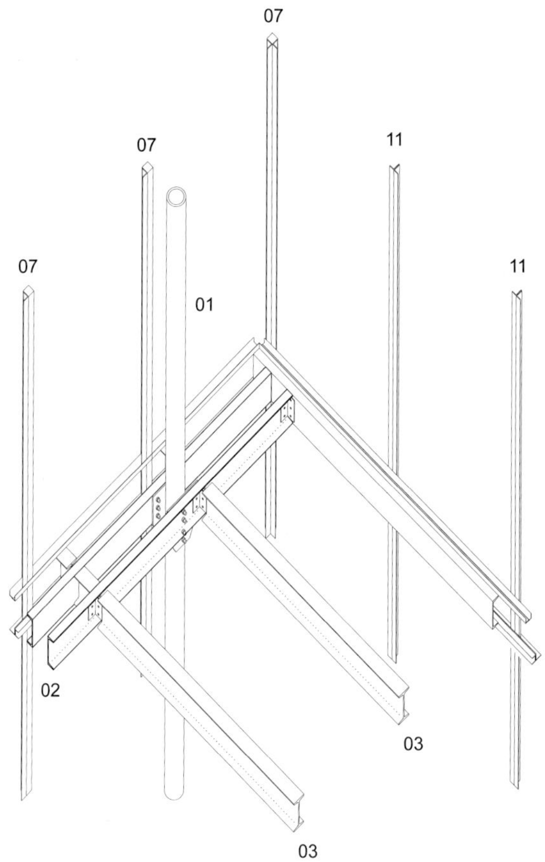

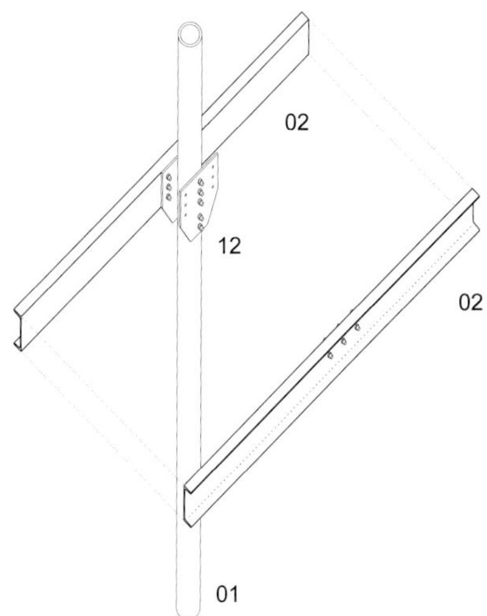

01. Round steel columns.
02. Main girders. Double-channel steel profiles.
03. Floor joists. Channels and I-beams.
04. Steel deck. *Truscon* Ferroboard.
05. Floor. *Thermax* fiber board finished in linoleum.
06. False ceiling, steel channels, and fiber board.
07. Façade structure. 2x2" wood studs and steel angles.
08. Façade exterior. Insulation board, building paper, and exterior covering of corrugated aluminum.
09. Façade interior. Insulation board finished in *Fabrikoid*.
10. *Truscon* projected steel windows.
11. Window mullions. Double steel angles.
12. Special piece in the original design. Steel plate capital to stiffen the girder-column joint.

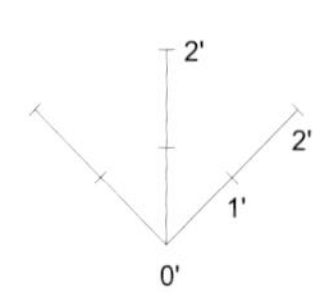

Figure 7.12. A. Lawrence Kocher and Albert Frey. Aluminaire House 1930 (Built). Axonometric views of the construction system. Scale 1/8"=1'-0".

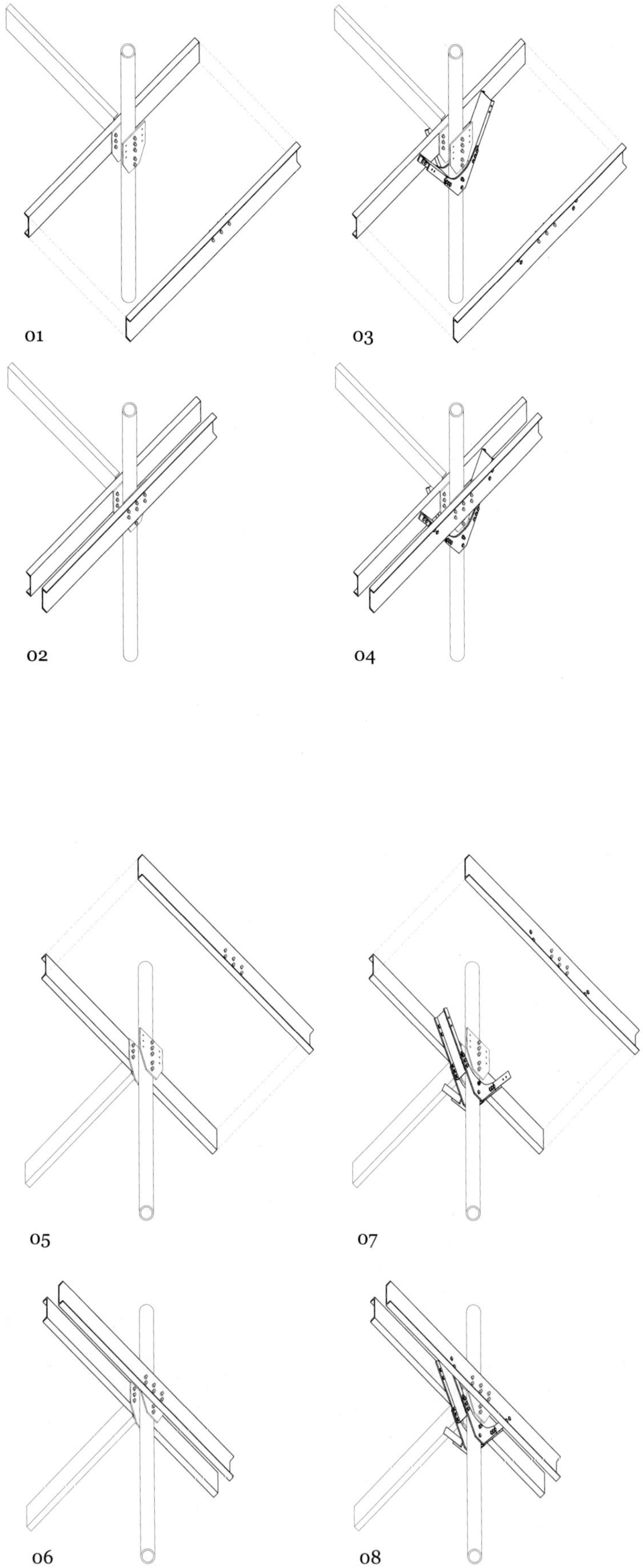

Figure 7.13. A. Lawrence Kocher and Albert Frey. Aluminaire House 1930 (Built). Axonometric views of the structural system. Scale 3/8”=1’-0”.
01–02. Original column-beam connection. Top view.
03–04. Modified column-beam connection. Top view.
05–06. Original column-beam connection.Bottom view.
07–08. Modified column-beam connection. Bottom view.

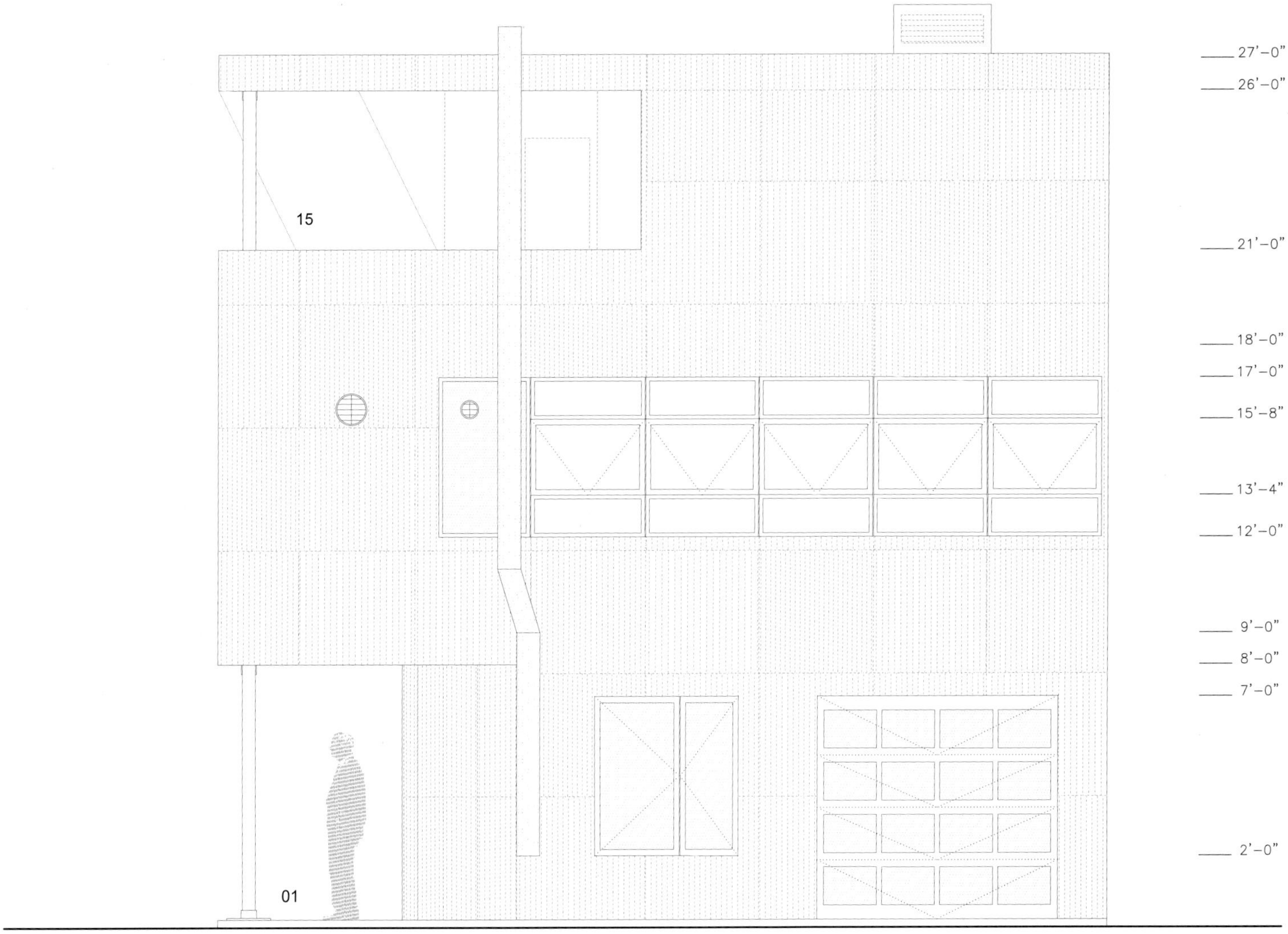

01. Access porch.
02. Vestibule.
03. Boiler room.
04. Garage.
05. Storage under the stair.
06. Dumbwaiter.
07. Dining room.
08. Living room.
09. Kitchen.
10. Bedroom.
11. Bathroom.
12. Exercise room.
13. Library-auxiliary bed room.
14. Bathroom.
15. Terrace.
16. Terrace gardens.

Figure 7.14. A. Lawrence Kocher and Albert Frey. Aluminaire House 1930 (Built). Elevation. Scale 3/16"=1'-0".

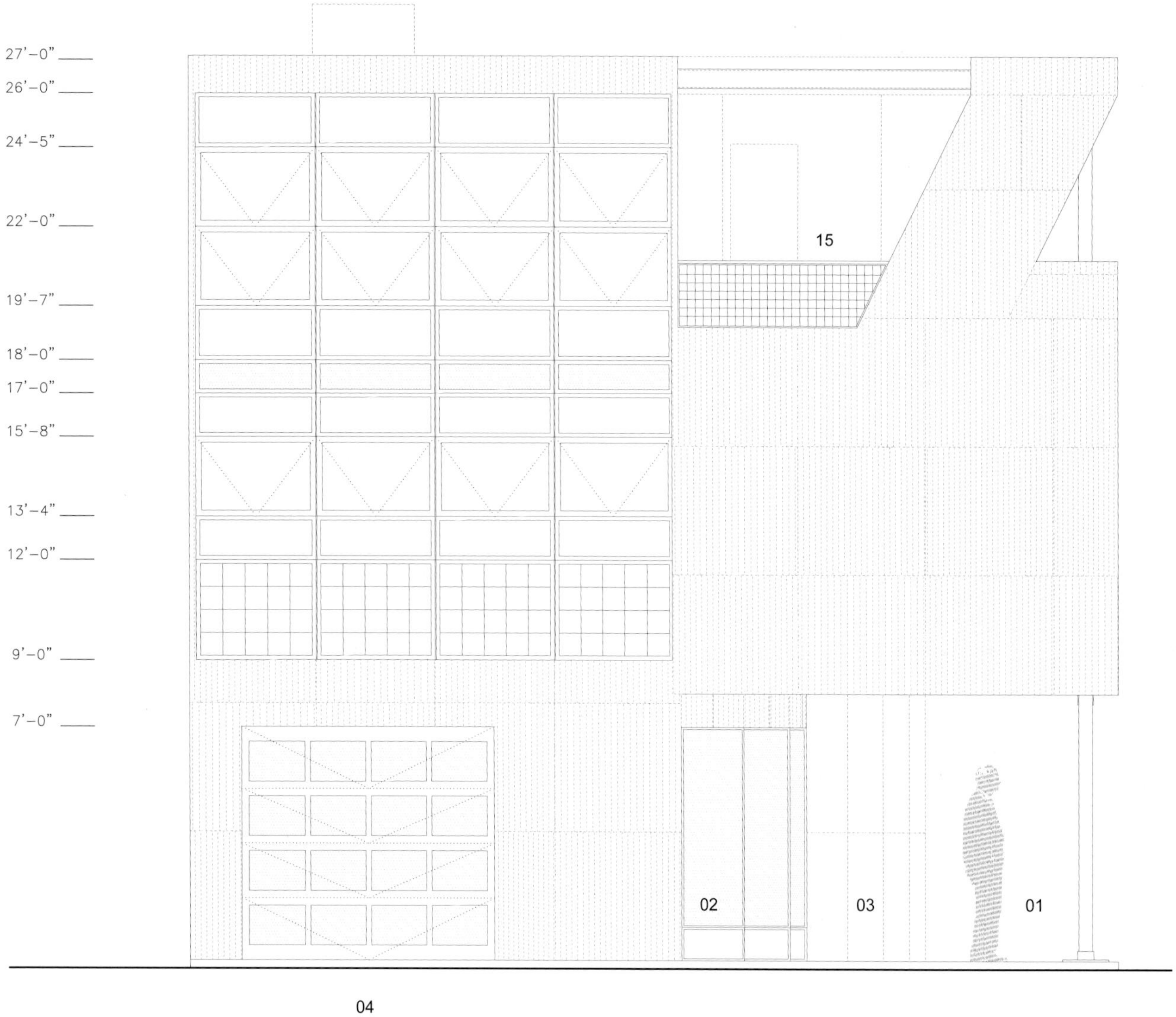

01. Access porch.
02. Vestibule.
03. Boiler room.
04. Garage.
05. Storage under the stair.
06. Dumbwaiter.
07. Dining room.
08. Living room.
09. Kitchen.
10. Bedroom.
11. Bathroom.
12. Exercise room.
13. Library-auxiliary bed room.
14. Bathroom.
15. Terrace.
16. Terrace gardens.

Figure 7.15. A. Lawrence Kocher and Albert Frey. Aluminaire House 1930 (Built). Elevation. Scale 3/16"=1'-0".

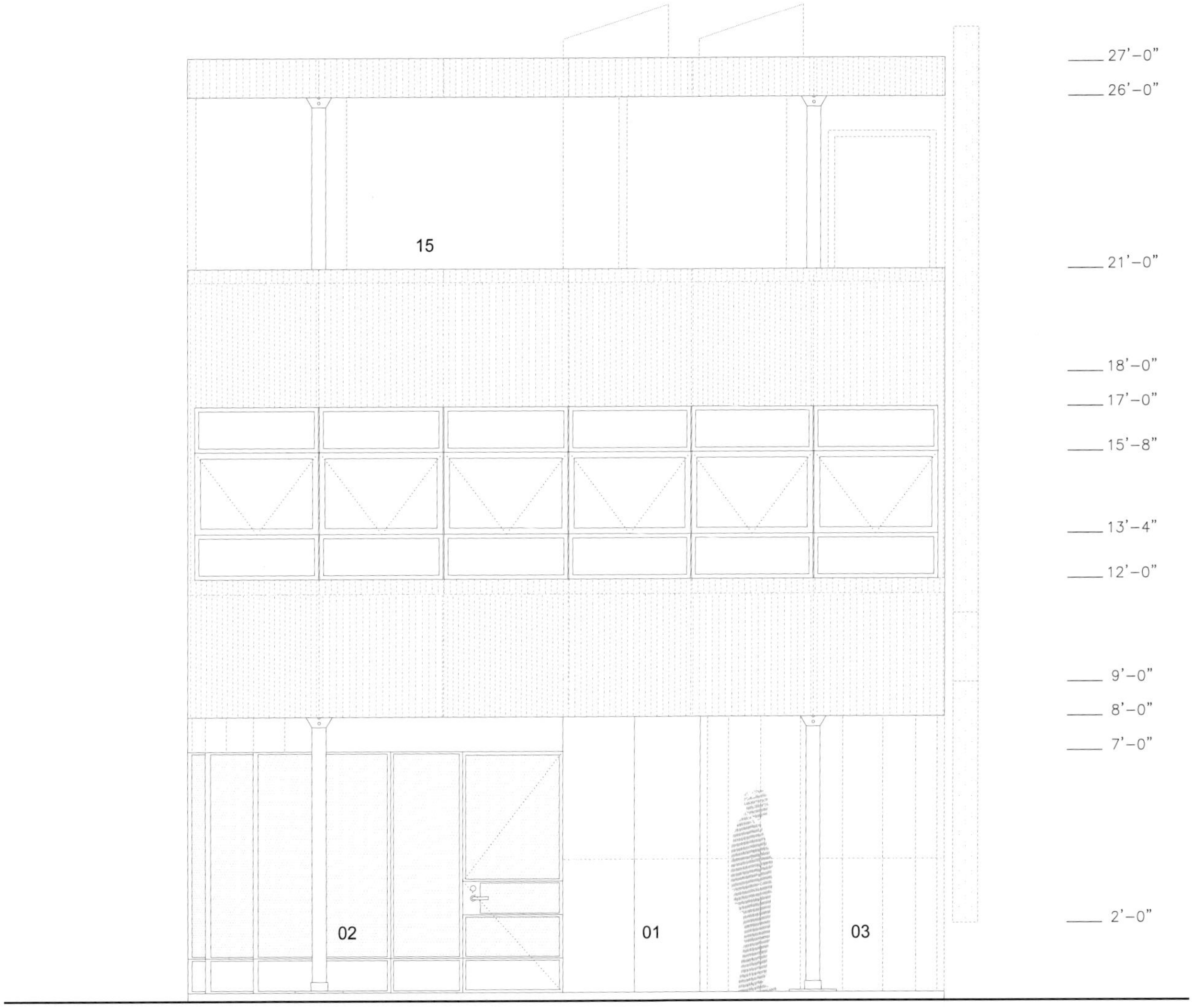

01. Access porch.
02. Vestibule.
03. Boiler room.
04. Garage.
05. Storage under the stair.
06. Dumbwaiter.
07. Dining room.
08. Living room.
09. Kitchen.
10. Bedroom.
11. Bathroom.
12. Exercise room.
13. Library-auxiliary bed room.
14. Bathroom.
15. Terrace.
16. Terrace gardens.

Figure 7.16. A. Lawrence Kocher and Albert Frey. Aluminaire House 1930 (Built). Elevation. Scale 3/16"=1'-0".

0' 2' 5'

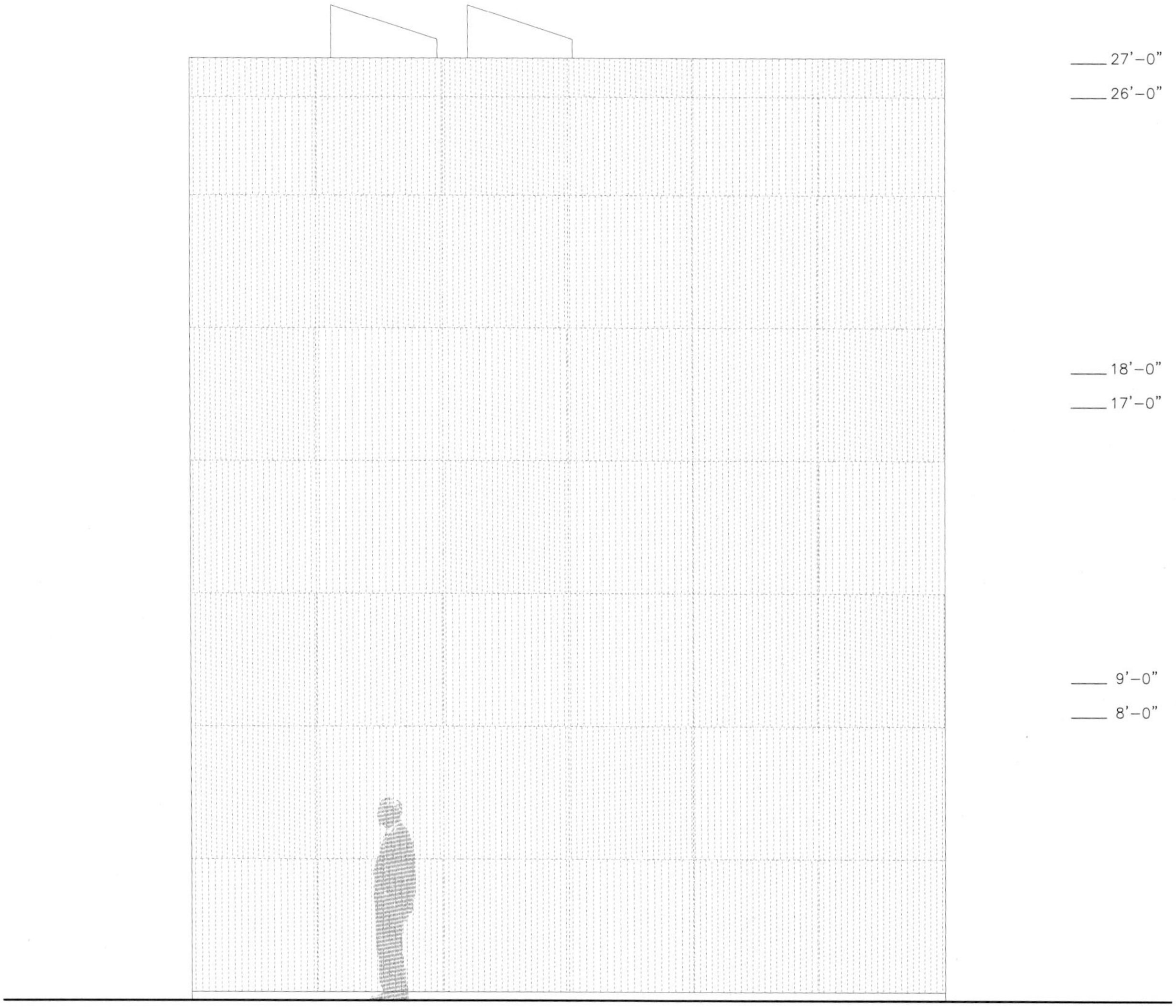

Figure 7.17. A. Lawrence Kocher and Albert Frey. Aluminaire House 1930 (Built). Elevation. Scale 3/16"=1'-0".

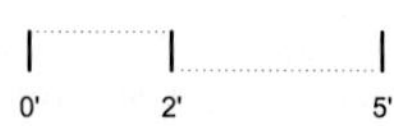

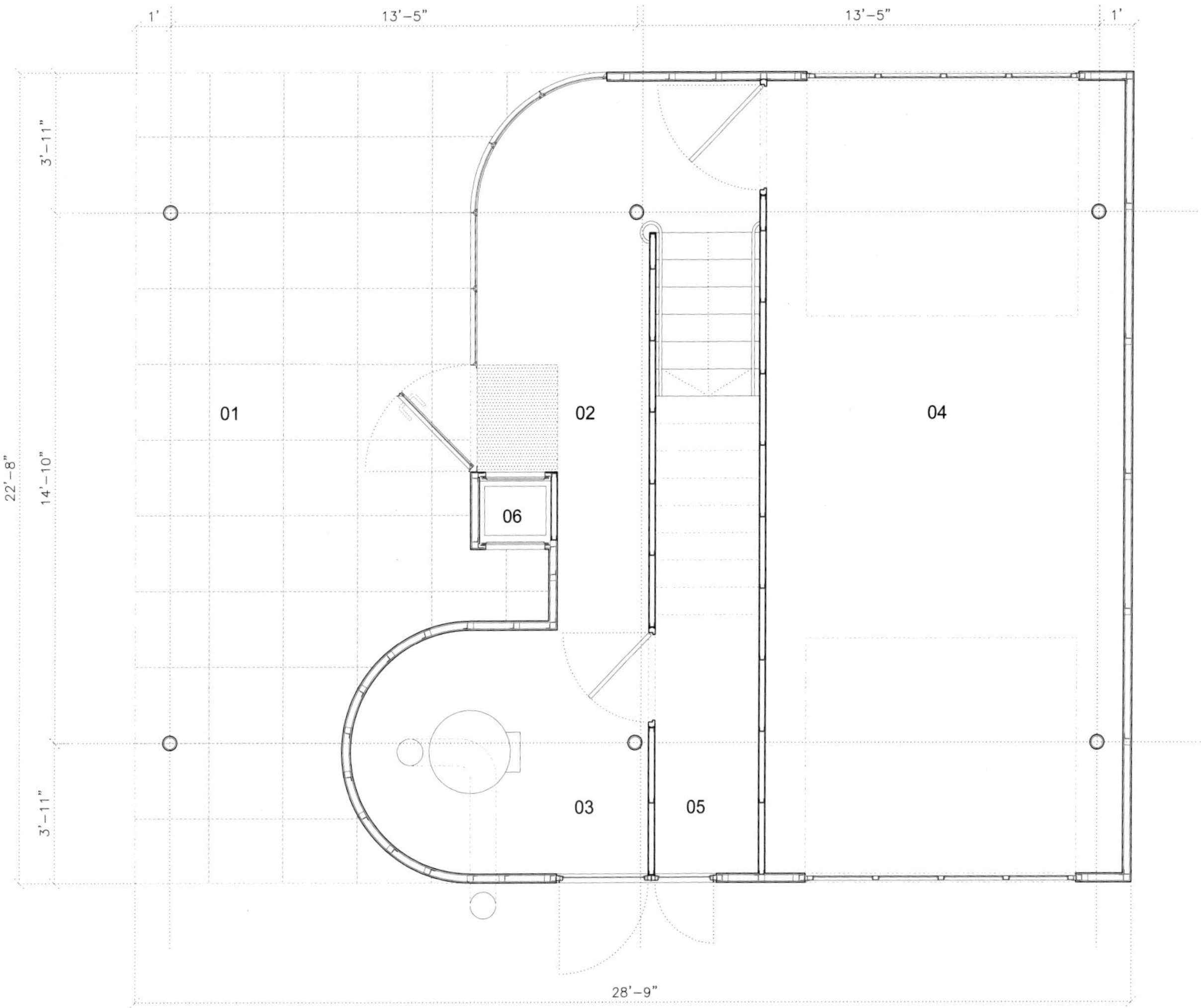

01. Access porch.
02. Vestibule.
03. Boiler room.
04. Garage.
05. Storage under the stair.
06. Dumbwaiter.

Figure 7.18. A. Lawrence Kocher and Albert Frey. Aluminaire House 1930 (Built). First floor plan. Scale 3/16"=1'-0".

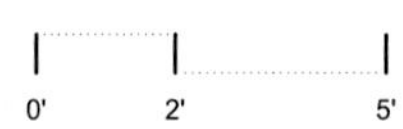

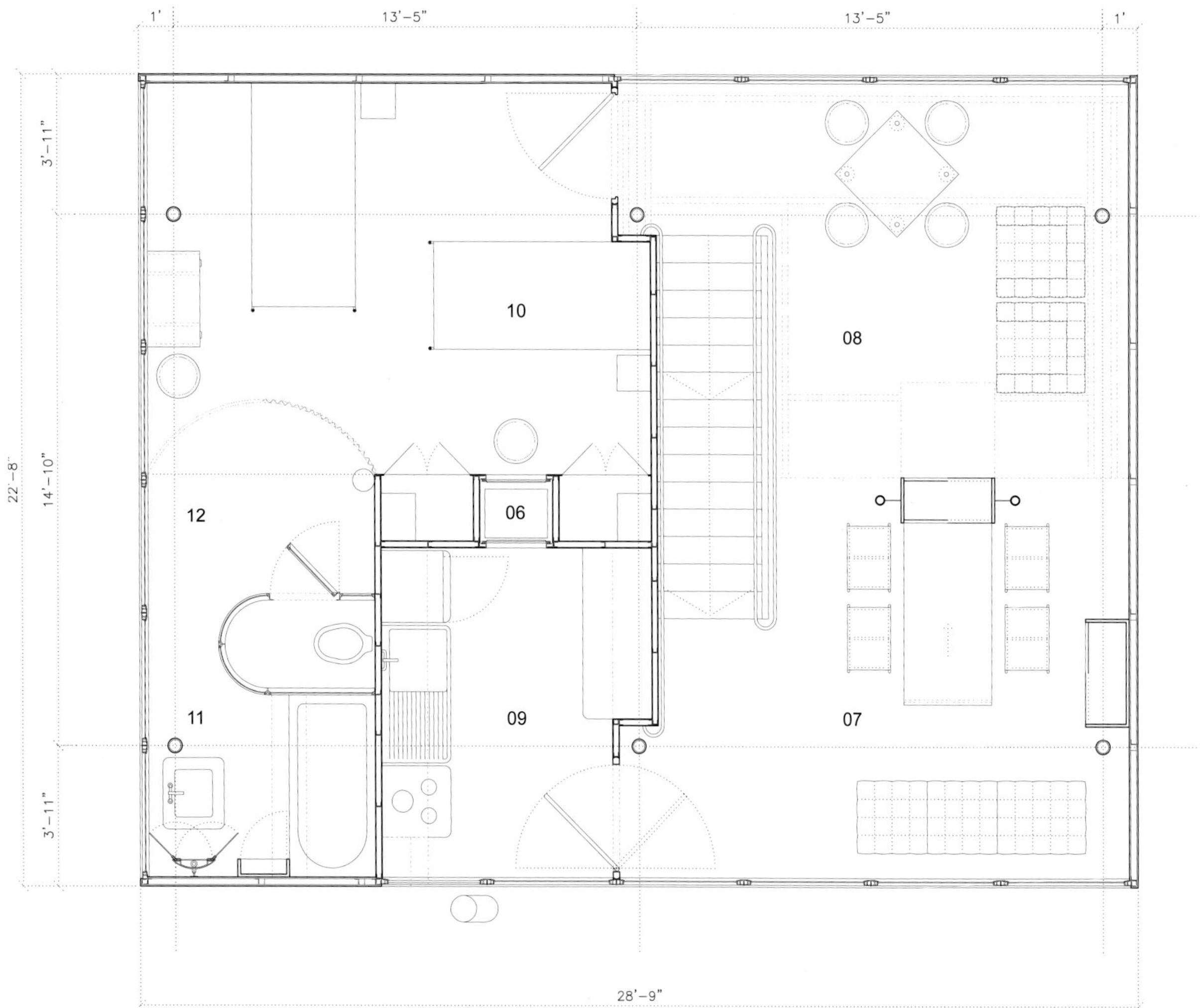

06. Dumbwaiter.
07. Dining room.
08. Living room.
09. Kitchen.
10. Bed room.
11. Bath room.
12. Exercise room.

Figure 7.19. A. Lawrence Kocher and Albert Frey. Aluminaire House 1930 (Built). Second floor plan. Scale 3/16"=1'-0".

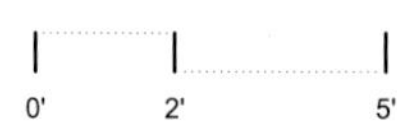

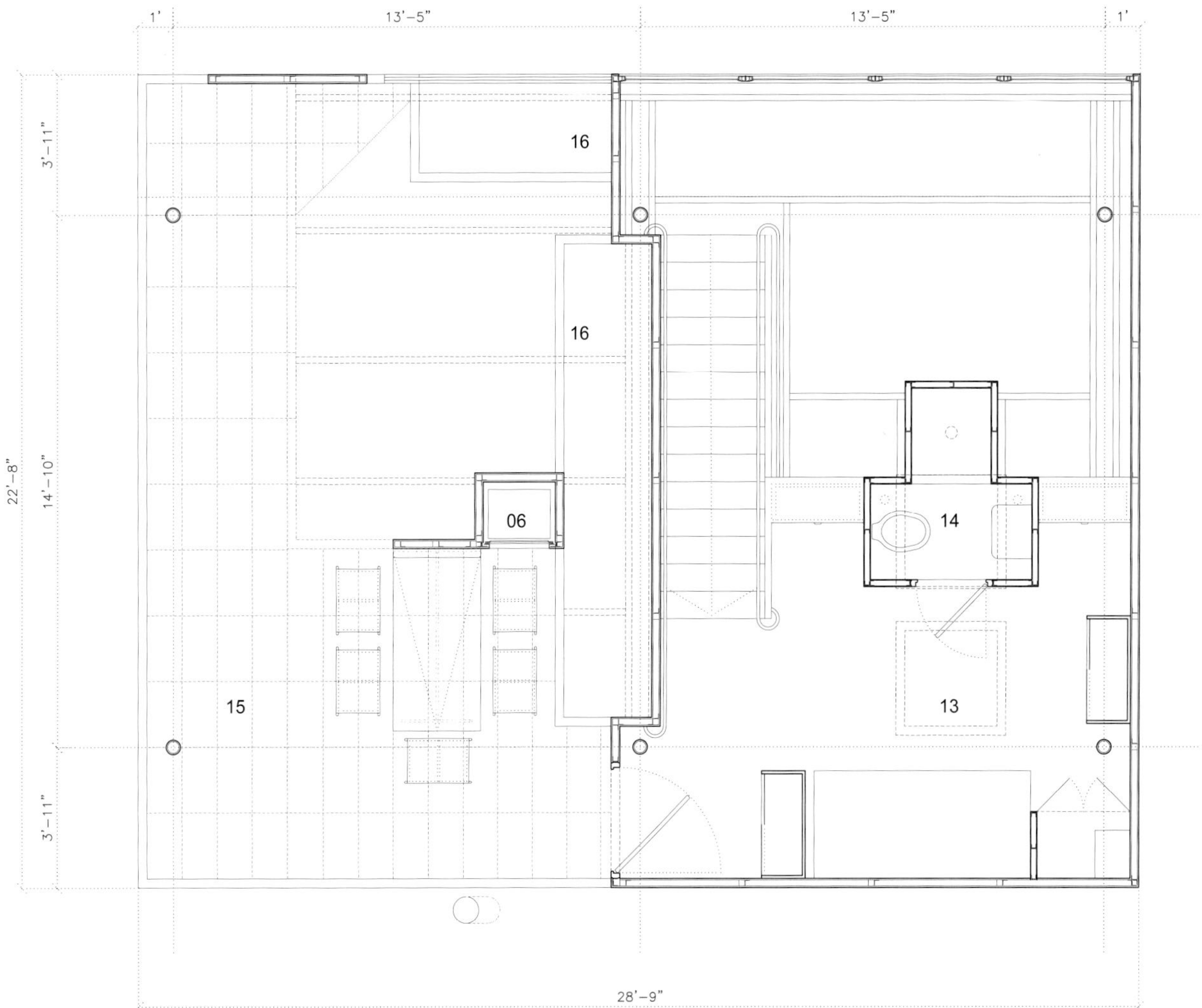

06. Dumbwaiter.
13. Library-auxiliary bed room.
14. Bath room.
15. Terrace.
16. Terrace gardens.

Figure 7.20. A. Lawrence Kocher and Albert Frey. Aluminaire House 1930 (Built). Third floor plan. Scale 3/16"=1'-0".

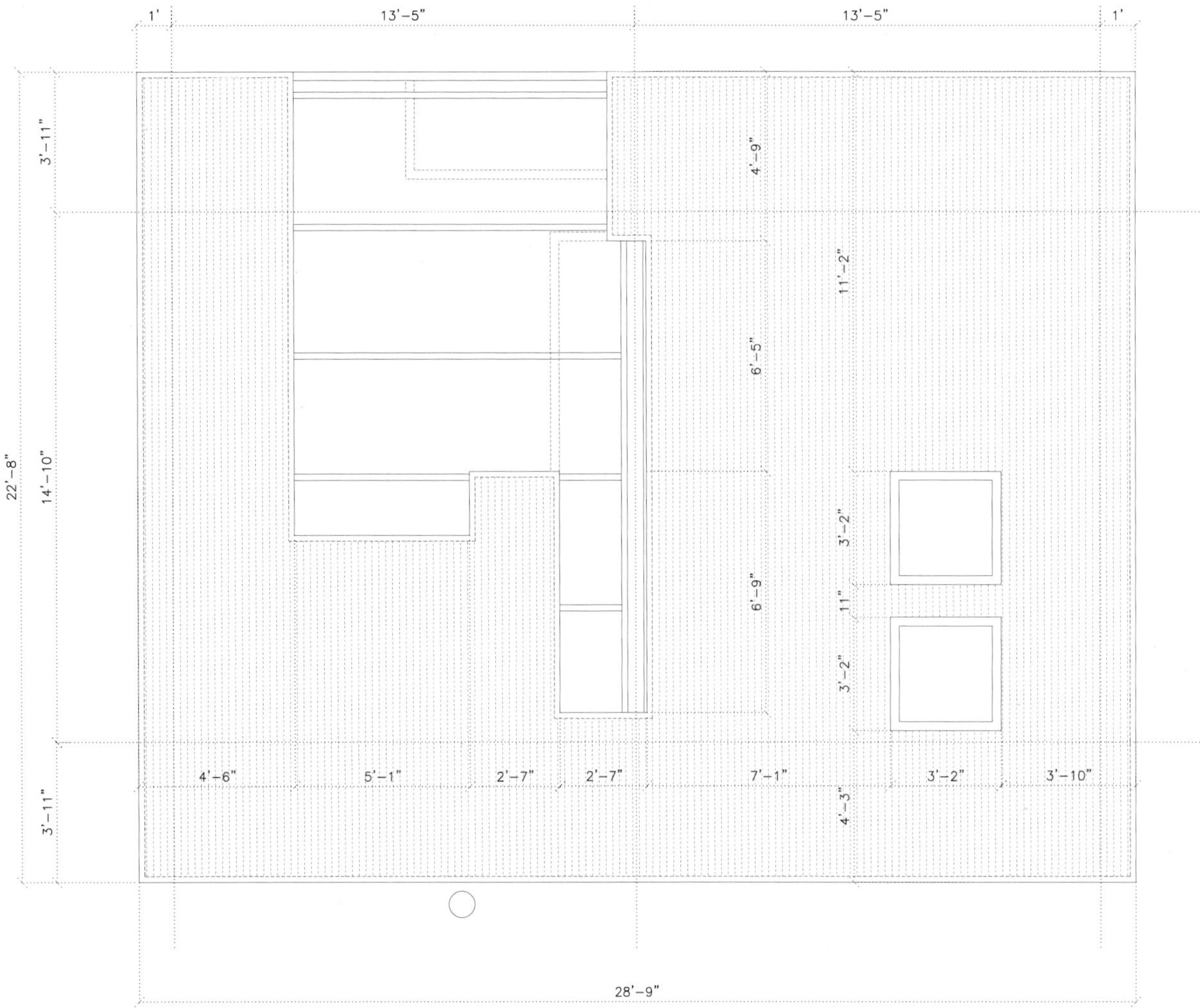

Figure 7.21. A. Lawrence Kocher and Albert Frey. Aluminaire House 1930 (Built). Roof plan. Scale 3/16"=1'-0".

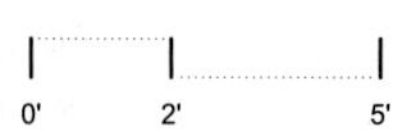

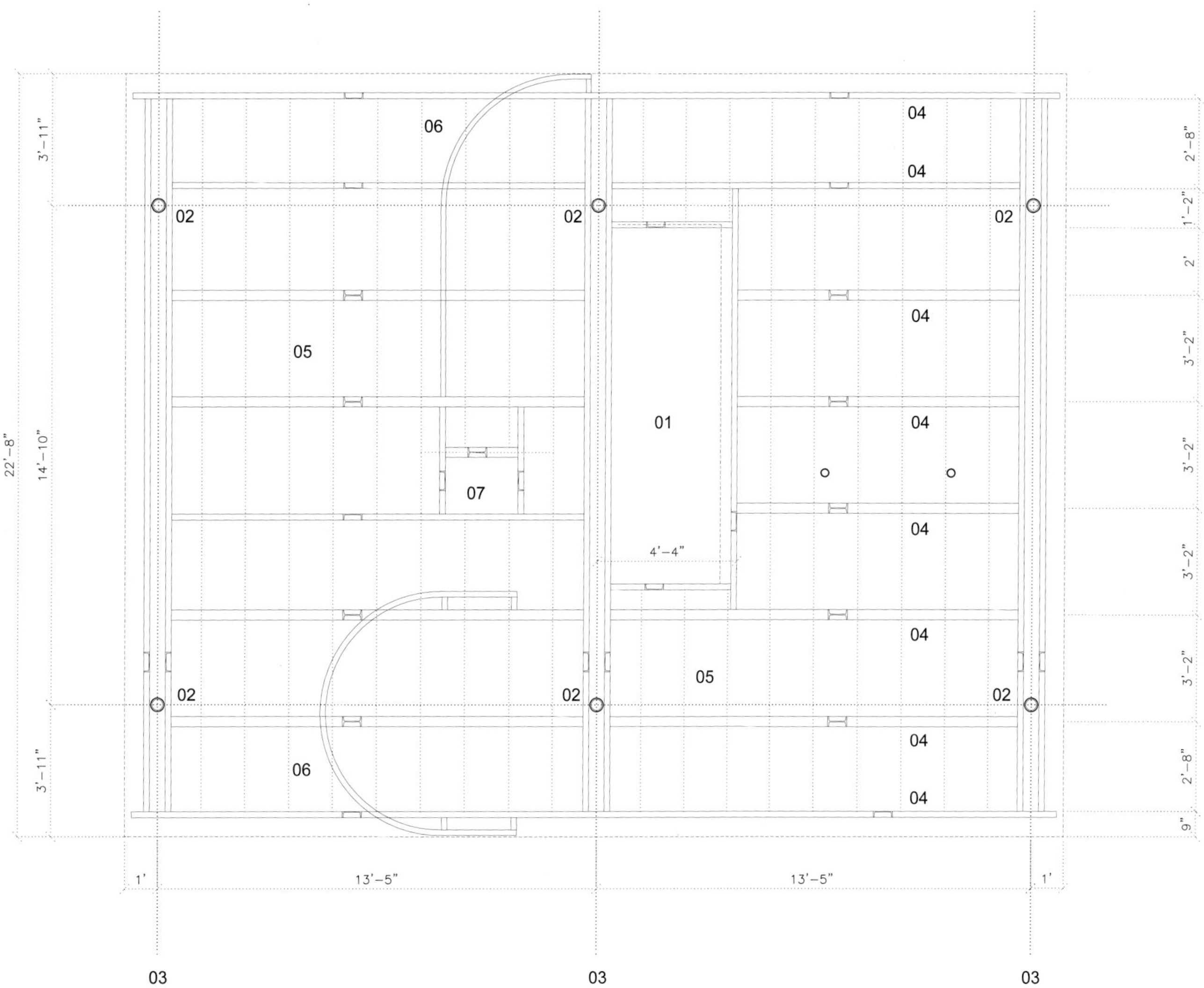

01. Stair position.
02. Round steel columns.
03. Main girders. Double-channel steel profiles.
04. Floor joists. Channels and I-beams.
05. Steel deck. *Truscon* Ferroboard.
06. Special profiles for round shapes in first floor. Channels and I-beams.
07. Dumbwaiter position.

Figure 7.22. A. Lawrence Kocher and Albert Frey. Aluminaire House 1930 (Built).
Framing plan second floor. Scale 3/16"=1'-0".

0' 2' 5'

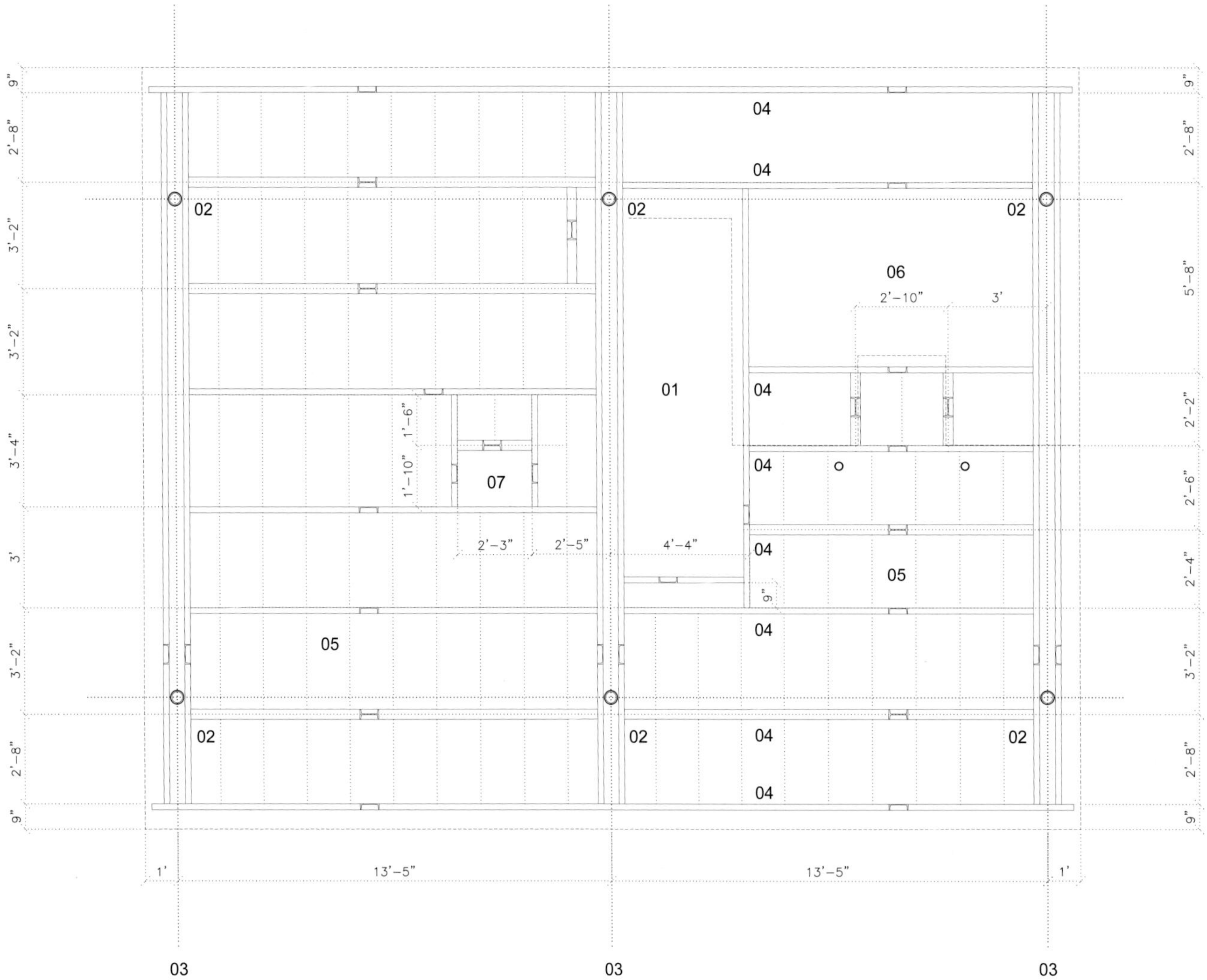

01. Stair position.
02. Round steel columns.
03. Main girders. Double-channel steel profiles.
04. Floor joists. Channels and I-beams.
05. Steel deck. *Truscon* Ferroboard.
06. Double height over living room.
07. Dumbwaiter position.

Figure 7.23. A. Lawrence Kocher and Albert Frey. Aluminaire House 1930 (Built). Framing plan third floor. Scale 3/16"=1'-0".

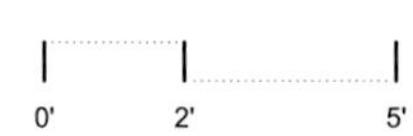

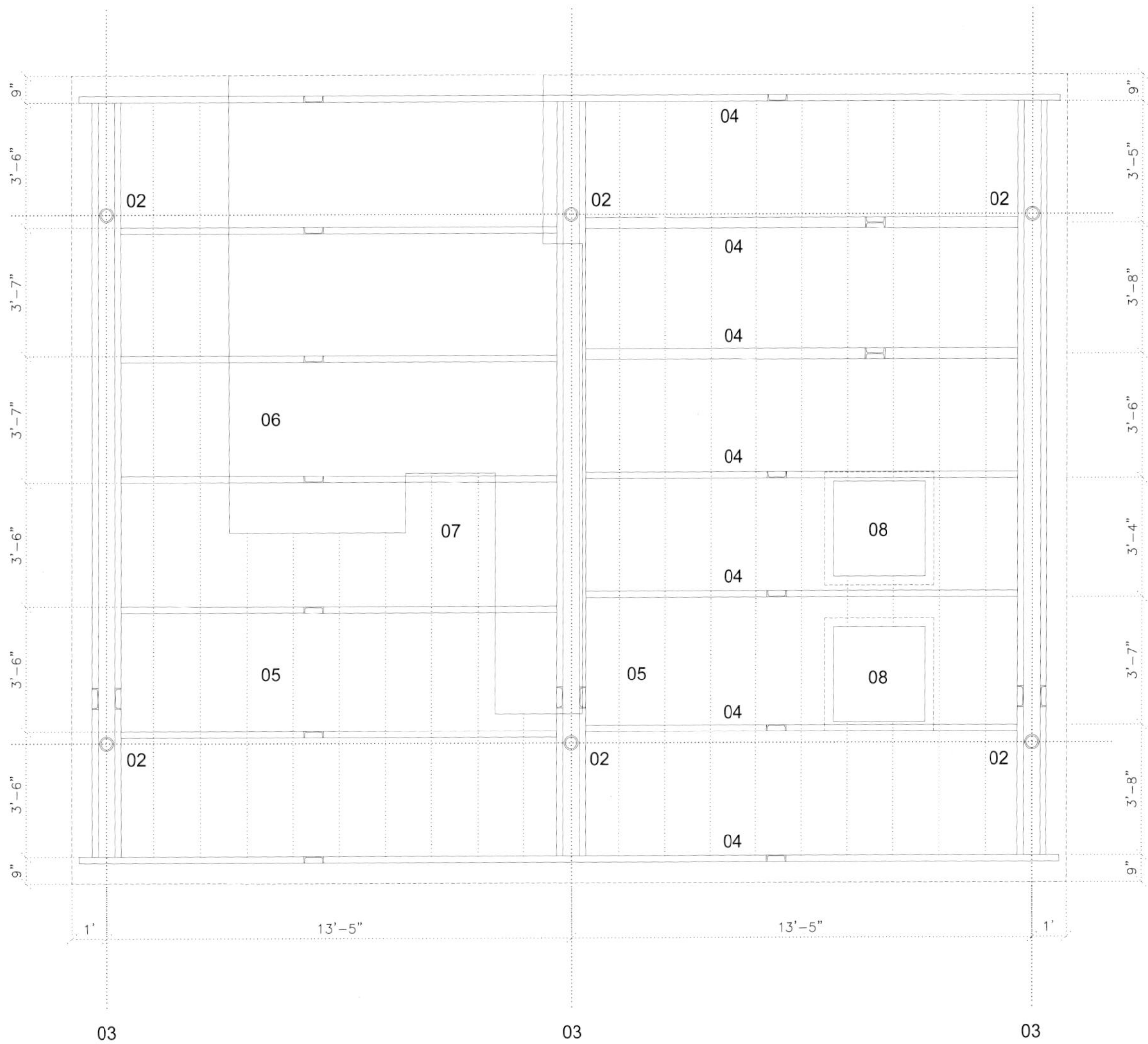

01. Stair position.
02. Round steel columns.
03. Main girders. Double-channel steel profiles.
04. Floor joists. Channels and I-beams.
05. Steel deck. *Truscon* Ferroboard.
06. Double height over terrace.
07. Dumbwaiter position.
08. Skylights.

Figure 7.24. A. Lawrence Kocher and Albert Frey. Aluminaire House 1930 (Built). Framing plan roof. Scale 3/16"=1'-0".

0' 2' 5'

EXPERIMENTAL WEEKEND HOUSE 1932 (UNBUILT).

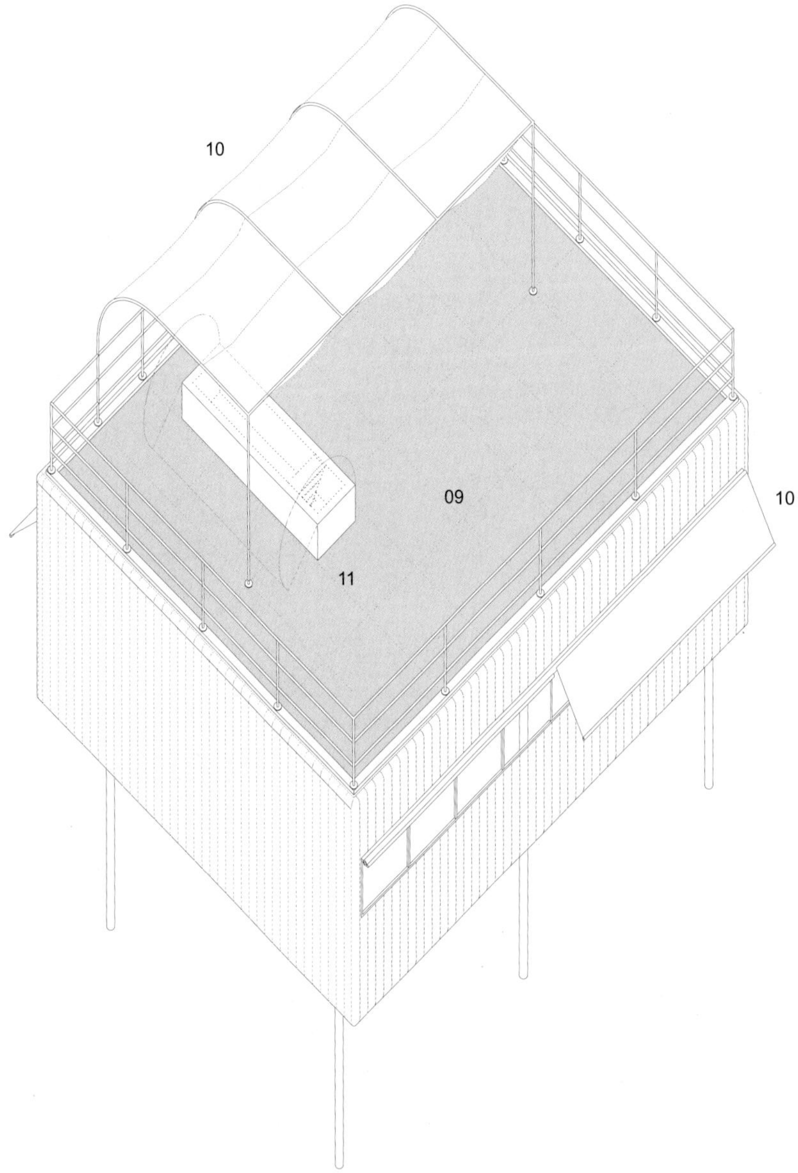

01. *Bessler* fold-away stair connecting with first floor.
02. Dinning room.
03. *Bessler* fold-away stair connecting with roof terrace.
04. Kitchen.
05. Bathroom.
06. Living room (day); main bedroom (night).
07. Living room (day); bedroom (night).
08. Storage closets.
09. Roof terrace.
10. Canvas canopy and awnings.
11. Box to house bessemer stair.

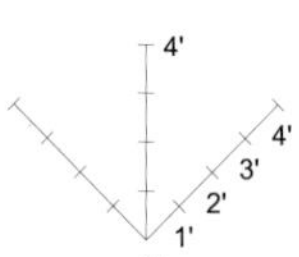

Figure 7.25. A. Lawrence Kocher and Albert Frey. Experimental Weekend House 1932 (Unbuilt). Axonometric view of the exterior envelope. Scale 3/8"=1'-0".

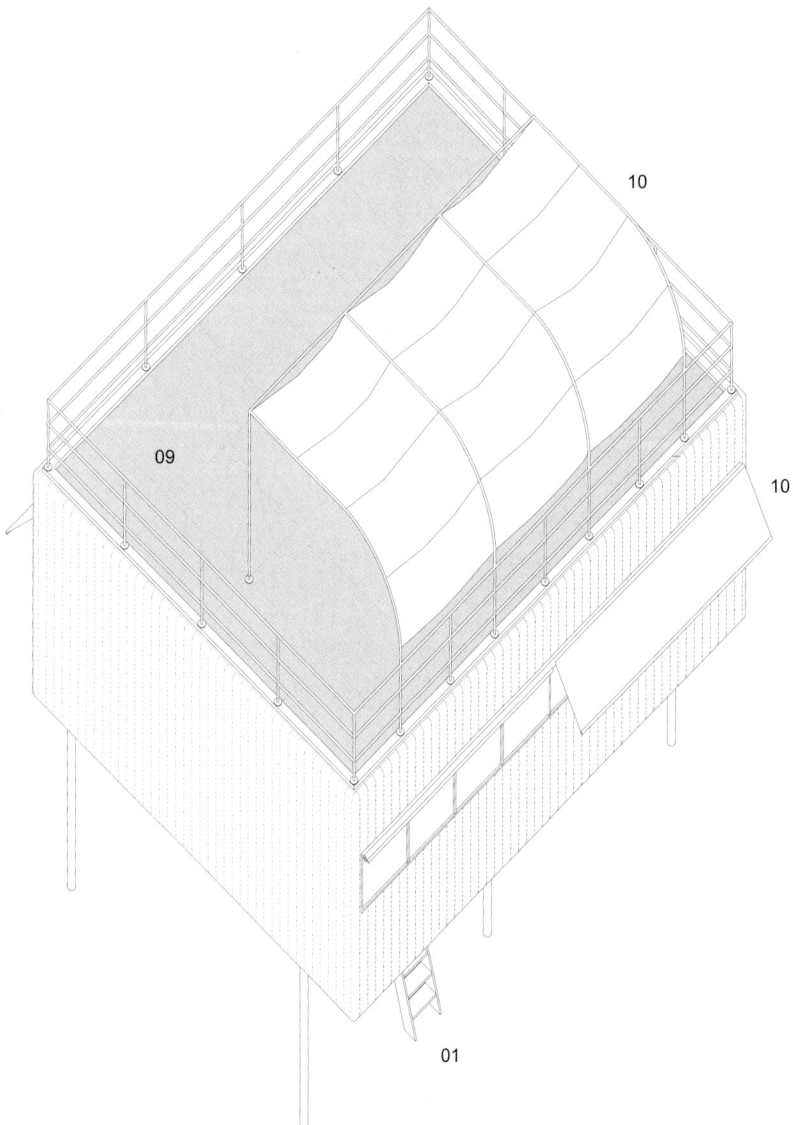

01. *Bessler* fold-away stair connecting with first floor.
02. Dinning room.
03. *Bessler* fold-away stair connecting with roof terrace.
04. Kitchen.
05. Bathroom.
06. Living room (day); main bedroom (night).
07. Living room (day); bedroom (night).
08. Storage closets.
09. Roof terrace.
10. Canvas canopy and awnings.
11. Box to house bessemer stair.

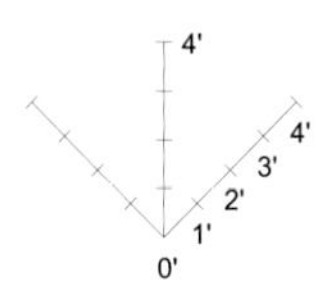

Figure 7.26. A. Lawrence Kocher and Albert Frey. Experimental Weekend House 1932 (Unbuilt). Axonometric view of the exterior envelope. Scale 3/8"=1'-0".

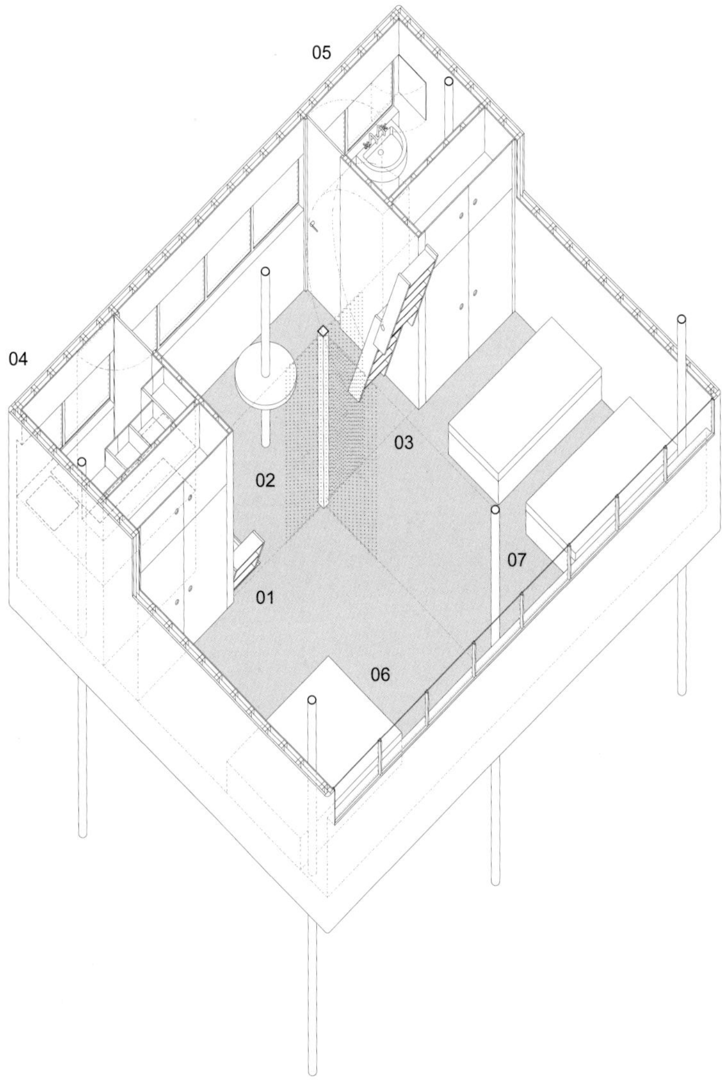

01. *Bessler* fold-away stair connecting with first floor.
02. Dinning room.
03. *Bessler* fold-away stair connecting with roof terrace.
04. Kitchen.
05. Bathroom.
06. Living room (day); main bedroom (night).
07. Living room (day); bedroom (night).
08. Storage closets.
09. Roof terrace.
10. Canvas canopy and awnings.
11. Box to house bessemer stair.

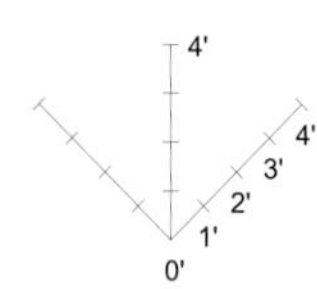

Figure 7.27. A. Lawrence Kocher and Albert Frey. Experimental Weekend House 1932 (Unbuilt). Cut-away axonometric view showing all internal spaces. Scale 3/8"=1'-0".

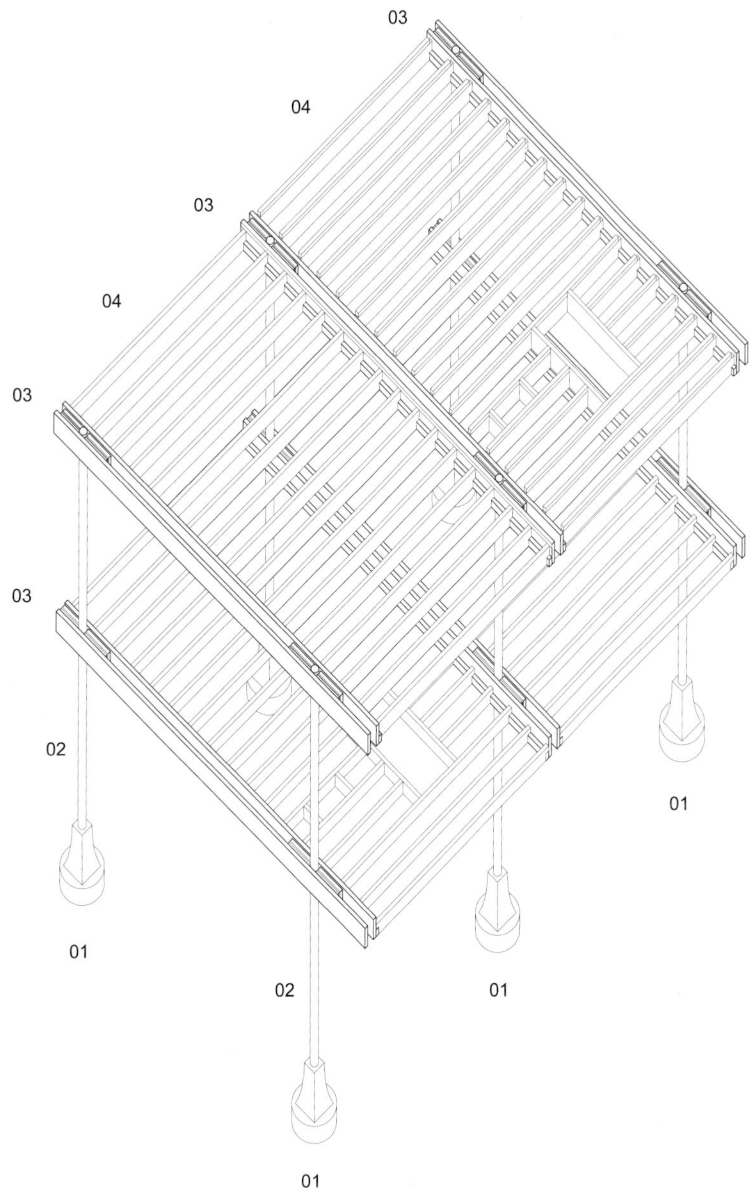

01. Reinforced concrete footings.
02. Round steel columns.
03. Main girders. Double timber beams.
04. Timber floor joists.

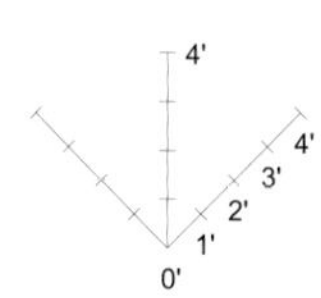

Figure 7.28. A. Lawrence Kocher and Albert Frey. Experimental Weekend House 1932 (Unbuilt). Axonometric view of the structural system. Scale 3/8"=1'-0".

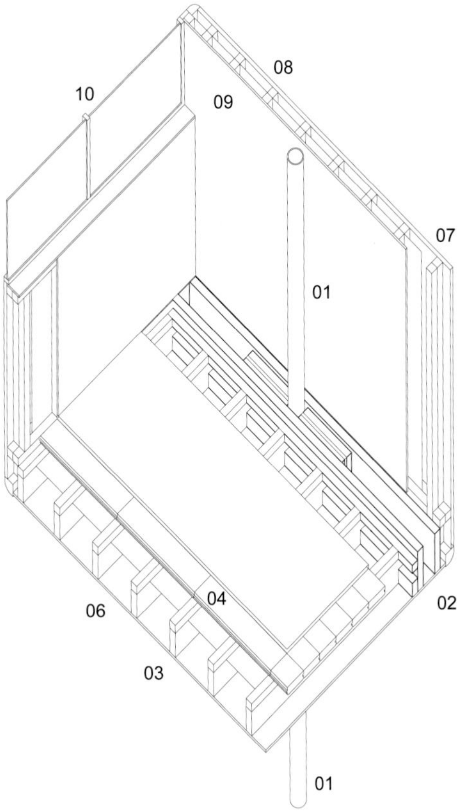

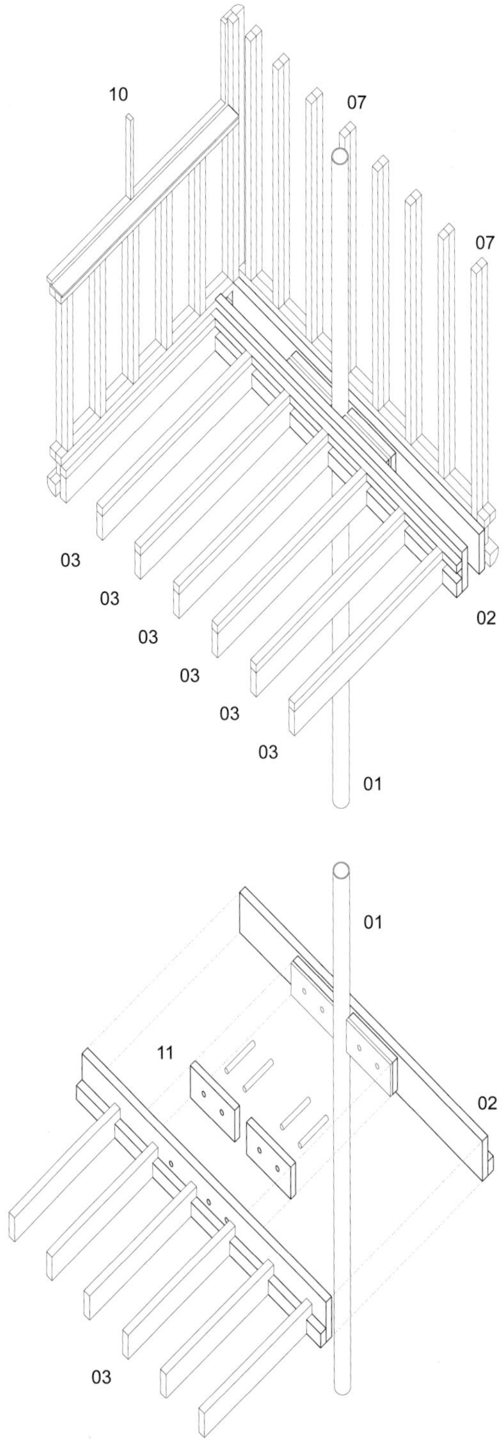

01. Round steel columns.
02. Main girders. Double timber beams.
03. Timber floor joists.
04. Wood deck.
05. Floor. *Thermax* fiber board finished in linoleum.
06. False ceiling, fiber board.
07. Façade structure. 2x2" wood studs with aluminum sheet inbetween.
08. Façade exterior. Insulation board, building paper, and exterior covering of adhered canvas.
09. Façade interior. Insulation board finished in *Fabrikoid*.
10. Wood window frames.
11. Wood column-girder connection piece.

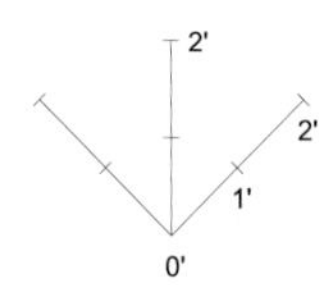

Figure 7.29. A. Lawrence Kocher and Albert Frey. Experimental Weekend House 1932 (Unbuilt). Axonometric view of the constructive system. Scale 1/8"=1'-0".

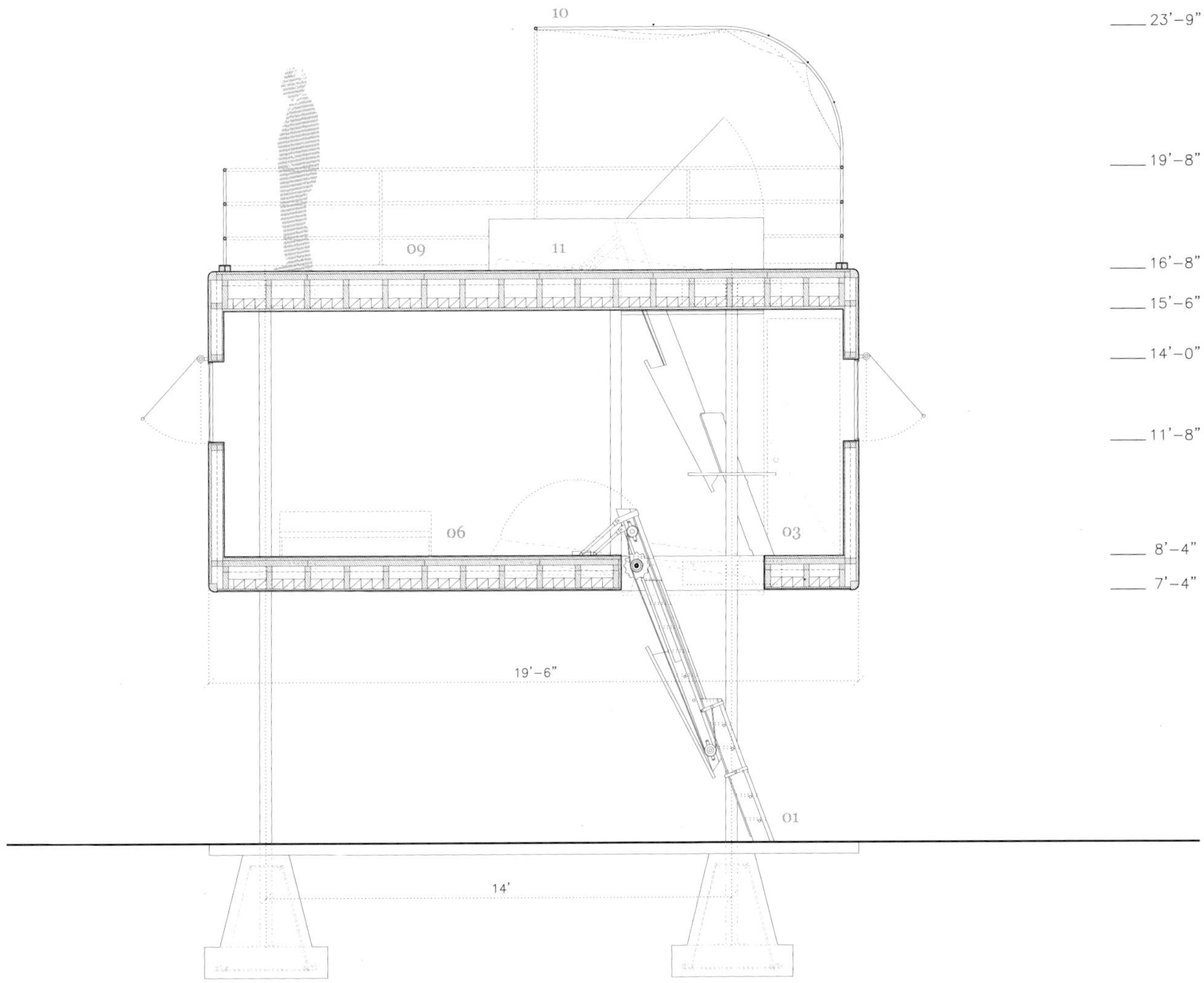

01. *Bessler* fold-away stair connecting with first floor.
02. Dinning room.
03. *Bessler* fold-away stair connecting with roof terrace.
04. Kitchen.
05. Bathroom.
06. Living room (day); main bedroom (night).
07. Living room (day); bedroom (night).
08. Storage closets.
09. Roof terrace.
10. Canvas canopy and awnings.
11. Box to house *Bessler* stair.

Figure 7.30. A. Lawrence Kocher and Albert Frey. Experimental Weekend House 1932 (Unbuilt). Section. Scale 3/16"=1'-0".

0' 2' 5'

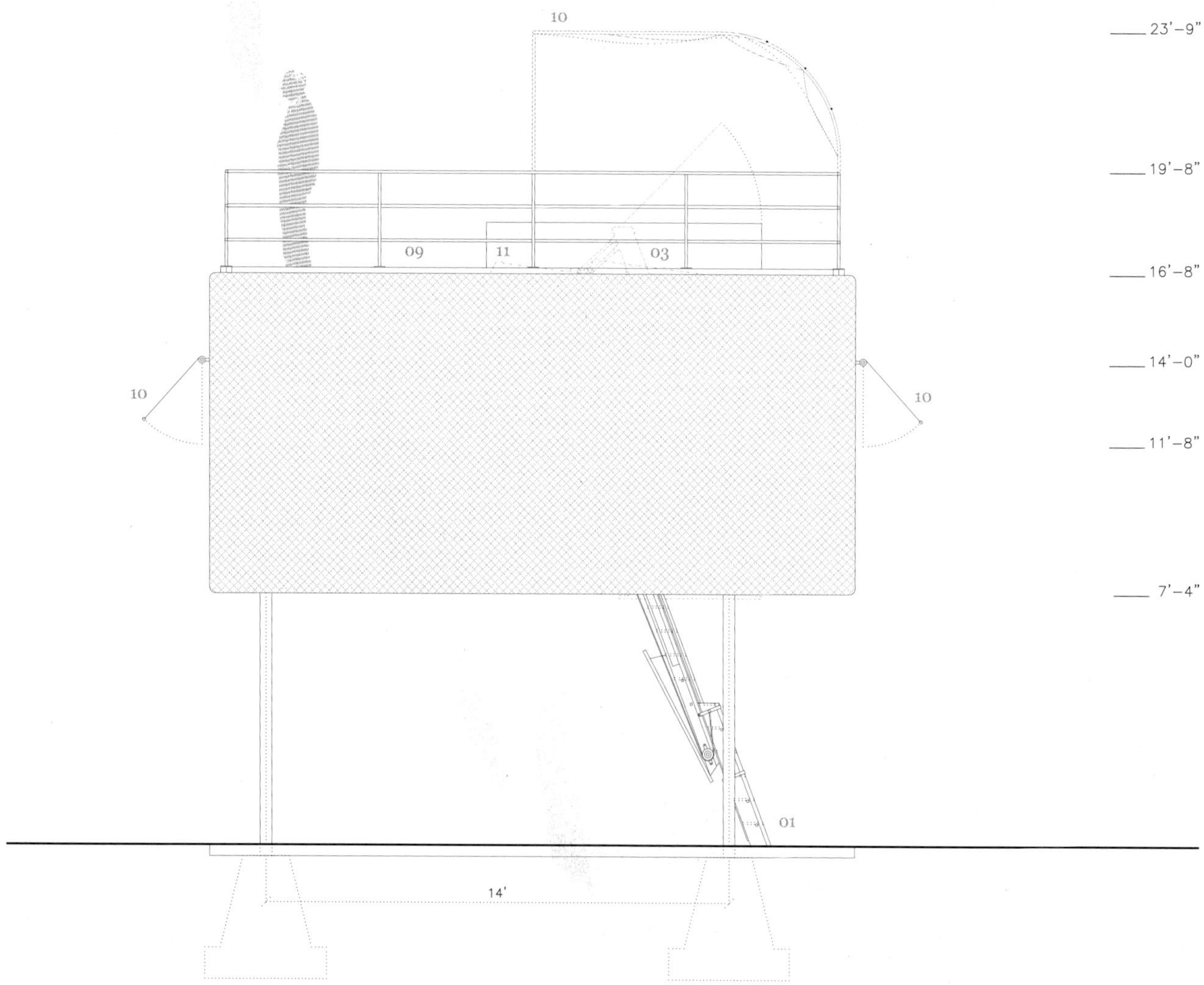

01. *Bessler* fold-away stair connecting with first floor.
02. Dinning room.
03. *Bessler* fold-away stair connecting with roof terrace.
04. Kitchen.
05. Bathroom.
06. Living room (day); main bedroom (night).
07. Living room (day); bedroom (night).
08. Storage closets.
09. Roof terrace.
10. Canvas canopy and awnings.
11. Box to house *Bessler* stair.

Figure 7.31. A. Lawrence Kocher and Albert Frey. Experimental Weekend House 1932 (Unbuilt). Elevation. Scale 3/16"=1'-0".

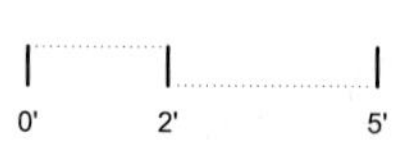

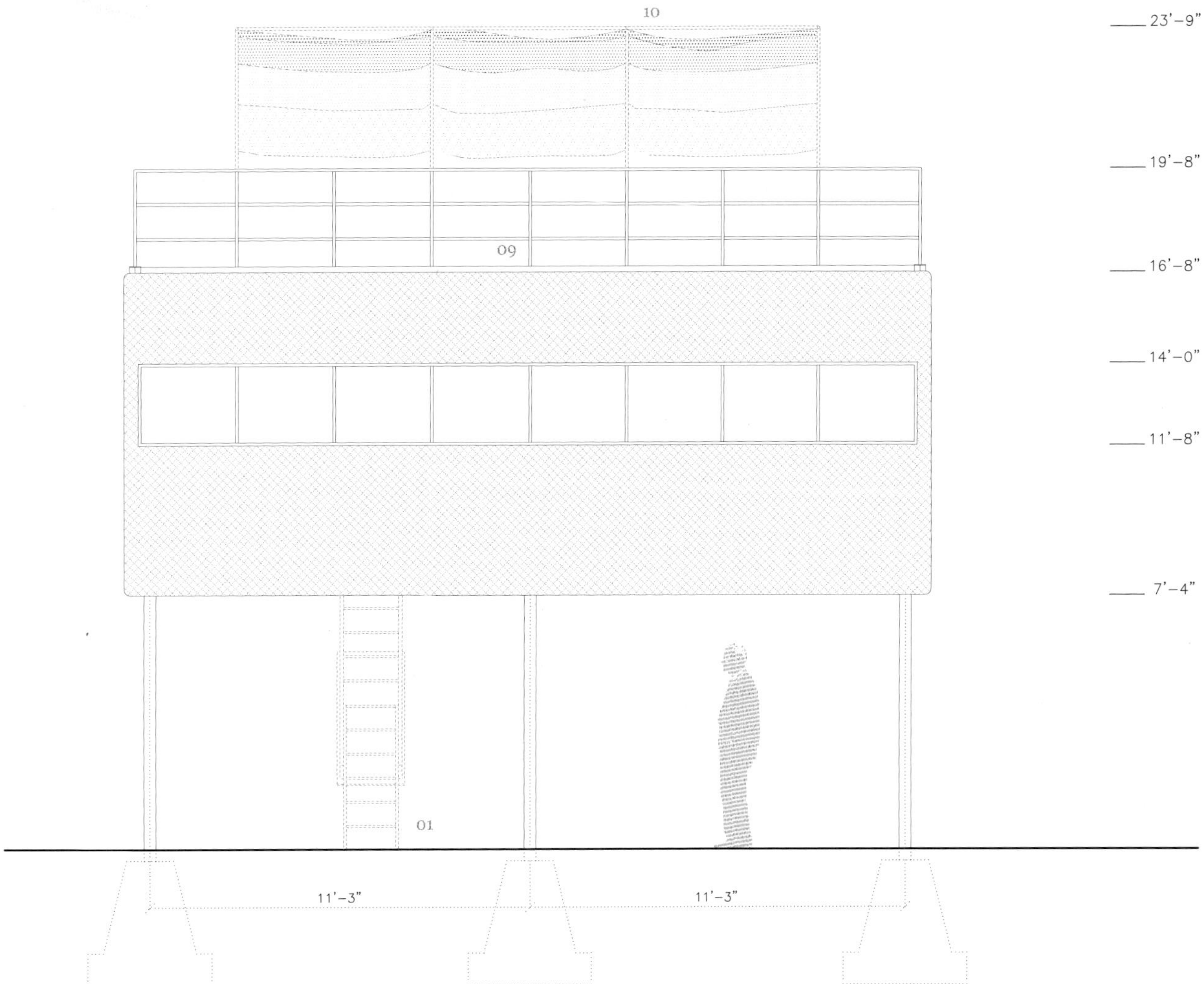

01. *Bessler* fold-away stair connecting with first floor.
02. Dinning room.
03. *Bessler* fold-away stair connecting with roof terrace.
04. Kitchen.
05. Bathroom.
06. Living room (day); main bedroom (night).
07. Living room (day); bedroom (night).
08. Storage closets.
09. Roof terrace.
10. Canvas canopy and awnings.
11. Box to house *Bessler* stair.

Figure 7.32. A. Lawrence Kocher and Albert Frey. Experimental Weekend House 1932 (Unbuilt). Elevation. Scale 3/16"=1'-0".

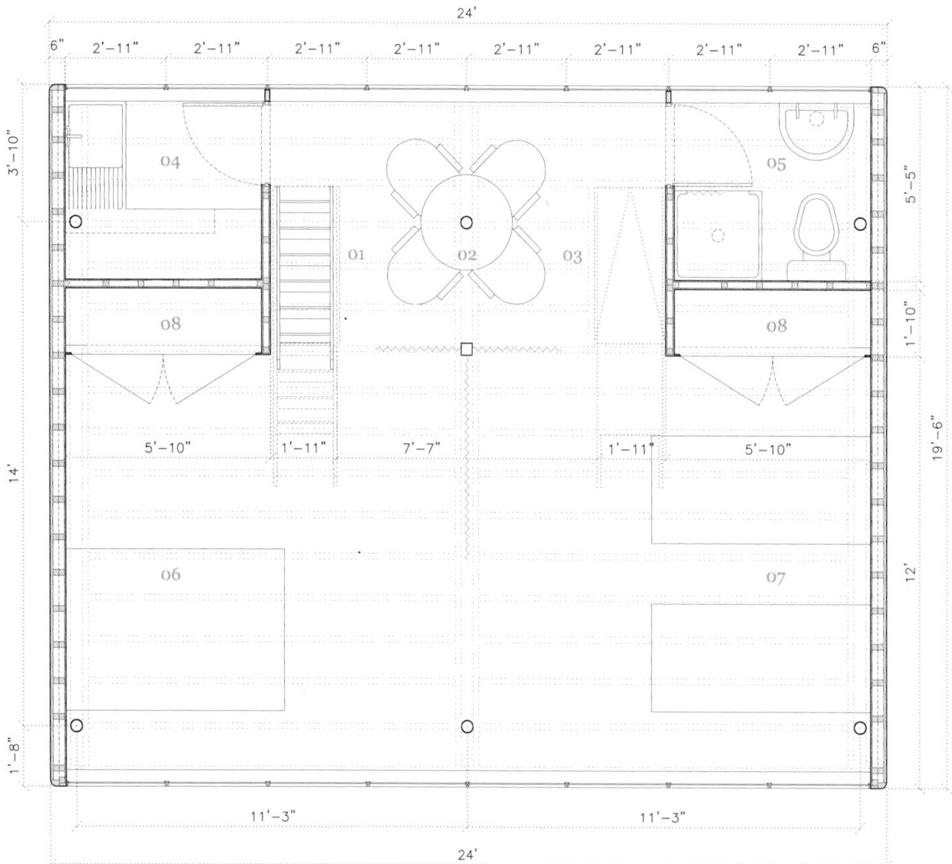

01. *Bessler* fold-away stair connecting with first floor.
02. Dinning room.
03. *Bessler* fold-away stair connecting with roof terrace.
04. Kitchen.
05. Bathroom.
06. Living room (day); main bedroom (night).
07. Living room (day); bedroom (night).
08. Storage closets.

Figure 7.33. A. Lawrence Kocher and Albert Frey. Experimental Weekend House 1932 (Unbuilt). Second floor plan. Scale 3/16"=1'-0".

KOCHER CANVAS WEEKEND HOUSE, 1934–1935 (BUILT)

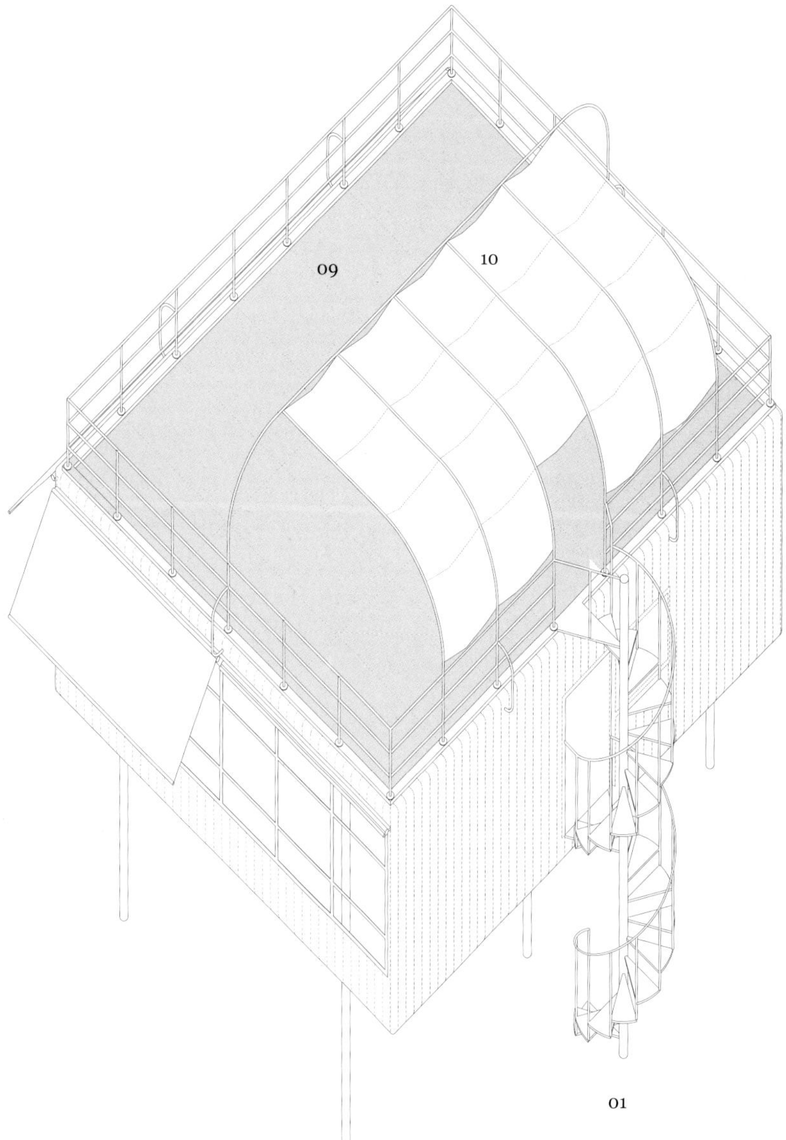

01. Prefab cast-iron spiral stair.
02. Dinning room.
03. Kitchen.
04. Bathroom.
05. Living room (day); bedroom (night).
06. Living room (day); main bedroom (night).
07. Storage closets and cabinets.
08. Boiler room.
09. Roof terrace.
10. Canvas roof canopy.
11. Drainage pipe.

Figure 7.34. A. Lawrence Kocher and Albert Frey. Kocher Canvas Weekend House, 1934–1935 (Built). Axonometric view of the external envelope. Scale 3/8"=1'-0".

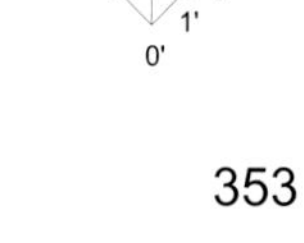

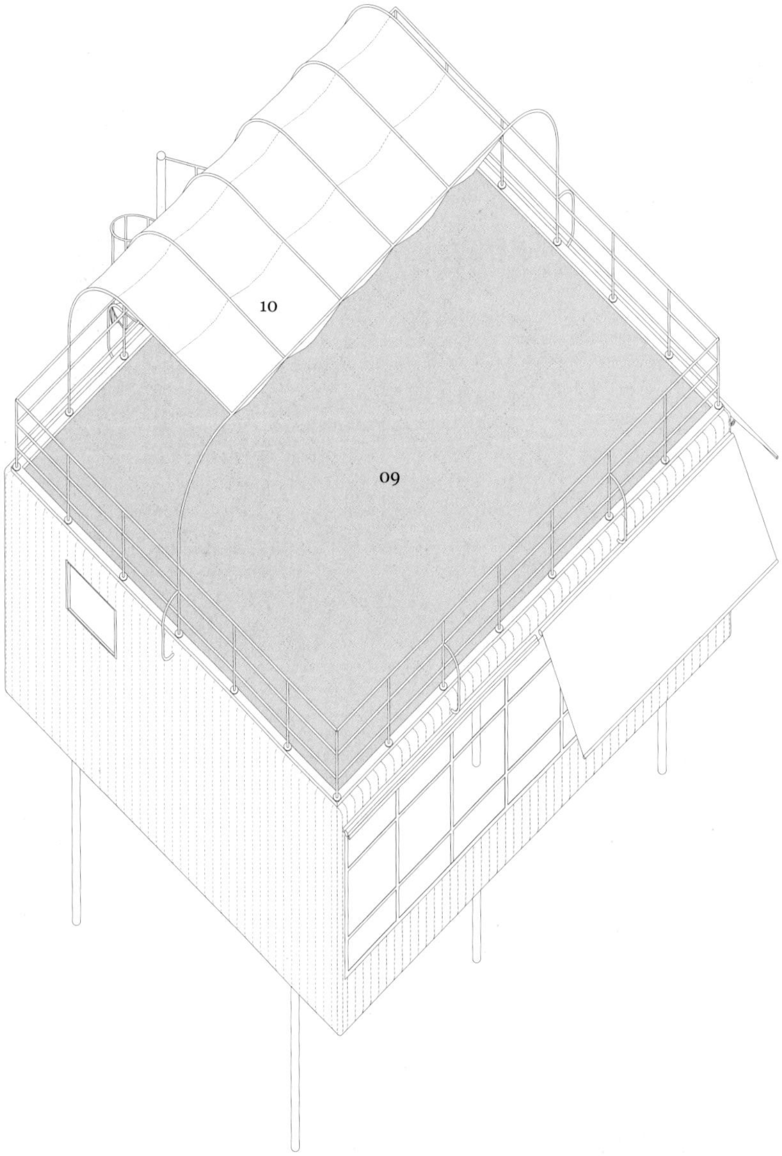

01. Prefab cast-iron spiral stair
02. Dinning room.
03. Kitchen.
04. Bathroom.
05. Living room (day); bedroom (night).
06. Living room (day); main bedroom (night).
07. Storage closets and cabinets.
08. Boiler room.
09. Roof terrace.
10. Canvas roof canopy.
11. Drainage pipe.

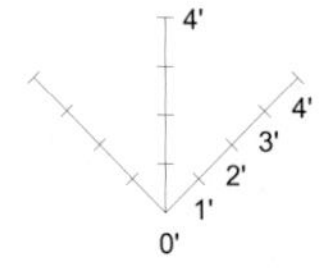

Figure 7.35. A. Lawrence Kocher and Albert Frey. Kocher Canvas Weekend House, 1934–1935 (Built). Axonometric view of the external envelope. Scale 3/8"=1'-0".

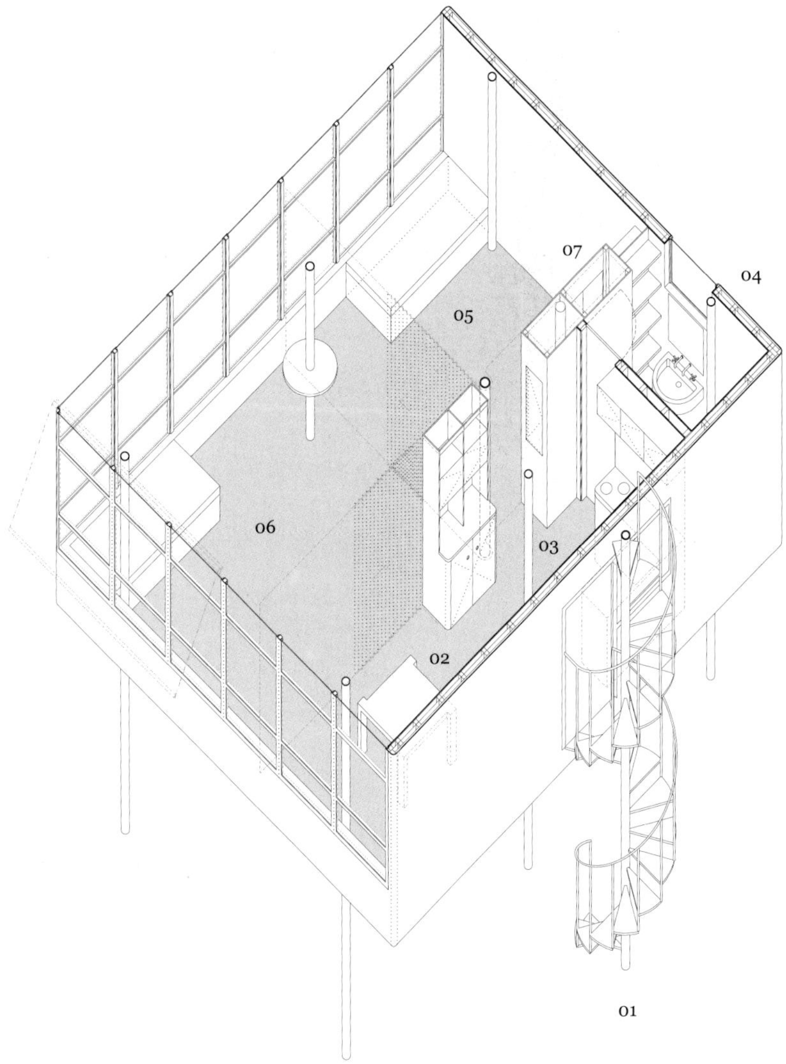

01. Prefab cast-iron spiral stair
02. Dinning room.
03. Kitchen.
04. Bathroom.
05. Living room (day); bedroom (night).
06. Living room (day); main bedroom (night).
07. Storage closets and cabinets.
08. Boiler room.
09. Roof terrace.
10. Canvas roof canopy.
11. Drainage pipe.

Figure 7.36. A. Lawrence Kocher and Albert Frey. Kocher Canvas Weekend House, 1934–1935 (Built). Cut-away axonometric view. Scale 3/8"=1'-0".

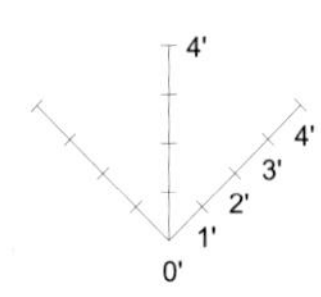

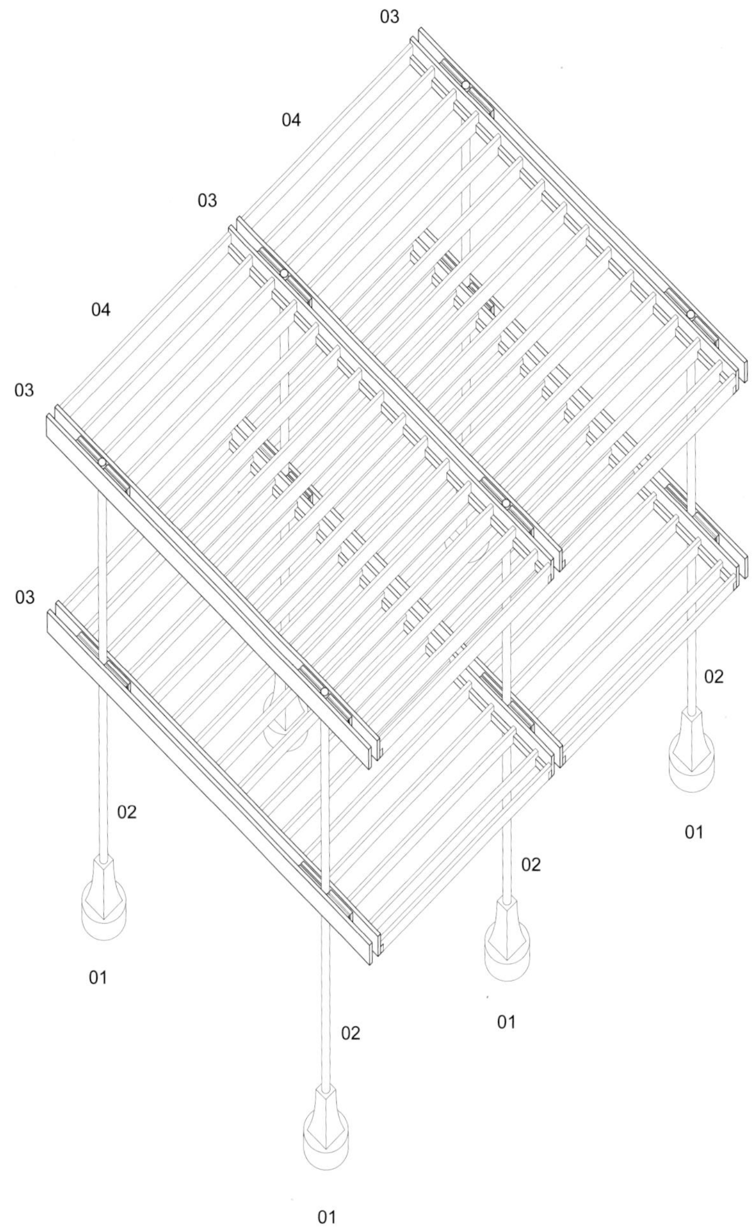

01. Reinforced concrete footings.
02. Round steel columns.
03. Main girders. Double timber beams.
04. Timber floor joists.

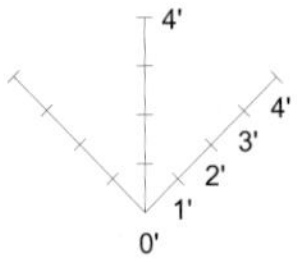

Figure 7.37. A. Lawrence Kocher and Albert Frey. Kocher Canvas Weekend House, 1934–1935 (Built). Axonometric view of the structural system. Scale 3/8"=1'-0".

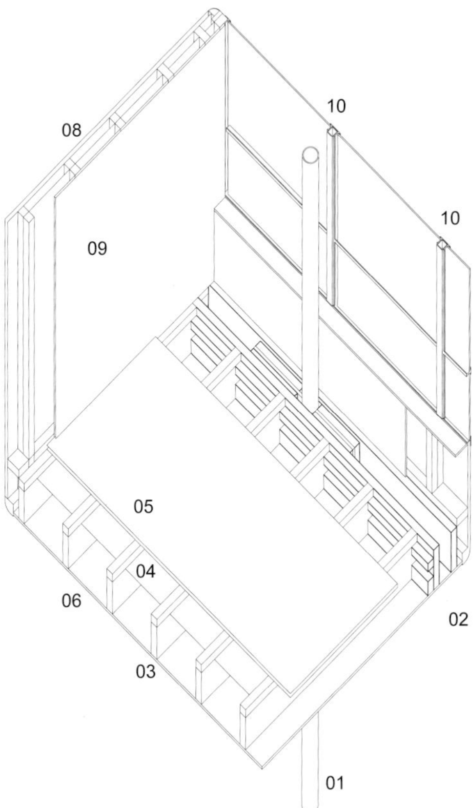

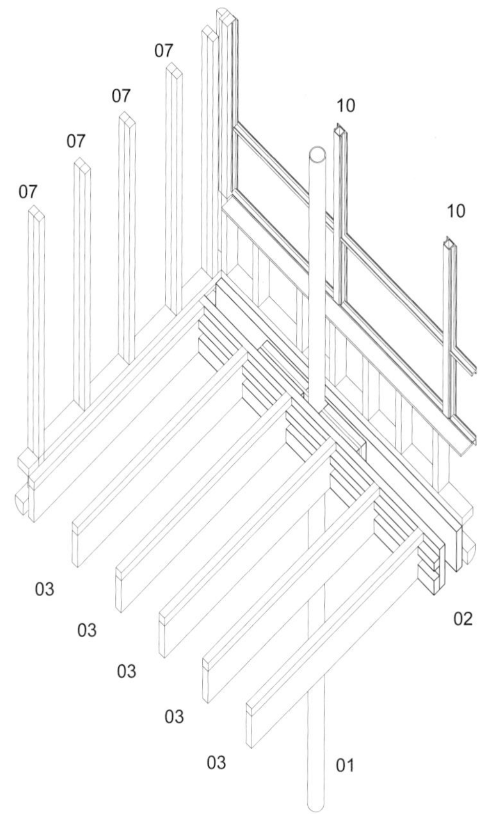

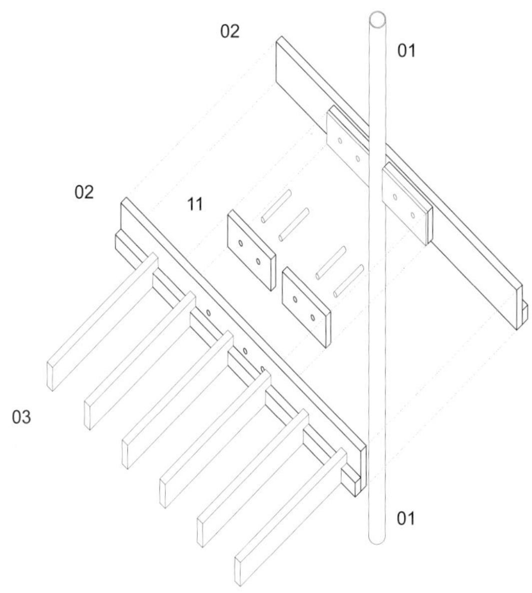

01. Round steel columns.
02. Main girders. Double timber beams.
03. Timber floor joists.
04. Aluminum sheet on top of floor joists..
05. Floor. *Thermax* fiber board finished in linoleum.
06. False ceiling, fiber board.
07. Façade structure. 2x2" wood studs with aluminum sheet in between.
08. Façade exterior. Insulation board, building paper, and exterior covering of adhered canvas.
09. Façade interior. Insulation board finished in *Fabrikoid*.
10. Steel window frames.
11. Wood column-girder connection piece.

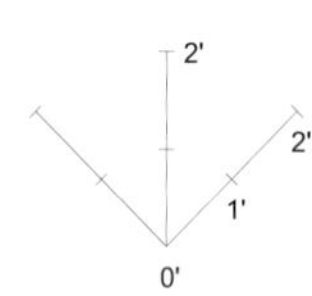

Figure 7.38. A. Lawrence Kocher and Albert Frey. Kocher Canvas Weekend House, 1934–1935 (Built). Axonometric view of the constructive system. Scale 1/8"=1'-0".

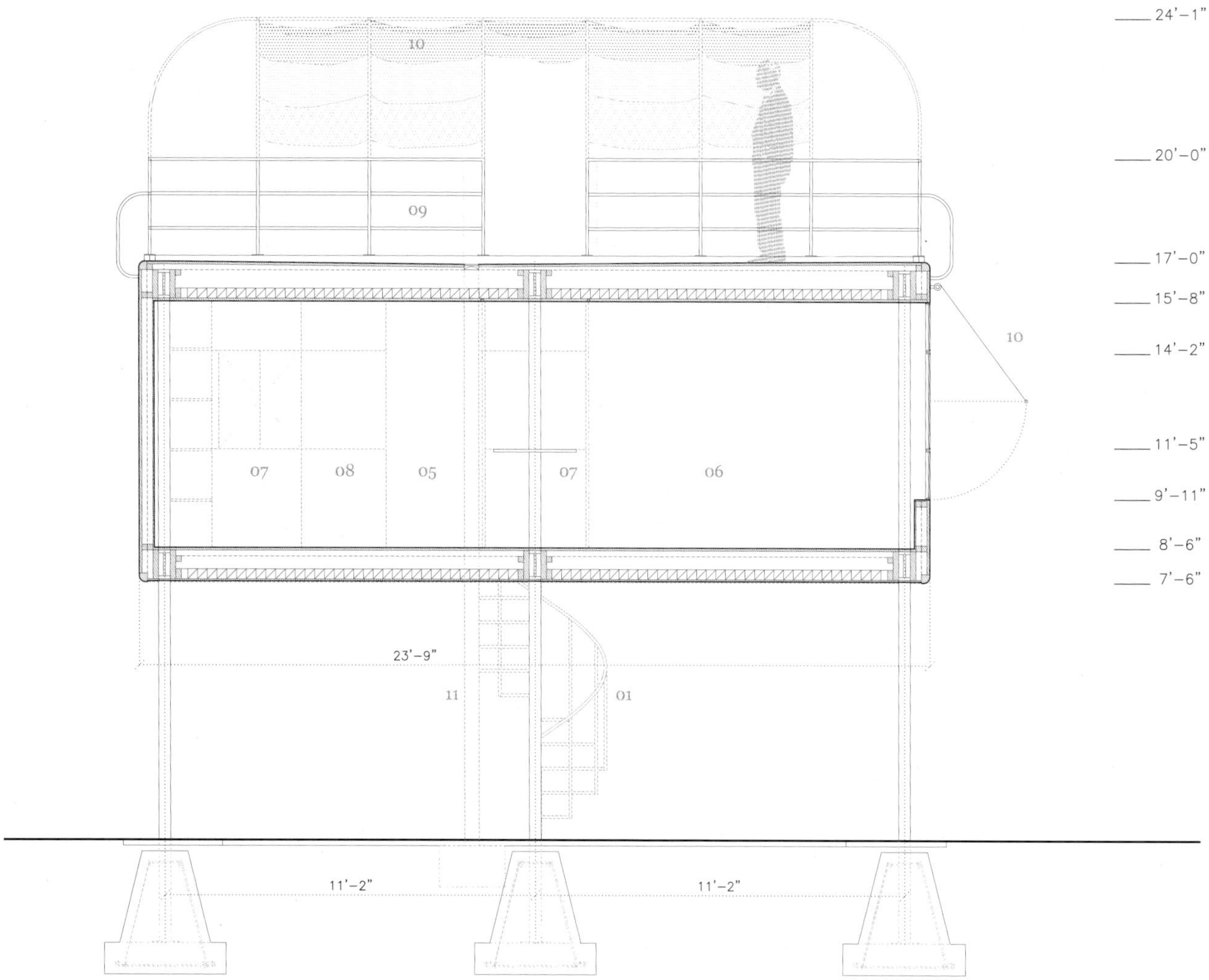

01. Prefab cast-iron spiral stair
02. Dinning room.
03. Kitchen.
04. Bathroom.
05. Living room (day); bedroom (night).
06. Living room (day); main bedroom (night).
07. Storage closets and cabinets.
08. Boiler room.
09. Roof terrace.
10. Canvas roof canopy.
11. Drainage pipe.

Figure 7.39. A. Lawrence Kocher and Albert Frey. Kocher Canvas Weekend House, 1934–1935 (Built). Section. Scale 3/16"=1'-0".

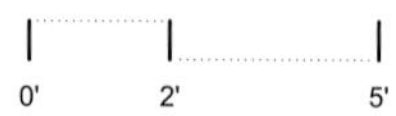

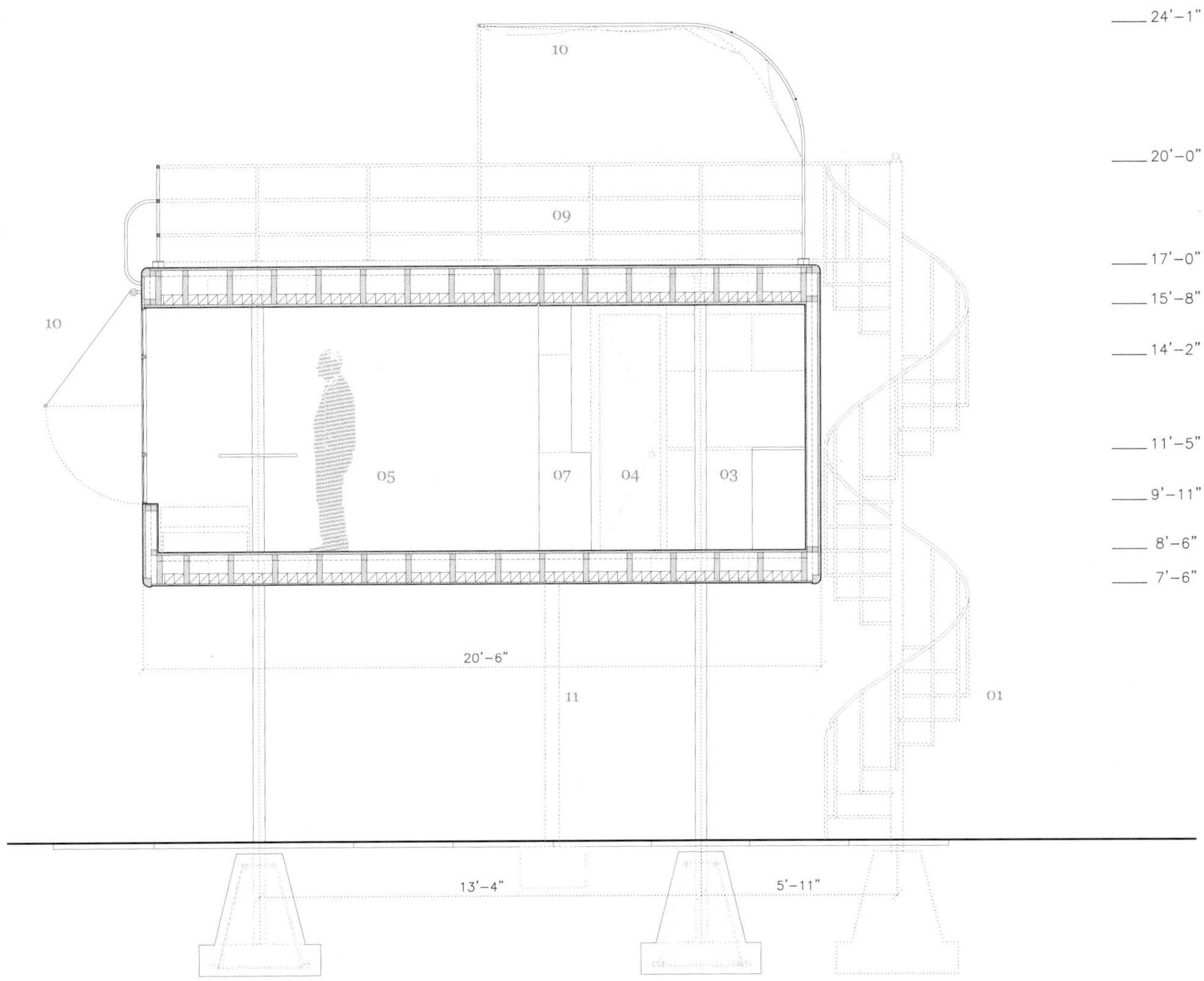

01. Prefab cast-iron spiral stair
02. Dinning room.
03. Kitchen.
04. Bathroom.
05. Living room (day); bedroom (night).
06. Living room (day); main bedroom (night).
07. Storage closets and cabinets.
08. Boiler room.
09. Roof terrace.
10. Canvas roof canopy.
11. Drainage pipe.

Figure 7.40. A. Lawrence Kocher and Albert Frey. Kocher Canvas Weekend House, 1934–1935 (Built). Section. Scale 3/16"=1'-0".

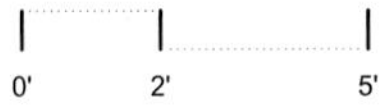

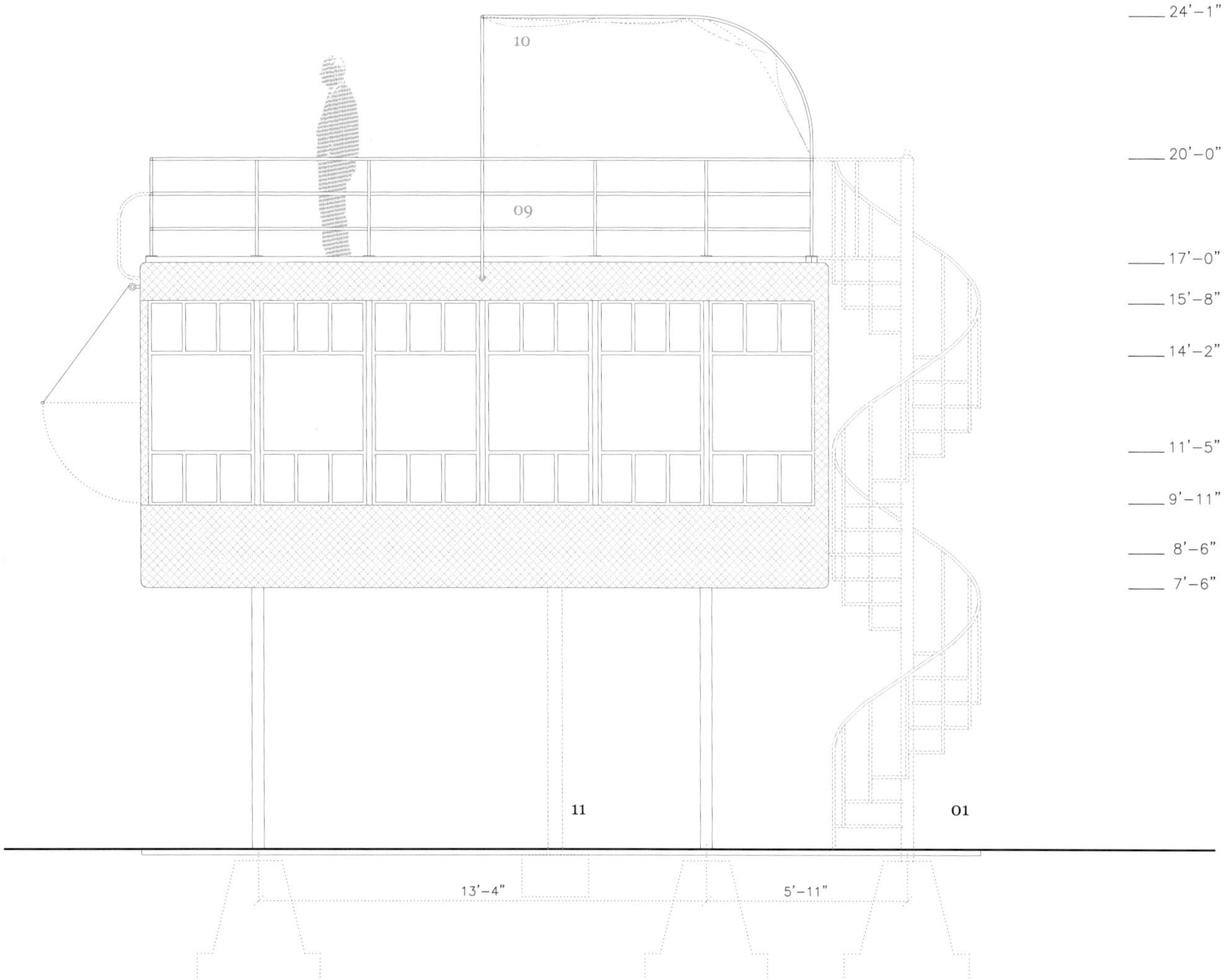

01. Prefab cast-iron spiral stair
02. Dinning room.
03. Kitchen.
04. Bathroom.
05. Living room (day)-bedroom (night).
06. Living room (day)-main bedroom (night).
07. Storage closets and cabinets.
08. Boiler room.
09. Roof terrace.
10. Canvas roof canopy.
11. Drainage pipe.

Figure 7.41. A. Lawrence Kocher and Albert Frey. Kocher Canvas Weekend House, 1934-35 (Built). Elevation. Scale 3/16"=1'-0".

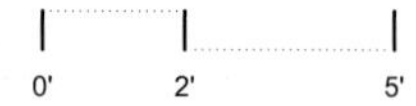

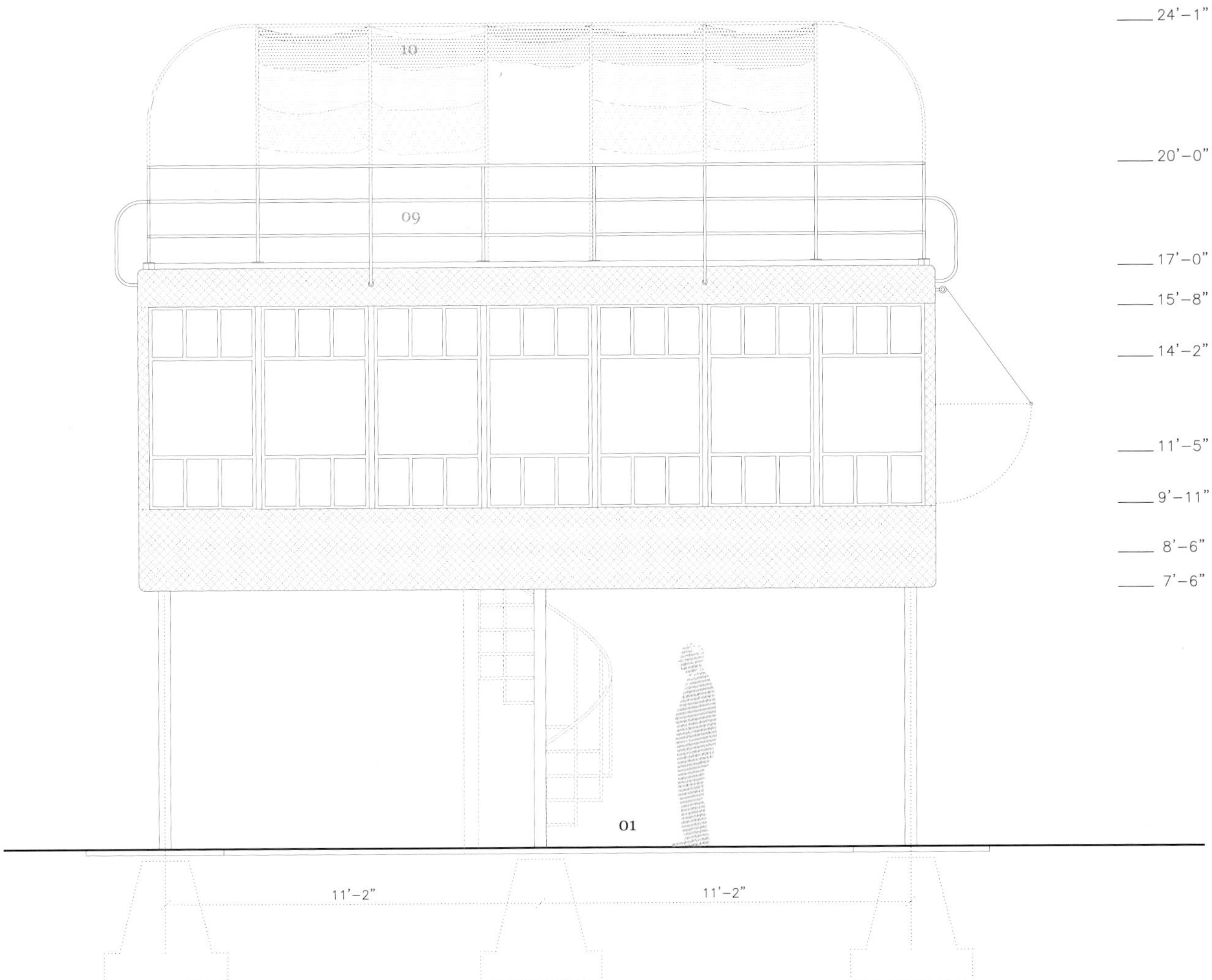

01. Prefab cast-iron spiral stair
02. Dinning room.
03. Kitchen.
04. Bathroom.
05. Living room (day)-bedroom (night).
06. Living room (day)-main bedroom (night).
07. Storage closets and cabinets.
08. Boiler room.
09. Roof terrace.
10. Canvas roof canopy.
11. Drainage pipe.

Figure 7.42. A. Lawrence Kocher and Albert Frey. Kocher Canvas Weekend House, 1934-35 (Built). Elevation. Scale 3/16"=1'-0".

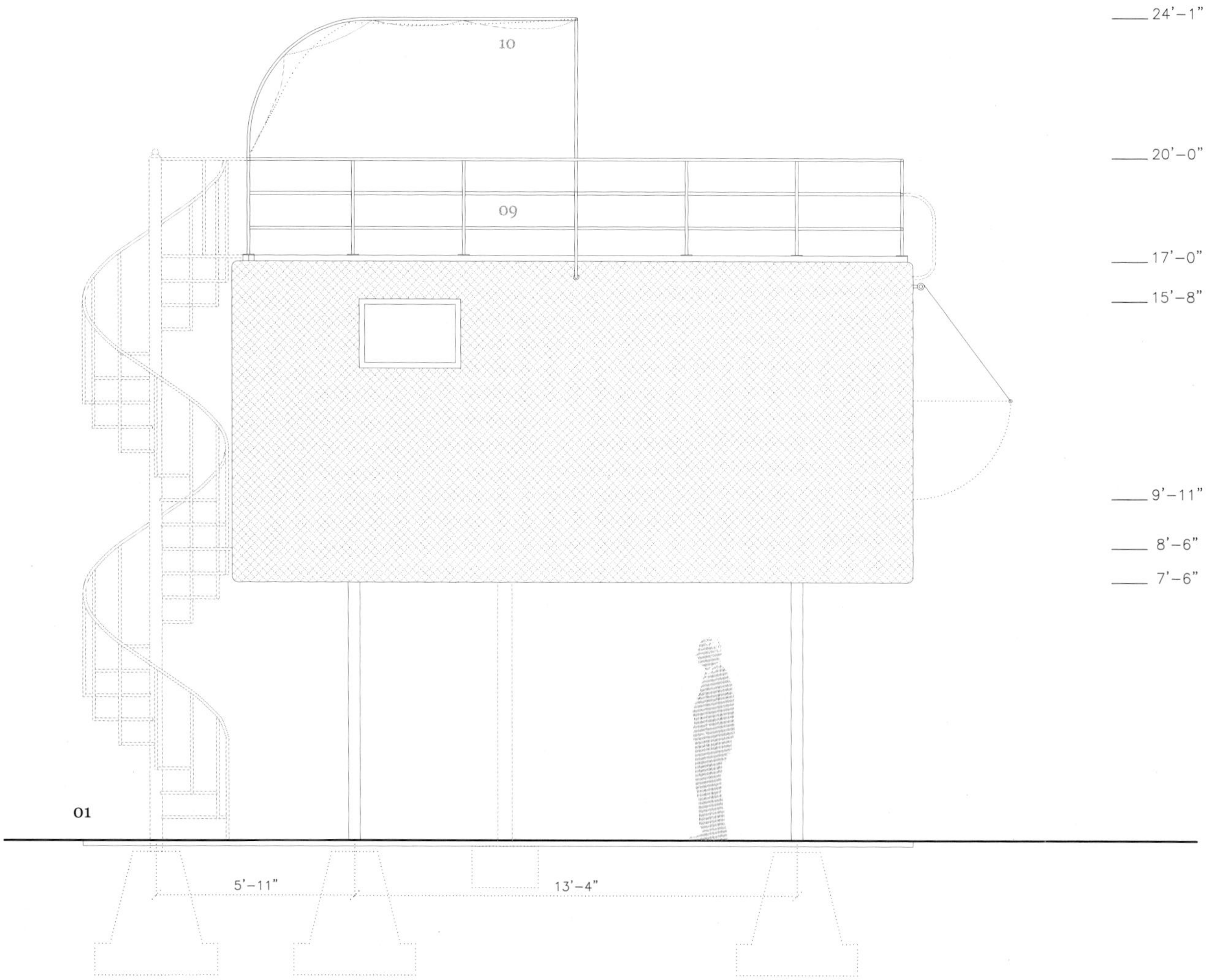

01. Prefab cast-iron spiral stair
02. Dinning room.
03. Kitchen.
04. Bathroom.
05. Living room (day); bedroom (night).
06. Living room (day); main bedroom (night).
07. Storage closets and cabinets.
08. Boiler room.
09. Roof terrace.
10. Canvas roof canopy.

Figure 7.43. A. Lawrence Kocher and Albert Frey. Kocher Canvas Weekend House, 1934–1935 (Built). Elevation. Scale 3/16"=1'-0".

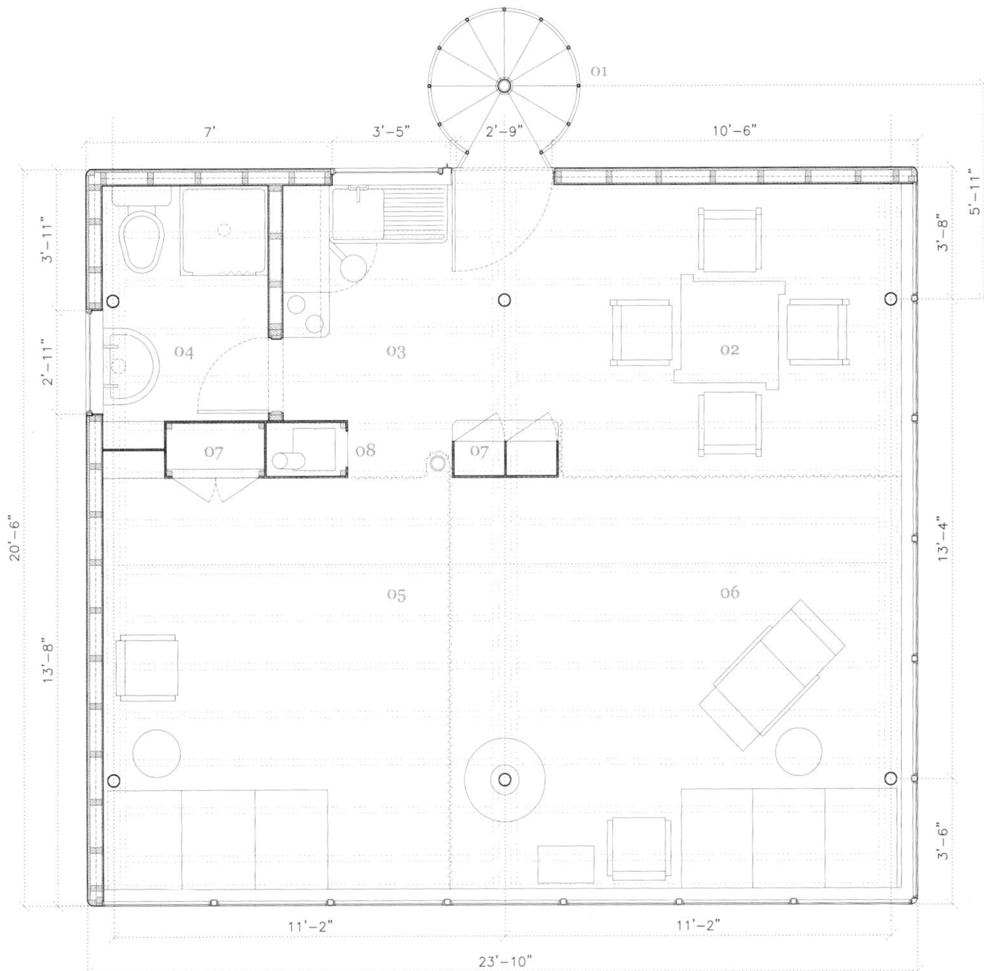

01. Prefab cast-iron spiral stair
02. Dinning room.
03. Kitchen.
04. Bathroom.
05. Living room (day); bedroom (night).
06. Living room (day); main bedroom (night).
07. Storage closets and cabinets.
08. Boiler room.

Figure 7.44. A. Lawrence Kocher and Albert Frey. Kocher Canvas Weekend House, 1934–1935 (Built). First floor plan. Scale 3/16"=1'-0".

0' 2' 5'

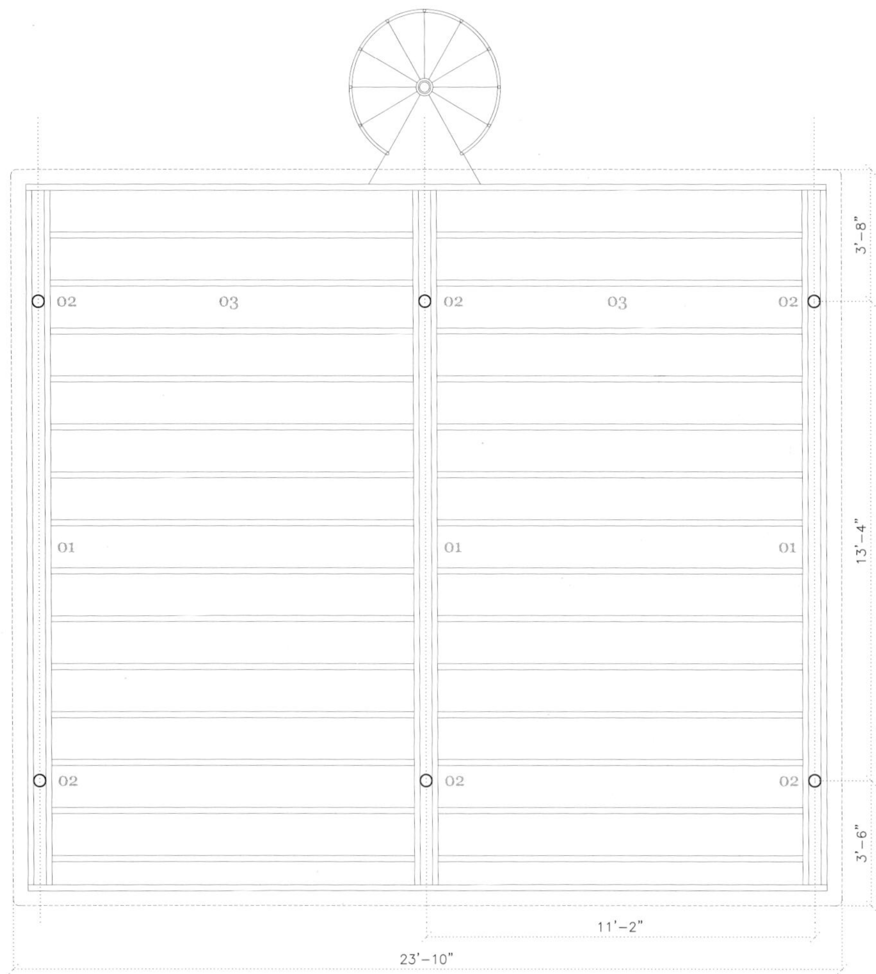

01. Main girders. Double timber beams.
02. Round steel columns.
03. Timber floor joists.

Figure 7.45. A. Lawrence Kocher and Albert Frey. Kocher Canvas Weekend House, 1934–1935 (Built). Framing plan. Scale 3/16"=1'-0".

0' 2' 5'

FLORIDA WEEKEND HOUSE, 1937–1939 (UNBUILT)

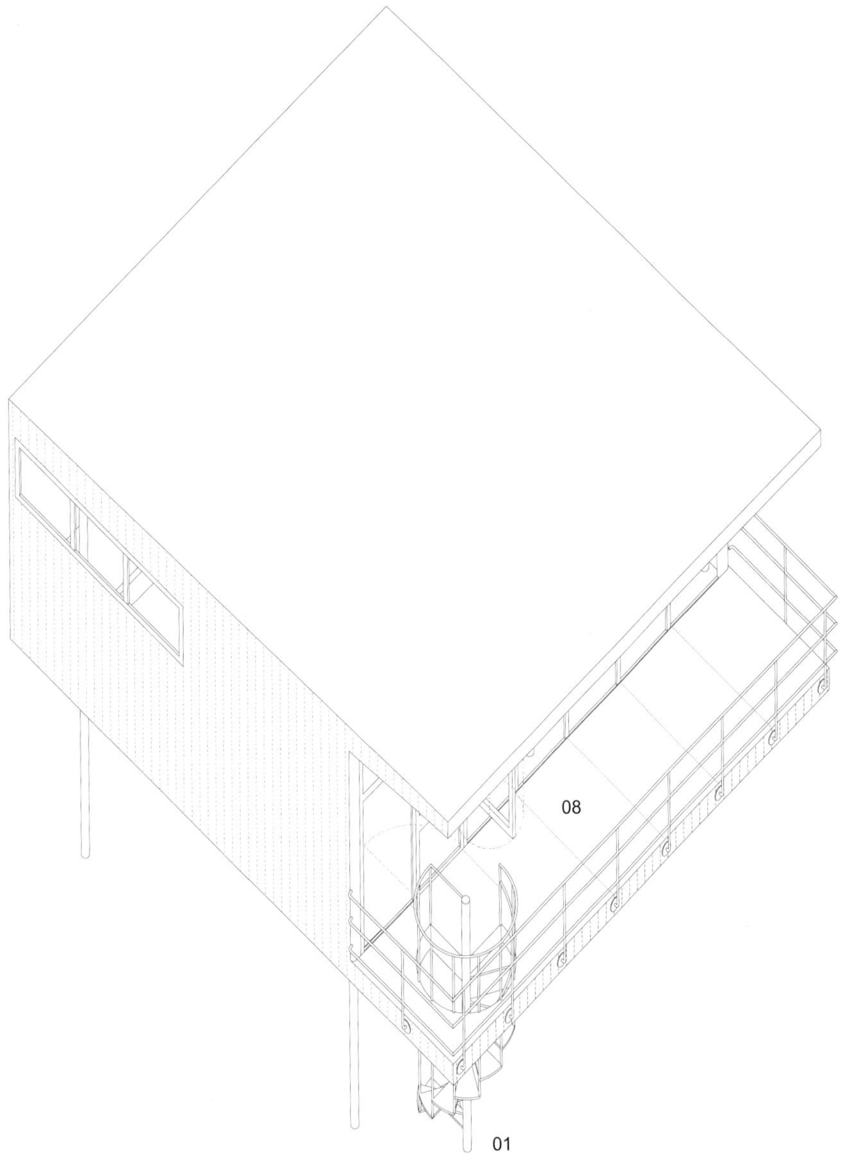

01. Prefab cast-iron spiral stair
02. Dinning room.
03. Kitchen.
04. Bathroom.
05. Living room (day); bedroom (night).
06. Living room (day); main bedroom (night).
07. Storage closets and cabinets.
08. Terrace.

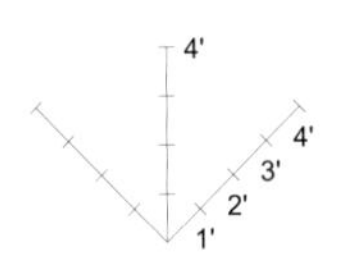

Figure 7.46. A. Lawrence Kocher. Florida Weekend House, 1937–1939 (Unbuilt). Axonometric view of the external envelope. Scale 3/8"=1'-0".

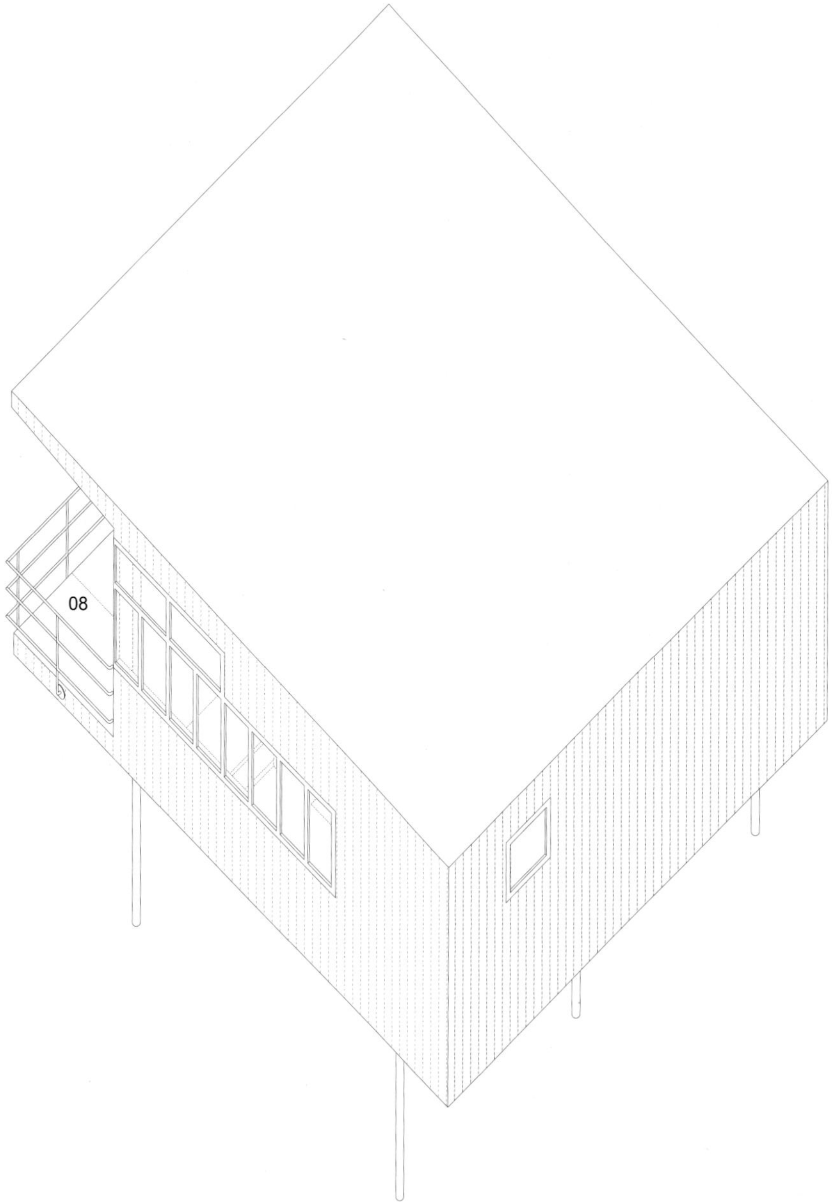

01. Prefab cast-iron spiral stair
02. Dinning room.
03. Kitchen.
04. Bathroom.
05. Living room (day)-bedroom (night).
06. Living room (day)-main bedroom (night).
07. Storage closets and cabinets.
08. Terrace.

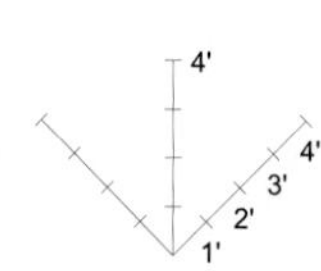

Figure 7.47. A. Lawrence Kocher. Florida Weekend House, 1937-39 (Unbuilt). Axonometric view of the external envelope. Scale 3/8"=1'-0".

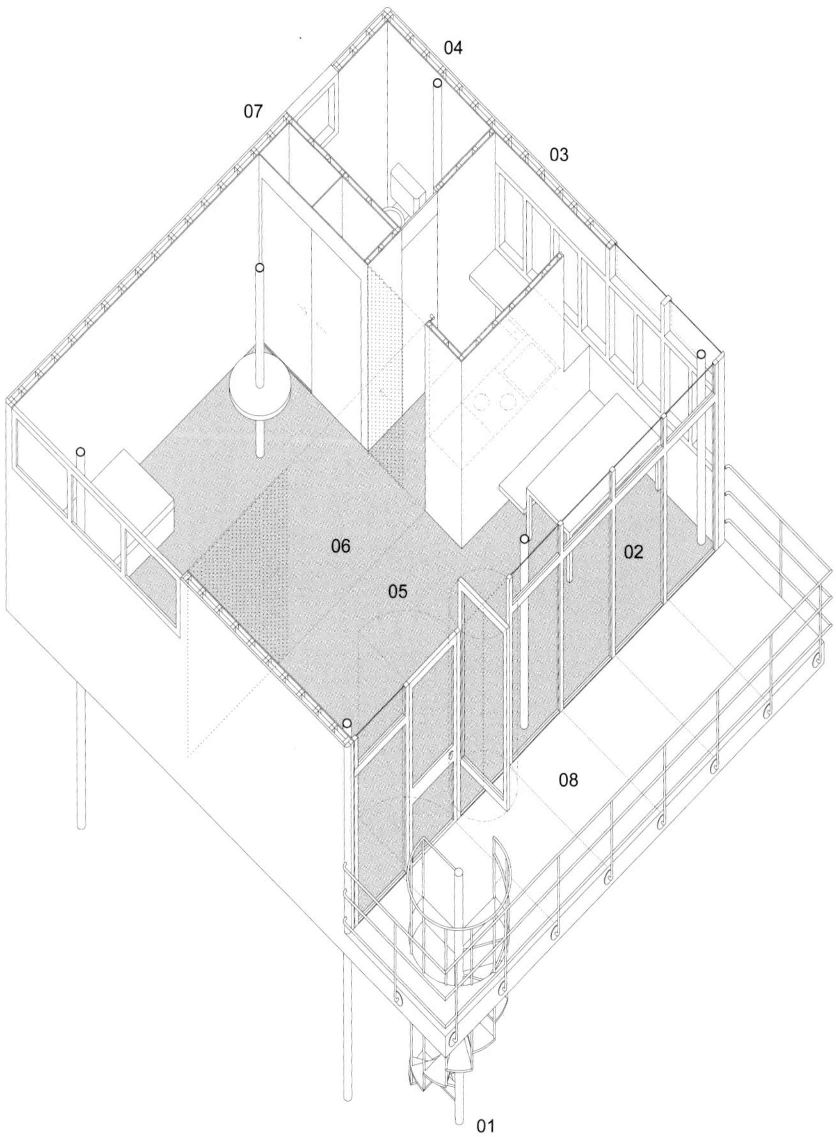

01. Prefab cast-iron spiral stair
02. Dinning room.
03. Kitchen.
04. Bathroom.
05. Living room (day); bedroom (night).
06. Living room (day); main bedroom (night).
07. Storage closets and cabinets.
08. Terrace.

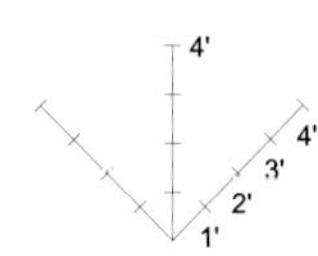

Figure 7.48. A. Lawrence Kocher. Florida Weekend House, 1937–1939 (Unbuilt). Cut-away axonometric view. Scale 3/8"=1'-0".

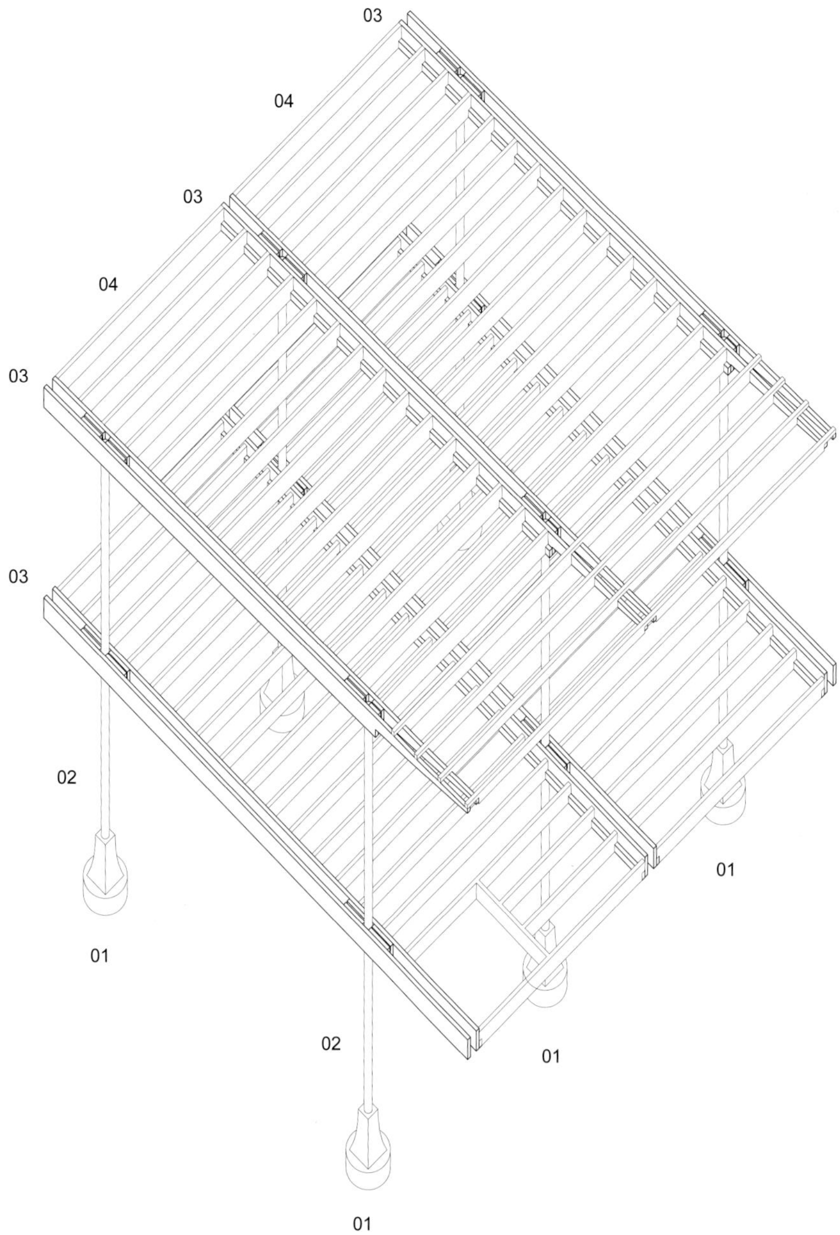

01. Reinforced concrete footings.
02. Round steel columns.
03. Main girders. Double timber beams.
04. Timber floor joists.

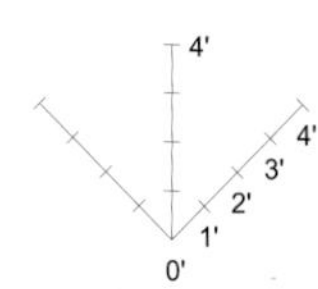

Figure 7.49. A. Lawrence Kocher. Florida Weekend House, 1937–1939 (Unbuilt). Axonometric view of the structural system. Scale 3/8"=1'-0".

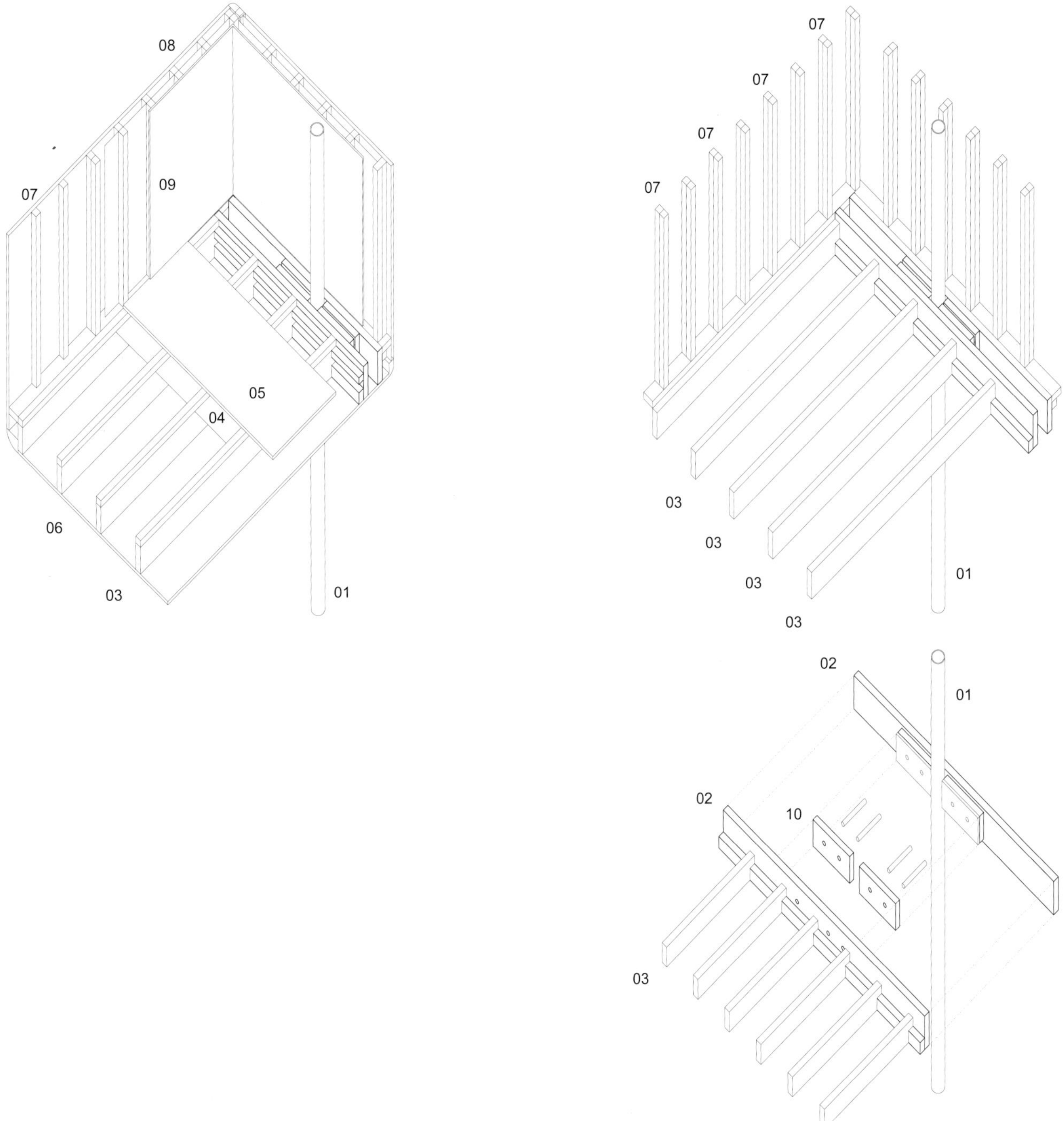

01. Round steel columns.
02. Main girders. Double timber beams.
03. Timber floor joists.
04. Aluminum sheet on top of floor joists.
05. Floor. *Thermax* fiber board finished in linoleum.
06. False ceiling, fiber board.
07. Façade structure. 2x2" wood studs with aluminum sheet in between.
08. Façade exterior. Insulation board, building paper, and exterior covering of adhered canvas.
09. Façade interior. Insulation board finished in *Fabrikoid.*
10. Wood column-girder connection piece.

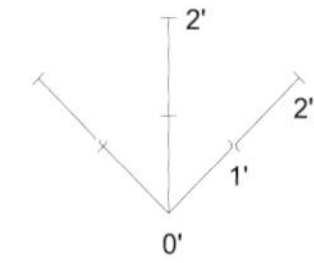

Figure 7.50. A. Lawrence Kocher. Florida Weekend House, 1937–1939 (Unbuilt). Axonometric view of the constructive system. Scale 1/8"=1'-0".

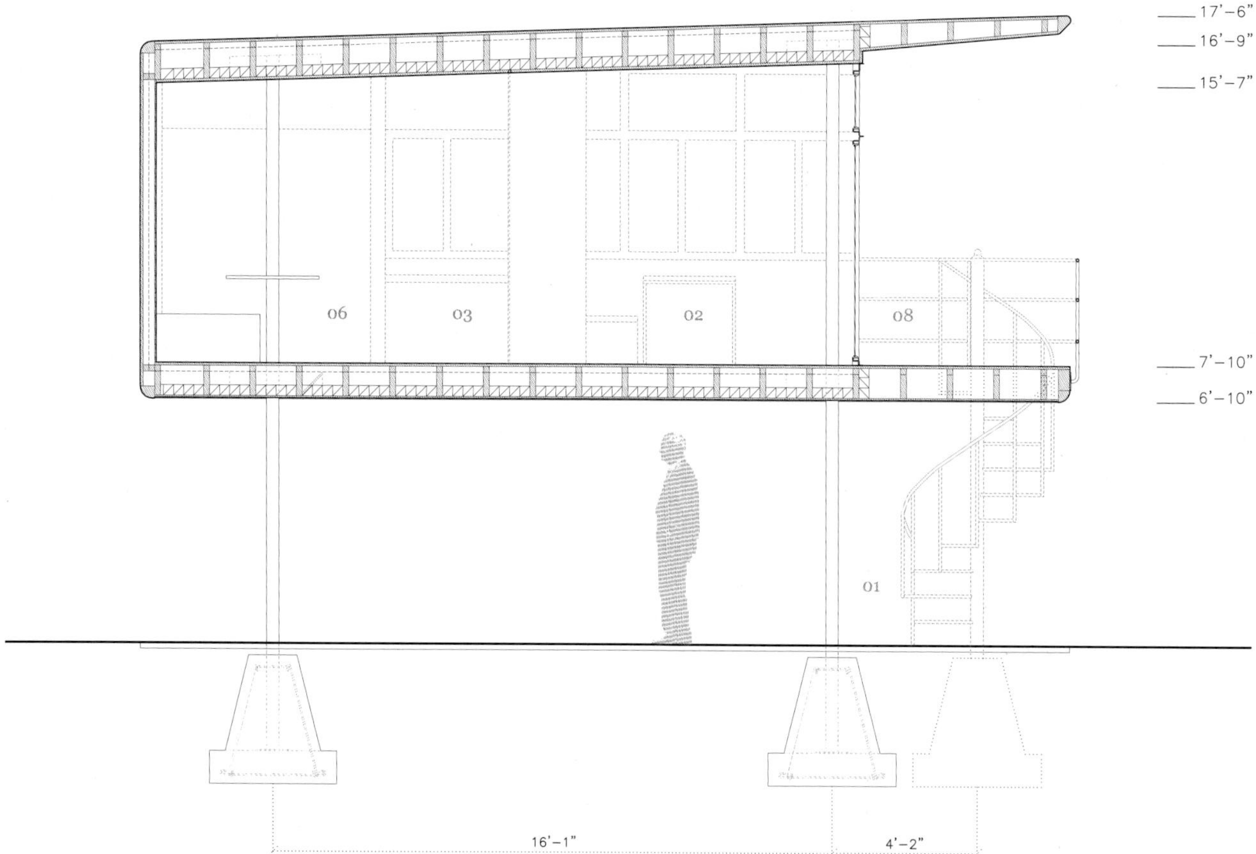

01. Prefab cast-iron spiral stair
02. Dinning room.
03. Kitchen.
04. Bathroom.
05. Living room (day); bedroom (night).
06. Living room (day); main bedroom (night).
07. Storage closets and cabinets.
08. Terrace.

Figure 7.51. A. Lawrence Kocher. Florida Weekend House, 1937–1939 (Unbuilt). Section. Scale 3/16"=1'-0".

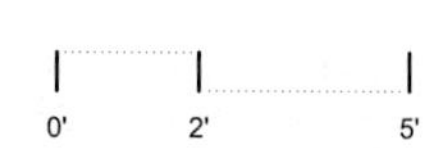

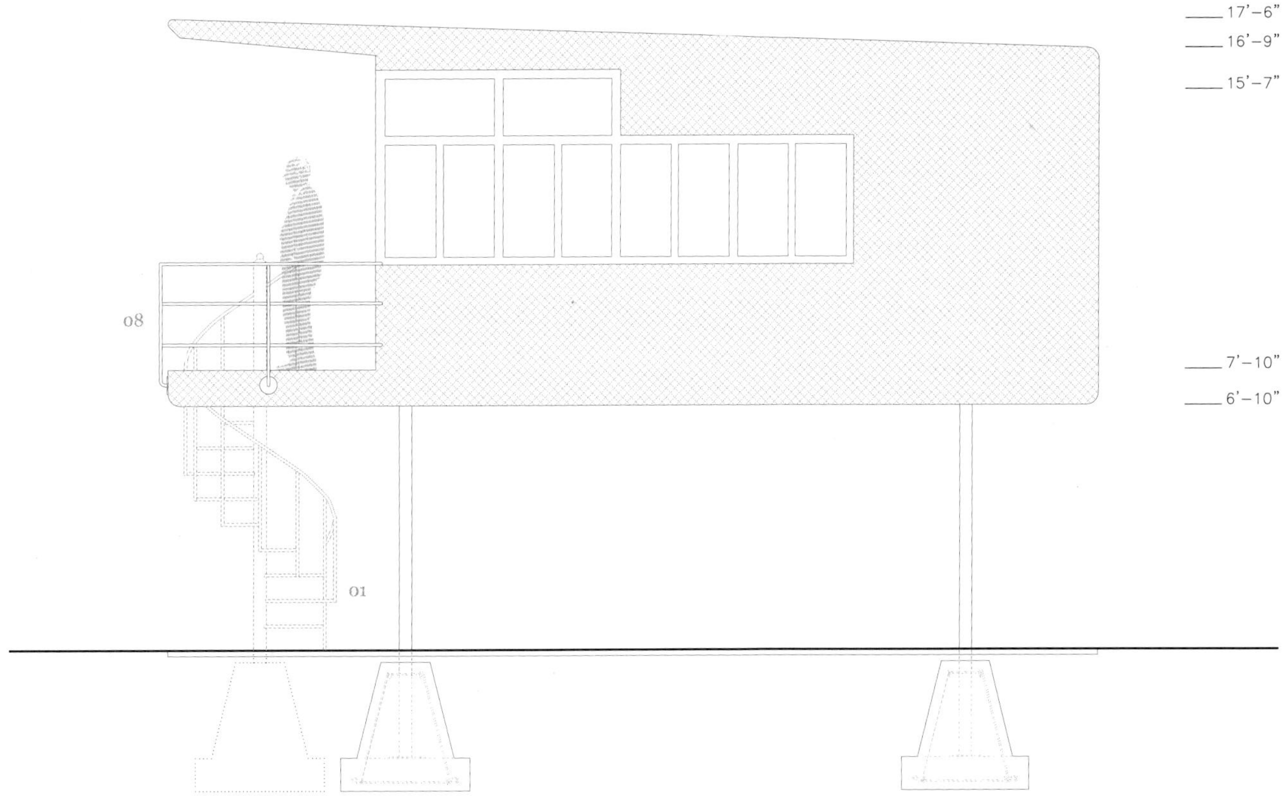

01. Prefab cast-iron spiral stair
02. Dinning room.
03. Kitchen.
04. Bathroom.
05. Living room (day); bedroom (night).
06. Living room (day); main bedroom (night).
07. Storage closets and cabinets.
08. Terrace.

Figure 7.52. A. Lawrence Kocher. Florida Weekend House, 1937–1939 (Unbuilt). Elevation. Scale 3/16"=1'-0".

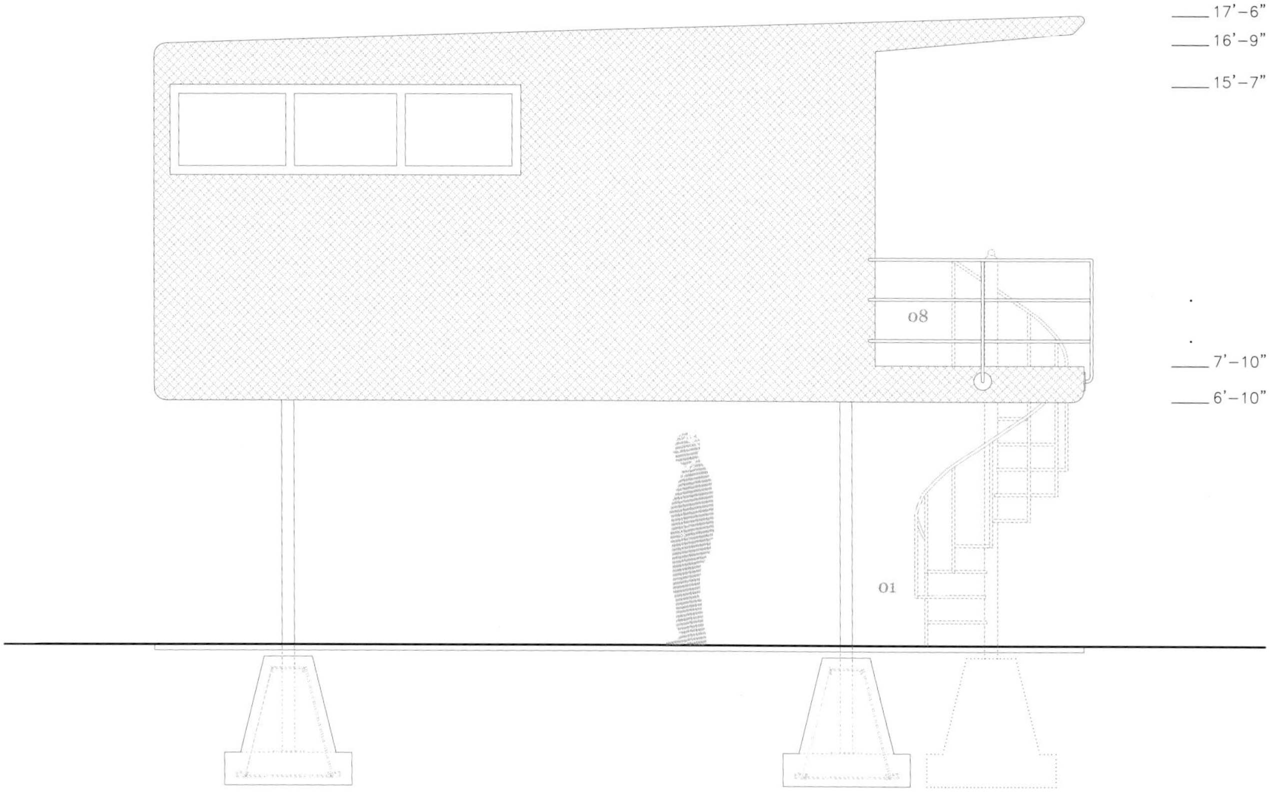

01. Prefab cast-iron spiral stair
02. Dinning room.
03. Kitchen.
04. Bathroom.
05. Living room (day); bedroom (night).
06. Living room (day); main bedroom (night).
07. Storage closets and cabinets.
08. Terrace.

Figure 7.53. A. Lawrence Kocher. Florida Weekend House, 1937–1939 (Unbuilt). Elevation. Scale 3/16"=1'-0".

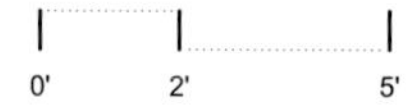

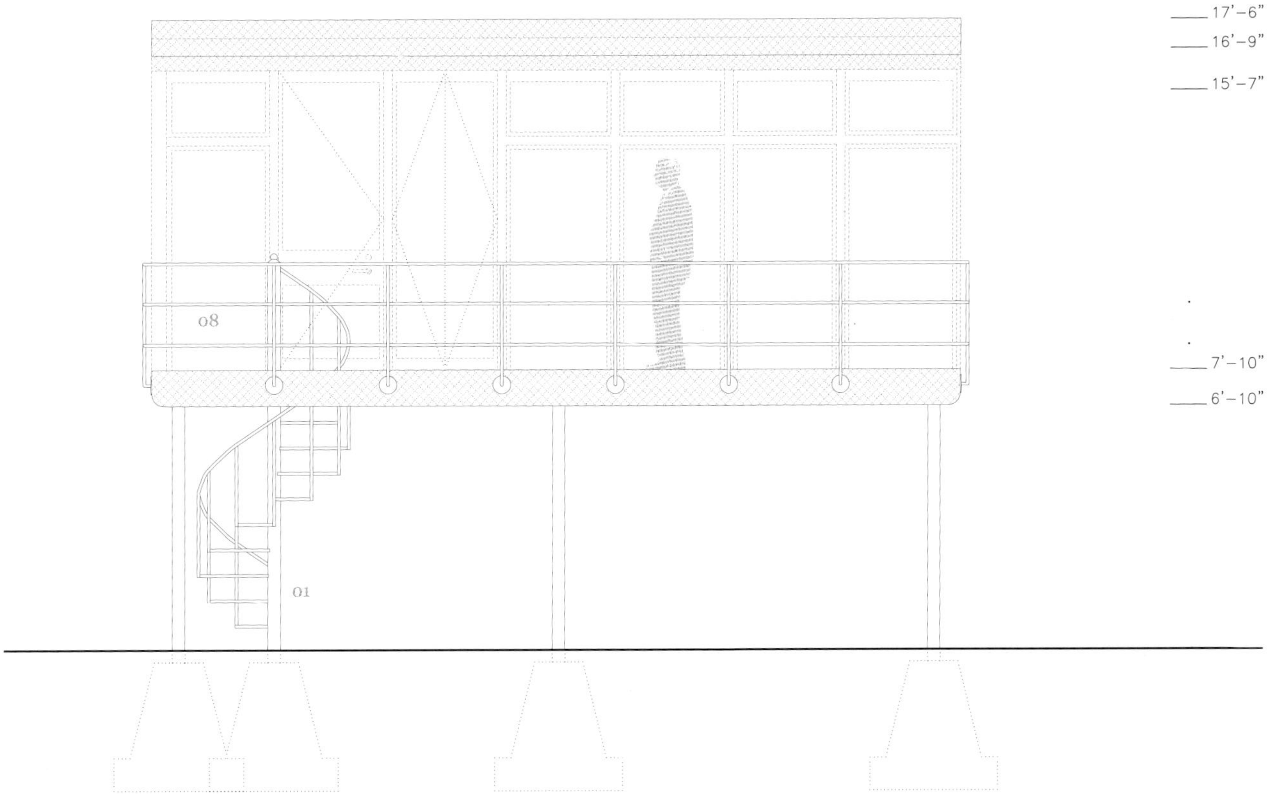

01. Prefab cast-iron spiral stair
02. Dinning room.
03. Kitchen.
04. Bathroom.
05. Living room (day); bedroom (night).
06. Living room (day); main bedroom (night).
07. Storage closets and cabinets.
08. Terrace.

Figure 7.54. A. Lawrence Kocher. Florida Weekend House, 1937–1939 (Unbuilt). Elevation. Scale 3/16"=1'-0".

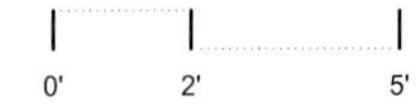

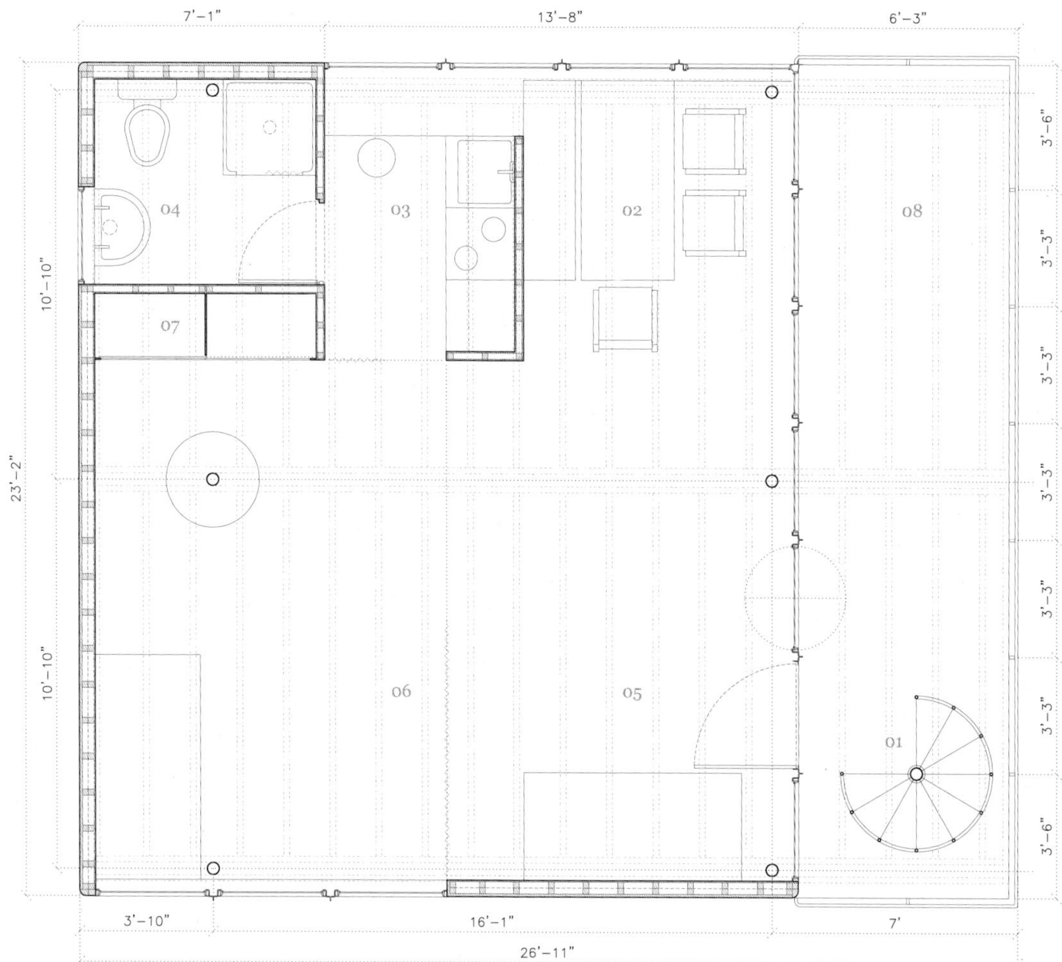

01. Prefab cast-iron spiral stair
02. Dinning room.
03. Kitchen.
04. Bathroom.
05. Living room (day); bedroom (night).
06. Living room (day); main bedroom (night).
07. Storage closets and cabinets.
08. Terrace.

Figure 7.55. A. Lawrence Kocher. Florida Weekend House, 1937–1939 (Unbuilt).
First floor plan. Scale 3/16"=1'-0".

BIBLIOGRAPHY

Ackerman, J. S. (1990) *The Villa. Form and Ideology of Country Houses*. Princeton, NJ: Princeton University Press.

Ashby, W. (1934) Farmhouse Plans. *Farmers Bulletin*, No. 1738. Washington D.C: U.S. Department of Agriculture.

Banham, R. (1965) A Home is not a House. *Art in America*. Vol 2. P 70–79.

Banham, R. (1978) Taking It with You. *New Society* 45, no. 826, August.

Banham, R. (1986) *A Concrete Atlantis. U.S. Industrial Building and European Modern Architecture*. Cambridge: The MIT Press.

Banham, R. (1996) *A Critic Writes: Selected Essays by Reyner Banham*. Berkeley: University of California Press.

Bannister, T.C. (1954) *The Architect at Mid-Century: Evolution and Achievement. report of the Commission for the Survey of Education and Registration of the American Institute of Architects*. New York: Reinhold.

Basalla, G. (1988) *The Evolution of Technology*. Cambridge: Cambridge University Press.

Belasco W. J. (1991) *Americans on the Road*. Cambridge: MIT Press.

Bemis, A. F. (1936) *The Evolving House, Volume III: Rational Design*. Cambridge, Massachusetts: The MIT Press.

Bercaw, L. O: Hannay, A. M.: Colvin, E. M. (1934) *Bibliography on land settlement: with particular reference to small holdings and subsistence homesteads*. Washington, D.C.: U.S. Dept. of Agriculture.

Bosworth, F. H: Jones, R.C. (1932) *A Study of Architectural Schools*. New York: Charles Scribner's Sons.

Brown, J. (1940) *Public Relief*, 1929–1939. New York: Henry Holt and Company

Bruder, J. (2018) *Nomadland: Surviving America in the Twenty-First Century*. New York: W. W. Norton & Company.

Bryson, N. (1990) *Looking at the Overlooked. Four essays on still life painting*. Cambridge, Ma: Harvard University Press.

Burns, T. (2015) *Useful Fictions: How Popular Mechanics Builds Technological Literacy through Magazine Cover Illustration*. Doctoral Dissertation. Texas Tech University. Published online Feb 6, 2018. https://issuu.com/tomkburns/docs/burns_dissertationreview.

Chandler, L. V. (1970) *America's Greatest Depression, 1929-1941*. New York: HarperCollins College Division.

Cohen, L. (2003) *A Consumer's Republic: The Politics of Mass Consumption in Postwar America*. New York: Alfred A. Knopf.

Cohen, L. (2003) "A Consumers' Republic: The Politics of Mass Consumption in Postwar America," *Journal of Consumer Research*, vol. 31, June.

Cornell, D: Zeuler R.L. (2017) *Albert Frey and Lina Bo Bardi. A Search for Living Architecture*. Munich-London-New York: Palm Springs Art Museum, DelMonico Books, Prestel.

Dalbey, M. (1990) *Building for Progressive Education: A. Lawrence Kocher and the Black Mountain College*. Thesis (M. Arch. Hist.) University of Virginia.

Davies, C. (2005) *The Prefabricated Home*. London: Reaktion Books.

Denzer, A. (2013) *The Solar House: Pioneering Sustainable Design*. New York: Rizzoli, 2013.

Dewey, J. (1902) *The School and Society and The Child and the Curriculum*. Chicago: The University of Chicago Press.

Díaz, A: Mocholí, G. (2012) Les Maisons Loucheur. La máquina para habitar se industrializa. *Proyecto, Progreso, Arquitectura*. May. Seville: University of Seville.

Díaz, E. (2014) *The Experimenters: Chance and Design at Black Mountain College*. Chicago: University of Chicago Press.

Dickstein, M. (2009) *Dancing in the Dark. A Cultural History of the Great Depression*. New York: W. W. Norton & Company.

Faber, W. M: Wolfe, T. (1933) *Proceedings of the National Conference on Low Cost Housing*. Cleveland: The Cleveland Engineering Society.

Field, W. (1942). A Re-examination into the Invention of the Balloon Frame. *Journal of the Society of Architectural Historians*, II/4 October, 3–29.

Ford, J: Ford, K. M. (1940) *The Modern House in America*. New York: Architectural Book Publishing Co. Inc.

Frey, A. (1939) *In Search of a Living Architecture*. New York: Architectural Book Publishing Company Inc.

Frisch, K. von (1974) *Tiere als Baumeister.* Frankfurt: Ullstein.

Galati, G. (2011) Modelos no lineares, historia del arte y de los nuevos medios. *Adversus, revista de semiótica.* VIII, 21. December.

Gebhard, D. (1965) *A Guide to Architecture in Southern California*. Los Angeles: Los Angeles County Museum of Art/LACMA.

Giedion, S. (1928) *Bauen in FrankReich, Bauen in Eisen, Bauen in Eisenbeton*. Leipzig: Klinkhardt & Biermann.

Giedion, S. (1948) *Mechanization Takes Command: A Contribution to Anonymous History.* Oxford: Oxford University Press.

Glaab, C. N.: Brown, T. (1983) *A History of Urban America*. New York: Macmillan Pub Co.

Glick, P. M. (1935) The Federal Subsistence Homesteads Program. *Yale Law Journal*, Vol. 44, June.

Golub, J. (1998) *Albert Frey. Houses 1 + 2*. New York: Princeton Architectural Press.

Gombrich, E. H. (1986) *Aby Warburg, an intellectual biography*. Chicago: The University of Chicago Press-Phaidon.

Goodman, A. (2017) Making Prefabrication American. The Work of A. Lawrence Kocher. *Journal of Architectural Education* 71. No 1. January.

Gowans, A. (1964) *Images of American Living: Four Centuries of Architecture and Furniture as Cultural Expression*. Philadelphia/New York: J.B. Lippincott Company.

Herbert, G. (1972) The Portable Colonial Cottage. *Journal of the Society of Architectural Historians*, Vol. 31, No. 4. December.

Hitchcock, H. R. (1929) *Modern Architecture: Romanticism and Reintegration*. New York: Payson & Clarke Ltd.

Hitchcock, H. R: Johnson, P. (1932) *The International Style; Architecture Since 1922*. New York: W.W Norton and Co. Inc.

Hoskins, W.G. (1953) The Rebuilding of Rural England, 1570–1640. *Past & Present*. 4, 44–59.

Hosmer Jr., C. B. (1980) "Preservation Comes of Age: From Williamsburg to the National Trust, 1926-1949," *Bulletin of the Association for Preservation Technology*, Vol. 12, No. 3. 20–27.

Hounshell, D. A. (1984) *From the American System to Mass Production, 1800-1932: The Development of Manufacturing Technology in the United States*. Baltimore: John Hopkins University Press.

Houston, R. E. (1927) Ford Production Department, August 3rd. www.mtfca.com/encyclo/fdprod.htm.

Hudnut, J. (1943) Architecture after the Peace, *Magazine of Art*, no. 36, April.

Hunnicutt, B. (2010) *Work Without End: Abandoning Shorter Hours for the Right to Work*. Philadelphia, PA: Temple University Press.

Isaacs, R. R. (1983). *Walter Gropius: Der Mensch und Sein Werk*. Berlin: Mann.

Jackson, J. B. (1984). The Movable Dwelling and How It Came to America. In: Jackson, J. B. (1997) *Landscape in Sight. Looking at America*. New Haven-London: Yale University Press.

Jackson, N. (1996) *The Modern Steel House*. London: Routledge.

Jackson, N. (1998). Aluminaire House, USA (Kocher and Frey). In: Cunningham, A. (editor) (1998) *Modern Movement Heritage*. London: E & FN Spon. 136–144.

Jakle, J. A.: Sculle, K. A: Rogers, J. S. (1996) *The Motel in America*. Baltimore: Johns Hopkins University Press.

Jandl, H.W. (1991) *Yesterday's Houses of Tomorrow*. Washington D.C.: The Preservation Press.

Jandl, H. W. (1991) With Heritage So Shiny: America's First All-Aluminum House. *Association for Preservation Technology (APT) Bulletin: The Journal of Preservation Technology*, Vol. 23, No. 2, Preserving What's New, 38–43.

Kelly, J. (2015) "Vulgar Modernism: J. M. Richards, Modernism and the Vernacular in British Architecture," *Architectural History*, Vol. 58. 229–259.

Kentgens-Craig, M. (2001) *The Bauhaus and America: First Contacts, 1919–1936*. Cambridge, MA: MIT Press.

Kocher, A. L. (1920) *The Early Architecture of Lancaster County, Pennsylvania: being an account of the origin and development of architectural forms in Lancaster County during the eighteenth century*. Lancaster, Pa.: Lancaster County Historical Society.

Kocher, A. L. (1920) Early Architecture of Pennsylvania (The). Part I. *Architectural Record*. Vol 48, No 6. December. 513–530.

Kocher, A. L. (1921) Early Architecture of Pennsylvania (The). Part II. *Architectural Record*. Vol 49, No 1. January. 30–47.

Kocher, A. L. (1921) Early Architecture of Pennsylvania (The). Part III. *Architectural Record*. Vol 49, No 2. February. 134–155.

Kocher, A. L. (1921) Early Architecture of Pennsylvania (The). Part IV. *Architectural Record*. Vol 49, No 3. March. 232–248.

Kocher, A. L. (1921) Early Architecture of Pennsylvania (The). Part V. *Architectural Record*. Vol 49, No 4. April. 310–330

Kocher, A. L. (1921) Early Architecture of Pennsylvania (The). Part VI. *Architectural Record*. Vol 49, No 5. May. 408–422

Kocher, A. L. (1921) Early Architecture of Pennsylvania (The). Part VII. *Architectural Record*. Vol 49, No 6. June. 518–535

Kocher, A. L. (1921) Early Architecture of Pennsylvania (The). Part VIII. *Architectural Record*. Vol 50, No 1. July. 27–43.

Kocher, A. L. (1921) Early Architecture of Pennsylvania (The). Part IX. *Architectural Record*. Vol 50, No 2. August. 147–157.

Kocher, A.L. (1921) Early Architecture of Pennsylvania (The). Part X. *Architectural Record*. Vol 50, No 3. September. 215–226.

Kocher, A.L. (1921) Early Architecture of Pennsylvania (The). Part XI. *Architectural Record*. Vol 50, No 5. November. 397–406

Kocher, A. L. (1921) Hand Books of Samuel Rhoads, Carpenter–Builder. *Architectural Record*, Vol 50, No 6, December. 507–09.

Kocher, A. L. (1922) Early Architecture of Pennsylvania (The). Part XII. *Architectural Record*. Vol 51, No 6. June. 507–520.

Kocher, A. L. (1922) Early Architecture of Pennsylvania (The). Part XIII. *Architectural Record*. Vol 52, No 2. August. 121–132.

Kocher, A. L. (1922) Early Architecture of Pennsylvania (The). Part XIV. *Architectural Record*. Vol 52, No 5. November. 435–444.

Kocher, A. L. (1924) The Library of the Architect. *Architectural Record*. Vol 56, No 2. August. 123–128.

Kocher, A. L. (1924) The Library of the Architect. Part II. *Architectural Record*. Vol 56, No 3. September. 218–224.

Kocher, A.L. (1924) The Library of the Architect. Part III. *Architectural Record*. Vol 56, No 4. October.

Kocher, A. L. (1924) The Library of the Architect. Part IV. *Architectural Record*. Vol 56, No 5. November.

Kocher, A. L. (1925) The Library of the Architect. Part V. *Architectural Record*. Vol 57, No 1. January. 29.

Kocher, A. L. (1925) The Library of the Architect. Part VI. *Architectural Record*. Vol 57, No 2. February. 125.

Kocher, A. L. (1925) The Library of the Architect. Part VII. *Architectural Record*. Vol 57, No 3. March. 221.

Kocher, A. L. (1925) The Library of the Architect. Part VIII. *Architectural Record*. Vol 57, No 4. March. 317.

Kocher, A.L. (1926) The Country House, Are We Developing an American Style? *Architectural Record*. Vol 60, No 5. November. 385.

Kocher, A. L. (1927) The Country House. An Analysis of the Architect's Method of Approach. *Architectural Record*. Vol 62, No 5. November. 337.

Kocher, A. L. (1928) Color in Early American Architecture, with Special

References to the Origin and Development of House Painting, *Architectural Record*, Vol 64, No 4. October. 278–290.

Kocher, A. L.: Ziegler, G. (1929) Sunlight Towers. *Architectural Record,* Vol 65. March. 307–310.

Kocher, A. L.: Ziegler, G. (1929) An Architect's Office, A. Lawrence Kocher and Gerhard Ziegler, Architects, *Architectural Record*, Vol. 66, No. 3. September. 262–268.

Kocher, A. L. (1930) Keeping the Architect Educated. *Architectural Record.* Vol 67. January. 45–46.

Kocher, A. L. (1930) A Multi-floor Prison. *Architectural Record.* Vol 67. January. 96.

Kocher, A. L. (1930) The Restoration of Old Buildings. *Architectural Record.* Vol 67. February. 174–175.

Kocher, A. L. (1930) Drawings of Sunlight Towers. *Architectural Record.* Vol 67. March. 286–288.

Kocher, A. L. (1930) Make Grandstands Safe. Editorials. *Architectural Record.* Vol 68. July. 75.

Kocher, A. L. (1930) How Architects May Cultivate Businesses. *Architectural Record.* Vol 68. October. 290–292.

Kocher, A. L.: Frey, A. (1931) Planning the House Garage. *Architectural Record.* Vol 69. January. 52–57.

Kocher, A. L.: Frey, A. (1931) Windows. *Architectural Record*, Vol 69. February. 126–137.

Kocher, A. L.: Frey, A. (1931) Clothes Closets. *Architectural Record*, Vol 69. March. 237–243.

Kocher, A. L.: Frey, A. (1931) Real State Subdivisions for Low-Cost Housing. *Architectural Record.* Vol 69. April. 323–327.

Kocher, A. L.: Frey, A. (1931) Stairways, Ramps, Escalators. *Architectural Record*, Vol 70. July. 43–48.

Kocher, A. L.: Frey, A. (1932) Dimensions: Part One. Kitchens. *Architectural Record.* Vol 71. January. 49–54.

Kocher, A. L.: Frey, A. (1932) Dimensions. Part Two. Bedrooms, Bathrooms. *Architectural Record*, vol 71. February. 123–128.

Kocher, A. L.: Frey, A. (1932) Design and Drafting Problems, Seating Heights and Spacing Table Sizes and Heights. *Architectural Record*, vol 71. April. 261–267.

Kocher, A. L.: Frey, A. (1932) Model of Farmhouse of Low Cost. *Architectural Record*, vol 71. May. 297.

Kocher, A. L.: Frey, A. (1932) Design and Drafting Problems, Planning Offices for Economy. *Architectural Record.* Vol 72. September. 197–202.

Kocher, A. L.: Frey, A. (1933) New Materials and Improved Construction Methods. *Architectural Record.* Vol 73. April. 281–289.

Kocher, A. L.: Frey, A. (1933) Wood Frame House. *Architectural Record*, vol 73. April. 304.

Kocher, A. L.: Ziegler, G. (1933) House of Rex Stout Near Danbury, Connecticut. *Architectural Record*, vol 73. April. 288.

Kocher, A. L.: Ziegler, G. (1933) House of Rex Stout Fairfield County, Conn. *Architectural Record*, vol 74. July. 45–49.

Kocher, A. L: Ziegler, G. (1933) House of Rex Stout Near Danbury, Connecticut. *House and Garden* 64. 42–43.

Kocher, A. L.: Frey, A. (1934) Low Cost Farmhouse. *Architectural Record.* Vol 75, No 1. January. 30.

Kocher, A. L.: Frey, A. (1934) Weekend House. *Architectural Record.* Vol 75, No 1. January. 34.

Kocher, A. L.: Frey, A. (1934) Subsistence Farmsteads. *Architectural Record.* Vol 75. April. 350–356.

Kocher, A. L.: Frey, A. (Compilers). (1934) Check List for New Construction and Modernization of Houses including Dimensions of Essential Equipment and Furniture. *Architectural Record*, vol 76. October. 257–286.

Kocher, A. L.: Frey, A. (1935) Real Estate Office and Apartment Building for Dr. J.J. Kocher. Palm Springs, California. *Architectural Record.* Vol 78. October. 267–275.

Kocher, A. L.: Frey, A. (1936) Designers. Bedroom Interior. *Architectural Record.* Vol 79. February. 101.

Kocher, A. L.: Frey, A. (1936) Ralph-Barbarin House Near Stamford, Conn. *Architectural Record.* Vol 79. April. 296–297.

Kocher, A. L.: Frey, A. (1936) Kitchen Apartment at Palm Springs, California. *Architectural Record.* Vol 80. October. 318.

Kocher, A. L.: Ziegler, G. (1936) Sun Light Towers Apartment. New York City. *Architectural Record.* Vol 80. October. 321.

Kocher, A. L.: Frey, A. (1936) A Community Exhibition Building Proposed for Darien, Conn. *Architectural Record.* Vol 80. December. 425.

Kocher, A. L.. (1936) Prefabrication and Architecture: An Introduction. In: Bemis, A. F. (editor) (1936) *The Evolving House: Rational Design, vol. III.* Cambridge, MA: Technology Press, MIT. 33–35.

Kocher, A. L.. (1937) Furniture. in: John Mc Andrew, *Aalto: Architecture and Furniture*. New York City: MoMA.

Kocher, A. L. (1939) "New Type of Study Faces Architects," *New York Times*, May 7.

Kocher, A. L. (1942) *Homes to Enrich Our National Standard of Living.* New York: Revere Copper and Bass Inc.

Kocher A. L: Dearstyne, H. (1954) *Shadows in Silver: A Record of Virginia, 1850-1900, in Contemporary Photographs Taken by George and Huestis Cook, With Additions from the Cook Collection.* New York: Charles Scribner's Sons.

Kocher, A. L. (1956) The New House for Family Living: Architect's Own House, New York. *Architectural Record* 119, May. 86–102.

Kocher A. L: Dearstyne H. (1961) *Colonial Williamsburg: Its Buildings and Gardens; A Descriptive Tour of the Restored Capital of the British Colony of Virginia.* Williamsburg, VA: Colonial Williamsburg.

Koenig, G. (2017) *Albert Frey*. Cologne: Taschen.

Lamprecht, B. M., Neutra, R. J., Goessel, P., Neutra, D., & Shulman, J. (2000). *Richard Neutra: Complete Works*. Köln: Taschen.

Leggett, J. (1939) The Trailer Grows Up. *Popular Mechanics*. August.

Lonberg-Holm, K. (1930) The Week-End House. *Architectural Record*, Vol. 68, No. 2. August. 177.

Lord, R.: Johnstone, P. H., Eds. (1942) *A place on earth; a critical appraisal of subsistence homesteads.* Washington, D.C.: United States Department of Agriculture, Bureau of Agricultural Economics.

Loudon, J. C. (1846) *An Encyclopedia of Cottage, Farm, and Villa Architecture and Furniture.* London: Longman, Brown, Green, & Longmans.

Martí Aris, C. (1993) *Las variaciones de la identidad.* Barcelona: Ediciones del Serbal-Demarcación de Barcelona del COAC.

McAndrew, J. Ed. (1940) *Guide to Modern Architecture: Northeast States.* New York: Museum of Modern Art/MoMA.

McDonald, T. C. (2007) The Fundamental Practice of Fieldwork at Colonial Williamsburg. In: *Perspectives in Vernacular Architecture*, Special 25th Anniversary Issue: Vernacular Architecture Forum, Vol. 13, No. 2. 26–53.

McElvaine, R. (1993) *The Great Depression: America 1929-1941*. New York City: Times Books.

McInnis, M. D.: Nelson, L. P. (2019) *Educated in Tyranny: Slavery at Thomas Jefferson's University*. Charlottesville: University of Virginia Press.

Moholy-Nagy, S. (1948) *Native Genius in Anonymous Architecture*. New York City: Horizon Press Inc.

Molesworth, H. (2015) *Leap Before You Look: Black Mountain College 1933–1957*. New Haven: Yale University Press.

Morton, J. F. (1958) A. Lawrence Kocher, Pioneer Architect. Thesis, College of William and Mary, Department of Fine Arts.

Mumford, E. P. (2000) *The CIAM Discourse on Urbanism, 1928-1960*. Cambridge, Massachusetts: The MIT Press.

Newhouse, V. (1989) *Wallace K. Harrison, Architect*. New York: Rizzoli.

Nabokov, P.: Easton, R. (1989) *Native American Architecture*. New York-Oxford: Oxford University Press.

Nesbitt, K. (Ed.) (1996) *Theorizing a New Agenda for Architecture. An anthology of architectural theory 1965-1995*. New York: Princeton Architectural Press.

Ockman J. Ed. (2012) *Architecture School: Three Centuries of Educating Architects in North America*. Cambridge, Massachusetts: The MIT Press.

Pai, H. (2002) *The Portfolio and the Diagram: Architecture, Discourse, and Modernity in America*. Cambridge, MA: MIT Press.

Pearlman, J. (2007) *Inventing American Modernism: Joseph Hudnut, Walter Gropius, and the Bauhaus Legacy at Harvard*. Charlottesville: University of Virginia Press.

Pitz, M.: Schneiderman, L. M. (2022) *Kaufmann's: The Family That Built Pittsburgh's Famed Department Store*. Pittsburgh: University of Pittsburgh Press.

Reist, A. L. (1975) *The Conestoga Wagon, Masterpiece of the Blacksmith*. Lancaster: Forry and Hacker.

Rob Zaleski, C. (2012) *Long Island Modernism. 1930-1980*. New York: W.W. Norton and Co. Inc.

Rosa, J. (1990) A. Lawrence Kocher Albert Frey. The Aluminaire House, 1930-31. *Assemblage,* No. 11 (April), The MIT Press. 58–69.

Rosa, J. (1990) *Albert Frey, Architect*. New York: Rizzoli International Publications.

Rodriguez Cheda, J. B. (2006) El aluminio en la construcción. *Tectonica 22. Aluminio*. Madrid: ATC Ediciones.

Roth, A. (1940) *The New Architecture. Presented in 20 examples*. Zurich: Verlag Dr. H. Girsberger.

Rudofsky, B. (1948) *The Prodigious Builders*. New York City: Harcourt Brace Jovanovich.

Rudofsky, B. (1964) *Architecture Without Architects: A Short Introduction to Non-pedigreed Architecture*. New York City: The Museum of Modern Art – Doubleday.

Sambrook, J. (2016) *The Eighteenth Century: The Intellectual and Cultural Context of English Literature 1700-1789*. Abingdon: Routledge.

Shanken, A. M. (2005) From the Gospel of Efficiency to Modernism: A History of Sweet's Catalogue, 1906-1947, *Design Issues*, vol. 21, no. 2. 28–47.

Shanken, A. M. (2006) Better Living: Toward a Cultural History of a Business Slogan, *Enterprise & Society*, vol. 7, no. 3. Cambridge University Press.

Shanken, A. M. (2009) *194X: Architecture, Planning, and Consumer Culture on the American Home Front*. Minneapolis: University of Minnesota Press.

Simon, M. J. Ed. (1945) *Solar Houses: An Architectural Lift of Living*. Toledo: Libbey-Owens-Ford.

Sperdy, G. (2019) *American Autopia: An Intellectual History of the American Roadside at Midcentury*. Charlottesville, VA: University of Virginia Press.

Sprague, P. E. (1981) The Origin of Balloon Framing. *Journal of the Society of Architectural Historians*, vol. 40, no. 4, 311–319.

Stephens, S. (2016) Lawrence Kocher, Renaissance Man. *Architectural Record*. April 1. https://www.architecturalrecord.com/articles/11585 lawrence-kocher-renaissance-man.

Stewart G. R. (1962) The Prairie Schooner Got Them There. *American Heritage*. February, Volume 13, Issue 2. 4–17.

Stiverson, C. Z. (1989) *Architecture and the Decorative Arts: The A. Lawrence Kocher Collection of Books at the Colonial Williamsburg Foundation*. West Cornwall, CT: Locust Hill Press.

Taylor, C. (2004). *Modern Social Imaginaries*. Durham: Duke University Press.

Wallis. A. D. (1991) *Wheel State. The Rise and Decline of Mobile Homes*. New York-Oxford. Oxford University Press.

Watkins, T. H. (1995) *The Great Depression. America in the 1930s*. New York: Back Bay Books.

Wattenberg, B. J. (1976) *The Statistical History of the United States: From Colonial Times to the Present*. New York: Basic Books Publishers.

White, R. B. (2001) *Home on the Road: The Motor Home in America*. Washington: Smithsonian Institution Scholarly Press.

Whitehill, W. M.: Nichols, F. D. (1976), *Palladio in America*. Milan: Electa Editrice.

Wilson M. O.: Dewitt, L.: Piper, C. (2019) *Thomas Jefferson, Architect: Palladian Models, Democratic Principles, and the Conflict of Ideals*. New Haven: Yale University Press.

Wilson, R. G. (1986) *The Machine Age in America 1918-1941*. New York: Harry N. Abrahams Inc.

Wilson, R. G. (1982) "International Style: The MoMA Exhibition," *Progressive Architecture*, February. 92–105.

Wilson, R. G.: Pilgrim, D. H.: Tashjian, D. (1986) *The Machine Age in America 1918-1941*. New York: Brooklyn Museum of Art-Harry N. Abrams, Inc.

Wodehouse, L. (1982) Kocher at Black Mountain. *Journal of the Society of Architectural Historians*, Vol. 41, No. 4 (Dec), 328–332.

Yorke, F. R. S. (1934) *The Modern House*. London: The Architectural Press,

Yorke, F. R. S. (1951) *The Modern House*. London: The Architectural Press.

Zaleski, C. R. (2012) *Long Island Modernism: 1930–1980*. New York: W.W. Norton and Co. Inc.

Zhaw Institute of Constructive Design. Editors (2019) *At Home in Steel: Residential Construction in Steel, Thoughts on Space and Structure*. Zurich: Park Books.

ILLUSTRATION
CREDITS

Images.

All illustrations from the John D. Rockefeller Jr. Library, Williamsburg, A. Lawrence Kocher Collection, except those noted below:

Palm Springs Art Museum. Albert Frey Collection. *1.2.*

Public Domain. Library of Congress, Prints & Photographs Division, [reproduction number, e.g., LC-B2-1234]. *1.43.*

Public Domain. U.S. Department of Agriculture, Farmers Bulletin, No. 1738, October 1934. *4.1, 4.2, 4.3, 4.4.*

Wurts Brothers Photography Collection, National Building Museum, Washington, D.C. *1.32.*

Private collection of the authors. *5.46, 5.48.*

Front page. Photo by Palmer Shannon. John D. Rockefeller Jr. Library, Williamsburg, A. Lawrence Kocher Collection.

Chapters' front illustrations, all from John D. Rockefeller Jr. Library, Williamsburg, A. Lawrence Kocher Collection.

Chapter 1. Kocher-Frey. Aluminaire House. Photo by Palmer Shannon.

Chapter 2. Kocher-Ziegler. Sunlight Towers. Typical floor plan.

Chapter 3. Kocher-Frey. Experimental Weekend House. Model photo.

Chapter 4. Kocher-Frey. Kocher Canvas Weekend House. Photo.

Chapter 5. Kocher. Black Mountain College Studies Building. Photo.

Chapter 6. Kocher. Clarence White School of Photography. New York. Rendering of the façade.

Chapter 7. Kocher-Frey. Aluminaire House. Structure detail.

Drawings.

LP. Luis Pancorbo Crespo / IM. Inés Martín Robles / XX. Xianwen Xu.

Drawings by LP, IM: *1.31, 7.6, 7.7, 7.14, 7.15, 7.16, 7.17, 7.18, 7.19, 7.20, 7.21, 7.22, 7.23, 7.24, 7.30, 7.31, 7.32, 7.33, 7.39, 7.40, 7.41, 7.42, 7.43, 7.44, 7.45, 7.51, 7.52, 7.53, 7.54, 7.55.*

Drawings by LP, IM, XX: *7.1, 7.2, 7.3, 7.4, 7.5, 7.8, 7.9, 7.10, 7.11, 7.12, 7.13, 7.25, 7.26, 7.27, 7.28, 7.29, 7.34, 7.35, 7.36, 7.37, 7.38, 7.46, 7.47, 7.48, 7.49, 7.50.*

Authors.

Luis Pancorbo Crespo and Inés Martín Robles are Associate Professors at the University of Virginia's School of Architecture, where they engage in teaching and scholarly work. Luis Pancorbo's research delves into the technical dimensions of architecture, particularly the role of industrial ruins and neglected landscapes in shaping architectural methodologies. He earned his Ph.D. with a dissertation titled *Albert Kahn Inc. Architecture as a Technical Object*. Prior to joining the University of Virginia in 2015, Luis served as *Profesor Asociado* at the School of Architecture of Madrid (ETSAM-UPM). Inés Martín Robles focuses her interest on Modern Spanish and Ibero-American architecture, exploring the interplay between tradition and memory in design. She holds a Ph.D. for her research in architectural project methodology.

They have authored numerous peer-reviewed articles in specialized journals and their co-authored book, *The Tradition in Julio Cano Lasso* (2020), examines the lasting impact of tradition in architectural practice. With 25 years of collaborative practice, they have earned recognition in the field, including 17 awards in international architectural competitions and 10 honors for their built projects. Their recent accolades include the prestigious AZ Awards in Canada, the AR Awards from the American Institute of Architects (AIA), and the ACSA Faculty Design Award. Their work has been featured in prominent international architectural publications, such as *C3, The Plan, Plot, AIT, Mark, Archicree, Arquitectura Viva, L'architecture d'aujourdhui, Frame, On Diseno, Azure, IW, Architect*, underscoring their influence on contemporary design discourse.

This investigation was partially funded by the Summer Research Grants of 2020 and 2021 from the University of Virginia's School of Architecture, with additional support for its publication in 2024 from the same institution. Special thanks to Dean Ila Berman, Dean Malo Hutson, and Associate Dean for Research Andrew Mondschein for their invaluable backing of this initiative.
We wish to extend our sincere gratitude to the staff of the John D. Rockefeller, Jr. Library, particularly to Marianne Martin, for their unwavering help throughout the entire research process.